Student's Book of College English

RHETORIC, READER, RESEARCH GUIDE, AND HANDBOOK

THIRTEENTH EDITION

DAVID SKWIRE
HARVEY S. WIENER

The City University of New York
LaGuardia Community College

PEARSON

Boston Columbus Indianapolis New York San Francisco Upper Saddle River
Amsterdam Cape Town Dubai London Madrid Milan Munich Paris Montréal Toronto
Delhi Mexico City São Paulo Sydney Hong Kong Seoul Singapore Taipei Tokyo

Senior Acquisitions Editor: Lauren Finn
Senior Development Editor: David Kear
Development Manager: Mary Ellen Curley
Senior Marketing Manager: Sandra McGuire
Senior Supplements Editor: Donna Campion
Production Manager: Eric Jorgensen
Project Coordination, Text Design, and Electronic
Page Makeup: Element-Thomson North America

Senior Cover Design Manager: Nancy Danahy
Cover Designer: Nancy Sacks
Cover Image: © Mikael Damkier/Alamy
Senior Manufacturing Buyer: Dennis Para
Printer/Binder: R. R. Donnelley/Crawfordsville
Cover Printer: Lehigh-Phoenix Color Corporation

Credits and acknowledgments borrowed from other sources and reproduced, with permission, in this textbook appear on the appropriate page within text.

This title is restricted to sales and distribution in North America only.

Library of Congress Cataloging-in-Publication Data
Skwire, David.
    Student's book of college English : rhetoric, reader, research guide, and handbook /
David Skwire, Harvey S. Wiener. — 13th ed.
        p. cm.
        Includes bibliographical references and index.
        ISBN-13: 978-0-205-17167-5
        ISBN-10: 0-205-17167-2
    1. English language—Rhetoric.   2. English language—Grammar—Handbooks, manuals, etc.
3. College readers.   4. Report writing.   I. Wiener, Harvey S.   II. Title.
        PE1408.S546 2011
        808'.0427—dc23   2011029907

10 9 8 7 6 5 4 3 2 —DOC— 15 14 13 12

ISBN-13: 978-0-205-17167-5
ISBN-10: 0-205-17167-2

A la Carte edition:
ISBN-13: 978-0-205-22919-2
ISBN-10: 0-205-22919-0

www.pearsonhighered.com

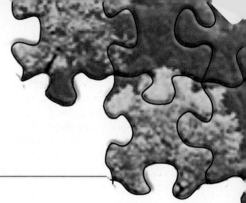

Detailed Contents

9 EXAMPLE 172

10 PROCESS 196

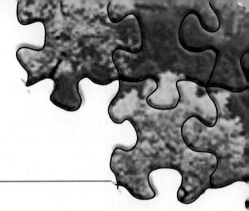

Thematic Contents

Love, Sweet Love

Gender Dynamics

Race, Equality, and Prejudice

Crime and Punishment

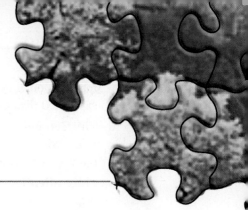

Preface

Changes give life; consistency sustains it. Although few traps are more insidious for an instructor than teaching a book—or a course—from memory, relying on a text's consistent philosophy from edition to edition has many rewards. Our thirteenth edition has changed and improved, yet the basic appeal of *Student's Book of College English* remains unchanged: It provides in a coherent package thorough instruction on all the issues likely to face students within First Year English—and then supplements that instruction with numerous essays, poems, visual texts, and works of fiction by students and professional writers.

One of the special, possibly unique, features of *Student's Book* is the mix wherever practicable of readings for use as models and readings for use as subjects for compositions. We believe that this mix significantly increases the versatility of the book and helps account for its success. We maintain this principle in the thirteenth edition. Users will find, for example, student and professional models of descriptive writing, but they will also find a short story that students can profitably analyze in writing their own descriptions.

We hope that clear prose and good sense also made their contributions to the success of earlier editions. We have tried to keep them constantly in mind while writing the current one.

What's New in the Thirteenth Edition

By making additions and improvements in the thirteenth edition of *Student's Book*, we aim to keep the text fresh and timely. Outstanding features of this revision include the following:

- **A new "In the World Around You" feature provides an example of each method of development** in a real-world context plus an activity to help students connect composition strategies they learn in college with the writing they see in the world around them (Ch. 7–15).

- **New coverage of developing thesis statements added to each method of development chapter** is reinforced by a new section in Chapter 3 to help students develop strong—as well as identify and revise weak—thesis statements (Ch. 3, 7–15).

- **Revised coverage of research** now starts with guidance on using the Internet and includes a new section on critically evaluating online sources, new material on limiting a topic and determining a research question, and an expanded discussion of developing a thesis (Ch. 20).

- **Thirteen new professional readings** have been added from authors such as John Grisham, David Brooks, and Stephanie Coontz, and five new student readings provide updated examples of different modes and writing strategies.

- **More attention to reading visual texts** includes detailed "Tips" for reading, evaluating, and using various types of visual texts as well as updated examples (Ch. 1).

- **Expanded coverage of revision** features a new section on revising to improve a thesis, provide supporting detail, clarify organization, and implement an appropriate structure as well as a new example of editing a student paper (Ch. 6).

- **A new formal writing prompt in each project chapter** provides teachers with additional assignment ideas and gives students more opportunities to practice the strategies they've been learning (Ch. 7–16).

- **Extended "Tips" provide more guidance for each method of development,** such as discussions of audience, purpose, prewriting, topic selection, outlining, supporting details, structure, revising, and proofreading (Ch. 7–15).

- **A heightened emphasis on outlining consists of** a new section on the benefits of outlining and guidance for correcting weaknesses in a formal outline as well as new outlines for selected student essays that highlight important points of their organization (Ch. 4, 11–13).

Other Features of *Student's Book*

In preparing the thirteenth edition, we have retained many time-tested features that help students improve their writing skills and produce good essays:

- **Comprehensive coverage of the writing process** addresses all aspects of writing, from prewriting and outlining to drafting and revising, while examples and annotations of student drafts help demystify writing.

- **A practical chapter on outlining** (Chapter 4), unique in rhetorics organized by rhetorical patterns, offers students a reliable strategy to help them progress from prewriting and their thesis statements into their rough drafts, helping them build coherence in their papers from the very first draft. Furthermore, in Chapter 20, *Student's Book* features outlining as a key part of the process of planning a research paper.

- **Two or more sample student essays in the modes chapters** offer twice as many student readings per rhetorical pattern than most other comparable rhetorics and expose students to a variety of options to consider as they plan and develop their own papers.

- **Over 90 readings** that include both classic and contemporary essays, photographs, cartoons, and Web-based writing provide students with material for response in their own writing as well as models for different rhetorical strategies.

- **Annotated professional samples** illustrate for students how active readers interact with texts.

- **Argument writing prompts, "Having Your Say,"** throughout the text ask students to think about a high-interest or controversial topic about which they have read and argue a position, strengthening their argumentation skills as a component of each chapter's writing assignments.

- **Critical Thinking activities, "Crosscurrents,"** at the end of the readings in each chapter in Part Two, encourage students to connect themes, ideas, and issues.

- **"Collaborative Learning" activities** create opportunities for students to learn in groups as they discuss reading selections and student samples.

- **Step-by-step, detailed treatment of the research paper** includes tips and Strategy Checklists for doing research and writing the research paper. "Frequently Asked Questions" about writing the research paper, coverage of MLA and APA documentation styles, and a fully annotated student research paper help students effectively solve some of their most troublesome research problems and learn the skills needed for research writing across the curriculum.

- **The Handbook** and **Glossary of Problem Words** in Part Six also offer exercises that allow students to practice and evaluate their progress.

- **"ESL Pointers: Tips for Non-Native Writers,"** a dedicated section in the Handbook, features helpful instruction and exercises in key trouble spots for students learning English as a second language.

- **The alternate thematic table of contents** for readings, visual texts, and student writing supports instructors who want another way to approach the reading selections.

Plan of the Book

In **Part One, "Getting Started: The Principles of Good Reading and Writing,"** we explore critical reading, prewriting strategies, drafting, and revising, and provide extensive practice on outlining, drafting, and developing a thesis. We show student writing at various stages of development and offer commentary to guide the reader's appreciation of how a paper progresses from start to finish.

Part Two, "Methods of Development," contains ten chapters, one devoted to each of the key rhetorical modes, beginning with description and narration, the working through example, process, comparison and contrast, classification and division, cause and effect, definition, and argumentation. Each of these chapters contains a discussion of how to write in the particular modes, professional and student examples and readings, and a large number of analytical and generative exercises ("For Writing or Discussion" questions follow every selection). Many readings in Part Two are new. We've tried to incorporate new readings that reflect the interests of today's student body. As a culminating chapter in Part Two, we provide full instruction in using mixed modes so that students see and practice how to integrate different rhetorical strategies in a single paper.

To add to the practicality of the book, all chapters in Part Two include a writing assignment with suggested writing topics and end with strategy checklists to serve as reminders and chapter summaries. Another popular feature in Part Two, "Crosscurrents," points out even more possibilities for writing topics by directing students' attention to thematic parallels between and among writing selections in different parts of the book.

Part Three, "Special Writing," includes a chapter on literary analysis and a chapter on writing essay exams, as well as an overview of business writing.

Part Four, "Research," gives considerable attention to essential research instruction. We include research with online databases, computerized card catalogs, and the Web, as well as significant coverage of the writing process, incorporating sources into one's own writing, avoiding plagiarism, and revising. The *MLA Style Manual and Guide to Scholarly Publishing*, Third Edition, and the *Publication Manual of the American Psychological Association*, Sixth Edition, guide our instruction in citation and documentation. Illustrated source samples of a book, a journal article, and a Web page help students see where to find citation information.

Part Five, "Style," includes three chapters: Chapter 22 helps students understand how to choose the right words to convey their meaning; Chapter 23 on effective sentences highlights those stylistic issues directly involved with creation of effective sentences; and Chapter 24 on stylistic problems and solutions offers students practical writing advice, including guidelines for avoiding sexist language. The style chapters are especially noteworthy, we believe, for the great number and variety of exercises.

Part Six, "Handbook, Glossary, and ESL Pointers," is easily accessible through alphabetical arrangement of entries, a colored bar at the end of the pages, and tabs with symbols that correspond to the list of Corrections Symbols and Abbreviations at the back of the book. The inside back cover contains guides to the text's planning, writing, and revising coverage, and a guide to the Handbook and Glossary, for quick reference. Student writers can find answers to most questions they have about grammar, sentences, punctuation, and mechanics in the Handbook and Glossary. Extensive exercises in Part Six enable students to demonstrate their command of the basics. A section called "ESL Pointers: Tips for Non-Native Writers" addresses many stumbling blocks faced by English-as-a-second-language student writers.

Supplements for Students and Instructors

- **Instructor's Manual.** The *Instructor's Manual*, revised by Angela R. Morales of Glendale College, features additional discussion on teaching strategies, including sample syllabi, portfolio instruction, and collaborative activities. In addition, the new manual contains an updated and expanded analysis of each essay.

- **MyCompLab Web site.** MyCompLab is an eminently flexible application that empowers student writers and teachers by integrating a composing space and assessment tools with multimedia tutorial services (such as online tutoring), and exercises for writing, grammar, and research. Students can use MyCompLab on their own, benefiting from self-paced diagnostics and a personal study plan that recommends the instruction and practice each student needs to improve his or her writing skills. Teachers can recommend it to students for self-study, use it to track student progress, or leverage the power of administrative features to be more effective and save time. The assignment builder and commenting tools, developed specifically for use in writing courses, bring instructors closer to their student writers, make managing assignments and evaluating papers more efficient, and put powerful assessments within reach. Students receive feedback linked directly to their own writing, which encourages critical thinking and revision and helps them to develop skills based on their individual needs. Learn more at www.mycomplab.com

- **Interactive E-book.** The e-book version of *Student's Book of College English* is also available in MyCompLab. This online version integrates the many resources of MyCompLab into the text to create an enriched, interactive learning experience for writing students.

- **CourseSmart E-book.** *Student's Book of College English* is also available as a CourseSmart e-textbook. This is an exciting new choice for students, who can subscribe to the same content online and search the text, make notes online, print out reading assignments that incorporate lecture notes, and bookmark important passages for later review. For more information, or to subscribe to the CourseSmart e-textbook, visit www.coursesmart.com.

Acknowledgments

We are proud and grateful for the more than thirty years that our textbook has served college writers throughout the country. Our deepest thanks go to the faculty, students, and, we are certain, some of those students' children who have honored us with their trust and attention.

The planning and preparation of this edition, as well as earlier editions, have benefited enormously from the essential insights of Lauren A. Finn, our editor, and the wise counsel of Eben W. Ludlow, our former editor, now retired. We want to express special appreciation to David B. Kear, our developmental editor, whose wide-ranging experience and attention to detail kept us focused. We would also like to thank editorial assistant Sandra Manzanares for all her support. And we owe a special debt of thanks to Eric Jorgensen, who guided us over the rough spots of production with calm and intelligence.

We are also grateful for the helpful advice of the reviewers of this edition: Jacob Bonnerup, Brown College; Rita A. Delude, Nashua Community College; Bart Ganzert, Forsyth Technical Community College; George E. Longenecker, Vermont Technical College; Devona Mallory, Albany State University; Linda Mobley, Bishop State Community College; Kelley Montford, Colorado Technical University; Renee Moore, Mississippi Delta Community College; Kristin L. Redfield, Forsyth Technical Community College; Tanya L. Reese, University of the District of Columbia; and Kristen Pearson Westrick, DeKalb Technical College.

DAVID SKWIRE
HARVEY S. WIENER

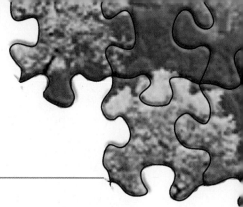

About the Authors

David Skwire, with degrees from the University of Wisconsin—Madison and Cornell University, taught composition, creative writing, and American literature at Cuyahoga Community College for twenty-five years. He also served on the faculties of Tufts University and Temple University. He acknowledges, however, that his job of most interest to students was a two-year stint as a writer of humorous greeting cards. In addition to his coauthorship of *Student's Book of College English*, he is author of the successful *Writing with a Thesis*. Now retired, Skwire lives near Cleveland.

Harvey S. Wiener taught for many years as professor of English at LaGuardia Community College. He has served in a variety of administrative positions, most recently as Vice President at Marymount Manhattan College. Dr. Wiener has directed the basic writing program at Pennsylvania State University and has taught at Teachers College, Columbia University, Brooklyn College, Queensborough Community College, and the State University of New York at Stony Brook. A Phi Beta Kappa graduate of Brooklyn College, Wiener holds a Ph.D. in Renaissance literature from Fordham University. He was founding president of the Council of Writing Program Administrators and was chair of the Teaching of Writing Division of the Modern Language Association.

Wiener is the author of many books on reading and writing for college students and their teachers, including *The Writing Room*. His book for parents, *Any Child Can Write*, was a Book-of-the-Month Club alternate. His most challenging writing assignment was a test to quality as Chief Writer for a network soap opera by developing the content for six weeks of episodes. He does not regret having lost the job to someone else.

PART ONE

Getting Started: The Principles of Good Reading and Writing

CHAPTER 1

Critical Reading

In this chapter you will

- examine the elements that contribute to critical reading

- apply the elements of critical reading to your own reading

- analyze a sample of critical reading in action

- learn to read for inquiry

- apply critical reading to visual images such as photographs, advertisements, graphs, tables, charts, cartoons, and Web sites

- learn the principles of collaborative learning and apply them

Why Read?

Even a few decades ago, the question "Why read?" would rarely have crossed anyone's mind. The essential way to gaining wisdom and enlightenment, to understanding issues and reacting wisely to world events, to filling time with pleasurable activity, was to read books, magazines, journals, and newspapers. Reading brought knowledge; reading brought delight; reading brought comfort and self-awareness.

In an age of multimedia, however, the question "Why read?" has urgency. After all, televisions, DVD players, computers, video game consoles, MP3 players, and cell phones all compete to fill our time with exciting visual and auditory presentations. We can watch and listen to an extraordinary range of information without turning a page of paper.

So, why read? One set of responses to this question is obvious, of course. We read traffic signs and warning signs. We read recipes and directions for putting together a toy or installing an air conditioner. We read menus and sales brochures. Furthermore, we also read in various electronic media. Television images frequently include words that we have to read. Text messaging on a cell phone involves reading and writing. E-mail, instant messages, blogs, and Web sites usually require us to decode written language. So, reading skills such as dealing with new vocabulary, figuring out the meaning of a message, and using inference regularly come into play. At the very least, being an attentive reader is important for survival as we go about our daily lives.

But beyond these practical instances, why should you try to improve your reading competence, especially in college, where you can address innumerable topics and questions through nonbook sources?

Much of the world's collected knowledge still resides in print that dwells in non-cyber libraries and bookstores. To maximize your learning experience, you'll have to read books handed down across centuries, do required textbook reading in your courses, and research newspapers and magazines that may not be online. These print media have a permanence that cyberspace often lacks.

What we have to say about reading in this chapter will help you read in any of the media demanded by your college programs. To be a successful college reader, you have to be a critical reader. Critical reading means reading actively.

Many college students are passive readers. They start reading with little advanced thought. They expect the words and sentences on a page to produce meaning without the reader's help. Passive readers do little to build a partnership with the writer and the text in order to understand what the writer says.

Active readers, critical readers, on the other hand, know that they have to work at getting meaning from words and sentences. They take conscious steps to engage what they read. The writer and the reader together create meaning.

TIPS for Reading Critically

■ **Have a reason for reading.**   Think in advance about what you expect to gain from your reading. Try to connect your purpose with the intellectual demands of the reading material and your expectations from it. You can read to learn new concepts and vocabulary. You can read to prepare for a class lecture or discussion or to learn someone's opinions on a controversial topic. You can read to stimulate your own writing for a required essay, to explore essential scholarship for a research paper, or to examine rhetorical and other writing strategies as an aid to honing your own skills. Without a purpose, you risk a passive stance as a reader, and that puts you at risk of never truly interacting with the words before you.

■ **Explore what you know about the topic before you read.**   Before you read anything below the title, try to connect the title with any related information you may have seen or heard. Look at any subtitles, photographs, illustrations, graphs, charts—and all the accompanying captions—before you begin reading. Think a moment about the author's name and about any information provided about the author. When you start reading, stop after you complete the first paragraph or two. Think again about how you can relate what you already know to the topic the writer is investigating.

- **As you read, record your responses.** Write down what the selection makes you think of or what it makes you feel. Write out any questions you have. Copy out phrases that stimulate, challenge, annoy, thrill, puzzle, or ignite you. Make notes in the margins of books you own.

- **Establish the writer's thesis.** All good readers try to determine the main point of a reading. Sometimes the writer will tell you very directly what the thesis is, and before the end of the first few paragraphs—sometimes at the end of the very first sentence—you'll know exactly what the piece is about. But in other cases, no single statement or statements will tell you the thesis precisely. Here you have to state the writer's thesis in your own words. The various sentences and paragraphs in an essay will contribute information that you must use to define the thesis yourself.

- **Pay attention to the words the writer chooses.** Words are alive with both denotative (the dictionary definition) and connotative (the implied or suggested definition) meanings. A writer naming a person who is about thirteen years old can use one of these words that, roughly speaking, would do the job: youngster, child, adolescent, teenager, kid, eighth grader, prepubescent, young adult. Critical readers always consider the implications of word choice and think about why a writer selects one word instead of another.

- **Determine the writer's purpose and audience.** Writers have many reasons for writing: to inform, to entertain, to challenge, to complain, to convince, to describe, to tell a story, to call for action—there are others certainly. As you read, you should be able to figure out the intended purpose. Related to the writer's purpose is the audience the writer has in mind, which influences the writing markedly. For example, to write about steps for preventing the spread of AIDS, a writer would use wholly different strategies if writing for eighth-grade kids in a suburban classroom, for social workers in Chicago, or for health care workers in Africa.

- **Consider the way that the writer has constructed the essay.** Look at the sentences to see if they relate to the main point. Look at the introductions and conclusions, the essay's opening and closing doors. Do they achieve their ends? Do they satisfy you? How do the parts of the essay hold together? Do all the ideas seem to relate to the central point? Do the sentences connect smoothly with each other? And how has the writer accomplished these near-magical feats? Attending to the structure of what you read will help you learn strategies for your own writing.

■ **Be aware of the writer's tone.**   *Tone* is the writer's attitude toward the subject. For example, one writer writing about the high incidence of guns in schools could approach the topic with shock and horror; another, with anger; another, analytically; another, clinically, simply describing or chronicling events; another, sentimentally, longing for the good old school days with no weapons and with well-behaved kids. Thoughtful readers always keep an eye on the tone. Like purpose and audience, it influences word choice, sentence structure, and style.

Critical Reading in Action

Look at the following selection and note in the margins the questions and comments that show how a critical reader treated the piece "The Shy, Egg-Stealing Neighbor You Didn't Know You Had." Note the steady interaction between the student and the essay regarding language and content—the student reader cross-examines the piece, acknowledges important or difficult words, and makes comments on the writing. In short, these comments reflect many of the strategies outlined in the previous section of this chapter.

LAWRENCE DOWNES

The Shy, Egg-Stealing Neighbor You Didn't Know You Had

Odd title—whose neighbor steals eggs? And if it's a neighbor, how could you not know you had it?

1 The suburbs, pretty as they may be, are <u>nobody's idea</u> of nature in balance. Sure, they are lush, green places where people and their vehicles get along with flowers, vegetables, songbirds and the littler mammals. But this harmony is enforced with an iron fist. It takes lots of chemicals, artificial irrigation and gas-powered trimming and mowing to keep such an arbitrary ecosystem under control.

True? Nobody's idea?

Fair? Urban "ecosystems" also arbitrary and must be controlled.

Nice word! Implies conscious uprising, people on the attack!

People refuse to control the intruders. "Distasteful" because we'd have to kill them somehow.

2 Leave it to nature to mount an <u>insurgency</u> against the tranquility of the <u>grass-and-pavement grid</u>. Canada geese and white-tail deer are the most brazen intruders, multiplying beyond all reason and refusing to be subdued. The best-equipped predators, people, sidestepped the job, finding it distasteful. Instead they adjust their garden netting, check for ticks and brood about the tendency of their fallen Eden to keep collapsing into chaos.

Writer's view of suburbs. Good image—"grass-and-pavement grid."

Here, "insurgency" is by geese and deer!

3   But what if that didn't always happen? What if Mother Nature decided not to run amok but to tidy up?

Questions raised: Expect writer to answer them.

4   Just such an amazing circumstance appears to be happening on the outskirts of Chicago. Research biologists there announced last month that they had stumbled across a possible answer to the problem of the proliferating suburban goose: the proliferating suburban coyote.

Coyotes are keeping goose population in check. How?

Good image: "Mother" Nature tidying up.

5   The researchers belong to the Cook County Coyote Project, which has spent nearly six years studying the habits of more than 200 coyotes in the northern and western Chicago suburbs. Among other things, they tried to determine what the growing numbers of these beasts might have had to do with another puzzling development: the sudden end of the goose explosion. The local population of Canada geese had soared in the 1980's and 90's, but by 2000 the increase had slowed to about only 1 percent a year. An unknown predator was assumed to be the reason.

Repetition of word "proliferating"— good balancing. One proliferation is a problem, the other a solution.

Sounds responsible. Google this?

Coyotes grow in numbers. Geese stop populating. What's the reason?

6   The coyote was not an obvious suspect, being small and skulky and unlikely to stand up to a wrathful Canada goose. Examinations of coyote scat had seldom found damning traces of eggshell. But then infrared cameras exposed the coyote as a nest robber, one that carefully cracks open a goose egg and licks it clean.

This is how it's done! Coyote cracks egg and sucks out insides—leaves no evidence.

Canada geese have mean tempers.

7   Evidence like this bolsters the conclusion that coyotes, in their own wily way, have become keystone predators in a land long emptied of wolves and mountain lions. The Cook County project's principal investigator, Prof. Stanley Gehrt of Ohio State University, speaks admiringly of his subjects, who have withstood more than 200 years of hunting, trapping and poisoning and are more entrenched in North America than ever. Every state but Hawaii has them. They have spread into suburbs and cities, forcing biologists to revise their definition of coyote habitat to this. Basically anywhere.

Expert testimony— professor knows the issues as project head.

Resourceful creatures!

Wily means cunning.

No wolves or mountain lions left to do the job.

Check on coyotes here in this state. Goes back to title "Shy, Egg-Stealing Neighbor."

8   Here is what is really strange: Humans have barely noticed. Egg-rustling, night-howling varmints are raising litters in storm drains, golf courses, parks and cemeteries. They are sometimes heard but seldom seen. In cities, they keep to themselves and work nights. There are coyotes, Professor Gehrt says, living in the Chicago Loop.

Transition refers to previous paragraph.

9   You could call that sneaky. Or you could call it discreet. Professor Gehrt said that one surprising discovery of the study was how little danger the coyote poses to his unwitting human neighbors. "The risk is quite low, as long as we don't monkey with their behavior," he said. If you assert yourself when you see one—by yelling, cursing and throwing sticks—it will respect your space and lie low. The coyote's tendency to avoid people—and more importantly, raccoons— has made rabies a nonissue, Professor Gehrt said, with only one case of coyote-to-human transmission ever recorded.

"Sneaky" and "discreet"— words for human activity contribute to coherence of essay.

Shih Tzu is a small dog, once a favorite of the Imperial Chinese court, now a favorite of wealthy suburbanites.

A little humor here. More use of "people" words ("well-mannered," "responsible").

Coyotes will behave, he said, as long as people do not feed them. Leave nothing tasty outside in an open trash can or food dish, and definitely <u>nothing small and fluffy</u> at the end of a leash. Professor Gehrt says with confidence that the sensible suburban toddler has little to fear from the suburban coyote, but he will not say the same for the suburban Shih Tzu.

The Cook County Coyote Project is the largest and most comprehensive of its kind, but it is just one study. It is probably not the time to call for coyote subsidies and captive-breeding programs for goose-plagued subdivisions. But any effort to learn more about these creatures—like a four-year coyote study being done in Westchester County by New York State and Cornell University—is highly welcome. It is intriguing to consider the possibility that such a shunned, <u>maligned</u> animal may be a misunderstood hero. The suburbs could use well-mannered, responsible predators, and house cats are clearly not up to the job.

10

Obviously a cat or dog—coyotes will go after them.

11

Maligned means badly treated.

Why maligned? What is coyote's history?

FOR WRITING OR DISCUSSION

1. What is the main point of Downes' piece?

2. How do the marginal notes demonstrate critical reading?

3. Where does the reader call attention to issues of language? Why does the reader raise these issues?

4. How does the comment about the title show an application of prior knowledge? Now that you've read the selection, how would you answer the question that the reader raised about the title?

5. What additional comments or questions would you raise about this piece?

Reading as Inquiry

One of the many dimensions of reading in our lives is how a particular selection can stimulate our thinking and urge us to read further in order to find more information, to test an assumption, or to challenge a writer's point. Reading as inquiry requires an inquiring mind, a mind that asks questions about the words and sentences on the page and wants to follow up in finding answers to those questions. Especially in a writing course, your readings can stimulate enough thought that you can generate topics you can write about. Thus, if you ask many questions of the invisible writer as you read, you can find yourself identifying a topic for next week's essay requirement or the starting point for a research paper required by your instructor. We've provided many readings in this text and hope that you can use some of them to generate topics for your writing assignments.

Look at the box below to see how one student used reading as inquiry to generate questions as he read "The Shy, Egg-Stealing Neighbor You Didn't Know You Had," and how those questions led to a variety of potential topics.

Questions	Possible Resulting Topics
What artificial procedures are needed to maintain suburban beauty and tranquility?	Lawn Chemicals and People's Health
	Birds and Bees and Insecticide
	Suburban Elegance: How to Maintain It
What is the Cook County Coyote Project?	Local Governments and Animal Control
	Bad Animals Are Good for Us
	Protecting against Coyotes
	Animal Control Measures in Our State
Are coyotes a threat to domestic animals?	Coyotes and Cats and Dogs
	Coyote Personality
What is the New York State and Cornell University study about?	Studying Coyotes in Upstate New York
	Coyote Problems in New York State
Why are coyotes considered maligned?	Battling Coyotes in the Last Two Decades
	Methods Used to Trap and Kill Coyotes

Notice how the questions generated by the reader have led to a variety of topic possibilities, some even remote from the essay. The point here is that if you read with an inquiring mind, you can produce topic ideas that are rooted in your own questions and interests. And then, these topic ideas can become springboards for further thought and research.

STRATEGY CHECKLIST: Reading Critically

Determine your purpose for reading.	Do I want to: ☐ Learn concepts and vocabulary? ☐ Understand the writer's opinion? ☐ Prepare for a class or exam? ☐ Gather information for a research project? ☐ Learn strategies to use in my own writing? ☐ Read for some other reason (what?)?
Explore what you already know about the topic.	☐ What do I know about the topic? ☐ What do the author information, title, and headings tell me? ☐ What do the illustrations and captions tell me? ☐ How do the first couple of paragraphs connect with what I already know?
As you read, take notes.	☐ Have I recorded ideas as I read? ☐ Have I noted key words? ☐ Have I noted challenging words and phrases?
Determine the writer's thesis.	☐ What is the main point of the reading? ☐ Have I restated the main point in my own words?
Pay attention to the language.	☐ Do I understand the denotation and connotation of words? ☐ Have I examined the writer's choice of words?
Determine the writer's purpose and audience.	☐ Why has the writer written the piece? ☐ Who is the writer's intended audience?
Consider the structure of the piece.	☐ How do the introduction and conclusion serve the essay? ☐ Do all sentences relate to the main idea? ☐ Do sentences follow one another logically?

Pay attention to the writer's tone.	☐ What is the writer's attitude to the subject? ☐ How does the language contribute to the tone?
Establish inquiry strategies.	☐ What questions has the piece generated in my mind? ☐ What possible topics of interest can I write about based on my inquiry?

EXERCISE

Examine the essay on pages 11–14, "A Hanging," by George Orwell (1903–1950). Orwell was a British citizen who at one point worked as a police officer in Burma, a colony in the British Empire and a province of India. A renowned essay writer, journalist, and social critic, Orwell searingly examines the relations between individual rights and oppressive governments in his novels *Animal Farm* and *1984*. Answer the questions below.

Before You Read

1. What purpose have you set for yourself before you read the text?
2. Before reading the entire essay, look at the note above about the author, look at the title of the selection, and read only the first two paragraphs. What thoughts are stimulated in your mind? What do you think this essay will be about? Where else have you read about or discussed similar issues?

During and After Your Reading

3. Write down thoughts as they occur to you. Use the margins, keeping in mind the notes in the margins of the piece by Lawrence Downes on pages 5–7. Underline, highlight, or copy challenging phrases and sentences.
4. State the writer's thesis in your own words. Where in the essay does the writer himself come closest to stating what you think is the thesis?
5. What is your view of the writer's use of language? Where do you find indelible images, snapshots of people and places through the use of color, sound, and action? What is the effect on the reader of the images in the first paragraph? The first sentence?
6. Why does Orwell never directly criticize capital punishment? Nonetheless, you are left with a very clear idea of where Orwell stands on the issue. How does he achieve that end? How does paragraph 10 serve the essay?
7. What is Orwell's purpose? How can you tell? Who do you believe is his intended audience? How can you tell?

8. Comment on the introduction (the first couple of paragraphs). Are they effective in bringing you into the scene as well as in revealing the topic of the essay? Why or why not? What is your reaction to the last paragraph? How does it provide dramatic closure to the essay? What strategies has Orwell used to connect the ideas smoothly from one sentence to the next, from one paragraph to the next?

9. What is the tone of the essay—Orwell's attitude toward his subject? Is he indifferent, humorous, astonished, saddened, ironic, sentimental, imperialistic—or something else? Defend your choice.

GEORGE ORWELL

A Hanging

It was in Burma, a sodden morning of the rains. A sickly light, like yellow tinfoil, was slanting over the high walls into the jail yard. We were waiting outside the condemned cells, a row of sheds fronted with double bars, like small animal cages. Each cell measured about ten feet by ten and was quite bare within except for a plank bed and a pot of drinking water. In some of them brown silent men were squatting at the inner bars, with their blankets draped round them. These were the condemned men, due to be hanged within the next week or two. 1

One prisoner had been brought out of his cell. He was a Hindu, a puny wisp of a man, with a shaven head and vague liquid eyes. He had a thick, sprouting moustache, absurdly too big for his body, rather like the moustache of a comic man on the films. Six tall Indian warders were guarding him and getting him ready for the gallows. Two of them stood by with rifles with fixed bayonets, while the others handcuffed him, passed a chain through his handcuffs and fixed it to their belts, and lashed his arms tight to his sides. They crowded very close about him, with their hands always on him in a careful, caressing grip, as though all the while feeling him to make sure he was there. It was like men handling a fish which is still alive and may jump back into the water. But he stood quite unresisting, yielding his arms limply to the ropes, as though he hardly noticed what was happening. 2

Eight o'clock struck and a bugle call, desolately thin in the wet air, floated from the distant barracks. The superintendent of the jail, who was standing apart from the rest of us, moodily prodding the gravel with his stick, raised his head at the sound. He was an army doctor, with a grey toothbrush moustache and a gruff voice. "For God's sake hurry up, Francis," he said irritably. "The man ought to have been dead by this time. Aren't you ready yet?" 3

Francis, the head jailer, a fat Dravidian in a white drill suit and gold spectacles, waved his black hand. "Yes sir, yes sir," he bubbled. "All iss satisfactorily prepared. The hangman iss waiting. We shall proceed." 4

"Well, quick march, then. The prisoners can't get their breakfast till this job's over." 5

6   We set out for the gallows. Two warders marched on either side of the prisoner, with their rifles at the slope; two others marched close against him, gripping him by arm and shoulder, as though at once pushing and supporting him. The rest of us, magistrates and the like, followed behind. Suddenly, when we had gone ten yards, the procession stopped short without any order or warning. A dreadful thing had happened—a dog, come goodness knows whence, had appeared in the yard. It came bounding among us with a loud volley of barks, and leapt round us wagging its whole body, wild with glee at finding so many human beings together. It was a large woolly dog, half Airedale, half pariah. For a moment it pranced round us, and then, before anyone could stop it, it had made a dash for the prisoner, and jumping up tried to lick his face. Everyone stood aghast, too taken aback even to grab at the dog.

7   "Who let that bloody brute in here?" said the superintendent angrily. "Catch it, someone!"

8   A warder, detached from the escort, charged clumsily after the dog, but it danced and gambolled just out of his reach, taking everything as part of the game. A young Eurasian jailer picked up a handful of gravel and tried to stone the dog away, but it dodged the stones and came after us again. Its yaps echoed from the jail walls. The prisoner, in the grasp of the two warders, looked on incuriously, as though this was another formality of the hanging. It was several minutes before someone managed to catch the dog. Then we put my handkerchief through its collar and moved off once more, with the dog still straining and whimpering.

9   It was about forty yards to the gallows. I watched the bare brown back of the prisoner marching in front of me. He walked clumsily with his bound arms, but quite steadily, with that bobbing gait of the Indian who never straightens his knees. At each step his muscles slid neatly into place, the lock of hair on his scalp danced up and down, his feet printed themselves on the wet gravel. And once, in spite of the men who gripped him by each shoulder, he stepped slightly aside to avoid a puddle on the path.

10   It is curious, but till that moment I had never realised what it means to destroy a healthy, conscious man. When I saw the prisoner step aside to avoid the puddle, I saw the mystery, the unspeakable wrongness, of cutting a life short when it is in full tide. This man was not dying, he was alive just as we were alive. All the organs of his body were working—bowels digesting food, skin renewing itself, nails growing, tissues forming—all toiling away in solemn foolery. His nails would still be growing when he stood on the drop, when he was falling through the air with a tenth of a second to live. His eyes saw the yellow gravel and the grey walls, and his brain still remembered, foresaw, reasoned—reasoned even about puddles. He and we were a party of men walking together, seeing, hearing, feeling, understanding the same world; and in two minutes, with a sudden snap, one of us would be gone—one mind less, one world less.

11   The gallows stood in a small yard, separate from the main grounds of the prison, and overgrown with tall prickly weeds. It was a brick erection like three sides of a shed, with planking on top, and above that two beams and a crossbar with the rope dangling. The hangman, a grey-haired convict in the white uniform of the prison, was waiting beside his machine. He greeted us with a servile crouch as we entered. At a word from Francis the two warders, gripping the prisoner more closely than ever, half led, half pushed him to the

gallows and helped him clumsily up the ladder. Then the hangman climbed up and fixed the rope round the prisoner's neck.

We stood waiting, five yards away. The warders had formed in a rough circle round the gallows. And then, when the noose was fixed, the prisoner began crying out on his god. It was a high, reiterated cry of "Ram! Ram! Ram! Ram!," not urgent and fearful like a prayer or a cry for help, but steady, rhythmical, almost like the tolling of a bell. The dog answered the sound with a whine. The hangman, still standing on the gallows, produced a small cotton bag like a flour bag and drew it down over the prisoner's face. But the sound, muffled by the cloth, still persisted, over and over again: "Ram! Ram! Ram! Ram! Ram!"   12

The hangman climbed down and stood ready, holding the lever. Minutes seemed to pass. The steady, muffled crying from the prisoner went on and on, "Ram! Ram! Ram!" never faltering for an instant. The superintendent, his head on his chest, was slowly poking the ground with his stick; perhaps he was counting the cries, allowing the prisoner a fixed number—fifty, perhaps, or a hundred. Everyone had changed colour. The Indians had gone grey like bad coffee, and one or two of the bayonets were wavering. We looked at the lashed, hooded man on the drop, and listened to his cries—each cry another second of life; the same thought was in all our minds: oh, kill him quickly, get it over, stop that abominable noise!   13

Suddenly the superintendent made up his mind. Throwing up his head he made a swift motion with his stick. "Chalo!" he shouted almost fiercely.   14

There was a clanking noise, and then dead silence. The prisoner had vanished, and the rope was twisting on itself. I let go of the dog, and it galloped immediately to the back of the gallows; but when it got there it stopped short, barked, and then retreated into a corner of the yard, where it stood among the weeds, looking timorously out at us. We went round the gallows to inspect the prisoner's body. He was dangling with his toes pointed straight downwards, very slowly revolving, as dead as a stone.   15

The superintendent reached out with his stick and poked the bare body; it oscillated, slightly. "*He's* all right," said the superintendent. He backed out from under the gallows, and blew out a deep breath. The moody look had gone out of his face quite suddenly. He glanced at his wristwatch. "Eight minutes past eight. Well, that's all for this morning, thank God."   16

The warders unfixed bayonets and marched away. The dog, sobered and conscious of having misbehaved itself, slipped after them. We walked out of the gallows yard, past the condemned cells with their waiting prisoners, into the big central yard of the prison. The convicts, under the command of warders armed with lathis, were already receiving their breakfast. They squatted in long rows, each man holding a tin pannikin, while two warders with buckets marched round ladling out rice; it seemed quite a homely, jolly scene, after the hanging. An enormous relief had come upon us now that the job was done. One felt an impulse to sing, to break into a run, to snigger. All at once everyone began chattering gaily.   17

The Eurasian boy walking beside me nodded towards the way we had come, with a knowing smile: "Do you know, sir, our friend (he meant the dead man), when he heard his appeal had been dismissed, he pissed on the floor of his cell. From fright—Kindly take one of my cigarettes, sir. Do you not admire my new silver case, sir? From the boxwallah, two rupees eight annas. Classy European style."   18

19   Several people laughed—at what, nobody seemed certain.

20   Francis was walking by the superintendent, talking garrulously: "Well, sir, all hass passed off with the utmost satisfactoriness. It was all finished—flick! like that. It iss not always so—oah, no! I have known cases where the doctor wass obliged to go beneath the gallows and pull the prisoner's legs to ensure decease. Most disagreeable!"

21   "Wriggling about, eh? That's bad," said the superintendent.

22   "Ach, sir, it iss worse when they become refractory! One man, I recall, clung to the bars of hiss cage when we went to take him out. You will scarcely credit, sir, that it took six warders to dislodge him, three pulling at each leg. We reasoned with him. 'My dear fellow,' we said, 'think of all the pain and trouble you are causing to us!' But no, he would not listen! Ach, he wass very troublesome!"

23   I found that I was laughing quite loudly. Everyone was laughing. Even the superintendent grinned in a tolerant way. "You'd better all come out and have a drink," he said quite genially. "I've got a bottle of whisky in the car. We could do with it."

24   We went through the big double gates of the prison, into the road. "Pulling at his legs!" exclaimed a Burmese magistrate suddenly, and burst into a loud chuckling. We all began laughing again. At that moment Francis's anecdote seemed extraordinarily funny. We all had a drink together, native and European alike, quite amicably. The dead man was a hundred yards away.

COLLABORATIVE LEARNING

One of the best ways to develop a critical reading style is to engage regularly in conversation about texts—you read and write, and we provide a series of collaborative exercises where you can benefit from the thoughts and ideas of fellow classmates. Collaboration requires an effort to reach consensus on an issue. *Consensus* is collective agreement or accord—a general concurrence after conversational give-and-take—with necessary acknowledgment of dissenting opinions. Through collaboration, you can benefit from the interactions in a group of people wrestling with a challenging topic or question.

Try this collaborative effort after reading "A Hanging." Form groups of five students and discuss the issue of capital punishment. Using Orwell's essay as a springboard, make a list of the pros and cons of taking the lives of accused criminals in the name of the state. As a group, try to reach consensus: If your group had the power, would it sustain or eliminate capital punishment? One person from each group should report back to the whole class. What is the general feeling of the class about this issue?

After you have heard all the groups' reports, look ahead to "Perspectives on the Death Penalty" in Chapter 15 and write an essay about capital punishment.

Reading Visual Images

"A picture is worth a thousand words." People use this saying not only to indicate the power and impact of a visual image, but also to suggest that words are a liability, that they cannot communicate as well as a single picture can. To sketch a scene verbally, the saying implies, we must use an endless supply of language (a thousand words!) to capture what a real-life scene, a photograph, a drawing, or an illustration can do much more simply through visual appeal.

But there is another way to understand the saying. Pictures without the viewer's use of words to explain, analyze, and interpret the image are pretty much worthless. Visual literacy—that is, the ability to understand and analyze images—depends on making meaning from what you see. When you look at a photograph, a cartoon, an illustration, an advertising promotion, you can't fully understand and appreciate it without language. "What am I seeing?" something in your brain asks. That's an old woman asking for a handout. The sun on that canvas is too bright. There's Snoopy lying on the roof of his doghouse again.

Always try to put thought into words when you read a visual image. Our powers as thinking, word-using human beings give us the ability to take as much as possible from a pictorial representation. A picture may be worth a thousand words—but think of the word *worth* in the adage to mean *valued at* or *deserving of* and you'll understand the point.

Finally, remember that you should view the visual image, like the written selection, as a rhetorical event. Creators of visuals consider the same rhetorical situations and often use the same strategies as creators of written documents. Issues like main idea, supporting details, and organization, to name just a few, always pertain to visual presentations as they do to essays and stories.

Reading a Photograph

Photos often accompany readings, and you want to be sure that you understand them fully. You have to read actively—examine the details, ask yourself questions about what you see, and try to put your responses into language. Accompanying captions can help significantly, so read them carefully.

 TIPS for Reading Photographs

- **Look carefully at the scene and the people or objects in it.** Who are the people in the photograph and what are they doing? Where is the image set? How do the figures interact with each other? What do the people's faces tell you about their physical and emotional state? Is the photo posed or spontaneous?

- **Determine the main point of the picture.** Try to determine the point that the photographer is making. Is the photo taking sides in an argument?

Capturing a scene difficult to put into words? Trying to upset you, make you happy, push you to action? Some photographs can excite the imagination and produce strong sentiment: the planting of the American flag on Iwo Jima in World War II, for example, the astronaut walk on the moon, the devastating pictures of men and women newly released from Nazi concentration camps.

■ **Read the caption.**   Many photographs include captions that identify the people and (or) the scene. Be sure to connect the caption with the photograph. What information does it provide? What information is missing from the caption? How can you explain the information that is missing?

■ **Consider the photograph in its context.**   Many photographs will accompany essays and articles in periodicals and books. What does the photograph contribute to the written selection? Why has the writer or publisher chosen to include it?

■ **Evaluate the technique of the photographer.**   Is the photo a close-up or taken from a distance? Is the photo in color or black and white? What angle has the photographer used: Is she looking up or down at some object?

Examining a Photo

Look at this picture. In a sentence explain the point of the picture— that is, what you think the picture is about.

You probably said something like, "A young person is carrying three cats in a large plastic container." But certainly there is more to the photograph than that, and only careful observation can help you flesh out other important information. The person is stepping through water with shoes and socks on: that implies some kind of urgent departure, perhaps the result of a flood or a hurricane. Trees immersed in water support that observation. The expression on the person's face is one of worry, even fear; and although you might identify the person as a young male,

Photo Courtesy: Chris Graythen/Getty Images News/Getty Images

there is little evidence in the photograph about the gender of the person. The writing on the T-shirt suggests other key elements, or at least helps you raise other questions. Is the word "Jesuit" merely a T-shirt decoration? Or does the word imply a religious or charitable commitment that might explain an apparently selfless act of animal rescue in a dangerous situation?

If this photograph accompanied some text, you might expect to find answers to these questions in the language of the selection. In any case, looking carefully at the visual will help you extract meanings you might have missed and, through your active engagement with the photograph, will contribute to your growth as a critical reader.

Reading Advertisements

In a world bombarded by media imagery and dedicated to consumerism, product advertisements have a powerful hold on society. Radio, television, movies, the Internet, newspapers, magazines, billboards—all these attractions offer a range of advertising possibilities for anyone with a message and willing to pay in order to share it with an audience. As an aware citizen-consumer, you should pay careful attention to the advertisements swirling around us.

Advertisers use images and words to persuade us to buy a product, admire a company, or support a point of view on an issue, among many other intentions. The ads themselves are rhetorical situations with the same kinds of goals that you find in an essay. Read advertisements in the same way that you read a page of print, trying to determine the main idea, purpose, point of view, supporting details, unity, coherence, and word choice.

 **TIPS** for Reading Advertisements

- **Examine the components of the advertisement.**   Identify the people and the setting. Are the people you see young or old? Is the setting indoors or outdoors? Is the object real or exaggerated? Why has the advertiser decided to use these elements?

- **Read the words in the advertisement carefully.**   You want to understand the language of the advertisement, of course, but you want to think about the word choice as well. How do the words interact with the visual elements? In the famous "Got milk?" ads with celebrities, for example, why does the advertiser say "Got" instead of "Do you have"? "Got milk" sticks in the mind. The word *got* is more colloquial, more a word of the people, so to speak, and the ad by its familiar idiomatic language intends to draw you into its world of famous people who always have milk available. You're in good company!

■ **Determine what the advertisement intends for you to do.**   Like the writers of argumentative essays (see Chapter 15), the creators of advertisements want to convince you of something. They also want you to take an action—buy this product, join this association, vote for this candidate. If you think carefully about what a flashy ad wants you to do, you can decide intelligently whether or not you ought to do it.

■ **Identify the elements that the advertisement uses to convince you.** Does it appeal to your emotions, fears, goals, dreams, or desires? For example, is the testimony of a famous person enough to convince you to buy a product? Is the ad trying to make you feel famous and important if you buy the product or take the suggested action? Is the ad in black and white when it could be in color? Black and white suggests a seriousness of purpose and a conservative bent.

■ **Consider the medium in which the advertisement appears.**   Advertisers choose their media very carefully, and an ad says as much about the people going to view it as it does about the product being advertised. Television and Internet advertising can draw on multiple techniques for a lively presentation designed to get you to do something, and these ads target audiences carefully. Ads during the Super Bowl are among the most popular, but they rarely appear on other shows. Beer makers in particular advertise during sports broadcasts: men watch sports, men are well-known beer drinkers, hence, the lively ads by Coors and Miller and Budweiser. Magazines and newspapers have fewer dazzling techniques available to them, yet print advertisers have a clear picture of whom they expect to read a particular periodical. The ads that you find in *Rolling Stone*, for example, rarely are the same as those in *Vanity Fair*. By reading certain magazines and newspapers, you become part of the audience the advertisers are aiming for.

■ **Raise questions about the advertisement and try to answer them.**   For example, ask yourself :

   ■ What is the main point of the advertisement?

   ■ Why was this advertisement created? What is its purpose?

   ■ What does it want me to do? Do I want to do what the ad is directing me toward? Do I need the product being advertised?

   ■ Why does this ad appear in this particular medium?

   ■ Whom is the ad aimed at?

   ■ What particular features of the ad are most compelling?

   ■ Why has the advertiser used the particular images that appear?

Examining an Advertisement

Look at the automobile advertisement below and, using the Tips for Reading Advertisements, analyze the ad and then answer the questions.

Why Is This Car Smiling?

Because it's an EPA SmartWay Certified vehicle. It's fuel-efficient,
produces fewer greenhouse gases and can save you money.
And that's enough to make anyone smile.

Find more reasons to smile at:

epa.gov/smartway/vehiclepsa

Courtesy of the EPA.

FOR WRITING OR DISCUSSION

1. What is the main point of this advertisement?

2. Who is the EPA? Why doesn't the advertisement spell out the name for which EPA is an abbreviation? Some people won't know what EPA stands for. Why has the advertiser risked producing an ad that not all readers will understand?

3. Why has the advertiser used this green color for the automobile in the ad? Why is there no brand label on the auto? Is it a Chevrolet, BMW, Volkswagen, or Cadillac—or doesn't it matter? Why or why not?

4. Whom does the ad expect to be smiling because of the smiling auto? Are you one of those people? Why or why not?

5. The ad obviously is boasting about good environmental conditions associated with an "EPA SmartWay Certified vehicle." What is the

purpose in using a made-up word like *SmartWay*? What does the URL (the Uniform Resource Locator) for the Web site accomplish in the ad?

6. *Details*, an American monthly men's magazine published by Condé Nast since 1982, is primarily a magazine devoted to fashion and lifestyle for young men. Why would the advertisers place this ad in such a magazine? In what other magazines might you expect to see this advertisement? Explain your answer.

7. Would you think of buying an "EPA SmartWay Certified vehicle"? Why or why not? Write an essay in which you analyze the advertisement and explain its appeal—or lack of appeal—to you or other consumers.

EXERCISE

Trace the elements of a long-term advertising campaign, such as the campaign for milk ("Got milk?"), diamonds ("A diamond is forever"), insurance (Geico's Gekko), Camel cigarettes (Joe Camel), cereal (Tony the Tiger), or some other campaign that has caught your eye over the years. Follow the guidelines on pages 17–18 to analyze the visual image you have chosen.

1. What does the campaign mean? Describe it and analyze it. What message is the advertiser attempting to convey?
2. Report on the total image as well as its parts. How do the parts of the image relate to the message the ad is attempting to convey?
3. What is the purpose of the advertising campaign—other than simply to get you to buy the product? What techniques has the creator of the image used? To whom is the campaign targeted? How do the words in the ads support the purpose and intended audience?

COLLABORATIVE LEARNING

Brainstorm in groups about the role of advertisements in our lives. Ask members of your group to share positive and negative views of advertising. What is the general consensus in each group: Have ads had an unquestionably positive or negative impact on our lives? After one person from each group reports to the full class, write a paper in which you explore the effects of advertisements in your life.

Reading Graphs, Tables, and Charts

To support their positions on a variety of topics across the disciplines, academic writers are making increasing use of visuals. As a reader, you need to pay close attention to visuals embedded in written texts since they often strengthen the writer's position.

TIPS for Reading Graphs, Tables, and Charts

- **Read the title, captions, and labels carefully.** To understand the meaning of numbers presented visually, you have to examine the surrounding language. Tables always include column headings. Graphs will often provide labels at key points in the visual presentation.

- **Turn the relations among the numbers into language.** Graphs, tables, and charts require interpretation, and the only way that you can understand their meanings is to apply your active reading skills. Why is one bar or part of a circle on a graph larger than another? What does that information tell you about other visual representations? How do the entries on a table compare and contrast with each other?

- **Consider why the writer included the graph, table, or chart.** In what ways does the visual representation support the essay or article that you're reading? Why has the writer chosen to include the graph or table in her presentation?

- **Be sure that you understand any symbols used in a graph.** Graphs sometimes include an explanation of the features used to represent the numbers. Check to see if there is a legend—that is, a key to explain the shapes or colors—on the graph, and use the information to interpret what the graph presents.

- **Be sure that you recognize the true value of the numbers.** As you will see on the graph estimating numbers of aliens, the numbers on the graph itself range from 3.5 to 12. But the word "Millions" at the bottom of the graph tells a different story. The number 12 means *12 million*; the number 3.5 means *3.5 million*. Be sure to check on the numerical indicators before you reach any conclusions about what the graph or table is saying.

A writer explaining the inconsistencies in estimating the number of illegal aliens in the United States, for example, would have to provide written evidence. But think about the added impact of the chart on the next page that the writer could insert into the essay.

Note how the graph and the table beneath it put important data in visual and verbal form. The horizontal bars show readers the relations among the various estimates of illegal aliens in our country; the labels to the left of the bars identify the various organizations providing these estimates; and the numbers to the right of the bars indicate the millions of people in each estimate. The table lists in declining order the cities with the largest illegal alien populations and provides the estimated numbers of aliens in each city.

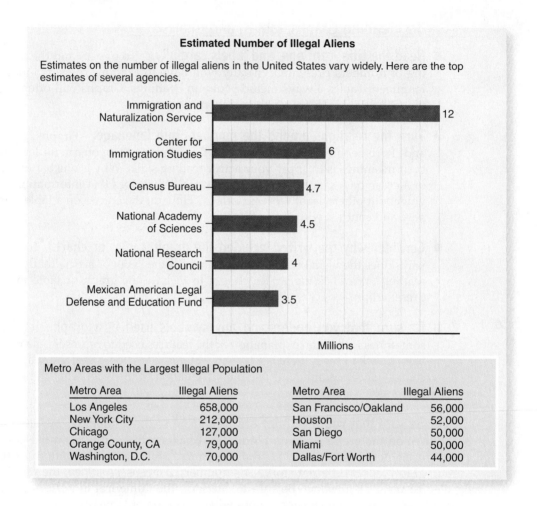

Estimated Number of Illegal Aliens

Estimates on the number of illegal aliens in the United States vary widely. Here are the top estimates of several agencies.

Agency	Millions
Immigration and Naturalization Service	12
Center for Immigration Studies	6
Census Bureau	4.7
National Academy of Sciences	4.5
National Research Council	4
Mexican American Legal Defense and Education Fund	3.5

Metro Areas with the Largest Illegal Population

Metro Area	Illegal Aliens	Metro Area	Illegal Aliens
Los Angeles	658,000	San Francisco/Oakland	56,000
New York City	212,000	Houston	52,000
Chicago	127,000	San Diego	50,000
Orange County, CA	79,000	Miami	50,000
Washington, D.C.	70,000	Dallas/Fort Worth	44,000

Reading Cartoons

Cartoons and comics provide amusement on both playful and serious issues. You probably have experience with the Sunday funny papers; comic books about Superman and Spiderman, for example, have added significantly to popular culture; and the Internet provides a range of cartoons on every imaginable subject.

Often called editorial cartoons, the comic drawings you will read in college and beyond often present a serious topic in a humorous fashion so that you see the ironies or absurdities in current issues—most often political, but also social and cultural. Cartoonists always expect you to come away from their drawings and captions with a fresh insight on life's realities.

TIPS for Reading Cartoons

- **Identify the figures in the cartoon.** Look at the characters carefully. Are they ordinary people? Celebrities? Politicians? Cartoonists will frequently use **caricature**—distorted or exaggerated drawings—to represent famous people that they expect you to recognize.

- **Read the caption and any other words in the cartoon.** The caption of the cartoon usually delivers the punch line to explain what the illustration is about. Be sure that you understand it and how it relates to the picture. Don't ignore other words that might appear in the picture itself.

- **Develop a thesis from the cartoon.** State the topic and the artist's opinion about it, as if the cartoon were an essay you were reading. As we said earlier in this book, visual representations are just as rhetorical as essays, and you have to consider rhetorical elements as you interpret what you see.

- **Consider the cartoonist's techniques.** Are the pen strokes heavy or light? Are the figures sketchy or full-blown? Are there any small details that contribute to the meaning of the cartoon? You want to think about how the artist's technique contributes to the effectiveness of the illustration.

- **Check the cartoonist on the Internet.** You can Google well-known cartoonists like Roz Chast, who has her own website (www.rozchast.com). Some cartoonists have their own Web sites. Find out what you can about the artist, and examine other drawings she has made. Also, look for political leanings that could influence your understanding of the cartoon.

- **Evaluate the fairness of the presentation.** The artist may have a particular axe to grind; or perhaps she is distorting one side of an argument in order to create more humor or to attack a person or issue. You want to ask yourself if the presentation is fair. Consider the opposite point of view, if possible, for a rounded sense of a complex matter.

Examining Cartoons

Note how the artist uses the editorial cartoon on the following page to appeal to your emotions and to condition your response to the threat of someone driving while using a cellular telephone.

The cartoon makes a humorous point about the serious issue of people who use cell phones when they drive. The artist shows the potential destruction that could result from automobile phone use: Some poor guy watching television

Cartoon by permission of Gary Varvel and Creators Syndicate, Inc.

sees the wall of his house damaged and an automobile in his living room. Instead of using his own phone to call in the car crash to the emergency network, the car driver is so engaged in his telephone use at the moment that he asks the fellow in the chair to make the call! Not even an auto accident compels him to hang up and report the disaster. The larger point here is that cell phone use while driving won't go away quickly because people insist on using their phones despite all dangers, even, as the cartoonist sees it, a car crash. (Read "Thumbs on the Wheel," p. 208, for a serious view of phone use in automobiles.)

Reading Web Sites

The key question for anyone who uses the Internet is how to determine whether a site is reliable and its information valid. Perhaps even more than with conventional print sources, you have to bring sharp powers of observation and evaluation to Web sites in order to find information and determine their dependability. Teachers, librarians, and researchers have suggested a range of items to take into account when you evaluate a Web site. These items focus on currency, reliability, and authority. When you call up a Web site, keep in mind these principles for evaluating it.

 TIPS for Reading and Evaluating Web Sites

- **Don't assume that all information found on the Internet is reliable.** Check to see if the information comes from a dependable source. Look at the URL. For example, Web site addresses that end with abbreviations like

.gov (government body), *.org* (nonprofit organization), and *.edu* (educational body) are often reliable and can serve as good starting points for online research. Many *.com* sites are reliable, but many are not.

■ **Look carefully at the author or sponsor of the Web site.** Check the sponsor's and author's credentials. Identify the author's connection to any organization, lobbying group, or commercial enterprise, or to some association with a political, social, or economic agenda that can influence the site.

■ **Examine visual as well as verbal elements.** Web designers integrate words and graphics, so you need to think about how they interact to give you information.

■ **Read sidebars, banners, and tabs for more information and related links.** These additional elements can help you find further information on the topic. Advertisements on the site can tell you a great deal about the intended users.

■ **Use your prior knowledge as a barometer of the information you find on the site.** The online information should seem consistent with your other reading.

■ **Determine the purpose of the site and its intended audience and point of view.** If these elements are hidden or not easily accessible, treat the site with skepticism.

■ **Look for an indication of the dates the site was prepared and revised.** You want to certify that information is current. Even if the preparation and revision dates seem recent, be sure that the material itself is as well.

■ **Be sure that the site indicates its sources of information.** You want to be able to validate the information at similar sources and assure that facts seem reasonable, reliable, and truthful.

■ **Check the site for an appropriate level of breadth and range.** Unfortunately, superficial approaches to important topics are abundant on Web sites, and you want to be certain that any site you use shows an understanding of the issues' complexity.

■ **Be sure that the site provides adequate evidence to corroborate assertions made.**

Examining a Web Site

Examine the Web site below, paying particular attention to the labels that point to important features of the site. Then, using the "Tips for Reading and Evaluating Web Sites" and the "Strategy Checklist" (page 27), answer the questions below.

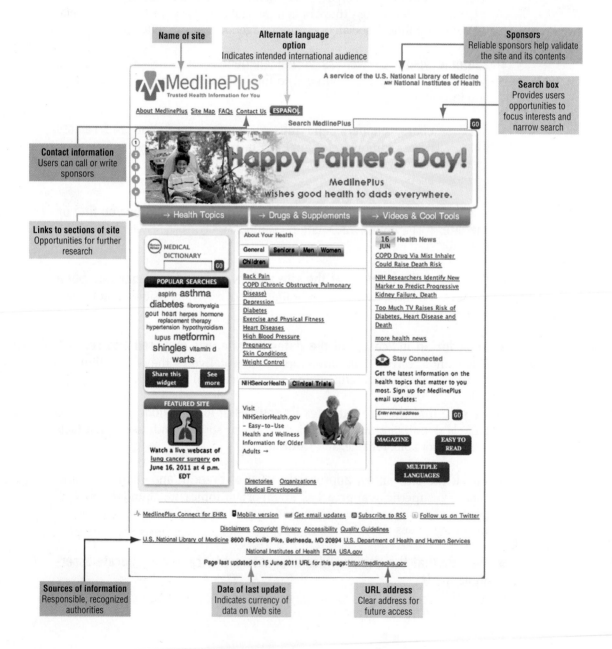

STRATEGY CHECKLIST: Reading and Evaluating Web Sites

Check the Web site address.	☐ What type of site is it—school (.edu), government (.gov), nonprofit (.org), or commercial (.com)?
Check the site sponsor and (or) author.	☐ Who is the sponsor of the site? ☐ Who is the author, if any is named? What are the author's credentials?
Examine the visual and verbal elements of the site.	☐ What does the site say? ☐ What visuals does the site use? ☐ How do visual and verbal elements work together?
Explore the banners, tabs, menus, and other links.	☐ How is the site organized? ☐ What parts does it have? ☐ What links does it have to other Web sites?
Determine the purpose of the site.	☐ What is the intent of the site? ☐ Who is its anticipated audience?
Evaluate the information presented.	☐ Does my prior knowledge of the topic support the information on the site? ☐ Does the site provide evidence for its assertions? ☐ Is the material up to date?

Critical Reading

Read the following selection and, using what you have learned in this chapter, draw on the various skills that will help you understand the piece fully. Take notes as you read. Note the use of visuals and the way that they support the text.

Christopher Caldwell is a senior editor at *The Weekly Standard*. He is a regular contributor to the *Financial Times* and *Slate*. His essays and reviews appear in the *New York Times*, *The Wall Street Journal*, and *The Washington Post*.

Answer the questions after you read.

CHRISTOPHER CALDWELL

Intimate Shopping: Should Everyone Know What You Bought Today?

1   **"Information,"** the apostles of cyberspace have been singing for more than a decade, "wants to be free." Well, maybe *your* information does. But in late November, the social networking Web site Facebook discovered that many of its 58 million members don't feel that way. On social networks, people can exchange photos, letters and information with people they know, and "friend" people they don't. Facebook has grown so big, so rich (its market value is estimated at $15 billion) and so addictive because it offers its users new ways to exchange information and intimacies with people they care about. In early November, Facebook's 23-year-old C.E.O., Mark Zuckerberg, rolled out an advertising program called Beacon. It would track users onto the sites of Facebook's commercial partners—Coca-Cola, the N.B.A., *The New York Times* and Verizon, among others—and keep their friends posted about what they were doing and buying there.

2   Did it ever. A Massachusetts man bought a diamond ring for Christmas for his wife from overstock.com and saw his discounted purchase announced to 720 people in his online network. What if it hadn't been for his wife? What if he had been buying acne cream? Por-

nography? A toupee? You could go on. Researchers at Computer Associates, an information-technology firm, discovered that Beacon was more invasive than announced. MoveOn.org started a petition movement against Beacon that rallied 75,000 Facebook subscribers.

3   Facebook designed Beacon so that members would be able to "opt out" by clicking in a pop-up window. But these windows were hard to see and disappeared very fast. If you weren't quick on the draw, your purchases

Michael Lewis/GalleryStock

were broadcast to the world, or at least to your network. Since people, too, sometimes want to be free, privacy advocates urged that Beacon be made an "opt in" program, which members would have to explicitly consent to join. In early December, Facebook agreed to this approach.

The Beacon fiasco gives a good outline of what future conflicts over the Internet will look like. Whether a system is opt-in or opt-out has an enormous influence on how people use it. He who controls the "default option"—the way a program runs if you don't modify it—writes the rules. Online, it can be tempting to dodge the need to get assent for things that used to require it. This temptation is particularly strong in matters of privacy. For instance, the "default option" of the pre-Internet age was that it was wrong to read others' mail. But Google now skims the letters of its Gmail subscribers, in hopes of better targeting them with ads, and the N.S.A. looks for terrorists not only in the traditional manner—getting warrants for individual wiretaps—but also by mining large telecommunications databases.

So it is with Facebook's Beacon. We used to live in a world where if someone secretly followed you from store to store, recording your purchases, it would be considered impolite and even weird. Today, such an option can be redefined as "default" behavior. The question is: Why would it be? The price in reputation for overturning this part of the social contract is bound to be prohibitively high.

For the owners of social-networking sites, it may be a price worth paying. Thanks to data-collection technology, your shopping choices and preferences have value. Who owns those choices? Common sense says that you do. If a company wants to use you to advertise its products, it can pay you, just as Nike pays Tiger Woods. But the idea that your preferences (not to mention your conversations about them) are your property rests on an implicit social contract. And the thing about implicit contracts is that people who can figure out ways to break them can often make a lot of money.

The concept of "implicit contracts" was developed in a landmark 1988 paper by the economists Andrei Shleifer and Lawrence Summers. Their subject—hostile corporate takeovers—seems far from cyberprivacy, but it is not. Shleifer and Summers showed that increases in share price following takeovers were not due to gains in efficiency, as the defenders of those buyouts claimed. There often were such gains, but they were not the source

NOTHING SACRED?
Percentage of Americans who ...

do not know that charities are allowed to sell their names to other charities without permission.

	72%

do not know that supermarkets are allowed to sell information about purchases to other companies.

	64%

believe that this (false) statement is true: "If a Web site has a privacy policy, it means the site won't share my information with other Web sites and companies".

	75%

Source: Annenberg Public Policy Center, 2005
Chart by Charles M. Blow

4

5

6

7

of the profits. The profits came from reneging on implicit contracts—like the tradition of overpaying older workers who had been overworked when young on the understanding that things would even out later. These contracts, because implicit, were hard to defend in court. But the assets they protected were real. To profit from them, buyout artists had only to put someone in place who could, with a straight face and a clean conscience, say, "I didn't promise nothin'!"

8   As commerce moves from Main Street to the Web, lots of businessmen are in that position. All bets are off, and entrepreneurs are seeking new ways to make money by trial and error. Sometimes they do so by adding value to the economy. Sometimes they do so by abrogating implicit contracts. Like managers newly seated after a hostile takeover a quarter-century ago, today's online innovators are not always skilled at telling the difference: "Your friendships are your own business? Golly, I wasn't here when they negotiated *that*."

9   Beacon was a clumsy attempt to reset the default on the common-sense understanding of discretion and to profit off the resetting. As in the 1980s, technological sophistication, entrepreneurial genius and gains to efficiency are a part of this story—but a larger part was the attempt to monetize and sell a vulnerable implicit contract. Facebook was thwarted, as the corporate raiders of years past were not, because it aimed not at pension plans and seniority-based pay scales but at something considerably more valuable—the unwritten rules of privacy that make civilized human interaction possible.

FOR WRITING OR DISCUSSION

1. What did your prior knowledge contribute to your approach to the selection before reading it? How did the title help? The brief statement about what the essay deals with? The information about the author? The photo? The graph?

2. What is the main point of the selection? State it in your own words.

3. What notes or marginal comments did you write as you read the piece?

4. What was the writer's purpose in writing this piece? Who do you think was his intended reader?

5. How well do the introduction and conclusion serve the selection?

6. What does the photograph add to the selection? The graph? Why did the writer include these visuals with his essay?

STRATEGY CHECKLIST: Reading and Interpreting Visuals

Look at the visual as a whole.	☐ What type of visual image is it—photograph, painting, drawing, cartoon, diagram, graph, chart, and so on?
	☐ Where is the setting—a park, an office, a laboratory, or someplace else?
	☐ What is the meaning of the visual?
	☐ What is the purpose of the visual—to inform, to describe, to analyze, or to persuade?
	☐ What rhetorical elements in addition to purpose should I consider—main idea, use of supporting details, organization, argument, point of view, and so on?
Read the caption or other accompanying text.	☐ What does the caption or other text say?
	☐ How does the text help me interpret the meaning and purpose of the visual?
	☐ What information is missing from the caption or text?
	☐ If the visual illustrates a reading selection, why did the writer include it? How does it help explain the reading?
Examine the different parts of the visual.	☐ What are the different parts of the visual—people, things, places, data?
	☐ What are the relations among the different parts?
	☐ If there are people, what are they doing? What do their gestures and expressions tell me?
	☐ How do these parts contribute to the meaning of the visual?
Consider the techniques used by the creator of the visual.	☐ Is the subject close or far away?
	☐ Is the scene natural or staged?
	☐ Are any elements exaggerated to produce an effect?
	☐ Is the visual a single image or a composite?
Evaluate the effectiveness of the visual.	☐ Does the visual accomplish its purpose?
	☐ Do words and images work well together?

For support in meeting this chapter's objectives, follow this path in MyCompLab: Resources ⇒ **Writing** ⇒ **Writing and Visuals.** Review the Instruction and Multimedia resources about **visual rhetoric;** then complete the Exercises and click on Gradebook to measure your progress.

CHAPTER 2

Active Writing

In this chapter you will

- limit a topic to a manageable range
- narrow a broad topic in stages
- determine your purpose and audience
- use prewriting to develop your paper
- analyze a student's first draft of an essay

In this chapter we will explore methods of getting started that many writers find extremely helpful when they have to produce a piece of work. And the first step for every writer is limiting the topic to a reasonable degree so that the task is not overwhelming and is possible to achieve, given the resources of time, word limitations, and available information.

Choosing a Good Topic

Choosing a subject isn't usually a big problem. If you choose to write about something on your own, you do so because you are interested in it and you want to share your thoughts with others. If you don't actually choose to write but are told to do so, your instructor will usually give you a general subject. For example, your history professor probably won't tell you simply to write a paper; he will assign a paper on the effects of Islamic culture on the Western world. Even when your assignment is an essay based on a personal experience, your instructor will give you a general subject: a memorable journey, an influential person, a goal, a hobby, a favorite magazine or newspaper.

Setting Limits on a Topic

Most subjects need to be limited, and that can create a problem. You need to decide what part of the subject you will write about. Consider the assignment about the effects of Islamic culture on the Western world. The topic is vast, and so you must limit it. Prewriting efforts (see pages 36–38) can help you identify one or two groups of ideas or facts that dominate your early thinking. You could choose one of them as your limited subject.

You can let your special interests determine how you limit the subject. If, for example, you have a good understanding of architecture, you may decide to explain how Islamic culture contributed to modern architecture by exploring geometric forms. Or you might write about the influence on modern sculpture of geometric form as design. If you're a nursing or pre-med student, you could trace the contributions of the Islamic world to medical science. If you're interested in politics, you might discuss the effects on early Islamic cultures of the lack of a centralized government, comparing these cultures with others of the same period. Your interests could lead to other subjects—from military strategies to love poems—and still fulfill the assignment. Any subject, then, can and must be limited before you begin to write, and your personal interests can often determine the way you limit it.

Much of the writing you will do for your college courses, in a wide range of disciplines, will require research. In Chapter 21 you'll learn how to use sources appropriately. You know how to use a few citation systems so that you can adapt your writing and documentation to your teacher's instructions. But remember, all good writing and all good research must begin with a limited topic.

Narrowing a Topic in Stages

Some writers find it useful to narrow a broad topic to a manageable one through a series of three or four steps, each step contracting the topic a little more. By moving from a general topic to more and more specific ones, the writer can shape the subject to suit her interests and meet the requirements of the assignment.

Suppose you wanted to write about the topic *crime in America*. Clearly the topic is too broad. Note how the writer moved progressively to more specific subject matter.

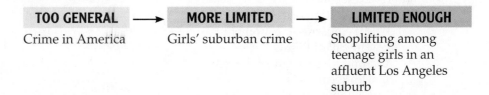

TOO GENERAL →	**MORE LIMITED** →	**LIMITED ENOUGH**
Crime in America	Girls' suburban crime	Shoplifting among teenage girls in an affluent Los Angeles suburb

The topic *crime in America* is much too general to address in an essay; even an expert on crime would have trouble writing an entire book about the topic as stated. The student narrowed the topic further by limiting the issue of crime to crimes committed in the suburbs by girls. That still is too general and raises many questions that the student writer must address before settling on the topic—what age group of girls, what kinds of crimes, in which suburbs? Finally, the writer produced a controllable topic that she could address to meet the terms of her assignment in the time allotted to her for writing. She could produce an essay that dealt effectively with teenage shoplifters in a prosperous Los Angeles suburb. The limited topic allows her to proceed efficiently.

In the following examples you can see how student writers limited their topics in stages.

TOO GENERAL →	MORE LIMITED →	LIMITED ENOUGH
Sports	High school football	What makes a good high school football coach
Women's fashions	New trends in women's fashions	Body decorations—body paint, body jewelry, removable tattoos—in women rock stars
Politics	The policies of the Democratic Party	Why I am a Democrat
Concerts	Promoting concerts	Promoting "nostalgia" concerts to the over-thirty set

EXERCISE   Limit the following broad topics, drawn from a wide variety of college courses.

Example

Broad topic	More limited	Still more limited
The Middle East	Democracy movements in the Middle East	The role of social media in Egypt's pro-democracy revolution in 2011

1. Rock concerts
2. Modern American painters
3. An embarrassing moment
4. The Bill of Rights
5. America's role in Afghanistan
6. Deadbeat dads
7. Olympic games
8. Women's magazines
9. Domestic violence
10. Teenage rock stars

Determining Your Purpose and Audience

Once you've limited your subject, you need to set your purpose and determine what audience you will write for, and doing so involves some related choices.

What Is Your Purpose? You must decide how you will treat your limited subject—that is, being clear about your purpose in writing. What will you do with it? Writing about your summer vacation, will you explain a process—for example, how to pitch a tent? Will you compare two campsites? Will you report an event—what happened when you unwittingly pitched your tent in a cow pasture? Will you argue that one can have an enjoyable yet inexpensive vacation by camping in state parks?

Each of these approaches will help you determine what to include and what to leave out of your essay, and each will produce a different paper.

Who Is Your Audience? You also must determine what kind of reader you are writing for. The answer to that question will affect the style and content of your paper, because the words a writer chooses and the facts a writer selects are largely determined by the audience, the people who will read the material.

In a paper about pitching a tent, just imagine how different the paper would look if you wrote it for Cub Scouts planning to sleep in the backyard, troopers training in unfamiliar terrain, sporting goods sales clerks who have to explain a new product to potential buyers, or out-of-shape senior citizens camping for the first time.

You may now be thinking that any discussion of audience is pointless because you know who your reader is—your English professor. In one sense, that's true, of course. But you'll write better papers if, instead of thinking of your English professor every time you begin to write, you imagine other specific kinds of readers. Define a reader. Are you writing for a group of experts on your subject? For your classmates? For the president of your company? For readers of the editorial page of the morning paper? Defining the reader not only helps you decide the style and exact content of your paper, but also makes for livelier reading.

Your treatment of the subject and your sense of the audience help determine the purpose of your paper. And the purpose controls the style and content of the paper—its organization, its facts, its diction, its tone.

EXERCISE   For each topic listed here, indicate the purposes a writer might have for writing about it. Look at the example. You may wish to limit the topic first.

Example

Topic: Teenage drivers

Possible purposes
1. To describe a harrowing drive with "wild man Bob," my sixteen-year-old cousin.
2. To explain how teenagers can save money on driving costs by following a few simple steps.
3. To compare and contrast male and female teenage drivers.
4. To classify types of sports car drivers I've observed in my job as a gas station attendant.

5. To argue in favor of allowing fourteen-year-olds to drive under special circumstances.
6. To convince teenagers of the dangers of drinking and driving.

Topics

1. Charities
2. Personal finance
3. Job hunting
4. Fever
5. Drug testing for athletes

COLLABORATIVE LEARNING

Divide the class into three groups and examine the topic and audience sets below. Beside each topic is a list of possible audiences a writer could address. What demands do you think each audience would make on the writer? What different issues would the writer have to address for each audience?

Topic	Possible audience
1. Relaxation techniques	a. Sixth graders in an inner-city public school
	b. High-pressured business executives
	c. Recovering heart attack patients
2. Baking chocolate chip cookies	a. Students at a training school for chefs
	b. First-time homemakers
	c. Kindergarteners
3. The advantages of swimming in improving fitness	a. Home swimming pool manufacturers
	b. Physical therapists
	c. Overweight, sedentary college students

Prewriting

Experienced writers use many strategies to limber up, so to speak, well before they start producing the connected sentences and paragraphs that make up a first draft. The label for these warm-up activities—**prewriting**—is a useful term: the prefix *pre-* reminds you that you have a good deal to do in advance of writing your paper. Many inexperienced writers fail because they leap too soon into producing their papers and do not take enough time with the various steps.

By practicing prewriting strategies—thinking and talking about your ideas, free association, list-making, brainstorming, keeping a journal, reporters' questions, subject trees or maps—you'll uncover a surprising number of possibilities for your topic. For example, if you're trying to get started on a paper about your summer vacation topic, your prewriting exercises might stimulate memories of dancing all night and then going for a swim at sunrise, or the day your old Toyota broke down on a muddy road, or eating your first fiery salsa, or meeting a village character, or watching the sun set over the ocean, or sleeping out under the stars. Any one of these memories could make a good paper.

Before committing to a topic, always return to your warm-up activities and examine them. You may see that one or two groups of ideas or facts dominate your thinking—that is, you may have jotted down more points about, say, the town oddball you met than about any other highlight of your vacation. In that case, your topic choice should be clear: Write about the village character. If you discover that you have a number of limited subjects you could write about, settle on one so that you can get on with writing the paper.

Use the strategies described in the "Strategy Checklist: Prewriting" to get started on ideas for your essay.

STRATEGY CHECKLIST: Prewriting

Discuss your ideas.	☐ What can I tell others about my topic? ☐ What ideas do my friends and family have?
Explore your topics on the Internet.	☐ What information can I find about my topic? ☐ How credible is the information I've found (see the "Strategy Checklist" on page 27)? ☐ What ideas have I found that might be useful?
Browse the library.	☐ Have I checked the online catalog? ☐ Have I checked the online database indexes? ☐ What kinds of books and articles are people writing about my topic? ☐ What issues have other people identified?

Free associate.	☐ Have I written nonstop for 15 or 20 minutes?
	☐ Have I come up with ideas worth pursuing?

Make a list.	☐ Have I compiled an informal list of ideas about my topic?

Brainstorm some questions.	☐ Have I raised questions about my topic?
	☐ Have I used the reporter's questions—who, what, where, when, why, and how—to stimulate my thinking?

Sketch or diagram your topic.	☐ Have I used a visual strategy on my topic?
	☐ Have I sketched a subject map or subject tree (see page 41)?

Keep a journal.	☐ Do I have a notebook or file for informal writing?
	☐ Have I used the journal to help me develop ideas?

Organizing Ideas

Try to organize your thinking somewhat. You've identified and limited your topic, and you have considered your *audience* and *purpose*. Now, as you zero in on your central idea (Chapter 3 deals with the all-important thesis statement), look at your written thoughts and eliminate any that seem off target. Cluster the thoughts that seem to go together. You might even try a rough outline of main topics as headings and subtopics numbered beneath them. Or you might draw arrows and make circles to join related ideas, or use scissors and paste to lay connected impressions near each other.

Writing with a computer enables you to move words, sentences, and paragraphs and to keep at hand many versions of your efforts. You can refer to often, and perhaps even salvage, thoughts you may have rejected.

Your attempts at grouping related material are important because they can help you develop an outline (Chapter 4), a key organizing strategy for many writers. Outlining is especially important when you deal with complex topics or with lots of research materials. Like a road map, your outline can help you find your way through new territory.

Bear in mind that the prewriting activities described here are not rigid prescriptions. They vary from writer to writer, and they do not necessarily follow each other in an exact sequence. Prewriting is a loosely defined process that you should adapt freely to your own needs as a writer and to the elements of the writing task at hand.

Writing Drafts

Here are some suggestions for writing a rough draft.

 **TIPS** for Writing a Rough Draft

- **Use your prewriting.** To begin the all-important drafting stage, use your prewriting. Read over your ideas on paper and your efforts at grouping your thoughts.

- **Write a first draft.** Then, without worrying about spelling, grammar, or punctuation, try to get your ideas down. Remember that you're only exploring here; you're not aiming for perfection. Your first draft is a rough copy that you will revisit later to make changes, additions, and deletions. Delete words and phrases that are dead ends. Insert new thoughts. Don't worry here about being neat or correct. Your goal at this stage is to write clear, connected sentences that address your topic. Your first draft may look like a finished copy when you print it out. But don't let a neat, clean page lull you into thinking that you've finished working!

- **Remember and obey two key words:** *Save* and *print*. Don't leave your computer without saving what you've written and printing it out. As you revise, you may want to use parts of your prior efforts.

- **Show it around.** Once you've produced a draft, show it to a friend, your roommate, or another member of your writing class. Drawing on peer review (see pages 113–116) can provide very useful guidance from fellow writers in your class. Sometimes your instructor will read and comment on an early draft to help you think about possible approaches to your next draft.

- **Revise.** Use the comments made on your papers to help you think about your revision and create your next draft. (Look ahead to Chapter 6.) You don't have to follow all the recommendations you receive or answer all the questions raised—but you must consider them.

- **Write more drafts.** As you revise your paper, developing intermediate drafts, you want to change any sentences that are off base, add necessary details to support a point, and fix key errors. Don't concentrate on grammatical errors in early drafts; do address these errors as you move closer to a final copy.

- **Use word processing features carefully.** Computers do have limitations. A spell checker wouldn't detect omitted words or incorrectly used but correctly spelled words, for instance.

One Student Writing: First Draft

In this chapter and in Chapter 6, you'll see how one student, John Fousek, went about limiting a subject and developing and revising a paper. Having been told to write a short paper on the topic "a friend," John did lots of advance thinking before he wrote. To explore his thoughts, he made a subject map about the topic (see page 41). As he considered this preliminary effort, he finally chose to write about his roommate, Jim, and began jotting down impressions on the computer about him. Because he knew his roommate well, however, John soon found that he would have too much material for a short paper and would have to limit his subject to one of Jim's characteristics. That was easy to do because John had argued with his roommate that morning and, still annoyed, could readily identify his major interest of the day: his roommate's irritating habits.

Next, John began to make a list of any of those habits that happened to occur to him. He ended up with quite a list:

- doesn't take out garbage
- slams doors on mornings
- leaves toothpaste open on sink
- doesn't tighten cap on shampoo
- uses my printer paper without replacing
- leaves wet towels on bathroom floor
- doesn't rinse dirty dishes
- uses my after-shave lotion
- wears my socks
- doesn't write down telephone messages

- doesn't do his share of cooking
- plays music when I'm studying
- opens bathroom door when I'm showering
- leaves drawers open
- never closes closet door
- never hangs up his coat
- doesn't remove muddy boots
- never empties dishwasher
- reads my e-mail

After studying the list, John saw that he could not develop every point; he had to eliminate some items. He concluded that two of Jim's shortcomings bothered him most: Jim's failure to close things and his failure to dispose of things. He eliminated all items on the list that did not pertain to those two failures and could now group his ideas:

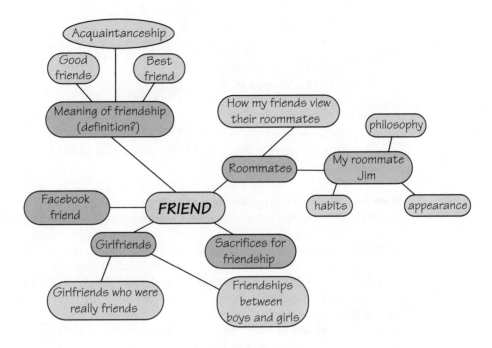

Subject Map

Not closing
- doesn't tighten cap on shampoo
- doesn't close bathroom door
- doesn't close drawers
- doesn't close closet door

Not disposing
- doesn't take out garbage
- leaves wet towels on bathroom floor
- doesn't empty dishwasher
- doesn't rinse dishes

Then John realized that even this limiting left him with too much to cover; finally, he decided to discuss in his paper only his roommate's failure to close things.

As John thought about how to organize his paper, he produced this rough outline:

Intro:
1. how much I like Jim—his personality, sharing, funny, honest
2. what I don't like: never closes things

Drawers

1.   kitchen drawer always messy and left open
2.   bedroom drawers and closets
3.   I'm embarrassed by it all

Bathroom

1.   leaves door open—shower area gets freezing cold
2.   forgets to close shampoo bottle—shampoo spills all over me, much wasted down drain

Note how the informal outline builds on the preceding grouped list titled "Not closing." The rough outline provides a working plan for the first draft of John's essay.

With his outline and prewriting as resources, John was able to arrange his ideas and write a draft of his paper. His first draft appears here.

John's rough draft is a good start. He states a thesis early in the paper. He presents concrete examples to support his irritation with Jim. He seems to have a good grasp of his topic. The paper has a beginning, a middle, and an end, and its ideas are related to each other. Note how John has raised questions for himself in the margins and spaces between lines.

First Draft

John Fousek

my roommate

1   My friend Jim really irritates me with his habbit of ~~not~~ never closing things that he opens up. Don't get me wrong. As roommates for the last couple of years Jim and I get along real well in our small apartment. As students we don't get to see each other a whole lot. We also both work and this cuts down on the time we spend together too. We share

check spelling
has a

responsibilities in the apartment. I clean and Jim cooks. He's generous,

Thesis statement OK?

We had a good relationship over the last two years.

good sense of humor and is honest. But boy his shortcoming of not

s   *its?*

closing things up burn me up. It's a real pain.

2   Jim must be allergic to dishes, he never remembers to rinse the dirty dishes after we eat a meal together. Smears of ketchup and clumps of chile or stew are on the plates after he dumps them in the sink and runs off to a soccer practice or the library. When I get to loading the dishwasher the stuff is impossible to scrape off. Our arrangement is when I load the

dishwasher he's suppose to empty the dishes when they're clean. Fat chance. He always forgets and too many times I've put dirty dishes in with the clean ones before realizing my misteak.

He has other bad habits.

Show what's in drawers

For example never closing a drawer. This embarasses me a lot, I am compulsive about being neat, Jim is a slob. He never thinks of organizing his drawers. He just dumps everything into his drawers and closets. In the kitchen everything is just dumped into the drawers and he's constantly banging silverware before every meal. This is when I'm usually studying and I prefer peace and quite to rattling kitchen items. *because* 3

Jim also often fails to close the bathroom door after using the facilities while I shower. Since the bathroom has become warm and steamy during the couse of my shower, the cold air annoys me, the idea that Jim has been so thoughtless bothers me. *chills* 4

Of course he leaves the kitchen drawers open along with the clothing drawers. Our apartment always looks like a bomb hit it. The appearance irritates my neat soul. I'm embarassed when friends visit us. *If he'd only organize the drawer* *check spelling* *Trite?* *in the first place he* 5

Fix this? Sounds funny

I get even madder at Jim's failure to close things in the bathroom he never closes the shampoo cap. This makes me lose my cool composure more than anything. I always When I'm in the shower I always grab the shampoo bottle by the cap a loose cap results in the agravation of shampoo on my toes instead of my hair. And because I am economically minded, moneywise, watching shampoo go down the drain really bothers me. *one sentence?* *comma?* *check spelling* *wouldn't be bothering me with his noise and* 6

Conclusion too short? Expand?

I try to overlook Jim's bad habbits but when he doesn't close things up especially when I get a cold blast of morning air in the shower it really irritates me. 7

But John's paper still needs revising and editing. John notes in the margin some issues he wants to think about when he revises, but there are many others he'll have to consider. His sentences are sometimes rambling and repetitive, and the writing is much too informal in spots. The ideas should be more smoothly connected, and some of the paragraphs should be joined. You no doubt noted errors in spelling and sentence structure. John must address all these issues as he develops successive drafts.

STRATEGY CHECKLIST: Getting Started with Writing

Choose a topic.	☐ Have I picked a topic that interests me? ☐ Have I started to limit the topic so I can manage it in the space and time I have for the assignment?
Determine purpose and audience.	☐ What is the purpose of my paper? ☐ Who is my audience?
Prewrite.	☐ Have I talked with others, browsed the Internet and library, free associated, made a list, brainstormed questions, sketched or diagrammed my topic, or made journal entries? ☐ Have I developed my ideas and limited my topic further? ☐ Have I organized my prewriting efforts to connect related ideas?
Write a rough draft.	☐ Have I written a rough draft? ☐ Have I ignored spelling, grammar, and punctuation concerns in order to get my ideas down?

EXERCISE   Examine John Fousek's prewriting activities and his first draft and then answer the following questions.

1. How did John's subject map help him limit his topic?
2. How does John's first list (page 40) compare and contrast with his second list (see page 41)? What specific features of the first list has John eliminated in the second? Why has he dropped so many details from the first list?
3. How does John's rough outline build on the list that he prepared, "Not closing"?
4. How does John's rough draft compare with his rough outline?

EXERCISE   Use the prewriting techniques explained on pages 36–38 for one of the following topics that interests you. From these warm-up activities, determine how you would limit the subject.

1. Iron Man
2. The environment
3. Friendship

4. The homeless
5. Television preachers
6. Volunteer work

7. Teenage drivers
8. Cell phones

9. Welfare-to-work programs
10. Being a politician

COLLABORATIVE LEARNING

Bring to class your prewriting efforts developed from the exercise above. Form groups of three students. In each group examine each other's prewriting. Answer the following questions for each student's work:

- In what ways does the prewriting show evidence of uncensored thought on the topic?
- Has the writer used the prewriting strategies to explore the topic effectively? How?
- What recommendations could you make so that the writer could get even better results from the prewriting effort?
- How does the prewriting activity help the writer limit the subject?

 Using your prewriting efforts, develop a first draft of your paper.

 For support in meeting this chapter's objectives, follow this path in MyCompLab: Resources ⇒ Writing ⇒ Writing Process ⇒ Planning. Review the Instruction and Multimedia resources about narrowing a topic, then complete the Exercises and click on Gradebook to measure your progress.

CHAPTER **3**

Finding and Supporting a Thesis

In this chapter you will

- identify the elements of a good thesis

- develop a thesis for your own papers

- analyze the relation between a topic and a thesis

- evaluate strong and weak thesis sentences

- use supporting details to back up a thesis

- analyze student and professional writing for their use of details to support a thesis

To be sure that you have the kind of central idea that will lead to an interesting and unified paper, you must state a thesis, and you must consider how to present appropriate and logical support for it.

A **thesis** is the position a writer takes on an arguable point—one on which more than one opinion is possible. It is the main idea the paper will support. The writer must convince the reader that this position or idea is valid.

Remember that your topic is not your thesis. Instead, your thesis is what you have to say about your topic. It is an opinion about, or an attitude toward, the topic, which you will attempt to support in your essay. It is a one-sentence summary of the idea the writer will defend. Here are two examples:

Topic	Thesis
Graduation requirements	Technical programs should require students to take some courses in the humanities.
Registration	A few simple changes would improve the registration procedure on our campus.

With few exceptions, the papers your instructors will ask you to write in college will benefit enormously from a thesis. A professor of American literature, for example, won't ask you to summarize *Huckleberry Finn*. She wants to know what conclusions you reached after reading the novel: *Mark Twain's* Huckleberry Finn *is an indictment of slavery*, let's say; or *Mark Twain, in* Huckleberry Finn, *criticizes the violence of the pre–Civil War South*. Until you can make that kind of statement, you aren't ready to write effectively because you don't have clearly in mind the point you will make. And if you aren't certain of what your idea is, you stand little chance of convincing a reader of its validity. It's important, therefore, to spend time thinking your idea through before you start writing. This will save time and grief in the long run.

Elements of a Good Thesis

There are several characteristics of a good thesis. When you are writing, you can use these tips to evaluate your thesis statements.

 **TIPS** for Evaluating a Thesis

- **You usually can state a good thesis in one complete sentence.** Even though you may find that you want to devote a paragraph or more to presenting the idea of your paper, until you can state your main idea in one sentence, you may not have it under control.

- **A good thesis almost always appears in the first (or sometimes second) paragraph of a college essay.** Like all good "rules," there are exceptions, and the recommendation that you write your thesis in the first paragraph of your essay is not carved in stone. Some writers won't state a thesis directly, expecting the reader to infer it. Some writers like to build slowly to a thesis and will take more than a couple of paragraphs to get to their main point. But for your own success in writing the many papers you'll have to produce in college, it's a very good idea to state your thesis in a single sentence in the first paragraph. Aim to build an introductory paragraph whose final sentence is your thesis statement.

- **A good thesis avoids stating the obvious.** If you're writing about the dangers of driving while intoxicated, which of these sentences serves as the better thesis, do you think?

  1. People who drink and then drive are dangerous.

  2. People convicted of drunk driving should have their licenses revoked after the first offense.

  Sentence 2 makes the better thesis. It states a topic and offers an opinion about it—and a challengeable one at that. You could argue that sentence 1 states topic and opinion—except that the point is so obvious that a reader could easily turn away in frustration. Sure, people who drive and drink are dangerous, and (although many violators exist, to be sure) everyone knows this as a fact. Your thesis always should avoid stating the obvious.

■ **A good thesis gives an opinion or attitude about the facts.** To say that Brutus stabbed Shakespeare's Julius Caesar on the Ides of March is to state a fact. A thesis, a statement *about* the fact, might read, *Brutus succeeded in killing Caesar on the Ides of March because Caesar had grown too arrogant and proud to protect himself.*

■ **A good thesis is limited.** The idea stated must be one that can be clearly explained, supported, and illustrated in the space called for. A long magazine article might have this as its thesis:

> Although, as a result of a controversial and aggressive promotional campaign, women professional golfers now make more money and receive greater recognition than they did ten years ago, they still do not make as much money, receive as much media coverage, or command as much respect as men professional golfers.

But this won't do for a two- or three-page paper; the writer could not develop the thesis fully in so short a space. A better thesis for a short paper might read, *The promotional campaign for the Women's Professional Golf Association has attracted money and attention for professional female golfers.* An even better thesis would be, *The promotional campaign for the Women's Professional Golf Association will offend members and fans who oppose commercialism in women's athletics.*

■ **A good thesis is appropriately focused.** Consider this thesis: *The reports in* Time *are entertaining and informative, but* Time *slants its reports to suit its political bias, and the vocabulary used by* Time *requires constant trips to the dictionary.* This thesis says three things about *Time*: the magazine's reports are entertaining and informative; the reports are slanted; the vocabulary of *Time* requires constant use of the dictionary. A writer who begins with such a thesis runs the risk of writing a three-part paper that has no central focus. The point of emphasis is not clear. To emphasize that the magazine's reports are entertaining and informative, the writer must subordinate the other points to that idea:

> Although the vocabulary used in *Time* requires constant trips to the dictionary and the reports are often slanted to suit a political bias, the reports are entertaining and informative.

To emphasize the shortcomings of the magazine, the writer should subordinate the entertaining and informative nature of the reports:

> Although the reports in *Time* are entertaining and informative, their vocabulary makes them hard to read, and the material is often slanted to suit a political bias.

■ **A good thesis is precise.** It lets the reader and the writer know exactly what the paper will contain. Words such as *good, interesting, impressive,* and *many* are too vague to do the job. They say nothing about the subject:

What is interesting or good to one person may appear dull or offensive to another. Don't say, "Agatha Christie's detective stories are good." Say, instead, "Agatha Christie's detective stories appeal to those who enjoy solving puzzles." Don't say, "My history class is interesting." Say, "My professor makes history easy to understand."

Stating Your Thesis

Rules for a good thesis are one thing; applying them is another. These tips will help you arrive at that perfectly stated thesis.

 **TIPS** for Developing a Thesis

- **Answer a question.** Sometimes, especially in essay examinations, the thesis statement is suggested by the question. Often, all you have to do is think of a one-sentence answer to the question, and you have your thesis statement.

Example question:	What is job enrichment? Is job enrichment an attempt by management to exploit workers?
Sample thesis statement:	Job enrichment, an effort to increase productivity by making the job more attractive, is an attempt by management to exploit laborers by motivating them to work harder.

In this thesis statement, the writer has both defined *job enrichment* and stated an opinion about the practice. The rest of the essay will give the reasons job enrichment, in this writer's opinion, is an attempt to exploit laborers.

- **Think about your subject.** Frequently, you have to work with a large-scale subject. As you know, it is up to you to limit the subject and decide what point you want to make about it (see pages 33–34). On some subjects–subsidizing college athletics, for example—you may already have a s' opinion. If you have information to back up that opinion, you hav lem. Just state your opinion and then begin thinking about ho it up. On other subjects, though, you may at first think yc Yet you might, for example, remember from history cl past outdistanced the United States in the production television sets to automobiles. Go to the library and the In on the subject. You may then form the opinion that one rea a major industrial power is that the economy had not, since the end of World War II, had to support a military machine. Now you have a thesis.

■ **Review your prewriting activities.** A valuable way to produce a thesis statement is to review your prewriting activities—free association, brainstorming, lists, and subject maps (see Chapter 2)—with an eye toward a central issue that may be brewing somewhere in your early, unedited thinking on a topic. Suppose that you're considering a paper on the subject of children's toys. It's near holiday time, you're a parent, and you've been giving lots of thought to toys lately. You've used free association to jot down anything that comes to mind on the topic. Your list might look like this:

Topic: Toys

1. Expense of toys

2. Shoddy construction: plastic parts don't fit together

3. Focus on violence: guns, destructive images

4. Too many batteries required

5. Sexist toys

6. Difficulty in putting together the parts of toys

7. Unclear, misleading assembly instructions

Considering your list, you note that three items (6, 7, and part of 2) relate to your frustrations with toy assembly. Putting together that kiddie gym really irritated you, didn't it? The more you think about that experience and others like it, the more you realize that item 7 on your list is the heart of the matter. The reason assembling toys is so difficult is that the instructions are unclear and misleading. There's your thesis statement: *Instructions accompanying disassembled toys are misleading.*

Here is the important message: *You must have a thesis statement clearly in mind as you plan the rest of the paper.*

It should be obvious by now that a thesis is different from a topic. A topic is simply the subject of your paper, whereas a thesis makes an assertion about the subject. For the topic *toys,* you saw how the writer developed the thesis statement. Having a topic in mind helps you produce a thesis. Merely placing a title at the top of your page to reflect your topic does not mean you have provided a thesis statement.

Thesis Statements: Strong or Weak?

The various topics listed stimulated the thesis statements in the table below. In each case the weak thesis lacks focus and direction and is usually too broad. The successful theses all provide a strong main idea for the writer to pursue in an essay requirement.

Topic	Weak Thesis	Strong Thesis	Explanation
Teenage drinking	A. Teenage drinking is a serious problem.	B. Local colleges have developed success-ful programs that help college freshmen learn to drink responsibly.	A is too broad; who would disagree, making the point too obvious as stated. B prods the reader's interest: a college-supported program for responsible teenage drinking? Really?
Beauty	A. Different people have different views on the meaning of beauty.	B. To me, beauty is not physical, internal, or structural. The most accurate definition of beauty is someone giving encouragement when you are in deep trouble.	Again, A is unchallengeable; why should a reader continue reading what she already knows is true? B, on the other hand, takes an unconventional view of beauty, and readers will want to know why the writer chooses this word to connect to encouragement.
College costs	A. College costs are rising all over the country and straining family budgets.	B. Tuition costs may be fixed, but attentive college students can help strapped families cut other costs in at least six ways.	The reader of thesis B will read on to learn what these cost-cutting steps will be. Thesis A states the obvious and is much too broad to serve in an essay for class. All over the country? Too much!
Describe a place you know	A. Our school cafeteria is an interesting place.	B. At lunch time in our school cafeteria the noise and nonstop activity are enough to give anyone a headache.	"Interesting" is not interesting for a reader. In B, the writer's focus—noise and action—is clear, and his opinion about it is provocative enough to entice readers to continue reading.
Compare the roles of women and men in a society	A. Men and women had different roles and responsibili-ties in nineteenth-century Western society in the United States.	B. Despite obvious differences in their gen-eral roles and responsi-bilities, when it comes to family relations and deal-ing with children, men and women in urban Chinese families have remarkably similar roles.	A tries to narrow the topic (nineteen[t]h century Western society in the United States), but the re[st] thesis statement is to[o] B turns the obvi[ous] similar resp[onse] families?[—] attention. B will not deal

EXERCISE   Look at the thesis sentences below. What is the topic of each? What is the writer's main point—what does the writer want to say about the topic? How do you think each writer will go about supporting the thesis?

1. The costs of prescription drugs have skyrocketed, creating problems for consumers of all ages.
2. People use the label "terrorist" indiscriminately and therefore make unfair judgments based on race, color, or religion.
3. Some parents will do, say, or pay anything to get their children into the "right" nursery school.
4. Innovation in American automobile manufacturers has taken a back seat to advances by foreign competitors.
5. Through a variety of creative programs and police vigilance, it is possible to cut down dramatically on drunk driving among teens.

EXERCISE   Consider the topics indicated below and write a thesis statement that the writer could develop successfully into an essay.

1. Steps to take in improving your vocabulary
2. Adding years to a person's life through proper exercise and nutrition
3. The pleasures and pains of rearing a child
4. The value of work-study programs in high school
5. Why texting has become a central activity in teenage life

EXERCISE   Look at the topics in the exercise on page 35. What thesis could you develop about each of them?

EXERCISE   Determine which of the following items are thesis statements and which are not. Also determine which thesis statements are too general or too lacking in unity to make a good paper. How does each statement meet the specifications for a thesis, as explained on pages 47–49? Revise the unacceptable thesis statements accordingly.

1. In a weak economy, employers do not hire quality workers.
2. Teenage drivers are a menace!
3. Americans are saving less and less money each year.
4. Curtailing drug use begins with education.
5. Readers now can download from their home computers many complete texts, including short stories, novels, and works of nonfiction.

RCISE   Return to the exercise on page 34. For any five topics you limited there, develop thesis statements that could be used successfully in a paper.

Supporting Your Thesis: Details

Once you've stated your thesis clearly, you need to consider how you will support it. The best way to convince a reader that your idea is worth considering is to offer details that back up your point and to present these details logically.

Chapter 15 presents the important topic of logic, and you no doubt will examine it fully later on. Here, it is important to know that logic involves the relation between the particulars and generalities as you present them in your paper. Logic is the process of reasoning inherent in your writing, and all readers expect a kind of clarity and intelligence that make the points and arguments understandable and easy to follow. Logical writing avoids what we call *fallacies*—that is, false notions, ideas founded on incorrect perceptions. We'll consider logic and logical fallacies in greater depth later in your course.

Using Sensory Details

In presenting details to support your point, you have many options. If you're drawing on your own personal experience, you can *provide examples* that illustrate your point. Examples drawn from experience rarely prove anything; however, they point out why you've made the generalization put forth in your thesis. When you use personal experiences to support a thesis, you should rely on **concrete sensory details**—colors, actions, sounds, smells, images of taste and touch. Details rooted in the senses make what you've experienced come alive for the reader. If you are narrating an event or describing a scene, concrete imagery will help your readers see things your way. Thus, if you're writing about the misleading instructions for assembling toys, you might show your frustration by describing your efforts to put together the offending kiddie gym—the hunt for an orange plastic tube, the pungent smell of epoxy glue, the rough silver hooks that don't fit the holes made for them, and the diagram labeled in Japanese characters and no English words. George Orwell's "A Hanging" is a brilliant example of how concrete sensory details can support a thesis. You read Orwell's essay on pages 11–14. In the paragraph repeated below, note the rich imagery that the writer creates through sensory detail:

> One prisoner had been brought out of his cell. He was a Hindu, a puny wisp of a man, with a shaven head and vague liquid eyes. He had a thick, sprouting moustache, absurdly too big for his body, rather like the moustache of a comic man on the films. Six tall Indian warders were guarding him and getting him ready for the gallows. Two of them stood by with rifles with fixed bayonets, while the others handcuffed him, passed a chain through his handcuffs and fixed it to their belts, and lashed his arms tight to his sides. They crowded very close about him, with their hands always on him in a careful, caressing grip, as though all the while feeling him to make sure he was there. It was like men handling

a fish which is still alive and may jump back into the water. But he stood quite unresisting, yielding his arms limply to the ropes, as though he hardly noticed what was happening.

Using Data: Statistics, Cases, and Expert Testimony

Other kinds of supporting details draw on **data**—statistics and cases that demonstrate a point. For example, if your thesis is *Driver education courses have had a dramatic effect on improving the car safety record of young teenagers*, you'd need to cite comparative data of teens who took the course and those who didn't. You also would need to show the decrease, let us say, in speeding violations, drunk driving, and fatal accidents. Your analysis of the data would help readers see how you interpret the details. You might focus on a particularly illuminating case— the record of a young driver, say, before and after a driver's education course.

In supporting your thesis, you also might want to present expert testimony as supporting details. **Expert testimony** means the words and ideas of respected thinkers on your subject. Depending on your topic, you'll find an array of experts, thoughtful researchers, and other authorities who have considered the same issue and who have shared their observations in a variety of sources. Thus, the books and magazines you read, the films and television programs you watch, the Web sites you visit, the radio stations you listen to, and the lectures and recitations in which you participate at school are all rich sources for details in an essay. For that thesis on assembling toys at home, for example, you might cite a Taiwanese manufacturer whom you saw on a business news film clip on the Public Broadcasting System and who talked about the problems in producing clear instructions for home toy assembly. You'd certainly want to quote from one or more sets of instructions to highlight their inadequacies. Perhaps an article in your local paper reported on a toy buyers' revolution, where dozens of angry parents dumped parts from unassembled kiddie gyms on the doorstep of a toy store because the parents couldn't figure out how to put the expensive toys together. Citing that article would strengthen your thesis.

Without adequate support, your thesis is merely an assertion—an opinion. Unsupported assertions never win readers' respect.

Note how the writer uses particular cases, relevant data, and expert testimony in these paragraphs:

> Several studies have found that cruising for curb parking generates about 30 percent of the traffic in central business districts. In a recent survey conducted by Bruce Schaller in the SoHo district in Manhattan, 28 percent of drivers interviewed while they were stopped at traffic lights said they were searching for curb parking. A similar study conducted by Transportation Alternatives in the Park Slope neighborhood in Brooklyn found that 45 percent of drivers were cruising.
>
> When my students and I studied cruising for parking in a 15-block business district in Los Angeles, we found the average cruising time was 3.3 minutes, and

the average cruising distance half a mile (about 2.5 times around the block). This may not sound like much, but with 470 parking meters in the district, and a turnover rate for curb parking of 17 cars per space per day, 8,000 cars park at the curb each weekday. Even a small amount of cruising time for each car adds up to a lot of traffic.

Over the course of a year, the search for curb parking in this 15-block district created about 950,000 excess vehicle miles of travel—equivalent to 38 trips, around the earth, or four trips to the moon. And here's another inconvenient truth about underpriced curb parking: cruising those 950,000 miles wastes 47,000 gallons of gas and produces 730 tons of the greenhouse gas carbon dioxide. If all this happens in one small business district, imagine the cumulative effect of all cruising in the United States.

—Donald Shoup

Shoup, a professor of urban planning at the University of California Los Angeles, asserts that significant pollution derives from people's driving around looking for parking spots. He supports his thesis with a variety of data, and by presenting in detail a study conducted by a colleague in Manhattan, Bruce Schaller, Shoup brings outside expert authority to the argument. (Schaller is president of a consulting firm widely known for its knowledge of transportation issues.) And Shoup cites the case of the Los Angeles business district that he and his students studied.

COLLABORATIVE LEARNING

Form five groups. Ask each group to propose the kinds of details a writer might provide to support the following theses. Have each group report to the whole class.

1. Hispanic Americans have contributed substantially to economic growth in our southern cities.
2. Lady Gaga's personal lifestyle, strange as it may be, should not enter into judgments about her music.
3. Textbooks across the elementary school curriculum present women in passive roles.
4. Dawn on the desert is a haunting display of light and shadow.
5. Caring for an aging parent can drain a family's resources.

EXERCISE

For any three thesis statements that you developed for the exercise on page 52, indicate the kinds of details you might use to support them.

Student Writing: Thesis and Details

As you read this student paper, see how the writer establishes the thesis and supports it in the essay.

Marginal comments highlight important points.

Title: a phrase from the essay's dialog

Generalization in first sentence draws reader's attention.

Thesis sentence states writer's opinion, is well limited, well focused, and precise.

Concrete sensory details support point of the paragraph.

Realistic dialog enlivens essay.

Strong sensory details further support thesis.

Thomas Healey
"You Must Be Crazy!"

It's easy to note the behavioral dark spots in those around us. My father is a skinflint; when I need a loan or simply extra cash, he turns a deaf ear to my pleading hysterics. Mom is excessively moody. When something bothers her she sulks for hours, never revealing what set her off, and we just have to wait until she gets over it. However, as a fairly normal teenager, I never thought of myself as having any particular character flaws. Yet, as I faced my brother Matthew at his bedroom door one spring afternoon last year, I became aware of the ugly features of anger and temper in my personality.

Though he's two years younger than I am, Matt and I share many things, including our clothes sometimes. But this time he had borrowed my new tan sweater and had returned it to my drawer with big grease stains on the sleeve and near the collar. "How did this happen?" I shouted, pointing to a large black spot. "Oh," he said casually, looking up from the *Sports Illustrated* he was reading on the brown rug near his bed, "I was fooling around with the Chevy. Oil dripped on everything."

I couldn't believe my ears. "You wore my good sweater to work on your stupid car? I don't believe you." My neck tightened and my hands grew wet and cold. I felt my eyelid twitch. Matt rubbed the arch of his left foot covered in a white sweat sock. Then he shrugged his shoulders. "Those are the breaks," he said, looking down again at his magazine.

It was probably that lack of concern that drove me wild. Lunging at him, I pushed him down to the floor. The more I pushed against him, the angrier I felt. Some strange power had overtaken my body and mind. When I looked at Matt's face suddenly, I heard him choking, and I realized that I had my elbow pressed against his throat. What was I doing? I jumped up as Matt lay sputtering. "You must be crazy!" he gasped in a voice I could barely hear. His frightened blue eyes stared at me in amazement. "You could have killed me."

1 Introduction builds up to the thesis; Healey will not write about his mother and father anywhere in the essay other than here in the introduction.

2 Transition: Words "Matt and I" remind readers of previous paragraph content.

3 Descriptive details help reader envision Matt.

4 Transition: "that lack of concern"

Words "drove me wild" establish frame for supporting detail in paragraph.

I remember looking at my hands and then back at Matt. He was right. 5
I was crazy—crazy with anger. If rage could turn me into such a monster
with my own brother, imagine what it could do under other conditions. "I'm
sorry," I said. "I'm really sorry."

At that moment I realized the full meaning of anger. It was a strong 6 **Conclusion connects to ideas expressed in thesis sentence.**
and dangerous emotion that could easily overpower a person who did not
work to keep it under control.

FOR WRITING OR DISCUSSION

1. What is the writer's topic? What is his thesis? What is the relation
   between the topic and the thesis? In what ways is the thesis limited,
   focused, and precise? What is the writer's opinion or attitude as
   expressed in the thesis?

2. How do the sentences in the introduction build to the thesis?

3. How has the writer used descriptive detail to advantage? Which
   sensory images do you find most convincing? How does the
   description of Matthew contribute to the thesis?

4. What is the writer's purpose in this essay?

5. What is your opinion of the conclusion—the last paragraph of the
   essay? How might you expand it from its two-sentence structure?
   Or do you find it satisfying as is? Why, or why not?

6. Write a paper in which you explore anger or some other "dark spot"
   in your personality or in the personality of someone you know well.

HAVING YOUR SAY

Is sibling rivalry—the competition between brothers and sisters in the
same family for attention and approval by parents and others—an ines-
capable consequence of living together in a family unit? Write an essay in
which you argue for one side or the other on this question. Support your
point of view with appropriate detail.

Now let's look at another student's paper. As you read, consider the
thesis, and notice how the writer's choices of supporting detail and audience
contribute to the development of the paper. Also, before you read, review the
"Strategy Checklist: Reading Critically" on pages 9–10.

Joseph Anderson
Getting Juiced

For the past two decades, the issue of performance-enhancing drugs has been unfortunately synonymous with the sports world. Many athletes feel that they need to get "juiced" for an extra boost. But the use of drugs to improve performance desecrates the integrity of sports, and the drugs are very dangerous as well.

Sports developed over the centuries to display a person's natural ability in pure competition. The use of performance enhancing drugs is not only a disgrace to the sports world; it's also a disgrace to the person using it. To earn victory based on dishonesty is wrong. All of an athlete's achievements aren't worth anything if the athlete has cheated. A good example of this dishonesty is the Barry Bonds record. Bonds set the single-season home run record in 2001 by sending 73 balls into orbit. It was an epic moment in major league baseball history. On August 7, 2007, Barry Bonds broke Hank Aaron's long standing career home run record. Would this make Barry Bonds the greatest home run hitter of all time? No! Bonds is an alleged steroid user and although he denies it, few people doubt he is innocent. Look at the way he has bulked up from a skinny newcomer into a mass of flesh and muscle. Only drugs could achieve such an incredible change. Hank Aaron's record should not be broken by a cheater.

Another example is the American cyclist Floyd Landis who lost his 2006 Tour de France title for a doping offense. He denied it then, but recently he has admitted to steroid use through his career. He has also accused the world-famous cyclist Lance Armstrong of similar drug use.

Not only are performance-enhancing drugs a disgrace to the sports world, they are also extremely dangerous. Performance-enhancing drugs have many destructive effects on the human body. Steroids are the most dangerous of them all. Steroids are muscle enhancers. While you are getting "bulked up," your heart is also getting "bulked up." The human heart is a muscle, and the more exposed to steroids the higher the risk that deadly attacks can occur. There are several steroid-related deaths that plague America each year. For example, the wrestler Davey Boy Smith died at the age of thirty-nine. The coroner said that scar tissue on his heart was a sure sign of steroid abuse. So that leaves the question, "Why take a drug that can potentially kill you?"

Performance-enhancing substances are a plague on the sports world. Those who use them risk death. Maybe we should establish mandatory performance-enhancing drug testing in all sports at all levels—professional, high school. Maybe such testing will wipe out the plague.

FOR WRITING OR DISCUSSION

1. What is the writer's thesis? Where does he state it?
2. What is the difference here between the thesis and the topic?
3. The introduction is only three sentences long. How effective is it? Would you expand it? How?
4. What details does the writer present in support of his idea that doping is a problem in athletics? Does he convince you on the basis of these details? Why or why not?
5. How does the writer support his idea of the dangers of performance enhancing substances? Does he convince you on the basis of those details? Why or why not?
6. Who is the audience for this paper? How do you know?
7. What is your opinion of the title of this essay?

COLLABORATIVE LEARNING

Brainstorm in groups about the use of performance-enhancing drugs. How serious a problem is it? What should we do about it? What is the general consensus in each group: Have drugs badly damaged the image of athletes and athletics? After one person from each group reports to the full class, write a paper in which you explore the issue of drugs in competitive sports.

Writers and Details

Read the pieces that follow, in which the writers provide convincing details to support the thesis, and then answer the questions that follow each selection. Examine "Strategy Checklist: Reading Critically" on pages 9–10 before you begin.

NICHOLAS D. KRISTOF

Love and Race

1   In a world brimming with bad news, here's one of the happiest trends: Instead of preying on people of different races, young Americans are falling in love with them.

2   Whites and blacks can be found strolling together as couples even at the University of Mississippi, once the symbol of racial confrontation.

3   "I will say that they are always given a second glance," acknowledges C.J. Rhodes, a black student at Ole Miss. He adds that there are still misgivings about interracial dating, particularly among black women and a formidable number of "White Southerners who view this race-mixing as abnormal, frozen by fear to see Sara Beth bring home a brotha."

4   Mixed-race marriages in the U.S. now number 1.5 million and are roughly doubling each decade. About 40 percent of Asian-Americans and 6 percent of blacks have married whites in recent years.

5   Still more striking, one survey found that 40 percent of Americans had dated someone of another race.

6   In a country where racial divisions remain deep, all this love is an enormously hopeful sign of progress in bridging barriers. Scientists who study the human genome say that race is mostly a bogus distinction reflecting very little genetic difference, perhaps one-hundredth of 1 percent of our DNA.

7   Skin color differences are recent, arising over only the last 100,000 years or so, a twinkling of an evolutionary eye. That's too short a period for substantial genetic differences to emerge, and so there is perhaps 10 times more genetic difference within a race than there is between races. Thus we should welcome any trend that makes a superficial issue like color less central to how we categorize each other.

8   The rise in interracial marriage reflects a revolution in attitudes. As recently as 1958 a white mother in Monroe, N.C., called the police after her little girl kissed a black playmate on the cheek; the boy, Hanover Thompson, 9, was then sentenced to 14 years in prison for attempted rape. (His appeals failed, but he was released later after an outcry.)

9   In 1963, 59 percent of Americans believed that marriage between blacks and whites should be illegal. At one time or another 42 states banned intermarriage, although the Supreme Court finally invalidated these laws in 1967.

10   Typically, the miscegenation laws voided any interracial marriages, making the children illegitimate, and some states included penalties such as enslavement, life imprisonment, and whippings. My wife is Chinese-American, and our relationship would once have been felonious.

11   At every juncture from the 19th century on, the segregationists warned that granting rights to blacks would mean the start of a slippery slope, ending up with black men marrying white women. The racists were prophetic.

12   "They were absolutely right," notes Randall Kennedy, the Harvard Law School professor and author of a dazzling new book, "Interracial Intimacies," to be published next month.

"I do think [interracial marriage] is a good thing. It's a welcome sign of thoroughgoing desegregation. We talk about desegregation in the public sphere: here's desegregation in the most intimate sphere."

These days, interracial romance can be seen on the big screen, on TV shows, and in the lives of some prominent Americans. Former Defense Secretary William Cohen has a black wife, as does Peter Norton, the software guru. The Supreme Court justice Clarence Thomas has a white wife. 13

I find the surge in intermarriage to be one of the most positive fronts in American race relations today, building bridges and empathy. But it's still in its infancy. 14

I was excited to track down interracial couples at Ole Miss, thinking they would be perfect to make my point about this hopeful trend. But none were willing to talk about the issue on the record. 15

"Even if people wanted to marry [interracially], I think they'd keep it kind of quiet," explained a minister on campus. 16

For centuries, racists warned that racial equality would lead to the "mongrelization" of America. Perhaps they were right in a sense, for we're increasingly going to see a blurring of racial distinctions. But these distinctions acquired enormous social resonance without ever having much basis in biology. 17

FOR WRITING OR DISCUSSION

1. What is Kristof's thesis? State it in your own words. How does paragraph 14 reinforce the thesis?

2. What are the varied cases that the writer presents to support his point? How do the data in paragraph 9 help support the thesis?

3. Where does Kristof use expert testimony to good effect?

4. Write an essay in which you explore interracial dating and (or) interracial marriage as it appears in your community—on campus or in your home town. What are the prevalent attitudes among your friends and family toward "love and race," to quote Kristof's title. What are your own attitudes toward the phenomenon?

LANGSTON HUGHES

Salvation

I was saved from sin when I was going on thirteen. But not really saved. It happened like this. There was a big revival at my Auntie Reed's church. Every night for weeks there had been much preaching, singing, praying, and shouting, and some very hardened sinners 1 had been brought to Christ, and the membership of the church had grown by leaps and bounds. Then just before the revival ended, they held a special meeting for children, "to bring the young lambs to the fold." My aunt spoke of it for days ahead. That night I was escorted to the front row and placed on the mourners' bench with all the other young sinners, who had not yet been brought to Jesus.

2   My aunt told me that when you were saved you saw a light, and something happened to you inside! And Jesus came into your life! And God was with you from then on! She said you could see and hear and feel Jesus in your soul. I believed her. I had heard a great many old people say the same thing and it seemed to me they ought to know. So I sat there calmly in the hot, crowded church, waiting for Jesus to come to me.

3   The preacher preached a wonderful rhythmical sermon, all moans and shouts and lonely cries and dire pictures of hell, and then he sang a song about the ninety and nine safe in the fold, but one little lamb was left out in the cold. Then he said: "Won't you come? Won't you come to Jesus? Young lambs, won't you come?" And he held out his arms to all us young sinners there on the mourner's bench. And the little girls cried. And some of them jumped up and went to Jesus right away. But most of us just sat there.

4   A great many old people came and knelt around us and prayed, old women with jet-black faces and braided hair, old men with work-gnarled hands. And the church sang a song about the lower lights are burning, some poor sinners to be saved. And the whole building rocked with prayer and song.

5   Still I kept waiting to see Jesus.

6   Finally all the young people had gone to the altar and were saved, but one boy and me. He was a rounder's son named Westley. Westley and I were surrounded by sisters and deacons praying. It was very hot in the church, and getting late now. Finally Westley said to me in a whisper: "God damn! I'm tired o' sitting here. Let's get up and be saved." So he got up and was saved.

7   Then I was left all alone on the mourners' bench. My aunt came and knelt at my knees and cried, while prayers and songs swirled all around me in the little church. The whole congregation prayed for me alone, in a mighty wail of moans and voices. And I kept waiting serenely for Jesus, waiting, waiting—but he didn't come. I wanted to see him, but nothing happened to me. Nothing! I wanted something to happen to me, but nothing happened.

8   I heard the songs and the minister saying: "Why don't you come? My dear child, why don't you come to Jesus? Jesus is waiting for you. He wants you. Why don't you come? Sister Reed, what is this child's name?"

9   "Langston," my aunt sobbed.

10   "Langston, why don't you come? Why don't you come and be saved? Oh, Lamb of God! Why don't you come?"

Now it was really getting late. I began to be ashamed of myself, holding everything up so long. I began to wonder what God thought about Westley, who certainly hadn't seen Jesus either, but who was now sitting proudly on the platform, swinging his knickerbockered legs and grinning down at me, surrounded by deacons and old women on their knees praying. God had not struck Westley dead for taking his name in vain or for lying in the temple. So I decided that maybe to save further trouble, I'd better lie, too, and say that Jesus had come, and get up and be saved. 11

So I got up. 12

Suddenly the whole room broke into a sea of shouting, as they saw me rise. Waves of rejoicing swept the place. Women leaped in the air. My aunt threw her arms around me. The minister took me by the hand and led me to the platform. 13

When things quieted down, in a hushed silence, punctuated by a few ecstatic "Amens," all the new young lambs were blessed in the name of God. Then joyous singing filled the room. 14

That night, for the last time in my life but one—for I was a big boy twelve years old—I cried. I cried, in bed alone, and couldn't stop. I buried my head under the quilts, but my aunt heard me. She woke up and told my uncle I was crying because the Holy Ghost had come into my life, and because I had seen Jesus. But I was really crying because I couldn't bear to tell her that I had lied, that I had deceived everybody in the church, that I hadn't seen Jesus, and that now I didn't believe there was a Jesus any more, since he didn't come to help me. 15

FOR WRITING OR DISCUSSION

1. What is the thesis of this selection? State it in your own words.

2. What specific sensory details help support the thesis?

3. Why does the narrator not stand as he was expected to early in the narrative?

4. Why at the end does he in fact rise? How do the people around him react when he finally stands? Why? Why does the narrator cry at night?

5. Write an essay about how people pressured you (or someone you know) to do something you weren't sure was right. Or, perhaps you would prefer to write about a religious experience that you had. Be sure to support your thesis with concrete sensory detail.

STRATEGY CHECKLIST: Stating and Supporting a Thesis

Think about your subject.	☐ Have I narrowed my topic? ☐ Do I have an opinion about my topic?
Review your prewriting activities.	☐ Have I found an issue? ☐ Do my prewriting activities suggest a thesis?
State your thesis.	☐ Is my thesis about a limited topic? ☐ Does my thesis express an opinion and attitude? ☐ Is my thesis focused? ☐ Is my thesis precise? ☐ Is my thesis a complete sentence? ☐ Have I revised my thesis as needed?
Support your thesis with appropriate details.	☐ Have I used concrete sensory details to support my thesis? ☐ Have I use statistics and/or specific cases to support my thesis? ☐ Have I use expert testimony to support my thesis?

For support in meeting this chapter's objectives, follow this path in MyCompLab: Resources ⇒ **Writing** ⇒ **Writing Process** ⇒ **Planning**. Review the Instruction and Multimedia resources about **developing a thesis**, then complete the Exercises and click on Gradebook to measure your progress.

CHAPTER **4**

Planning a Paper: Outlining

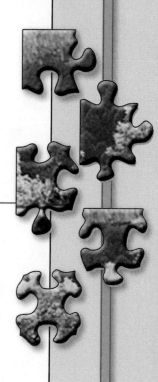

Proper planning is a key to writing a successful paper. As we saw in Chapter 2, John Fousek's two planning efforts—grouping related materials in lists and a rough outline—helped him to produce his drafts. Here we want to present outlining in greater detail as a valuable step in the writing process.

Why Outline?

When you do prewriting, often you're left with a page or two of notes and ideas, which are largely disorganized. Although your prewriting is essential for generating ideas on a topic, you need to bring to it a sense of order that will put you on the right track for developing your draft.

That's where outlining comes in.

In this chapter you will

- understand the value of outlining
- examine and create a rough outline
- learn the format of a formal outline for a complex paper and a short paper
- distinguish between topic and sentence outlines
- analyze one student's progress from prewriting to a formal outline to writing a paper
- develop sample outlines

- Outlining allows you to put your ideas in usable order.
- It allows you to establish and keep apart main ideas from supporting details.
- It helps you see at a glance how the parts of your paper relate to your thesis.
- And as you develop your outline, you can rethink how you will present information in your essay.

Outlines take many forms. Rough outlines provide an informal sketch of a paper without going into too much detail. Some people see rough outlining as identifying thought blocks and related ideas in a visual scheme. (See pages 76–77.) More formal outlining requires adherence to an agreed-upon format with clearly defined headings and subheadings and the use of Roman and Arabic numbers and upper- and lowercase letters. Formal outlines may present ideas as topics or in full sentences. You'll see all these kinds of outlines in this chapter.

Creating a Rough Outline

When you arrange your prewriting ideas in some kind of order, you have pretty much created a rough, or informal, outline. Linking related ideas, for example, and creating labels for them make good rough outlines. Think of the rough outline as an informal list, which you create as a convenience to you before you begin the more advanced aspects of developing your paper, including a formal outline. The rough outline does not follow a prescribed form, but it should have enough detail so that you can see the early shape and direction of your paper. In other words, the rough outline can help you decide preliminarily what you have to say and how to say it.

From prewriting notes, one student made the following rough outline for a paper on the value of television in today's society.

Rough Outline

THESIS: Television makes a valuable contribution in today's society.

1. **Introduction:** Why do people watch so much TV?

   Convenient and easy to use

   Addictive

   Little required effort

2. Television as excellent source of information

   Up-to-date news as it happens: wars, weather disasters, business news, science and medicine advances

   In-depth investigations: NOVA, 60 Minutes, etc.

3. Television as entertainer

   Comedy Central

   Concerts, dance programs, drama, movies (all appealing to different tastes)

4. Television teaches

   Children and Sesame Street

   College courses via television

   High school subjects review

5. **Conclusion:** Critics wrongly oppose television watching in the home.

Thesis (probably tentative)

Introduction: starting point for first paragraph

Supporting details for introduction

First general point

Supporting detail: possibilities for each general point

Next general point

Arabic numbers indicate possible sequence writer will use in draft

Last general point

Essay conclusion (to be developed in draft)

This informal outline can guide the writer in producing his rough draft. The writer includes a thesis, which makes an assertion about the topic. Undoubtedly, the thesis will change more than once, and some of the items under the numbered headings will change as the writer produces the first and subsequent drafts. Therefore, as the paper progresses, the rough outline itself will change—a good thing, to be sure. You should view any outline as a dynamic product, a work in progress, just as your drafts are works in progress. Even if you don't follow your original plan exactly, your outline is a first stab at unifying your thoughts and presenting them coherently.

Another less detailed but equally helpful rough outline appears on pages 76–77 as thought blocks and labels for them. Your rough outline might include the following items.

 **TIPS** for Making a Rough Outline

Include:

■ **Linked and labeled thought blocks.**

■ **A thesis statement.**

■ **An introduction or opening.**

■ **Ideas or main points in numbered sequence.**

■ **Possible supporting information for each main point.**

■ **A conclusion.**

EXERCISE   For any topic on page 34, develop a rough outline that you could use to write a paper on the subject.

Making a Formal Outline

A formal outline is a schematic presentation of your paper—a procedural diagram, if you will, in which you show the order of your topics and how they relate to each other. A formal outline gives a picture of the logical relations between the separate parts of the paper and the thesis or purpose. After your preliminary thinking on your topic and with your prewriting in hand, consider the formal outline as a road map to a territory you have just begun exploring but need clearer directions to navigate.

When you produce a formal outline, follow the conventions of its format, as presented on pages 69–70. After your prewriting, you should have an idea of your thesis. Thus, always begin your outline by stating your thesis or purpose. As we have pointed out before, you may want to modify your thesis as your outline takes shape, so don't be concerned if you haven't stated your thesis exactly the way you want it.

Establishing Main Divisions

After you state your thesis, your next task is to determine the main divisions of the paper as suggested by the thesis. In many cases, your choice of method of development (Part Two of this book) will determine the major sections. For example, if you wanted to write about why your brother decided not to go to college, what he is doing instead, and how his decision affected his personality, the sections of the paper seem clear, and you would use them as main headings in the outline format. Yes, you would still have to decide on what order to use in order to present the points in the paper, and what order to use for the supporting details under each point, but the three major parts of the paper are clear simply from the way you want to develop it.

In other papers, main divisions may not suggest themselves so clearly at the outset. As you examine your prewriting, try to see how some of what you've written falls into large blocks of thought. At your computer, you can experiment by grouping thoughts into blocks, saving your effort, and trying yet another plan. Some word-processing programs have templates for outlining. If you've written preliminary thoughts by hand, circles and arrows or marks in different colored pens or pencils can help you make visual links among related ideas that may be spread out over the page.

As the related thoughts come together, look at them as main points. If you can create a label for each thought block, you then can convert the label into a main heading. The main headings in your outline should match the number of blocks you have identified. If you see that your outline has more than five or so main points, reexamine it: You may be trying to do too much in your paper.

Adding Supporting Details

With thought blocks identified and labeled, you need then to think about the supporting details to place under each heading. The supporting points, of course, will pertain clearly to the main thought you stated in the heading. As you group these supporting points—some of which will appear in your prewriting, others to be invented as you produce the outline—they will become subheadings in your outline.

Once you've settled on your thought blocks, you will have to decide how to organize them. In a descriptive essay (Chapter 7), you generally move the reader from one place to the next, and once you decide where to begin (in a room, for example, front, back, sides, or middle), logic of place will assert itself.

But for most other essays, the arrangement of thought blocks is strictly the writer's option, with logic the prevailing factor for appropriate decisions.

Formatting a Formal Outline

Begin by stating the thesis or purpose. Then indicate all major divisions of the paper with Roman numerals. Mark the support for the major divisions with capital letters and additional support for those major divisions with Arabic numerals. If you are planning a very long paper, you may want to make further subdivisions. To do so, next use lowercase letters—*a, b, c*—and then Arabic numerals in parentheses—*(1), (2)*—then lowercase letters in parentheses—*(a), (b)*.

A standard formal outline for a complex paper has the following format.

Complex Paper Formal Outline

Thesis or Purpose: [State the thesis or purpose of your paper here.]

I. Major division

With *A*. level subdivision you must have *B*. at a minimum

  A. First-level subdivision

    1. Second-level subdivision

      With second-level subdivision at *1* you must also have *2* at a minimum

    2. Second-level subdivision

With third-level subdivision at *a*. you must also have *b*. at a minimum

      a. Third-level subdivision

      b. Third-level subdivision

        (1) Fourth-level subdivision

        With fourth-level subdivision at *(1)* you must also have *(2)* at a minimum

        (2) Fourth-level subdivision

  B. First-level subdivision

    1. Second-level subdivision

    2. Second-level subdivision

II. Major division

  A. First-level subdivision

    1 Second-level subdivision

    2. Second-level subdivision

  B. First-level subdivision

    1. Second-level subdivision

      a. Third-level subdivision

      b. Third-level subdivision

2. Second-level subdivision

   a. Third-level subdivision

   b. Third-level subdivision

      (1) Fourth-level subdivision

      (2) Fourth-level subdivision

         (a) Fifth-level subdivision

         (b) Fifth-level subdivision

Parentheses around Arabic number at fourth level

With fifth-level subdivision at (*a*) you must also have (*b*) at a minimum

Parentheses around lowercase letter at fifth level

An outline for a short paper usually includes several major divisions and sometimes two or three subdivisions for each major topic. Remember that a word or a phrase in an outline can be expanded into a sentence—even a paragraph—in your essay.

A typical outline format for a short paper looks like this:

Short Paper Formal Outline

Thesis or Purpose: [State the thesis or purpose of your paper here.]

I. Major division

  A. Subdivision

  B. Subdivision

II. Major division

  A. Subdivision

  B. Subdivision

  C. Subdivision

III. Major division

  A. Subdivision

  B. Subdivision

  C. Subdivision

First-level subdivisions only

Writing a Topic Outline

Formal outlines are of two types, *topic outlines* and *sentence outlines*. A **topic outline** is one in which the writer uses just a few words or phrases to indicate the topics and subtopics that the paper covers. Topic outlines are sufficient for many short papers, especially those that classify or present a process. Longer papers and those that develop theses often profit from sentence outlines.

Here is a topic outline for a short paper on how to change automobile license plates.

Topic Outline

Thesis: Changing auto license plates doesn't have to be a headache.

First major division at Roman numeral I.

I. Assemble materials

   A. Find screwdriver

   B. Find household oil

   C. Buy plastic screws

Second major division at Roman numeral II.

II. Remove old plates

   A. Oil screws to loosen rust

   B. Unscrew plates

   C. Discard metal screws

Third and fourth major divisions at Roman numerals III and IV.

III. Mount new plates

   A. Position plate with screw holes

   B. Screw on plate using plastic screws

IV. Break and discard old plates

Thesis sentence

Subdivisions to support major divisions, all at capital letters

EXERCISE

1. What is the first major division of the license plate outline? The second? The third?
2. What supporting information does the outline indicate as subdivisions for the major division "Remove old plates"?
3. Why does the fourth major division not have any subdivisions?
4. What thesis could you propose for the essay that this outline suggests?
5. In what order has the writer chosen to arrange the thought blocks indicated as major divisions?

Writing a Sentence Outline

Longer papers and those that develop theses often benefit from sentence outlines. To write a **sentence outline**, you must sum up in one sentence what you want to say on each major division and subdivision. The sentence doesn't merely indicate the topic; it states what you intend to say about the topic.

This kind of outline forces you to think through exactly what you want to say before you begin to write. By constructing a sentence outline, you will find out whether you really have support for your position.

Look at the formal sentence outline below as a model. The model effectively uses the accepted format and will help the writer produce a draft. Note that the writer presents first- through fourth-level subdivisions. Only the writer can determine how many divisions and subdivisions the paper needs, and there is no set number of required entries. Roman and Arabic tags correctly identify the divisions of the outline.

Model Sentence Outline

Thesis: My attitude toward the English language has changed from loathing to acceptance.

All major divisions relate clearly to thesis

I. At first, I hated the English language. *First major division*

Subdivisions A. and B. support major division I.

   A. Knowing very little English, I felt isolated. *First-level subdivision*

Arabic 1 and 2 support first-level subdivision A.

      1. I could not understand what people said to me. *Second-level subdivisions*

      2. I could not tell others what I thought or felt.

   B. The isolation I felt made me want to return to Greece. *First-level subdivision*

II. Now, six months later, I like the English language very much. *Second major division*

   A. The support of the Greek family I live with has helped me to accept English. *First-level subdivision*

      1. They gave me courage to try to use the language. *Second-level subdivision*

Third-level subdivisions supports second level at II.A.1.: "They gave me courage to try to use the language."

         a. They proved to me that they had learned the language. *Third-level subdivision*

         b. They proved to me that they could talk with others in English.

      2. They held conversations with me in English.

   B. The teachers in my English classes have helped me to accept the language. *Second-level subdivision after A.1. Subdivision for II.*

      1. They are approachable and helpful outside of class.

      2. They are good instructors in class.

         a. They explain material clearly.

Fourth-level subdivisions support third-level subdivision at II.B.2.b.: "They discuss a variety of subjects."

         b. They discuss a variety of subjects.

            (1) The variety increases my vocabulary.

            (2) The discussions improve my comprehension and speech.

III. I go out of my way now to assure my continuous contact with English.

    A. I study English regularly.

        1. I work with a tutor for one hour every day.

        2. I study grammar and vocabulary two hours every night.

    B. Since I meet few Greeks, I must speak English every day.

        1. I go to the supermarket to read and pronounce the names of consumer products.

            a. I love to say the weird names of candies and cereals.

                (1) Have you ever eaten Fiddle Faddle?

                (2) I have lots of fun with Captain Crunch, Sugar Frosted Flakes, and Count Chocula.

            b. I made friends with one of the stock boys who helps me when my English fails me.

        2. I always accept solicitation calls on the telephone just to practice my English.

Fourth-level subdivisions support third level subdivision at II.B.2.b: "They discuss a variety of subjects."

EXERCISE

1. What are the major divisions of the outline? Put a check mark beside each one. How do the major divisions relate to the thesis as stated as the first outline entry?
2. How do the items in I.A.1. and 2. relate to the item in I.A.? To the item in I.? To the thesis?
3. Look at the various items connected to III in the outline. Label each item appropriately as major division or first-, second-, third-, or fourth-level subdivision. Be prepared to explain why you chose the labels you did.
4. Using any one of the thought blocks labeled as a major division as well as the various subdivisions beneath it, try your hand at writing the paragraph that the outline suggests.

Correcting a Formal Outline

The following outline has many problems and inconsistencies that the writer must correct before she begins writing. Look at the annotations in the margin before doing the exercise.

No Arabic numeral for thesis

Weak Sentence Outline

1. *Thesis:* Both Christmas and Easter are religious holidays that provide an opportunity for secular pleasures.

   I. Both are religious holidays.

      A. Christmas observes the birth of Christ.

      B. Easter observes the Resurrection of Christ.

      C. Halloween is the eve of All Saints' Day.

First-level subdivision incorrect: Family meals are not religious

      D. Families eat meals together.

First-level subdivision incorrect: thesis allows only Christmas and Easter

   II. Both provide opportunities for secular pleasures.

      A. Christmas is a time for parties and gifts.

          1. Families decorate trees in a party atmosphere.

Second-level subdivision incorrect: Singing carols not a party or gift that II.A. states

          2. Children sing carols.

      B. Easter is a time for new clothes and egg hunts.

          1. The bunny rabbit is a symbol of Easter.

Second-level subhead does not support first level subdivision

          2. Baskets for eggs are beautifully decorated.

          3. The president of the United States sponsors an egg roll on the White House lawn.

Writer needs Arabic 4 to assert something about "new clothes" stated in II.B.

             a. Many children participate.

"a" requires "b" as well.

EXERCISE

1. Where could you put the current item I.D. so that it is in the correct place in the outline?
2. What would you do to correct the item at B.1.?
3. What could you add to create item II.B.3.b., which now is not in the outline?
4. Revise the outline thoroughly so that it conforms to the appropriate format and makes logical sense in terms of organization and use of details.

One Student Writing: From Prewriting to Essay

In an English class, one student, Alan Benjamin, received this assignment: Discuss the implications of the inscription on the pedestal of the statue in Shelley's poem "Ozymandias." We'll have more to say about approaches to literary analysis in Chapter 17; here we want to examine how the student developed a formal outline and how that outline led to the production of his essay.

First, read the brief poem "Ozymandias" so you'll know what stimulated the assignment.

PERCY BYSSHE SHELLEY

Ozymandias

I met a traveller from an antique land
Who said: Two vast and trunkless legs of stone
Stand in the desert. Near them, on the sand,
Half sunk, a shattered visage lies, whose frown,
And wrinkled lip, and sneer of cold command,
Tell that its sculptor well those passions read
Which yet survive, stamped on these lifeless things,
The hand that mocked them, and the heart that fed:[1]
And on the pedestal these words appear:
"My name is Ozymandias, king of kings:
Look on my works, ye Mighty, and despair!"
Nothing beside remains. Round the decay
Of that colossal wreck, boundless and bare
The lone and level sands stretch far away.

---

[1]The passions stamped on the broken face of the statue survive the hand (of the sculptor) that mocked them and the heart (of Ozymandias) that fed them.

Initial thinking about the assignment led the student to the prewriting effort on the next page.

Using his prewriting as a record of his preliminary thinking, Alan Benjamin tried to link related ideas visually using lines and boxes. As he considered the thought blocks suggested by his prewriting, he weighed how to organize them. He numbered related points so that he could see their interconnections. He did not link thoughts that seemed unrelated.

The next step on the road to preparing the outline and then writing the paper was to label the numbered blocks of thought. What words and phrases would best identify each cluster of information? The labels developed are

Prewriting

Such arrogance! Ozy's inscription then and now

Statue meant to challenge all who saw it—I am mighty, the rest of you puny

How was statue built in the first place?

People today who think they're powerful can learn from Ozy's fate—not from envy

"King of Kings"—Ozymandias thinks a lot of himself

"Sneer of cold command"—poet shows vanity and arrogance in having statue built in the first place

Ozy believes no one else will be able to match the magnificence of his works

Is Ozy a real figure in history?

Vanity today too—all material things crumble and yield disappointment if you put your faith in the material things

Where was Ozymandias' statue erected? Maybe at the gates of his capital city?

Where is this "antique land"?

Time eats away buildings and statues—look what's left of Ozymandias' vain effort to preserve his reputation and instill fear in people

"Despair"—Ozymandias' idea of despair comes from petty and foolish reasons. Now we have more realistic reasons for the origin of despair

preliminary and subject to considerable change as the outline takes shape; but you can see the first efforts on the next page. The numbers correspond to the numbered thought blocks Benjamin grouped (see page 77).

These labels and the thought blocks themselves serve as a rough outline and provide a good start for developing a formal outline. As the writer examined the labels and blocks of thought, he could identify the purpose he had in writing his paper. He wanted to contrast Ozymandias' views of despair as expressed in the poem with the meanings we bring to that word today. And as he weighed his purpose and the thought blocks he produced, he realized that the numbered clusters suggested the order that he would use. First he would present the king's notion of despair; then he would present the views we have of the term today based on the poem's assertions.

Labels for Thought Blocks

1. Meaning of despair different now from Ozymandias' day

2. Meaning of the statue to Ozymandias and his contemporaries

3. Meaning now

4. The petty and foolish vs. realistic reasons for despair

GROUPING THOUGHT BLOCKS

Such arrogance! Ozy's inscription then and now ①

Statue meant to challenge all who saw it–I am mighty, the rest of you puny ②

How was statue built in the first place?

People today who think they're powerful can learn from Ozy's fate—not from envy ③

"King of Kings"–Ozymandias thinks a lot of himself ②

"Sneer of cold command"–poet shows vanity and arrogance in having statue built in the first place ②

Ozy believes no one else will be able to match the magnificence of his works ②

Is Ozy a real figure in history?

Vanity today too—all material things crumble and yield disappointment if you put your faith in the material things ③

Where was Ozymandias' statue erected? Maybe at the gates of his capital city? ②

Where is this "antique land"?

Time eats away buildings and statues—look what's left of Ozymandias' vain effort to preserve his reputation and instill fear in people ③

"Despair"–Ozymandias' idea of despair comes from petty and foolish reasons. Now we have more realistic reasons for the origin of despair ④

Here is the outline developed from the preliminary materials that you just examined.

Outline

Thesis: The passing of time since Ozymandias ruled has altered greatly our view of the word <u>despair</u>.

I. In the poem "Ozymandias" by Percy Bysshe Shelley, the inscription "My name is Ozymandias, king of kings: / Look on my works, ye Mighty, and despair!" appears on a broken statue in the desert.

   A. King Ozymandias had one thing in mind with that inscription.

   B. Today the words take on a dramatically different meaning.

II. Vanity and arrogance motivated Ozymandias to build the statue of himself.

   A. The features of his face assert his self-importance.

     1. His "wrinkled lip and sneer of cold command" are apparent.

     2. The size of the statue is "colossal."

     3. He describes himself as "king of kings."

   B. We can imagine the site of the statue at the gates of the capital or its central square and people's reactions to it.

     1. Marble buildings gleam in the sunlight.

       a. We can visualize the palace, the treasury, and the temples.

       b. There are monuments to military victories.

     2. "Mighty" people come to see the wonders of Ozymandias' kingdom.

     3. "Look on my works, ye Mighty, and despair" the statue sneers.

       a. Despair because your creations will never equal mine.

       b. Despair because my works will make you see the insignificance of your own.

III. The passage of time has given a new dimension to Ozymandias' statement.

   A. Ozymandias' kingdom is now a desert.

      1. Time eats away marble.

      2. Buildings and statues crumble.

         a. Little remains of the statue of Ozymandias.

            (1) Two grotesque stone legs stick up in the air.

            (2) The statue has a "shattered visage."

         b. What remains is sand and desolation.

   B. The inscription on the pedestal takes on new significance.

      1. In one sense, it is meaningless.

         a. There are no more "works" left to look on.

         b. Ozymandias was silly in his pomposity.

      2. In another sense, the words have stronger and truer meaning than Ozymandias dreamed.

         a. Powerful people today can still despair as they look at Ozymandias' works.

         b. The despair people face will not be based on envy, however.

            (1) They will despair because they can see the fate of their own works.

            (2) They will despair because no matter how great their works are, the works won't matter.

            (3) They will despair because those who put their faith in material things are doomed to disappointment.

IV. With these contrasting views, there is more than enough despair to go around.

The paper developed from the formal outline appears next. As you read it, consider how the two relate to each other—and to the prewriting. How has the outline influenced the essay? What differences do you note?

Alan Benjamin
Enough Despair to Go Around

1   In Percy Bysshe Shelley's "Ozymandias," the poet reveals that these
words are inscribed on the pedestal of a broken statue in the desert: "My
name is Ozymandias, king of kings: / Look on my works, ye Mighty, and
despair!" What King Ozymandias had in mind when he chose those words
is dramatically different from the meaning they have now. The new meaning
comes not from Ozymandias but from the passage of time.

2   The still visible "wrinkled lip and sneer of cold command" suggest
the vanity and arrogance that motivated Ozymandias to have his statue
built in the first place. The "colossal" size of the statue and Ozymandias'
description of himself as "king of kings" add to the impression that he
thought a great deal of himself and wanted others to do the same. We
can imagine the statue being erected at the gates or in the central square
of King Ozymandias' great capital city. Marble buildings gleam in the
sunlight: the palace, the treasury, the temples, the monuments to military
victories. Powerful and "mighty" people from all over the known world
come to see the wonders of Ozymandias' kingdom. "Look on my works, ye
Mighty, and despair," sneers Ozymandias: Despair because your cre-
ations, your works, will never be able to equal the magnificence of mine;
despair because when you look at my works, you can only feel a sense of
the pitiful insignificance of your own.

3   Time passes. Time eats away marble. Buildings and statues crumble.
The glorious, thriving kingdom of Ozymandias is now a desert. Two grotesque stone legs stick up in the air, and together with a "shattered visage"
they are all that is left of the statue. Everything else is sand and desolation.
In one sense, the inscription on the pedestal has now become meaningless,
for there are no more "works" left to look on, and we can think only of how
silly Ozymandias must have been. In another sense, the words are filled
with a strong new meaning, stronger and far more true than Ozymandias
ever dreamed. Powerful and mighty people today can look at Ozymandias'
works and still despair. This time, however, they will despair not because
of envy, but because they can see the eventual fate of all their own works.
They will despair because, even if their own works surpass those of Ozymandias, it won't make any difference. They will despair now because they

can see that all material things crumble to dust and that people who put their faith in such things are doomed to futility and disappointment.

Ozymandias originally hoped that the despair would come from petty and foolish reasons. Today it can come from more intelligent and realistic reasons. But there is still more than enough despair to go around as "the lone and level sands stretch far away."

4

EXERCISE

1. How do both the outline and the essay fulfill the writer's statement of purpose? What is the writer's thesis in this essay? Where does the writer state it most clearly?
2. How did the labels for the blocks of thought in the prewriting influence the outline?
3. What three items in the prewriting did Alan Benjamin not include in the thought blocks? Why do you think he excluded these items?
4. The outline is obviously a sentence outline, yet in two places we read not sentences but only fragments. Where? Why does the writer use fragments here? How do the items appear in the essay itself?
5. Look at the four major headings and the various subheadings in the outline. How do they relate to the essay itself? What similarities do you note? How does the essay differ from the section of the outline to which it corresponds?

HAVING YOUR SAY

What do you think the inscription on the pedestal means in Shelley's poem "Ozymandias"? Reread the poem on page 75. Then make an assertion about the inscription and argue for your point with specific detail.

Preparing Your Formal Outline

Whether your outline is a topic or a sentence outline, it should include a statement of the thesis or purpose of the paper (depending on your teacher's instructions) and an indication by means of Roman numerals of the main points to be covered in the paper. Major and minor subdivisions, indicated by letters and Arabic numerals, respectively, should show how the main points will be developed.

Here are other points to observe in preparing an outline.

 **TIPS** for Writing a Formal Outline

- **Do not make single subdivisions.**   If you decide to subdivide a point, you must have at least two subdivisions. If there is a I, there must be a II; if there is an A, there must be a B. If you cannot think of two divisions, rephrase the heading so no division is necessary.

- **Use parallel grammatical forms for headings of equal importance.** Parallel forms help show the relation of headings to one another. If heading I reads "Assembling the ingredients," heading II should read "Mixing the ingredients," not "Mix the ingredients."

- **Make sure the divisions of an outline do not overlap and that you stick to a single principle of division.**   You should not, for example, discuss books in terms of fiction, nonfiction, and novels because novels are logically a subdivision of fiction. You should not discuss the branches of government in terms of legislative, judicial, executive, and crooked politicians because one might find crooked politicians in any of the branches.

- **Make sure headings and subheadings show a proper logical relation.** In discussing athletes, you should not establish Babe Ruth as one major division and baseball players as a second. You might, however, treat great home-run hitters as a major division and Babe Ruth and Hank Aaron as subdivisions.

One final reminder about outlines: They can be as helpful after you've written your paper as they are during the early stages of development. For example, if you choose to use only your prewriting activities or a rough outline as a guide to writing your first draft, a formal outline at this stage provides a visual scheme of how your ideas relate to each other logically.

As you develop your outline, ask yourself the questions in the "Strategy Checklist: Preparing a Formal Outline." Your answers to these questions can provide guidance as you write and revise your draft. You can determine if your major divisions relate logically to your thesis, and you can shift subdivisions or add new ones as necessary.

STRATEGY CHECKLIST: Preparing a Formal Outline

Prewrite.	☐ Did I record my random thoughts on the topic?
Identify thought blocks.	☐ Did I identify and label related blocks of thought? ☐ Did I use the labeled thought blocks to develop the major divisions of my outline? ☐ Do the major divisions advance my thesis?
Make a rough outline.	☐ Have I stated a thesis? ☐ Have I listed the main divisions of my paper? ☐ Have I noted possible supporting details for each main division or idea? ☐ Did I include an introduction and a conclusion?
Create a formal outline.	☐ Have I stated a thesis? ☐ Have I listed the main divisions of the paper using Roman numerals? ☐ Have I organized subdivisions using capital letters, Arabic numerals, lowercase letters, and Arabic numerals in parentheses? ☐ Have I avoided single subdivisions? ☐ Do my divisions and subdivisions make logical sense? ☐ Have I used parallel grammatical form for headings of equal importance? ☐ Is my outline a topic outline or a sentence outline?

EXERCISE   What strengths and weaknesses do you see in the following sentence outlines? Revise them so that they are more suitable to the writer's needs.

1. *Thesis:* Nationalism swept two major countries in Europe through the strength of dynamic leaders.

   I. In the last half of the nineteenth century, nationalism surfaced in Germany and Italy.

   II. Bismarck in Germany, and Cavour, Garibaldi, and Mazzini in Italy were the four key figures in nineteenth-century nationalism.
      A. Cavour, Garibaldi, and Mazzini combined their talents to unify Italy.
         1. Cavour was the "brains" of unification.
         2. Garibaldi was the "sword."
         3. Mazzini was the "spirit" of the revolution.
      B. Otto von Bismarck was the creator of a unified German state.
         1. He used "blood and iron" to unify the separate German states.
         2. He suppressed liberalism and democracy.
         3. His militaristic policies contributed to the outbreak of World War I.

2. *Thesis:* Getting a broken appliance repaired by sending it to a service center requires careful packing and mailing.

   I. Broken appliances can be repaired by service centers.
      A. It's generally easy to bring the appliance to a service unit if one exists in your city.
      B. Often, no such centers exist nearby.
         1. The manufacturer's center may be out of state.
         2. Local repair shops cannot do the work.
         3. Each company has its own designs and required parts.

   II. Mailing the appliance requires attention to important details.
      A. You can find the mailing address easily.
         1. Check the literature that accompanied the object.
         2. Telephone the store where you purchased the object to find out the address.
      B. The biggest job is packing up the object and mailing it off.
         1. Find a strong cardboard box and pack the appliance well in order to prevent shifting and breakage.
         2. Close the carton with strong tape.
         3. Print mailing and home addresses carefully.
         4. Write a letter providing essential information.
            a. Tell what is wrong with the appliance and where you bought it.

b. Address the envelope correctly and enclose the letter.

c. Tape the envelope to the outside of the carton.

5. The post office will weigh the package and tell you costs for mailing and insurance.

EXERCISE

One student jotted down the following information for an essay entitled "Linking Atlantic and Pacific: The Panama Canal." Read all of her data and then choose the two facts that represent the main headings (I and II). Then group the related facts under those headings in order to fill in the outline.

Disease, corruption, and lack of equipment caused the company to go bankrupt.

Actual construction cost $320 million.

The United States government eventually built the canal.

De Lesseps's company dug 76 million cubic yards of dirt.

Sanitation cost $20 million.

A French company owned by Ferdinand De Lesseps was the first to try to dig a canal through the Isthmus of Panama.

The United States government removed over 211 million cubic yards of earth.

The original French companies received $40 million.

The canal cost the United States about $390 million.

Ten million dollars was paid to Panama for rights.

EXERCISE

Write a formal topic or sentence outline of

1. John Fousek's paper on his roommate's irritating habits (see Chapter 2; pages 42–43).
2. Hugh Nicholes' paper "The Mechanics of Backyard Mechanics" on pages 94–95.

EXERCISE

For the topic you limited in the exercise on page 45, prepare an outline that will help you develop a draft paper.

EXERCISE

Look ahead to the formal outline (page 491) for the research paper. What does the outline tell you about how the writer will develop the paper?

COLLABORATIVE LEARNING

Bring to class the outline you produced for the previous exercise, an outline to help you develop a draft of a paper. Form groups of three or four and comment on each other's outlines. As you discuss the work of members in the group, address these questions:

- Does the outline indicate a clear thesis? If not, how can the writer improve it?
- Do the main categories indicate appropriate divisions for the paper?
- Do the subcategories logically support the main categories under which the writer has placed them?
- Does the outline follow the conventions of outline form?

For support in meeting this chapter's objectives, follow this path in MyCompLab: Resources ⇒ Writing ⇒ Writing Process ⇒ Planning. Review the Instruction and Multimedia resources about outlining; then complete the Exercises and click on Gradebook to measure your progress.

CHAPTER 5

Writing Your Paper: An Overview

Before we proceed in Part Two to developing different kinds of papers—comparison, classification, process, and others—we first need to discuss the characteristics common to almost all types of papers.

In this chapter you will

- examine model introductions and write a strong introduction for an essay

- examine the characteristics of strong body paragraphs

- analyze paragraphs with topic sentences

- use transitional expressions effectively

- develop methods for achieving unity and coherence in your writing

- write a strong conclusion for your essay

Writing a Strong Introduction

To start, you need a beginning, or an **introduction**. The introduction consists of one or more paragraphs that set the stage for the essay.

Stating the Thesis

The simplest introduction identifies the subject and states the thesis. This is not to say that the thesis statement you produced in your prewriting or placed at the top of your outline must necessarily appear in the same form in the actual introduction. For example, John Fousek's original thesis in Chapter 2, *My friend Jim really irritates me with his habit of never closing things that he opens up,* is stated differently in the introductory paragraph of his final draft in Chapter 6:

> But Jim has one shortcoming that irritates me: He doesn't close things.

Turn to Fousek's paper on pages 122–123 and note how his introduction builds to the thesis with interesting and pertinent information about his roommate, Jim, that sets the stage for the main point of the paper.

For yet another example, look ahead to the paper, "The Beginning of the End" (pages 394–395). Harriet McKay's original thesis statement in her outline for that paper was:

Although the ending of "Charles" by Shirley Jackson is a surprise, the author subtly presents clues throughout the story that enable one, on a second reading, to see that Jackson does prepare for the ending.

As you can see, in the final paper, she writes instead:

Until the last sentence of Shirley Jackson's "Charles," I had no idea that Charles, the terror of kindergarten, was an imaginary person created by Laurie and that Charles's little monster antics were really Laurie's own antics. The author fooled me completely, but I have to admit that she played fair. She gave her readers all the clues they needed to make a sensible guess about how the story would end.

What matters is to present the idea of the thesis in the most interesting manner possible.

Forecasting the Paper

Sometimes, in addition to identifying the subject and stating the thesis, the introduction lists the divisions of the rest of the paper.

Amid the growing pressure to study hard and make good grades, any student who admits to attending college to catch a mate risks alienation, hostility, and ridicule. I'm not sure that's fair. Although I firmly believe that students, while they are in college, should get the best education possible, I see no harm in their looking for a spouse at the same time. I believe college is an ideal place for an intelligent man or woman to look for a mate. For one thing, it's easy to meet eligible members of the opposite sex in college. Also, college provides a setting in which friendships can grow freely and naturally into love. Besides, an educated person surely wants a mate who shares his or her interests and tastes. What better place to find such a person than in college?

Here, the introduction identifies the subject—finding a mate while in college—and then states the thesis—*College is an ideal place for an intelligent man or woman to look for a mate.* The sentences following the thesis statement let you know how the writer will advance the argument in the body of the paper. You are prepared to expect the three reasons to be developed in such a way as to prove that college is an ideal place to find a mate.

Using Different Introductory Strategies

Although in short papers the one-paragraph introduction is most common, you are not limited to only one paragraph. Consider this four-paragraph introduction:

"I don't like to do my Christmas shopping early. I enjoy the bustle of last-minute crowds."

"Why should I start research for my term paper this early? I work best under pressure."

"I'll replace the washer on the bathroom sink Saturday when I have time to do it properly."

We recognize such statements for what they are—excuses for procrastination. We have, of course, been told from childhood that putting off until tomorrow what we can do today is bad practice, and we feel guilty about not following such good advice, so we make up excuses to justify our tendency to delay performing unpleasant tasks. But away with guilt. Away with excuses. Procrastination, far from being evil, can, in many cases, have positive effects.

The first three paragraphs give examples of the subject—procrastination. The fourth paragraph discusses the examples and then, about the time the reader probably expects a humdrum list of ways to avoid putting off tasks, offers a surprising thesis: *Procrastination may be a good thing.*

Many other kinds of introductions can start an essay effectively. You might, for example, occasionally try dramatizing a situation:

Sheila felt light-headed: Her eyes would not focus and there was a slight hum in her ears. Her hands, wet and clammy, shook so that she could hardly write. She could not concentrate. She wanted only to run, to be away from that terrible scene.

Sheila had not just witnessed some horrible accident that she must report. She is a freshman composition student who has been told to write her first in-class composition. Many students will recognize Sheila's symptoms. Perhaps the following tips about writing a composition under pressure will help alleviate their pain.

The scene described in the first paragraph attracts the reader's attention. The second paragraph explains the situation and anticipates the rest of the paper, which offers tips on writing under pressure. Another option is to use an anecdote to illustrate the subject:

> Mrs. Peters was busily talking to a neighbor over the telephone one afternoon when she experienced the sudden fear that her baby son had been hurt. She told her neighbor and ran to check the baby, supposedly napping in his crib upstairs. To her horror, she found the child unconscious on the floor. Evidently he had tried to climb out of the crib but, in the attempt, had fallen on his head. Mrs. Peters's "knowing" her baby was in danger is the kind of experience many of us have had at one time or another. Yesterday, for example, I dialed a friend, and just before his telephone could ring, he picked up the receiver to call me. Both of these incidents are illustrations of the kind of thought transference known as *telepathy*.

The two anecdotes in this introduction show how telepathy, the subject of the paper, functions. The remainder of the paper explains how telepathy works.

As you can see, introductions take various forms. In many cases, as in the preceding paragraph, the thesis sentence appears at the end of the introduction. The examples here by no means exhaust the possibilities, but they do illustrate some ways of approaching a subject. Whatever form you choose, it's important to remember that the introduction must interest your readers—after all, you do want them to read the remainder of the paper—and it should in some way prepare readers for what follows.

 TIPS   for Writing a Strong Introduction

Consider these options as you plan to write an introduction for your paper.

- **Build to your thesis.**   When you have a tentative thesis in place, you can build to it with a series of sentences. Your introduction should present the thesis in the most interesting manner possible. Spark your readers' interest and set a context for the thesis in your introduction.

- **Identify the paper's divisions.**   Let the reader know how you will treat the subject in the body of your paper.

- **Seek variety with more than one paragraph.**   Some topics benefit from a multi-paragraph introduction that builds to the thesis.

- **Tell an anecdote.**   A story relevant to your topic can appeal to readers and engage their interest.

- **Deal with the opposition.**   If you're writing about why sixteen-year-olds should have the right to vote, build to your thesis by explaining why some people oppose such a plan.

■ **Ask a challenging question.** You can stimulate your readers' interest with a thought-provoking question or series of questions that you will address in your essay.

■ **Inject some humor.** Often a humorous statement can win readers over as you prepare to build to the serious topic at hand.

■ **Quote a statement relevant to your topic.** Use a quote from books or current periodicals. *Bartlett's Familiar Quotations* or online quotation sites can be helpful resources.

■ **Provide dramatic data or statistics.** You can give important background to your topic by citing data. Consider the introductory data in the first sentence of this brief introduction to a paper about presidential campaign contributions on college campuses:

> At three major universities, Harvard, Stanford, and Columbia, more than 80 percent of the dollars in 2008 presidential campaign donations went to Democratic candidates. But these figures mask a strong conservative Republican base on college campuses.

■ **Avoid pitfalls.** Pay attention to approaches that can derail your essay with a weakness in your introduction:

- Balance the length of your introduction against the length of your body paragraphs. Don't make your introduction too long. Body paragraphs of about ten sentences suggest the length of introductory paragraphs at about four or five sentences.

- Don't identify the parts of your essay by name. Avoid writing, "In my introduction I will … " or "In my next paragraph I will…."

- Don't write to your readers as if they are sitting next to you. Avoid writing, "Now I will show you… " or "I want to explain this to you…."

- Don't apologize for anything, such as your lack of experience or limitations in writing about the topic. Avoid expressions like these: "My knowledge of this subject is limited" or "If I had more time I could have" or "People who know the area better than I do might disagree."

- Don't repeat yourself. An introduction is a vital part of your essay, not a space filler. Don't keep saying the same thing over and over because you haven't thought carefully enough about presenting your thesis. If you can't figure out how to develop your introduction, write only your thesis in a well-developed sentence or two.

EXERCISE   Decide whether the introductions below would be good first paragraphs for essays. Defend your opinions. Then make any corrections that you feel will improve the introductory paragraphs. In some cases, you may have to rewrite the paragraph completely. Use separate paper.

1. Swimming is an important activity for a healthy life. I was a swimmer in high school and college, and I will continue to swim as long as I am physically able. This essay will try to show how important swimming is and how swimmers benefit from swimming.

2. I do not know much about AIDS except what I have heard on TV. Physicians know more about this subject than I do, but I would like to consider the medical facts of the disease and some steps being taken to prevent its spread.

3. Michael Lemonick writes in *Scientific American* that "The basic proposition behind the science of climate change is so firmly rooted in the laws of physics that no reasonable person can dispute it." If that is the case, why is there so much controversy about the concept of global warming? Why do many scientists, politicians, and laymen deny that the earth is heating up? The naysayers offer many explanations for their position, but, as we can see, they are largely false.

4. A young boy cowers in the corner whenever he enters a room full of adults. A little girl refuses to talk with her teacher, the school nurse, or the principal. A five-year-old boy refuses assistance from a park attendant as he tries to climb onto the jungle gym. A red-haired, big-eyed seven-year-old girl would rather eat lunch alone than join a group of "grown-ups." Are these children simply cautious? No, they are the fearful victims of child abuse. Fortunately, a national campaign to alert the public about the horrors of child abuse is now under way.

5. In this essay, I will write about my summer vacation house. My first paragraph will show what the house looks like. Then I will tell about our annual Fourth of July party there and how I learned that love makes the world go round.

Writing the Body Paragraphs

The **body** of a paper provides support for the thesis presented in the introduction. Body paragraphs develop the writing plan or outline and should lead readers logically from one section to another without causing confusion.

Writing Topic Sentences

One method of leading your reader is to write clear topic sentences for each paragraph. A **topic sentence** is to a paragraph what a thesis is to a paper: it expresses the central idea of the paragraph. The remainder of the paragraph gives support for the topic sentence.

Stated Topic Sentences

Topic sentences generally appear at the beginning of a paragraph, but they can appear anywhere in a paragraph.

Topic Sentence at the Beginning

Mrs. Jackson, my landlady's mother, is very nosy. No matter how many times I descend the stairs in one day, I always find Mrs. Jackson peeking out her front door. Usually she makes some statement or asks some question: "You really get around a lot. I guess you're going to the grocery now, huh?" I must give an explanation, denial, or confirmation of her guess—rather loudly, I might add, because of her hearing problem. Whenever company calls, they too are detained and cross-examined on the first floor. "Who are you going to see?" "Are you a relative?" "I guess you've known her a long time." Never does a visitor get up the stairs without first conversing with Mrs. Jackson.

Topic Sentence at the End

He drank noisily and chewed with his mouth open. He made loud, vulgar comments to the waitress, who had difficulty hiding her anger as other customers turned to stare. His idea of conversation was to regale his date with statistics about the World Series or facts about his expensive new car—especially its expense. *An hour with Bruce in the city's most costly restaurant made Jane wish she had dined at home alone on a tuna fish sandwich.*

Topic Sentence in the Middle

A fire-warning detector will "smell" smoke and sound an alarm; a guided missile will "see" and pursue a radar echo or the hot engines of a bomber; a speed governor will "feel" when a shaft is spinning too fast and act to restrain it. *But ... quotation marks are appropriate in all such cases, because these machines do not have minds and they do not perceive the world as human beings do.* Information from our eyes, ears, and other senses goes to our brains, and of some of it (by no means all) we are aware as a vivid part of our conscious experience, showing us the world we inhabit.

—Nigel Calder, *The Mind of Man*

On rare occasions, writers do not state the topic sentence directly at all; instead, they imply it:

Implied Topic Sentence

Often when I find some passage in a book especially impressive—especially bright, say, or especially moving—I find myself turning to the dust jacket, if the author's picture is there, to communicate, to say a kind of "Well done." Coretta Scott King's photograph, soft, shadowed, and lovely, is on the jacket of her book *My Life with Martin Luther King, Jr.* I must have turned to it a dozen times in the reading of this book.

Here, the paragraph's central idea—that Coretta Scott King's book *My Life with Martin Luther King, Jr.* is especially impressive—is so clear that a statement of it is unnecessary; indeed, to state it directly would mar the grace of the paragraph. Implied topic sentences are tricky, though; use them cautiously. An idea that seems quite clear to you may not be as clear to your reader.

In summary, a topic sentence states the central idea of the paragraph. Wherever you decide to put your topic sentence, keep your readers in mind. They should not experience any confusion in following your thought. The central idea of every paragraph must be clear enough to lead readers easily from one point of your paper to another.

One Student Writing: Topic Sentences

In the following student paper, Hugh Nicholes classifies a group of his friends. Notice how the topic sentences move the classification along.

Hugh Nicholes
The Mechanics of Backyard Mechanics

Introduction states similarities among friends and sets frame for thesis.

1   Among my circle of friends and acquaintances, whose ages range from twenty to thirty-five, there is a general point of similarity. They are all short of funds and they depend on cars for transportation. Consequently, they all attempt to maintain and repair their own cars when possible. These backyard mechanics fall into three amusing categories: the putterer, the gas station mechanic, and the gadgeteer.

Thesis sentence: Friends who repair their own cars ("backyard mechanics") fall into three categories.

Topic sentence of second paragraph: introduces first kind of backyard mechanic that this paragraph will present. Note effective link between topic sentence and thesis sentence.

The putterer, as his title suggests, approaches his work in an aimless, often ineffective manner. Although he will undertake almost any job and stick with it until it is completed, he does so with considerable trepidation, and for good reason. It generally takes him ages to complete a job unless he gets help. His almost complete ignorance of machinery is well balanced by an insufficiency of tools. He works on the theory that if he makes no major alterations, he can do no major damage, and he may accomplish something while fooling around. He may be identified by his conversation: "Say, good buddy, why don't you drop over and have a beer or two with me? By the way, I'm doing a little work on my car. You used to do this sort of thing; maybe you've got some ideas?"

2

Supporting details establish qualities of the "putterer."

Topic sentence of third paragraph.

The gas station mechanic replaces components; he never tries to repair anything that can be unbolted and forced off a more general assembly. Often he replaces many components before he finds the one that was actually defective. This technique frequently costs more money than he can afford. He has a fair number of tools and some mechanical knowledge. He works on the theory that anything can be replaced by reversing the process of removal. His typical comment on his repairs is, "Damn! I guess the problem wasn't electrical. Can you lend me twenty bucks? I think I need a new carburetor."

3

Supporting details explain the category "gas station mechanic."

Topic sentence of fourth paragraph.

Supporting details explain the "gadgeteer."

The gadgeteer is a study in improvisation. His command of theory is good, his experience is adequate, but his application is dubious. He generally has a nearly sufficient number of tools, but he relies on tape, string, and wire. His basic theory of operation reads as follows: "If some-thing doesn't work, it may as well be experimented upon; the worst that can happen is it gets broken, which is what is wrong in the first place. A car will run without many of its components." His generally does. When speaking of his repairs, he usually sounds slightly doubtful: "All I did was twist this strut around so this thing off an old Ford truck would fit, and now it runs like a top. I think." Of the three groups, this type has the most fun with his car.

4

Topic sentence of final paragraph. Note important link to thesis sentence.

My best friend, Robert, has gone through all three stages, which shows that placement in a category is not permanent. In fact, one may change categories at any time for any reason, and, in the case of the putterer and the gas station mechanic, that would be a good thing to do.

5

FOR WRITING OR DISCUSSION

1. What is the thesis of the paper?

2. Do the topic sentences give you a good idea of the nature of each type of mechanic? Why, or why not?

3. Which type of mechanic is the best? In what paragraph is this type described? Should he have been described earlier? Why, or why not?

4. Does the audience for the paper need to know much about cars to appreciate the descriptions of each type? Why, or why not?

5. What does the topic sentence of the last paragraph contribute to your impression of the three types?

COLLABORATIVE LEARNING

Form groups and examine the following short paragraphs, both of which lack a topic sentence. As a group, develop a logical topic sentence for each. Then report your topic sentence and compare it with those written by other groups.

1. Jason's room is always in a shambles because he never bothers to pick up after himself. His clothes, schoolbooks, and other papers are on the floor, on his bed, and every place else. He never bothers to take dishes back to the kitchen. He just lets them pile up, and he won't lift a finger to tidy up his room until he is literally threatened. Jason is so lazy that when he is watching television, rather than change the channel, he'll just watch the same station all evening, even if he doesn't like the programs. He even walks around with his shoes untied because he is too lazy to bend over and tie them. Sometimes I think he may be too lazy to breathe.

2. Many students enter college with poor reading and writing skills. During their first year of college they need special courses designed to elevate their language competence, although they should have achieved a reasonably high level in high school. In addition, teachers often criticize first-year college students for their inability to think critically. What, college teachers wonder, have students done during four years of high school? What books have they read? What writing have they done? Have they not analyzed books, films, events?

Writing Transitions

Another way to help readers follow your thoughts is to use **transitions,** words or phrases that show the logical connections between ideas. Transitional words like *and, but, however, therefore, next,* and *finally* act as signals. They say to a reader, "Here's an additional point," or "A contrast is coming up," or "Now, I'm drawing a conclusion." Transitions make connections between ideas clear and therefore easy to follow. Consider, for example, the following pairs of sentences.

Awkward:	My nephew is a brat. I love him.
Better:	My nephew is a brat, *but* I love him.
Awkward:	The magician showed the audience that the hat was empty. He pulled a rabbit from it.
Better:	*First* the magician showed the audience that the hat was empty. *Then* he pulled a rabbit from it.

Here are some examples of transitions.

Common Transitional Expressions

To show space relations

above, adjacent to, against, alongside, around, at a distance from, at the, below, beside, beyond, encircling, far off, forward, from the, in front of, in the rear, inside, near the back, near the end, nearby, next to, on, over, surrounding, there, through the, to the left, to the right, up front

To show time relations

afterward, at last, before, earlier, first, former, formerly, further, furthermore, immediately, in the first place, in the interval, in the meantime, in the next place, in the last, later on, latter, meanwhile, next, now, often, once, previously, second, simultaneously, sometime later, subsequently, suddenly, then, therefore, third, today, tomorrow, until now, when, years ago, yesterday

To indicate something added to what has come before

again, also, and, and then, besides, further, furthermore, in addition, last, likewise, moreover, next, nor, too

To give examples or to intensify points

after all, as an example, certainly, for example, for instance, indeed, in fact, in truth, it is true, of course, specifically, that is

To show similarities

alike, in the same way, like, likewise, resembling, similarly

To show contrasts

after all, although, but, conversely, differ(s) from, difference, different, dissimilar, even though, granted, however, in contrast, in spite of, nevertheless, notwithstanding, on the contrary, on the other hand, otherwise, still, though, unlike, while this may be true, yet

To indicate cause and effect

accordingly, as a result, because, consequently, hence, since, then, therefore, thus

To conclude or summarize

finally, in brief, in conclusion, in other words, in short, in summary, that is, to summarize

I do not need to tell you how important the election is. *Nor* do I need to remind you to vote tomorrow.

Laura is always on one kind of diet or another. *Yet* she never seems to lose any weight.

Medicare can be a blessing to elderly people. The difficulty of filling out all the required forms, *however*, sometimes makes them wonder how blessed they are.

I have been a thrifty stay-at-home most of my life. It was a surprise to my children, *therefore*, when I went off to Europe first class last summer.

Avoiding Too Many Transitions

Used sensibly, transitions contribute to the smoothness of your paper. However, too many transitions can be as distressing to a reader as too few. This example overuses transitional words:

The children wanted to see the animals in my woods. *However*, they made too much noise. *In the first place*, all twenty of them shouted. *Moreover*, they screamed. *Furthermore*, they threw rocks into the streams. *Therefore*, birds, frogs, even bugs went rushing to the hills. *As a result*, the children saw no animals. *Nor* should they have expected to see animals after making so much noise. *Nevertheless*, I was sorry that they thought they might see what only hours of silence and days of watching ever bring to sight.

Now look at how the paragraph actually appears in *The Inland Island* by Josephine Johnson:

"Where are all your animals?" the little children cried, running … through the woods—twenty little children, panting, shouting, screaming, throwing rocks into the streams. Birds, frogs, even bugs went rushing to the hills. How sad that the children thought they might see what only hours of silence, days of watching ever bring to sight.

Clearly, Johnson's paragraph is far better. All those transitions in the first paragraph do not help it flow; rather, they get in the way. Use transitions, then, but use them only to signal a logical connection that would not otherwise be obvious.

Using Sentences and Paragraphs as Transitions

In making connections between ideas, you are not limited to single words and short phrases. Often the topic sentence serves both as a transition and as an indicator of the central idea of a paragraph.

> *Besides making life difficult for his parents,* Charles sent his first-grade teacher home with a nightly headache.
> *Although the Puritans observed a strict code of behavior,* their lives were often filled with great joy.

In sentences of this kind, the introductory adverbial phrase or clause (shown here in italics) points back to the preceding paragraph to provide a transition. At the same time, the rest of the sentence points forward to the subject matter of the paragraph for which it is the topic sentence.

Occasionally, an entire paragraph may serve as a transition. It's sometimes a good idea to stop—at a logical point, of course—and sum up what you've said so far before going on to another point. The good **transitional paragraph**, like the transitional topic sentence, points back to what has gone before and points forward to what is yet to come. Note the successful use of these transitional paragraphs:

> Thus, granting Professor Maly time to do a thorough and conscientious new edition of her book will add to her professional standing, bring a bit of valuable attention and some money to the college, and result in a book more helpful than ever in teaching students how to write clear English. These considerations are, I think, justification for the professional leave she has requested, but I have other reasons for recommending that her request for leave be granted.
> So much for the preparation of the surface. Now we are ready to paint.
> Thus, Jackie Robinson had to confront a long tradition of bigotry in the major leagues. How did he meet this challenge?
> With all these arguments in favor of state-run lotteries, opponents of such lotteries can still raise some valid points.

EXERCISE See the excerpt from John Fousek's paper on pages 118–119. How would you revise the over-coordinated sentence?

Developing Paragraphs: Unity and Coherence

In addition to leading your reader from one paragraph to another, you need to be certain that the paragraphs themselves are logically and adequately developed. A **paragraph**—a group of related sentences developing a single topic—must be unified, coherent, and complete.

Paragraph Unity

A paragraph must be **unified**—that is, all the sentences in the paragraph must develop one idea, the one contained in the topic sentence. Anything that doesn't contribute to the idea should be omitted from the paragraph. One of the following two paragraphs appears exactly as it was written by Lewis Thomas, a skilled essayist whose paragraphs are beautifully unified. Which paragraph do you think Thomas wrote?

Paragraph 1

[1]Viewed from the distance of the moon, the astonishing thing about the earth ... is that it is alive. [2]The photographs show the dry, pounded surface of the moon in the foreground, dead as an old bone. [3]Aloft, floating free beneath the moist, gleaming membrane of bright blue sky, is the rising earth, the only exuberant thing in this part of the cosmos. [4]If you could look long enough, you would see the swirling of the great drifts of white cloud, covering and uncovering the half-hidden masses of land. [5]If you had been looking for a very long, geologic time, you could have seen the continents themselves in motion, drifting apart on their crustal plates, held afloat by the fire beneath. [6]It has the organized, self-contained look of a live creature, full of information, marvelously skilled in handling the sun.

Paragraph 2

[1]Viewed from the distance of the moon, the astonishing thing about the earth ... is that it is alive. [2]The great technological advances that made it possible for man to walk on the moon also made it possible to send photographs back to earth. [3]Such are the miracles of modern science that you sat in your living room and watched the astronauts romp, enjoying their gravity-less freedom. [4]Soon, however, you saw something much more important, the photographs of the moon. [5]The photographs show the dry, pounded surface of the moon in the foreground, dead as an old bone. [6]It is so dead you marvel that poets for centuries have hymned its praises. [7]On the other hand, aloft, floating free beneath the moist, gleaming membrane of bright blue sky, is the rising earth, the only exuberant thing in this part of the cosmos. [8]If you could look long enough, you would see the swirling of the great drifts of white cloud, covering and uncovering the half-hidden masses of land. [9]If you had been looking for a very long, geologic time, you could have seen the continents themselves in motion, drifting apart on their crustal plates, held afloat by the fire beneath. [10]It has the organized, self-contained look of a live creature, full of information, marvelously skilled in handling the sun.

The first paragraph is the paragraph taken from Lewis Thomas. In the second—and longer—one, sentences 2, 3, 4, and 6 obviously do not advance Thomas' idea that the earth is alive. Instead, they distract the reader, and the paragraph loses its central idea in the confusion.

 **TIPS** for Achieving Paragraph Unity

- **Give each paragraph a controlling idea by means of a topic sentence.**

- **Check each sentence in a paragraph to see that it supports the main idea.**

- **Revise or eliminate any sentence that distracts from the main idea.**

Paragraph Coherence

A paragraph must have **coherence**; it must stick together. This means the sentences must be smoothly integrated. You can't expect your readers to follow your thought if the sentences do not follow some intelligible order. Is the following paragraph orderly? Can you follow the writer's thought?

> Yesterday was one big disaster. When I found my right rear tire flat as a board, I laid my head on the steering wheel and wept. The burned bacon didn't help, either; especially after that cold shower, I needed a hot meal. I had worked so hard on my paper I didn't think it was fair that the professor gave me a "D" on it. Sleeping through the alarm always starts my day off wrong. And now I've got to write a 20-page term paper for history. I should have stayed in bed.

Using a simple **chronological order** can make this paragraph coherent:

> Yesterday was one big disaster. I slept through the alarm. Late, I rushed to the bathroom. No more hot water. Teeth chattering from a cold shower, I decided to cook a hot breakfast—and burned the bacon. I gulped down some cold shredded wheat and dashed to my car. By running two traffic lights, I made it to my English class on time and eagerly waited for the professor to return our papers. I had worked hard and was sure I had made at least a "B," if not an "A." Then I saw a big red "D" at the top of my paper. It didn't seem fair. I went on to my history class, and the professor assigned a 20-page term paper. I decided to cut my remaining classes and go home. When I got to my car and found the right rear tire flat as a board, I laid my head on the steering wheel and wept. I should have stayed in bed.

You can achieve order in a number of other ways as well. One of these lies in the use of **space order**—from left to right, from top to bottom, or, as in the following example, from near to far.

It was a rimy morning, and very damp. I had seen the damp lying on the outside of my little window, as if some goblin had been crying there all night, and using the window for a pocket-handkerchief. Now I saw the damp lying on the bare hedges and spare grass, like a coarser sort of spiders' webs; hanging itself from twig to twig and blade to blade. On every rail and gate, wet lay clammy, and the marsh-mist was so thick, that the wooden finger on the post directing people to our village—a direction which they never accepted, for they never came there—was invisible to me until I was quite close under it…. The mist was heavier yet when I got out upon the marshes, so that instead of my running at everything, everything seemed to run at me….

—Charles Dickens, *Great Expectations*

You can sometimes **enumerate reasons** by listing them in regard to an action or belief (italics added):

I have sought love, *first*, because it brings ecstasy—ecstasy so great that I could often have sacrificed all the rest of life for a few hours of this joy. I have sought it, *next*, because it relieves loneliness—that terrible loneliness in which one shivering consciousness looks over the rim of the world into the cold unfathomable lifeless abyss. I have sought it, *finally*, because in the union of love I have seen, in a mystic miniature, the prefiguring vision of the heaven that saints and poets have imagined. That is what I sought, and though it might seem too good for human life, that is what—at last—I have found.

—Bertrand Russell, "What I Have Lived For"

You can give coherence to a paragraph by means of **cause and effect:**

This sentiment of retaliation is, of course, exactly what impels most offenders to do what they do. Except for racketeers, robbers, and professional criminals, the men who are arrested, convicted, and sentenced are usually out to avenge a wrong, assuage a sense of injury, or correct an injustice as they see it. Their victims are individuals whom they believe to be assailants, false friends, rivals, unfaithful spouses, cruel parents—or symbolic figures representing these individuals.

—Karl Menninger, *The Crime of Punishment*

Perhaps one of the most useful logical relations you can use to achieve coherence within a paragraph is the **comparison** of one thing to another:

In science fiction, which is the literature of extrapolation, there is to be found the recurrent theme of the omniscient computer which ultimately takes over the ordering of human life and affairs. Is this possible? I believe it is not; but I also believe that the arguments commonly advanced to refute this possibility are the wrong ones…. It is said, for example, that computers [unlike humans] "only do what they are told," that they have to be programmed for every computation they undertake. But I do not believe that I was born with an innate ability to solve quadratic equations or to identify common members of the British flora; I, too,

had to be programmed for these activities, but I happened to call my program-
mers by different names, such as "schoolteacher," "lecturer," or "professor."

—W. T. Williams, "Computers as Botanists"

You can achieve coherence by using **parallel structure**. Note the use of semicolons to achieve parallelism in this paragraph, all written to support the word
black at the beginning.

Black: the dead locust limb that scrapes my bedroom window; crows, hundreds
of them, perched like clothespins in the branches of a bare tree; the crooked lines
of tar that fill the cracks on a concrete highway; the tip of Buddy's nose when it
is wet; seven black swans, floating on a leaf-flecked pond; twisted Italian tobies
in a yellow box; leeches squirming in a white earthen jar; burned gunpowder
from my shotgun on the flannel cleaning rag; the lacquered Eaglerock biplane at
Rogers Field; tiny cloves stuck in a baked Virginia ham; licorice in elastic sticks
and lozenges and squares; cloud shadows on fields of ripening grain.

Another strategy for achieving coherence is **repetition**. In the paragraph
below by Mark Twain, the words "I know" help integrate the sentences smoothly.

I know how a prize watermelon looks when it is sunning its fat rotundity
among pumpkin vines and "simblins"; I know how to tell when it is ripe without "plugging" it; I know how inviting it looks when it is cooling itself in a tub
of water under the bed, waiting; I know how it looks when it lies on the table
in the sheltered great floor space between house and kitchen, and the children
gathered for the sacrifice and their mouths watering; I know the crackling sound
it makes when the carving knife enters its end, and I can see the split fly along in
front of the blade as the knife cleaves its way to the other end; I can see its halves
fall apart and display the rich red meat and the black seeds, and the heart standing up, a luxury fit for the elect; I know how a boy looks behind a yard-long slice
of that melon, and I know how he feels; for I have been there. I know the taste
of the watermelon which has been honestly come by, and I know the taste of the
watermelon which has been acquired by art.

—Mark Twain, *Autobiography*

Pronouns help achieve coherence. They refer readers to a previously noun
(the antecedent) and help the writer connect the ideas without having to name
the nouns again and again.

The Deadbeat Dad has emerged as our principal cultural model for ex-fathers,
for obviously failed fathers. As a cultural category, the Deadbeat Dad has
become our primary symbol of the growing failure of fatherhood in our society.
We demonize him in part because he reminds us of our fatherlessness. He
represents loss. He forces us to reduce our expectations. Consequently, we vilify
him, we threaten him—we demand that he pay—largely because he so clearly
embodies the contemporary collapse of good-enough fatherhood.

—David Blankenhorn, *The Deadbeat Dad*

Use any of these methods—or any others that work—to achieve coherence. The important thing is to achieve it—to make the relation between and among sentences clear to the reader.

 **TIPS** for Achieving Paragraph Coherence

- **Be sure that your sentences follow each other logically.**

- **Use appropriate—but not excessive—transitions.**

- **Order details appropriately through chronological or spatial order or though a list.**

- **Show causes and effects clearly.**

- **Compare one thing to another.**

- **Use parallel structure.**

- **Use repetition.**

- **Link ideas with pronouns.**

Writing a Strong Conclusion

A good **conclusion** gives a sense of finality, which you can achieve in one of several ways.

The easiest way to conclude a paper is to mention again its major ideas. The following example concludes a paper in which the writer explains membership in a book club:

> Interesting reading, the exchange of ideas, and new friends—these were my reasons for joining a book club. I have not been disappointed.

Some conclusions merely restate the thesis, although in different words to avoid monotony.

> There's an explanation for everything, it's true, but some explanations are more readily acceptable than others. That's the way it is.
>
> —George E. Condon

Some conclusions interpret the significance of the material presented in the body of the paper.

Since these personality characteristics depend on the growth of the layers of the little egg from which the person developed, they are very difficult to change.

Nevertheless, it is important for the individual to know about these types, so that he can have at least an inkling of what to expect from those around him, and can make allowances for the different kinds of human nature, and so that he can become aware of and learn to control his own natural tendencies, which may sometimes guide him into making the same mistakes over and over again in handling his difficulties.

—Eric Berne

An anecdote sometimes effectively concludes a paper. Following is the conclusion to a paper about the rewards given Dr. Jonas Salk for his polio vaccine:

Probably the greatest tribute Dr. Salk received was unwittingly paid by a small boy whose father, having shown his son the research center, told him that Dr. Salk invented the polio vaccine. The boy, looking puzzled, said, "Daddy, what's polio?"

Quotations and questions can serve to conclude papers. Both devices are used in this conclusion to a paper urging support of the United Torch Drive:

Samuel Johnson defined a patron as "one who looks with unconcern on a man struggling for life in the water, and when he has reached ground encumbers him with help." Shall we be merely patrons of the needy?

Some of the most effective conclusions attempt to set a broader, more general context for the topic. Such a conclusion helps the reader see that the limited topic you have advanced has relevance beyond your immediate concerns in the paper. By developing a larger application for the topic, you provide a new significance for it.

A student writer produced this thesis sentence in an effort to show the different shades of meaning for the word "excitement":

Excitement means one thing to a seven-year-old and something quite different to a girl in her teens.

In the first body paragraph the writer tells of the excitement she felt on a day her whole third-grade class visited her house to see the backyard cherry tree in bloom. In the next paragraphs she tells of a political demonstration she participated in and the excitement and fear of being jostled in a crowd and then knocked to the ground by people fleeing the police. Here is the conclusion to the essay:

In both instances I experienced excitement; one moment simple and innocent, and the other complex and explosive. Since such different situations aroused the same kind of emotion, I wonder if our emotions are reliable at all until we have a full chance to test them with time and experience.

I have to laugh when I hear my thirteen-year-old neighbor say she loves her high school boyfriend. Does she have any idea of what the word means? Love is an emotion, and to rely on an early or untested experience for the definition is ridiculous. Still, many young people marry at seventeen or eighteen, claiming deep love for their partners. Then, of course, in too many cases, the divorce courts spring into action just a short time after. Decisions based on emotions must be very carefully made so that we understand the full range of meaning we attach to any special feeling.

—Sarah Fogel

The conclusion establishes a new, general context; the writer's experiences lead her to believe that only maturity allows us true perspective on emotion. The essay itself is about excitement; the conclusion deals with an altogether different emotion, love; yet the example in the conclusion works very well to help the writer make her larger point.

 **TIPS** for Writing a Strong Conclusion

- **Refer to the major ideas in the paper.**

- **Restate the thesis in different words.**

- **Interpret the significance of the ideas presented.**

- **Use a lively anecdote.**

- **Present a quotation.**

- **Raise a question.**

- **Establish a new context for the topic.**

EXERCISE   For the draft of your own paper, examine the introduction, body, and conclusion in light of the guidelines explored in this chapter. What changes, additions, or deletions should you make in the draft? Revise your paper and submit it to your instructor and classmates for their comments and suggestions.

 For support in meeting this chapter's objectives, follow this path in MyCompLab: Resources ⇒ Writing ⇒ Writing Process ⇒ Drafting. Review the Instruction and Multimedia resources about writing introductions, body paragraphs, and conclusions; then complete the Exercises and click on Gradebook to measure your progress.

CHAPTER 6

Revising, Editing, and Proofreading Your Paper

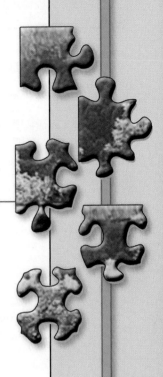

As good as John Fousek's first draft is (see Chapter 2, pages 42–43), like all papers, it needs revising and editing. These two interrelated terms identify critical stages in the development of a successful paper.

When you **revise**, you rethink the ideas and concepts in your paper and change them to reflect your new thoughts. Revision means literally *looking again*. In revising your paper, you want to present and explore any fresh insights you've developed, make necessary changes in focus and direction for your topic, and add essential details. You may have to scrap whole sentences and paragraphs or shift them around for better organization.

In this chapter you will

- develop skills for revising your thesis, improving supporting details and organization, and focusing on purpose and audience

- develop skills for revising your introduction, body paragraphs, and conclusion

- use peer review as part of your draft writing activity

- develop your skills for editing and proofreading your paper

You may have to change your thesis or alter your supporting details. And sometimes you have to start all over.

When you revise, you also make changes in language and expression. You reshape sentences for clarity and emphasis, you improve the style, you attend to appropriate word choice, diction, and sentence structure. When you **edit**, you review your writing for errors in grammar, punctuation, and spelling. Frequently, the efforts work hand in hand, especially as you draw closer to your final draft; you revise and edit at the same time.

As a specialized part of editing, **proofreading** (see pages 119–121) allows you to concentrate on errors you might have missed as well as typos or other mistakes on your final draft.

In your first effort to produce another draft, focus on the content of your essay. Try to make your paper as clear as possible. Check on organization and development of ideas. Examine your introduction and conclusion. Consider the unity, coherence, and completeness of your paragraphs. Where should you add information? What unexplored feature of your topic could you open for your readers' advantage? How could you connect related thoughts in different parts of your paper?

Revising Your Paper

Ask yourself these questions as you embark on your first attempt at revision.

- How could you improve your thesis?
- Do you have sufficient detail to back up your thesis—or do you need to cut any information that does not suit the focus of your paper as stated in your thesis?
- Could you reorganize the parts of your paper for greater effect?
- How can you assure that you accomplish your purpose? Have you defined and addressed your audience appropriately?
- Do your introduction, body paragraphs, and conclusion provide suitable structure for the ideas presented in the essay?

Revising to Improve Your Thesis

You've seen in Chapter 3 how to produce a successful thesis, and you want to review that chapter and do the thesis-writing exercises explored there. Here we want to reemphasize the importance of not viewing your thesis as written in stone. As you develop your paper, your thoughts may take you on a track that you never anticipated. In such a case you have some options:

- Revise your thesis so that it addresses the issues you have raised.
- Move your thesis to a more strategic position in your essay.
- Eliminate from your essay any ideas that do not adhere to the thesis you intended.
- Start all over with a new thesis.

You can see how John Fousek's thesis evolved through the various drafts of his paper.

First draft thesis	Intermediate draft thesis	Final draft thesis
(See page 114)	(See page 116)	(See page 122)
My friend Jim really irritates me with his habit of not closing things that he opens up.	I like Jim very much but he has one habit that I see as an annoying shortcoming. Jim doesn't close things.	But Jim has one shortcoming that irritates me: He doesn't close things.

John's first draft thesis appears as the very first sentence in his introduction. As he revised his paper, he moved the thesis to the last sentence of the introductory paragraph. You can see above how he changed the language of his thesis from draft to draft.

Revising for Appropriate Supporting Detail

As you revise, you need to be sure that the detail you're providing is appropriate to your thesis. As you will see, in revising his paper "My Roommate," John Fousek added a number of sensory details to help the reader see exactly what items his roommate Jim did not close. (See pages 116–117.) For example, the sentence "Spoons and knives clink together as he pokes through the nearest open drawer looking for things in the mess" adds an intense visual image to paragraph 3 in the intermediate draft. The verb "clink" contributes a sound to the image; and the word "pokes" lets readers see the action clearly: We actually can visualize Jim at the open drawer digging in a mess of silverware. But John also saw that he had extraneous detail. He had to eliminate the whole of paragraph 2, beginning with "Jim must be allergic to dishes... ." This paragraph—a strong one, to be sure—about Jim's failure to scrape dishes or empty the dishwasher no longer suited John's new focus in his paper, which is to present Jim's failure to close things. No doubt Jim's weakness regarding the dishes was annoying; however, it did not suit the new focus of the paper and the writer had to eliminate it.

In his essay "Getting Juiced" (pages 58–59), Joseph Anderson states his thesis clearly—the dishonesty and danger in using drugs to enhance sports performance. Note how the supporting details about baseball celebrity Barry Bonds in paragraph 2, and, in paragraphs 4 and 5, details about the cyclist Floyd Landis and the wrestler Davey Boy Smith add heft to the writer's point. Without the details, the writer's point is simply an unsupported opinion.

Revising for Better Organization

It's one thing to have a paper with strong details and a clear thesis; it's another to have the information in the paper arranged so that readers easily can follow its logic. You should have spent some time in developing an organizational strategy by means of an outline for your essay, and the outline should guide you to present your thoughts clearly. Nevertheless, when you write a draft of your paper, you must be sure that the sentences and paragraphs make sense in their current order. Would moving a section of the paper strengthen its presentation? Would a few sentences in one paragraph sound better in another? Would moving sentences around make your ideas more logical? In John Fosek's intermediate draft (page 116), you'll see that paragraph 4 now incorporates paragraph 3 from the first draft (page 115). John's complaint about Jim's not closing the bathroom door works better as part of a more general observation about the failure to close items in the bathroom.

Revising for Purpose and Audience

After you have a first draft, you want to look very carefully at your writing to see whether or not you have made your purpose and audience apparent. In regard to purpose, you must be sure that the way you wanted to treat your topic is obvious. If someone were to ask you, "What exactly are you trying to accomplish in your paper?" would you be able to answer the question simply and directly? If so, what parts of your paper most effectively make your purpose clear?

In regard to audience, you want to put yourself in your reader's place to see if any words or ideas do not strike home. Have you defined terms if you are using highly technical language? What assumptions have you made about your audience that your writing reflects?

Revising for Suitable Structure: Introduction, Body Paragraphs, Conclusion

As you revise, be sure that you have considered the key structural elements of your essay and the way they contribute to the success of your paper.

Your **introduction** is the window to the rest of your essay. On pages 87–91 we've described a variety of approaches that you might take in developing your introduction; when you revise your paper keep those options in mind.

In John Fousek's essay, note how the introduction evolved as the writer revised draft after draft.

Introduction: First Draft

My friend Jim really irritates me with his habbit of never closing things that he opens up. Don't get me wrong. As roommates for the last couple of years Jim and I get along real well in our small apartment. As students we don't get to see each other a whole lot. We also both work and this cuts down on the time we spend together too. We share responsibilities in the apartment. I clean and Jim cooks. He's generous, good sense of humor and is honest. But he has a lot of shortcomings that really burns me up. He can be a real pain.

Introduction: Final Draft

My roommate, Jim, and I have shared a small apartment for the past two years. On the whole, we get along very well. We are both students, and we both work, so we don't spend much time together; but when we do, we cooperate. Jim, who is good at it, does most of the cooking; I do most of the cleaning. We find the arrangement satisfactory. And I like Jim. He is generous, witty, honest. Our two-year association has, for the most part, been a good one. But Jim has one shortcoming that irritates me: He doesn't close things.

In John's first draft introduction, he began with his thesis statement. As he thought about the paper, John felt that the thesis was too abrupt as a starting point. He decided to build to the thesis with the background information about Jim and their cordial relationship. He cut the first sentence and created a new thesis that ended the introductory paragraph. His revisions tweaked the language for the final draft introduction; he tightened some of the sentences, removed some unnecessary language, and thereby improved his introduction significantly so that it achieved its goal of building to the thesis and setting the stage for the main point of the paper.

The **body paragraphs** in any essay must contribute to the thesis by providing information that supports the topic. In your revision, you need to assure that your paragraphs achieve that goal. Also, you want to be sure that your body paragraphs themselves have clear topics, usually expressed in a topic sentence. (You saw in Chapter 5 the various placements for a topic sentence in a paragraph.) The topic in each paragraph must relate clearly to your thesis. As you may recall, you achieve *unity*—all sentences in a paragraph developing one idea—and *coherence*—all sentences in a paragraph smoothly integrated and following one another logically—in the way your paragraphs build upon the topic. (See pages 100–104.) As you revise, be sure to check carefully on how the sentences in your paragraphs relate to the topic sentence of the paragraph and how the sentences stick together in an intelligible order. Your use of transitions here is important, and you want to be sure that you have used linking words wisely but sparingly.

John made a number of revisions in his body paragraphs, as you can see from the drafts on pages 114, 116, and 118. We have already noted how he eliminated completely the second body paragraph of the first draft. Now look at the evolution of paragraph 3 from the initial draft to the intermediate draft, which you will read on pages 116–117, to the final draft.

Paragraph 3: First Draft

For example never closing a drawer. This embarasses me a lot, I am complusive about being neat, Jim is a slob. He never thinks of organizing his drawers. He just dumps everything into his drawers and closets. In the kitchen everything is just dumped into the drawers and he's constantly banging silverware before every meal. This is when I'm usually studying and I prefer peace and quite to rattling kitchen items.

Paragraph 2 (Paragraph 3 In First Draft): Intermediate Draft

For example, he never, or almost never, closes drawers or closet doors. I may be compulsive about being neat but he's a complete slob. It never seems to have entered his mind to organize a drawer.

Paragraph 3 in the first draft has become paragraph 2 in the intermediate draft. John realized the unnecessary repetition in his first draft of paragraph 2 and reduced it sharply—by half, from 70 words to 35, five sentences to three. The new paragraph in the intermediate draft has little more than a topic sentence indicating that Jim doesn't close things and provides little useful supporting information for the assertion. From a bloated paragraph, John produced an excessively deflated one. Wisely, he rejected this paragraph in his next try.

In the final draft observe how John once again has expanded his ideas into a substantial body paragraph, full of details but empty of repetition. The details support the topic sentence and reinforce the thesis with specific references to Jim's sloppiness and his habit of never closing drawers.

Body Paragraph: Final Draft

Jim, for example, almost never closes a drawer or a closet door, and his failure to do so is often a source of embarrassment to me. The problem is that I am compulsively neat, and Jim, I'm sorry to say, is a slob. It seems never to have occurred to him that the contents of a drawer could be organized. When he does his laundry, he just empties his bag of clean clothes into a drawer—white socks, underwear, a rainbow of t-shirts with college crests, pajamas, graying handkerchiefs. When the drawer is full, he begins filling the next one. Then when he needs clean socks or a shirt, he rolls the contents of the drawer around until he finds what he wants, often leaving rejected items hanging over the edge of the drawer. His clothes closet is just as messy as the drawers. He does the same kinds of things in the kitchen. Spatulas, flatware, eggbeaters, knives clink together as he pokes through the nearest open drawer to find his favorite tool for beating eggs or mincing onions. If he'd organized the drawer in the first place, the rattle of kitchenware wouldn't disturb my study time before every meal. Since Jim doesn't close drawers or closets, our apartment usually looks like the site of a rummage sale at closing time. The appearance offends my neat soul and embarrasses me when friends visit us.

The **conclusion** of your essay is an essential component of the whole paper: it creates for your reader the final impression of your written work. Don't always settle just for a restatement of the main ideas or for a paraphrase of your thesis.

John Fousek changed his conclusion significantly from draft to draft.

Conclusion: First Draft

I try to overlook Jim's bad habbits but when he doesn't close things up especially when I get a cold blast of morning air in the shower it really irritates me.

Conclusion: Intermediate Draft

Jim is such a great guy, and I know his failure to close things is a minor bad habbit, and I try to overlook it. However, it does tend to irritate me, especially when cold air hits me right after I'm out of the shower.

Conclusion: Final Draft

When that frigid air blasts my wet body, my irritation with Jim reaches its peak. Nevertheless, because he is such a great guy and because I know his failure to close things is, in the scheme of human problems, just a minor bad habit, I try to overlook it. I shut my mouth and take a deep breath. In fact, by learning to deal with this annoyance I think I've learned a little about how to handle the frustrations of some of my friends' strange habits in general. I keep a good sense of humor and I hold my temper. After all, I'd rather have opened closets and drawers than a door closed on friendship.

In his first attempt, his conclusion is merely a restatement of his thesis with another example as support. The intermediate draft adds words but little else of import. But the conclusion in the final draft brings the main point of the essay to a close and then applies John's experience with Jim in a new context: how John is better able now "to handle the frustrations of some of my friends' strange habits in general." And the final sentence provides a neat closing to both the conclusion and the essay itself.

Peer Review: Learning from Other Students

John shaped his first draft by working first with another student in a peer-critiquing session in class.

Some teachers build peer review sessions into regular writing instruction. In **peer review**, you and your classmates comment on each other's drafts. Sometimes you work in small groups and offer comments and suggestions orally. Or, you can write comments directed at specific questions posed by fellow writers or by your teacher on a peer-response checklist. The following sample guide will help you and your classmates make useful comments about each other's drafts.

PEER EVALUATION GUIDE

- What is the thesis of the paper? Does the introduction introduce it successfully?
- What is the writer's purpose? Audience?
- Has the writer organized the essay effectively? Can you follow the ideas easily?
- Do details provide enough support for the main idea in each paragraph? Do transitions connect ideas smoothly?
- Has the writer produced an effective conclusion to the essay?
- What is the best part of the essay?
- What recommendations can you make for improvement?

Look again at John Fousek's first draft of his essay "My Roommate" and then the Peer Evaluation Guide that one of his fellow students filled out after reading the draft. John then used some of these comments as he wrote his intermediate draft.

First Draft

John Fousek

1   My friend Jim really irritates me with his habbit of not never closing things that he opens up. Don't get me wrong. As roommates for the last couple of years Jim and I get along real well in our small apartment. As students we don't get to see each other a whole lot. We also both work and this cuts down on the time we spend together too. We share responsibilities in the apartment. I clean and Jim cooks. He's generous, good sense of humor and is honest. But boy his shortcoming of not closing things up burn me up. It's a real pain.

2   Jim must be allergic to dishes, he never remembers to rinse the dirty dishes after we eat a meal together. Smears of ketchup and clumps of chile or stew are on the plates after he dumps them in the sink and runs off to a soccer practice or the library. When I get to loading the dishwasher the stuff is impossible to scrape off. Our arrangement is when I load the dishwasher he's suppose to empty the dishes when they're clean. Fat chance. He always forgets and too many times I've put dirty dishes in with the clean ones before realizing my misteak.

3   He has other bad habits.

4   For example never closing a drawer. This embarasses me a lot, I am compulsive about being neat, Jim is a slob. He never thinks of organizing his drawers. He just dumps everything into his drawers and closets. In the

kitchen everything is just dumped into the drawers and he's constantly banging silverware before every meal. This is when I'm usually studying and I prefer peace and quite to rattling kitchen items.

Jim also often fails to close the bathroom door after using the facilities while I shower. Since the bathroom has become warm and steamy during the couse of my shower, the cold air annoys me, the idea that Jim has been so thoughtless bothers me.

5

Of course he leaves the kitchen drawers open along with the clothing drawers. Our apartment always looks like a bomb hit it. The appearance irritates my neat soul. I'm embarassed when friends visit us.

6

I get even madder at Jim's failure to close things in the bathroom he never closes the shampoo cap. This makes me lose my cool composure more than anything. I always When I'm in the shower I always grab the shampoo bottle by the cap a loose cap results in the agravation of shampoo on my toes instead of my hair. And because I am economically minded, moneywise, watching shampoo go down the drain really bothers me.

7

I try to overlook Jim's bad habbits but when he doesn't close things up especially when I get a cold blast of morning air in the shower it really irritates me.

8

SAMPLE PEER EVALUATION

- **What is the thesis of the paper? Does the introduction introduce it successfully?** Your thesis is that your roommate doesn't close things and that it annoys you. I like the intro because it shows that you really like the guy and that he's not a total nerd. But is intro upside down? Your thesis comes first? Why?
- **What is the writer's purpose? Audience?** To show in detail what the not closing things looks like. Your audience is the kids in the class and the professor. (Right?)
- **Has the writer organized the essay effectively? Can you follow the ideas easily?** No problem. But the dirty dishes part doesn't have anything to do with closing things.
- **Do details provide enough support for the main idea in each paragraph? Do transitions connect ideas smoothly?** The ideas flow so I think the transitions are good. You have good details, like the dumping things in the drawers
- **Has the writer produced an effective conclusion to the essay?** It is a little short, but it's okay. I mean that you can tell that it's a conclusion that goes back to your thesis. And "cold blast of air in the morning shower" is good.
- **What is the best part of the essay?** The bathroom examples—funny! I've had toe shampoos too. And I like the open drawers part.
- **What recommendations can you make for improvement?**
  1. Show more details, like what's in the drawers and how they're dumped in. Maybe describe the bathroom, too? And show what Jim looks like?
  2. I agree with your question. Watch slang and trite words. like "like a bomb hit it" and "burn me up."

These comments from one of John's classmates will be very helpful as John attends to the next draft. Certainly, the paper could benefit from more precisely stated details. And, as the student reviewer suggests, the writing is too conversational. John thought more about his topic and the comments and suggestions his classmate provided. Another friend and John's teacher offered further insights about the first draft.

Before you read a draft written by one of your classmates, look at the Peer Evaluation Guide and keep the questions in mind so that you can provide detailed comments that will help the writer with the next draft.

Before you revise your own essay, examine the Peer Evaluation Guide filled out by one of your classmates. Consider carefully the responses that your reader provided. You don't have to accept all the points made, but you do have to think about the observations and recommendations that may help you improve the next draft of your paper.

COLLABORATIVE LEARNING

Exchange drafts with another student in the class and write comments about the student's paper. Ask the other student to write comments on your paper as well. The purpose of your comments is to help the writer produce the next draft. Focus most of your comments on the questions about thought, content, and essay form. Do not make extensive comments about errors in grammar, spelling, and punctuation.

One Student Writing: Revising and Editing

Back at the computer, John developed his next draft, shown following.

We've pointed out some of the advances in John's paper, and you probably saw others. He tightened the introduction and sharpened the thesis sentence. (See Chapter 3, pages 87–88.) Following his classmate's advice on the Peer

---

INTERMEDIATE DRAFT
My Roommate

1　　Jim and I have been sharing an apartment for the last two years and we get along pretty well. We are both students. We both work. We don't spend a lot of time together. When we are together, we cooperate with chores. Jim does the cooking because he's good at it, and I do the cleaning. Jim is fun to be with and he has many good qualities. He is honest, generous, and a fun guy. We had a good relationship over the last two years. I like Jim very much but he has one habit that I see as an annoying shortcoming. Jim doesn't close things.

needed?

For example, he never, or almost never, closes drawers or closet   2
doors. I may be compulsive about being neat but he's a complete slob. It
never seems to have entered his mind to organize a drawer.

His clothes closet is just as messy, he does the same thing in the   3
kitchen when he's cooking. If he'd organize the drawer in the first place the
noisy silverware wouldn't bother me. Spoons and knives clink together as he
pokes through the nearest open drawer looking for things in the mess. Our
apartment usually looks like a messy rummage sale. I really get embarrassed
when any of my friends visit and they see the place looking so messy.

I'm bothered even more by Jim's failure to close bathroom objects,   4
for example, he never closes the shampoo cap. This makes me lose
my cool composure more than anything. When I'm showering, I always
grab the shampoo bottle by the cap. a loose cap always results in
shampoo on my toes and not in my hair, which at this point is soaking wet. Because I am economically minded, moneywise watching
a green puddle of shampoo going down the drain wasted every day
really upsets me. Jim forgets to close the bathroom door after using
the facilities while I shower. The bathroom has grown warm and steamy
during the couse of my shower, the cold morning air chills me. Jim's
thoughtlessness is very annoying.

Jim is such a great guy, and I know his failure to close things is a   5
minor bad habit, and I try to overlook it. However, it does tend to irritate
me, especially when cold air hits me right after I'm out of the shower.

Evaluation Guide, John eliminated the paragraph about dishes in the dishwasher, and he also eliminated some colloquial expressions. He provided additional concrete language; "a green puddle of shampoo" is a good image.

Improvements aside, you probably saw as well several areas for John to
explore in further revision and editing. John's paper would benefit significantly
from even more sensory language (see pages 53–54). In paragraph 1, better
coordination and subordination would link related thoughts and eliminate the
bumpy ride from sentence to sentence. In addition, some of John's sentences
still ramble a bit and ideas are repeated, as in the last few sentences of the third
paragraph. Note how many times John refers to messy conditions; the repetitive language needs revision and editing here. Some of the ideas throughout
the essay should be reordered or more smoothly connected (or both), and
some of the paragraphs should be joined. John's first and last paragraphs, vital
elements in any paper, could be strengthened (see Chapter 5).

Editing

Although John made handwritten changes to correct some mistakes on his intermediate draft, his sentences contain many structural errors—particularly run-ons and fragments. In the revision process, some of these errors may disappear simply because new or reorganized sentences will replace some of those sentences with mistakes. Nevertheless, a pattern of errors emerges here, and John must address them as he revises, edits, and proofreads in successive drafts.

Learning from Your Instructor's Comments

Your instructor may read an early draft of your writing and (or) your final copy. In either case, she no doubt will use a system of marking symbols (like those at the end of this book), as well as marginal comments and final summary remarks to suggest changes and corrections for you to consider. Pay careful attention to any comments you receive. Just as you attended to your classmate's comments on the Peer Evaluation Guide, when you revise your work again, think through your instructor's suggestions as you make the changes and corrections that your instructor indicates. If you are responding to comments on a final draft, you should answer any questions and rewrite any segments you've been asked to.

Reproduced here are the last two paragraphs of John Fousek's intermediate draft, together with his teacher's marginal comments and symbols. Note especially his instructor's summary comments at the end of the paper.

INTERMEDIATE DRAFT
FINAL PARAGRAPHS WITH INSTRUCTOR'S COMMENTS

cs

I'm bothered even more by Jim's failure to close bathroom objects, for example, he never closes the shampoo cap. This makes me lose my good composure more than anything. When I'm showering. I always grab the shampoo bottle by the cap. A loose cap always results in shampoo on my toes and not in my hair, which at this point is soaking wet. Because I am economically minded, moneywise watching a green puddle of shampoo going down the drain wasted every day really upsets me. Jim forgets to close the bathroom door after using the facilities while I shower. The bathroom has grown warm and steamy during the course of my shower, the cold morning air chills me. Jim's thoughtlessness is very annoying.

Jim is such a great guy, and I know his failure to close things is a minor bad habit, and I try to overlook it. However, it does tend to irritate me, especially when cold air hits me right after I'm out of the shower.

frag sp
The "wise" ending is questionable in making adjectives. Do you need "moneywise" at all here?

Too much coordination in this sentence. Revise?

Good! You corrected a run-on.

cs

You've certainly made Jim's habits real for us. Everybody knows an "I don't close things" person. (I admit it—I'm one myself!) Limiting the topic to one specific shortcoming focuses the paper well. I like sensory images like "banging silverware" (par. 2) and "warm and steamy" (next-to-last par.).

Consider these points as you revise:

1. Provide more details in par. 2. Show us the mess in the drawers. What's in them? What do they look like?

2. Slang and colloquial expressions can be bothersome. Don't get too stuffy now, but do strive for a slightly more formal writing style. Look especially at "pretty well" and "fun guy."

3. Smooth out transitions and logic as I've indicated in the margin.

4. Proofread carefully for those run-ons, comma splices, and fragments—these can be major problems on a final draft. See relevant sections in the Handbook (at the end of <u>Student's Book</u>) for review and practice.

5. The conclusion lacks impact. Can you interpret the significance of your experience with Jim? Go beyond the immediate experiences you share with the readers here.

Good try for an intermediate draft, John. Revise! Revise! Revise!

EXERCISE   Read the excerpt from John Fousek's paper on page 118 and make the grammatical and spelling changes that respond to the marginal symbols written by John's teacher.

Proofreading

Proofreading is the part of the editing process in which you reread your paper particularly for errors. This step in the writing process is best accomplished at two stages.

First, proofread your draft after you make revisions and edit before you produce the final copy for submission. At this point, check for problems in grammar, syntax, spelling, and usage. Proofread the paper a second time just before you turn it in to catch mistakes you may have overlooked. At this stage, you can make minor revisions neatly on the final copy. However, if you discover major problems that require extensive reworking, you should produce another copy. Do not submit for evaluation a paper containing numerous changes and corrections.

You'll find the following pointers useful as you proofread.

TIPS   for Careful Proofreading

■ **When you proofread, read slowly.**   Your purpose is to check for errors, and quick readings make errors hard to find.

- **Use a ruler, a blank sheet of paper, or an index card below each line.** This will help you focus so that you are not distracted by words farther down the page.

- **Proofread after you have made revisions and editing changes.** Do not try to revise and proofread at the same time. Except for glaring errors, which you should correct as you find them, revision and editing call for concentration on thought and meaning. If you attend to errors when you revise, you won't be focusing on issues related to the content and clarity of your paper. Thus, treat proofreading as a separate activity, after you're satisfied with your writing and revising.

- **Be familiar with the types of errors that you tend to make and keep them in mind as you proofread.** If you tend to write run-on sentences or fragments, proofread your paper for those mistakes especially. Thoughtful students keep a record of their own errors and consult it before proofreading. At the very least, you should look over any comments and corrections that your instructor or your peers have written on other papers you wrote.

- **Be sure to remove wrong words or extra letters on your computer-generated draft when you make spelling changes.** Also remember to reformat your text if necessary and to examine your paragraphing: all paragraphs must be indented. Use the cursor as a proofreading aid by moving it from word to word as you proofread; this step will help you slow down your reading.

- **If you must make minor revisions on a final copy, use blue or black ink, not pencil.** Cross out errors neatly with one line and insert changes directly above the mistake or in the margin, if you need more room. Remember, extensive changes on a draft mean that you must do another draft before submitting it. Use a caret (^) for insertions.

She admonished ^her^ brother for being late.

EXERCISE   Proofread the following paragraph and make corrections as needed.

For most people a job only represent a way too get the money needed, the bills each month, or a place were people get bored eigth hours a day, for other's it means a chance to show of there skills. For many its the first door to financial freedom, in some ways have a job can give you wonderful oportunities to socialize in you're nieghborhood and to learn something that could help you get better job in the future.

STRATEGY CHECKLIST: Revising and Editing Your Drafts

Revise for thought and content.	☐ Does my thesis state the topic clearly and give my opinion about the topic? ☐ Is my thesis sufficiently limited? ☐ Does my thesis cover the evidence and detail that I intend to use to support my idea? ☐ Have I provided sufficient details to support my assertions? ☐ Have I used precise and appropriate language? ☐ Have I varied my sentence structure? ☐ Have I eliminated unnecessary words? ☐ Are my thoughts unified? Do my ideas relate to each other? ☐ Is my writing coherent? Do my ideas flow logically? ☐ Are my purpose and audience clear?
Revise for essay form.	☐ Have I followed my outline? If not, can I revise my outline so that I still have presented the ideas sensibly? ☐ Have I used a conscious organization plan for presenting my points? ☐ Will my introduction engage readers? ☐ Does each paragraph's topic clearly relate to my thesis? ☐ Does my conclusion grow naturally from the ideas stated in the thesis and developed in the essay? ☐ Do my transitions logically connect paragraphs and thoughts within paragraphs?
Edit and proofread for grammar, usage, and mechanics.	☐ Have I avoided run-on sentence errors and sentence fragments? ☐ Do my subjects and verbs agree? ☐ Are my verb tenses correct? ☐ Are my pronoun references clear? ☐ Have I avoided sexist language? ☐ Have I used punctuation to enhance sentence meanings? ☐ Have I used quotation marks correctly to indicate someone else's words? ☐ Have I checked the spelling of difficult words in a dictionary?

One Student Writing: Final Draft

After reading his paper over several times, discussing it with friends and his writing teacher, making revisions, and producing new drafts, John finally submitted the following paper to his instructor.

Final Draft

My Roommate, Jim

1   My roommate, Jim, and I have shared a small apartment for the past two years. On the whole, we get along very well. We are both students, and we both work, so we don't spend much time together; but when we do, we cooperate. Jim, who is good at it, does most of the cooking; I do most of the cleaning. We find the arrangement satisfactory. And I like Jim. He is generous, witty, honest. Our two-year association has, for the most part, been a good one. But Jim has one shortcoming that irritates me: He doesn't close things.

2   Jim, for example, almost never closes a drawer or a closet door, and his failure to do so is often a source of embarrassment to me. The problem is that I am compulsively neat, and Jim, I'm sorry to say, is a slob. It seems never to have occurred to him that the contents of a drawer could be organized. When he does his laundry, he just empties his bag of clean clothes into a drawer—white socks, underwear, a rainbow of t-shirts with college crests, pajamas, graying handkerchiefs. When the drawer is full, he begins filling the next one. Then when he needs clean socks or a shirt, he rolls the contents of the drawer around until he finds what he wants, often leaving rejected items hanging over the edge of the drawer. His clothes closet is just as messy as the drawers. He does the same kinds of things in the kitchen. Spatulas, flatware, eggbeaters, knives clink together as he pokes through the nearest open drawer to find his favorite tool for beating eggs or mincing onions. If he'd organized the drawer in the first place, the rattle of kitchenware wouldn't disturb my study time before every meal. Since Jim doesn't close drawers or closets, our apartment usually looks like the site of a rummage sale at closing time. The appearance offends my neat soul and embarrasses me when friends visit us.

3   The irritation I experience because of open drawers and closets, however, is nothing compared with the irritation that Jim's failure to close things in the bathroom produces. Jim's failure to tighten the cap on the shampoo

bottle, for example, causes me to completely lose my composure when I am showering. Because I am in the habit of grasping the shampoo bottle by its cap, a loose cap results in the annoyance of shampoo on my toes instead of in my hair. And because I am a frugal sort, I hate seeing a green puddle of unused shampoo oozing down the drain each day. Jim also often fails to close the bathroom door after using the facilities while I shower. Since the bathroom has become warm and steamy during the course of my shower, the cold draft of morning air chills and distresses me, and the idea that he has been so thoughtless bothers me.

When that frigid air blasts my wet body, my irritation with Jim reaches its peak. Nevertheless, because he is such a great guy and because I know his failure to close things is, in the scheme of human problems, just a minor bad habit, I try to overlook it. I shut my mouth and take a deep breath. In fact, by learning to deal with this annoyance I think I've learned a little about how to handle the frustrations of some of my friends' strange habits in general. I keep a good sense of humor and I hold my temper. After all, I'd rather have opened closets and drawers than a door closed on friendship.

4

EXERCISE How does John's intermediate draft compare and contrast with the first draft? What advice did he take from the peer critique? What other changes did he make?

EXERCISE How does John's final draft compare and contrast with his intermediate draft? What additions has he made? How has he improved the level of detail in the intermediate draft? How has he improved the structure of his paragraphs? Where has he eliminated unnecessary words and sentences? How has he corrected grammatical errors?

A Brief Note on Style

Your paper should be readable. Of course, a polished style doesn't just happen when some English teacher calls for it, and Part Five of this book focuses on style at some length. You might find it helpful to look at that part now.

For support in meeting this chapter's objectives, follow this path in MyCompLab: Resources ⇒ Writing ⇒ Writing Process ⇒ Revising. Review the Instruction and Multimedia resources about revising, editing, and proofreading; then complete the Exercises and click on Gradebook to measure your progress.

PART TWO

Methods of Development

CHAPTER **7**

Description

When most students receive an assignment like "Write a **description** of a person, place, or thing" (a car, a wedding, a painting, or a temper tantrum), their first impulse is often to describe what the person, place, or thing looks like. Although many excellent descriptions do just that, in deciding on your subject and how to treat it, you don't need to limit your choices so severely. Most good descriptive writing appeals to the reader's senses, and sight is only one of our five senses. A piece of descriptive writing generally will explore more than one of the senses: the glories of franks and beans could involve sight and smell as well as taste, for example. Strong specific writing (see pages 53–55) is filled with life, and sensory appeal is likely to be built right in.

In this chapter you will

- identify the strategies for writing a descriptive paper

- analyze student essays of description

- identify a topic and write your own descriptive paper

- explore descriptive writing from the world around you

- analyze descriptive writing by professionals

TIPS   for Writing a Descriptive Essay

- **Select a meaningful topic.**   What place stands out in your mind as a dynamic enough spot to write about? Can you revisit it? Perhaps there's a person you know well or remember vividly whom you'd like to make alive for readers in an essay.

- **Do prewriting.**   Use a strategy that works for you in generating ideas about the person or place that you want to describe. Look back to pages 36–38 for some prewriting approaches, such as making a list, doing nonstop writing, making a scratch outline, drawing a subject tree, and other approaches. The key to prewriting is to help you liberate some ideas and to remind you that the best writing always moves through a series of steps or stages.

- **Draft a thesis statement.**   Periodically, shopkeepers need to take inventory. The procedure is vital to business survival, but if you try to include every piece of information you have on your subject in a descriptive essay, you are inviting disaster.

The writer who takes inventory may begin this way:

> My friend Judy is twenty years old. She is a solid C student. She has black hair, brown eyes, and weighs 115 pounds. Her family is comfortably middle class. Judy is very nearsighted but is vain about her appearance and often does not wear her glasses. She's been my friend for many years, and I like her.

This paragraph is simply a random collection of stray descriptive facts. No logic or principle seems to be at work here except the desire to get everything in—to take inventory. A descriptive essay needs a thesis. You must think of your paper not as "A Description of Judy" but as an attempt to prove that "Judy is terribly vain," or "Many people think that Judy is self-centered, but she has many fine qualities," or "Judy has no remarkable traits of any kind, and I wonder why she has been my best friend for so many years." Therefore, you must choose only the descriptive details that are connected to your thesis; if it will break your heart to omit a colorful but irrelevant detail, you must change your thesis to make the detail relevant. Sometimes, of course, a simple change in phrasing can turn a seemingly irrelevant detail into something significant, and your thesis can remain unchanged. Notice how a thesis and a few additional phrases can transform the mess about Judy into a coherent start for a potentially effective paper.

> There is nothing at all special about my friend Judy. Judy is such a completely ordinary twenty-year-old woman that I often wonder how our friendship has lasted so long and stayed so warm.
>
> Just for starters, consider these totally ordinary facts about her. Physically, she has absolutely undistinguished black hair and brown eyes, stands an average 5 feet 4 inches, and weighs an average 115 pounds. Scholastically, she is a solid C student. By solid I *mean* solid. In two years at college, I can't recall her once getting a daring C– or an exciting C+. Her family—you guessed it— is comfortably middle class, not too rich and not too poor. Even in her little flaws, Judy is just what you'd expect. Like so many people of her age, she tends to be vain about personal appearance and all too frequently tries to get by without her glasses, even though she's very nearsighted.

■ **Think about appropriate details.**   Remember that your reader is not familiar with the person or place you want to describe. To make it come alive, you must marshal an appropriate amount of concrete sensory detail that shows your subject clearly in the context of the opinion you've expressed about it. You might want to keep a sense chart in order to record sensory impressions that you'll later integrate into your essay.

Don't tell your reader that a room is old and neglected: indicate the squeaky floorboard next to the door, the lint collected in the coils of the radiator, the window propped up with a sooty stick of wood. If you do the job with details, the sense of age and neglect will come through. The more precise the detail, the greater its potential for arousing the attention of your reader. Nothing should be beneath your notice. The condition of a man's fingernails, the name of the store where a woman buys her clothes, or a broken traffic light on a street corner can convey as much information about a man, a woman, or a neighborhood—and convey it more interestingly—than any number of generalized comments.

■ **Consider your audience and purpose.** Will you be sharing your paper with your classmates? You should decide just what impression you want to give them about whatever you're describing, and you also have to consider your word choice. You'll need to explain any technical terms.

■ **Arrange details thoughtfully.** This suggestion means that you should have some way of determining what comes first and what comes next. The particular organizing principle you select makes little difference as long as it helps create a coherent paper. In describing a snowstorm, for instance, you might organize by **time,** presenting the storm from the first hesitant flakes through the massive downfall to the Christmas-card quietness at the end of the storm. In describing a landscape, you might organize by **space,** beginning with the objects farthest from the observer and working your way closer. A physical description of a person could go from top to bottom or bottom to top.

■ **Write an engaging introduction.** You want to build your introduction so that it culminates successfully in your thesis statement. Note how Nick Fiscina lays the groundwork for his thesis in the brief introduction to his essay, which you will find on page 128.

■ **Write a conclusion that brings the essay to a successful close.** Your last paragraph of the descriptive essay should reinforce your thesis by reminding readers why you chose the topic and reasserting your opinion about it. You can set a new context for your essay.

■ **Revise your drafts until you're satisfied with your paper.** You must view your initial attempt to produce your descriptive essay as a work in progress. Share your draft with fellow classmates; ask your teacher to read it and make recommendations; rely on your roommate, parents, friends, siblings to give you insights about where you could improve your essay. Is anything unclear to your reader? Does your draft need more details? Are the details arranged logically?

■ **Proofread carefully.** Don't hand in a final draft unless you've checked carefully for your own typical errors, especially run-ons and fragments.

ASSIGNMENT: DESCRIPTION

Write a descriptive essay in which you show readers clearly some person or place that you remember. If you can revisit the place or view the person again, so much the better. Use concrete sensory detail to include images of color and action, sound, smell, touch, and taste. If you cannot easily decide on a topic for your description paper, you might want to try one or more of these suggestions.

1. An office party
2. A religious leader
3. A loyal pet
4. A street corner
5. An afternoon schoolyard
6. People waiting in a line
7. Sloppy eaters
8. Doctor's waiting room
9. Restaurant waiters
10. Bad drivers
11. A school cafeteria
12. An amusement park
13. A hospital room
14. The contents of a wallet or pocketbook
15. Summer nights
16. A natural disaster
17. A morning at the beach
18. My best friend
19. The biology lab
20. A favorite food

Student Writing: Description

In the selection below, a student uses description to explore the relation between his father's working life and his own. Annotations in the margin point to key features of the essay, particularly the elements of description that enhance the writing.

Nick Fiscina
Dad's Disappointment

1   As a kid of fifteen, I'll never forget the first time I worked along with my father in the attic of our old house one hot summer afternoon. Dad spent most of his life as a construction worker, and I saw then how disappointing this existence was to him.

Thesis statement.

2   As we worked together to finish the attic by putting up insulation on the bare wooden beams of the roof, the smell of dust and perspiration filled the air. In the large gray room bits of paint and plaster hung loose on the walls. As if in another world, Dad lifted a large black bag of insulation onto his left shoulder and lumbered to the wooden ladder. Climbing it, he raised up the insulation in his large hands, brown and scarred, and waited without a word for me to staple the substance in place. His fingers held

Transition to opening paragraph: "As we worked together to finish the attic."

Sensory details.
Examples:
Sight: bare
wooden
beams; large
hands, brown
and scarred;
snowy-white
layer of powder
Sound: staples
clicked loudly
Smell: dust and
perspiration
Touch: burned
and scratched.

Transition to
previous para-
graph: "grim,
silent efforts."

Sensory details
communicate an
immediate sense
of the subject.

the material firmly as the staples clicked loudly, joining the insulation to the roof beams. Dad's nails were broken and dirty and small freckles spread beneath the graying hairs on the backs of his hands. As he held the insulation without talking, streams of burning dust fell on us, covering our arms and faces, and in the curly strands of black hair that hung on Dad's forehead there was a snowy-white layer of fine powder. Although it burned and scratched me, nothing bothered Dad's toughened, tanned skin.

As I watched his grim, silent efforts, it passed through my mind that   3
my father had a teaching degree from a university in the old country, Italy. I asked him, maybe too harshly as I think about this moment so many years ago, why he got into construction work if he had qualifications as a teacher. He remained silent for a long time. His massive arms hung at his sides and circles of sweat stained his brown shirt. After a while a voice filled with defeat broke into the dust-filled air. "Well, you see, Nicola," he said, "in life you make the best you can with what you have. I have to work with my hands to keep the family going." It really surprised me that my father should have such an attitude. This man I often hated for his angry temper and harsh words seemed very human to me. When I looked into his hard brown eyes gazing sadly past me, and watched the crow's feet at the corners wrinkle in a squint, I saw that he had accepted the life of a construction worker with disappointment in spite of success at it.

A family man myself with two young boys of my own, I've now had my   4
fill of construction work. I earn a living at it, but I too feel its disappointments. The conditions are harsh, the work is hard, and there is no security. I shudder to think of my sons writing an essay like this about me fifteen years from now. I can't accept my father's view of things: simply making the best you can with what you have. I want something better and more challenging, and I'm willing to sacrifice what I have to achieve it. That's why I'm enrolled in this community college course for medical technology, which, I believe, will be a more fulfilling career. Though I still nail insulation to roof beams and do other jobs with my hands, I look forward to a better life for my family and me.

Spoken words
animate the
subject.

Closing sentence
to paragraph
3 captures the
essence of the
moment.

Conclusion links
to introduc-
tion and thesis
sentence.

FOR WRITING OR DISCUSSION

1. What is the writer's thesis? Does he keep the thesis in mind through the body of the paper? How do you know?
2. What details of the writer's father do you find particularly compelling and original? To which senses do the images you like seem to appeal?

3. How has the writer managed to convey his father's disappointment other than in the direct statement in the opening paragraph?

4. How is this essay an example of descriptive detail arranged chronologically?

5. The closing paragraph moves off the topic of the writer's father and focuses on the writer himself. What is your reaction to this conclusion? Does it violate the thesis, or does it apply the thesis to a new frame of reference? Support your opinion.

6. Write a short descriptive paper focusing on some relative who, through his or her words or actions, gave you some special insight into that person's character. Use concrete sensory detail to give the reader a snapshot of your relative.

The student essay that follows describes a memorable scene. Answer the questions after you read.

Thomas Albanese
High School Practice

1   All my life I have loved baseball. As a kid I used to stand at the iron school-yard gates and watch the ninth graders zip around the bases. Spring, summer, and fall I still sit glued to the television and suffer with the Yankees as Rodriguez goes limp at the plate. In my high school days I always looked forward to the start of baseball practice in my high school gym. What I liked most about senior practice was the excitement of all my friends around me in the locker room and the exercise activity on the gym floor.

2   As I dressed in the locker room, I was excited to see the guys who played on the team with me in the previous year. Bob on my left dressed hurriedly to rush out to the gym; as team captain, he rapped on the metal lockers and yelled, "Let's get the lead out! Cut the talk and let's move!" Richard on my right stuffed his red flannel shirt and his copy of *Hamlet* into the locker as he dressed, talking continuously about winning a school championship.

3   When I looked around me, I saw the new players too, trying out for the team for the first time. They struggled with their uniforms. They were so nervous they could not even put their yellow sweats on straight. Then I saw Coach O'Neill flying out of his office. Even he looked wound up for the on-coming season which would last until June and the championship games. As he dashed out the door to the gym he looked at me and smiled as if to say, "Isn't it great to be back with the team again?"

Then, when all the fun in the locker room was over, we charged out onto the newly shellacked floor of the gym. We stood in the shadow of a basketball backboard waiting for the coach to finish checking the new bats and uniforms. I could not help thinking how I felt like a big brother to all the new guys on the team. I looked at the brown painted stands half-way pushed out, but before we even got near to sit down, Coach O'Neill grabbed the silver whistle dangling from his neck and blew it hard.

4

Sternly, he called us all together. His gray eyes looked mean as he barked out the drills we had to do. Then we started calisthenics because the coach said they would make us loose. As I did my push-ups to Coach O'Neill's crisp "One-two-three-four," I saw the yellow floor with its black stripes from the basketball court. Blood rushed up to my head, making me feel weak, but I still continued. Next we ran laps around the gym. As I ran I could see the huge window panes on the far wall of the gym, and the light of the sun blinded me every time I looked up. An open window brought a cool March breeze and the smell of the earth into the gym. After a loud blast from a whistle, the coach told us to stop running and take a rest. Five minutes later we ended the workout with wind sprints in the hallway so as to make room in the gym for the football team on its workout session. These activities in the gym made me feel happy and healthy.

5

Because I have so much fun in the gym, to me exercise is a wonderful part of living. I was surprised to hear on the television news about "Flabby Americans" and of the poor physical condition so many people today are in because of little activity. Maybe some better workouts in high school would start more people on physical fitness programs. My friends in public school say that gym teachers leave uninterested students pretty much alone to sit and talk on the sidelines as long as there is no trouble. But I think that this is wrong: physical education teachers should be convincing all those sideline talkers that participating is the greatest part of sports.

6

FOR WRITING OR DISCUSSION

1. What is the writer's topic? What is his attitude toward the topic?
2. Which descriptive details do you find most vivid or original?
3. What is the subject of the first body paragraph? The second?
4. How does the introduction lay the groundwork for the thesis sentence?
5. What new frame of reference does the conclusion establish?

Description
in the World Around You

Descriptive writing appears in many contexts, including magazine and newspaper feature stories, laboratory reports, advertisements, and brochures, such as the one shown here. All descriptive writing uses sensory details—appeals to sight, hearing, taste, smell, and touch, but always with an eye toward the main point being made.

This brochure uses many elements of effective descriptive writing:

Introduction — The brochure engages the reader quickly by pointing to the major reasons that divers should come to the Florida Keys.

Thesis — The brochure's main idea is that the Florida Keys are the world's most popular dive destination.

Specific details — Language tempts readers: "consistently clear water"; "hordes of tropical fish"; "immense schools of grunts and snapper off Davis Ledge and Alligator Reef."

Audience — The audience is potential vacationers to the Florida Keys, specifically divers and snorkelers. Brochure details focus on their interests

Organization — The authors have organized this section around the major sights divers will see.

Arrangement of details — The brochure describes potential dive sights, including sunken ships, corals, and fish. The striking photo provides further visual details.

Conclusion — The brochure concludes by saying the Keys "have it all!"

Your Turn

Go online and search for additional brochures, for vacation spots, automobiles, or other items. Select a brochure and write a short analysis of how the brochure uses description to convey the message. Were the descriptions effective? Did they entice you to visit the location or purchase the item? Why or why not?

DIVING & SNORKELING

The beauty and diversity of the underwater experience in the Florida Keys have made this the world's most popular dive destination. In fact, the Keys have been protected by designation as the nation's only tropical marine preserve, the *Florida Keys National Marine Sanctuary*.

Key Largo is home of the famed *John Pennekamp Coral Reef State Park*, the *Key Largo National Marine Sanctuary* and the 510 foot U.S.S. *Spiegel Grove* — one of the largest wrecks in divable U.S. waters. *Molasses Reef* is the world's most popular dive site for it's consistently clear water, amazing hordes of tropical fish and easy access. With out-stretched arms seemingly welcoming scuba enthusiasts, the submerged *Statue of Christ of the Abyss* is a Key Largo icon.

The entire Florida Keys are rich with wreck dive opportunities, including the 327 foot U.S. Coast Guard Cutters *Bibb* and *Duane* off Key Largo, the 287 foot freighter *Eagle* off Islamorada, the 188 foot *Thunderbolt* off Marathon, the 210 foot *Adolphus Busch, Sr.* off the Lower Keys and Key West's favorite wrecks, the 187 foot *Cayman Salvager* and the perfectly upright *Joe's Tug*. All of these ships are within easy depth ranges for sport divers and now host incredible resident populations of marine life. And we'll soon be adding to our underwater armada with the sinking of the 524 foot USAF *Vandenberg* in 2008.

Yet, it is the natural reefs of the Florida Keys that inspire the greatest awe among visiting divers. From the immense schools of grunts and snapper off *Davis Ledge* and *Alligator Reef* in Islamorada, to the dramatic coral canyons of Marathon's *Sombrero Reef* and *Coffin's Patch*, to the lush beauty and incredible diversity of the Lower Keys' famed *Looe Key National Marine Sanctuary*, to the majesty of the spur and groove coral formations decorating Key West's *Sambo Reefs*, the Florida Keys and Key West have it all!

Introduction

Thesis

Specific details

Conclusion

Audience is people who snorkel

Critical Reading: Description

As with any piece that you read, you want to engage in critical reading (see Chapter 1). Observe the marginal notes in this selection. They show how the reader stayed alert to the various issues of language and content, raising questions and making comments that helped her understand the brief essay. Let the comments guide you as you think through the selections in this chapter on description.

ESMERALDA SANTIAGO

A Blanco Navidad for New Yorikans

Spanish for "White Christmas."

1   It's Christmas Eve in my sister Alicia's apartment in the Parkchester section of the Bronx. In the living room, her stereo plays the brassy, conga-driven rhythms

Sad.

of *salsa* and *merengue*, or the plaintive strains of Puerto Rican *aguinaldos*. The music is loud, and, unable to hold a conversation, I ask my brother to dance.

Another sound. The room is alive!

Charlie leads me to the left, to the right, in circles, avoiding the other couples and our two-year-old nephew, who stands in the middle of the room bawling for his mother.

2   When it gets too hot, we step out to the sidewalk. The snow Americans write songs about seems imminent. A white Christmas is pretty, but for me it brings to mind my other life in Puerto Rico. There, the air doesn't force me to hunch my shoulders and draw my head, turtle-like, into my coat. There,

Three Kings Day on January 6—major holiday in PR.

Christmas Eve is for midnight mass and small gifts. The big gifts will come later, when the Three Magi have made their way to the island upon their trusty camels.

3   But I'm here now, in the land of Santa Claus and overnight delivery of presents bought over the Internet. I, 4 of my 11 siblings, and our mother, live in New York. None of our spouses is Puerto Rican, and our children and grandchildren have been born and raised in the United States. In our New York–based family there are 25 people, with whom we celebrate our

Christmases

American Christmas by trying to recreate *Las Navidades* as we knew them on the island.

"translucent jiggle of a honey-colored flan"—original picture!

4   And here, as there, we cook. Spicy ginger and cloves embedded in coconut rice. Oregano and garlic crusted over a pork shoulder, its crunchy skin smoky and brown. We evoke *Las Navidades* in the translucent jiggle of a honey-colored flan, in the sugar syrup that hardens into a crackle over the top and down the sides of the custard. It's in the fresh, unhulled pigeon peas and

"New Yorikans"—a newly coined word for Puerto Ricans who live in New York.

Image of sound. Spanish dance music.

What does aguinaldos mean? Some kind of song or singer?

It's going to snow.

Some differences between Christmas in NY and PR.

Big family, assimilated into American culture in NY.

Good images— color, sound, smell, taste, touch.

Spanish words.

Foods help bring Puerto Rican Christmas to NY. Old custom in PR.

in the bunches of spiny, fragrant recao leaves bought at the marketa. It's in the banana leaves roasted over the open flame of a gas burner until they're the color of Spanish olives. When Mami spoons grated plantain on the leaf, and Delsa tops it with a dollop of ground meat and spices, _Las Navidades_ are in every grain of salt they've poured, in every garlic clove they've mashed.

The gift-giving that used to take place on Jan. 6 now happens at the stroke of midnight on Christmas Eve. The children, who have fallen asleep curled up on the sofa or an easy chair, are roused and placed in front of the tree. One of us passes over the packages to eager hands. No one opens a gift until everything has been distributed. Then the sound of paper tearing, the squeals of delight, the hugs and hand-slapping and laughter drown out the sounds of the stereo, where someone has thought to put on the Spanish version of "Silent Night."

5

Adapted American custom against backdrop of Spanish version of "Silent Night."

A thick rice soup.

Afterwards, the presents are put in piles in the corners so we can continue the celebration. We're hungry again, so Mami makes a chicken _asopao_ while the sisters tidy the kitchen. Those of us not cleaning up huddle in small groups, talking. Mostly, we make plans for the next party, on New Year's Eve, because for us, like in Puerto Rico, _Las Navidades_ doesn't end on Dec. 25.

6

Again PR in the U.S.

Good visual images.

Snow brings the writer back fully to NY from her Puerto Rican _Navidad_.

The _asopao_ eaten, the sleepy children are gathered, the presents are stuffed into shopping bags, and we scatter to our individual homes. The street is deserted and quiet, every surface covered in white. Within minutes, the sidewalk bears the traces of our footsteps heading in different directions. Before I climb into my car, I stare at the flakes dancing under the street lamp. Then I hunch my shoulders and pull my head into my coat, astonished that, while I wasn't looking, my _Navidad_ in New York has become Christmas, dusted with snow.

7

Same image as in paragraph 2. Weather differences are important to Santiago.

FOR WRITING OR DISCUSSION

1. What is the thesis of this piece? How do the marginal comments help you arrive at the thesis, which the writer does not state in the essay?

2. How does the title help set up the purpose of the selection?

3. Where has Santiago made effective comparisons?

4. Which images do you find most original? Which help you best appreciate this Puerto Rican Christmas in America?

5. In your opinion, which elements of descriptive writing outlined on pages 125–127 does the selection best demonstrate?

6. Write an essay on a holiday that you celebrate with your family. Make the scene come alive with concrete sensory details of color, sound, smell, taste, and touch.

ROGER ANGELL

On the Ball

1   It weighs just over five ounces and measures between 2.86 and 2.94 inches in diameter. It is made of a composition-cork nucleus encased in two thin layers of rubber, one black and one red, surrounded by a hundred and twenty-one yards of tightly wrapped blue-gray wool yarn, forty-five yards of white wool yarn, fifty-three more yards of blue-gray wool yarn, a hundred and fifty yards of fine cotton yarn, a coat of rubber cement, and a cowhide (formerly horsehide) exterior, which is held together with two hundred and sixteen slightly raised red cotton stitches. Printed certifications, endorsements, and outdoor advertising spherically attest to its authenticity. Like most institutions, it is considered inferior in its present form to its ancient archetypes, and in this case the complaint is probably justified: on occasion in recent years it has actually been known to come apart under the demands of its brief but rigorous active career. Baseballs are assembled and hand-stitched in Taiwan (before this year the work was done in Haiti, and before 1973 in Chicopee, Massachusetts), and contemporary pitchers claim that there is a tangible variation in the size and feel of the balls that now come into play in a single game; a true peewee is treasured by hurlers, and its departure from the premises, by fair means or foul, is secretly mourned. But never mind: any baseball is beautiful. No other small package comes as close to the ideal in design and utility. It is a perfect object for a man's hand. Pick it up and it instantly suggests its purpose; it is meant to be thrown a considerable distance—thrown hard and with precision. Its feel and heft are the beginning of the sport's critical dimensions; if it were a fraction of an inch larger or smaller, a few centigrams heavier or lighter, the game of baseball would be utterly different. Hold a baseball in your hand. As it happens, this one is not brand new. Here, just to one side of the curved surgical welt of stitches, there is a pale-green grass smudge, darkening on one edge almost to black—the mark of an old infield play, a tough grounder now lost in memory. Feel the ball, turn it over in your hand; hold it across the seam or the other way, with the seam just to the side of your middle finger. Speculation stirs. You want to get outdoors and throw this spare and sensual object to somebody, or, at the very least, watch somebody else throw it. The game has begun. . . .

FOR WRITING OR DISCUSSION

1. What are the two meanings of the essay's title, "On the Ball"?

2. When were you certain that the subject being discussed is a baseball?

3. Notice the number of facts in the first two sentences. What purpose do the facts serve in the development of the description?

4. What is meant by the sentence that begins, "Like most institutions, it is considered inferior in its present form . . ."? What does the sentence show about

the author's attitude toward contemporary manufacturing techniques? How does the sentence telling where baseballs were once made support that attitude?

5. What is the thesis of the selection?

6. At what point does the selection cease to be factual and become a matter of opinion?

7. At what point does the writer bring the reader into the description? Why does he do so?

8. Do the sentences beginning with "Hold a baseball in your hand" make you feel the ball? Why or why not?

9. Write a paper describing a single small object—for example, a football, a TV remote, a kitchen utensil, a cell phone. Try to use both factual and personal details to make your reader see or feel the object as you do.

JOAN DIDION
Marrying Absurd

To be married in Las Vegas, Clark County, Nevada, a bride must swear that she is eighteen   1
or has parental permission and a bridegroom that he is twenty-one or has parental permission. Someone must put up five dollars for the license. (On Sundays and holidays, fifteen dollars. The Clark County Courthouse issues marriage licenses at any time of the day
or night except between noon and one in the afternoon, between eight and nine in the
evening, and between four and five in the morning.) Nothing else is required. The State of
Nevada, alone among these United States, demands neither a premarital blood test nor
a waiting period before or after the issuance of a marriage license. Driving in across the
Mojave from Los Angeles, one sees the signs way out on the desert, looming up from that
moonscape of rattlesnakes and mesquite, even before the Las Vegas lights appear like a
mirage on the horizon: "GETTING MARRIED? Free License Information First Strip Exit."
Perhaps the Las Vegas wedding industry achieved its peak operational efficiency between
9:00 p.m. and midnight of August 26, 1965, an otherwise unremarkable Thursday which
happened to be, by Presidential order, the last day on which anyone could improve his
draft status merely by getting married. One hundred and seventy-one couples were pronounced man and wife in the name of Clark County and the State of Nevada that night,
sixty-seven of them by a single justice of the peace, Mr. James A. Brennan. Mr. Brennan
did one wedding at the Dunes and the other sixty-six in his office, and charged each
couple eight dollars. One bride lent her veil to six others. "I got it down from five to
three minutes," Mr. Brennan said later of his feat. "I could've married them en masse, but
they're people, not cattle. People expect more when they get married."

2   What people who get married in Las Vegas actually do expect—what, in the largest sense, their "expectations" are—strikes one as a curious and self-contradictory business. Las Vegas is the most extreme and allegorical of American settlements, bizarre and beautiful in its venality and in its devotion to immediate gratification, a place the tone of which is set by mobsters and call girls and ladies' room attendants with amyl nitrite poppers in their uniform pockets. Almost everyone notes that there is no "time" in Las Vegas, no night and no day and no past and no future (no Las Vegas casino, however, has taken the obliteration of the ordinary time sense quite so far as Harold's Club in Reno, which for a while issued, at odd intervals in the day and night, mimeographed "bulletins" carrying news from the world outside); neither is there any logical sense of where one is. One is standing on a highway in the middle of a vast hostile desert looking at an eighty-foot sign which blinks "Stardust" or "Caesar's Palace." Yes, but what does that explain? This geographical implausibility reinforces the sense that what happens there has no connection with "real" life; Nevada cities like Reno and Carson are ranch towns, Western towns, places behind which there is some historical imperative. But Las Vegas seems to exist only in the eye of the beholder. All of which makes it an extraordinarily stimulating and interesting place, but an odd one in which to want to wear a candlelight satin Priscilla of Boston wedding dress with Chantilly lace insets, tapered sleeves and a detachable modified train.

3   And yet the Las Vegas wedding business seems to appeal to precisely that impulse. "Sincere and Dignified Since 1954," one wedding chapel advertises. There are nineteen such wedding chapels in Las Vegas, intensely competitive, each offering better, faster, and, by implication, more sincere services than the next: Our Photos Best Anywhere, Your Wedding on a Phonograph Record, Candlelight with Your Ceremony, Honeymoon Accommodations, Free Transportation from Your Motel to Courthouse to Chapel and Return to Motel, Religious or Civil Ceremonies, Dressing Rooms, Flowers, Rings, Announcements, Witnesses Available, and Ample Parking. All of these services, like most others in Las Vegas (sauna baths, payroll-check cashing, chinchilla coats for sale or rent), are offered twenty-four hours a day, seven days a week, presumably on the premise that marriage, like craps, is a game to be played when the table seems hot.

4   But what strikes one most about the Strip chapels, with their wishing wells and stained-glass paper windows and their artificial bouvardia, is that so much of their business is by no means a matter of simple convenience, of late-night liaisons between show girls and baby Crosbys. Of course there is some of that. (One night about eleven o'clock in Las Vegas I watched a bride in an orange minidress and masses of flame-colored hair stumble from a Strip chapel on the arm of her bridegroom, who looked the part of the expendable nephew in movies like *Miami Syndicate*. "I gotta get the kids," the bride whimpered. "I gotta pick up the sitter, I gotta get to the midnight show." "What you gotta get," the bridegroom said, opening the door of a Cadillac Coupe de Ville and watching her crumple on the seat, "is sober.") But Las Vegas seems to offer something other than "convenience"; it is merchandising "niceness," the facsimile of proper ritual, to children who do not know how else to find it, how to make the arrangements, how

to do it "right." All day and evening long on the Strip, one sees actual wedding parties, waiting under the harsh lights at a crosswalk, standing uneasily in the parking lot of the Frontier while the photographer hired by The Little Church of the West ("Wedding Place of the Stars") certifies the occasion, takes the picture: the bride in a veil and white satin pumps, the bridegroom usually in a white dinner jacket, and even an attendant or two, a sister or a best friend in hot-pink *peau de soie*, a flirtation veil, a carnation nosegay. "When I Fall in Love It Will Be Forever," the organist plays, and then a few bars of Lohengrin. The mother cries; the stepfather, awkward in his role, invites the chapel hostess to join them for a drink at the Sands. The hostess declines with a professional smile; she has already transferred her interest to the group waiting outside. One bride out, another in, and again the sign goes up on the chapel door: "One Moment please—Wedding."

I sat next to one such wedding party in a Strip restaurant the last time I was in Las   5
Vegas. The marriage had just taken place; the bride still wore her dress, the mother her corsage. A bored waiter poured out a few swallows of pink champagne ("on the house") for everyone but the bride, who was too young to be served. "You'll need something with more kick than that," the bride's father said with heavy jocularity to his new son-in-law; the ritual jokes about the wedding night had a certain Panglossian character, since the bride was clearly several months pregnant. Another round of pink champagne, this time not on the house, and the bride began to cry. "It was just as nice," she sobbed, "as I hoped and dreamed it would be."

FOR WRITING OR DISCUSSION

1. What is the significance of Didion's title for this essay? How does the title relate to her thesis? Do you agree with the title? Is marriage in Las Vegas absurd?

2. Why does the writer provide information about August 26, 1965?

3. This piece appeared in the 1960s. In what ways is it still relevant? What do you know about marriage ceremonies in Las Vegas today? Do the wedding chapels as Didion described them still exist? You might research the topic online.

4. Didion calls Las Vegas "bizarre and beautiful in its venality." Which images in the essay support her view? Where do you find original uses of sensory language?

5. Write an essay about a wedding you attended. If you noted any absurd elements, use them as supporting detail for a thesis built around what you consider absurd activity, even at a conventional wedding. Be sure to use concrete sensory details.

MAXINE HONG KINGSTON
"My Mother Has Cooked for Us"

1   My mother has cooked for us: raccoons, skunks, hawks, city pigeons, wild ducks, wild geese, black-skinned bantams, snakes, garden snails, turtles that crawled about the pantry floor and sometimes escaped under refrigerator or stove, catfish that swam in the bathtub. "The emperors used to eat the peaked hump of purple dromedaries," she would say. "They used chopsticks made from rhinoceros horn, and they ate ducks' tongues and monkeys' lips." She boiled the weeds we pulled up in the yard. There was a tender plant with flowers like white stars hiding under the leaves, which were like the flower petals but green. I've not been able to find it since growing up. It had no taste. When I was as tall as the washing machine, I stepped out on the back porch one night, and some heavy, ruffling, windy, clawed thing dived at me. Even after getting chanted back to sensibility, I shook when I recalled that perched everywhere there were owls with great hunched shoulders and yellow scowls. They were a surprise for my mother from my father. We children used to hide under the beds with our fingers in our ears to shut out the bird screams and the thud, thud of the turtles swimming in the boiling water, their shells hitting the sides of the pot. Once the third aunt who worked at the laundry ran out and bought us bags of candy to hold over our noses; my mother was dismembering skunk on the chopping block. I could smell the rubbery odor through the candy.

2   In a glass jar on a shelf my mother kept a big brown hand with pointed claws stewing in alcohol and herbs. She must have brought it from China because I do not remember a time when I did not have the hand to look at. She said it was a bear's claw, and for many years I thought bears were hairless. My mother used the tobacco, leeks, and grasses swimming about the hand to rub our sprains and bruises.

3   Just as I would climb up to the shelf to take one look after another at the hand, I would hear my mother's monkey story. I'd take my fingers out of my ears and let her monkey words enter my brain. I did not always listen voluntarily, though. She would begin telling the story, perhaps repeating it to a homesick villager, and I'd overhear before I had a chance to protect myself. Then the monkey words would unsettle me; a curtain flapped loose inside my brain. I have wanted to say, "Stop it. Stop it," but not once did I say, "Stop it."

4   "Do you know what people in China eat when they have the money?" my mother began. "They buy into a monkey feast. The eaters sit around a thick wood table with a hole in the middle. Boys bring in the monkey at the end of a pole. Its neck is in a collar at the end of the pole, and it is screaming. Its hands are tied behind it. They clamp the monkey into the table; the whole table fits like another collar around its neck. Using a surgeon's saw, the cooks cut a clean line in a circle at the top of its head. To loosen the

bone, they tap with a tiny hammer and wedge here and there with a silver pick. Then an old woman reaches out her hand to the monkey's face and up to its scalp, where she tufts some hairs and lifts off the lid of the skull. The eaters spoon out the brains."

Did she say, "You should have seen the faces the monkey made"? Did she say, "The people laughed at the monkey screaming"? It was alive? The curtain flaps closed like merciful black wings. 5

"Eat! Eat!" my mother would shout at our heads bent over bowls, the blood pudding awobble in the middle of the table. 6

She had one rule to keep us safe from toadstools and such: "If it tastes good, it's bad for you," she said. "If it tastes bad, it's good for you." 7

We'd have to face four- and five-day-old leftovers until we ate it all. The squid eye would keep appearing at breakfast and dinner until eaten. Sometimes brown masses sat on every dish. I have seen revulsion on the faces of visitors who've caught us at meals. 8

"Have you eaten yet?" the Chinese greet one another. 9

"Yes, I have," they answer whether they have or not. "And you?" 10

I would live on plastic. 11

FOR WRITING OR DISCUSSION

1. What is Kingston's main point? Although the selection is rich in acutely observed details, Kingston is not writing description for its own sake. How do the details support the main idea?

2. What instances of sensory language do you find most vivid and original? What details make you see the scene exactly as Kingston sees it?

3. What does Kingston suggest about her mother by means of the descriptions of what she cooked for the family?

4. What is your reaction to the monkey feast description?

5. Write a descriptive essay about an unusual meal you have eaten. Make the details you record serve a clearly stated thesis.

Reading and Writing About Poetry

Use this poem by a contemporary writer to stimulate your thinking about descriptive language and to help you write description.

MARK STRAND

Black Sea

One clear night while the others slept, I climbed
the stairs to the roof of the house and under a sky
strewn with stars I gazed at the sea, at the spread of it,
the rolling crests of it raked by the wind, becoming

5   like bits of lace tossed in the air. I stood in the long
whispering night, waiting for something, a sign, the approach
of a distant light, and I imagined you coming closer,
the dark waves of your hair mingling with the sea,
and the dark became desire, and desire the arriving light.

10 The nearness, the momentary warmth of you as I stood
on that lonely height watching the slow swells of the sea
break on the shore and turn briefly into glass and disappear . . .
Why did I believe you would come out of nowhere? Why with all
that the world offers would you come only because I was here?

FOR WRITING OR DISCUSSION

1. What is the main point of Strand's poem?

2. What does the sea make him think of? How does it stimulate his thoughts?

3. Which appeals to the senses can you identify here? How do the comparisons in lines 5 and 12 contribute to the meaning of the poem?

4. In what ways is this a love poem? A poem about nature?

5. Write a descriptive essay in which you show how some phenomenon in nature reminds you of an important person in your life—a friend, a parent, a love, a child.

6. Write your own poem about nature and how it connects to a person in your life.

CROSSCURRENTS

Esmeralda Santiago in "A Blanco Navidad for New Yorikans" (pages 134–135) and Maxine Hong Kingston in "My Mother Has Cooked for Us" (pages 140–141) both describe their family's food. What similar strategies have the writers used to present their descriptions? How do their strategies differ?

COLLABORATIVE LEARNING

Form groups of five students and discuss the student models: "Dad's Disappointment" (pages 128–130) and "High School Practice" (pages 130–131). How do the papers demonstrate the principles of descriptive writing? What recommendations would you make for improving the essays? Discuss your group's conclusions with the rest of the class.

STRATEGY CHECKLIST: Writing and Revising Your Descriptive Paper

Plan the paper.	☐ Have I used prewriting to explore ideas for a subject?
	☐ Will I describe a person, a place, or an object?
	☐ How can I limit the topic so that it is focused and meaningful?
	☐ Have I thought about the kinds of details I can use?
	☐ Have I thought carefully about my purpose in writing?
	☐ Do I have my audience clearly in mind?
	☐ Have I considered using an outline to organize my ideas?
Write a first draft.	☐ Have I established a clear thesis that states the topic and expresses an opinion?
	☐ Have I supported my thesis with sensory detail—appeals to sight, hearing, taste, smell, and touch?
	☐ Have I organized details logically—in space or time order or by some other principle that gives structure to my description?
Revise and edit the paper.	☐ Have I avoided taking inventory of a random collection of facts?
	☐ Have I established the topic in a lively introduction to capture and hold the reader's attention?
	☐ Have I used transitions when necessary to link ideas?
	☐ Does my conclusion tie together the points of the description?
Proofread the paper.	☐ Have I proofread for grammar, spelling, and mechanics?

 **PEARSON mycomplab**

For support in meeting this chapter's objectives, follow this path in MyCompLab: Resources ⇒ Writing ⇒ Writing Purposes ⇒ Writing to Describe. Review the Instruction and Multimedia resources about writing descriptions; then complete the Exercises and click on Gradebook to measure your progress.

CHAPTER **8**

Narration

"Last night, as I was driving home from work, I stopped for the light at Fifty-fifth and Main. I was just sitting there minding my own business when, all of a sudden...."

"You'll never guess what the kids did today."

"That reminds me of the time...."

We all tell stories, and for many reasons. Usually we tell stories just to share our daily experience with others. Frequently, however, we tell stories to make a point. At other times, we tell stories that illustrate ideas. A pastor, for example, does not merely say that repentance will bring forgiveness; he reads the story of the prodigal son from the Bible. Or we tell stories to make people laugh. Whatever the case, we enjoy telling and hearing stories, and you have been telling and hearing them all your life. So the assignment to write a narrative paper should be one you will enjoy.

A **narrative** is a story. To *narrate* means "to tell, to give an account of." Narratives take many forms. A novel is a narrative. So is a short story. A biography is a narrative because it tells the story of a person's life. Historical narrative traces events over time. Often a narrative is a brief story included in a longer work to illustrate an idea.

A **narrative paper** tells a story, usually of a personal experience, that makes a point or supports a thesis. The purpose of a narrative paper is to recreate an experience in such a way that your readers can imaginatively participate in it and share it with you.

Writing Your Narrative Paper

As you plan and write your paper, keep the following principles in mind.

TIPS for Writing a Narrative Essay

- **Limit the subject.** Almost any experience you have had can serve as subject matter for a narrative paper.

  But you must limit the subject, and, in a narrative paper, time usually determines the limits of your subject. Your goal is to tell a story so dramatically and so completely that your readers can share the experience. A subject such as your summer as a camp counselor, therefore, is too broad—unless you want to write a book. But you could tell about the time a skunk got into your RV. Even one day in the city provides too much material for a complete and dramatic story. But some part of that day—the hour you spent watching a pair of cardinals in the park teach their baby how to fly—can make a good story. It's probably no exaggeration to say that the subject cannot be too limited.

- **Have a thesis.** The experience you narrate is not as important as its significance to you. Why did the experience matter to you? Why do you want to tell about it? Did it change you in some way? Did it embarrass you? Did it make you happy? Sad? Was it thrilling? Frustrating? Did it lead to a decision? Did you learn something about yourself or about others or about the world around you? Were you disappointed? Any little event in your life—even taking out the garbage—can make good subject matter for a narrative paper if you determine the significance of the experience and tell the story well.

  The student essay "The Death of Santa Claus" on pages 150–152, for example, tells of the painful way one little girl learned the truth about Santa. As you read the story, you'll surely find it touching, amusing, and sad. You may feel that the older brother, Clay, was unnecessarily cruel. The reason you have these feelings is that the author saw the significance of her experience and narrated it so skillfully that you share it with her.

  The significance of your experience—your interpretation of it, what it meant to you—is your thesis. The thesis of "The Death of Santa Claus," for example, is *Because of the manner in which I discovered that there is no Santa Claus, Christmas lost its joy and sense of magic.* You don't have to state the thesis directly in your paper all the time, but you should certainly know what it is because the significance of the experience is exactly what you want to convey to your audience.

- **Use specific details.** In every chapter of this book, we urge you to use specific details because they give life to your writing, and the narrative paper is no exception. If your story is about being frightened out of your wits the first time you spent a night alone in your aunt's hundred-year-old house, it matters that cobwebs hung from the ceiling, that no lamp in the room was bright enough to illuminate the corners, that the stairs creaked and the wind moaned. Remember, a narrative re-creates an experience for your readers. In most cases, you can make your readers feel what you felt if you use specific details. What you learned in the last chapter about descriptive writing will help you considerably here and elsewhere when you need to marshal concrete sensory language.

A word of caution, however. The details you use, like everything else in your paper, should support your thesis. Extraneous details, no matter how vivid, always feel like padding and frustrate readers.

■ **Identify time, place, and people.**   Most narratives benefit greatly by telling readers as soon as possible where and when the story takes place. Although Jarrett David Lee Jackson identifies the precise date—month, day, year—of his narrative (he has an important reason for doing so, as you will see when you read his essay on pages 153–155), we're not recommending that level of exactness as an important aspect of your story. Rather, the month and time of year alone are sufficient in drawing the reader into the events. Phrases like "on a blustery November morning" or "one warm Sunday afternoon last spring" make it easy for readers to set the scene in their minds. Also, you should not skip identifying where your story takes place. There's a magic in naming places—and people as well—and readers respond to their specificity. In this selection from "Se Habla Español" (see pages 161–163), the writer names exact places with which the reader can easily identify: "We'd been on vacation in Washington, D.C., visiting the Smithsonian, the Capitol, and the home of Edgar Allan Poe. In the Volkswagen on the way home…." Without naming, the sentences are duds: "We'd been on vacation and visited many interesting places. In the car on the way home…."

In "The Death of Santa Claus" (pages 150–152), by the second sentence we know the time—Christmas Eve—and names of the writer's brothers, Clay, Brian, and Kevin. The names help bring us into the moment directly.

■ **Use language that sounds natural.**   Your readers should feel that an intelligent, articulate friend is telling them a story. The language of a narrative, therefore, should sound conversational, which means you should avoid two extremes—the pompous and the inarticulate.

> As, for the first time, I entered the portals of the edifice that housed my new employer and donned the attire specified for my position, I felt apprehensive.

> Like, man, that first day, ya know, was like… well, when I put that waiter's jacket on, ya know, I was scared.

Try, instead, something like this:

> I was nervous that first day on the job. When I put on my white waiter's jacket, my hands trembled.

These sentences sound natural, and they give a conversational tone to the narrative.

Another way to give a natural sound to your narrative is to use direct quotations when appropriate (see "Quotation Marks," pages 602–603).

> "Are you having a good time?" she asked.
> "Not really," I replied, "but I don't want to spoil the party for you and the kids."

Direct quotations give a sense of reality to the narrative, sometimes by helping set a scene. Direct quotations are also good for revealing the personality and feelings of the characters in your narrative. Don't feel, however, that you must fill your paper with them. For example, "Se Habla Español" (see pages 161–163) contains few direct quotations, but the narrative sounds natural and dramatic.

■ **Introduce your narrative.**   Your introduction may set the scene for the narrative:

> It was in Burma, a sodden morning of the rains. A sickly light, like yellow tinfoil, was slanting over the high walls into the jail yard. We were waiting outside the condemned cells, a row of sheds fronted with double bars, like small animal cages. Each cell measured about ten feet by ten and was quite bare within except for a plank bed and a pot of drinking water. In some of them brown silent men were squatting at the inner bars, with their blankets draped round them. These were the condemned men, due to be hanged within the next week or two.
> —George Orwell, "A Hanging"

Sometimes an introduction gives the background—the facts that led to the experience being narrated:

> In 1969, I was a senior on the Luther Burbank High School basketball team. The school is on the south side of San Antonio, in one of the city's many barrios. After practice one day our coach announced that we were going to spend the following Saturday scrimmaging with the ball club from Winston Churchill High, located in the city's rich, white north side.
> —Rogelio R. Gomez, "Foul Shots"

Indeed, sometimes a narrative paper doesn't even have an introduction. In this case, the writer simply begins with the first event of the story:

> "There's a gun at your back. Raise your hands and don't make a sound," a harsh voice snarled at me. I raised my hands.

Despite these many options, your narrative no doubt will benefit from an introduction that leads to a thesis statement. In a narrative essay about a day as a volunteer worker on a collective farm, the writer opens with this introduction:

The day starts when I rise at four in the morning and fumble in the darkness for my work clothes. I remember to take my blue sunhat. Dawn has not yet broken over Kibbutz Ein Zurim. Yet I know that the members of this Israeli commune are beginning their tasks this fall day. Today, the picking of pears with a steel ladder and plastic basket awaits me; inexperienced, I am both excited and worried about the job.

Note how the writer builds successfully to her thesis statement. The first three sentences set the scene for the reader, and we can in our minds join the writer as she wakes early, dresses, and worries excitedly about the day ahead of her. The thesis promises that the body paragraphs will show us the excitement and the worry that she feels.

■ **Sequence your body paragraphs.** The body of the narrative paper also differs from that of most other papers in that its organization only can be chronological. It is possible to begin with the present and then portray an earlier episode:

> As I sit in my soft leather easy chair that I keep in front of the fireplace this time of year and gaze at brightly burning pine logs, I remember a Christmas ten years ago when I was not so comfortable.

But the heart of the narrative—what happened ten years ago—should proceed chronologically. Since you want your readers to share the events as you experienced them, you must present the events in the order that they occurred: First this, then that, and later something else. And you should let your readers know, by means of transitions, what the chronology is. Transitions are, of course, important to any piece of writing, but the kinds of transitions that indicate the passage of time are essential to a narrative paper:

> then, next, soon, later
> at four o'clock, a few minutes later, on the way back, the next morning
> After I removed the bullets …
> I must have been asleep a couple of hours when a shout awakened me.

■ **Conclude your narrative.** Finally, the narrative's conclusion as well is different from other conclusions. In some narratives, the thesis of the paper appears for the first time in the conclusion. The writer tells a good story in the introduction and body and then states the significance of the story at the end of the paper:

> At last I admitted to myself that the raccoons had won. I was tired of getting up in the middle of the night to gather the garbage they scattered about the backyard. I was tired of trying to find a garbage can that they could not open. I was, in fact, tired of the country. As I crept wearily back

to my bedroom, I knew *the raccoons had taught me a valuable lesson: I did not belong in the country; I belonged in a high-rise apartment in the heart of the city.* And that's just where I moved two weeks later.

At other times, when the main point of the narrative is sufficiently clear within the piece, the conclusion may imply the thesis without restating it, or it may take up other ideas stated or hinted at in the narrative. In the essay "Se Habla Español" (pages 161–163), you might state writer Tanya Maria Barrientos' thesis like this: "I am a natural born Guatemalan living in America who feels alienated from my heritage because I never learned my native language, Spanish." Note how her conclusion, which she spreads over three paragraphs (the last two only one sentence each in length), generalizes from her own life to those of others who may be in the same predicament:

> There must be other Latinas like me. But I haven't met any. Or, I should say, I haven't met any who have fessed up. Maybe they are secretly struggling to fit in, the same way I am. Maybe they are hiring tutors and listening to tapes behind locked doors, just like me. I wish we all had the courage to come out of our hiding places and claim our rightful spot in the broad Latino spectrum. Without being called hopeless gringas. Without having to offer apologies or show remorse.
>
> If it will help, I will go first.
>
> *Aquí estoy.* Spanish-challenged and *pura* Latina.

■ **Consider your audience and purpose.** Imagine the person who will read your narrative. Does she need further information about the setting and time of your story? Will you need to define any specialized vocabulary? Note in the introduction to the essay about picking pears (page 148) how the writer subtly defines the Hebrew word *kibbutz* as "this Israeli commune"—some readers might not have known what a kibbutz is. If your purpose is to draw a serious conclusion from your narrative, be sure that your point is clear.

■ **Revise your drafts until you're satisfied with your paper.** Try to find as many readers as possible for the early drafts of your paper. Reread Chapter 6 for many tips on how to revise your essay. Work with fellow classmates; pay careful attention to your teacher's recommendations; ask your readers about how you could improve your essay. Is anything unclear to your reader? Does your draft need more details? Are the details arranged clearly?

■ **Proofread carefully.** Don't hand in a final draft unless you've checked carefully for your own typical errors, especially run-ons and fragments. Watch your use of upper- and lowercase letters in identifying places by name.

In any event, the conclusion for a narrative paper should do what all good conclusions do: give the paper a sense of completeness.

ASSIGNMENT: NARRATION

Write a narrative essay about a memorable event. Be sure that your reader can follow the sequence easily. Make use of vivid and concrete sensory details and images. If you are having trouble deciding on a topic for your narrative paper, you might find it helpful simply to choose one of the following proverbs, quotations, or commonsense statements and then write a narration supporting or attacking it.

1. Money can't buy happiness.
2. Money is the root of all evil.
3. I never met a man I didn't like.
4. If you can't take the heat, get out of the kitchen.
5. When the going gets tough, the tough get going.
6. You can't tell a book by its cover.
7. If at first you don't succeed, try, try again.
8. There's no such thing as a bad boy.
9. Nobody knows the trouble I've seen.
10. A penny saved is a penny earned.
11. Small children, small problems; big children, big problems.
12. Spare the rod and spoil the child.
13. Hell hath no fury like a woman scorned.
14. Good fences make good neighbors.
15. A stitch in time saves nine.

Student Writing: Narration

Read the following narrative by a student writer. Annotations highlight narrative strategies and essay development.

Alycia Hatten
The Death of Santa Claus

Introduction: brief (one sentence long), yet clearly implies thesis, which controls contents of paper.

1   I will never forget that heartbreaking Christmas Eve when my oldest brother murdered Santa Claus.

2   Clay was eleven that year; I was seven, Brian five, and Kevin four. Clay had always been the leader. Brian, Kevin, and I had always done everything he told us to do, and we always believed everything he said: if Clay said it, then it was the gospel truth. Clay, naturally, had come to expect us to look up to him.

Limited subject: "that heartbreaking Christmas Eve" confines topic in time and establishes narrative sequence.

Important background details.

Narrative
chronology
begins here.

That Christmas Eve was cold and rainy, so we children had been in the house all day. Although we tried to be good so Santa would visit us that night, we grew restless and irritable as the day wore on. Our mother, too, became irritable because, in addition to answering our questions and trying to think of ways to keep us amused, she had worked all day preparing for the Christmas feast our three uncles and four aunts would share with us the next day.

I don't know where I got the nerve, but that afternoon, for the first time in my life, I challenged Clay's authority. It was about four o'clock, and, at my mother's suggestion, I had turned to my coloring book. I had almost finished coloring the picture of a little girl, and I was especially proud of the costume I had given her. At that time, I believed pink and purple to be the two loveliest colors possible, and I had given the little girl a pink dress and purple shoes.

Just as I was putting the finishing touches on the shoes, Clay came into the den from the kitchen and began to inspect my work. "That's dumb," he said. "Who ever heard of purple shoes?" And picking up a black crayon, he began coloring my beautiful purple shoes black.

"Mommie," I screamed, "Clay's messin' up my picture and he says I'm dumb! You can, too, have purple shoes, can't you?"

My mother could usually settle an argument so gently that we were seldom aware it had been settled. This time, however, she rushed into the den from the kitchen, wiping flour dust from her hands, and snapped, "Clay, put that crayon back where you found it and leave your sister alone!" To me she said, "There's nothing to cry about. I've always liked purple shoes."

Clay dropped the black crayon and, turning on the TV, sat down to watch. Since my mother had confirmed my taste in colors, I finished my picture and forgot about the incident.

A few minutes later, my father came home, and we all had an early supper. My mother resumed her baking and discovered that she would need more candied citrus to finish her last batch of cookies. Perhaps because she knew Clay was hurt and she wanted us to become friends again, she told Clay and me to put on our raincoats and go to the corner store to get the citrus.

"Why does she have to go with me?" Clay whined.

3

4 **Time transition: "that afternoon"; "about four o'clock."**

Specific details appeal to sense of sight: "pink dress and purple shoes."

5

6

7 **Sharp image of mother: sensory details appeal to sight, sound, and touch.**

8

9 **Transitions continue to advance the chronological sequence: "A few minutes later."**

10

11   "It'll be good for your sister to get out of the house for a while. Besides, she's getting to be a big girl, and you can teach her to count the change," my mother replied.

12   Clay and I set out on our journey. I babbled all the way. Clay said hardly a word, but I was too happy to be going to the grocery with him to notice. On the way back I said to Clay, "Let's run home so we won't miss any of the 'Santa Claus Is Coming to Town' special."

13   Clay said, "No, I'm not runnin' home to see that stupid program, and there ain't a Santa Claus anyway."

14   I stopped dead in my tracks and said, "What do you mean there ain't a Santa Claus? Mommie just took us to Halle's yesterday to see him and we have pictures of him at home, and Mommie and Daddy don't tell lies, and I'm gonna tell on you when we get home." I could hardly wait to get home so I could tell my mother about Clay's awful lie.

15   "Your brother's just teasing you, and if he doesn't stop, Santa's going to leave him a big bag of ashes," my mother reassured me. Brian, Kevin, and I laughed with relief! I went into the den and started watching "Santa Claus Is Coming to Town."

16   When the commercial came on, Clay said, "Come on, I'll prove it to you." He went to Daddy's desk and got his flashlight. Then we went downstairs to the basement. Clay said, "Come over here to this big locker and I'll show you your toys."

17   We went to the locker, and Clay pulled open the door while I looked in with the flashlight. And there they were: most of the toys I had asked Santa for were in the locker!

18   I went to bed that night heartbroken. I felt as if someone had died. The next morning, even the presence of the bicycle I had dreamed of couldn't cheer me up. I didn't feel the sense of magic and the happiness that I had come to associate with Christmas morning. And I haven't ever again, not since Clay killed Santa Claus.

FOR WRITING OR DISCUSSION

1. Do the title and the first paragraph of the narrative reveal too much of the story? Why, or why not?

2. The writer uses strong words like *murdered*, *died*, and *killed* to suggest the way she felt when learning the truth about Santa. What do these words reveal about her understanding of her brother's behavior?

3. The thesis of the narrative is not directly stated. Should it be?

4. Identify four expressions that indicate the passage of time.

5. What do the direct quotations reveal about Clay and his sister?

6. How do the following details serve the narrative?

   "That Christmas Eve was cold and rainy…." (paragraph 3)

   "I had given the little girl… purple shoes." (paragraph 4)

   "…[S]he rushed into the den…, wiping flour dust from her hands…." (paragraph 7)

7. Write a narrative paper about the time you learned the truth about some myth (Santa Claus, the Easter bunny, the tooth fairy) of your childhood. Or, write a narrative about the difficulty you have or had in giving up some cherished belief.

Here is another student narrative. Note the use of concrete detail.

Jarrett David Lee Jackson
My Father's House

When I walk into my father's house every day, I always wonder if my parents should have stayed together and how my life would have changed because of it. It just seems funny to me that seven years ago my parents and my sister and I were one big happy family. 1

My father still lives at our old house with his new wife. I still think of all the memories I have in that house, and I also think about all the memories that he's making with a new family. I remember falling up the stairs for some reason. My sister found it amusing to see me bleeding and crying. It hurts every time I walk up to the door, knowing I have to knock instead of just using my key to get in. I don't even have a key to my father's house. Maybe he's just forgetful, or maybe he just doesn't want me to have one. 2

Every time I come to the house, I remember that horrible night. 3

4   The date was July 14, 1994. It's strange after all these years that I can remember the exact date. I remember to read all that day to keep my mind off of the past. I usually stay alone, too, choosing to isolate myself.

5   I remember cooking dinner that night. It had been a long, bad day at school, and I remember only wanting to go outside. I asked my mother if I could go outside and play. She gave me a hurt, empty look, like she didn't know what to say. Her face was full of hurt and disgust for something, but I didn't know what. She told me no and also to ask my father when he got home. She turned her back to me and rubbed her forehead and bloodshot eyes as if she wanted to cry but was holding it in.

6   I'd never seen my mother that bothered by something, but I didn't know what it was. I went to my older, wiser sister to see if she knew what was wrong with our mother. I knew she didn't really know *everything*, but it always made me feel better if my sister and I both didn't know what was going on. My sister got me through many, many problems in my life, but even she couldn't help me through this one.

7   My father drifted through the door at about 6:30. Usually he was home by 5:30. I had seen him late about three times in my whole life. I greeted him at the door with a hello. He said hello back with a very serious face. I was scared to ask him what was wrong, so I just told him that dinner was ready. He said okay, but it was like he wasn't even talking to me. After he hung up his coat, he walked right past me like I wasn't even there.

8   About 8:00, I went to my room to watch television and play a game or two. My mother was in the shower. My mother usually takes her nightly shower about nine or ten o'clock, so she was kind of early. My father slipped into the room and sat down on my bed. He told me to pause the game and come to their bedroom. I would have asked why, but I was looking in his face and he looked dead serious, so I just followed orders and went to their bedroom. My sister immediately followed. She pushed me, and we started playing, but then I caught a glimpse of my father's face and stopped. My sister sat down on the other side of the bed. I tried to think what I might have done in the past couple of days that I might have gotten into serious trouble for.

9   My father sat on the bed and said he loved us, but he got real nervous for some reason. Then my mother came in from the shower with her robe on. Her eyes showed that she was hurt or had been crying. She sat down in a chair next to the bed, but far away from my father. He tried to let us down easy about the situation. He explained

how people fall out of love with one another, but still care for one another. I didn't
understand. Who was he talking about? Was this some sort of life lesson I had to learn
that day? I got scared and sick to my stomach as I feared the worst.

"*We're getting a divorce.*" The most devastating words I have ever heard. Out of   10
my father's mouth? My heart dropped down to my feet. I couldn't move from the bed.
My sister was crying so hard I couldn't hear anything else. My mother grabbed hold
of me, trying to say she was sorry between her sobs. Everyone was crying but my
father and me. I maintained eye contact with him. I couldn't break contact with him for
fear I would look weak in one of those situations where I must not appear weak.

"How could you do this to us?" I asked, fighting back tears.   11

"Well, son, it can't be explained. It just happened," he answered in a mellow tone.   12

My father is a strong, stony man, and I really didn't expect too much emotion to   13
pour forth. He was also a loud man, but he maintained his hushed, mellow tone. He
explained that he was moving out and that I would have to become the man of the
house. It was a responsibility I knew I wasn't ready for, but I had to accept. I knew I
would try to be a man to the best of my boyish abilities.

My father slept on the couch that last night together. The house was extremely   14
silent. I didn't hear any snoring or even breathing. I was in my room thinking about
being the man of the house, of remaining strong for what remained of our family. I
got up to talk with my father, but when I got to the top of the stairs I stopped. A dead
silence filled the house as I realized I couldn't ask him for any help again. I felt that he
was taking the easy way out by divorcing my mother. I right then promised myself that
I would be a better father and man than he was. I would always try my hardest and at
eleven years old I would step up and become a better man than my father.

I'll never forget that day because while it was the lowest point in my life, it was also   15
a breakthrough for me. It was my day, an enlightenment of some sort. Oddly enough, I
still love my father, but in my heart I know I will be a better man than he has been, a better
husband, father, and man. I understand that love is forever and can never be "divorced."

FOR WRITING OR DISCUSSION

1. What is the writer's thesis? Where in the essay do you find it stated most
   clearly?
2. Where does the writer use sensory language most vividly?
3. Write a narrative paper about a personal discovery after you experienced an
   intense moment with your parents or other family members.

Narrative
in the World Around You

The telling of stories figures widely in our culture: rarely does a day go by without our efforts to tell a story or listen to one. Popular sitcoms are visual narratives usually told in clear chronology. Theatrical productions depend heavily on narrative. Travelogues on screen or in books detail narrative events at places of interest.

Despite instant cable news and Internet streams of current events, many people throughout the world read newspapers regularly. Newspaper reporting depends heavily on narrative: getting a story straight means identifying time, place, and people; including relevant details; presenting issues in comprehensible sequence; and focusing on a clearly defined thesis.

In this excerpt from a newspaper story about surrogate parents, note how the reporter uses narrative strategies to inform the reader about essential elements in the story.

Introduction — The bold letters, large type, eye-catching headline engage the reader right away.

Thesis — Surrogate babies created with few guiding rules.

Limited subject — The Kehoe baby narrative makes point about unregulated surrogacy.

Specific details — The article identifies by name the place and the people involved.

Natural language — Phrases include "showed off baby pictures" and "worrying and wondering what had happened."

Organization — A clear chronology helps readers follow the sequence of events; very short paragraphs aid newspaper readers in a hurry.

Quotations — The exact words of the people involved add life to the narrative.

Definition of terms — A key term is defined for those who might not know its meaning.

Audience and purpose — The article is abbreviated by the *New York Times* and appears in *Times Digest*. The audience is people who don't have time to read the original version, which runs to several columns. The purpose is to tell general readers about flawed surrogate arrangements by narrating one particular case.

Story with a point — The Kehoe experience is not the main point of the narrative. The writer uses the case of the Kehoe Michigan twins to make the larger point about unregulated surrogacy.

Your Turn

Go online to see how narrative figures in a web site of your choice. Check recent Facebook or Twitter entries of people you know to see how the telling of stories contributes to their posting. Write a brief essay on your findings.

Building a Baby, with Few Set Rules

STEPHANIE SAUL

Unable to have a baby of her own, Amy Kehoe became her own general contractor to manufacture one. For Ms. Kehoe and her husband, Scott, the idea seemed like their best hope after years of infertility.

Working mostly over the Internet, Ms. Kehoe handpicked the egg donor, a pre-med student at the University of Michigan. From the Web site of California Cryobank, she chose the anonymous sperm donor, an athletic man with a 4.0 high school grade-point average.

On another Web site, surromomsonline.com, Ms. Kehoe found a gestational carrier who would deliver her baby.

Finally, she hired the fertility clinic, IVF Michigan, which put together her creation last December.

"We paid for the egg, the sperm, the in vitro fertilization," Ms. Kehoe said as she showed off baby pictures at her home near Grand Rapids, Mich. "They wouldn't be here if it weren't for us."

On July 28, the Kehoes announced the arrival of twins, Ethan and Bridget, at University Hospital in Ann Arbor. Overjoyed, they took the babies home on Aug. 3 and prepared for a welcoming by their large extended family.

A month later, a police officer supervised as the Kehoes relinquished the swaddled infants in the driveway.

Bridget and Ethan are now in the custody of the surrogate who gave birth to them, Laschell Baker of Ypsilanti, Mich. Ms. Baker had obtained a court order to retrieve them after learning that Ms. Kehoe was being treated for mental illness.

"I couldn't see living the rest of my life worrying and wondering what had happened, or what if she hadn't taken her medicine, or what if she relapsed," said Ms. Baker, who has four children of her own.

Now, she and her husband, Paul, plan to raise the twins.

The creation of Ethan and Bridget tested the boundaries of the field known as third-party reproduction, in which more than two people collaborate to have a baby. Five parties were involved: the egg donor, the sperm donor, Ms. Baker and the Kehoes. And two separate middlemen brokered the egg and sperm.

About 750 babies are born each year in this country through gestational surrogacy, and twice that many surrogacies are attempted. Most are less complicated than the arrangement that resulted in the birth of Ethan and Bridget.

But as the dispute over the Michigan twins reveals, surrogacy arrangements that go badly can have profound implications, particularly for the children. Surrogacy is largely without regulation, with no authority deciding who may obtain babies through surrogacy or who may serve as a surrogate, according to interviews and court records.

157

Readings for Writing

These professional examples of narration are typical of the narratives you will be reading and writing. Notice as you read how each selection tells a good story but also makes a significant point.

CAROL K. LITTLEBRANT

Death Is a Personal Matter

1   My father sleeps. I sit writing … trying to get something on paper I know is there, but which is as elusive and slippery as the life that's ending before me.

2   My father has cancer. Cancer of the sinuses, and as the autopsy will show later, of the left occipital lobe, mastoid, cerebellum.

3   His head lies at an awkward angle on the pillow because of a lump on his neck grown to grapefruit size—the visible sign that, for some reason, was not considered worthy of biopsy for ten doctor-to-doctor-running months. The invisible is worse.

4   My imagination enters the chamber of horrors of overgrown sinus passages, and I wince at the thought of the excruciating pain my father has borne for so long. Occasionally the pain rips through the veil of drugs and, still asleep, he reaches out a skinny white arm and grips the bed railing with a hand, gnarled, but still warm and amazingly strong.

5   I watch his rickety body shudder from the bombarding agonies. I cry and pray and gently wipe the glistening sweat from his forehead, sit again and watch, not quite sure what I am watching for. I have no measure of previous days and nights. I have only been here a few hours.

A Painful Burden

6   When I came in, he didn't know me. I wrote my name on a card with the words, "I'm here, Dad." And he tried to understand, but couldn't. Later, when a friend arrived, he managed introductions of the lovely lady "who looks just like my daughter" to "my good friend, Oskar." Then, joking and being gracious, he made Oskar and me laugh, enjoy ourselves and feel comfortable. And we felt love. Now it is night, and I do not know whether the fitful sleep is appropriate and whether tomorrow he will wake and have time to joke and be gracious again.

7   I have not seen my father for nine months, when the lump was still a secret below his ear. A few months later I heard about it and headaches, and then from time to time all the diagnoses of arthritis, a cyst, sinusitis … even senility. Then finally—the lump now a painful burden to be carried—he was subjected to nine days of tests of bowels, bladder, blood. And on the last day a hollow needle was inserted into the growth; the cells gathered, magnified, interpreted and pronounced cancer. Immediate surgery and/or cobalt treatment indicated.

They were told, my mother and father, the day after his 75th birthday party. Then, after 8
panic and the trauma of an old World War I rifle that would not fire, with my mother—
ordered outside the bedroom—hearing click, click, click… and a plastic bag, tucked
around my father's face in one last act of stricken, singular loyalty and cooperation by my
mother, to be clawed away at the last moment… and spilled pills… and falling… and
weeping… and holding each other… and finally giving in, my father reluctantly left his
own bed and was taken to the hospital.

"Let Me Alone"

And after the trauma of no dentures, no hearing aid and one unexpected cobalt treat- 9
ment, triumphant that his mind functioned and his voice was firm, he stated unfalteringly:
"Let me alone. No more treatments. I am 75. I have had an excellent life. It is time for me
to die in my own way." His decision was not met with approval.

These things I learned later, but now I hear him moan and watch his face contort 10
and his bony fingers press his forehead. And I go down the night corridors of the hospital and ask for another shot for my father. All the nurses look at me, and I at them. We
do not speak. It is not necessary. The air is filled with the serene mystery of tacit agreements. Another doctor is in charge now, and the orders written on the chart are clear
and kind.

After the shot is given, my father's breathing changes. There are longer intervals 11
between each breath. I time them with my own breathing, and feel the suspense as I
wait to exhale and take another breath. But even now I do not know I am here for the
end. I am not familiar with dying. I pray again he will not suffer long. I anticipate weeks
because his heart is that of a lion.

I pet him, and hold his hand and kiss it. I wipe away the urine from between his 12
wasted legs, knowing he would be terribly embarrassed if he knew. But I am grateful to
minister to him with love at the end of his life.

In the morning, another friend comes in to relieve me. I go for breakfast. A head nurse 13
severely scolds me for wearing a cotton nightgown smock over my slacks as certainly not
appropriate to wear in my father's room. I shrug and order coffee.

Later on, washed and clean, my father rests peacefully on his side. I take his hand. 14
He wakens, and now with only one eye functioning, but it blue and clear, he smiles a
sweet gentle smile, and says, "Holy smokes… it's Carol." The last child has come and he
is happy. Then for a moment he looks puzzled… Carol all the way from Buffalo?… and
then he understands. He tells me he would like to rest now and squeezes my hand. His
eyes close, and as though a shade were being pulled back from his face, the pain moves
from chin to nose to forehead and disappears. He sleeps and breathes softly. I smile at his
peace. I leave.

My mother returns to the hospital to take my place. The phone rings 30 minutes later. 15
Gently and quietly my father has died with her last kiss upon his lips.

Joyous Freedom

16   As the family drives back to the hospital, I sense a great elation as if someone were flying with arms flung out in total freedom. I chuckle because the joyous, almost glee-fully alive, feeling, is so strong. Yes, old man … Pop … I'm glad for you. Enjoy, enjoy and Godspeed.

17   Death is not easy under any circumstances, but at least he did not suffer tubes and IVs and false hope, and we did not suffer the play-acting, the helpless agonies of watching a loved one suffer to no purpose, finally growing inured to it all or even becoming irritated with a dying vegetable that one cannot relate to any longer. In the end, I have learned, death is a very personal matter between parent and offspring, husbands and wives, loving neighbors and friends, and between God or symbols of belief and the dying ones and all who care about them.

18   There comes a point where it is no longer the business of the courts, the American Medical Association, the government. It is private business. And I write now publicly only because it needs to be said again, and my father would have agreed.

19   So, Pop, I say it for you, for all of us still here. Wish us well and God bless.

FOR WRITING OR DISCUSSION

1. What is the thesis of this piece?

2. Littlebrandt is writing about a complex and controversial subject. Where does she seem to give serious consideration to the position of those who may differ with her views?

3. What is the writer's attitude toward the medical profession? In what ways are her views both positive and negative?

4. What purposes do the many details about the nature of the father's illness serve in the essay?

5. Explain the meaning of "Wish us well …" in paragraph 19.

6. We all celebrate or commemorate the landmarks in our lives—births, marriages, deaths. Write a narrative showing how a person or group of people faced one of these major events.

TANYA BARRIENTOS
Se Habla Español

The Man on the Other End of the phone line is telling me the classes I've called about are 1
first-rate: native speakers in charge, no more than six students per group. I tell him that
will be fine and yes, I've studied a bit of Spanish in the past. He asks for my name and
I supply it, rolling the double "r" in "Barrientos" like a pro. That's when I hear the silent
snag, the momentary hesitation I've come to expect at this part of the exchange. Should I
go into it again? Should I explain, the way I have to half a dozen others, that I am Guatemalan by birth but *pura gringa* by circumstance?

This will be the sixth time I've signed up to learn the language my parents speak to 2
each other. It will be the sixth time I've bought workbooks and notebooks and textbooks
listing 501 conjugated verbs in alphabetical order, in hopes that the subjunctive tense
will finally take root in my mind. In class I will sit across a table from the "native speaker,"
who will wonder what to make of me. "Look," I'll want to say (but never do). "Forget the
dark skin. Ignore the obsidian eyes. Pretend I'm a pink-cheeked, blue-eyed blonde whose
name tag says 'Shannon.'" Because that is what a person who doesn't innately know the
difference between *corre*, *corra*, and *corrí* is supposed to look like, isn't it?

I came to the United States in 1963 at age 3 with my family and immediately stopped 3
speaking Spanish. College-educated and seamlessly bilingual when they settled in west
Texas, my parents (a psychology professor and an artist) wholeheartedly embraced the
notion of the American melting pot. They declared that their two children would speak
nothing but *inglés*. They'd read in English, write in English, and fit into Anglo society
beautifully.

It sounds politically incorrect now. But America was not a hyphenated nation back 4
then. People who called themselves Mexican Americans or Afro-Americans were considered dangerous radicals, while law-abiding citizens were expected to drop their cultural
baggage at the border and erase any lingering ethnic traits.

To be honest, for most of my childhood I liked being the brown girl who defied 5
expectations. When I was 7, my mother returned my older brother and me to elementary school one week after the school year had already begun. We'd been on vacation
in Washington, D.C., visiting the Smithsonian, the Capitol, and the home of Edgar Allan
Poe. In the Volkswagen on the way home, I'd memorized "The Raven," and I would recite
it with melodramatic flair to any poor soul duped into sitting through my performance. At
the school's office, the registrar frowned when we arrived.

"You people. Your children are always behind, and you have the nerve to bring them 6
in late?"

"My children," my mother answered in a clear, curt tone, "will be at the top of their 7
classes in two weeks."

The registrar filed our cards, shaking her head. 8

9   I did not live in a neighborhood with other Latinos, and the public school I attended attracted very few. I saw the world through the clear, cruel vision of a child. To me, speaking Spanish translated into being poor. It meant waiting tables and cleaning hotel rooms. It meant being left off the cheerleading squad and receiving a condescending smile from the guidance counselor when you said you planned on becoming a lawyer or a doctor. My best friends' names were Heidi and Leslie and Kim. They told me I didn't seem "Mexican" to them, I took this as a compliment. I enjoyed looking into the faces of Latino store clerks and waitresses and, yes, even our maid and saying *"Yo no hablo español."* It made me feel superior. It made me feel American. It made me feel white. I thought if I stayed away from Spanish, stereotypes would stay away from me.

10   Then came the backlash. During the two decades when I'd worked hard to isolate myself from the stereotype I'd constructed in my own head, society shifted. The nation changed its views on ethnic identity. College professors started teaching history through African American and Native American eyes. Children were told to forget about the melting pot and picture America as multicolored quilt instead. Hyphens suddenly had muscle, and I was left wondering where I fit in.

11   The Spanish language was supposedly the glue that held the new Latino community together. But in my case it was what kept me apart. I felt awkward among groups whose conversations flowed in and out of Spanish. I'd be asked a question in Spanish and I'd have to answer in English, knowing this raised a mountain of questions. I wanted to call myself Latina, to finally take pride, but it felt like a lie. So I set out to learn the language that people assumed I already knew.

12   After my first set of lessons, I could function in the present tense. *"Hola, Paco. ¿Qué tal? ¿Qué color es tu cuaderno? El mío es azul."* My vocabulary built quickly, but when I spoke, my tongue felt thick inside my mouth—and if I needed to deal with anything in the future or past, I was sunk. I enrolled in a three-month submersion program in Mexico and emerged able to speak like a sixth-grader with a solid C average. I could read Gabriel García Márquez with a Spanish-English dictionary at my elbow, and I could follow 90 percent of the melodrama on any given telenovela. But true speakers discover my limitations the moment I stumble over a difficult construction, and that is when I get the look. The one that raises the wall between us. The one that makes me think I'll never really belong. Spanish has become a litmus test showing how far from your roots you've strayed.

13   My bilingual friends say I make too much of it. They tell me that my Guatemalan heritage and unmistakable Mayan features are enough to legitimize my membership in the Latin American club. After all, not all Poles speak Polish. Not all Italians speak Italian. And as this nation grows more and more Hispanic, not all Latinos will share one language. But I don't believe them.

14   There must be other Latinas like me. But I haven't met any. Or, I should say, I haven't met any who have fessed up. Maybe they are secretly struggling to fit in, the same way I am. Maybe they are hiring tutors and listening to tapes behind locked doors, just like me. I wish we all had the courage to come out of our hiding places and claim our rightful

spot in the broad Latino spectrum. Without being called hopeless gringas. Without having to offer apologies or show remorse.

If it will help, I will go first.   15

Aquí estoy. Spanish-challenged and *pura* Latina.   16

FOR WRITING OR DISCUSSION

1. What is the thesis of this selection?

2. What narrative elements can you identify? Tell Barrientos' story (or stories) in your own words.

3. Why does the writer give her essay a Spanish title—especially since this piece is about not being able to speak Spanish? Where have you seen the words "*Se habla español*" before?

4. The writer has used many Spanish words and phrases throughout the piece. Identify them and explain their meaning. Why has she chosen this strategy of integrating Spanish words into an English essay?

5. Why is learning Spanish so important to Barrientos?

6. Write an essay about the importance of language for a person's identity. Do you believe that it is necessary for people to be able to speak the language of their ethnic heritage?

GREG SARRIS
"You Don't Look Indian"

I have heard that someone said to American Indian writer Louise Erdrich, "You don't look Indian." It was at a reading she gave, or perhaps when she received an award of some kind for her writing. Undoubtedly, whoever said this noted Erdrich's very white skin, her green eyes and her red hair. She retorted, "Gee, you don't look rude."   1

You don't look Indian.   2

How often I too have heard that. But unlike Erdrich, I never returned the insult, or challenged my interlocutors. Not with words anyway. I arranged the facts of my life to fit others' conceptions of what it is to be Indian. I used others' words, others' definitions. That way, if I didn't look Indian, I might still be Indian.   3

Well, I don't know if I am Indian, I said, or if I am, how much. I was adopted. I know my mother was white—Jewish, German, Irish. I was illegitimate. Father unknown. It was back in the fifties when having a baby without being married was shameful. My mother uttered something on the delivery table about the father being Spanish. Mexican maybe. Anyway, I was given up and adopted, which is how I got a name. For awhile things went   4 well. Then they didn't. I found myself with other families, mostly on small ranches where I milked cows and worked with horses. I met a lot of Indians—Pomo Indians—and was taken in by one of the families. I learned bits and pieces of two Pomo languages. So if you ask, I call myself Pomo. But I don't know … My mother isn't around to ask. After she had me, she needed blood. The hospital gave her the wrong type and it killed her.

5   The story always went something like that. It is true, all of it, but arranged so that people might see how I fit. The last lines—about my mother—awe people and cause them to forget, or to be momentarily distracted, from their original concern about my not looking Indian. And I am illegitimate. That explains any crossing of borders, anything beyond the confines of definition. That is how I fit.

6   Last year I found my father. Well, I found out his name—Emilio. My mother's younger brother, my uncle, whom I met recently, remembered taking notes from his sister to a "big Hawaiian type" on the football field. "I would go after school while the team was practicing," my uncle said. "The dude was big, dark. They called him Meatloaf. I think his name though was Emilio. Try Emilio."

7   To have a name, even a nickname, seemed unfathomable. To be thirty-six years old and for the first time to have a lead about a father somehow frightened me. You imagine all your life; you find ways to account for that which is missing, you tell stories, and now all that is leveled by a name.

8   In Laguna Beach I contacted the high school librarian and made arrangements to look through old yearbooks. It was just after a conference there in Southern California, where I had finished delivering a paper on American Indian education. I found my mother immediately, and while I was staring for the first time at an adult picture of my mother, a friend who was with me scanned other yearbooks for an Emilio. Already we knew by looking at the rows and rows of white faces, there wouldn't be too many Emilios. I was still gazing at the picture of my mother when my friend jumped. "Look," she said. She was tilting the book, pointing to a name. But already, even as I looked, a dark face caught my attention, and it was a face I saw myself in. Without a doubt. Darker, yes. But me nonetheless.

9   I interviewed several of my mother's and father's classmates. It was my mother's friends who verified what I suspected. Emilio Hilario was my father. They also told me that he had died, that I missed him by about five years.

10   I had to find out from others what he couldn't tell me. I wanted to know about his life. Did he have a family? What was his ethnicity? Luckily I obtained the names of several relatives, including a half-brother and a grandfather. People were quick about that, much more so than about the ethnicity question. They often circumvented the question by telling stories about my father's athletic prowess and about how popular he was. A few, however, were more candid. His father, my grandfather, is Filipino. "A short Filipino man," they said. "Your father got his height from his mother. She was fairer." Some people said my grandmother was Spanish, others said she was Mexican or Indian. Even within the family, there is discrepancy about her ethnicity. Her mother was definitely Indian, however. Coast Miwok from Tomales Bay just north of San Francisco, and just south of Santa Rosa, where I grew up. Her name was Rienette.

During the time my grandmother was growing up, probably when her mother— 11
Rienette—was growing up too, even until quite recently, when it became popular to be
Indian, Indians in California sometimes claimed they were Spanish. And for good reason.
The prejudice against Indians was intolerable, and often only remnants of tribes, or even
families, remained to face the hatred and discrimination. My grandmother spoke Spanish. Her sister, Juanita, married a Mexican and her children's children are proud *Chicanos*
living in East Los Angeles. Rienette's first husband, my grandmother and her sister's father,
was probably part Mexican or Portuguese—I'm not sure.

The story is far from complete. But how much Indian I am by blood is not the question 12
whose answer concerns me now. Oh, I qualify for certain grants, and that is important.
But knowing about my blood heritage will not change my complexion any more than it
will my experience.

In school I was called the white beaner. This was not because some of my friends 13
happened to be Mexican, but because the white population had little sense of the local
Indians. Anyone with dark hair and skin was thought to be Mexican. A counselor once
called me in and asked if my family knew I went around with Mexicans. "Yes," I said.
"They're used to it." At the time, I was staying with an Indian family—the McKays—and
Mrs. McKay was a mother to me. But I said nothing more then. I never informed the coun-
selor that most of my friends, the people she was referring to, were Indian—Pomo Indian.
Kashaya Pomo Indian. Sulfur Bank Pomo Indian. Coyote Valley Pomo Indian. Yokaya Pomo
Indian. Point Arena Pomo Indian. Bodega Bay Miwok Indian. Tomales Bay Miwok Indian.
And never mind that names such as Smith and Pinola are not Spanish (or Mexican) names.

As I think back, I said nothing more to the counselor not because I didn't want to 14
cause trouble (I did plenty of that), but because, like most other kids, I never really knew
a way to tamper with how the authorities—counselors, teachers, social workers, police—
categorized us. We talked about our ethnicity amongst ourselves, often speculating who
was more or less this or that. So many of us are mixed with other groups—white, Mexican,
Spanish, Portuguese, Filipino. I know of an Indian family who is half Mexican and they
identify themselves as Mexicans. In another family of the same admixture just the opposite
is true. Yet for most of the larger white community, we were Mexican, or something.

And here I am with blue eyes and fair skin. If I was a white beaner, I was, more gener- 15
ally, a kid from the wrong side of the tracks. Hood. Greaser. Low Brow. Santa Rosa was a
much smaller town then, the lines more clearly drawn between the haves and the have-
nots, the non-colored and the colored. Suburban sprawl was just beginning; there was
still the old downtown with its stone library and old Roman-columned courthouse. On
the fringes of town lived the poorer folk. The civil rights movement had not yet engendered the ethnic pride typical of the late sixties and early seventies.

I remember the two guys who taught me to box, Manuel and Robert. They said they 16
were Portuguese, Robert part Indian. People whispered that they were black. I didn't
care. They picked me out, taught me to box. That was when I was fourteen. By the time
I was sixteen, I beat heads everywhere and every time I could. I looked for fights and
felt free somehow in the fight. I say I looked for fights, but really, as I think about it,
fights seemed to find me. People said things, they didn't like me, they invaded my space.

I had reason. So I fought. And afterwards I was somebody. Manny said I had a chip on my shoulder, which is an asset for a good fighter. "Hate in your eyes, brother," he told me. "You got hate in your eyes."

17   I heard a lot of "Indian" stories too. We used to call them old-time stories, those about Coyote and the creation. Then there were the spook stories about spook men and women and evil doings. I knew of a spook man, an old guy who would be sitting on his family's front porch one minute and then five minutes later, just as you were driving uptown, there he'd be sitting on the old courthouse steps. The woman whose son I spent so much time with was an Indian doctor. She healed the sick with songs and prayer; she sucked pains from people's bodies. These are the things my professors and colleagues wanted to hear about.

18   I was different here too. I read books, which had something to do with my getting into college. But when I started reading seriously—about the middle of my junior year in high school—I used what I read to explain the world; I never engaged my experience to inform what I was reading. Again, I was editing my experience, and, not so ironically, I found meaning that way. And, not so ironically, the more I read the more I became separated from the world of my friends and what I had lived. So in college when I found people interested in my Indian experience as it related to issues of ecology, personal empowerment, and other worldviews, I complied and told them what I "knew" of these things. In essence I shaped what I knew to fit the books and read the books to shape what I knew. The woman who was a mother to me came off as Castaneda's Don Juan. Think of the "separate reality" of her dream world, never mind what I remember about her—the long hours in the apple cannery, her tired face, her clothes smelling of rotten apples.

19   Now, as I sort through things, I am beginning to understand why I hated myself and those people at the university; how by sculpting my experience to their interests, I denied so much of my life, including the anger and self-hatred that seeps up from such denial. I wanted to strike back, beat the hell out of them; I imagined them angering me in some way I could recognize—maybe an insult, a push or shove—so that I could hurt them. Other times I just wanted them to be somewhere, perhaps outside the classroom, on a street, in a bar, where they came suddenly upon me and saw me fighting, pummelling somebody. Anger is like a cork in water. Push it down, push it down, and still it keeps coming to the surface.

FOR WRITING OR DISCUSSION

1. How does the writer's illegitimacy explain "any crossing of borders, anything beyond the confines of definition"?

2. What stereotypes did Sarris have to endure as he was growing up?

3. What steps does the writer take to uncover his personal family history? How do you explain his efforts?

4. Assume that Sarris could have one meeting with his father or mother. Write a narrative about that meeting. Or, as an alternate assignment, write a narrative about the first meeting between a child and a long-lost parent.

KATE CHOPIN
The Story of an Hour

Knowing that Mrs. Mallard was afflicted with a heart trouble, great care was taken to break to her as gently as possible the news of her husband's death.   1

It was her sister Josephine who told her, in broken sentences; veiled hints that revealed in half concealing. Her husband's friend Richards was there, too, near her. It was he who had been in the newspaper office when intelligence of the railroad disaster was received, with Brently Mallard's name leading the list of "killed." He had only taken the time to assure himself of its truth by a second telegram, and had hastened to forestall any less careful, less tender friend in bearing the sad message.   2

She did not hear the story as many women have heard the same, with a paralyzed inability to accept its significance. She wept at once, with sudden, wild abandonment, in her sister's arms. When the storm of grief had spent itself she went away to her room alone. She would have no one follow her.   3

There stood, facing the open window, a comfortable, roomy armchair. Into this she sank, pressed down by a physical exhaustion that haunted her body and seemed to reach into her soul.   4

She could see in the open square before her house the tops of trees that were all aquiver with the new spring life. The delicious breath of rain was in the air. In the street below a peddler was crying his wares. The notes of a distant song which some one was singing reached her faintly, and countless sparrows were twittering in the eaves.   5

There were patches of blue sky showing here and there through the clouds that had met and piled one above the other in the west facing her window.   6

She sat with her head thrown back upon the cushion of the chair, quite motionless, except when a sob came up into her throat and shook her, as a child who has cried itself to sleep continues to sob in its dreams.   7

She was young, with a fair, calm face, whose lines bespoke repression and even a certain strength. But now there was a dull stare in her eyes, whose gaze was fixed away off yonder on one of those patches of blue sky. It was not a glance of reflection, but rather indicated a suspension of intelligent thought.   8

There was something coming to her and she was waiting for it, fearfully. What was it? She did not know; it was too subtle and elusive to name. But she felt it, creeping out of the sky, reaching toward her through the sounds, the scents, the color that filled the air.   9

Now her bosom rose and fell tumultuously. She was beginning to recognize this thing that was approaching to possess her, and she was striving to beat it back with her will—as powerless as her two white slender hands would have been.   10

When she abandoned herself a little whispered word escaped her slightly parted lips. She said it over and over under her breath: "free, free, free!" The vacant stare and the look of terror that had followed it went from her eyes. They stayed keen and bright. Her pulses beat fast, and the coursing blood warmed and relaxed every inch of her body.   11

She did not stop to ask if it were or were not a monstrous joy that held her. A clear and exalted perception enabled her to dismiss the suggestion as trivial.   12

13   She knew that she would weep again when she saw the kind, tender hands folded in death; the face that had never looked save with love upon her, fixed and gray and dead. But she saw beyond that bitter moment a long procession of years to come that would belong to her absolutely. And she opened and spread her arms out to them in welcome.

14   There would be no one to live for her during those coming years; she would live for herself. There would be no powerful will bending hers in that blind persistence with which men and women believe they have a right to impose a private will upon a fellow-creature. A kind intention or a cruel intention made the act seem no less a crime as she looked upon it in that brief moment of illumination.

15   And yet she had loved him—sometimes. Often she had not. What did it matter! What could love, the unsolved mystery, count for in face of this possession of self-assertion which she suddenly recognized as the strongest impulse of her being!

16   "Free! Body and soul free!" she kept whispering.

17   Josephine was kneeling before the closed door with her lips to the keyhole, imploring for admission. "Louise, open the door! I beg; open the door—you will make yourself ill. What are you doing, Louise? For heaven's sake open the door."

18   "Go away. I am not making myself ill." No; she was drinking in a very elixir of life through that open window.

19   Her fancy was running riot along those days ahead of her. Spring days, and summer days, and all sorts of days that would be her own. She breathed a quick prayer that life might be long. It was only yesterday she had thought with a shudder that life might be long.

20   She arose at length and opened the door to her sister's importunities. There was a feverish triumph in her eyes, and she carried herself unwittingly like a goddess of Victory. She clasped her sister's waist, and together they descended the stairs. Richards stood waiting for them at the bottom.

21   Some one was opening the front door with a latchkey. It was Brently Mallard who entered, a little travel-stained, composedly carrying his grip-sack and umbrella. He had been far from the scene of accident, and did not even know there had been one. He stood amazed at Josephine's piercing cry; at Richards' quick motion to screen him from the view of his wife.

22   But Richards was too late.

23   When the doctors came they said she had died of heart disease—of joy that kills.

FOR WRITING OR DISCUSSION

1. What is Chopin's main point here? What does the title contribute to the story?

2. How do you account for Mrs. Mallard's feelings toward her husband? Chopin's story was written in 1892. What might the period suggest in terms of attitudes of married men and women toward each other?

3. How do the paragraphs that come before paragraph 11 prepare you for the exultant "free, free, free!" uttered by Mrs. Mallard? For example, what do paragraphs 3–6 contribute to the story?

4. What do the doctors think killed Mrs. Mallard? What really killed her? What is the irony, then, in the last line of the story?

5. What narrative strategies do you identify here? How does the sequence of events play a particularly important role in the story?

6. How would the story turn out, do you think, if it were Mr. Mallard who incorrectly learned of the death of his wife? How, given the basic premise of "The Story of an Hour," do you think he would react? How might he react upon seeing his wife alive?

7. Write an essay in which you analyze and explain Mrs. Mallard's feelings toward her husband.

Reading and Writing About Poetry

Note how the nineteenth century author of *The Red Badge of Courage* uses a simple narrative structure to make a profound point. Answer the questions that follow the poem.

STEPHEN CRANE
I Saw A Man Chasing The Horizon

I saw a man chasing the horizon;
Round and round they sped.
I was disturbed at this;
I accosted the man.

"It is futile," I said,
"You can never—"
"You lie," he cried,
And ran on.

FOR WRITING OR DISCUSSION

1. What is the sequence of events in this poem? Why can you consider it a narrative?

2. Who is the speaker in this poem? What does he see a man doing? What does he try to tell the man?

3. What do you think Crane means by the word *horizon*?

4. What would you say is the main point of the poem? Do you agree with it?

5. Write a narrative essay about your trying to convince someone to do something that the person ultimately refused to do.

STRATEGY CHECKLIST: Writing and Revising Your Narrative Paper

Plan the paper.	☐ Have I used prewriting to explore ideas for a subject? ☐ Have I thought about my purpose for writing—that is, will my narrative make a point? ☐ Do I have my audience clearly in mind? ☐ Have I limited my topic? ☐ Have I considered using an outline to organize my ideas?
Write a first draft.	☐ Have I established a clear thesis to state the topic and express an opinion? ☐ Have I supported my thesis with concrete sensory details? ☐ Have I used natural sounding language in quotations from people I'm writing about? ☐ Have I established a clear sequence of events?
Revise and edit the paper.	☐ Does my introduction capture the reader's attention by setting the scene or providing background? ☐ Do my body paragraphs develop the action of the narrative in a clear sequence of events? ☐ Have I used transitions when necessary to link events in time? ☐ Does my conclusion tie together the points of the narrative by returning to the thesis in some way?
Proofread the paper.	☐ Have I checked carefully for correct punctuation of dialogue? ☐ Have I proofread for grammar, spelling, and mechanics?

CROSSCURRENTS

Both "'You Don't Look Indian'" by Greg Sarris (pages 163–166) and "My Father's House" by Jarrett David Lee Jackson (pages 153–155) deal with relations between parents and children. How do the ideas in the selections relate to each other? What do you think Sarris would have said to Jackson?

COLLABORATIVE LEARNING

In groups of five students each, compare and contrast the two student pieces, "The Death of Santa Claus" (pages 150–152) and "My Father's House" (pages 153–155) as models of narrative essays. Use the "Strategy Checklist: Writing and Revising Your Narrative Paper" as a touchstone for your comments.

 For additional help with writing, reading, and research, go to
www.mycomplab.com

CHAPTER 9

Example

In this chapter you will

- identify the strategies for writing an example paper

- analyze student example essays

- identify a topic and write your own example paper

- explore the use of examples from the world around you

- analyze the use of examples in writing by professionals

An example—or **illustration**—represents, or sometimes shows, the primary nature of the larger group to which it belongs: A rattlesnake is an example of a reptile; kidnapping is an example of crime; a Cadillac is an example of General Motors products. An **example paper** relies almost solely on examples to support the thesis, and learning to manage this kind of paper well will help prepare you for all the varieties of papers you will have to write.

Nearly all good writing depends heavily on examples or illustrations as an important means of supporting ideas—and for sound reasons. Examples give concreteness and, therefore, clarity to ideas. Because concreteness and clarity are essential to good writing, example often shapes even the smallest sentence sequence:

> To convince a reader, good writers usually offer support for their generalizations. In the Declaration of Independence, for example, Thomas Jefferson cited twenty-eight violations of basic human rights to support his assertion that George III was a tyrant.

Similarly, examples can develop an entire paragraph:

> History and legend tell us that some of the greatest scientific discoveries are the result of inspirations caused by chance occurrences. Three brief examples can demonstrate this point. First, Archimedes' noticing the rise of the water level as he submerged himself in a tub led to the formulation of the laws of liquid displacement, the foundation of many of the laws of modern physics. Second, Sir Isaac Newton discovered the law of gravity because an apple fell on his head while he was sitting under a tree. Third, after being caught in a strong current of hot rising air while flying his gas balloon, George Alexander Whitehead thought about the occurrence and developed the fundamental principles of meteorology. These and other incidents show that many of the greatest scientific developments spring from lucky accidents that stimulate work in a specific direction.

Writing Your Example Paper

Writers can shape sentences and paragraphs by means of example, but our concern in this chapter is to look at an entire paper developed by example. In such a paper, the writer offers well-developed examples to support a thesis. The success of the paper will depend largely on the quality of these illustrations and on their arrangement. We have some suggestions.

 **TIPS** for Writing an Example Essay

- **Be specific.** Remember, the purpose of an example is to give concreteness and clarity to an idea, and you won't get either with vague language (see pages 516–520). Notice the concrete language and the specific details in the following passage:

> I spent a good part of my life close to nature as a migratory worker, lumberjack, and placer miner. Mother Nature was breathing down my neck, so to speak, and I had the feeling that she did not want me around. I was bitten by every sort of insect, and scratched by burrs, foxtails and thorns. My clothes were torn by buck-brush and tangled manzanita. Hard clods pushed against my ribs when I lay down to rest, and grime ate its way into every pore of my body. Everything around me was telling me all the time to roll up and be gone. I was an unwanted intruder. I could never be at home in nature the way trees, flowers and birds are at home . . . I did not feel at ease until my feet touched the paved road.
>
> The road led to the city, and I knew with every fiber of my being that the man-made world of the city was man's only home on this planet, his refuge from an inhospitable nonhuman cosmos.
>
> —Eric Hoffer, "Cities and Nature"

Now, consider how much less vivid and therefore less interesting is the following version of Hoffer's passage:

> I lived and worked outdoors for several years, and the experience taught me that the city is the preferable habitat for man. In nature, I always felt dirty and uncomfortable. Nature was inhospitable to me. I was an alien there and never felt comfortable until I turned again toward the city, the only appropriate environment for man.

Obviously, good examples use specific details expressed in concrete language.

- **Make certain that your examples are really examples, and that your generalization, or thesis, is one that examples can support.** As noted earlier, an example is a single item selected from many to show the nature or character of the group, or it is one of many specific instances in which a generalization proves to be true. If Maria is the only woman in your school who has dyed her hair green, you cannot generalize that green hair is a fad in your school and then cite the one case as an example, no matter how vividly you describe Maria's new hair color. You can, however, use Maria's green hair as an example of her eccentricity if she really is eccentric—if she exhibits several other odd characteristics. An example is one of many, and a generalization is that which is usually or frequently or generally true of its subject.

■ **Play fair.**   When the subject allows, you should try to select examples that represent an honest cross-section of your subject. If you want to show, for instance, that most of the teachers in a particular school are boring lecturers, try to find examples of some who are young, some who are middle-aged, and some who are nearing retirement. Again, some of your examples should be women and some men, some perhaps single and some married. Your examples should also indicate a fair distribution among departments. You don't want your examples to suggest that all boring lecturers are middle-aged, married men who wear glasses and teach English. Rather, you want to show that boring teachers pop up everywhere and too often in this particular school, reflecting many backgrounds and subject areas—and even ways of being boring.

Of course, you don't always have to use several examples to make your point. Often, a good way to develop a thesis is to use one **extended example**. Even so, you should select the example according to the same rules of fairness that apply to the selection of numerous examples. It must truly represent an honest cross-section of the subject. One extended example can serve to support a thesis if the example is fully and convincingly developed. More often than not, however, you can build a stronger argument with several short examples. In this case, you need to give order to your examples, and this brings us to our last tip on writing an example paper.

■ **Think about the arrangement of your examples.**   Sometimes the best arrangement is chronological. The examples in the paragraph on pages 172–173 about scientific discoveries, for instance, are presented in chronological order—from the ancient to the modern world. At other times, a spatial order works best. In supporting a thesis about the restaurants in your town, you might offer examples from several sections of the town, and those examples could be arranged geographically from north to south, east to west.

Or consider this: Many writers like to save their best example for last in order to achieve a dramatic conclusion. Others like to use their best example first to awaken interest. Certainly, the first and last are likely to get the most attention from a reader. Since some examples are more dramatic and convincing than others, you would do well to bury the weaker ones in the middle of the paper. Of course, if all your examples are equally excellent, you have nothing to worry about.

- **Consider your audience and purpose.** Who will read your paper—aside from your instructor, of course? Make sure that you have provided enough information so that your examples are convincing. Keep an eye on any technical vocabulary and define words accordingly.

- **Revise your drafts.** Reread Chapter 6 for many tips on how to revise your essay. Ask classmates if your examples support your thesis successfully. When you revise, take into account all the feedback you have received.

- **Proofread carefully.** You should be aware of your own usual errors. Edit carefully for them after you are satisfied with your revision; but don't forget to proofread in any case. Errors have a way of avoiding attention, and you want to be sure that you've given your best effort to locating mistakes that may have slipped by.

ASSIGNMENT: EXAMPLE

Write an essay that you support with the use of examples. Be sure that your thesis establishes a generalization that provides the premise for your examples. Make a visual plan to help you develop your paper, if you need one. If you are having difficulty deciding on a topic for your example paper, you might find some help among these suggestions. Use examples to support or attack one of the following statements.

1. Watching the news does not guarantee that viewers learn the whole story.
2. Students on college campuses are turning more and more conservative in their politics.
3. Some television commercials are more entertaining than most of the scheduled programs.
4. The senior year in high school was more fun than hard work.
5. Many dangers await the desert hiker.
6. Teenagers do not know how to manage money.
7. Student government teaches important values.
8. Religion leaves many serious problems unsolved.
9. The United States has become the world's police force.
10. Computer dating is more popular now than ever.
11. Hazing rituals are unfortunate features of high school sports.
12. The chores on a farm are endless!
13. Not all problems can be solved— we just have to live with them.
14. Some modern conveniences have turned out to be very inconvenient.
15. Affirmative action has (has not) benefited America.

Student Writing: Example

See what you think of the quality and arrangement of examples in the following student papers. Annotations for the first paper will help focus your attention on key elements in writing example essays.

Monica Branch

Keep It Simple

1   I have eaten some incredible food in my time. My family has always liked to celebrate important occasions by going out to fancy restaurants, so graduations, engagements, college acceptances, anniversaries, and so on are times to try venison with cranberry gravy, or lobster Newburg, or pasta with a cream sauce and seven different kinds of unpronounceable mushrooms. So, I have eaten some fabulous meals over the years, and I have loved virtually all of them. But the more gourmet food I sample, the more I become convinced that the very best food is the simplest.

2   Consider barbecued spareribs. They are simple, unassuming, messy finger food. But purchased from the smoke-filled corner rib joint, served over a slice of white bread to catch the sauce, with a side of crisp fries and a paper cup of soggy coleslaw, dripping with fat, calories, and character, there is absolutely nothing better.

3   There is nothing better except for maybe real, homemade macaroni and cheese (not the kind that comes in a box with a packet of orange powder). Give me a brutally cold winter day. Let me feast my eyes on that beautiful, crunchy, brown top, fresh from the oven. We're talking joy. We're talking peace. We're talking love.

4   And then there's the fluffernutter! A huge glob of peanut butter and a huger glob of marshmallow fluff on the softest white bread around—it sounds like nothing, but it is the perfect sandwich. It wraps sweet, salty, crunchy, and smooth into one convenient package. The incredible stickiness is a delight as well.

5   There are Oreo cookies, ants on a log (celery sticks decorated with cream cheese and raisins), packaged chicken soup with ring-shaped noodles, southern fried steak, cold leftover pizza, bright orange French dressing, cinnamon toast, oatmeal with brown sugar, dill pickles, and a thousand other marvelous, simple foods. I love them all.

6   So, the next time my family and I have something special to celebrate, I will happily go to the fanciest restaurant they can find, but my love and respect for simple, ordinary, better-than-anything foods will never cease. And I'll be down at the rib joint when they're ready to go.

Annotations (margin notes):

Introduction: Provides background information that builds to the thesis. Paper is not about "incredible food," yet with this information writer establishes reason for choosing her thesis.

Thesis presents generalization that examples can illustrate.

Transition: "Consider..." links first body paragraph to thesis.

First example to support thesis. Concrete details provide sensory image for reader.

Sensory appeals to sight and sound.

Second example.

More specific language to provide images for reader.

Third example: Examples represent a good cross-section of the subject.

Last body paragraph lists other examples to supplement three examples developed in previous body paragraphs.

Conclusion: Returns to the idea of the thesis and reminds reader of "incredible food" introduction.

Researched Student Writing: Example

As you will see in Part 4 of this book, one of the key assignments your instructors will require is the formal research paper, and *Student's Book of College English* explores in depth the steps you need to take to prepare your research paper effectively. But even at this early stage in your developing skills as a writer, you know that using source material to support your thesis is an excellent way to strengthen your point.

In the paper that follows, note how the writer integrates quotations and paraphrases into the essay. Note further how the writer cites sources directly in the essay and how those sources appear fully in a list of works cited at the end of the paper. When you finish reading, answer the questions.

Laura Merkner
Children of Television

The topic of children and television has been controversial for years. Many   1
people worry that children will be affected negatively by television messages that involve violence, drugs, and sexuality. But, is all TV bad for children? Viewing experts say television programs could be deemed appropriate for a younger viewing audience if there is educational value in the program, if the program promotes non-violent behavior, and if the parents are monitoring what their child is watching. These three factors could lead to children watching more appropriate programs on television.

2   Children between the ages of four and sixteen are usually the most influenced by what they watch on television. According to TV Turnoff Network, an organization that promotes "More Reading, Less TV," when children between the ages of four and six were asked if they would rather watch TV or spend time with their fathers, more than fifty percent of the youngsters opted for the TV ("Facts and Figures"). These figures might be appalling, but the survey doesn't say *what* the young children would rather watch on TV. Some television programs for children could actually be considered beneficial for them. Some shows such as *Sesame Street* and *Mr. Rogers' Neighborhood* are considered educational since they help children learn fundamental skills such as counting, colors, and friendship. The Federal Communications Commission (FCC) has even identified for television networks what programs are considered educational. According to the FCC, educational, or core programs, must be "at least 30 minutes in length, be aired between the hours of 7:00 a.m. and 10:00 p.m., and be a regularly scheduled weekly program." Each television station must also "air at least three hours of their core programming per week, must provide parents and consumers with advance information about core programs being aired, and define the type of programs that qualify as core programs" ("Children's"). For example, the popular children's cartoon *Dragon Tales* is on for thirty minutes at 1:30 p.m. every day, so this wholesome show does qualify as a core program for PBS. So, if parents monitor what their children watch and are looking for educational programs, the FCC has laid out some basic guidelines to make this process easier.

3   Another guideline to make children's viewing habits safer is to not allow them to watch shows that promote violence. In 1966, Rosemary Lee Potter made a rather surprising discovery concerning a violent television show. Potter was working on a National Defense Educational Act for her graduate school program and was observing a first-grade class and teacher. The teacher gave the children puppets in order to help them with their verbal behavior. The children used the puppets to act out scenes, but what was surprising was that the children were usually narrating scenes from the popular *Batman* program that was aired weekly on the television set at home. Because of the increased enthusiasm in reading and speaking prompted by this show, the teacher developed reading material related to the caped crusader and his adventures. When the teacher tried out this reading material, Potter observed that "The children paid unusually close attention to detail, listened more closely to other readers, read complex sentences, and attacked unknown and difficult words with

great confidence." The reason why this is such a surprising discovery is because the *Batman* series could be considered a rather violent television show. Each week Batman must face an adversary and must physically, and sometimes mentally, beat his opponent in order to triumph as the victor. In each episode, there are often many kicks and punches used while Batman defeats his adversary. The program itself involves violence, but it does seem to promote a non-violent attitude. Batman typically only uses violence when it is necessary. Even though this could be considered a very violent television show, the kids were able to take something positive out of it. The teacher was able to use the fun and adventurous nature of Batman in order to help her students become excited about learning. Nothing that makes children excited about learning could be considered bad.

Some people, however, would disagree with that statement. Some believe that if a child is watching television, then nothing good can come of it. The TV Turnoff Network gives us another astonishing figure: In 1961, five percent of American children were obese, but in 2003, this percentage increased by over ten percent ("Facts and Figures"). This tells us that the obesity in children is increasing, and we already know that weight gain is linked to inactivity of the body. If children are watching TV many hours a day, then their body is inactive for just as many hours, and then the child will more than likely be gaining weight. The TV Turnoff Network also informs us that television "slows the metabolism and promotes an unhealthy lifestyle" ("Give TV"). So, if a child is gaining weight because he is watching too much TV, then yes, TV is a problem. However, if the child is watching an excessive amount of TV, then the problem might go deeper than his TV habits. Obesity in America is a growing epidemic but it is the parents' job to police what their kids are doing. If parents believe that their child is taking too much time watching TV and sitting on the couch, then the parent may want to suggest a healthier alternative for entertainment.

It is frightening to think about how teenage violence has progressed throughout the years, but TV should not be considered the only culprit. The programs on television can positively affect the younger generation if the program is educational, if the program is not excessively violent, and if the parents monitor what their kids are watching. Television can be a positive tool, since as Potter points out, "One of the best ways to offset the difficulties TV poses to children is to intervene in their viewing process by making constructive use of the massive TV experience" (Potter iv). If television is used in a positive and constructive manner, then there is no reason why parents should worry about their children sitting down and watching some television.

Works Cited

"Children's Educational Television." *Federal Communications Commission*. Federal
    Communications Commission, 1990. Web. 1 Dec. 2005.

"Facts and Figures about Our TV Habit." *TV Turnoff Network*. TV Turnoff Network
    Real Vision, 2003. Web. 1 Dec. 2005.

"Give TV the Hiking Boot." *TV Turnoff Network*. TV Turnoff Network Real Vision,
    2001. Web. 7 Dec. 2005.

Potter, Rosemary Lee. *The Positive Use of Commercial Television with Children*.
    Columbus: Avon, 1976. Print.

FOR WRITING OR DISCUSSION

1. What is the thesis of Merkner's essay?

2. Which data do you find particularly effective? Why?

3. How does the case of Potter's observations of a first-grade class support the
   writer's thesis? How is it an instance of an extended example?

4. Other than convenience, why do you think Merkner may have chosen mostly
   electronic sources for her research? What does the Web offer that books do not?
   What do books offer that Web sites do not?

5. Write an essay in which you consider the statement at the end of the third
   paragraph: "Nothing that makes children excited about learning could be
   considered bad." Use specific examples to support the thesis.

HAVING YOUR SAY

What do you think is responsible for the increased violence shown by many
teenagers across the country? What role do television and the movies play? Home
environment? Neighborhood? Genetic makeup? Write an example essay in which
you treat only those elements that you think contribute to teenage violence. Be
sure to do some research in the library and on the Web. Cite your sources as your
teacher instructs. You might want to look ahead to Chapter 20.

Example
in the World Around You

It's hard to imagine our inability to use examples in our everyday lives. When we tell what went wrong at the office or the adorable antics of a toddler or the recent horror films we've seen, we pepper our conversation with instances to back up our points. Elements in print or on television or on the Web draw regularly on examples to demonstrate, illustrate, explain, and support our assertions. In this Web site, note the use of examples to indicate the range of answers to the question posed in the title.

Title and Introduction — Attract the reader's attention with related questions.

Specific details — Three specific examples show views on video game addiction.

Fair play — Examples show a cross section of the responses to the question at hand.

Examples — The website provides three specific examples, each in its own paragraph with clear transitions and supporting details.

Arrangement of examples — from strong believer to potential believer to non believer.

Audience and purpose — The audience is fairly educated Web users interested in balanced views of technology addiction. (Web site URL is http:// www. techadiction.ca).

Your Turn

Look at a Web site related to another form of addiction—drugs, smoking, the Internet, alcohol, or overeating, for example. Write an essay about how the site uses examples and draws on some of the strategies identified in this chapter.

Video Game Addiction: Is it a "real" disorder?

Home
How to Help Children Addicted to Video Games
Download Self-Help Workbook
Education Corner
Tip of the Month
Blog
Support Forum
FAQS
Therapy
TechAddiction Interviews
News
Videos & Images
Useful Links
About TechAddiction

Video Game Addiction - Is It A "Real" Disorder?

Is video game addiction a "real" psychological disorder that deserves to be recognized as such? According to the American Psychological Association, video game addiction is not a mental disorder (at least for now).

Depending on whom you ask however, the answers you get will vary considerably. A mother with a teen who neglects his studies, rarely goes out with friends, and plays WoW in excess of 6 hours per day will likely believe that video game addiction is all too real. A gamer who occasionally finds himself spending too much time playing video games may believe that video game addiction is possible but quite rare. Someone who has never played video games may laugh at the idea of video game addiction and completely dismiss the entire concept.

And then we have the psychologists - of which I am one. Unfortunately (or depending on how you look at it, fortunately) we don't always agree on the causes, symptoms, and effects of various psychological and emotional issues. For example, there is considerable disagreement on the effects of violent video games.

TechAddiction has a commitment to providing (hopefully) non-biased information about video game addiction, internet addiction, and computer addiction - and makes conclusions based on actual clinical practice with clients and also on the latest scientific studies in respected, peer-reviewed journals.

As such, this article summarizes a recent journal article published in the International Journal of Mental Health Addiction arguing against the concept of video game addiction - and also several follow-up papers that take issue with some of the arguments.

The goal is not to present a case for or against the inclusion of video game addiction as a clinical diagnosis, but to present a balanced take on the issue.

Note: For the complete arguments, make sure to check out the full published articles.

Critical Reading: Example

Look at the marginal notes in this selection. They point to content and language issues to which an active critical reader pays attention. Note how the reader raises questions and makes comments that build understanding of the essay. You should apply thinking like this as you read the various selections in this book—and in your other courses. Answer the questions after you have read the piece and the surrounding commentary.

VERLYN KLINKENBORG

Inside the Mind's Eye, a Network of Highways

Mind's Eye: Phrase for the imagination, what you see in your head as you think.

1 It occurred to me the other day, on an old familiar stretch of highway out West, to think of all the old familiar stretches of highway in my life. Not as a metaphor or a way of seeing where I've gotten in life—the answer, in asphalt, being exactly nowhere—but just for the fun of it.

Repetition asserts importance of phrase to the thesis.

2 If I had a more graphic imagination, I would draw all those strips of road side by side in an oversized scrapbook or cut them out of the folding maps and glue them into a single discontinuous journey. For a while, for instance, I drove across Massachusetts and back again every week to teach. I did the same up the border of New York and Vermont. These days, I drive two routes through the Hudson Valley every week.

He means a visual imagination — but he can't lay out drawings of these highways in a scrapbook.

3 These roads I can see in my mind if I just close my eyes. They are so grooved into me that I doubt they will ever fade. Other roads—regular routes once upon a time—still come back to me in patches, like parts of the highway between Keams Canyon, on the Hopi Reservation, and Flagstaff, Ariz.

Different kinds of roads have different effects on his mind.

4 But some deeply familiar routes have long since worn away almost completely, leaving behind only the feeling of what it's like to be a child pressed against the door as the car makes a right-angle turn. That always happened somewhere on the drive to my grandparents' house in northwest Iowa. Was it in Boyden or Cherokee?

Even familiar routes fade from the memory.

5 I drove that old route a year ago, and it seemed to me as though I had never seen it before, though to be fair, my family last made that trip more than 40 years past, in a 1963 white Ford Galaxy.

Another example of "familiar stretch of highway."

6 The thought of all these highways occurred to me somewhere between Crow Agency, Mont., and the Wyoming border, part of a longer drive from Billings to Sheridan. In the last dozen years, I've driven that stretch of highway—I90—dozens of times. It's a daydreamer's road, a big, wide freeway cutting through a big, wide country.

Metaphor means comparison: Writer won't compare highway travel with travel down the road of life's achievements. He wants to look at roads he's traveled simply for the fun of it.

3 "grooved"— powerful word shows permanence of image.

5 "that old route": transition.

Repetition again— emphasizes the point.

7   The road rolls up out of the lowland along the Yellowstone River—past the refineries and the Billings live-stock auction—into a great sweep of wheat land, across the Crow Reservation over a shoulder of the Rosebud Mountains and down into the Tongue River drainage.

The route of this drive and examples of what he sees.

The area is changing but the roads remain constant.

8   Whenever I think of that road, that's usually the direction I'm heading, north to south, always surprised to find the Wyoming welcome sign farther off than I remember; always surprised to see how little has changed in a West where everything is changing as fast as it can.

9   There are times on that highway when I feel motionless even at 80 miles an hour. Often, the car begins to buck whenever it gets crosswise to the wind, which has no impediments out there. When I first began making that trip, it still had the feel of a mythic journey, pushing backward in time.

Mythic means imaginary or like a myth. The words echo the first four words in the title.

The land creates and then erodes the myths.

10   It wasn't the Crow Reservation that made me feel that way or the signs for Little Bighorn. It was the lay of the land, the rimrock, the grasses, the antelope racing across the plains. And there have been night drives when it felt as if every mile had to be won against my own fatigue. But if I spend enough time in the West the myths erode, and what I'm left with is an actual landscape.

11   In a dry year, a vast swath of wheat burns black. Another year, the radio is suddenly full of Christian stations, a mixture of salvation rock and home-town choirs coming over the air. One trip, a golden eagle nearly lands on the hood of the car. On another, I wake up from my daydream and find myself closing in fast on a sugar-beet truck headed for Western Sugar in Billings, a single light flashing slowly on its tail. The beets look prehistoric, like lumps of matter waiting to be formed.

Examples of "actual landscape."

Similar phrase in par. 11: "wheat burns black."

12   I'm still only an occasional traveler on this road, of course. I've missed the blizzards that shut it down from time to time, though I've caught more than enough of the thunderstorms, black as a burned wheatfield in the sky, that scour the ridges and the flats. A couple of months ago, I drove all the way from Hardin to Garryowen under the arc of the most violent rainbow I've ever seen, a dense wall of color shimmering overhead.

More examples of "land elements" creating a myth in his mind— "the illusion of frozen beasts."

13   This last time, I left Sheridan after a hard autumn frost. In the pastures along the highway, the horses seemed to have frozen solid overnight. They held themselves absolutely motionless, broadside to the rising sun, in all of the classic postures available to their kind. One stood with eyes closed, ears pricked backward. Another lay with front legs folded under, its neck arched so that only its muzzle touched the ground. Some stood clumped together in frozen bands amid frozen herds of cattle.

Transition.

14   There was no breeze to sweep their tails or manes. Mile after mile; pasture after pasture, the illusion held, as if I were driving through a land of cryogenic beasts.

The sun dismisses the illusion.

15   Then the morning sun took hold, and they all came to life again.

FOR WRITING OR DISCUSSION

1. What is Klinkenborg's thesis?

2. How has he used examples to make his point? Which examples do you find most visual?

3. Which marginal comments did you find most helpful? Why? What other comments might you have added?

4. Read "What I've Learned From Men," following, by Barbara Ehrenreich. Make your own marginal comments to demonstrate your active critical reading of the selection.

5. Write a brief essay on roads, streets, or highways that you have traveled by car, bicycle, or foot. Write a thesis about these roadways and use examples to support your point.

Readings for Writing

The selections that follow demonstrate how writers can use efffective examples to make a point.

BARBARA EHRENREICH

What I've Learned from Men

For many years I believed that women had only one thing to learn from men: how to get the attention of a waiter by some means short of kicking over the table and shrieking. Never in my life have I gotten the attention of a waiter, unless it was an off-duty waiter whose car I'd accidentally scraped in a parking lot somewhere. Men, however, can summon a maître d' just by thinking the word "coffee," and this is a power women would be well advised to study. What else would we possibly want to learn from them? How to interrupt someone in mid-sentence as if you were performing an act of conversational euthanasia? How to drop a pair of socks three feet from an open hamper and keep right on walking? How to make those weird guttural gargling sounds in the bathroom? 1

But now, at mid-life, I am willing to admit there are some real and useful things to learn from men. Not from all men—in fact, we may have the most to learn from some of the men we like the least. This realization does not mean that my feminist principles have gone soft with age: what I think women could learn from men is how to get *tough*. After more than a decade of consciousness-raising, assertiveness training, and hand-to-hand combat in the battle of the sexes, we're still too ladylike. Let me try that again—we're just too *damn* ladylike. 2

3   Here is an example from my own experience, a story that I blush to recount. A few years ago, at an international conference held in an exotic and luxurious setting, a prestigious professor invited me to his room for what he said would be an intellectual discussion on matters of theoretical importance. So far, so good. I showed up promptly. But only minutes into the conversation—held in all-too-adjacent chairs—it emerged that he was interested in something more substantial than a meeting of minds. I was disgusted, but not enough to overcome 30-odd years of programming in ladylikeness. Every time his comments took a lecherous turn, I chattered distractingly; every time his hand found its way to my knee, I returned it as if it were something he had misplaced. This went on for an unconscionable period (as much as 20 minutes); then there was a minor scuffle, a dash for the door, and I was out—with nothing violated but my self-esteem. I, a full-grown feminist, conversant with such matters as rape crisis counseling and sexual harassment at the workplace, had behaved like a ninny—or, as I now understand it, like a lady.

4   The essence of ladylikeness is a persistent servility masked as "niceness." For example, we (women) tend to assume that it is our responsibility to keep everything "nice" even when the person we are with is rude, aggressive, or emotionally AWOL. (In the above example, I was so busy taking responsibility for preserving the veneer of "niceness" that I almost forgot to take responsibility for myself.) In conversations with men, we do almost all the work: sociologists have observed that in male–female social interactions it's the woman who throws out leading questions and verbal encouragements ("So how did you *feel* about that?" and so on) while the man, typically, says "Hmmmm." Wherever we go, we're perpetually smiling—the on-cue smile, like the now-outmoded curtsy, being one of our culture's little rituals of submission. We're trained to feel embarrassed if we're praised, but if we see a criticism coming at us from miles down the road, we rush to acknowledge it. And when we're feeling aggressive or angry or resentful, we just tighten up our smiles or turn them into rueful little moues. In short, we spend a great deal of time acting like wimps.

5   For contrast, think of the macho stars we love to watch. Think, for example, of Mel Gibson facing down punk marauders in "The Road Warrior" . . . John Travolta swaggering his way through the early scenes of "Saturday Night Fever" . . . or Marlon Brando shrugging off the local law in "The Wild One." Would they simper their way through tight spots? Chatter aimlessly to keep the conversation going? Get all clutched up whenever they think they might—just might—have hurt someone's feelings? No, of course not, and therein, I think, lies their fascination for us.

6   The attraction of the "tough guy" is that he has—or at least seems to have—what most of us lack, and that is an aura of power and control. In an article, feminist psychiatrist Jean Baker Miller writes that "a woman's using self-determined power for herself is equivalent to selfishness [and] destructiveness"—an equation that makes us want to avoid even the appearance of power. Miller cites cases of women who get depressed just when they're on the verge of success—and of women who do succeed and then bury their achievement in self-deprecation. As an example, she describes one company's periodic meetings to recognize outstanding salespeople: when a woman is asked to say a few words about her achievement, she tends to say something like, "Well, I really don't know how it happened.

I guess I was just lucky this time." In contrast, the men will cheerfully own up to the hard work, intelligence, and so on, to which they owe their success. By putting herself down, a woman avoids feeling brazenly powerful and potentially "selfish"; she also does the traditional lady's work of trying to make everyone else feel better ("She's not really so smart, after all, just lucky").

So we might as well get a little tougher. And a good place to start is by cutting back on the small acts of deference that we've been programmed to perform since girlhood. Like unnecessary smiling. For many women—waitresses, flight attendants, receptionists—smiling is an occupational requirement, but there's no reason for anyone to go around grinning when she's not being paid for it. I'd suggest that we save our off-duty smiles for when we truly feel like sharing them, and if you're not sure what to do with your face in the meantime, study Clint Eastwood's expressions—both of them.   7

Along the same lines, I think women should stop taking responsibility for every human interaction we engage in. In a social encounter with a woman, the average man can go 25 minutes saying nothing more than "You don't say?" "Izzat so?" and, of course, "Hmmmm." Why should we do all the work? By taking so much responsibility for making conversations go well, we act as if we had much more at stake in the encounter than the other party—and that gives him (or her) the power advantage. Every now and then, we deserve to get more out of a conversation than we put into it: I'd suggest not offering information you'd rather not share ("I'm really terrified that my sales plan won't work") and not, out of sheer politeness, soliciting information you don't really want ("Wherever did you get that lovely tie?"). There will be pauses, but they don't have to be awkward for *you*.   8

It is true that some, perhaps most, men will interpret any decrease in female deference as a deliberate act of hostility. Omit the free smiles and perky conversation-boosters and someone is bound to ask, "Well, what's come over *you* today?" For most of us, the first impulse is to stare at our feet and make vague references to a terminally ill aunt in Atlanta, but we should have as much right to be taciturn as the average (male) taxi driver. If you're taking a vacation from smiles and small talk and some fellow is moved to inquire about what's "bothering" you, just stare back levelly and say, the international debt crisis, the arms race, or the death of God.   9

There are all kinds of ways to toughen up—and potentially move up—at work, and I leave the details to the purveyors of assertiveness training. But Jean Baker Miller's study underscores a fundamental principle that anyone can master on her own. We can stop acting less capable than we actually are. For example, in the matter of taking credit when credit is due, there's a key difference between saying "I was just lucky" and saying "I had a plan and it worked." If you take the credit you deserve, you're letting people know that you were confident you'd succeed all along, and that you fully intend to do so again.   10

Finally, we may be able to learn something from men about what to do with anger. As a general rule, women get irritated: men get *mad*. We make tight little smiles of ladylike exasperation; they pound on desks and roar. I wouldn't recommend emulating the full basso profundo male tantrum, but women do need ways of expressing justified anger clearly, colorfully, and, when necessary, crudely. If you're not just irritated, but *pissed off*, it might help to say so.   11

12   I, for example, have rerun the scene with the prestigious professor many times in my mind. And in my mind, I play it like Bogart. I start by moving my chair over to where I can look the professor full in the face. I let him do the chattering, and when it becomes evident that he has nothing serious to say, I lean back and cross my arms, just to let him know that he's wasting my time. I do not smile, neither do I nod encouragement. Nor, of course, do I respond to his blandishments with apologetic shrugs and blushes. Then, at the first flicker of lechery, I stand up and announce coolly, "All right, I've had enough of this crap." Then I walk out—slowly, deliberately, confidently. Just like a man.

13   Or—now that I think of it—just like a woman.

FOR WRITING OR DISCUSSION

1. Specifically, what changes in their usual behavior does the writer think would be beneficial for women?

2. Is the writer guilty of stereotyping men and women? Why or why not?

3. Why is the frequent use of humor so effective?

4. Write a paper using examples either to describe or to demonstrate the falsity of a common male or female stereotype (the "strong, silent type," the "jock," the "dumb blonde," the "schoolmarm," and so on).

JOHN GRISHAM
Boxers, Briefs and Books

1   I WASN'T always a lawyer or a novelist, and I've had my share of hard, dead-end jobs. I earned my first steady paycheck watering rose bushes at a nursery for a dollar an hour. I was in my early teens, but the man who owned the nursery saw potential, and he promoted me to his fence crew. For $1.50 an hour, I labored like a grown man as we laid mile after mile of chain-link fence. There was no future in this, and I shall never mention it again in writing.

2   Then, during the summer of my 16th year, I found a job with a plumbing contractor. I crawled under houses, into the cramped darkness, with a shovel, to somehow find the buried pipes, to dig until I found the problem, then crawl back out and report what I had found. I vowed to get a desk job. I've never drawn inspiration from that miserable work, and I shall never mention it again in writing, either.

3   But a desk wasn't in my immediate future. My father worked with heavy construction equipment, and through a friend of a friend of his, I got a job the next summer on a highway asphalt crew. This was July, when Mississippi is like a sauna. Add another 100 degrees for the fresh asphalt. I got a break when the operator of a Caterpillar bulldozer was fired;

shown the finer points of handling this rather large machine, I contemplated a future in the cab, tons of growling machinery at my command, with the power to plow over anything. Then the operator was back, sober, repentant. I returned to the asphalt crew.

I was 17 years old that summer, and I learned a lot, most of which cannot be repeated in polite company. One Friday night I accompanied my new friends on the asphalt crew to a honky-tonk to celebrate the end of a hard week. When a fight broke out and I heard gunfire, I ran to the restroom, locked the door and crawled out a window. I stayed in the woods for an hour while the police hauled away rednecks. As I hitchhiked home, I realized I was not cut out for construction and got serious about college.

4

My career sputtered along until retail caught my attention; it was indoors, clean and air-conditioned. I applied for a job at a Sears store in a mall. The only opening was in men's underwear. It was humiliating. I tried to quit, but I was given a raise. Evidently, the position was difficult to fill. I asked to be transferred to toys, then to appliances. My bosses said no and gave me another raise.

5

I became abrupt with customers. Sears has the nicest customers in the world, but I didn't care. I was rude and surly and I was occasionally watched by spies hired by the company to pose as shoppers. One asked to try on a pair of boxers. I said no, that it was obvious they were much too small for his rather ample rear end. I handed him an extra-large pair. I got written up. I asked for lawn care. They said no, but this time they didn't offer me a raise. I finally quit.

6

Halfway through college, and still drifting, I decided to become a high-powered tax lawyer. The plan was sailing along until I took my first course in tax law. I was stunned by its complexity and lunacy, and I barely passed the course.

7

Around the same time, I was involved in mock-trial classes. I enjoyed the courtroom. A new plan was hatched. I would return to my hometown, hang out my shingle and become a hotshot trial lawyer. Tax law was discarded overnight.

8

This was 1981; at the time there was no public-defender system in my county. I volunteered for all the indigent work I could get. It was the fastest way to trial, and I learned quickly.

9

When my law office started to struggle for lack of well-paying work—indigent cases are far from lucrative—I decided to go into yet another low-paying career: in 1983, I was elected to a House seat in the Mississippi State Legislature. The salary was $8,000, which was more than I made during my first year as a lawyer. Each year from January through March I was at the State Capitol in Jackson, wasting serious time, but also listening to great storytellers. I took a lot of notes, not knowing why but feeling that, someday, those tales would come in handy.

10

Like most small-town lawyers, I dreamed of the big case, and in 1984 it finally arrived. But this time, the case wasn't mine. As usual, I was loitering around the courtroom, pretending to be busy. But what I was really doing was watching a trial involving a young girl who had been beaten and raped. Her testimony was gut-wrenching, graphic, heartbreaking and riveting. Every juror was crying. I remember staring at the defendant and wishing I had a gun. And like that, a story was born.

11

12   Writing was not a childhood dream of mine. I do not recall longing to write as a student. I wasn't sure how to start. Over the following weeks I refined my plot outline and fleshed out my characters. One night I wrote "Chapter One" at the top of the first page of a legal pad; the novel, "A Time to Kill," was finished three years later.

13   The book didn't sell, and I stuck with my day job, defending criminals, preparing wills and deeds and contracts. Still, something about writing made me spend large hours of my free time at my desk.

14   I had never worked so hard in my life, nor imagined that writing could be such an effort. It was more difficult than laying asphalt, and at times more frustrating than selling underwear. But it paid off. Eventually, I was able to leave the law and quit politics. Writing's still the most difficult job I've ever had—but it's worth it.

FOR WRITING OR DISCUSSION

1. What is Grisham's thesis? How does the thesis lend itself to the use of examples?

2. What is the writer's purpose? Who do you think is his audience?

3. Which examples best support the thesis? Which do you find liveliest and rich in sensory detail?

4. Identify some of the transitions Grisham has used in the essay. How effective are they? In what ways do they help you follow the arrangement of details?

5. Grisham is a best-selling author of novels about the law, some of which have become movies. Check him out on the Internet to identify some of his accomplishments. What is your reaction to what he says in the conclusion to this essay? In what ways does he reflect what many writers in general feel about their craft? How do these remarks reflect your own attitude toward writing?

6. Write an example essay in which you present some of the jobs you or someone you know has held. Be sure to establish a thesis that will unify your examples.

JUDY BRADY

I Want a Wife

1   I belong to that classification of people known as wives. I am A Wife. And, not altogether incidentally, I am a mother.

2   Not too long ago a male friend of mine appeared on the scene fresh from a recent divorce. He had one child, who is, of course, with his ex-wife. He is obviously looking for another wife. As I thought about him while I was ironing one evening, it suddenly occurred to me that I, too, would like to have a wife. Why do I want a wife?

I would like to go back to school so that I can become economically independent, support myself, and, if need be, support those dependent upon me. I want a wife who will work and send me to school. And while I am going to school I want a wife to keep track of the children's doctor and dentist appointments. And to keep track of mine, too. I want a wife to make sure my children eat properly and are kept clean. I want a wife who will wash the children's clothes and keep them mended. I want a wife who is a good nurturant attendant to my children, who arranges for their schooling, makes sure that they have an adequate social life with their peers, takes them to the park, the zoo, etc. I want a wife who takes care of the children when they are sick, a wife who arranges to be around when the children need special care, because, of course, I cannot miss classes at school. My wife must arrange to lose time at work and not lose the job. It may mean a small cut in my wife's income from time to time, but I guess I can tolerate that. Needless to say, my wife will arrange and pay for the care of the children while my wife is working.

I want a wife who will take care of *my* physical needs. I want a wife who will keep my house clean. A wife who will pick up after me. I want a wife who will keep my clothes clean, ironed, mended, replaced when need be, and who will see to it that my personal things are kept in their proper place so that I can find what I need the minute I need it. I want a wife who cooks the meals, a wife who is a *good* cook. I want a wife who will plan the menus, do the necessary grocery shopping, prepare the meals, serve them pleasantly, and then do the cleaning up while I do my studying. I want a wife who will care for me when I am sick and sympathize with my pain and loss of time from school. I want a wife to go along when our family takes a vacation so that someone can continue to care for me and my children when I need a rest and change of scene.

I want a wife who will not bother me with rambling complaints about a wife's duties. But I want a wife who will listen to me when I feel the need to explain a rather difficult point I have come across in my course of studies. And I want a wife who will type my papers for me when I have written them.

I want a wife who will take care of the details of my social life. When my wife and I are invited out by my friends, I want a wife who will take care of the babysitting arrangements. When I meet people at school that I like and want to entertain, I want a wife who will have the house clean, will prepare a special meal, serve it to me and my friends, and not interrupt when I talk about the things that interest me and my friends. I want a wife who will have arranged that the children are fed and ready for bed before my guests arrive so that the children do not bother us. I want a wife who takes care of the needs of my guests so that they feel comfortable, who makes sure that they have an ashtray, that they are passed the hors d'oeuvres, that they are offered a second helping of the food, that their wine glasses are replenished when necessary, that their coffee is served to them as they like it.

And I want a wife who knows that sometimes I need a night out by myself.

8   I want a wife who is sensitive to my sexual needs, a wife who makes love passionately and eagerly when I feel like it, a wife who makes sure that I am satisfied. And, of course, I want a wife who will not demand sexual attention when I am not in the mood for it. I want a wife who assumes the complete responsibility for birth control, because I do not want more children. I want a wife who will remain sexually faithful to me so that I do not have to clutter up my intellectual life with jealousies. And I want a wife who understands that *my* sexual needs may entail more than strict adherence to monogamy. I must, after all, be able to relate to people as fully as possible.

9   If, by chance, I find another person more suitable as a wife than the wife I already have, I want the liberty to replace my present wife with another one. Naturally, I will expect a fresh, new life; my wife will take the children and be solely responsible for them so that I am left free.

10   When I am through with school and have a job, I want my wife to quit working and remain at home so that my wife can more fully and completely take care of a wife's duties.

11   My God, who *wouldn't* want a wife?

FOR WRITING OR DISCUSSION

1. What is the thesis of this essay?
2. How does Brady use the rhetorical strategy of example? Which examples do you find most compelling in support of Brady's argument?
3. What is the effect on the reader of the multiple examples Brady provides? How successful is she in supporting her argument?
4. How has the writer achieved a humorous effect in the essay? In what ways do you detect anger or frustration beneath the surface of the humor?
5. Write an essay called "I Want a Husband." Write the essay from the point of view of a *male* seeking a husband, and provide examples in the way Brady has. You can choose a humorous or a serious tone, based on your purpose.

HAVING YOUR SAY

Brady wrote this essay many years ago at the height of the women's movement in America. Have demands on women in our society changed or remained the same from those indicated in the essay? Select one side or the other and write an argumentative paper in which you support your point with specific details.

Reading and Writing About Poetry

In this poem, Edna St. Vincent Millay uses examples to build toward a dramatic point. Read "Lament" and then answer the questions that follow.

EDNA ST. VINCENT MILLAY

Lament

Listen, children:
Your father is dead.
From his old coats
I'll make you little jackets;
I'll make you little trousers
From his old pants.
There'll be in his pockets
Things he used to put there,
Keys and pennies
Covered with tobacco;
Dan shall have the pennies
To save in his bank;
Anne shall have the keys
To make a pretty noise with.
Life must go on,
And the dead be forgotten;
Life must go on,
Though good men die;
Anne, eat your breakfast;
Dan, take your medicine;
Life must go on;
I forget just why.

FOR WRITING OR DISCUSSION

1. What point is Millay trying to make about the death of a family member?
2. How does the poet use examples to make her point? What is the effect of the sensory details such as "Keys and pennies/Covered with tobacco"?
3. Which sensory images do you find most compelling and original?
4. What is the effect of the title? The last line of the poem?
5. Write an example essay in which you indicate how you or someone close to you explained difficult events to a child, such as a serious accident, the need to move to a different city or neighborhood, or the death of a loved one. Use concrete sensory details. Be sure to use more than one example.

STRATEGY CHECKLIST: Writing and Revising Your Example Paper

Plan the paper.	☐ Have I used prewriting to explore ideas for a subject? ☐ Have I limited my topic so that my examples will support it effectively? ☐ Have I concentrated on using specific examples to support my thesis? ☐ Have I thought carefully about my purpose in writing? ☐ Do I have my audience clearly in mind? ☐ Have I considered using an outline to organize my ideas?
Write a first draft.	☐ Have I established a clear thesis that my examples support? ☐ Have I supported my thesis with honest examples that represent a cross-section of my subject? ☐ Have I arranged the examples in logical order—in space or time order or by order of importance?
Revise and edit the paper.	☐ Does my introduction capture and hold the reader's attention? ☐ Have I used transitions when necessary to link ideas? ☐ Does my conclusion tie the examples together?
Proofread the paper.	☐ Have I proofread for grammar, spelling, and mechanics?

CROSSCURRENTS

One of the main premises in Barbara Ehrenreich's "What I've Learned from Men" (pages 185–188) is that what women could learn from men is "how to get tough" and that the tough guy's attraction is that he seems to have, or does have, "an aura of power and control." How would Ehrenreich react to John Grisham in "Boxers, Briefs and Books" (pages 188–190)? Would she see him as weak or maintaining "an aura of power and control"? Are Grisham's experiences related to gender or to something else, do you think? Could a woman have written a piece like "Boxers, Briefs and Books"? Explain your answer.

COLLABORATIVE LEARNING

In groups of five, discuss the student essays "Keep It Simple" (pages 176–177) and "Children of Television" (pages 177–180) as models of example essays. Comment on the thesis, the quality of the examples (are they specific, fair, and arranged in a clear and effective order, for instance), the introduction and the conclusion, and any other elements that draw your attention. Also consider the audiences to whom the writers have directed their papers. Do thesis, purpose, and details make the point successfully? What recommendations could you make to improve the essays?

 For additional help with writing, reading, and research, go to www.mycomplab.com

Process

The **process** paper indicates a series of actions, changes, or functions that bring about an end or a result. The most familiar kind of process paper is the "how-to" paper, a step-by-step set of instructions on how to do or make something—how to change a tire, how to bake a cake, how to do aerobic exercise, how to assemble a bicycle. Some process papers explain how something is done, not necessarily a procedure the reader or even the writer can perform—how viruses attack cells, how a cellular phone works, how companies design video games, for example. Some process papers identify the steps to take to correct a problem, right a wrong, improve conditions: how to end poverty, for example, or how to stop teenage alcohol abuse.

Writing Your Process Paper

Follow these guidelines for writing process papers:

TIPS   for Writing a Process Essay

- **Choose carefully the kind of process you will write about—showing how to carry out a process or explaining a process that you don't expect a reader to carry out.**   If you're an expert at some task, you can draw on your personal experiences to explain the process. But because you're an expert doesn't mean that your reader will easily understand the materials you need, the language of the activity, or even the appropriate sequence of events. In most cases you have to state the obvious, as Michael Wollan does in his process paper "Coffee Time" (pages 201–203): you will note that he reminds his readers to wash the percolator (a term he defines) before beginning. Experienced coffee makers might dismiss this as needless advice, but someone who has never perked coffee before had better acknowledge and follow the step. The point here is that if you're writing for an audience who may not know how to carry out the process you're explaining and is looking to you for careful guidance, you have to make sure that you omit no important steps.

On the other hand, you might choose to explain a process that you don't expect someone to carry out, and that explanation requires additional strategies. If you know from experience how to take apart a clock, for example, and want to explain how it's done without expecting someone to perform the intricate task, you'll need to follow the suggestions in the previous paragraph, of course. Leave nothing out. Assume that your readers have little knowledge of the task at hand. But you may be interested in a process whose steps you yourself do not know—how double-entry bookkeeping works, or what steps we can take to reduce greenhouse gases, for instance. In these cases, you'll need to do research so that you understand the process fully enough to explain it to someone else. And here, too, you must make a thorough go of it so readers don't come away puzzled about any steps.

Finally, if you want to recommend steps in a process not yet implemented, you have to be clear about why no one has initiated those steps already and what the objections to them might be. If, for example, your plan to reduce traffic midtown in a congested city is to create new one-way streets, prevent taxis from using all lanes in rush hours, and raising taxes on car use in the city center, you'd have to find out why transportation directors might not have implemented your suggested process already; and you'd have to respond to their opposition.

■ **Make certain that the explanation is complete and accurate.** If, for example, you want to describe the process for baking a cake, you would mislead your reader if you omitted the instruction to grease and flour the pan. It's surprisingly easy to leave out important steps. You will be writing about a process you know extremely well, and you probably perform some steps—such as greasing a pan—without consciously thinking about them.

■ **Maintain strict chronological order as needed.** Tell your reader what to do first, what to do second, and so on. Once the cake is in the oven, it is too late to say that one must stir walnuts into the batter.

Not all process papers require chronological arrangement. In the student paper "Preparing for the First Day of Classes" (pages 204–205), Omprakash K. Pansara has implied a chronological arrangement with the transitions "The first step … ," "The second step … ," "The third step … ." In truth, the chronology in the steps he is recommending is not really significant. Buying books and supplies could precede creating an organized schedule. Going to orientation could precede purchasing supplies and books. The point is that, depending on your topic, you may have some flexibility in how you arrange the steps. In Michael Wollan's essay (pages 201–203), the chronology of how to make coffee is very important, and the writer carefully indicates the steps in the order one must follow them.

■ **If a particular kind of performance is called for in any part of the process, indicate its nature.**   Should the batter be stirred vigorously or gently? Should an applicant for a job approach the interviewer humbly, aggressively, nonchalantly? Besides indicating the nature of the action, you should also tell the reader why such action is called for. Readers are more likely to follow instructions if they understand the reasons for them.

■ **Group the steps in the process.**   A process may include many steps, but you usually can group them in their chronological order under logical headings.

Suppose you want to explain how to make a favorite dish—stir-fried shrimp, for example. You could develop paragraphs around two headings as part of a rough outline as shown following. Because they often require such precise steps in strict order, process papers lend themselves to outlining. You should develop an outline (see Chapter 4) as a check on the accuracy of your presentation.

   A.   Assembling ingredients
        1. Raw shrimp
        2. Oil
        3. Red and green peppers
        4. Almonds
        5. Hot chiles
        6. Orange rind
        7. Orange juice
        8. Cornstarch

   B.   Assembling utensils
        1. Wok
        2. Sharp kitchen knife with small blade
        3. Cooking fork
        4. Wooden spoon
        5. Measuring cup and measuring spoons

Other headings to organize steps logically for this topic might include "C. Mixing ingredients" and "D. Cooking ingredients." A number of steps may be involved in each of the divisions A, B, C, and D, but reading the steps in paragraphs that address the groups separately is far less over-whelming and confusing to readers than beginning with step 1 and ending with step 19. What steps would you include under the "C" and "D" headings for a process paper on making stir-fried shrimp?

■ **Pay careful attention to your audience.** Who will read your process paper? Who do you anticipate as your main audience? For example, a paper explaining a quick way to change the oil in a car would use one approach to address a group of experienced auto mechanics but quite another one to address car owners eager to save on repair costs but unfamiliar with the parts of an automobile.

■ **Define terms that might be unfamiliar to the reader or that have more than one meaning.** To most of us, *conceit* means extreme self-love, but to a literary scholar, it means an elaborate and extended metaphor. The scholar, when writing instructions for first-year students on analyzing a poem, would have to define the term for readers.

■ **Have a thesis.** It's possible just to present a clear set of instructions and stop. But the most interesting process papers do have theses. Few of us read car manuals or recipe books for pleasure, but we might well read the student paper "Coffee Time" (pages 201–203) more than once, just for the fun of it. Part of the fun comes from the thesis, which gives the paper focus and charm. It's a good idea, then, to try for a thesis.

■ **Anticipate difficulties.** One way to prevent difficulties for your readers is to warn them in advance when to expect problems:

This step requires your constant attention.
Now you will need all the strength you can muster.
You'd better have a friend handy to help with this step.

Another way to anticipate difficulties is to give readers advice on how to make the process easier or more pleasant. It's possible to apply organic garden insecticides without using a face mask, but you've learned that the unpleasant odors can cause severe coughing and sneezing even if the products are considered harmless. Naturally, you want to warn your readers about how to avoid possible side effects.

Finally, consider using a visual—a drawing, a diagram, a photograph. (See Chapter 1.) Wollan's essay "Coffee Time" might have provided a labeled drawing of a coffee percolator if he felt that the illustration would make readers understand his essay more clearly. You'll see on pages 206–207 how effective visuals can be in explaining a process.

■ **Tell the reader what to do if something goes wrong.**   In many processes, one can follow the instructions faithfully and still encounter problems. Prepare your reader for such cases.

> If, at this point, the pecan pie is not firm when you test the center, reduce the heat to 250 degrees and cook it 15 minutes longer.
> If, even after careful proofreading, you find a misspelled word at the last minute, carefully cross out the word and neatly print the correction by hand.

■ **Use other rhetorical strategies as needed.**   It's hard to write a process paper without drawing on some of the other writing strategies explored in this book. Narrative, for example, will help you frame the chronological sequence of steps to take in the process you're explaining. You may need to use descriptive details to identify some object. If you look ahead to the chapters on cause and effect (13) and definition (14), you might find explanations there that will help you develop your topic. The point is that you should mix rhetorical approaches as needed to write the best process paper that you can.

■ **Weigh your options for an introduction and a conclusion.**   An introduction to a how-to paper, in addition to presenting the thesis, might state when and by whom the process would be performed. It could also list any equipment needed for performing the process, and it might briefly list the major headings or divisions of the process. Don't forget about the need for a conclusion. You want the last thought in your reader's mind to be about the process as a whole, not about the comparatively trivial final step.

■ **Revise your drafts.**   Process papers require careful revision. When you review your initial draft, be sure that you have included all necessary ingredients and shown the steps in appropriate order. Revise to address any omissions or confusions. Check your essay against any outline that you may have developed. Try to see the steps in your mind's eye before you produce your final draft: Will someone be able to follow the steps that you suggest and achieve the desired result? Reread Chapter 6 for many tips on how to revise your essay. Peer review can be very helpful here: See if one of your early readers thinks he or she can duplicate the process that you're analyzing. When you revise, take into account all the feedback you have received.

■ **Proofread carefully.**   Edit your paper carefully for your own usual errors. Review pages 119–120 for proofreading tips.

ASSIGNMENT: PROCESS

Write an essay to explain a process. Explain how to do or make something that a reader can duplicate; or how something is made or done, even though you do not expect a reader to be able to carry out; or how to fix or change something like a problem or an injustice. Look at the student models (pages 201–205) and the "Tips for Writing a Process Essay." If you cannot easily decide on a topic for your process paper, you might want to use one of these suggestions as a topic idea:

1. How to be a working parent
2. How to use an iPad
3. How to achieve peace in the Middle East
4. How to teach math concepts to preschoolers
5. How to adopt a child in your city or state
6. How a steam engine works
7. How to get an A in English
8. How to make your favorite sandwich
9. How to prevent juvenile crime
10. How to manage stress
11. How to read an e-book
12. How a lightbulb works
13. How to enjoy a concert
14. How to waste time
15. How to listen to music
16. How World War II began
17. How to help a candidate win an election
18. How to deal with terrorists
19. How to deal with natural disaster
20. How to fix a flat tire

Student Writing: Process

Following are process papers by student writers. How has each writer given clear instructions on performing the task? Annotations on the first paper highlight features of the essay. Answer the questions after you read.

Coffee Time
Michael Wollan

Drip coffee is all the rage nowadays. Pour some water into a drip coffeemaker, put ground coffee in a filter below the water, flip a switch, and watch some hot stuff pretending to be coffee dribble into a glass container. That's not real coffee. And that brown fluid you're drinking from a McDonald's paper cup and have filled from a big urn, that's not real

1 Introduction: Negatives help set up thesis in next paragraph.

coffee either. Neither is the hot drink that bubbles on a heating unit at even the best restaurants, nor the bitter, lemon peel-tainted thimbles of muddy liquid called espresso. And the stuff made from a spoonful of crystals added to boiling water—how could anybody call that coffee?

Clearly stated thesis.

2   As a passionate coffee drinker, I know that only one kind is truly worthy of the name. It's percolated coffee, and I'm going to tell all you confused and deceived coffee drinkers just how to make it. In case you don't know, a percolator is a metal pot with a spout and a lid that contains a glass bubble on the top. A tube fits inside the pot; on it will sit a round metal container that holds the coffee. A cover with multiple tiny holes encloses the container.

Definition of *percolator*, key term in essay, for readers unfamiliar with the object.

3   Some people think that perked coffee is hopelessly out of date (you probably don't even have a percolator in your kitchen), but it's really so retro that it's avant garde. Brewing good coffee in a percolator requires patience and skill, but the first sip tells you it was all worth the effort. To begin, wash the percolator thoroughly to remove any bits of used black grounds from the last brew that can ruin this one. Next, decide on how many cups you want to make. For each cup of coffee, use two level tablespoons of ground coffee and six ounces of cold water. (Some stubborn coffee lovers will add salt or eggshells to the ground coffee in order to improve the taste, but these are unneeded additions, mostly for showoffs who swear that even the best grinds need help from human tinkering.) Pour the water into the pot and put the coffee into the small basket with the hole in the center. Cover the basket with the perforated lid. Attach the basket to the metal stand; then place the whole assembly into the water-filled percolator. Put the lid with the small glass dome on top of the coffee pot. Finally, place it on the stove.

Transition: "To begin" starts chronological arrangement.

Specific details support the steps and enliven the explanation.

Transition: "Finally,"

Next step in process. Transition sentence "The best way to brew coffee ..." moves process along.

4   The best way to brew coffee is with a medium gas flame, not electric heat. When boiling begins, the percolator will groan and rumble like distant thunder. The heat forces liquid up the tube. The liquid hits the glass slowly at first and then with rhythmic plop-plop-plops. The water falls downward through the perforated lid, through the ground coffee, and back into the

Simile: "groan and rumble like distant thunder" helps reader see process through concrete sensory detail.

Simile: "swill could serve only as black paint."

base of the pot. Lower the flame as soon as you hear the first tiny noises against the glass, or the liquid will splatter all over the stove. Or, it could quickly boil down, and the resulting swill could serve only as black paint for your backyard fence. Over a small flame the coffee will perk gently, gradually turning brown. The rich, intoxicating aroma of coffee beans now will hang in the air. In exactly seven minutes after the boil, your perked coffee will be ready.

Writer explains potential problems: liquid could splatter or boil down.

Don't contaminate it with milk or cream or sugar or tiny pink envelopes of artificial sweetener or by using a weird concoction made from vanilla or almond or raspberry (ugh!) flavored beans. Drink your coffee black, full strength. Some people think that it helps to treat yourself to this magnificent potion as a reward after a great event, like the end of finals week, or getting a date with the dark-haired gem in your bio class, or passing your driver's test after three flunks. But it really doesn't matter when you drink freshly brewed percolated coffee. For those in the know, it is its own reward.

5 Conclusion maintains light and humorous mood and returns to the thesis by reinforcing excellence of brewed coffee.

FOR WRITING OR DISCUSSION

1. What is the thesis of this essay? How does it relate to the title?

2. The essay is clearly more than just a step-by-step guide to making coffee. What was the writer's purpose in writing this essay? Who is his intended audience?

3. What elements make this a strong process paper? Could you make coffee from the way Wollan tells how to do it? Why or why not?

4. How has the writer used sensory detail to advantage? Where does humor come into play? What other rhetorical strategies does the writer draw on to explain the process?

5. Choose a simple task performed in the kitchen or some other room of your house or apartment and write a paper to explain how to do it. Decide on your audience and purpose before you begin writing, and make the process come alive so that your readers can duplicate it. Use sensory details and, if appropriate to your thesis and purpose, try your hand at some humor.

Omprakash K. Pansara
Preparing for the First Day of Classes

1   What is the best way of preparing for the first day of classes? Freshmen have different goals, and they attend colleges to acquire them. Students are often excited and often fail to prepare for the first day, and as a result, they often find difficulties. To avoid a hard time on the first day, they should prepare themselves by following the simple steps of organizing their schedules, buying supplies and books, and attending orientations.

2   The first step in preparing for the first day of classes is to create an organized schedule. First, students should choose classes according to their majors. They can go to the college Web site to get information, so they can see prerequisites and know what classes to take. Then students should decide to take classes taught by good, helpful teachers. They can question students who have already taken these courses, or they can check some websites such as *Ratemyprofessors.com*. Furthermore, students can directly e-mail the teachers or meet them during their office hours. Next, students should try to make appropriate schedules, keeping in mind such issues as conflicting job schedules and problems getting a ride to campus. Finally, they can register for classes. In short, choosing classes and making suitable schedules are important for the first day of classes.

3   The second step is to buy supplies and books. First, students should e-mail teachers or check the school's official website for required purchases. For example, if a student is taking a college algebra class, he or she is required to have a graphing calculator. Headphones and Internet access are required for online classes. Students should also make a list of supplies that they need to buy, including notebooks, papers, index (flash) cards, pens, pencils, erasers, and USB flash drives. Next, it's a good idea to check the prices for supplies and books in campus bookstores, off-campus bookstores, and online, where inexpensive and quality supplies and books are available. Purchasing required items is essential for being ready for the first day of classes.

The third important step is to attend an orientation. New students 4
frequently become confused about where things are located on campus;
therefore, it is essential to attend an orientation for a campus tour. At
orientation, students learn the locations of major school facilities including
libraries, computer labs, and cafeterias, as well as financial-aid, regis-
tration, counseling, and cashier's offices. Orientations also show how to
use academic e-mail accounts and how to read campus news using the
school's website with assigned usernames and passwords.

In conclusion, students often have difficulties on the first day of 5
classes, but they will find it easier if they follow these simple procedures of
organizing their schedules, purchasing essential materials, and attending
orientation. They will enjoy studying and will have a good time if they are
well prepared. These students are often successful students because they
are ready for their first day of the classes.

FOR WRITING OR DISCUSSION

1. What is the writer's thesis? Which details best support it?
2. Where does the writer explain a process most clearly?
3. What is your reaction to the introduction and conclusion? Are they
   engaging, wordy, repetitive, thought-provoking—or something else?
   What suggestions could you make to improve them?
4. Where has the writer indicated necessary materials?
5. Write a process essay called "Preparing for the First Day of … ."
   Fill in the blank with a word or phrase that you can explain in a
   series of steps. You might use "a new job," "military service," or
   "being married," for example.

Process
in the World Around You

Web sites offer step by step procedures for getting into college, improving your health, or preparing dinner, just to name a few. Television airs many do-it-yourself programs, such as *Extreme Makeover* and *This Old House*. Videos on YouTube will show you how to step dance, how to play guitar, or how to do hundreds of other activities. Check any retailer and you'll find a remarkable number of books or DVDs explaining everything from how to look more beautiful to how to create gardens in tiny spaces.

This selection, clearly a how-to piece, appeared in a regular segment called "Ask Men's Health: Life's Questions, Answered" from the magazine *Men's Health*. Note how the writer draws on a number of process-writing strategies identified in this chapter.

How something is done – Since most people drive, checking a blind spot is a process they would benefit from, but might not know how to do.

Complete and accurate – The feature shows how to check all the mirrors, and includes guidance on how to test your success.

Chronological order – The author uses numbers to indicate the sequence in which the steps should be carried out.

Audience – The audience is drivers, and the author uses terms drivers would be familiar with, like "driver's side mirror." The author does not use complex automotive or spatial terms.

Thesis – The introductory paragraph has a clear thesis, indicating that you can eliminate blind spots if you follow this method.

Anticipating difficulties – By including both "good positioning" and "bad positioning" diagrams, the author helps the reader to identify and correct potential problems.

Visuals – The diagrams help you understand the steps in the process, and see what the text describes.

Your Turn

Find a Web site that shows how to solve another automotive problem, such as how to pass a vehicle safely on the road, how to change oil, or how to change a flat tire. Write an essay summarizing the main steps in the process.

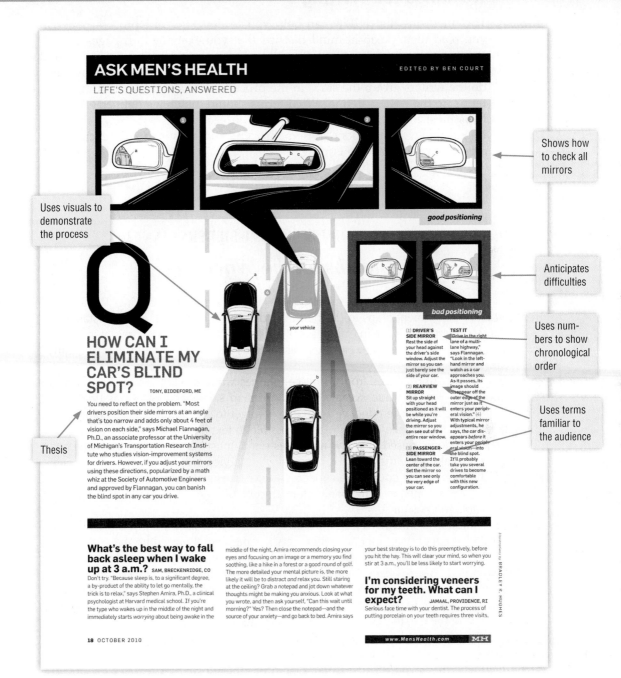

good positioning

bad positioning

Shows how to check all mirrors

Uses visuals to demonstrate the process

Anticipates difficulties

Uses numbers to show chronological order

Uses terms familiar to the audience

Thesis

Q

HOW CAN I ELIMINATE MY CAR'S BLIND SPOT?

TONY, BIDDEFORD, ME

You need to reflect on the problem. "Most drivers position their side mirrors at an angle that's too narrow and adds only about 4 feet of vision on each side," says Michael Flannagan, Ph.D., an associate professor at the University of Michigan's Transportation Research Institute who studies vision-improvement systems for drivers. However, if you adjust your mirrors using these directions, popularized by a math whiz at the Society of Automotive Engineers and approved by Flannagan, you can banish the blind spot in any car you drive.

your vehicle

(1) DRIVER'S SIDE MIRROR
Rest the side of your head against the driver's side window. Adjust the mirror so you can just barely see the side of your car.

(2) REARVIEW MIRROR
Sit up straight with your head positioned as it will be while you're driving. Adjust the mirror so you can see out of the entire rear window.

(3) PASSENGER-SIDE MIRROR
Lean toward the center of the car. Set the mirror so you can see only the very edge of your car.

TEST IT
"Drive in the right lane of a multi-lane highway," says Flannagan. "Look in the left-hand mirror and watch as a car approaches you. As it passes, its image should disappear off the outer edge of the mirror just as it enters your peripheral vision." (4) With typical mirror adjustments, he says, the car disappears before it enters your peripheral vision—into the blind spot. It'll probably take you several drives to become comfortable with this new configuration.

What's the best way to fall back asleep when I wake up at 3 a.m.? SAM, BRECKENRIDGE, CO

Don't try. "Because sleep is, to a significant degree, a by-product of the ability to let go mentally, the trick is to relax," says Stephen Amira, Ph.D., a clinical psychologist at Harvard medical school. If you're the type who wakes up in the middle of the night and immediately starts *worrying* about being awake in the middle of the night, Amira recommends closing your eyes and focusing on an image or a memory you find soothing, like a hike in a forest or a good round of golf. The more detailed your mental picture is, the more likely it will be to distract *and* relax you. Still staring at the ceiling? Grab a notepad and jot down whatever thoughts might be making you anxious. Look at what you wrote, and then ask yourself, "Can this wait until morning?" Yes? Then close the notepad—and the source of your anxiety—and go back to bed. Amira says your best strategy is to do this preemptively, before you hit the hay. This will clear your mind, so when you stir at 3 a.m., you'll be less likely to start worrying.

I'm considering veneers for my teeth. What can I expect? JAMAAL, PROVIDENCE, RI

Serious face time with your dentist. The process of putting porcelain on your teeth requires three visits,

www.MensHealth.com MH

Readings for Writing

The selections that follow can help you to develop your process paper. As you read them, keep in mind the tips that you examined on pages 196–200. For example, are the explanations clear, complete, and accurate, and how do the writers achieve these goals? Is the order of activities easy to follow? How do the writers group the steps in the process for easier understanding? What terms do the writers define? What terms should they have defined? And, perhaps most important, what is the thesis in each case? What does the writer intend for the instructions to demonstrate? The questions after each reading ask you to address these issues.

MARK A. SHIFFRIN AND AVI SILBERSCHATZ

Thumbs on the Wheel

1   President Obama has forbidden federal employees from texting while driving. The federal Transportation Department plans to do the same for commercial-truck and Interstate-bus drivers. And support is building in Congress for legislation that would require states to out-law texting or e-mailing while driving. Such distractions cause tens of thousands of deaths each year.

2   But the way to stop people from using cellphones while driving is not to make it a crime. Too many drivers value convenience more than safety and would assume they wouldn't get caught. A more effective approach is to get telecommunications companies to tweak technology to make it difficult or impossible to text and drive.

3   When a cellphone is used in a moving car, its signal must be handed off from one cell tower to the next along the route. This process tells the service provider that the phone is in motion. Cellphone towers could be engineered to not transmit while a phone is traveling. After a phone had stopped moving for a certain amount of time —three minutes, maybe— it would be able to transmit again.

4   Another solution would be to install hardware in cars and software in cellphones that would disable some phone functions when cars are moving. It would be the electronics equivalent of putting a guard on a knife handle or a grill over the blades of a fan.

5   This would, of course, affect passengers in moving cars as well as drivers. The inconvenience would arguably be worth it. But it is also easy to imagine technology that would allow only passengers to use their phones—by tethering them to devices, placed on the passenger side of the car, that would override the system.

6   Just as the text function could be disabled from a moving vehicle, so could the talk function be limited—at least when used without hands-free operating technology like Bluetooth. Given the evidence suggesting that even hands-free operation is

dangerously distracting to drivers, we may need to ask whether all cellphone use should be technologically impeded in moving cars. There is nothing unreasonable in expecting drivers to park before making calls.

While texting behind the wheel is a problem today, innovations may give rise to other risky behaviors within a few years, if not months. The best solutions will come not from lawmakers plugging holes in the dike, but from the engineers finding ways to make products safer.   7

FOR WRITING OR DISCUSSION

1. What is the thesis of this brief essay?
2. In what ways is this a process essay? What are the steps that the writers recommend? What order of arrangement have they used for the steps in the process?
3. What is the writers' conclusion? Do you agree with it? What "other risky behaviors" can you imagine in the future?
4. Write an essay about your own use of texting and the steps you might recommend to cut its use in the automobile.

MILDRED ARMSTRONG KALISH

Wash Day

Nowadays, with computerized washing machines and automatic water temperature controls, we don't give the family wash a second thought. I note that my children and grandchildren change clothing from the skin out every single day and throw every item, including the bath towel used only once, into the hamper. I'm sure they would be amazed to learn that in my day men, women, and children put on clean clothes on Monday morning and were expected to wear them for the entire week, because laundering those clothes was a major undertaking, with every member of the family called upon to contribute.   1

Though Monday was the official wash day throughout the farm community and in the town of Garrison, preparations usually started Sunday night, when all of the dirty clothes were collected, sorted, and given special scrutiny. The boys were expected to empty the pockets of their shirts and "overhauls"—the ubiquitous bibbed pants made of blue denim. All men and boys wore them; women and girls almost never did. Mama would turn the pant and shirt pockets inside out and brush away the chaff, dirt, alfalfa seeds, and barley beards. All the clothes were then put to soak in a large galvanized tub of cool water.   2

3   If we were in Garrison, the next step was for a couple of the Big Kids to bring the copper oval-shaped boiler up from the cellar and place it on the Monarch kitchen range. Here was where real cooperation began. We Little Kids would pump cistern water into three-gallon galvanized buckets and the boys would carry them, two at a time, to fill both the boiler and the reservoir that was permanently attached to the kitchen range. We used cistern water—which is rainwater collected and stored in a cistern usually thirty to forty feet deep and lined with stones—because rainwater, unlike well water, is soft. In fact, there is a saying in Iowa that the well water is so hard you have to bite it out of the cup. Everyone uses it for drinking and for cooking, because it tastes fabulous and makes great coffee. But since it doesn't allow suds to form and is harsh on the skin, hair, and clothing, soft cistern water is always used for washing.

4   The laundry soap was also prepared on Sunday night. Using a tin cabbage slicer, Grandpa shredded one and a half bars of P&G, Fels Naphtha, or our own homemade brown soap into a green marbleized graniteware pan kept exclusively for this purpose. After adding a little water to the pan, he placed it on the back of the warm kitchen range and by morning we would have plenty of soft soap ready for the washing machine.

5   Since the stove had to be kept fired up to heat the wash water, wash day always meant beans for supper, because we could leave them to cook untended on the back of the hot stove. So while Grandpa made the soap, Grandma and I picked over a couple of pounds of navy beans. After discarding the tiny rocks and shriveled beans that we always found, we placed the remainder in a big iron pot. The next morning we would throw in a couple of carrots, an onion, a small slab of bacon or a ham hock, and a few potatoes. Except for an occasional stir, the bean pot required no further attention.

6   Once the wash water was brought to a boil Monday morning, the heavy, awkward, round wooden washing machine was moved into the kitchen and Grandpa filled it with the water from the boiler and added the soft soap. All the clothes were washed in the same water, and were washed in order of whiteness and cleanliness: white clothes and bed linens first, followed by hand and dish towels, then the colored clothes, and finally the men's work socks, shirts, and overalls. In order to operate the washing paddles, once a batch of clothes was put in, someone alternately pushed and pulled a shoulder-high lever which was attached under the tub by some intricate arrangement of worm gears. Push-pull, push-pull, push-pull: fifteen minutes for every load. We all took turns at this task until it was time to leave for school, and then Grandpa manned the lever.

7   Sometime around 1936 when Roosevelt's Rural Electrification Act made life easier for farmers, Grandpa purchased a Maytag washing machine. We were thrilled to have it. Of course, we still washed all of the clothes in a single tub of water, but the chore of push-pull, push-pull was eliminated. That square, brushed aluminum Maytag did duty in our family for over twenty years (though for the last half dozen it was used only to wash dog beds).

8   Once the clothes were clean, using a wooden wash stick—best described as an unpainted broomstick—we lifted them out of the steaming water and put them through the

hard rubber rollers of the hand-turned wringer, from whence they fell into a tub of cool rinse water. After being rinsed, they had to be wrung out again. Rinsing and wringing was a two-person activity. One person turned the handle of the wringer, while another rinsed the clothes by hand and fed them through the rubber rollers which ejected them into the wicker wash basket below.

Then the whole process started over again with the next load of clothes, which was placed in that same wash water, followed by the third, fourth, and fifth loads, until all were washed, rinsed, and wrung out.   9

A much-admired accomplishment in those days was the ability to make smooth starch. Here is how you made and used it. First of all, you prepared a paste by adding cold water to the dry, powdery starch and stirred it until it had the consistency of thin toothpaste. Then you stirred this mixture constantly while you poured boiling water into it. If you stopped stirring or pouring, even briefly, you created a lumpy, unusable mess. For the final step, after pouring this starchy liquid into a dishpan half filled with cool water, you dipped the freshly washed shirt fronts, collars and cuffs, aprons, blouses, dresses, and tablecloths into it and hung them out to dry.   10

We considered it a badge of honor to get all the wash on the line by ten o'clock in the morning, and to hang the clothes according to the strict method dictated by the house-wives of the community. Sheets and pillowcases, handkerchiefs and towels had to be hung just so, the edges pulled taut between thumbs and forefingers. We called this procedure pressing by hand, for if done properly, it saved a lot of ironing later. We turned all the col-ored clothes inside out to discourage fading. We hung shirts, blouses, and undershirts by the tails; we hung pants and shorts from the belt line; we pinned all socks in pairs by the toes; and we hung all like items together.   11

Is there any sense in trying to make the modern-day reader understand the immense satisfaction we experienced in viewing our bright, clean wash arranged in such a meticu-lous fashion on the clothesline? Heaven knows we had more than enough to do without this added display of superhousewifery. But the whole ritual was a matter of pride.   12

There was a rumor in Garrison that a wily housewife, whose husband drove a long-haul semitruck, resulting in frequent and erratic absences, chose the clothesline method for signaling her handsome, blond lover. When her husband was in residence, she pinned the belt of his pants to the line; when he was absent, she pinned the legs of the pants to the line so they hung upside down. I never knew whether this was true or not, but it did make for good gossip.   13

There were a few years when the women in Garrison hung their panties and bras inside a pillowcase to conceal them from the eyes of any lascivious males who happened to pass by while these unmentionables were drying. But people made fun of the practice and it was soon abandoned. I don't recall that we ever engaged in that bit of silly primness on the farm.   14

In the summertime the clothes would sometimes dry so fast that by the time we got the second basket out to the line, the first batch was already dry. We removed the clothes from   15 the line as soon as they dried, being careful not to wrinkle the sweet-smelling, deliciously warm, sun-dried garments. We, meaning Grandma, Mama, my little sister, and I, would immediately put the sheets and pillowcases back on the beds, looking forward to the time when we could lie down on them. To crawl between crisp sheets, warm and fresh from the sun and air, at the end of a bone-wearying day, is one of the true soul-restoring luxuries of life, which hardly anyone of the current generation will ever know.

16   If the weather presented us with a quick drying day, we did the ironing as soon as we brought the clothes indoors, using the three heavy flatirons that had been heating on the back of the stove. Otherwise, we dipped a small vegetable brush in water, sprinkled the clothes to be ironed, rolled them tightly, placed them in the wash basket, and ironed them on Tuesday.

17   In the winter, to limit our exposure to the freezing weather, we carefully folded the wet sheets, pillowcases, and towels, shook the wrinkles out of the shirts and blouses, and warmed the clothespins in the oven before dashing outdoors to hang the clothes on the line. Sometimes the clothes would freeze stiff before we ever got the clothespins on them. However, we pinned them on the line anyway, for the wind usually evaporated the ice and they would flap fairly dry before too long. If they didn't dry, however, the great heater that served the living and dining rooms had to be stoked with chunks of oak, and then we had to remove the frozen items from the line and dry them on long wooden sticks placed on the backs of wooden chairs. These two-by-two-inch sticks were twelve feet long and did double duty as frames for quilting at another time. Sometimes it would take two days to get the whole wash dry.

18   At the end of wash day we had to drain and clean the washing machine and move it back to its proper place. But if it was summer, we emptied the wash water into buckets and took them out to the outhouse where we used the dirty but soap-laden water to scrub down the oak seats and the floor. Remember: Waste not; want not.

FOR WRITING OR DISCUSSION

1. What is the writer's thesis in this selection? How does the last sentence comment on the thesis?

2. How does the first paragraph establish an appropriate context for the rest of the selection?

3. Kalish identifies a number of processes that she explains to readers. Which one do you find most interesting or engaging? Which specific details make the process especially clear for you?

4. Where does the writer define terms? Why does she take time to provide these definitions?

5. Write an essay about a process in which some of your family participates together—cooking a meal, cleaning the house, raking leaves, visiting the supermarket.

NIKKI GIOVANNI
Campus Racism 101

There is a bumper sticker that reads: TOO BAD IGNORANCE ISN'T PAINFUL. I like that. 1
But ignorance is. We just seldom attribute the pain to it or even recognize it when we see
it. Like the postcard on my corkboard. It shows a young man in a very hip jacket smoking
a cigarette. In the background is a high school with the American flag waving. The caption
says: "Too cool for school. Yet too stupid for the real world." Out of the mouth of the young
man is a bubble enclosing the words "Maybe I'll start a band." There could be a postcard
showing a jock in a uniform saying, "I don't need school. I'm going to the NFL or NBA."
Or one showing a young man or woman studying and a group of young people saying, "So
you want to be white." Or something equally demeaning. We need to quit it.

I am a professor of English at Virginia Tech. I've been here for four years, though for 2
only two years with academic rank. I am tenured, which means I have a teaching position
for life, a rarity on a predominantly white campus. Whether from malice or ignorance,
people who think I should be at a predominantly Black institution will ask, "Why are you
at Tech?" Because it's here. And so are Black students. But even if Black students weren't
here, it's painfully obvious that this nation and this world cannot allow white students to
go through higher education without interacting with Blacks in authoritative positions. It
is equally clear that predominantly Black colleges cannot accommodate the numbers of
Black students who want and need an education.

Is it difficult to attend a predominantly white college? Compared with what? Being 3
passed over for promotion because you lack credentials? Being turned down for jobs because you are not college-educated? Joining the armed forces or going to jail because you
cannot find an alternative to the streets? Let's have a little perspective here. Where can you
go and what can you do that frees you from interacting with the white American mentality?
You're going to interact; the only question is, will you be in some control of yourself and
your actions, or will you be controlled by others? I'm going to recommend self-control.

What's the difference between prison and college? They both prescribe your behavior 4
for a given period of time. They both allow you to read books and develop your writing.
They both give you time alone to think and time with your peers to talk about issues. But
four years of prison doesn't give you a passport to greater opportunities. Most likely that
time only gives you greater knowledge of how to get back in. Four years of college gives
you an opportunity not only to lift yourself but to serve your people effectively. What's
the difference when you are called nigger in college from when you are called nigger in
prison? In college you can, though I admit with effort, follow procedures to have those
students who called you nigger kicked out or suspended. You can bring issues to public attention without risking your life. But mostly, college is and always has been the future. We,
neither less nor more than other people, need knowledge. There are discomforts attached
to attending predominantly white colleges, though no more so than living in a racist world.
Here are some rules to follow that may help:

5   *Go to class.* No matter how you feel. No matter how you think the professor feels about you. It's important to have a consistent presence in the classroom. If nothing else, the professor will know you care enough and are serious enough to be there.

6   *Meet your professors.* Extend your hand (give a firm handshake) and tell them your name. Ask them what you need to do to make an A. You may never make an A, but you have put them on notice that you are serious about getting good grades.

7   *Do assignments on time.* Typed or computer-generated. You have the syllabus. Follow it, and turn those papers in. If for some reason you can't complete an assignment on time, let your professor know before it is due and work out a new due date—then meet it.

8   *Go back to see your professor.* Tell him or her your name again. If an assignment received less than an A, ask why, and find out what you need to do to improve the next assignment.

9   Yes, your professor is busy. So are you. So are your parents who are working to pay or help with your tuition. Ask early what you need to do if you feel you are starting to get into academic trouble. Do not wait until you are failing.

10   *Understand that there will be professors who do not like you;* there may even be professors who are racist or sexist or both. You must discriminate among your professors to see who will give you the help you need. You may not simply say, "They are all against me." They aren't. They mostly don't care. Since you are the one who wants to be educated, find the people who want to help.

11   *Don't defeat yourself.* Cultivate your friends. Know your enemies. You cannot undo hundreds of years of prejudicial thinking. Think for yourself and speak up. Raise your hand in class. Say what you believe no matter how awkward you may think it sounds. You will improve in your articulation and confidence.

12   *Participate in some campus activity.* Join the newspaper staff. Run for office. Join a dorm council. Do something that involves you on campus. You are going to be there for four years, so let your presence be known, if not felt.

13   You will inevitably run into some white classmates who are troubling because they often say stupid things, ask stupid questions—and expect an answer. Here are some comebacks to some of the most common inquiries and comments:

14   **Q:** What's it like to grow up in a ghetto?
15   **A:** I don't know.

16   **Q:** (from the teacher): Can you give us the Black perspective on Toni Morrison, Huck Finn, slavery, Martin Luther King, Jr., and others?
17   **A:** I can give you my perspective. (Do not take the burden of 22 million people on your shoulders. Remind everyone that you are an individual, and don't speak for the race or any other individual within it.)

18   **Q:** Why do all the Black people sit together in the dining hall?
19   **A:** Why do all the white students sit together?

20   **Q:** Why should there be an African-American studies course?
21   **A:** Because white Americans have not adequately studied the contributions of Africans and African-Americans. Both Black and white students need to know our total common history.

Q: Why are there so many scholarships for "minority" students?   22

A: Because they wouldn't give my great-grandparents their forty acres and the mule.   23

Q: How can whites understand Black history, culture, literature, and so forth?   24

A: The same way we understand white history, culture, literature, and so forth. That is why   25
we're in school: to learn.

Q: Should whites take African-American studies courses?   26

A: Of course. We take white-studies courses, though the universities don't call them that.   27

Comment: When I see groups of Black people on campus, it's really intimidating.   28

Comeback: I understand what you mean. I'm frightened when I see white students   29
congregating.

Comment: It's not fair. It's easier for you guys to get into college than for other people.   30

Comeback: If it's so easy, why aren't there more of us?   31

Comment: It's not our fault that America is the way it is.   32

Comeback: It's not our fault, either, but both of us have a responsibility to make changes.   33

It's really very simple. Educational progress is a national concern; education is a private   34
one. Your job is not to educate white people; it is to obtain an education. If you take the
racial world on your shoulders, you will not get the job done. Deal with yourself as an
individual worthy of respect, and make everyone else deal with you the same way. College
is a little like playing grown-up. Practice what you want to be. You have been telling your
parents you are grown. Now is your chance to act like it.

FOR WRITING OR DISCUSSION

1. The title is an immediate shock to most readers. Why? What is the effect of the
   "101" in the title?

2. Giovanni establishes her credentials (paragraph 2). Why does she do this? How
   does it contribute to the point of the essay?

3. Why does she make a comparison between prison and college? Is this an
   effective comparison—or do you think it a bit over-the-top? Explain your
   position.

4. What rules does the writer propose for black students who attend white
   colleges? Could these rules apply to any students, no matter what their race, or
   do you think they are particularly race-based? Why?

5. What is the effect on the essay of the recommended responses to "stupid"
   questions and comments black students may hear on campus?

6. Write a process essay in which you give advice to white students attending
   a predominantly black college, or any other college in which they are a
   minority.

SUSAN DOUGLAS

Remote Control: How to Raise a Media Skeptic

1   "Mommy, Mommy, come here now! Hurry, you're gonna miss it. It's Barbie's High-Steppin' Pony, and its legs really move! Hurreeeeey!"

2   "No!" I bark, as I'm wiping the dog barf up from the carpet, stirring the onions again so they don't burn, and slamming the phone down on a caller from Citibank who wants to know how I'm doin' today. It is 5:56 p.m., and I'm in no mood. "I don't come for commercials, and besides, the horse doesn't really move—they just make it look that way."

3   "Oh yeah?" demands my daughter, sounding like a federal prosecutor. "It can too. It's not like those old ones where you told me they faked it—this one really does move."

4   So now I have to go see and, indeed, the sucker takes batteries, and the stupid horse moves—sort of. "See, Mommy, the commercials don't always lie."

5   Moments like this prompt me to wonder whether I'm a weak-kneed, lazy slug or, dare I say it, a hypocrite. See, I teach media studies, and, even worse, I go around the country lecturing about the importance of media literacy. One of my talking points is how network children's programming is, ideologically, a toxic waste dump. Yet here I am, just like millions of parents during that portion of the day rightly known as hell hour—dinnertime—shoving my kid in front of Nickelodeon so my husband and I can get dinner on the table while we whisper sweet nothings like "It's your turn to take her to Brownies tomorrow" and "Oh, I forgot to tell you that your mother called three days ago with an urgent message."

6   We let her watch Nickelodeon, but I still pop in to ridicule Kool-Aid commercials or to ask her why Clarissa's parents (on *Clarissa Explains It All*) are so dopey. I am trying to have it both ways: to let television distract her, which I desperately need, and to help her see through its lies and banalities. I am very good at rationalizing this approach, but I also think it isn't a bad compromise for overworked parents who believe Barbie is the anti-Christ[1] yet still need to wash out grotty lunch boxes and zap leftovers at the end of the day.

7   It's best to be honest up front: My house is not media proofed. I am not one of those virtuous, haloed parents who has banished the box from the home. I actually believe that there are interesting, fun shows for my daughter to watch on TV. (And I'm not about to give up *ER*.)

8   But I'm also convinced that knowing about television, and growing up with it, provides my daughter with a form of cultural literacy that she will need, that will tie her to her friends and her generation and help her understand her place in the world. So instead of

---

[1]In the days before the return of Christ to the world, the Christian religion believes, an evil person, the *Antichrist*, will appear.

killing my TV, I've tried to show my daughter basic nonsense-detecting techniques. Don't think your choices are either no TV or a zombified kid. Studies show that the simple act of intervening—of talking to your child about what's on television and why it's on there—is one of the most important factors in helping children understand and distance themselves from some of the box's more repugnant imagery.

I recommend the quick surgical strike, between throwing the laundry in and picking up the Legos. Watch a few commercials with them and point out that commercials lie about the toys they show, making them look much better than they are in real life. Count how many male and female characters there are in a particular show or commercial and talk about what we see boys doing and what we see girls doing. Why, you might ask, do we always see girls playing with makeup kits and boys playing with little Johnny Exocet missiles? Real-life dads change diapers, push strollers, and feed kids, but you never see boys doing this with dolls on commercials. Ask where the Asian and African-American kids are. Point out how most of the parents in shows geared to kids are much more stupid than real-life parents. (By the way, children report that TV shows encourage them to talk back to their folks.) Tell them that all those cereals advertised with cartoon characters and rap music (like Cocoa Puffs and Trix) will put giant black holes in their teeth that only a dentist with a drill the size of the space shuttle can fix. 9

One of the best words to use when you're watching TV with your kids is *stupid*, as in "Aren't Barbie's feet—the way she's always forced to walk on her tiptoes—really stupid?" or "Isn't it stupid that Lassie is smarter than the mom on this show?" (My favorite Barbie exercise: Put your kitchen timer on for a minute and make your daughter walk around on her tiptoes just like Barbie; she'll get the point real fast.) *Cool*—a word that never seems to go out of style—is also helpful, as in "Isn't it cool that on *Legends of the Hidden Temple* (a game show on Nickelodeon) the girls are as strong and as fast as the boys?" Pointing out what's good on TV is important too. 10

See, I think complete media-proofing is impossible, because the shallow, consumerist, anti-intellectual values of the mass media permeate our culture. And we parents shouldn't beat ourselves up for failing to quarantine our kids. But we can inoculate them—which means exposing them to the virus and showing them how to build up a few antibodies. So don't feel so guilty about letting them watch TV. Instead, have fun teaching them how to talk back to it rather than to you. 11

FOR WRITING OR DISCUSSION

1. What process is Douglas trying to explain? How successful is she in accomplishing her goal?

2. What is Douglas' thesis? How does she use an introduction to build to the thesis? What do the words in the title, "Remote Control," contribute to the essay?

3. What specific techniques does the writer offer her daughter in order to help the child develop a critical eye for television viewing?

4. What is your reaction to such words and phrases as, "indeed, the sucker takes batteries," "toxic waste dump," "hell hour," and "zap leftovers at the end of the day"? Why does Douglas use such informal, even slang, expressions? Who do you think is her intended audience?

5. Write a process essay in which you indicate how you would explain to a child how to be cautious about some essentially pleasure-giving act—riding a bicycle or a horse, playing in the street, or eating junk food, for example. Or, write a process paper on how you would help a child learn to be critical about watching television.

HAVING YOUR SAY

Television: Is it good or bad for children? Write an essay in which you argue one side or the other of this controversial topic.

Reading and Writing About Poetry

How will the world end? Robert Frost builds on contemporary theories to create a deceptively simple poem. Read "Fire and Ice" and answer the questions that follow.

ROBERT FROST

Fire and Ice

Some say the world will end in fire,
Some say in ice.
From what I've tasted of desire
I hold with those who favor fire.
But if it had to perish twice,
I think I know enough of hate
To say that for destruction ice
Is also great
And would suffice.

FOR WRITING OR DISCUSSION

1. What scientific notions of the possible destruction of the world does Frost draw on? What does fire symbolize? Ice? What emotions does Frost connect to each of these states of temperature?

2. In the last line, how does the understatement—saying something less than the writer really means or less strongly than the situation calls for—contribute to the poem?

3. What role do comparison and contrast play in the poem? (See Chapter 11.)

4. Why do you think Frost takes five lines to explain destruction by ice and only two lines to explain destruction by fire?

5. Write a process essay that is opposite to Frost's point. That is, write a paper to explain how the world will survive and avoid destruction.

STRATEGY CHECKLIST: Writing and Revising Your Process Paper

Plan the paper.	☐ Have I chosen a process that I understand thoroughly?
	☐ Will I explain a process that I expect readers to perform, or will I explain how something is done or made without expecting readers to perform the action?
	☐ Have I thought carefully about my purpose in writing?
	☐ Do I have my audience clearly in mind?
	☐ Have I used an outline to organize my ideas?
	☐ Have I addressed any issues raised by readers about my outline?
Write a first draft.	☐ Have I done any necessary research if I'm explaining a complex process?
	☐ Have I made the process interesting with an introduction that engages readers?
	☐ Have I developed a thesis?
	☐ Have I explained the process completely and accurately—in chronological order, where necessary?
	☐ Have I provided reasons for performing some steps, where necessary?
	☐ Have I identified all the steps in the process and grouped them logically?

Revise and edit the paper.	☐ Have I identified all necessary materials and equipment?
	☐ Have I defined unfamiliar terms for the reader?
	☐ Have I anticipated any problems people performing the process might face?
	☐ Have I adapted my language and instructions for the person who is performing the action or someone just trying to understand it?
Proofread the paper.	☐ Have I proofread for grammar, spelling, and mechanics?

CROSSCURRENTS

Both "Wash Day" (pages 209–212) by Mildred Armstrong Kalish and "Remote Control: How to Raise a Media Skeptic" (pages 216–218) by Susan Douglas provide snapshots of children and parents. What generalizations can you draw from the two pieces about the appropriate relations between parents and children? How are the selections alike? How are they different?

COLLABORATIVE LEARNING

Develop an outline for the topic that you will write about for your process paper. In groups of three students, read each other's outlines. What suggestions can the group make about the development of each paper? Use the outlines to comment on the thesis, purpose, and details. What suggestions can you make for improving the outlines and, therefore, the draft that should follow?

For support in meeting this chapter's objectives, follow this path in MyCompLab: Resources ⇒ Writing ⇒ Writing Purposes ⇒ Writing to Inform. Review the Instruction and Multimedia resources about instructions for felling a tree, then complete the Exercises and click on Gradebook to measure your progress.

CHAPTER 11

Comparison and Contrast

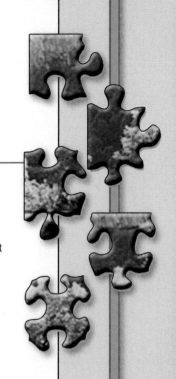

A *comparison* shows the similarities between two or more things; a *contrast* shows the differences between two or more things. Used interchangeably, if imprecisely, each term often includes the other. Asked to compare, you'll probably contrast automatically as well. Asked to contrast, you can't escape comparing too. Many teachers use the unambiguous term **comparison–contrast** to signal the task of showing likenesses and differences. No matter what the term, the most common kinds of essay questions on examinations call for comparison and contrast. It is important, then, to master the techniques of this method of development.

In this chapter you will

■ identify the strategies for writing a comparison–contrast paper

■ analyze student comparison–contrast essays

■ identify a topic and write your own comparison–contrast paper

■ explore the use of comparison and contrast in writing from the world around you

■ analyze the use of comparison–contrast in writing by professionals

Writing Your Comparison–Contrast Paper

Everyone uses comparisons, sometimes to explain the unfamiliar, and sometimes just to establish a superficial similarity: "He is as slow as a snail," for example. But to produce a good comparison–contrast paper, the writer must apply logical principles to the consideration of similarities and differences.

TIPS for Writing a Comparison–Contrast Essay

■ **Compare and contrast according to a single principle.** You might compare automobiles and airplanes as means of transportation, or you might compare them as causes of air pollution. The principle in the first instance might be ease of travel; in the second, pollution. In each case, the principle determines the similarities and differences discussed in the paper. If you're concerned with ease of travel, you won't mention the variety of colors that both airplanes and automobiles can be painted. If you're concerned with pollution, you won't mention the comfort of adjustable seats.

In a sense, this means developing a thesis. However, you usually must establish a principle for comparison–contrast before you can arrive at a thesis: the meaning of the similarities and differences. Having examined the similarities and differences according to the principle of ease of travel, you might establish as a thesis that travel by air is more convenient than travel by automobile.

■ **Compare and contrast according to a single purpose.**   One useful purpose is to clarify. For an audience that knows little about soccer, for example, you could make the game understandable by comparing it to football, a game with which more American audiences are familiar. A foreign student might explain the courtship and wedding customs of his or her country by contrasting them to their American equivalents.

A second purpose of comparison–contrast is to show the superiority of one thing over another: Spiffy Peanut Butter is a better buy than Spunky Peanut Butter, say; or living in a high-rise apartment is easier than living in a house; or travel by air is more convenient than travel by automobile.

A third purpose of comparison–contrast is to use the two items as examples of a generalization. Toni Cade Bambara and Toni Morrison show in their writings that African-Americans want to be thought of as individuals rather than as stereotyped representatives of causes or groups.

■ **Be fair with your comparison–contrasts.**   If you see an exception to the comparison you have made, mention it. This is known as *qualification*, and often it can win the reader's respect and confidence.

■ **Follow an established pattern of organization.**   You can organize a comparison–contrast paper in different ways: subject by subject, point by point, or a combination of the two. Review the student papers on the following pages.

■ **Avoid the obvious.**   Strive to select items for comparison–contrast that do not seem on the surface to be similar or different. Apples and oranges seem very different—hence, the famous saying "It's like comparing apples and oranges"— but you could make a good case for their similarities: healthful fruits, satisfying snacks, low-cost options for tight budgets. Don't try to compare items that everyone would agree were similar or to contrast items that obviously differ greatly. Everyone knows that operatic music and country music are vastly different, so a paper contrasting the two would not engage readers. However, if you tried to show how these two different musical forms were actually quite similar in many respects, you'd have an interesting topic to write about.

■ **Check the logic of your presentation.**   Especially in the alternating patterns of development (see pages 226–227), be sure that you follow the same order in writing about the two objects you've chosen to compare. In comparing the outcomes of World War I and World War II in regard to economics and social programs, if you discuss the economics of World War I first, you should also start with World War I when you write about social programs. Switching the order can be distracting for your readers.

■ **Revise your drafts.** Be sure to check your drafts against any outline or informal plan that you have established for the comparison and contrast essay. Reread Chapter 6 for suggestions about how to revise your papers. Ask classmates if your comparisons are clear and if they support your thesis successfully.

■ **Proofread carefully.** Edit carefully for your own usual errors after you are satisfied with your revision; but don't forget to proofread as well.

ASSIGNMENT: COMPARISON AND CONTRAST

Write an essay that compares and (or) contrasts two activities, ideas, people, historical events, objects, places, or issues that interest you. Use the tips on pages 221–223 and the student models on pages 225–229 as guides. If you are having difficulty deciding on a topic for your comparison–contrast paper, the following suggestions might be helpful. Bear in mind that the number of comparison–contrast topics is almost infinite, and these just begin to scratch the surface. These suggestions are intended more to start your own thoughts flowing than to be specific, final topics.

1. Any past-versus-present topic: cars, sports teams or athletes, places you've lived, girlfriends or boyfriends, movie stars, musical styles, clothes, ways of celebrating a holiday, a change in your attitude toward someone or something, attitudes before and after 9/11.

2. What you thought something was going to be like and what it was actually like: a country, a town, college life, a job, a book, a romantic attachment, a marriage, a divorce, a tourist attraction.

3. A which-is-better topic: two competing products, cultures, newscasters, restaurants, television sitcoms, business establishments, seasons of the year, cats versus dogs, breeds of dog, methods of disciplining children.

4. Two contrasting types of people: teachers, police officers, drivers, salespeople, political leaders, "dates," hairstylists, servers at restaurants.

5. Two contrasting (but sometimes confused) emotions or character traits: love and infatuation, courage and recklessness, pride and arrogance, snobbery and good taste, fear and terror.

6. Two contrasting views on a controversial issue: dealing with terrorists, compulsory drug testing for high school athletes, abortion, SUV drivers, censorship, pornography, to name a few possibilities.

Student Writing: Comparison–Contrast

Subject-by-Subject Pattern

For short papers, one of the clearest patterns of organization—for comparison *or* contrast—is the **subject-by-subject pattern** or **block method.** If you select this pattern, you first discuss one side of the subject completely, and then you discuss the other side. You must, of course, stress the same points in discussing each side of the subject; otherwise there will be no comparison. The diagram below will help you visualize the block method.

The following student outline and paper use the subject-by-subject pattern of organization.

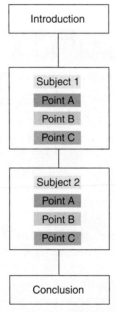

Subject-by-Subject Pattern

Carey Byer

Outline for "In the Swim"

<u>Thesis</u>: Swimming provides benefits without the hazards of jogging.

   I. The dangers of running as exercise

     A. Works lower body instead of upper body

     B. Muscle strain

    C. Bad for recovering patients

    D. Straining exercise

II. Advantages of swimming

    A. Less strain while improving muscle strength

    B. Increase flexibility

    C. Improved circulation

    D. Mental relaxation

Carey Byer
In the Swim

1   The jogging craze continues to sweep the country. In fancy nylon suits or in simple jeans and T-shirts, men and women everywhere jog to build stamina, tone muscles, take off unwanted pounds, strengthen the heart, and just to feel good. Yet jogging is probably the worst form of self-torture a person can inflict upon the body. Swimming, on the other hand, provides physical and mental well-being without the unnecessary hazards of running.

2   Although running is popular for its improvement of muscle strength and endurance, there are many negative points to consider. First, running concentrates on the lower body, helping people develop strong leg muscles but ignoring the upper body, the arms and chest, the parts important for what we do the most. Another disadvantage is that runners frequently strain muscles and pull ligaments in their legs, which are painful and can keep a person off his or her feet for days. Also, running on hard surfaces like cement and asphalt has really bad effects on the knees, ankles, and back.

3   For people recovering from illness, running is simply too vigorous an activity. Those requiring exercise after a heart attack, stroke, or surgery are in no shape to start running—it is just too strenuous. Despite some of its benefits, running is an intense, straining exercise. Feet pound on the pavement, jarring all the internal organs. One could hardly call running a relaxing activity.

4   Swimming, on the other hand, puts much less strain on the body, while still improving fitness. Swimming—like running—improves muscle strength and

endurance, stamina and balance. Swimming increases flexibility much more than running does, and also improves upper and lower body strength. Suspension of the body in the water supports the back. Swimming is also the best exercise for building stamina among the ill or recovering. Warm water improves circulation and relaxation, and cool water reduces swelling, lowers blood pressure, and decreases the pain of strains and bruises.

5   Finally, another important benefit of swimming is its proven effect on mental relaxation. The water and the rhythmical breathing and movement of swimming are extremely soothing and help people relax easily. Thus a person is free to allow the mind to wander instead of having to focus complete attention on exercise.

6   With all the facts we now have about the correlation between regular exercise and the prevention of heart diseases and other illnesses, more and more people are exercising. Inactivity is out, fitness is in. People play tennis and racquetball, run, jump rope, do aerobics, ride bicycles, and find many other ways to become physically active. Yet the many positive effects of swimming on the body and mind may soon make it the most popular exercise in the country.

FOR WRITING OR DISCUSSION

1. What is the writer's thesis?
2. Which details best support the writer's assertions about running? Swimming?
3. What transitions connect elements in the body paragraphs? Between paragraphs?
4. What suggestions would you make to the writer before producing the next draft?
5. Write a paper in which you compare and contrast two activities, exercises, or sports that you know. Use the block method.

Point-by-Point Pattern

A second pattern of development is the **point-by-point** or **alternating pattern**. Although this pattern is most frequently used in writing long papers, it is by no means restricted to them. In this pattern, the writer establishes one or more points of comparison or contrast and then applies those points to each side of a subject. We can represent this pattern in a diagram.

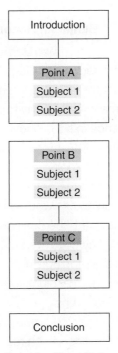

Point-by-Point Pattern

The following student outline and essay use the point-by-point method of organization.

Benjamin Simonovich

Outline for "Two Jobs"

<u>Thesis</u>: I can make a difference working at the Animal Municipal Center as opposed to working at Wendy's.

  I. Dealing with customers

     A. Wendy's

     B. Animal Municipal Center

  II. Work environment

     A. Wendy's

     B. Animal Municipal Center

  III. Interactions with fellow employees

     A. Wendy's

     B. Animal Municipal Center

Benjamin Simonovich

Two Jobs

1   As I drag myself into a blistering 110-degree room where the walls are melting, twenty hamburgers are flipping on a 200-degree stove, potatoes are deep frying, and one order after another hits me, I feel like my frustration will never stop. I sit back and wonder, "Did I make a difference in someone's life today?" The answer always is "No." But having worked at the Animal Municipal Center a year later proved that I could make a change in someone's life. Seeing people drifting in incomplete tears over a lost pet, then seeing their joy once the pet is found is unforgettable. The factors that helped me progress from meaningless work to knowing I mattered in someone's life at the Animal Municipal Center were the customers, the work environment, and the social interactions at work with my coworkers.

2   At Wendy's, I was constantly apologizing to every customer stating, "I'm training—sorry." Just their facial expressions told me "Hurry up and give me my food." My contact with the customers at Wendy's was practiced, plain, and fast. But at the Animal Municipal Center, I really got to know the customers. They showed me that their pets were a part of their families, which really pushed me into doing my job one hundred percent. This was a totally different story from Wendy's where I didn't really get involved with the customers except giving them their food. What difference was I making in these people's lives at Wendy's if I wasn't even getting to know the customer at all? At the Animal Municipal Center, my days were made by a simple adoption, a lost pet or injured pet, or the aftermath of having to kill a sick, helpless animal. Even though some days were slow, I was occupied by the dogs' barking in the cage area all day.

3   At Wendy's the work requirements were awful, not at all like those at the Center. Every day I had to wear an uncomfortable uniform at Wendy's where the requirements were for a black Wendy's hat, green shirt, black pants, and black shoes, and I had to wear all this no matter what the weather and despite the indoor heat. Every day I had to put up with annoying flies buzzing around salad, fries, burger bits, chicken nuggets, and frosty mix all over the floor. There was no such unpleasantness at the Animal Municipal Center. I could wear my casual clothing to work, which made me feel really comfortable instead of being stuck in an unpleasant uniform all day. I had my own desk with a computer, file cabinet, my own stapler, paper clips, and paper.

I felt like a professional. The environment at the Animal Municipal Center gave me the drive to wake up eager in the morning, whereas Wendy's made me dread each day.

My coworkers at Wendy's were really hard to communicate with since most of them spoke no English. The only thing I knew how to translate was the word for the food I needed for a customer. The workers would always laugh and chatter in their own language, but I would never know what they were saying. It made me and the other English-speaking workers feel left out instead of part of the team. One experience at Wendy's really showed the type of disrespect one could get at work. I was taking orders at the drive-through in the mid-afternoon, and during a little intermission, the coworkers started asking me questions, and then all of a sudden, someone pulled my pants down to my ankles. The others howled with laughter, but I was embarrassed and angry, which ultimately led to my quitting that very day. But from my first day at the Animal Municipal Center, I was at ease and already having fun, which made me want to come to work to see my second family while making money at the same time. At the Animal Municipal Center, I was part of a huge family that was always growing.

Now as I amble into work at the Animal Municipal Center a nice breeze of air-conditioning hits me. There are no hot stoves and sizzling burgers. The barking of the dogs plays as music for my eight-hour day; and being able to walk these dogs that have been abandoned by their owners and help the people that love them makes the job worthwhile.

FOR WRITING OR DISCUSSION

1. Identify the writer's thesis. How does it prepare the reader for the comparison–contrast essay that follows?

2. What elements in the paper make the basis for the comparison between Wendy's and the Animal Municipal Center?

3. Which details best show the writer's frustrations at working at Wendy's?

4. Which details best show the writer's pleasure in working at the Animal Municipal Center?

5. Write an essay in which you compare and contrast two jobs. You can write about two paying or volunteer jobs that you have had or two tasks that you had to perform.

Comparison and Contrast in the World Around You

Comparison and contrast is a fundamental mode of human thought. We compare Kanye West's latest album to his previous release. Students compare this teacher to that; food lovers argue over the taste of one chili con carne over another; movie goers contrast *The Hangover* and *The Hangover Part II*.

So it should be no surprise that comparison and contrast infuses the books and magazines we read, the Web sites we visit, and the advertisements we respond to. Examine this piece from *National Geographic* to see how the strategies we've pointed out in this chapter help make a striking presentation.

Title and Introduction — They immediately establish the terms of the contrast, wolves in Yellowstone National Park in the past and present.

Single principle — The state of Yellowstone is considered only in regard to its character before and after the introduction of wolves.

Details — The language is rich in specific details: "elk overbrowsed the streamside willows…"; "A healthy fear of wolves also keeps elk from lingering at streamsides."

Visuals — Vibrant colors paint the landscape. Non-predators like elk dominate the scene. The drawing reinforces the "before" of the comparison.

Single purpose — The piece attempts to show that wolves have had a favorable impact on Yellowstone.

Organization — The block method is used—readers see on the left the effects prior to wolves being introduced and on the right the effects after their introduction.

Your Turn

Visit two contrasting Web sites on the same current issue: global warming, voting rights for teenagers, gay marriage, the death penalty, or some other contemporary challenge. Prepare a side-by-side presentation like the one from *National Geographic*. Follow the rhetorical principles reviewed in this chapter.

Before & After Wolves

Restoring wolves to Yellowstone after a 70-year absence as a top predator—especially of elk—set off a cascade of changes that is restoring the park's habitat as well.

YELLOWSTONE WITHOUT WOLVES 1926-1995 ▸

ELK overbrowsed the streamside willows, cotton-woods, and shrubs that prevent erosion. Birds lost nesting space. Habitat for fish and other aquatic species declined as waters became broader and shallower and, without shade from streamside vegetation, warmer.

ASPEN trees in Yellow-stone's northern valleys, where elk winter, were seldom able to reach full height. Elk ate nearly all the new sprouts.

COYOTE numbers climbed. Though they often kill elk calves, they prey mainly on small mammals like ground squirrels and voles, reducing the food available for foxes, badgers, and raptors.

ART BY FERNANDO G. BAPTISTA, NG STAFF;
AMANDA HOBBS, NG STAFF
SOURCES: ROBERT L. BESCHTA AND
WILLIAM J. RIPPLE, OREGON STATE
UNIVERSITY; DOUGLAS W. SMITH,
YELLOWSTONE NATIONAL PARK

YELLOWSTONE WITH WOLVES 1995-PRESENT ▸

ELK population has been halved. Severe winters early in the reintroduction and drought contributed to the decline. A healthy fear of wolves also keeps elk from lingering at streamsides, where it can be harder to escape attack.

ASPENS The number of new sprouts eaten by elk has dropped dramatically. New groves in some areas now reach 10 to 15 feet tall.

COYOTES Wolf predation has reduced their numbers. Fewer coyote attacks may be a factor in the resurgence of the park's pronghorn.

WILLOWS, cottonwoods, and other riparian vege-tation have begun to stabi-lize stream banks, helping restore natural water flow. Overhanging branches again shade the water and welcome birds.

BEAVER colonies in north Yellowstone have risen from one to 12, now that some stream banks are lush with vegetation, especially willows (a key beaver food). Beaver dams create ponds and marshes, supporting fish, amphibians, birds, small mammals, and a rich insect population to feed them.

CARRION Wolves don't cover their kill, so they've boosted the food supply for scavengers, notably bald and golden eagles, coyotes, ravens, magpies, and bears.

Aspens

Coyote

Elk

Willow

Title and Introduction state terms of comparison and contrast

Single purpose: positive effect of wolves

Specific details

Block method: first before, then after

231

Readings for Writing

As you read the selections that follow, notice the comparison–contrast patterns at work. In addition, some selections will provide opportunities for you to develop your own comparison–contrast essays.

MARK TWAIN (SAMUEL L. CLEMENS)

The Professional

1   The face of the water [of the Mississippi River, where the author was a steamboat pilot] in time became a wonderful book—a book that was a dead language to the uneducated passenger but which told its mind to me without reserve, delivering its most cherished secrets as clearly as if it uttered them with a voice. And it was not a book to be read once and thrown aside, for it had a new story to tell every day. Throughout the long twelve hundred miles there was never a page that was void of interest, never one that you could leave unread without loss, never one that you would want to skip, thinking you could find higher enjoyment in some other thing. There never was so wonderful a book written by man, never one whose interest was so absorbing, so unflagging, so sparklingly renewed with every reperusal. The passenger who could not read it was charmed with a peculiar sort of faint dimple on its surface (on the rare occasions when he did not overlook it altogether) but to the pilot that was an *italicized* passage; indeed it was more than that, it was a legend of the largest capitals with a string of shouting exclamation-points at the end of it, for it meant that a wreck or a rock was buried there that could tear the life out of the strongest vessel that ever floated. It is the faintest and simplest expression the water ever makes, and the most hideous to a pilot's eye. In truth, the passenger who could not read this book saw nothing but all manner of pretty pictures in it, painted by the sun and shaded by the clouds, whereas to the trained eye these were not pictures at all, but the grimmest and most dead-earnest of reading matter.

2   Now when I had mastered the language of this water, and had come to know every trifling feature that bordered the great river as familiarly as I knew the letters of the alphabet, I had made a valuable acquisition. But I had lost something, too. I had lost something which could never be restored to me while I lived. All the grace, the beauty, the poetry, had gone out of the majestic river! I still keep in mind a certain wonderful sunset which I witnessed when steamboating was new to me. A broad expanse of the river was turned to blood; in the middle distance the red hue brightened into gold, through which a solitary log came floating, black and conspicuous; in one place a long, slanting mark lay sparkling upon the water; in another the surface was broken by boiling, tumbling rings, that were as many-tinted as an opal; where the ruddy flush was faintest, was a smooth spot that was covered with graceful circles and radiating lines, ever so delicately traced; the shore on our left was densely wooded, and the somber shadow that fell from this forest was broken in one place by a long, ruffled trail that shone like silver; and high above the forest wall

a clean-stemmed dead tree waved a single leafy bough that glowed like a flame in the unobstructed splendor that was flowing from the sun. There were graceful curves, reflected images, woody heights, soft distances; and over the whole scene, far and near, the dissolving lights drifted steadily, enriching it every passing moment with new marvels of coloring.

3

I stood like one bewitched. I drank it in, in a speechless rapture. The world was new to me, and I had never seen anything like this at home. But as I've said, a day came when I began to cease from noting the glories and the charms which the moon and the sun and the twilight wrought upon the river's face; another day came when I ceased altogether to note them. Then, if that sunset scene had been repeated, I should have looked upon it without rapture, and should have commented upon it, inwardly, after this fashion: "This sun means that we are going to have wind tomorrow; that floating log means that the river is rising, small thanks to it; that slanting mark on the water refers to a bluff reef which is going to kill somebody's steamboat one of these nights, if it keeps on stretching out like that; those tumbling 'boils' show a dissolving bar and a changing channel there; the lines and circles in the slick water over yonder are a warning that that troublesome place is shoaling up dangerously; that silver streak in the shadow of the forest is the 'break' from a new snag, and he has located himself in the very best place he could have found to fish for steamboats; that tall dead tree, with a single living branch, is not going to last long, and then how is a body ever going to get through this blind place at night without the friendly old landmark?"

No, the romance and beauty were all gone from the river. All the value any feature of it had for me now was the amount of usefulness it could furnish toward compassing the safe piloting of a steamboat. Since those days, I have pitied doctors from my heart. What does the lovely flush in a beauty's cheek mean to a doctor but a "break" that ripples above some deadly disease? Are not all her visible charms sown thick with what are to him the signs and symbols of hidden decay? Does he ever see her beauty at all, or doesn't he simply view her professionally and comment upon her unwholesome condition all to himself? And doesn't he sometimes wonder whether he has gained most or lost most by learning his trade?

4

FOR WRITING OR DISCUSSION

1. What pattern of development does Twain use to contrast the beginner's view of the river to the seasoned professional's view?

2. In paragraph 1, Twain uses *analogy*—a special kind of comparison—to describe the river as if it were a book. Identify the words and phrases used to show this analogy.

3. In which sentence or sentences does Twain first state the thesis? Where does he restate the thesis?

4. Do you agree with Twain that increased knowledge interferes with simple emotional pleasure? Why, or why not?

5. Write a paper about how you once felt about some person, place, or idea, emphasizing the contrast between past and present.

SUZANNE BRITT

That Lean and Hungry Look

1 Caesar was right. Thin people need watching. I've been watching them for most of my adult life, and I don't like what I see. When these narrow fellows spring at me, I quiver to my toes. Thin people come in all personalities, most of them menacing. You've got your "together" thin person, your mechanical thin person, your condescending thin person, your tsk-tsk thin person, your efficiency-expert thin person. All of them are dangerous.

2 In the first place, thin people aren't fun. They don't know how to goof off, at least in the best, fat sense of the word. They've always got to be doing. Give them a coffee break, and they'll jog around the block. Supply them with a quiet evening at home, and they'll fix the screen door and lick S & H green stamps. They say things like "there aren't enough hours in the day." Fat people never say that. Fat people think the day is too damn long already.

3 Thin people make me tired. They've got speedy little metabolisms that cause them to bustle briskly. They're forever rubbing their bony hands together and eyeing new problems to "tackle." I like to surround myself with sluggish, inert, easygoing fat people, the kind who believe that if you clean it up today, it'll just get dirty again tomorrow.

4 Some people say the business about the jolly fat person is a myth, that all of us chubbies are neurotic, sick, sad people. I disagree. Fat people may not be chortling all day long, but they're a hell of a lot *nicer* than the wizened and shriveled. Thin people turn surly, mean and hard at a young age because they never learn the value of a hot-fudge sundae for easing tension. Thin people don't like gooey soft things because they themselves are neither gooey nor soft. They are crunchy and dull, like carrots. They go straight to the heart of the matter while fat people let things stay all blurry and hazy and vague, the way things actually are. Thin people want to face the truth. Fat people know there is no truth. One of my thin friends is always staring at complex, unsolvable problems and saying, "The key thing is. . . ." Fat people never say that. They know there isn't any such thing as the key thing about anything.

5 Thin people believe in logic. Fat people see all sides. The sides fat people see are rounded blobs, usually gray, always nebulous and truly not worth worrying about. But the thin person persists. "If you consume more calories than you burn," says one of my thin friends, "you will gain weight. It's that simple." Fat people always grin when they hear statements like that. They know better.

6 Fat people realize that life is illogical and unfair. They know very well that God is not in his heaven and all is not right with the world. If God was up there, fat people could have two doughnuts and a big orange drink anytime they wanted it.

7 Thin people have a long list of logical things they are always spouting off to me. They hold up one finger at a time as they reel off these things, so I won't lose track. They speak slowly as if to a young child. The list is long and full of holes. It contains tidbits like "get a grip on yourself," "cigarettes kill," "cholesterol clogs," "fit as a fiddle," "ducks in a row," "organize" and "sound fiscal management." Phrases like that.

8 They think these 2,000-point plans lead to happiness. Fat people know happiness is elusive at best and even if they could get the kind thin people talk about, they wouldn't

want it. Wisely, fat people see that such programs are too dull, too hard, too off the mark. They are never better than a whole cheesecake.

Fat people know all about the mystery of life. They are the ones acquainted with the night, with luck, with fate, with playing it by ear. One thin person I know once suggested that we arrange all the parts of a jigsaw puzzle into groups according to size, shape and color. He figured this would cut the time needed to complete the puzzle at least by 50 percent. I said I wouldn't do it. One, I like to muddle through. Two, what good would it do to finish early? Three, the jigsaw puzzle isn't the important thing. The important thing is the fun of four people (one thin person included) sitting around a card table, working a jigsaw puzzle. My thin friend had no use for my list. Instead of joining us, he went outside and mulched the boxwoods. The three remaining fat people finished the puzzle and made chocolate, double-fudged brownies to celebrate.   9

The main problem with thin people is they oppress. Their good intentions, bony torsos, tight ships, neat corners, cerebral machinations and pat solutions loom like dark clouds over the loose, comfortable, spread-out, soft world of the fat. Long after fat people have removed their coats and shoes and put their feet up on the coffee table, thin people are still sitting on the edge of the sofa, looking neat as a pin, discussing rutabagas. Fat people are heavily into fits of laughter, slapping their thighs and whooping it up, while thin people are still politely waiting for the punch line.   10

Thin people are downers. They like math and morality and reasoned evaluation of the limitations of human beings. They have their skinny little acts together. They expound, prognose, probe and prick.   11

Fat people are convivial. They will like you even if you're irregular and have acne. They will come up with a good reason why you never wrote the great American novel. They will cry in your beer with you. They will put your name in the pot. They will let you off the hook. Fat people will gab, giggle, guffaw, gallumph, gyrate and gossip. They are generous, giving and gallant. They are gluttonous and goodly and great. What you want when you're down is soft and jiggly, not muscled and stable. Fat people know this. Fat people have plenty of room. Fat people will take you in.   12

FOR WRITING OR DISCUSSION

1. Tell why you agree or disagree with this statement: "In 'That Lean and Hungry Look,' Britt is mostly contrasting fat and thin people just for laughs. She is a good deal more serious, however, about contrasting two opposing philosophies of life."

2. What pattern of organization does Britt use to make the contrasts?

3. Using the comparison–contrast technique of Britt's essay, write a paper in which you attempt to refute the author's position—that is, defend the thin person's view.

HAVING YOUR SAY

What is your view of the effects of being thin or being overweight on a person's personality? Write a comparison–contrast essay, supporting your point with specifics.

DAVID BROOKS
The Medium Is the Medium

1   Recently, book publishers got some good news. Researchers gave 852 disadvantaged students 12 books (of their own choosing) to take home at the end of the school year. They did this for three successive years.

2   Then the researchers, led by Richard Allington of the University of Tennessee, looked at those students' test scores. They found that the students who brought the books home had significantly higher reading scores than other students. These students were less affected by the "summer slide"—the decline that especially afflicts lower-income students during the vacation months. In fact, just having those 12 books seemed to have as much positive effect as attending summer school.

3   This study, along with many others, illustrates the tremendous power of books. We already knew, from research in 27 countries, that kids who grow up in a home with 500 books stay in school longer and do better. This new study suggests that introducing books into homes that may not have them also produces significant educational gains.

4   Recently, Internet mavens got some bad news. Jacob Vigdor and Helen Ladd of Duke's Sanford School of Public Policy examined computer use among a half-million 5th through 8th graders in North Carolina. They found that the spread of home computers and high-speed Internet access was associated with significant declines in math and reading scores.

5   This study, following up on others, finds that broadband access is not necessarily good for kids and may be harmful to their academic performance. And this study used data from 2000 to 2005 before Twitter and Facebook took off.

6   These two studies feed into the debate that is now surrounding Nicholas Carr's book, "The Shallows." Carr argues that the Internet is leading to a short-attention-span culture. He cites a pile of research showing that the multidistraction, hyperlink world degrades people's abilities to engage in deep thought or serious contemplation.

7   Carr's argument has been challenged. His critics point to evidence that suggests that playing computer games and performing Internet searches actually improve a person's ability to process information and focus attention. The Internet, they say, is a boon to schooling, not a threat.

8   But there was one interesting observation made by a philanthropist who gives books to disadvantaged kids. It's not the physical presence of the books that produces the biggest impact, she suggested. It's the change in the way the students see themselves as they build a home library. They see themselves as readers, as members of a different group.

9   The Internet-versus-books debate is conducted on the supposition that the medium is the message. But sometimes the medium is just the medium. What matters is the way people think about themselves while engaged in the two activities. A person who becomes a citizen of the literary world enters a hierarchical universe. There are classic works of literature at the top and beach reading at the bottom.

10 A person enters this world as a novice, and slowly studies the works of great writers and scholars. Readers immerse themselves in deep, alternative worlds and hope to gain some lasting wisdom. Respect is paid to the writers who transmit that wisdom.

A citizen of the Internet has a very different experience. The Internet smashes hierarchy and is not marked by deference. Maybe it would be different if it had been invented in Victorian England, but Internet culture is set in contemporary America. Internet culture is egalitarian. The young are more accomplished than the old. The new media is supposedly savvier than the old media. The dominant activity is free-wheeling, disrespectful, antiauthority disputation. 11

These different cultures foster different types of learning. The great essayist Joseph Epstein once distinguished between being well informed, being hip and being cultivated. The Internet helps you become well informed—knowledgeable about current events, the latest controversies and important trends. The Internet also helps you become hip—to learn about what's going on, as Epstein writes, "in those lively waters outside the boring mainstream." 12

But the literary world is still better at helping you become cultivated, mastering significant things of lasting import. To learn these sorts of things, you have to defer to greater minds than your own. You have to take the time to immerse yourself in a great writer's world. You have to respect the authority of the teacher. 13

Right now, the literary world is better at encouraging this kind of identity. The Internet culture may produce better conversationalists, but the literary culture still produces better students. 14

It's better at distinguishing the important from the unimportant, and making the important more prestigious. 15

Perhaps that will change. Already, more "old-fashioned" outposts are opening up across the Web. It could be that the real debate will not be books versus the Internet but how to build an Internet counterculture that will better attract people to serious learning. 16

FOR WRITING OR DISCUSSION

1. What is Brooks' thesis? In which paragraph do you find the best statement of the writer's thesis?

2. What do you think is Brooks' purpose here? What audience does he have in mind? (The essay first appeared in *The New York Times*.) How does Brooks' use of informal language—words like "maven," "kids," and "piles of research," for example—affect his intended audience and purpose?

3. What comparison–contrast strategies does the writer use? Who is Nicholas Carr? (Google him.)

4. What does Brooks mean by the title "The Medium Is the Medium"? An early critic of the media, Marshall McLuhan (Google him), coined the phrase "The medium is the message," and later the playful "The medium is the massage." How do these phrases influence Brooks' point of view, do you think?

5. What advantages does Brooks see in the literary world? The Internet world?

6. Write an essay in which you respond to the last paragraph of Brooks' essay.

Youthful Imagination: Two Stories for Comparison and Contrast

SHIRLEY JACKSON

Charles

1   The day my son Laurie started kindergarten he renounced corduroy overalls with bibs and began wearing blue jeans with a belt; I watched him go off the first morning with the older girl next door, seeing clearly that an era of my life was ended, my sweet-voiced nursery-school tot replaced by a long-trousered, swaggering character who forgot to stop at the corner and wave good-bye to me.

2   He came home the same way, the front door slamming open, his cap on the floor, and the voice suddenly become raucous shouting, "Isn't anybody *here*?"

3   At lunch he spoke insolently to his father, spilled his baby sister's milk, and remarked that his teacher said we were not to take the name of the Lord in vain.

4   "How was school today?" I asked, elaborately casual.

5   "All right," he said.

6   "Did you learn anything?" his father asked.

7   Laurie regarded his father coldly. "I didn't learn nothing," he said.

8   "Anything," I said. "Didn't learn anything."

9   "The teacher spanked a boy, though," Laurie said, addressing his bread and butter. "For being fresh," he added, with his mouth full.

10 "What did he do?" I asked. "Who was it?"

11 Laurie thought. "It was Charles," he said. "He was fresh. The teacher spanked him and made him stand in a corner. He was awfully fresh."

12 "What did he do?" I asked again, but Laurie slid off his chair, took a cookie, and left, while his father was still saying, "See here, young man."

13 The next day Laurie remarked at lunch, as soon as we sat down, "Well, Charles was bad again today." He grinned enormously and said, "Today Charles hit the teacher."

14 "Good heavens," I said, mindful of the Lord's name, "I suppose he got spanked again?"

15 "He sure did," Laurie said. "Look up," he said to his father.

16 "What?" his father said, looking up.

17 "Look down," Laurie said. "Look at my thumb. Gee you're dumb." He began to laugh insanely.

18 "Why did Charles hit the teacher?" I asked quickly.

19 "Because she tried to make him color with red crayons," Laurie said. "Charles wanted to color with green crayons so he hit the teacher and she spanked him and said nobody play with Charles but everybody did."

The third day—it was Wednesday of the first week—Charles bounced a see-saw on to the head of a little girl and made her bleed, and the teacher made him stay inside all during recess. Thursday Charles had to stand in a corner during story-time because he kept pounding his feet on the floor. Friday Charles was deprived of blackboard privileges because he threw chalk. 20

On Saturday I remarked to my husband, "Do you think kindergarten is too unsettling for Laurie? All this toughness, and bad grammar, and this Charles boy sounds like such a bad influence." 21

"It'll be all right," my husband said reassuringly. "Bound to be people like Charles in the world. Might as well meet them now as later." 22

On Monday Laurie came home late, full of news. "Charles," he shouted as he came up the hill; I was waiting anxiously on the front steps. "Charles," Laurie yelled all the way up the hill, "Charles was bad again." 23

"Come right in," I said, as soon as he came close enough. "Lunch is waiting." 24

"You know what Charles did?" he demanded, following me through the door. "Charles yelled so in school they sent a boy in from first grade to tell the teacher she had to make Charles keep quiet, and so Charles had to stay after school. And so all the children stayed to watch him." 25

"What did he do?" I asked. 26

"He just sat there," Laurie said, climbing into his chair at the table. "Hi, Pop, y'old dust mop." 27

"Charles had to stay after school today," I told my husband. "Everyone stayed with him." 28

"What does Charles look like?" my husband asked Laurie. "What's his other name?" 29

"He's bigger than me," Laurie said. "And he doesn't have any rubbers and he doesn't ever wear a jacket." 30

Monday night was the first Parent-Teachers meeting, and only the fact that the baby had a cold kept me from going; I wanted passionately to meet Charles's mother. On Tuesday Laurie remarked suddenly, "Our teacher had a friend come to see her in school today." 31

"Charles's mother?" my husband and I asked simultaneously. 32

"Naaah," Laurie said scornfully. "It was a man who came and made us do exercises, we had to touch our toes. Look." He climbed down from his chair and squatted down and touched his toes. "Like this," he said. He got solemnly back into his chair and said, picking up his fork, "Charles didn't even do exercises." 33

"That's fine," I said heartily. "Didn't Charles want to do exercises?" 34

"Naaah," Laurie said. "Charles was so fresh to the teacher's friend he wasn't *let* do exercises." 35

"Fresh again?" I said. 36

"He kicked the teacher's friend," Laurie said. "The teacher's friend told Charles to touch his toes like I just did and Charles kicked him." 37

"What are they going to do about Charles, do you suppose?" Laurie's father asked him. 38

39   Laurie shrugged elaborately. "Throw him out of school, I guess," he said.

40   Wednesday and Thursday were routine; Charles yelled during story hour and hit a boy in the stomach and made him cry. On Friday Charles stayed after school again and so did all the other children.

41   With the third week of kindergarten Charles was an institution in our family; the baby was being a Charles when she cried all afternoon; Laurie did a Charles when he filled his wagon full of mud and pulled it through the kitchen; even my husband, when he caught his elbow in the telephone cord and pulled telephone, ashtray, and a bowl of flowers off the table, said, after the first minute, "Looks like Charles."

42   During the third and fourth weeks it looked like a reformation in Charles; Laurie reported grimly at lunch on Tuesday of the third week, "Charles was so good today the teacher gave him an apple."

43   "What?" I said, and my husband added warily, "You mean Charles?"

44   "Charles," Laurie said. "He gave the crayons around and he picked up the books afterward and the teacher said he was her helper."

45   "What happened?" I asked incredulously.

46   "He was her helper, that's all," Laurie said, and shrugged.

47   "Can this be true, about Charles?" I asked my husband that night. "Can something like this happen?"

48   "Wait and see," my husband said cynically. "When you've got a Charles to deal with, this may mean he's only plotting."

49   He seemed to be wrong. For over a week Charles was the teacher's helper; each day he handed things out and he picked things up; no one had to stay after school.

50   "The P.T.A. meeting's next week again," I told my husband one evening. "I'm going to find Charles's mother there."

51   "Ask her what happened to Charles," my husband said. "I'd like to know."

52   "I'd like to know myself," I said.

53   On Friday of that week things were back to normal. "You know what Charles did today?" Laurie demanded at the lunch table, in a voice slightly awed. "He told a little girl to say a word and she said it and the teacher washed her mouth out with soap and Charles laughed."

54   "What word?" his father asked unwisely, and Laurie said, "I'll have to whisper it to you, it's so bad." He got down off his chair and went around to his father. His father bent his head down and Laurie whispered joyfully. His father's eyes widened.

55   "Did Charles tell the little girl to say *that*?" he asked respectfully.

56   "She said it *twice*," Laurie said. "Charles told her to say it *twice*."

57   "What happened to Charles?" my husband asked.

58   "Nothing," Laurie said. "He was passing out the crayons."

59   Monday morning Charles abandoned the little girl and said the evil word himself three or four times, getting his mouth washed out with soap each time. He also threw chalk.

My husband came to the door with me that evening as I set out for the P.T.A. meeting. 60
"Invite her over for a cup of tea after the meeting," he said. "I want to get a look at her."

"If only she's there," I said prayerfully. 61

"She'll be there," my husband said. "I don't see how they could hold a P.T.A. meeting 62
without Charles's mother."

At the meeting I sat restlessly, scanning each comfortable matronly face, trying to 63
determine which one hid the secret of Charles. None of them looked to me haggard
enough. No one stood up in the meeting and apologized for the way her son had been
acting. No one mentioned Charles.

After the meeting I identified and sought out Laurie's kindergarten teacher. She had 64
a plate with a cup of tea and a piece of chocolate cake; I had a plate with a cup of tea
and a piece of marshmallow cake. We maneuvered up to one another cautiously, and
smiled.

"I've been so anxious to meet you," I said. "I'm Laurie's mother." 65

"We're all so interested in Laurie," she said. 66

"Well, he certainly likes kindergarten," I said. "He talks about it all the time." 67

"We had a little trouble adjusting, the first week or so," she said primly, "but now he's 68
a fine little helper. With occasional lapses, of course."

"Laurie adjusts very quickly," I said. "I suppose this time it's Charles's influence." 69
"Charles?" 70

"Yes," I said laughing, "you must have your hands full in that kindergarten, with 71
Charles."

"Charles?" she said. "We don't have any Charles in the kindergarten." 72

SAKI (H. H. MUNRO)
The Open Window

"My aunt will be down presently, Mr. Nuttel," said a very self-possessed young lady of 1
fifteen; "in the meantime you must try and put up with me."

Framton Nuttel endeavored to say the correct something which should duly flatter 2
the niece of the moment without unduly discounting the aunt that was to come.
Privately he doubted more than ever whether these formal visits on a succession of total
strangers would do much towards helping the nerve cure which he was supposed to be
undergoing.

"I know how it will be," his sister had said when he was preparing to migrate to this 3
rural retreat; "you will bury yourself down there and not speak to a living soul, and your

nerves will be worse than ever from moping. I shall just give you letters of introduction to all the people I know there. Some of them, as far as I can remember, were quite nice."

4   Framton wondered whether Mrs. Sappleton, the lady to whom he was presenting one of the letters of introduction, came into the nice division.

5   "Do you know many of the people round here?" asked the niece, when she judged that they had had sufficient silent communion.

6   "Hardly a soul," said Framton. "My sister was staying here, at the rectory, you know, some four years ago, and she gave me letters of introduction to some of the people here."

7   He made the last statement in a tone of distinct regret.

8   "Then you know practically nothing about my aunt?" pursued the self-possessed young lady.

9   "Only her name and address," admitted the caller. He was wondering whether Mrs. Sappleton was in the married or widowed state. An undefinable something about the room seemed to suggest masculine habitation.

10   "Her great tragedy happened just three years ago," said the child; "that would be since your sister's time."

11   "Her tragedy?" asked Framton; somehow in this restful country spot tragedies seemed out of place.

12   "You may wonder why we keep that window wide open on an October afternoon," said the niece, indicating a large French window that opened on to a lawn.

13   "It is quite warm for the time of the year," said Framton; "but has that window got anything to do with the tragedy?"

14   "Out through that window, three years ago to a day, her husband and her two young brothers went off for their day's shooting. They never came back. In crossing the moor to their favorite snipe-shooting ground they were all three engulfed in a treacherous piece of bog. It had been that dreadful wet summer, you know, and places that were safe in other years gave way suddenly without warning. Their bodies were never recovered. That was the dreadful part of it." Here the child's voice lost its self-possessed note and became falteringly human. "Poor aunt always thinks that they will come back someday, they and the little brown spaniel that was lost with them, and walk in at that window just as they used to do. That is why the window is kept open every evening till it is quite dusk. Poor dear aunt, she has often told me how they went out, her husband with his white waterproof coat over his arm, and Ronnie, her youngest brother, singing 'Bertie, why do you bound?' as he always did to tease her, because she said it got on her nerves. Do you know, sometimes on still, quiet evenings like this, I almost get a creepy feeling that they will all walk in through that window—"

15   She broke off with a little shudder. It was a relief to Framton when the aunt bustled into the room with a whirl of apologies for being late in making her appearance.

16   "I hope Vera has been amusing you?" she said.

17   "She has been very interesting," said Framton.

18   "I hope you don't mind the open window," said Mrs. Sappleton briskly; "my husband and brothers will be home directly from shooting, and they always come in this way.

They've been out for snipe in the marshes today, so they'll make a fine mess over my poor carpets. So like you menfolk, isn't it?"

She rattled on cheerfully about the shooting and the scarcity of birds, and the prospects for duck in the winter. To Framton it was all purely horrible. He made a desperate but only partially successful effort to turn the talk on to a less ghastly topic; he was conscious that his hostess was giving him only a fragment of her attention, and her eyes were constantly straying past him to the open window and the lawn beyond. It was certainly an unfortunate coincidence that he should have paid his visit on this tragic anniversary.   19

"The doctors agree in ordering me complete rest, an absence of mental excitement, and avoidance of anything in the nature of violent physical exercise," announced Framton, who labored under the tolerably widespread delusion that total strangers and chance acquaintances are hungry for the least detail of one's ailments and infirmities, their cause and cure. "On the matter of diet they are not so much in agreement," he continued.   20

"No?" said Mrs. Sappleton, in a voice which only replaced a yawn at the last moment. Then she suddenly brightened into alert attention—but not to what Framton was saying.   21

"Here they are at last!" she cried. "Just in time for tea, and don't they look as if they were muddy up to the eyes!"   22

Framton shivered slightly and turned towards the niece with a look intended to convey sympathetic comprehension. The child was staring out through the open window with a dazed horror in her eyes. In a chill shock of nameless fear Framton swung round in his seat and looked in the same direction.   23

In the deepening twilight three figures were walking across the lawn towards the window; they all carried guns under their arms, and one of them was additionally burdened with a white coat hung over his shoulders. A tired brown spaniel kept close at their heels. Noiselessly they neared the house, and then a hoarse young voice chanted out of the dusk: "I said, Bertie, why do you bound?"   24

Framton grabbed wildly at his stick and hat; the hall door, the gravel drive, and the front gate were dimly noted stages in his headlong retreat. A cyclist coming along the road had to run into the hedge to avoid imminent collision.   25

"Here we are, my dear," said the bearer of the white mackintosh, coming in through the window, "fairly muddy, but most of it's dry. Who was that who bolted out as we came up?"   26

"A most extraordinary man, a Mr. Nuttel," said Mrs. Sappleton; "could only talk about his illnesses, and dashed off without a word of goodby or apology when you arrived. One would think he had seen a ghost."   27

"I expect it was the spaniel," said the niece calmly; "he told me he had a horror of dogs. He was once hunted into a cemetery somewhere on the banks of the Ganges by a pack of pariah dogs, and had to spend the night in a newly dug grave with the creatures snarling and grinning and foaming just above him. Enough to make anyone lose their nerve."   28

Romance at short notice was her speciality.   29

FOR WRITING OR DISCUSSION

1. In what ways could you classify these pieces as "surprise ending" stories? How does each writer achieve the surprise? What clues to the outcome do you notice in each case before you reach the ending?

2. In what ways are the children in the stories similar? Different? How do the adults affect the outcome—the parents in Laurie's case, the aunt and Mr. Nuttel (note the man's name!) in the niece's case?

3. The last line of each story is well known. How do the last lines capture the heart of the stories?

4. Write a paper comparing and/or contrasting Jackson's short story with Saki's. You may use one or more of the preceding questions to guide you in limiting your subject.

Love, Sweet Love: Two Poems for Comparison and Contrast

The comparison–contrast paper is especially effective as a means of writing about literature. When you examine one literary work along with another, the comparison often provides fresh insights into both works. If, for example, you read the following two poems separately, you would probably not derive the same meaning from them as did the student who compares them in "Two Kinds of Love." The annotations on the student's essay will help you see the pattern at work.

WILLIAM SHAKESPEARE

Sonnet 29

When, in disgrace with Fortune and men's eyes,
I all alone beweep my outcast state,
And trouble deaf heaven with my bootless[1] cries,
And look upon myself and curse my fate,
Wishing me like to one more rich in hope,
Featured like him, like him with friends possessed,
Desiring this man's art, and that man's scope,
With what I most enjoy contented least;

5

---
[1]Futile.

Yet in these thoughts myself almost despising,
Haply[2] I think on thee, and then my state,
Like to the lark at break of day arising
From sullen earth, sings hymns at heaven's gate;
For thy sweet love remembered such wealth brings
That then I scorn to change my state with kings.

10

---

[2]By chance.

WILLIAM SHAKESPEARE

Sonnet 130

My mistress' eyes are nothing like the sun;
Coral is far more red than her lips' red;
If snow be white, why then her breasts are dun;
If hairs be wires, black wires grow on her head.
I have seen roses damasked, red and white,   5
But no such roses see I in her cheeks;
And in some perfumes is there more delight
Than in the breath that from my mistress reeks.
I love to hear her speak; yet well I know
That music hath a far more pleasing sound.   10
I grant I never saw a goddess go:
My mistress, when she walks, treads on the ground.
And yet, by heaven, I think my love as rare
As any she belied with false compare.

Julie Olivera
Two Kinds of Love

Shakespeare's Sonnet 29, "When, in disgrace with Fortune and men's eyes," and Sonnet 130, "My mistress' eyes are nothing like the sun," both strike me as very fine love poems. Both offer great tributes to the loved person. Love comes in all shapes and sizes, however, and I think the feelings expressed in "My mistress' eyes" are more realistic and more trustworthy. I'd rather be the woman that poem was written for than the other woman.

"When, in disgrace," begins by describing a situation in which the poet feels totally depressed. Totally is no exaggeration. He hasn't had any

1 Introduction and thesis: Writer establishes framework for comparison–contrast.

Purpose clear: To show superiority of one poem over
2 the other.

Transition and
introduction to
first subject in
comparison.

Quotations
from poem
advance brief
summary of
Sonnet 29.

good "fortune," people look down on him, he is jealous of other people, heaven is "deaf" to his prayers. He has little or no hope. He has few, if any, friends. The things he enjoys most mean nothing to him. He even comes close to hating himself. The second part of the poem very beautifully says that even in a foul mood like that if he just happens to "think on thee," he cheers up. He realizes, in fact, that he is one of the luckiest men in the world. He has her love, and her love makes him richer than a king in all that really matters. "For thy sweet love remembered such wealth brings/ That then I scorn to change my state with kings."

Fair explanations:
Writer identifies
sonnet's
strengths even
though she likes
this poem less
than the other
poem she will
discuss.

3

Writer's interpre-
tation of "When,
in disgrace."

Well, I'd be flattered, of course, and I might even wipe away a tear, but I'm not sure how much I would trust him. Love is a great inspiration to fall back on if one's life starts going to pieces, but it also has to exist on a day-to-day basis, through all the normal wear and tear, through all the boredom and nothing-special times. If I save a drowning person, he might say with complete sincerity that he loves and adores me, but that is no real basis for a lifelong relationship. If it takes bad times to make the poet realize how much he loves his lady, what starts happening to the love when times aren't so bad?

Analogy helps
writer support
her point about
love as defined
in the poem.

4

Transition to
second subject of
comparison and
clear pattern of
organization.

In "My mistress' eyes," the poet is not depressed, but confident and cheerful. He is in love just as much, but this time with a real person, not a goddess or miracle worker. If anything bothers him, it is people who have to depend on illusions and lies to make their loves seem worthwhile. He still wouldn't trade places with a king, yet he knows and gladly accepts that other women are better-looking, and that they have nicer voices, and even that they have sweeter-smelling breath. He doesn't have to turn his lady into something she isn't in order to love her.

Summary and
interpretation of
Sonnet 130.

5

In this paragraph,
writer develops
contrast between
the two poems.

I think this expression of love is by far the more valid one. People want to be loved for what they are, imperfections and all. If someone says he loves me, I want to feel he loves me rather than an unrealistic mental image he has of me. If all he loves is the image, the love is an insult. In direct contrast, the poet in "When, in disgrace" seems to love the woman for what she does for him, while the poet in "My mistress' eyes" loves her simply for what she is.

6

Conclusion:
a strong
restatement of
the thesis.

Between the stickiness and sweetness of the first poem and the realism of the second, I have to choose the second. Both poems are fine, but one is written for rare moods, and the other is written for a lifetime.

FOR WRITING OR DISCUSSION

1. What pattern of development does the writer use? How would you outline the paper?

2. Has the writer produced a unified comparison–contrast paper, or has she written two separate essays on two separate poems? Explain your answer.

3. In your view, do the poems present two opposing attitudes? The writer assumes they were written about two different women. Could they have been written about the same woman?

4. Write a paper in which you compare and contrast the two sonnets by Shakespeare. Follow the guidelines on writing a comparison–contrast essay explored in this chapter.

STRATEGY CHECKLIST: Writing and Revising Your Comparison–Contrast Paper

Plan the paper.	☐ Have I used prewriting to explore ideas for a subject? ☐ Have I determined a single principle by which to compare and contrast? ☐ Will I show similarities, or differences, or a combination of the two? ☐ Have I chosen a pattern of development that suits my subject? ☐ Have I thought carefully about my purpose in writing? ☐ Do I have my audience clearly in mind? ☐ Have I used an outline to organize my ideas?

Write a first draft.	☐ Have I developed a clear thesis?
	
	 ☐ Have I provided enough support for my thesis?
	
	 ☐ Have I used the patterns of development appropriately?
	    ■ Subject-by-subject (block) pattern: See page 224.
	    ■ Point-by-point (alternating) pattern: See page 226.

Revise and edit the paper.	☐ Does my introduction establish the purpose for my comparison?
	☐ Do my points suit the purpose I have established?
	☐ Have I cut any points that do not support my thesis?
	☐ Should I add more points to support my thesis?
	☐ Have I checked my paper against my outline to make sure it is arranged logically?
	☐ Does my conclusion bring my paper to a logical ending?
Proofread the paper.	☐ Have I proofread for grammar, spelling, and mechanics?

CROSSCURRENTS

Judy Brady and Barbara Ehrenreich present views on the relations between men and women and the differences between the sexes. Write an essay in which you compare and contrast the essential points in "I Want a Wife" (pages 190–192) and "What I've Learned from Men" (pages 185–188).

COLLABORATIVE LEARNING

In groups of three to five students, discuss the student essays "In the Swim" (pages 225–226) and "Two Jobs" (pages 228–229). Look particularly at the relations between the outlines presented and the essays themselves. In what ways did the writers use the outlines successfully in developing the papers? What suggestions can the group make for improving the outlines? The essays?

For support in meeting this chapter's objectives, follow this path in MyCompLab: Resources ⇒ Writing ⇒ Writing Purposes ⇒ Writing to Compare or Contrast. Review the Instruction and Multimedia resources about writing to compare, then complete the Exercises and click on Gradebook to measure your progress.

CHAPTER **12**

Classification and Division

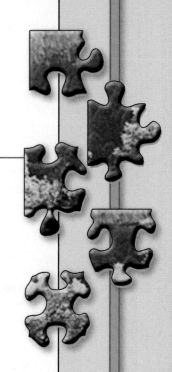

Classification and division are among humanity's most advanced, yet most basic, modes of thought. These thinking skills allow us to see relations among parts and so make the world around us more comprehensible.

Classification and Division in Action

Saturday night is just around the corner, and you've decided to spend a quiet evening at home—cook some pasta, make a salad, stream a movie onto your computer, and pick up the latest Stephen King book for a little nighttime terror before bed. If you're walking, biking, driving, or taking a bus, you're already plotting the most efficient route. Maybe in your dorm room you take a look first online at Netflix for a movie rental, then it's a trip to Pathmark Supermarket, and finally a visit to the local library.

At Netflix you see different groups of films at the site—new releases, comedies, adventure classics, romances, and others. You decide on *The Hangover*—you've seen it at least twice before, but its antics seem to be the perfect antidote to Stephen King. So you jump to the comedies section and click to select it. There's a two-for-one special—well, maybe you'll be bored the third time around with Zach Galifianakis, Ed Helms, and Bradley Cooper and company—so you click over to the adventure classics section; your friend Miguel has been raving about *Saving Private Ryan*, a World War II film that he loves. You arrange for streaming both films.

When you get to Pathmark, your first stop is at the produce area for the makings of a small salad, then to the boxes of macaroni and spaghetti piled high in the pasta section (it's linguine tonight, you've decided), and then over to the shelves marked "Sauces" for a jar of Ronzoni's marinara sauce. Finally, you go to the frozen food section, check out the ice-cream bin, and pick Ben and Jerry's Cherry Garcia.

In this chapter you will

- distinguish between classification and division as rhetorical modes

- identify a topic and write your own classification paper

- analyze student classification essays

- identify the strategies for writing a classification paper

- explore the use of classification in writing from the world around you

- analyze the use of classification in writing by professionals

Off to the library then; inside this branch has a section called New Releases near the checkout desk. You look for the King book and note that one copy is in the group of books to rent with a daily fee and another copy in the group of free books—from which you grab your copy and head home.

Using Division (or Analysis)

When you established your method for picking up the various items you needed for Saturday night at home, you used *division*, maybe even unconsciously. You considered the whole map of your town or neighborhood and divided it into separate units to make your trip easier. The dorm room computer, the supermarket, the library—these are the sections of your larger surrounding geography. When you divide, you break down something (here, your town or neighborhood) into parts or sections. Your purpose in dividing was for ease of transport and so you divided the entity into units that served your purpose. Clearly, many other possibilities exist for dividing the neighborhood you live in, all depending on the purpose for the division. You could separate the neighborhood by the way people vote in elections; by the ethnic makeup of various sections; by the architectural varieties of buildings; by the lawns and flower gardens and what they look like; and by the school districts and the businesses—the options are numerous.

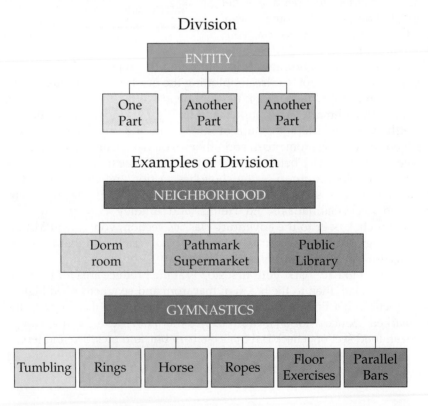

In the process of division—which, incidentally, many people call *analysis*— you break down an entity into its discrete parts, all based on some organizing principle. Division moves from the general to the specific; you look at a large category and try to understand it better by seeing what makes it up. When you analyze a Big Mac, a rock song, a television program, a magazine ad, or a poem, you divide it into distinct elements in order to understand the parts and how they contribute to the whole.

Using Classification

As you scooted around from your dorm room, to the supermarket, to the library, you used a different, but related, thinking skill. When you searched for movies, pasta, vegetables, ice cream, and a King thriller, you relied on *classification*.

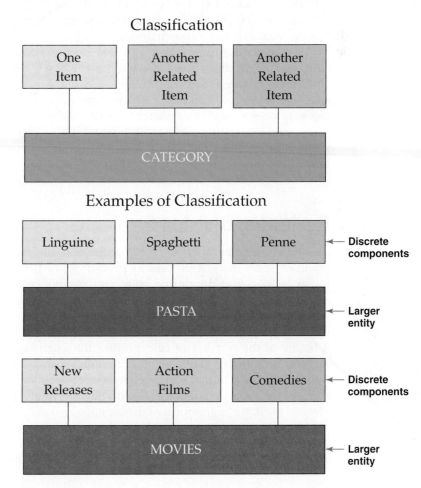

To locate specific items, you had to identify the large group into which someone had placed them. Classification creates large entities from discrete components.

How Are Classification and Division Different?

Do you see the differences? *Division* moves from the larger group to the smaller parts. *Classification* moves from the smaller parts to the larger group. Division and classification as rhetorical strategies often work hand in hand and overlap considerably.

If you wanted to write about preparing for your Saturday night at home, as we've revealed it here, you might explain how you *divided* your surroundings into entities that let you move easily from one stop to the other. Then you'd explain how *classification* at your various stops helped you set up an evening of leisure according to your own design.

To take another example, if you wanted to write about violence on television, you might *divide* the topic into news shows, daytime soap operas, and children's programs. Selecting one or more of these, you might then *classify* the soaps, for example. You might identify categories of violence that you saw on the soap operas, such as violence against children; violence among husbands, wives, and lovers; and violence at the workplace. Each category would require supporting detail to make your classification stick—but we'll have more to say later about how to write your classification essay.

Reviewing Division Strategies

As you've seen, another name for division is *analysis*. When you analyze—a poem or short story, a process or procedure, or the reasons for some behavior or action—you divide the issue into components. In analysis by *division*, you break down a subject usually thought of as a single unit into each one of its parts. An analysis of a stereo system, for example, requires naming and describing each of its components. An analysis of a breakfast cereal requires a listing of the number of calories and the grams of protein, carbohydrates, fat, and sodium in a single serving. An analysis of a process—how to change a lightbulb or how to make iron ore into steel—requires discussing the separate steps of the process. So, in fact, if you have written a process paper, you have already used one major form of division.

If you wrote a literary analysis using comparison–contrast strategies (see pages 245–247), you used division to break the piece of literature into the components that concerned you before you showed similarities and differences.

When you write a cause-and-effect paper, often called *causal analysis* (see Chapter 13), division will help you separate an entity—an event, an action, or a consequence—into components.

We deal, therefore, with analysis (division) in other sections of this book. This chapter focuses on *classification*.

Writing Your Classification Paper

As you have seen, **classification** is the process by which we categorize members of a large group—ideas, people, plants, animals, books, pasta, films, and so on—on the basis of a single principle. Classification enables us to cope with a large body of material by organizing it into smaller, more workable categories. Besides, we all like to classify. We do it naturally. Students classify their professors as boring or stimulating. Homemakers classify their cooking utensils, perhaps as those used often and those used occasionally, and place them in drawers and cupboards accordingly. But whether used for fun or for profit, classification has certain requirements, many of which you have already used in developing outlines.

 TIPS for Writing a Classification Essay

- **Determine the basis for classification and then apply it consistently.** To classify automobiles, you would not want to establish as the categories "foreign cars," "expensive cars," and "sedans" because these classes do not have the same basis of classification. The first class is based on country of origin, the second on price, and the third on body style. A member of one class would be likely to overlap into others. A Rolls-Royce or a Mercedes, for example, could fit into any of the three classes. Logic would require selection of a single basis of classification such as price and then sticking to the issue of price with subclasses like "expensive," "medium-priced," and "low-priced." Likewise, if you were going to classify the courses you are taking according to level of interest, you shouldn't establish as the categories "dull," "moderately interesting," and "difficult." The class "difficult" violates the principle of classification—level of interest, in this case.

- **Define terms that might be unfamiliar to your audience or that are used in a special way.** A writer using technical terms like *mesomorph, ectomorph,* and *endomorph* to describe human body types would need to define those terms. Even familiar terms like *mature* and *immature* or *realistic* and *unrealistic* may often require definitions because their interpretations can vary. Similarly, suppose you invent names for your categories. You might, for instance, classify joggers as red-faced wobblers, short-legged two-steppers, and long-legged striders. You must share with your reader your understanding of these made-up terms.

■ **Decide whether you need only describe each category fully or whether you need to add clarifying examples.** A classification of people as overweight, underweight, and normal, for example, would require merely a complete description of each type. Readers could, on the basis of the description, decide which category the various people they meet belong to. On the other hand, a classification of the present Supreme Court justices as liberals or conservatives, besides giving the characteristics of liberal and conservative justices, should also give the names of the justices who belong to each category and some explanation of why they appear in each group.

■ **Have a thesis.** In one sense, of course, the classification itself provides the basis for a thesis. If you assert that there are three classes of teachers or four classes of pet owners or five classes of social drinkers and can support your assertion, you have a thesis. But as usual, your thesis should express your opinion about or attitude toward your subject. You could show, for example, that one of the categories is preferable to the others, or that all of the categories are silly or despicable or admirable. Having a thesis gives force and interest to your categories.

■ **Establish some kind of order.** In some cases, you can order your categories according to time, from earliest to latest. Or, depending on your thesis, several other possibilities for ordering the categories present themselves. You might order the categories from worst to best, best to worst, least enjoyable to most enjoyable, or weakest to strongest, for example. In most listings, you may have more interesting comments to make about some classes than about others. Arrange your classes so that the less interesting ones are in the middle of your paper. Hook your readers with a strong first category and leave them satisfied with an even stronger last category. The practice of ordering categories will make an important contribution to your classification papers.

■ **Revise your drafts.** As you revise, be sure that the basis for your classification is clear and consistent. Make sure that your details support the categories you have established. Reread Chapter 6 for suggestions about on how to revise your papers.

■ **Proofread carefully.** Edit your essay for your own usual errors after you are satisfied with your revision. Be sure to proofread as well.

ASSIGNMENT: CLASSIFICATION

Write a classification essay in which you break a broad or complex topic into categories according to some logical organizing principle. Be sure to show the special features of each category and also, where appropriate, how the features of each group vary among the categories. Use the tips on pages 253–254 and the student model on pages 256–257 as guides. The following list of subjects may offer you some ideas for a topic for your classification paper. Notice how some subjects can easily be limited further than they are: "Summer jobs" could be limited to summer jobs at resorts, "Outstanding teachers" to outstanding physical education teachers, and so on.

1. Tyrants
2. Attitudes toward Christmas
3. Campus parties
4. Outstanding teachers
5. Summer jobs
6. Major classes of love
7. Automobiles
8. Male or female chauvinists
9. Types of chili (or pizza or burgers)
10. Natural disasters
11. People at a sporting event
12. TV preachers
13. Good drugs
14. Concert goers
15. Voters
16. Holiday gifts
17. Terrorism
18. Shoppers
19. The contents of my handbag (or bookbag or briefcase)
20. Great leaders

Student Writing: Classification

Examine this student's outline and classification essay; use the annotations to guide your reading.

Yvonne C. Younger
Outline for "Tomorrow, Tomorrow"

Thesis: There are many ways to avoid doing anything at all.

I. Classic procrastination

  A. Typical of teenagers

  B. Lying face up and staring at ceiling

  C. No effort needed

  D. Guilt not avoided

II. Childish style

    A. Typical of college students

    B. Play games when responsibilities arrive

    C. Procrastinators show themselves as energetic, not lazy

    D. Costly toys and games for a good time

III. Responsible procrastination

    A. Organized, responsible adults

    B. Find other less unappealing work

    C. Too busy then to do unpleasant chores

    D. Procrastinator is working anyway!

IV. Artistic procrastination

    A. Like classic procrastination

    B. Lying on couch—but awaiting inspiration

    C. Impressive work-avoidance if done properly

    D. Procrastinator still suspected of merely lying on the couch

Yvonne C. Younger
Tomorrow, Tomorrow

1   Up and at 'em. Make hay while the sun shines. Seize the bull by the horns. Never put off 'til tomorrow what can be done today. Just do it. There are scores of ways for people to tell others to get up, get out, and get going. Fortunately, there are just as many ways to completely avoid doing anything at all.

Introduction: Begins to establish the context for classification.

2   Over the past few years I have made a serious and concentrated study of the varied ways to procrastinate. I have discovered that there are as many ways to avoid work as there are people who wish to avoid working. Happily for the length of this essay, however, I have determined that all kinds of procrastination can be divided into four major groups: the classic, the childish, the responsible, and the artistic.

Thesis includes writer's assertion and purpose.

Topic divided; categories identified indicate basis for classification.

First category includes example to explain "classic" procrastination.

The classic type of procrastination is particularly typical of teen-agers. It involves lying face up on a flat surface of the procrastinator's choice—beds, sofas, and floors are popular. The procrastinator then pro-ceeds to count ceiling tiles, trace the path of a wandering spider, or simply gaze at a fixed point off in the distance. The advantage of this procrastina-tion style is that it requires no effort. The disadvantage is that there is noth-ing to distract the work-avoider from the guilt he or she feels at not doing what must be done.

3

Second category and examples.

Procrastinating in the childish style is standard for college students. Faced with an essay to write, a problem set to complete, or a stack of bills to pay, childish procrastinators are overcome with the desire to play. Video games, Legos, and Frisbees are some common tools of this method. The popularity of this style stems at least partly from its ability to convince others that deep down the procrastinator is amusing and energetic, not lazy. Its single drawback is the expense of equipping oneself with enough games and toys to have a really good time.

4

Third category: "responsible" procrastination with illustrative examples.

Those who procrastinate responsibly are liable to be adults with a reputation for being organized and "together." Their approach to avoiding work is to find other, different, less unappealing work to do. To put off filing their taxes, followers of this style will scrub floors, bake endless batches of cookies, alphabetize their CD collections, and even color-code their sock drawers. The advantage of this style is that one is simply too busy to be working at unpleasant chores. The grave disadvantage is that one ends up working anyway.

5

Artistic procrastination is for the creative spirit. On the surface it resembles classic procrastination almost exactly. The work-avoider lies on the couch all day, staring into the distance. However, when accused of procrastinating, the artistic procrastinator looks offended and either explains that he or she is waiting for inspiration to strike, or looks tor-tured and complains that no one understands artistic struggle and true suffering. The best part of this procrastination method is how impressive it can be if done properly. The worst part is that, no matter how con-vincingly it is done, one will always be suspected of simply lying on the couch.

6
Last category: Most interesting group placed last in the essay.

Conclusion links to introduction and thesis.

7   Each type of procrastination has its advantages and disadvantages. Each style is also remarkably good for ignoring and avoiding work. Try them all; perfect your favorite, and never work again.

FOR WRITING OR DISCUSSION

1. What determines the order in which the first three classes are presented?
2. Should the fourth class have been saved for last, or should it have been presented earlier? Why or why not?
3. Which classes make most effective use of specific details? Which class uses specific details least effectively?
4. Where does the essay briefly turn to comparison–contrast writing? Why?
5. Does the author seem to favor any one class above the others? Is there a thesis?
6. Write a classification paper, choosing an undesirable type or person or practice as your subject: spoiled brats, incompetent parents, nags, worriers, bigots, drinkers, smokers, and so on.

HAVING YOUR SAY

Many cultures and societies view procrastination as evil, the devil's work. Yet doing nothing has a large group of followers in our age. What is your view of procrastination? Write an essay in which you take a position on one side or the other of this topic.

Classification
in the World Around You

For thirty years, the U.S. Department of Agriculture has issued guidelines for an appropriate diet for people to stay healthy. The Department uses classification to identify food groups, their essential elements, and the manner in which people should use the groups to advantage. The well-known food guide called "My Pyramid: Steps to a Healthier You" draws on the principles of classification explored in this chapter.

Basis of classification — The presentation takes discrete components, the various food groups, and organizes them under the larger entity of foods for a healthful diet.

Thesis — The food group pyramid identifies food categories—grains, vegetables, fruits, milk, and meat and beans—and their essential elements.

Category descriptions — Every group includes specific details: "dark green veggies like broccoli, spinach, and other dark leafy greens"; "fish, beans, peas, nuts, and seeds."

Visuals — Each color represents a different classification, and the color coordinates with the elements in each group. Drawings of food objects are clarifying examples. The figure ascending the steps highlights the need for exercise.

Order — The categories go from least to most complex food groups, visually from left to right.

Definition of terms — Most language is familiar to readers; "sodium," in parentheses, serves as alternative to "salt"

Your Turn

Check the Web for other classification schemes represented verbally and visually. Look for classifications of automobiles, financial investments, heath plans, or mental or physical illnessed. Make sure that you're looking at a large group broken down into smaller groups so that users will understand them. You might want to look at other food groups diagrams to see which presentation better uses the classification scheme.

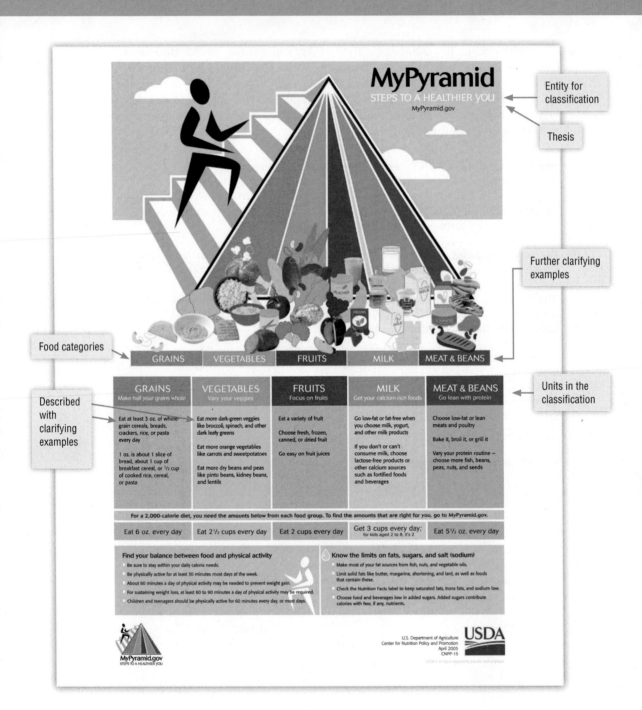

Entity for classification

Thesis

Further clarifying examples

Food categories

Units in the classification

Described with clarifying examples

MyPyramid
STEPS TO A HEALTHIER YOU
MyPyramid.gov

| GRAINS | VEGETABLES | FRUITS | MILK | MEAT & BEANS |

GRAINS	VEGETABLES	FRUITS	MILK	MEAT & BEANS
Make half your grains whole	Vary your veggies	Focus on fruits	Get your calcium-rich foods	Go lean with protein
Eat at least 3 oz. of whole-grain cereals, breads, crackers, rice, or pasta every day 1 oz. is about 1 slice of bread, about 1 cup of breakfast cereal, or ½ cup of cooked rice, cereal, or pasta	Eat more dark-green veggies like broccoli, spinach, and other dark leafy greens Eat more orange vegetables like carrots and sweetpotatoes Eat more dry beans and peas like pinto beans, kidney beans, and lentils	Eat a variety of fruit Choose fresh, frozen, canned, or dried fruit Go easy on fruit juices	Go low-fat or fat-free when you choose milk, yogurt, and other milk products If you don't or can't consume milk, choose lactose-free products or other calcium sources such as fortified foods and beverages	Choose low-fat or lean meats and poultry Bake it, broil it, or grill it Vary your protein routine — choose more fish, beans, peas, nuts, and seeds

For a 2,000-calorie diet, you need the amounts below from each food group. To find the amounts that are right for you, go to MyPyramid.gov.

| Eat 6 oz. every day | Eat 2½ cups every day | Eat 2 cups every day | Get 3 cups every day; for kids aged 2 to 8, it's 2 | Eat 5½ oz. every day |

Find your balance between food and physical activity
- Be sure to stay within your daily calorie needs.
- Be physically active for at least 30 minutes most days of the week.
- About 60 minutes a day of physical activity may be needed to prevent weight gain.
- For sustaining weight loss, at least 60 to 90 minutes a day of physical activity may be required.
- Children and teenagers should be physically active for 60 minutes every day, or most days.

Know the limits on fats, sugars, and salt (sodium)
- Make most of your fat sources from fish, nuts, and vegetable oils.
- Limit solid fats like butter, margarine, shortening, and lard, as well as foods that contain these.
- Check the Nutrition Facts label to keep saturated fats, trans fats, and sodium low.
- Choose food and beverages low in added sugars. Added sugars contribute calories with few, if any, nutrients.

MyPyramid.gov
STEPS TO A HEALTHIER YOU

U.S. Department of Agriculture
Center for Nutrition Policy and Promotion
April 2005
CNPP-15

USDA

Readings for Writing

As you read the following essays, consider how the writers have observed the strategies of classification discussed in this chapter.

JARED SANDBERG

A Brief, Handy Guide to Those Odd Birds in the Upper Branches

Bosses, like birds, come in a wide variety of colorful species, and learning how to iden-   1
tify yours can be instructive and fun. To assist you, I offer "A Field Guide to Bosses," with
apologies to winged friends and special thanks to contributing boss-watchers.

Time-Wasting Sapsucker: This boss mistakes activity for productivity. Can be seen   2
pounding head against the wall like a woodpecker and encouraging others to do same.
A stickler for punctuality, he'll retaliate against latecomers with passive-aggressive
scheduling. Can damage homes as well. Habitat: under your skin. Call: "I have a new
project for you." Says one retired history professor: "No meaningful creative ability, poor
social skills," but leaves a lot of droppings. Not to be confused with the Yellow-Bellied
Fence Sitter, whose preferred habitat is uncertainty.

Winking-Eyed Rooster: A morning person, this cocky strutter manages by fear. He picks   3
on everyone but favors young and weak. Prone to sarcastic clapping. Diets on negatives,
pointless rules and supercilious displays of power. Greets friends by fake-boxing. Habitat:
the spotlight. Call: "Whodda Man?" "Very easy to spot," says software engineer Robert
Czarnecki. "Just listen for shouting."

Pigeon-Toed Thrasher: Common in all climes. Poor long-distance vision and weak   4
sense of direction makes migration impossible. Flits from task to task. Multiple top priorities. Scatters e-mails when alarmed. Mimics every opinion to be right about something.
Like other thrashers, "lots of commotion and precious little accomplishment," says orni-
thologist Charles Duncan. Habitat: thickets. Call: "I knew it!"

Really Red-Faced Cardinal: Ferocious in defense of his place in the pecking order, this   5
boss is so territorial he'll attack his own reflection in windows. Still upset about something that happened decades ago. Prefers unthreatening cohorts and limits their contact
with outsiders. Nostril flare and spitting distinguishes him from a Tanager (see below).
Habitat: behind closed doors. Call: throaty, unpublishable exclamations.

Micro-Tanager: Common control freak that circles the floor and hovers over desks.   6
Has firm, stifling grip. Hoards credit for herself. "She can't let go of things," says the
professor. "She can't believe that any of us are going to do the job the way it needs to
be done." Misdirects others to keep everyone guessing. Habitat: other people's business.
Call: a clipped "I better do it."

Sharp-Tongued Grouse: Grumbler; displays permanent disappointment. Beaten down   7
by superiors and unimpressed with staffers. Feathers always ruffled. "Nothing is ever

good enough," says one research librarian. Stays low to the ground and makes no secret about how he'd run the place, but is too chicken to tell it to bosses. Thinks he's proved himself and shouldn't have to work for advancement. Makes you write your own performance review but never submits it. Habitat: pharmacies and ledges. Call: a plaintive, whining moan.

8   *Puff-Chested Nuthatch:* This boss is a nimble climber. Considered an excellent self-promoter who tells underlings to work hard so he can look good. Desperately tries to be chairman's wingman. Spends "all his time preening his personal image," says spotter Richard Clark. Distinguished from the similar Sharp-Elbowed Loon in that he's not good with names or hallway chatter and is more self-forgiving. Blames lapses on his secretary and thinks she doesn't know it. Habitat: the mirror on his office door. Call: overzealous laughter at CEO's bad jokes, interspersed with a rhythmic "Absolutely."

9   *Eleven-Fingered Vulture:* Loves to chew out people in public. Grabs prime office space from freshly fledged colleagues. Tiny head relative to his body. Tan and leathery, he winters in Boca time-share. "You wouldn't want one as a pet," says Mr. Duncan. Habitat: racquetball courts. Call: "Not much of an athlete, are ya?"

10   *Two-Faced Snipe:* This boss's courtship ritual involves huge promises that are never kept. He will abandon any toady under his wing he suspects is disloyal or ascending. Shows charm but often backstabs and sets up others for failure. Prefers cover of dense brush to open fields. "Virtually no one is safe," says the research librarian, "from verbal lacerations." Eats off of other people's plates. Habitat: mud. Call: a conspiratorial, "C'mere a minute . . ."

11   *Once-Crested Bufflehead:* Walks like a boss, talks like a boss but is really a quack. Had a great idea once and won't let you forget it. Coasts on his own hot air. Gathers periodicals for the men's room. Lengthy pauses during his long tales make you think he's a liar. Says one Los Angeles lawyer: "This boss has advanced as far as he will ever go." Habitat: threadbare laurels. Call: "Once, when I . . ."

12   *Sage Dove:* Tame and approachable, this variety nods while walking. Bright, gregarious and a touch irreverent, solicits opinions from his flock. Commands respect from and for his direct reports. Defers to their expertise. Habitat: out on a limb for you. Call: a reassuring coo. "I'd try to seek out folks like him," says Howard Karten, who last spotted one 30 years ago. "Sadly, they're few and far between—a true *rara avis*."

FOR WRITING OR DISCUSSION

1. What does Sandberg mean by "odd birds"? Why does he say that he is offering readers "A Field Guide to Bosses"? He obviously builds his presentation around an extended metaphor—bosses as birds. Does the metaphor work? Explain your response.

2. What categories does the writer establish in his scheme of classification?

3. Many of the entries that provide supporting detail for each category are sentence fragments. Why has the writer used so many fragments?

4. Obviously, this is a humorous piece. How does the writer accomplish the humor? How does naming the groups after birds contribute to the comic effect?

5. The writer builds his comic presentation on real characteristics of people in charge. Where is Sandberg most accurate in his classification? What bosses do you recognize in these categories?

6. This piece, originally a column in the *Wall Street Journal*, obviously has no conclusion. Why? What would you write in a conclusion for this selection?

7. Write your own classification essay called "A Field Guide to _____" and fill in the blank with some entity you wish to classify—teachers, workers, movies, sports figures, fellow students, or actors, for example. Try your hand at humor, using animals, plants, or some other natural phenomenon to help identify the groups you establish.

JOHN HOLT

Three Kinds of Disciplines

A child, in growing up, may meet and learn from three different kinds of disciplines. The first and most important is what we might call the Discipline of Nature or of Reality. When he is trying to do something real, if he does the wrong thing or doesn't do the right one, he doesn't get the result he wants. If he doesn't pile one block right on top of another, or tries to build on a slanting surface, his tower falls down. If he hits the wrong key, he hears the wrong note. If he doesn't hit the nail squarely on the head, it bends, and he has to pull it out and start with another. If he doesn't measure properly what he is trying to build, it won't open, close, fit, stand up, fly, float, whistle, or do whatever he wants it to do. If he closes his eyes when he swings, he doesn't hit the ball. A child meets this kind of discipline every time he tries to do something, which is why it is so important in school to give children more chances to do things, instead of just reading or listening to someone talk (or pretending to). This discipline is a great teacher. The learner never has to wait long for his answer; it usually comes quickly, often instantly. Also it is clear, and very often points toward the needed correction; from what happened he cannot only see that what he did was wrong, but also why, and what he needs to do instead. Finally, and most important, the giver of the answer, call it Nature, is impersonal, impartial, and indifferent. She does not give opinions, or make judgments; she cannot be wheedled, bullied, or fooled; she does not get angry or disappointed; she does not praise or blame; she does not remember past failures or hold grudges; with her one always gets a fresh start, this time is the one that counts. 1

The next discipline we might call the Discipline of Culture, of Society, of What People Really Do. Man is a social, a cultural animal. Children sense around them this culture, this network of agreements, customs, habits, and rules binding the adults together. They want to understand it and be a part of it. They watch very carefully what people around them 2 are doing and want to do the same. They want to do right, unless they become convinced they can't do right. Thus children rarely misbehave seriously in church, but sit as quietly as they can. The example of all those grownups is contagious. Some mysterious ritual is going on, and children, who like rituals, want to be part of it. In the same way, the little children that I see at concerts or operas, though they may fidget a little, or perhaps take a nap now and then, rarely make any disturbance. With all those grownups sitting there, neither moving nor talking, it is the most natural thing in the world to imitate them. Children who live among adults who are habitually courteous to each other, and to them, will soon learn to be courteous. Children who live surrounded by people who speak a certain way will speak that way, however much we may try to tell them that speaking that way is bad or wrong.

3　　　　The third discipline is the one most people mean when they speak of discipline—the Discipline of Superior Force, of sergeant to private, of "You do what I tell you or I'll make you wish you had." There is bound to be some of this in a child's life. Living as we do surrounded by things that can hurt children, or that children can hurt, we cannot avoid it. We can't afford to let a small child find out from experience the danger of playing in a busy street, or of fooling with the pots on the top of a stove, or of eating up the pills in the medicine cabinet. So, along with other precautions, we say to him, "Don't play in the street, or touch things on the stove, or go into the medicine cabinet, or I'll punish you." Between him and the danger too great for him to imagine we put a lesser danger, but one he can imagine and maybe therefore wants to avoid. He can have no idea of what it would be like to be hit by a car, but he can imagine being shouted at, or spanked, or sent to his room. He avoids these substitutes for the greater danger until he can understand it and avoid it for its own sake. But we ought to use this discipline only when it is necessary to protect the life, health, safety, or well-being of people or other living creatures, or to prevent destruction of things that people care about. We ought not to assume too long, as we usually do, that a child cannot understand the real nature of the danger from which we want to protect him. The sooner he avoids the danger, not to escape our punishment, but as a matter of good sense, the better. He can learn that faster than we think. In Mexico, for example, where people drive their cars with a good deal of spirit, I saw many children no older than five or four walking unattached on the streets. They understood about cars, they knew what to do. A child whose life is full of the threat and fear of punishment is locked into babyhood. There is no way for him to grow up, to learn to take responsibility for his life and acts. Most important of all, we should not assume that having to yield to the threat of our superior force is good for the child's character. It is never good for *anyone's* character. To bow to superior force makes us feel impotent and cowardly for not having had the strength or courage to resist. Worse, it makes us resentful and vengeful. We can hardly wait to make someone pay for our humiliation, yield to us as we were once made to yield. No, if we cannot always avoid using the Discipline of Superior Force, we should at least use it as seldom as we can.

4　　　　There are places where all three disciplines overlap. Any very demanding human activity combines in it the disciplines of Superior Force, of Culture, and of Nature.

The novice will be told, "Do it this way, never mind asking why, just do it that way, that is the way we always do it." But it probably *is* just the way they always do it, and usually for the very good reason that it is a way that has been found to work. Think, for example, of ballet training. The student in a class is told to do this exercise, or that; to stand so; to do this or that with his head, arms, shoulders, abdomen, hips, legs, feet. He is constantly corrected. There is no argument. But behind these seemingly autocratic demands by the teacher lie many decades of custom and tradition, and behind that, the necessities of dancing itself. You cannot make the moves of classical ballet unless over many years you have acquired, and renewed every day, the needed strength and suppleness in scores of muscles and joints. Nor can you do the difficult motions, making them look easy, unless you have learned hundreds of easier ones first. Dance teachers may not always agree on all the details of teaching these strengths and skills. But no novice could learn them all by himself. You could not go for a night or two to watch the ballet and then, without any other knowledge at all, teach yourself how to do it. In the same way, you would be unlikely to learn any complicated and difficult human activity without drawing heavily on the experience of those who know it better. But the point is that the authority of these experts or teachers stems from, grows out of their greater competence and experience, the fact that what they do *works*, not the fact that they happen to be the teacher and as such have the power to kick a student out of the class. And the further point is that children are always and everywhere attracted to that competence, and ready and eager to submit themselves to a discipline that grows out of it. We hear constantly that children will never do anything unless compelled to by bribes or threats. But in their private lives, or in extra-curricular activities in school, in sports, music, drama, art, running a newspaper, and so on, they often submit themselves willingly and wholeheartedly to very intense disciplines, simply because they want to learn to do a given thing well. Our Little-Napoleon football coaches, of whom we have too many and hear far too much, blind us to the fact that millions of children work hard every year getting better at sports and games without coaches barking and yelling at them.

FOR WRITING OR DISCUSSION

1. What are the names of the three kinds of disciplines?
2. Identify the topic sentence in each paragraph.
3. In what kind of discipline are parents and teachers least active? Why?
4. What kind of discipline does the author like least? What are the reasons for his dislike? Is he completely opposed to it?
5. What is the purpose of the last paragraph?
6. Choose some kind of behavior as your subject and write a classification paper titled "Three Kinds of _____." Possible subjects could be nervousness, exercise, studying, arguing, driving, shopping, praying, and so on.

AMARTYA SEN

A World Not Neatly Divided

1   When people talk about clashing civilizations, as so many politicians and academics do now, they can sometimes miss the central issue. The inadequacy of this thesis begins well before we get to the question of whether civilizations must clash. The basic weakness of the theory lies in its program of categorizing people of the world according to a unique, allegedly commanding system of classification. This is problematic because civilizational categories are crude and inconsistent and also because there are other ways of seeing people (linked to politics, language, literature, class, occupation, or other affiliations).

2   The befuddling influence of a singular classification also traps those who dispute the thesis of a clash: To talk about "the Islamic world" or "the Western world" is already to adopt an impoverished vision of humanity as unalterably divided. In fact, civilizations are hard to partition in this way, given the diversities within each society as well as the linkages among different countries and cultures. For example, describing India as a "Hindu civilization" misses the fact that India has more Muslims than any other country except Indonesia and possibly Pakistan. It is futile to try to understand Indian art, literature, music, food, or politics without seeing the extensive interactions across barriers of religious communities. These include Hindus and Muslims, Buddhists, Jains, Sikhs, Parsees, Christians (who have been in India since at least the fourth century, well before England's conversion to Christianity), Jews (present since the fall of Jerusalem), and even atheists and agnostics. Sanskrit has a larger atheistic-literature than exists in any other classical language. Speaking of India as a Hindu civilization may be comforting to the Hindu fundamentalist, but it is an odd reading of India.

3   A similar coarseness can be seen in the other categories invoked, like "the Islamic world." Consider Akbar and Aurangzeb, two Muslim emperors of the Mogul dynasty in India. Aurangzeb tried hard to convert Hindus into Muslims and instituted various policies in that direction, of which taxing the non-Muslims was only one example. In contrast, Akbar reveled in his multiethnic court and pluralist laws, and issued official proclamations insisting that no one "should be interfered with on account of religion" and that "anyone is to be allowed to go over to a religion that pleases him."

4   If a homogeneous view of Islam were to be taken, then only one of these emperors could count as a true Muslim. The Islamic fundamentalist would have no time for Akbar; Prime Minister Tony Blair, given his insistence that tolerance is a defining characteristic of Islam, would have to consider excommunicating Aurangzeb. I expect both Akbar and Aurangzeb would protest, and so would I. A similar crudity is present in the characterization of what is called "Western civilization." Tolerance and individual freedom have certainly been present in European history. But there is no dearth of diversity here, either. When Akbar was making his pronouncements on religious tolerance in Agra, in the 1590's, the Inquisitions were still going on; in 1600, Giordano Bruno was burned at the stake, for heresy, in Campo dei Fiori in Rome.

5   Dividing the world into discrete civilizations is not just crude. It propels us into the absurd belief that this partitioning is natural and necessary and must overwhelm all other

ways of identifying people. That imperious view goes not only against the sentiment that "we human beings are all much the same," but also against the more plausible understanding that we are diversely different. For example, Bangladesh's split from Pakistan was not connected with religion, but with language and politics.

Each of us has many features in our self-conception. Our religion, important as it may be, cannot be an all-engulfing identity. Even a shared poverty can be a source of solidarity across the borders. The kind of division highlighted by, say, the so-called "antiglobalization" protesters—whose movement is, incidentally, one of the most globalized in the world—tries to unite the underdogs of the world economy and goes firmly against religious, national, or "civilizational" lines of division. 6

The main hope of harmony lies not in any imagined uniformity, but in the plurality of our identities, which cut across each other and work against sharp divisions into impenetrable civilizational camps. Political leaders who think and act in terms of sectioning off humanity into various "worlds" stand to make the world more flammable—even when their intentions are very different. They also end up, in the case of civilizations defined by religion, lending authority to religious leaders seen as spokesmen for their "worlds." In the process, other voices are muffled and other concerns silenced. The robbing of our plural identities not only reduces us; it impoverishes the world. 7

FOR WRITING OR DISCUSSION

1. Sen argues against classification, yet his essay does have a structure. What is it? How does he classify?

2. What, according to Sen, is the basic weakness of the thesis of clashing civilizations? What does "singular classification" mean? Why is classifying people in terms of their civilization "crude and inconsistent"?

3. Why does Sen worry particularly about the use of singular classification by political leaders?

4. Write an essay about "singular classifications" that you observe on your current campus, at your high school, or in your neighborhood.

CASS R. SUNSTEIN

How Polarizing Is the Internet?

In 1995 the technology specialist Nicholas Negroponte predicted the emergence of "the Daily Me"—a newspaper that you design personally, with each component carefully screened and chosen in advance. For many of us, Negroponte's prediction is coming true. As a result of the Internet, personalization is everywhere. If you want to read essays arguing that climate change is a fraud and a hoax, or that the American economy is about to collapse, the technology is available to allow you to do exactly that. If you are bored and upset by the topic of genocide, or by recent events in Iraq or Pakistan, you can avoid those 1 subjects entirely. With just a few clicks, you can find dozens of Web sites that show you are quite right to like what you already think.

2   Actually you don't even need to create a Daily Me. With the Internet, it is increasingly easy for others to create one for you. If people know a little bit about you, they can discover, and tell you, what "people like you" tend to like—and they can create a Daily Me, just for you, in a matter of seconds. If your reading habits suggest that you believe that climate change is a fraud, the process of "collaborative filtering" can be used to find a lot of other material that you are inclined to like. Every year filtering and niche marketing becomes more sophisticated and refined. Studies show that on Amazon, many purchasers can be divided into "red-state camps" and "blue-state camps," and those who are in one or another camp receive suitable recommendations, ensuring that people will have plenty of materials that cater to, and support, their predilections.

3   Of course self-sorting is nothing new. Long before the Internet, newspapers and magazines could often be defined in political terms, and many people would flock to those offering congenial points of view. But there is a big difference between a daily newspaper and a Daily Me, and the difference lies in a dramatic increase in the power to fence in and to fence out. Even if they have some kind of political identification, general-interest newspapers and magazines include materials that would not be included in any particular Daily Me; they expose people to topics and points of view that they do not choose in advance. But as a result of the Internet, we live increasingly in an era of enclaves and niches—much of it voluntary, much of it produced by those who think they know, and often do know, what we're likely to like. This raises some obvious questions. If people are sorted into enclaves and niches, what will happen to their views? What are the eventual effects on democracy?

4   To answer these questions, let us put the Internet to one side for a moment and explore an experiment conducted in Colorado in 2005, designed to cast light on the consequences of self-sorting. About 60 Americans were brought together and assembled into a number of groups, each consisting of five or six people. Members of each group were asked to deliberate on three of the most controversial issues of the day: Should states allow same-sex couples to enter into civil unions? Should employers engage in affirmative action by giving a preference to members of traditionally disadvantaged groups? Should the United States sign an international treaty to combat global warming?

5   As the experiment was designed, the groups consisted of "liberal" and "conservative" enclaves—the former from Boulder, the latter from Colorado Springs. It is widely known that Boulder tends to be liberal, and Colorado Springs tends to be conservative. Participants were screened to ensure that they generally conformed to those stereotypes. People were asked to state their opinions anonymously both before and after 15 minutes of group discussion. What was the effect of that discussion?

6   In almost every case, people held more-extreme positions after they spoke with like-minded others. Discussion made civil unions more popular among liberals and less popular among conservatives. Liberals favored an international treaty to control global warming before discussion; they favored it far more strongly after discussion. Conservatives were neutral on that treaty before discussion, but they strongly opposed it after discussion. Liberals, mildly favorable toward affirmative action before discussion,

became strongly favorable toward affirmative action after discussion. Firmly negative about affirmative action before discussion, conservatives became fiercely negative about affirmative action after discussion.

The creation of enclaves of like-minded people had a second effect: It made both liberal groups and conservative groups significantly more homogeneous—and thus squelched diversity. Before people started to talk, many groups displayed a fair amount of internal disagreement on the three issues. The disagreements were greatly reduced as a result of a mere 15-minute discussion. In their anonymous statements, group members showed far more consensus after discussion than before. The discussion greatly widened the rift between liberals and conservatives on all three issues.

The Internet makes it exceedingly easy for people to replicate the Colorado experiment online, whether or not that is what they are trying to do. Those who think that affirmative action is a good idea can, and often do, read reams of material that support their view; they can, and often do, exclude any and all material that argues the other way. Those who dislike carbon taxes can find plenty of arguments to that effect. Many liberals jump from one liberal blog to another, and many conservatives restrict their reading to points of view that they find congenial. In short, those who want to find support for what they already think, and to insulate themselves from disturbing topics and contrary points of view, can do that far more easily than they can if they skim through a decent newspaper or weekly newsmagazine.

A key consequence of this kind of self-sorting is what we might call enclave extremism. When people end up in enclaves of like-minded people, they usually move toward a more extreme point in the direction to which the group's members were originally inclined. Enclave extremism is a special case of the broader phenomenon of group polarization, which extends well beyond politics and occurs as groups adopt a more extreme version of whatever view is antecedently favored by their members.

Why do enclaves, on the Internet and elsewhere, produce political polarization? The first explanation emphasizes the role of information. Suppose that people who tend to oppose nuclear power are exposed to the views of those who agree with them. It stands to reason that such people will find a disproportionately large number of arguments against nuclear power—and a disproportionately small number of arguments in favor of nuclear power. If people are paying attention to one another, the exchange of information should move people further in opposition to nuclear power. This very process was specifically observed in the Colorado experiment, and in our increasingly enclaved world, it is happening every minute of every day.

The second explanation, involving social comparison, begins with the reasonable suggestion that people want to be perceived favorably by other group members. Once they hear what others believe, they often adjust their positions in the direction of the dominant position. Suppose, for example, that people in an Internet discussion group tend to be sharply opposed to the idea of civil unions for same-sex couples, and that they also want to seem to be sharply opposed to such unions. If they are speaking with people who are also sharply opposed to these things, they are likely to shift in the direction of even sharper opposition as a result of learning what others think.

The final explanation is the most subtle, and probably the most important. The starting point here is that on many issues, most of us are really not sure what we think. Our lack

7

8

9

10

11

12

of certainty inclines us toward the middle. Outside of enclaves, moderation is the usual path. Now imagine that people find themselves in enclaves in which they exclusively hear from others who think as they do. As a result, their confidence typically grows, and they become more extreme in their beliefs. Corroboration, in short, reduces tentativeness, and an increase in confidence produces extremism. Enclave extremism is particularly likely to occur on the Internet because people can so easily find niches of like-minded types—and discover that their own tentative view is shared by others.

13   It would be foolish to say, from the mere fact of extreme movements, that people have moved in the wrong direction. After all, the more extreme tendency might be better rather than worse. Increased extremism, fed by discussions among like-minded people, has helped fuel many movements of great value—including, for example, the civil-rights movement, the antislavery movement, the antigenocide movement, the attack on communism in Eastern Europe, and the movement for gender equality. A special advantage of Internet enclaves is that they promote the development of positions that would otherwise be invisible, silenced, or squelched in general debate. Even if enclave extremism is at work—perhaps *because* enclave extremism is at work—discussions among like-minded people can provide a wide range of social benefits, not least because they greatly enrich the social "argument pool." The Internet can be extremely valuable here.

14   But there is also a serious danger, which is that people will move to positions that lack merit but are predictable consequences of the particular circumstances of their self-sorting. And it is impossible to say whether those who sort themselves into enclaves of like-minded people will move in a direction that is desirable for society at large, or even for the members of each enclave. It is easy to think of examples to the contrary—the rise of Nazism, terrorism, and cults of various sorts. There is a general risk that those who flock together, on the Internet or elsewhere, will end up both confident and wrong, simply because they have not been sufficiently exposed to counterarguments. They may even think of their fellow citizens as opponents or adversaries in some kind of "war."

15   The Internet makes it easy for people to create separate communities and niches, and in a free society, much can be said on behalf of both. They can make life a lot more fun; they can reduce loneliness and spur creativity. They can even promote democratic self-government, because enclaves are indispensable for incubating new ideas and perspectives that can strengthen public debate. But it is important to understand that countless editions of the Daily Me can also produce serious problems of mutual suspicion, unjustified rage, and social fragmentation—and that these problems will result from the reliable logic of social interactions.

FOR WRITING OR DISCUSSION

1. What is Sunstein's thesis? What is the significance of "the Daily Me"?

2. What two basic categories does the writer establish in regard to "personalization"?

3. In what ways does the Colorado experiment of 2005 contribute to the essay? How does the experiment classify modes of thinking?

4. How does the Internet polarize people into groups?

5. What are "enclaves" and "niches"? How do they serve the strategy of classification?

6. What dangers does Sunstein see for self-sorting as permitted by the Internet?

7. What is the function of the conclusion in this essay? How does it serve to summarize two essential positions regarding the Internet?

8. Write an essay on what you see as the strengths or weaknesses of the Internet. Try to classify the elements in your position and then provide examples of each.

Reading and Writing About Poetry

Robert Frost writes playfully about a classification scheme that turns into an understated assertion of regard.

ROBERT FROST

The Rose Family

The rose is a rose,
And was always a rose.
But the theory now goes
That the apple's a rose,
And the pear is, and so's
The plum, I suppose.
The dear only knows
What will next prove a rose.
You, of course, are a rose—
But were always a rose.

FOR WRITING OR DISCUSSION

1. Frost has taken a literal classification system and used it to reach a larger assertion, which comes off as wonderful and humorous understatement. The botanical category Rosacaea includes the fruits named in lines 4–6. How does Frost use this fact to structure the poem?

2. What is the purpose of the last two lines? The title?

3. What do lines 7–8 mean?

4. In what ways is "The Rose Family" a love poem?

5. Write a classification essay in which you establish a broad category and explain what should and should not be included in the group. For example, you might want to classify teachers, cousins, rock music, film idols, or novels.

STRATEGY CHECKLIST: Writing and Revising Your Classification Paper

Plan the paper.	☐ Have I used prewriting to identify a topic for classification?
	☐ Have I determined a basis for my classification that allows a logical grouping?
	☐ Have I thought carefully about my purpose in writing the classification essay?
	☐ Do I have my audience clearly in mind?
	☐ Have I used an outline to identify groups and suggest examples in each group?
Write a first draft.	☐ Have I written a thesis that expresses an opinion about the topic I will develop through classification?
	☐ Have I identified the reason for the classification in my introduction?
	☐ Have I explained each category with sufficient examples and details?
	☐ Have I determined an effective order for the categories: time order, least to most important, most to least important, best to worst, worst to best?
Revise and edit the paper.	☐ Have I sought peer feedback to assure that my categories make sense?
	☐ Have I checked to see that categories do not overlap?
	☐ Should I add any examples, details, or categories to improve my paper?
	☐ Should I eliminate any examples, details, or categories to improve my paper?
Proofread the paper.	☐ Have I proofread for grammar, spelling, and mechanics?

CROSSCURRENTS

John Holt's "Three Kinds of Discipline" (pages 263–265) and Susan Douglas's "Remote Control: How to Raise a Media Skeptic" (pages 216–217) both deal with rearing children. What would Holt say to Douglas? What would she say to him?

COLLABORATIVE LEARNING

Read or reread the professional essays included in this chapter: "A Brief, Handy Guide to Those Odd Birds in the Upper Branches," "Three Kinds of Disciplines," "A World Not Neatly Divided," and "How Polarizing Is the Internet?" Which of the essays does your group think better embodies the principles of good classification papers? What elements do you point to as contributing to the success of the essays? In what ways does the best essay reflect the points on pages 253–254?

For additional help with writing, reading, and research, go to www.mycomplab.com

CHAPTER **13**

Cause and Effect

In this chapter you will

- identify the strategies for writing a cause-and-effect paper

- analyze student cause-and-effect essays

- identify a topic and write your own cause-and-effect paper

- explore the use of cause and effect in writing from the world around you

- analyze the use of cause and effect in writing by professionals

Many of the papers you write in college will require analysis of causes or circumstances that lead to a given result: Why does the cost of living continue to rise? Why do people with symptoms of cancer or heart disease put off consulting a doctor? In questions of this type, the **effect** or result is given, at least briefly. Your job is to analyze the causes that produce the effect.

Other assignments will require that you discuss the results of a particular case: What are the positive and negative effects of legalizing lotteries? What are the effects of giving direct legislative power to the people? What is the effect of noise pollution on our bodies? In questions of this type, the **cause** is given, and you must determine the effects that might result or have resulted from the cause.

Writing Your Cause-and-Effect Paper

Cause-and-effect papers do not call for the rigid structure demanded of classification and process papers. Nevertheless, writers must meet some logical demands.

 TIPS for Writing a Cause-and-Effect Essay

- **Do not confuse cause with process.** A process paper tells *how* an event or product came about; a cause-and-effect paper tells *why* something happened.

■ **Avoid the *post hoc* fallacy.** That a man lost his billfold shortly after walking under a ladder does not mean that walking under the ladder caused his loss. Similarly, that a woman lost her hearing shortly after attending a loud rock concert does not prove that her deafness is a direct result of the band's decibel level. (See the discussion of *post hoc* fallacies in Chapter 15 on pages 325–326.)

■ **Understand your options for writing a cause-and-effect paper.** As we've pointed out, you can look at an event, a situation, or an activity and ask why it happened. Or you can look at an event, a situation, or an activity and ask what happened or will happen as a result of it:

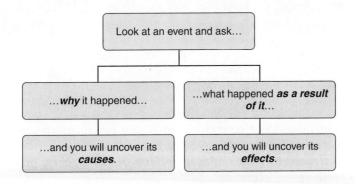

If you wanted to write about the **causes** of World War II, for example, early prewriting activity might produce the following:

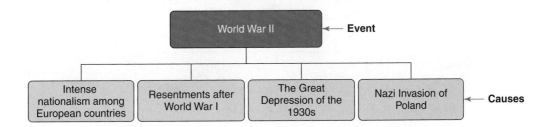

In writing about these causes, you'd expand on each of them, providing specific detail to support each point. Sometimes to explain an event you will find that the causes are connected. One cause brings about a result, which in turn becomes another cause that brings about another result—a kind of chain reaction. All of these *linked causes* finally produce the effect that you are analyzing. In explaining the causes of war, Sigmund Freud, the renowned psychologist, suggested these linked causes:

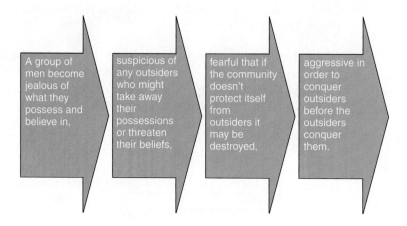

A group of men become jealous of what they possess and believe in,

suspicious of any outsiders who might take away their possessions or threaten their beliefs,

fearful that if the community doesn't protect itself from outsiders it may be destroyed,

aggressive in order to conquer outsiders before the outsiders conquer them.

The causes clearly are connected: each one produces an effect, which then becomes a cause for something else to happen.

If you wanted to write about the **effects** of WWII, early prewriting activity might produce the following:

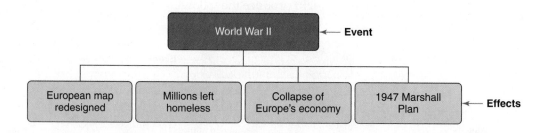

World War II ← **Event**

European map redesigned

Millions left homeless

Collapse of Europe's economy

1947 Marshall Plan ← **Effects**

Here, too, you would expand each effect with supporting details.

- **Write a clearly focused thesis.** Once you decide on your approach, be sure that you develop a thesis that covers the causes or effects that you're writing about. The thesis sentences below come from student essays that you will read later in the chapter. Notice how each one clearly suggests its approach to the essay.

Thesis	Essay Approach
External factors as well as some bad personal decisions all contributed to my school problems.	The writer will identify the causes for his lack of school success.
Banning same-sex marriage is unconstitutional, for reasons faulty and unjustifiable, and defeat is necessary to uphold American values.	The writer will identify the faulty and unjustifiable causes for people's beliefs in banning same-sex marriage and the reasons that defeating such a ban is necessary in regard to American values.

- **Pay careful attention to your purpose in writing.** You can view almost any event or situation in terms of what brought it about and what will happen as a result of it. As a writer, you want to be sure that you know what your intent is so that you can pursue the appropriate causes or effects of your selected topic. Explaining both causes *and* effects requires careful pruning of ideas. Given the length requirements of your paper, the time that you have to complete it, and the demands of your topic, you want to be sure to cover enough—but not too much—territory. You'll note in Richard Yee's paper on same-sex marriages on pages 282–284 that he balances causes and effects carefully so as not to overreach in his essay.

- **Tread lightly with "what might happen" approaches.** It's one thing to look at an event and present causes or effects that you can support with accurate details because the event occurred some time in the past and the root causes are available for scrutiny. It's another thing to present possible effects—ones that have not occurred but that you *think* might occur. If you are presenting possible effects, make sure that you invest them with strong logic or research or past behaviors—or a combination of these elements. If you think that a meteor's landing on the earth will bring thousands of little green aliens, you'd be skating on very thin ice. On the other hand, if you said that a meteor landing on earth would cause an intense sulfurous odor that might sicken people nearby, you'd be reflecting a more accurate possibility; such an outcome occurred when a meteor landed in Peru in 2007.

- **Do not oversimplify causes.** Getting a good night's sleep before an exam doesn't cause a student to receive the highest grade in the class. The rest certainly won't do any harm, but familiarity with the material covered on the exam, intelligence, and an ability to write also have something to do with the grade. Almost all effects worth writing about have more than one cause.

- **Do not oversimplify effects.** Even though it may be true that many people lose money by gambling on lotteries, that does not mean legalizing lotteries will result in nationwide bankruptcy.

■ **Follow an established pattern of organization.**   Once you have determined the causes or effects that you wish to discuss, you can organize your paper in several ways. In a paper devoted primarily to cause, the simplest way to open is to identify the effect in the introduction, then to develop the reasons for that effect in the body of the paper. If, for example, you want to explain a recent rise in the cost of living, you might begin with an indication of the rise (effect)—the cost of living has risen dramatically during the past three years and promises to go even higher in the coming year—before dealing with the causes. Similarly, a paper devoted primarily to effect usually begins with a description of the cause. If your subject is the probable effects of a proposed tax increase, you might begin with a description of the proposal itself (cause) before discussing effects.

In some cases, as when cause and effect are of approximately equal concern, you may want to present one dramatic instance of an effect to open the paper. For example, you might begin a paper on ocean pollution with a description of the infamous 2010 oil spill in the Gulf of Mexico, a striking example of oil pollution. The rest of the introduction would lead into the causes, or sources, of ocean pollution in general. The first major division of what follows might list several important causes other than oil spillage, and the second major division might detail the effects of those causes: extermination of sea life, danger to public health, and so on.

ASSIGNMENT: CAUSE AND EFFECT

Write a cause-and-effect essay in which you examine an event, a situation, an activity, or an idea for its causes and (or) effects. What brought about the event? What consequences resulted from it? Use the tips on pages 274–278 and the student models on pages 280–284 as guides. If you cannot easily decide on a topic for your cause-and-effect paper, you might want to try one or more of the following suggestions. You can treat most of the subjects as material for a cause-only, effect-only, or cause-and-effect paper.

1. One of your personality quirks
2. Effects of going to college
3. Why people smoke cigarettes despite their proven dangers
4. A change of mind about something or someone
5. The popularity of Christian bands in mainstream music
6. Results of the loss of Democratic Party seats in Congress in the 2010 midterm elections
7. Growth or decrease in the popularity of a style of music
8. Same-sex marriage
9. Growth or decrease in the popularity of a clothing style

10. Street gangs
11. Why sexism remains a problem
12. Global warming
13. Teaching preschoolers to read
14. Emphasis on computers in American schools
15. Why teenagers drink alcohol
16. Blind dates
17. Excessively strict or lenient parents
18. Internet spam
19. Election fraud
20. World hunger

Student Writing: Cause and Effect

The student's outline and the annotations on this paper will help you see key features of this cause-and-effect essay.

Richard S. Smith

Outline for "Cause for Failure"

Thesis: External factors as well as bad personal decisions all contributed to my school problems.

I. Difficulties at home with Mother

    A.   Didn't keep after me

    B.   Little energy after her hard day's work

    C.   Furious at our failures

II. Friends no help

    A.   Not the studying kind

    B.   Cut classes regularly

    C.   No diplomas

III. No connection between school and life

    A.   Algebra and Civil War instruction boring

    B.   Didn't know what educated person was

    C.   Always wanted immediate payoff

IV. Finding a job

    A.   Stockboy getting nowhere

    B.   No other jobs

    C.   No education, no diploma

V. Finally getting an education

    A.   Passed high school equivalency

    B.   Business major now at community college

Richard S. Smith
Cause for Failure

1   I was never a good student and never thought twice about it until I had to face the reality of putting together a life for myself. When I try to understand my years of failure in school, I can come up with some answers, now that I'm finally in college and serious about my work. External factors as well as some bad personal decisions all contributed to my school problems.

Introductory paragraph presents thesis.

2   In the first place, things were not easy at home. I'm not trying to lay the blame of my past failures on my home life—I hate people who are constantly making excuses for themselves because other people created trouble for them. Nevertheless, I know that family tensions didn't help my school record. For much of my childhood five of us lived in a small, dark apartment on Sutter Avenue. My father died when I was five, and my mother's energy after a day of packing chemicals at a local factory was too low for her to keep after me. After dinner, her eyelids drooping with exhaustion, she would stretch out on an old brown sofa before the television, and my sisters and I would sit beside her. We never heard a word about doing homework or opening our books. At report card time she was always furious with our failures, but I think she knew that she just had no strength to push us forward. She couldn't even find the strength to push herself.

Transition "In the first place" opens second paragraph as writer states the first cause.

Cause developed with images and explanation.

3   My friends were no help either. They certainly were not the studying kind. On spring afternoons we would cut high school classes regularly, smoking and rapping in my friend Jerry's old Ford or dribbling lay-ups at the basketball courts in Hillcrest Park. I read a survey by the U.S. Department of Education that showed that fewer than two-thirds of my generation's high school students ever graduated, but in my group of eight students not one of us received a diploma. And we couldn't have cared less!

Next cause introduced. Word "either" serves as transition that lends coherence to paper.

Cause developed with details.

Another cause identified: "most important reason" establishes principle of arrangement in essay.

Perhaps the most important reason for my failures, though, was that I 4
never saw (or maybe it's more accurate to say that I never allowed myself
to see) a connection between what we did at our scratched wooden desks
and what was waiting for us beyond our high school days. I don't think that
I ever believed Mrs. Allen's pages of algebra homework or Mr. Delaney's
boring lectures on the Civil War had any real meaning for me. What did
this have to do with my life? I had no concept then of what an educated
person was supposed to know or understand. Everything to me had to
have an immediate payoff. What good would knowing an equation or the
Emancipation Proclamation do for me?

Writer identifies effects of his failure in school as he builds toward conclusion.

And then I tried to find a job. I worked for a few years as a stockboy 5
without getting anywhere. Lugging up cartons of Coke and boxes of toilet
tissue from the basement of Foodtown was not my idea of a future. I tried
finding other jobs without success. In my case, I suppose it was both the
lack of a diploma and the lack of an education that held me back. I started
studying for the high school equivalency exam and passed it on the first try.

As a business major now at my community college, I know that there 6
are no guarantees about my life from now on, but at least a college degree
may open doors that people slammed in my face before. And I'm trying to
see myself as getting educated. Maybe those courses in social science
and literature will shape my thinking and help me later on.

FOR WRITING OR DISCUSSION

1. What is the thesis of Smith's paper?
2. What pattern of organization does the writer use in this essay?
3. Are the causes the writer gives reasonable explanations for his school failures? Defend your response.
4. What images does the writer provide to help you envision the scene?
5. Think of your own pattern of successes and failures at school and write a paper that analyzes its causes.

Researched Student Writing: Cause and Effect

Note how the writer uses details drawn from source materials to produce a forceful cause and effect essay on same-sex marriage. Since Richard Yee wrote this piece, California rescinded approval of marriage for gay men and women.

Five states other than Massachusetts—New York, Connecticut, New Hampshire, Vermont, and Iowa—in addition to Washington, D.C., now allow same-sex marriage.

Richard Yee

Banning Same-Sex Marriage: An Attack on the American Institution

1   In its relatively short lifetime, the United States of America has faced numerous issues concerning discrimination and equality, conquering differences in race, religion, and gender. Today, the American people confront yet another field of controversy: sexual orientation. Homosexuality, once considered an unspeakable topic, has gradually found its way into television, cinema, and modern society and presently struggles to find its place in the nation's legal system. Massachusetts and California are currently the only states that allow the marriage of homosexuals; other states prohibit gay marriage or permit only civil unions. A proposed constitutional amendment banning same-sex marriage nationwide is now the subject of heated debate. Advocates are concerned about the protection of tradition and society, but from a legal and ethical standpoint, the proposition is erroneous and unjust. Banning same-sex marriage is unconstitutional, for reasons faulty and unjustifiable, and defeat is necessary to uphold American values.

2   Proponents of the ban, including President George W. Bush, argue that gay marriage threatens the sanctity of marriage. They claim that marriage is strictly a religious tradition intended to be between a man and a woman, and allowing homosexuals to take part would destroy the sacred institution and eventually society as a whole. Not only is this position a drastic exaggeration, it conflicts with the separation of church and state described in the federal constitution, which ensures the division of religion and government. While marriage may have originated in religion, it has since become a social custom and a basic human right. As Allen Snyder notes, a provision limiting marriage to a group of people on the sole basis of religion would violate the First Amendment (1). Moreover, the notion that gay marriage would lead to the breakdown of marriage and society is a foolish overstatement. Massachusetts and other parts of the world have shown no signs of total destruction since legalizing same-sex marriage. Extending the institution of marriage to homosexuals does not prevent heterosexuals from marrying, nor does it harm the structure of society. Banning it is unconstitutional, and the fears of allowing it are irrational.

3   Supporters of the amendment also argue that the main purpose of marriage is to encourage procreation, something homosexuals are incapable of. Joanna

Grossman counters that, under this definition, opposite-sex couples who are infertile or choose not to have children should not engage in marriage as well (3). Others claim that the best setting for raising children is in a family with opposite-sex parents. However, as Grossman rebuts, many conventional families consist of neglectful or incompetent parents, and no evidence indicates that a gay couple would be better or worse parents than a straight couple (3). In fact, Andrew Sullivan describes same-sex marriage as "pro-family, uniting those gay family members with their siblings and parents in the unifying ritual of civil marriage" (78). It does not endanger traditional marriage, but rather strengthens it by expanding the institution to encompass additional members. According to Sullivan, homosexuals do not intend to steal or demolish marriage; they only desire to participate in a celebrated practice that calls for "fidelity, responsibility and commitment" (78). Those who suggest gays do not satisfy the qualifications for marriage have apparently forgotten about love, the true reason marriage exists.

4   Yet the ban's greatest problem is not its unconstitutionality or unwarranted motives, but rather its disregard for what America stands for. This nation has strived to promote the equality of opportunity and personal liberty of all, regardless of sex, race, or creed; sexual orientation, a major component of one's individuality, should be no different. It would be un-American to restrict the rights of a particular group of people merely because of who they are. If an act does not harm or negatively affect anyone in any way, then no legitimate reason exists to prohibit it. Hence, forbidding same-sex marriage is a blatant form of discrimination, overlooking widely shared American values. Homosexuals are American citizens and deserve to be treated like American citizens. They have the right to pursue happiness even if the manner in which they do so differs from the social norm. Instead of devising ways to divide America through its differences, a true patriot would unite the nation by embracing its differences. One does not need to agree with or accept homosexuality in order to respect it. By attacking same-sex marriage, one is disrespecting homosexuality as a whole, and, in a way, disrespecting America.

5   Those who oppose gay marriage have made passionate cases from various perspectives, but they all fail under the weight of reason. Limiting marriage for the purpose of protecting its sanctity is a violation of the federal constitution, and the supposed intentions and objectives of those favoring heterosexuals are close-minded and inconsistent. Giving homosexuals the right to marry poses no threat to heterosexual marriage, nor does it jeopardize the fabric of society. Not only does

same-sex marriage benefit society by spreading the joy and obligations of marriage, it is necessary to preserve the fundamental values and beliefs of the nation. As seen in the past, original intentions cease to matter in a continually changing world. What cannot change, however, are the basic principles that make up the foundation of society, and such change is exactly what this constitutional ban will do. What is at stake here is not the institution of marriage, but the institution of America. Denying citizens the right to pursue happiness may not lead to the downfall of civilization, but it would certainly halt centuries of social progress.

Works Cited

Grossman, Joanna. "Are Bans on Same-Sex Marriage Constitutional?" *FindLaw.* Thomson Reuters, 20 Nov. 2003. Web. 18 Jan. 2010.

Snyder, Allen. "Banning Same-Sex Marriage Violates Church-State Separation." *OpEdNews.com.* OpEdNews, 14 Mar. 2004. Web. 18 Jan. 2010.

Sullivan, Andrew. "If at First You Don't Succeed . . . ." *Time,* 26 July 2004: 78. Print.

FOR WRITING OR DISCUSSION

1. What is the writer's thesis? Which sentence in the essay best states the thesis? How does the title reinforce it?

2. What reasons does the writer give for people who would ban same-sex marriage? In what ways is this an effort to deal with causes?

3. What does Yee indicate as results of not banning gay marriage?

4. What does Yee see as the greatest problem of any ban on same-sex marriage? In what ways is his explanation an effort to explore what might result from such a ban?

5. Select an important social issue such as teenage drinking, legalizing marijuana use, or lowering the voting or driving age, for example, and write an essay explaining why we should change the current laws or keep them intact. Make your dominant approach causes and (or) effects.

HAVING YOUR SAY

What is your view on whether gay people and others of untraditional sexual orientation require special treatment under the law? You might want to read the Supreme Court decision written by Justice John Paul Stevens in the *Romer v. Evans* case [116 S. Ct. 1620 (1996)], as well as the dissenting opinion by Justice Antonin Scalia.

Cause and Effect in the World Around You

The way that we understand the events in our lives and in years and centuries past relies heavily on cause and effect analysis. From the time they learn to talk, young children bombard adults with why, daddy? or why, mommy? questions. As adults we struggle to find motivations for puzzling or delightful or deplorable happenings from the mundane to the bizarre. Why did eight-year old Johnny eat those worms? Why did Bill Gates, the Microsoft mogul, donate millions for technology in the schools? Why did terrorists bomb the Trade Center in New York City on September 11, 2001? And we also seek to root out the effects of occurrences. What happened to the worm-eating child? What resulted from the Gates investment in education? What were the results of the 9–11 bombing?

In thinking through events like these, cause and effect strategies move us ahead. We want answers, and the answers help us prepare for future events. In this selection from an on-line Web site, note how the sponsors draw on some of the elements we have examined in this chapter.

Thesis — The main point of the piece is to explore the effects of second-hand smoke. The title reinforces the thesis, as does the second paragraph.

Organization — The writer has identified the effect in the introduction and has then enumerated the effects to explain it.

Effects, not process — This is not a "how-to quit smoking" article, which, of course, is easy to find in magazines, brochures, and videos. The content of the site tries to get at the effects of second-hand smoke.

Multiple effects — Although the effects are not linked, note how the writer does not oversimplify them. The piece identifies several different effects.

Details — The bulleted list draws attention to the basic effects of second-hand smoke; the rest of the Web site expands on the general point with appropriate details.

Audience and purpose — The selection focuses on adults who smoke. A section for parents helps them see what effects second-hand smoke could have on their children. The writer wishes to deal with only effects of second-hand smoking, not its causes.

Your Turn

Go on line to find a site that explores the *causes* of smoking. Write an essay in which you identify the major causes of smoking.

- Home
- Use the Step-by-Step Quit Guide
- Talk to an Expert
- Find Tools to Help You Quit
- Learn About Topics Related to Quitting
  - Benefits of Quitting
  - Depression Basics
  - Medications to Help You Quit
  - • Secondhand Smoke
    - Protecting Your Family
    - Secondhand Smoke Quiz
  - Stress and Smoking
  - Withdrawal

Secondhand Smoke

 SHARE

Health consequences for everyone

Secondhand smoke is the combination of smoke from the burning end of a cigarette and the smoke breathed out by the smoker. When you stand near a smoker or go to a restaurant or home where smoking is allowed, you breathe secondhand smoke.

Secondhand smoke is dangerous. There is no safe amount of secondhand smoke. Breathing secondhand smoke for a short time can hurt your body. Over time, secondhand smoke causes death and disease in kids and adults—even if they do not smoke. — **Thesis**

- Secondhand smoke causes cancer. It has more than 50 chemicals that are known to cause cancer in adults. Secondhand smoke causes lung cancer in people who have never smoked themselves.

- Secondhand smoke causes heart disease. Even a short time in a smoky room has immediate harmful effects on the body. Breathing secondhand smoke makes it more likely that you will get heart disease, have a heart attack, and die early. — **Multiple effects**

- Secondhand smoke can cause breathing problems, like coughing, extra phlegm, wheezing, and shortness of breath.

Babies and kids are hurt by secondhand smoke

Audience is adults who smoke, and might have children

Because their bodies are growing, the poisons in secondhand smoke hurt babies and young kids more than adults.

Babies whose mothers smoke while pregnant are more likely to die from SIDS (sudden infant death syndrome) than babies who do not breathe secondhand smoke. Babies who are exposed to secondhand smoke after birth are also more likely to die from SIDS.

Mothers who breathe secondhand smoke while pregnant are more likely to have a baby weighing 5½ pounds or less. Babies who are born this small are weaker and have a higher risk for many serious health problems.

Babies whose moms smoke while pregnant or who breathe secondhand smoke after birth have weaker lungs than other babies. This increases their risk of many health problems.

Kids whose parents smoke around them get bronchitis and pneumonia more often.

Secondhand smoke causes kids who already have asthma to get more frequent and severe attacks. — **Effects, not process**

Secondhand smoke causes lung problems, including coughing, too much phlegm, wheezing, and breathlessness among school-aged kids.

Kids exposed to secondhand smoke are at increased risk for ear infections. They are also more likely to need surgery to get ear tubes for drainage.

Learn how you can protect your family from secondhand smoke.

For more information, read:
NCI Factsheet, Secondhand Smoke: Questions and Answers
CDC, Secondhand Smoke What It Means To You (PDF)

Source: U.S. Department of Health and Human Services. The Health Consequences of Involuntary Exposure to Tobacco Smoke: A Report of the Surgeon General. Atlanta, GA: U.S. Department of Health and Human Services, Centers for Disease Control and Prevention, Coordinating Center for Health Promotion, National Center for Chronic Disease Prevention and Health Promotion, Office on Smoking and Health, 2006.

Next: Protecting Your Family ❯

Quit Smoking **TODAY!** we can help

"I used to smoke 2 packs a day. Now, I don't even think about lighting up."

Readings for Writing

The readings that follow illustrate different cause-and-effect combinations.

BOB HERBERT

Tweet Less, Kiss More

I was driving from Washington to New York one afternoon on Interstate 95 when a car came zooming up behind me, really flying. I could see in the rearview mirror that the driver was talking on her cellphone. 1

I was about to move to the center lane to get out of her way when she suddenly swerved into that lane herself to pass me on the right—still chatting away. She continued moving dangerously from one lane to another as she sped up the highway. 2

A few days later, I was talking to a guy who commutes every day between New York and New Jersey. He props up his laptop on the front seat so he can watch DVDs while he's driving. 3

"I only do it in traffic," he said. "It's no big deal." 4

Beyond the obvious safety issues, why does anyone want, or need, to be talking constantly on the phone or watching movies (or texting) while driving? I hate to sound so 20th century, but what's wrong with just listening to the radio? The blessed wonders of technology are overwhelming us. We don't control them; they control us. 5

We've got cellphones and BlackBerrys and Kindles and iPads, and we're e-mailing and text-messaging and chatting and tweeting—I used to call it Twittering until I was corrected by high school kids who patiently explained to me, as if I were the village idiot, that the correct term is tweeting. Twittering, tweeting—whatever it is, it sounds like a nervous disorder. 6

This is all part of what I think is one of the weirder aspects of our culture: a heightened freneticism that seems to demand that we be doing, at a minimum, two or three things every single moment of every hour that we're awake. Why is multitasking considered an admirable talent? We could just as easily think of it as a neurotic inability to concentrate for more than three seconds. 7

Why do we have to check our e-mail so many times a day, or keep our ears constantly attached, as if with Krazy Glue, to our cellphones? When you watch the news on cable television, there are often additional stories being scrolled across the bottom of the screen, stock market results blinking on the right of the screen, and promos for upcoming features on the left. These extras often block significant parts of the main item we're supposed to be watching. 8

A friend of mine told me about an engagement party that she had attended. She said it was lovely: a delicious lunch and plenty of Champagne toasts. But all the guests had their cellphones on the luncheon tables and had text-messaged their way through the entire event. 9

ready with this hyperactive behavior, this techno-tyranny and nonstop fre- need to slow down and take a deep breath.

posed to the remarkable technological advances of the past several years. I go back to typewriters and carbon paper and yellowing clips from the news- . I just think that we should treat technology like any other tool. We should control it, bending it to our human purposes.

12   Let's put down at least some of these gadgets and spend a little time just being ourselves. One of the essential problems of our society is that we have a tendency, amid all the crazi-ness that surrounds us, to lose sight of what is truly human in ourselves, and that includes our own individual needs—those very special, mostly nonmaterial things that would fulfill us, give meaning to our lives, enlarge us, and enable us to more easily embrace those around us.

13   There's a character in the August Wilson play "Joe Turner's Come and Gone" who says everyone has a song inside of him or her, and that you lose sight of that song at your peril. If you get out of touch with your song, forget how to sing it, you're bound to end up frus-trated and dissatisfied.

14   As this character says, recalling a time when he was out of touch with his own song, "Something wasn't making my heart smooth and easy."

15   I don't think we can stay in touch with our song by constantly Twittering or tweeting, or thumbing out messages on our BlackBerrys, or piling up virtual friends on Facebook.

16   We need to reduce the speed limits of our lives. We need to savor the trip. Leave the cellphone at home every once in awhile. Try kissing more and tweeting less. And stop talk-ing so much.

17   Listen.

18   Other people have something to say, too. And when they don't, that glorious silence that you hear will have more to say to you than you ever imagined. That is when you will begin to hear your song. That's when your best thoughts take hold, and you become really you.

FOR WRITING OR DISCUSSION

1. What is Herbert's thesis? Which sentence in the essay comes closest to expressing it?

2. What is the purpose of the two anecdotes in the opening paragraphs?

3. What does the writer mean by the title, "Tweet Less, Kiss More"?

4. In what ways is this a cause-and-effect essay?

5. Herbert writes, "We need to slow down and take a deep breath." What does he mean by this statement? Why might you agree or disagree with this point?

6. Write an essay in which you explain what you see as the causes for the ever-present use of texting, tweeting, checking Facebook, or other available technologies among members of today's societies?

HAVING YOUR SAY

Texting while driving is apparently a great hazard, causing automobile accidents and fatalities across the country, despite laws against it. What do you think we should do to prevent it? Or, perhaps you believe that we should continue to allow it. Write an essay in which you take a position on the use of texting while driving an automobile.

CARLL TUCKER

On Splitting

One afternoon recently, two unrelated friends called to tell me that, well, their marriages hadn't made it. One was leaving his wife for another woman. The other was leaving her husband because "we thought it best."

As always after such increasingly common calls, I felt helpless and angry. What had happened to those solemn vows that one of the couples had stammered on a steamy August afternoon three years earlier? And what had happened to the joy my wife and I had sensed when we visited the other couple and their two children last year, the feeling they gave us that here, in this increasingly fractionated world, was a constructive union?

I did not feel anger at my friends personally: Given the era and their feelings, their decisions probably made sense. What angered me was the loss of years and energy. It was an anger similar to that I feel when I see abandoned foundations of building projects—piled bricks and girders and a gash in the ground left to depress the passerby.

When our grandparents married, nobody except scandalous eccentrics divorced. "As long as we both shall live" was no joke. Neither was the trepidation brides felt on the eves of their wedding days. After their vows, couples learned to live with each other—not necessarily because they loved each other, but because they were stuck, and it was better to be stuck comfortably than otherwise.

Most of the external pressures that helped to enforce our grandparents' vows have dissolved. Women can earn money and may enjoy sex, even bear children, without marrying. As divorce becomes more common, the shame attendant on it dissipates. Some divorcés even argue that divorce is beneficial, educational; that the second or third or fifth marriage is "the best." The only reasons left to marry are love, tax advantages, and, for those old-fashioned enough to care about such things, to silence parental kvetching.[1]

In some respects, this freedom can be seen as social progress. Modern couples can flee the corrosive bitterness that made Strindberg's marriages nightmares.[2] Dreiser's Clyde Griffiths might have abandoned his Roberta instead of drowning her.[3]

---

[1] Complaining.
[2] August Strindberg (1849–1912) was a Swedish dramatist.
[3] The reference is to Dreiser's 1925 novel, *An American Tragedy*.

spects, our rapidly rising divorce rate and the declining marriage rate (as
e couples opt to forgo legalities and simply live together) represent a loss.
e of spending a lifetime with a person is seeing each other grow and change.
, it is not possible to see history in the bathroom mirror—gray hairs, crow's
not a change of mind or temperament. Yet, living with another person, it is
impossible not to notice how patterns and attitudes change and not to learn—about yourself and about time—from those perceptions.

8   Perhaps the most poignant victim of the twentieth century is our sense of continuity.
People used to grow up with trees, watch them evolve from saplings to fruit bearers to
gnarled and unproductive grandfathers. Now, unless one is a farmer or a forester, there
is almost no point to planting trees because one is not likely to be there to enjoy their
maturity. We change addresses and occupations and hobbies and lifestyles and spouses
rapidly and readily, much as we change TV channels. In our grandparents' day one committed oneself to certain skills and disciplines and developed them. Carpenters spent lifetimes learning their craft; critics spent lifetimes learning literature. Today, the question
often is not "What do you do?" but "What are you into?" Macrame one week, astrology the
next, health food, philosophy, history, jogging, movies, EST—we flit from "commitment"
to "commitment" like bees among flowers because it is easier to test something than to
master it, easier to buy a new toy than to repair an old one.

9   I feel sorry for what my divorced friends have lost. No matter how earnestly the former spouses try to "keep in touch," no matter how generous the visiting privileges for the
parent who does not win custody of the children, the continuity of their lives has been
broken. The years they spent together have been cut off from the rest of their lives; they
are an isolated memory, no more integral to their past than a snapshot. Intelligent people,
they will compare their next marriages—if they have them—to their first. They may even,
despite not having a long shared past, notice growth. What I pray, though, is that they do
not delude themselves into believing, like so many Americans today, that happiness is only
measurable moment to moment and, in their pursuit of momentary contentment, forsake
the perspectives and consolation of history.

10   There is great joy in watching a tree grow.

FOR WRITING OR DISCUSSION

1. What causes does Tucker give for the increase in divorce? Does the writer
   clearly approve or disapprove of any of these causes?

2. According to Tucker, what are the most negative effects of divorce? Are there
   any possible good effects?

3. Explain how the writer tries to link the rise in divorce rates to general trends in
   American lifestyles.

4. Explain what Tucker means in the last sentence of the essay.

5. Write a paper analyzing the effects of some major decision you've made in your
   life, such as marriage, divorce, or choice of school, job, or place of residence.

MOHAN SIVANAND

Why I Write Wrong

The day I discovered Grammar Check in my new word processor, I was delighted. Grammar Check (GC) is supposed to help you guard against making mistakes in English, including those that would make the best of writers blush.   1

Oops. I can already see a wiggly green line under *writers* in my previous sentence. That's Grammar Check at work. The green wiggly underline is the digital equivalent of a referee throwing a flag.   2

Let's see what's wrong. GC suggests that I change *writers* to *writer's*. As in *writer's block*, I suppose—and that's not much help, is it? Meanwhile, I spot a curvaceous red line under *wiggly* itself. This time it's GC's cousin Spell Check blowing the whistle. Suggested change: *wiggle*.   3

But back to the causes of writer's blush. Grammar Check is very precise. By pressing F7 on the keyboard and clicking on Options then Settings, you can instruct your machine to watch out for Commonly Confused Words, Clichés, Contractions, Jargon, Wordiness, Gender-Specific Words and much, much more.   4

Strange. Not a single wiggle line appeared in the previous sentence despite the wordiness and all those capitals. GC, however, is not happy with my beginning that paragraph with *But*, and recommends I change it to *Nevertheless*.   5

"If you're so smart," I say aloud to GC, "here's something you can't mess around with." I type in a well-known line from Shakespeare: "Friends, Romans, countrymen, lend me your ears; I come to bury Caesar, not to praise him."   6

Oh, dear! GC suggests I change *countrymen* to *fellow citizens*. Friends, Romans, fellow citizens? That is an unkind cut.   7

Maybe I've been unfair. Shakespeare, after all, was a poet. I try a line of prose: "Sorrow came—a gentle sorrow—but not at all in the shape of any disagreeable consciousness."   8

Problem again: wiggle line under *came*. "Verb confusion (no suggestions)," says GC's warning box. "You're the one who is confused," I type. "Jane Austen was the most clear-headed of writers, and she never needed no Grammar Check or Microsoft Word." (Know something? GC hasn't yet spotted my double negative. But cousin SC wants me to change *Austen* to *Austin*. Ah, man, that's smart!)   9

Wait a second. I see a new green wiggle line under *man*. "Gender-Specific Language," I'm warned. The alternatives suggested in place of *man* are *operate* or *staff*.   10

If grammar is a tricky thing, Grammar Check is a downright booby trap. GC must be at a very early stage in its evolution. Something like jellyfish on the scale of living things. ("Likes jellyfish," GC insists.)   11

Nevertheless—although you've paid good money for it—you can always switch off Grammar Check. Better still, throw it out the Windows.   12

G OR DISCUSSION

ys is this a cause-and-effect essay?

vanand's thesis?

rding to the writer, is the effect of Grammar Check and Spell Check on his prose? What would result if the writer followed the instructions of these two language helpers that are part of his word-processing program?

4. How does the writer achieve humor in his piece?

5. Write your own short, humorous cause-and-effect essay called "Why I _____ Wrong." Fill in the blank with a word or phrase of your choice. For example, you might consider using a word like *eat*, *sing*, *talk*, *dance*, *drive*, or *do homework*. Explain the cause of your "wrong" act and indicate some of the consequences of your behavior. Keep a light and humorous tone.

HAVING YOUR SAY

Have computers made our lives simpler or more complicated? Choose one side of the issue and write an essay to support your point of view.

BRENT STAPLES

What Adolescents Miss When We Let Them Grow Up in Cyberspace

1 My 10th-grade heartthrob was the daughter of a fearsome steelworker who struck terror into the hearts of 15-year-old boys. He made it his business to answer the telephone—and so always knew who was calling—and grumbled in the background when the conversation went on too long. Unable to make time by phone, the boy either gave up or appeared at the front door. This meant submitting to the first-degree for which the girl's father was soon to become famous.

2 He greeted me with a crushing handshake, then leaned in close in a transparent attempt to find out whether I was one of those *bad* boys who smoked. He retired to the den during the visit, but cruised by the living room now and then to let me know he was watching. He let up after some weeks, but only after getting across what he expected of a boy who spent time with his daughter and how upset he'd be if I disappointed him.

3 This was my first sustained encounter with an adult outside my family who needed to be convinced of my worth as a person. This, of course, is a crucial part of growing up. Faced with the same challenge today, however, I would probably pass on meeting the girl's father—and outflank him on the Internet.

Thanks to e-mail, online chat rooms and instant messages—which permit private, real-time conversations—adolescents have succeeded at last in shielding their social lives from adult scrutiny. But this comes at a cost. The paradox is that teenagers nowadays are both more connected to the world at large than ever, and more cut off from the social encounters that have historically prepared young people for the move into adulthood. 4

The Internet was billed as a revolutionary method of enriching our social lives and expanding our civic connections. This seems to have worked well for elderly people and others who were isolated before they got access to the World Wide Web. But a growing body of research is showing that the heavy use of the Net actually isolates younger socially connected people who are unwittingly allowing time online to replace face-to-face interaction with their families and friends. 5

Online shopping, checking e-mail and Web surfing—mainly solitary activities—have turned out to be more isolating than watching television, which friends and family often do in groups. Researchers have found that the time spent in direct contact with family members drops by as much as half for every hour we use the Net at home. 6

This should come as no surprise to two-career couples who have seen their domestic lives taken over by e-mail and wireless tethers that keep people working around the clock. But a startling body of research from the Human-Computer Interaction Institute at Carnegie Mellon has shown that heavy Internet use can have a stunting effect outside the home as well. Studies show that gregarious, well-connected people actually lose friends, and experience symptoms of loneliness and depression, after joining discussion groups and other activities. People who communicated with disembodied strangers online found the experience empty and emotionally frustrating but were nonetheless seduced by the novelty of the new medium. As Prof. Robert Kraut, a Carnegie Mellon researcher, told me recently, such people allowed low-quality relationships developed in virtual reality to replace higher-quality relationships in the real world. 7

No group has embraced this socially impoverishing trade-off more enthusiastically than adolescents, many of whom spend most of their free hours cruising the Net in sunless rooms. This hermetic existence has left many of these teenagers with nonexistent social skills—a point widely noted in stories about the computer geeks who rose to prominence in the early days of Silicon Valley. 8

Adolescents are drawn to cyberspace for different reasons than adults. As the writer Michael Lewis observed in his book *Next: The Future Just Happened*, children see the Net as a transformational device that lets them discard quotidian identities for more glamorous ones. Mr. Lewis illustrated the point with Marcus Arnold, who, as a 15-year-old, adopted a pseudonym a few years ago and posed as a 25-year-old legal expert for an Internet information service. Marcus did not feel the least bit guilty, and wasn't deterred, when real world lawyers discovered his secret and accused him of being a fraud. When asked whether he had actually read the law, Marcus responded that he found books "boring," leaving us to conclude that he had learned all he needed to know from his family's big-screen TV. 9

Marcus is a child of the Net, where everyone has a pseudonym, telling a story makes it true and adolescents create older, cooler, more socially powerful selves any time they 10 wish. The ability to slip easily into a new, false self is tailor-made for emotionally fragile adolescents, who can consider a bout of acne or a few excess pounds an unbearable tragedy.

11   But teenagers who spend much of their lives hunched over computer screens miss the socializing, the real world experience that would allow them to leave adolescence behind and grow into adulthood. These vital experiences, like much else, are simply not available in a virtual form.

FOR WRITING OR DISCUSSION

1. What does Staples mean in the title by the phrase "Grow Up in Cyberspace"? How is the phrase an example of a metaphor?
2. What is the purpose of the personal anecdote at the beginning of the essay?
3. How does the writer support his point that heavy Internet use "can have a stunting effect outside the home"?
4. How does Staples use expert testimony in this essay? Are the cited sources reliable? How do you know?
5. Why, according to the writer, are adolescents drawn to cyberspace?
6. How does the last paragraph serve as a statement of Staples' thesis?
7. Write an essay on how cyberspace can be a *positive* influence on adolescents.

Reading and Writing About Poetry

Examine the poem below for its cause-and-effect implications.

A.E. HOUSMAN

"Is my team ploughing…"

'Is my team ploughing,
That I was used to drive
And hear the harness jingle
When I was man alive?'

Ay, the horses trample,
The harness jingles now;
No change though you lie under
The land you used to plough.

'Is football playing
Along the river shore,
With lads to chase the leather,
Now I stand up no more?'

Ay, the ball is flying,
The lads play heart and soul,
The goal stands up, the keeper
Stands up to keep the goal.

'Is my girl happy,
That I thought hard to leave,
And has she tired of weeping
As she lies down at eve?'

Ay, she lies down lightly,
She lies not down to weep:
Your girl is well contented.
Be still, my lad, and sleep.

'Is my friend hearty,
Now I am thin and pine,
And has he found to sleep in
A better bed than mine?'

Yes, lad, I lie easy,
I lie as lads would choose;
I cheer a dead man's sweetheart,
Never ask me whose.

FOR WRITING OR DISCUSSION

1. Who are the speakers in this poem?
2. What causes and effects does the poem draw on?
3. How has the poet created a humorously ironic poem out of a conversation between a dead man and his living friend?
4. Why is the first speaker curious about all the situations that he questions— whether his team of horses is still working the land, whether his friends are still playing soccer, and so on?
5. Write an essay in which you examine the causes and effects in the poem.

STRATEGY CHECKLIST: Writing and Revising Your Cause-and-Effect Paper

Plan the paper.	☐ Have I used prewriting to explore topics?
	☐ Have I identified a topic that I can develop through causal analysis?
	☐ Am I prepared to explain *why* something happened instead of *how* it happened?
	☐ Will my topic lend itself to either causes or effects, or a combination of both?
	☐ Have I thought carefully about my purpose in writing?
	☐ Do I have my audience clearly in mind?
	☐ Have I used an outline to organize my ideas?

Write a first draft.	☐ Have I developed a clear thesis that expresses an opinion about the topic I will develop through cause-and-effect analysis?
	☐ Have I written an introduction that presents the topic and makes clear my focus?
	☐ Have I avoided oversimplifying causes and effects?
	☐ Have I used an appropriate pattern of development in the body paragraphs:
	■ Effects of a single event?
	■ Causes of a single event?
	■ A chain of events (effects) resulting from a particular action or idea?
	■ A chain of events (causes) leading to an outcome?
	■ Causes of an event *and* effects of that event?
	☐ Does my conclusion revisit the thesis and provide an appropriate perspective on the causal issue I'm presenting?

Revise and edit the paper.	☐ Have I sought peer feedback to see whether my causes and effects make sense?
	☐ Are my causes and effects logical in the context of my topic?
	☐ Have I avoided the *post hoc* fallacy (one event preceding another doesn't mean that the first one caused the second)?
	☐ Have I missed any causes or effects?
	☐ Have I included multiple causes or causal chains, if appropriate?
	☐ Have I mistaken causes for effects or vice versa?
Proofread the paper.	☐ Have I proofread for grammar, spelling, and mechanics?

CROSSCURRENTS

Housman's "Is My Team Ploughing?" (pages 294–295), Orwell's "A Hanging" (pages 11–14), and Littlebrandt's "Death Is a Personal Matter" (pages 158–160) each treat the issue of death from a different perspective. What social and moral considerations arise in these pieces? What philosophy of living and dying emerges in each?

 For additional help with writing, reading, and research, go to www.mycomplab.com

Definition

In this chapter you will

- identify the strategies for writing a definition paper

- analyze student formal and informal definition essays

- identify a topic and write your own definition paper

- explore the use of definition from the world around you

- analyze the use of definition in writing by professionals

From time to time, you may have found yourself in a shouting match with friends over a question such as, Which is the all-time great concert group—the Beatles, the Rolling Stones, Queen, or Pink Floyd? Eventually, some wise soul says, "Hey, wait a minute. What's your idea of a great concert group?" The speaker has demanded a **definition** of the term that has sparked the debate. You may find that one person's standard for "great" is how many albums the group sold. Another may appreciate how the group subtly improvises on a theme. And another may insist that "great" means having long-lasting effect on music worldwide. Then you realize, perhaps, either that your respective ideas of a great group are so different that you can't have a discussion or that, once you understand each other's terms, you have no real disagreement.

When writing, you won't have the advantage of another person's asking what you mean. If you want to appear reasonable when you present an idea, you sometimes have to define terms.

Often, a dictionary won't be much help. It may be a good place to start, but at times a dictionary definition won't explain a term fully. Take that word *great*, for example. A dictionary tells you that it means "remarkable or outstanding in magnitude, degree, or extent," and so it does; but how does such a definition help you distinguish between one rock group and another? To do so, you could begin with a dictionary definition, to be sure, but you must let your reader know what you believe the positive or desirable qualities of a rock group are. You must provide an **extended definition.**

As you have no doubt learned on your own, much of your course work— in psychology, history, sociology, biology, and so on—depends on extended definitions. So you know that certain terms, then, require a more elaborate definition than a dictionary gives. The burden is on the writer to explain the meaning of the term. Sometimes in a long paper you have to write an extended definition that may take up one or two paragraphs. Occasionally, a definition can become the paper itself.

The following kinds of terms often need defining:

Words and Terms for Definition

- *Judgmental words*—words that reflect opinions—need definition. Whether subjects being discussed are *good, better, best; bad, worse, worst; beautiful, ugly; friendly, unfriendly; wise, foolish; fair, unfair;* and so on, is a matter of opinion.
- *Specialized terms*—terms with a special meaning to a given group—need definition. Almost every professional or occupational group uses terms that the members of the group understand but that require explanation for those outside the group—for example, *psychosis,* a psychological term; *neoclassicism,* a literary term; *writ,* a legal term; and *gig,* a show-business term.
- *Abstractions*—general words like *love, democracy, justice, freedom,* and *quality*—need definition.
- *Controversial terms* like *male chauvinist, nuclear buildup,* and *affirmative action* need definition.
- *Slang terms* like *bro, phat, cool, the 'hood, bling,* and *hot* may need definition for many audiences.

Writing Your Definition Paper

You can present your extended definition in one of two ways—formally or informally.

Beginning a Formal Definition

A **formal definition** contains the three parts of a dictionary definition: (1) the term itself—the word or phrase to be defined; (2) the class—the large group to which the object or concept belongs; and (3) the differentiation—those characteristics that distinguish it from all others in its class.

TERM	→	CLASS	→	DIFFERENTIATION
A garden		is a small plot of land		used for the cultivation of flowers, vegetables, or fruits.
Beer		is a fermented alcoholic beverage		brewed from malt and flavored with hops.
Lunch		is a meal		eaten at midday.

To write an extended formal definition, you first need to develop a one-sentence definition of the term. Keep the following cautions in mind:

 **TIPS** for Writing One-Sentence Definitions

- **Make sure to include the class.** Don't write, "Baseball is when nine players. . . ." Write instead, "Baseball is a *sport* in which nine players. . . ."

- **Restrict the class.** Speak of a sonnet not as a kind of literature but as a kind of poem.

- **Include no important part of the term itself or its derivatives in the class or differentiation.** Don't say that "a definition is that which defines."

- **Make certain that the sentence defines and does not simply make a statement about the term.** "Happiness is a Madonna concert" doesn't have the essential parts of a definition of happiness.

- **Provide adequate differentiation to clarify the meaning.** Don't define a traitor as "one who opposes the best interests of his or her country." That definition doesn't exclude the well-meaning person who misunderstands the country's best interests and opposes from ignorance. Try instead, "A traitor is one who opposes the best interests of his or her country with malicious intent."

- **Don't make the definition too restrictive.** Don't define a matinee as "a drama presented during the day." That definition doesn't include other forms of entertainment, such as ballets or concerts, which also could be held in daytime.

EXERCISE   Using a dictionary whenever necessary, write one-sentence formal definitions for the following terms.

1. Politics
2. Joy
3. Intelligent design
4. Philosophy
5. Democracy
6. Terrorist
7. Cold fusion
8. Chauvinism
9. Hanukkah
10. Inflation

11. Chivalry
12. Marriage
13. Fear
14. Love
15. Compromise
16. Solar power
17. Loyalty
18. Social network
19. Partying
20. Lacrosse

Drafting Your Formal Definition Paper

Once you have composed a one-sentence formal definition, its three parts can become the major divisions of your paper. The introduction to your paper might contain the term and its one-sentence definition. That sentence could become the thesis for your paper. Or, in addition to providing a one-sentence definition, you could also express an attitude toward the term. In the paper on pages 303–304, student writer Frederick Spense expresses his attitude in this way: "Equality ought to be a philosophy and set of laws in which all people are given the same opportunity to achieve their own individual potential."

The next division of your paper could discuss the class, and the final division, the differentiation. In these discussions, you can make your idea clear by using specific details, by making comparisons and using analogies, by giving examples or telling anecdotes, and sometimes by tracing the history of the term. Often you will be able to quote or refer to the definitions others have given the term. This technique is particularly useful if experts disagree over the meaning of the term. An especially effective tool is *exclusion*, showing what the term is *not*:

> *Gourmet* cooking does not mean to me the preparation of food in expensive wines; it does not mean the preparation of exotic dishes like octopus or rattlesnake; it does not mean the smothering of meat with highly caloric sauces. *Gourmet* cooking to me means the preparation of any food—whether black-eyed peas or hollandaise sauce—in such a way that the dish will be as tasty and attractive as it can be made.

In advancing your discussion of class and differentiation, you can use any rhetorical method or combination of methods of development you have studied. In fact, what makes definition such an interesting rhetorical challenge is that you can draw on most of the familiar patterns of essay development. For example, suppose you wanted to define the term *happiness*. You could use a variety of approaches, as indicated here.

Approaches to a Definition Essay Topic
Defining the Term Happiness

Possible approach	Mode of development
Provide accurate sensory details to describe the face and actions of a happy person you know.	Description (Chapter 7)
Tell a story about a moment when you were truly happy.	Narration (Chapter 8)
Provide several illustrations (examples) of happiness.	Example (Chapter 9)
Explain how to be happy or unhappy.	Process (Chapter 10)

Possible approach	Mode of development
Compare one state of happiness with another; contrast happiness with sadness.	Comparison–Contrast (Chapter 11)
Divide happy people into groups or categories.	Classification (Chapter 12)
Explain the conditions necessary for true happiness or the outcomes of happiness in a person's life.	Cause and Effect (Chapter 13)
Argue that happiness is not achievable in America today.	Argumentation (Chapter 15)

Writing an Informal Definition Paper

Although many terms lend themselves to the three-part formal definition, some are better explained by **informal definition**. What is a good teacher, for example? Or a bad marriage? Or an ideal home? Clearly, one can define such topics only in a subjective or personal way; your purpose is to show what the term means to you. In such instances, it is probably wise to avoid a rigid formal definition. Make your conception of the term clear by describing the subject as fully as you can. By the time readers finish the paper, they should understand what the term means to you.

As with formal definitions, you can use any method or combination of methods of development that you have studied to create an informal definition. Examples and anecdotes are especially good for explaining a term. So are comparison, process, classification, and cause and effect. The idea is to use whatever techniques come in handy to put the idea across.

ASSIGNMENT: DEFINITION

Write an extended definition (formal or informal according to your instructor's directions) of a word, phrase, or concept that you believe requires explanation beyond its denotative meaning. If you write a formal definition, use a one-sentence formal definition as a starting point. If you write an informal definition, choose a term of significant personal meaning to you. Use the tips on pages 299–302 and the student models on pages 303–306 as guides. Consider these words and terms as possible topics for your extended definition paper. Do library or online research, as needed.

1. Evolution
2. Happiness
3. Homelessness
4. Affirmative action
5. Shopping malls
6. Laziness
7. Wealth
8. Leadership
9. Astrology
10. Religion
11. Success
12. Political correctness
13. Depression
14. Hope
15. Virus
16. Friends
17. White-collar crime
18. America
19. "Wannabes"
20. Fun

Student Writing: Formal Definition

In the paper that follows, the student writer derives a formal definition of the term *equality* from his reading of "Harrison Bergeron." (Kurt Vonnegut's short story appears later in the chapter, pages 315–319.) Mr. Spense contrasts his understanding of *equality* with that of the futuristic society represented in Vonnegut's story.

Frederick Spense
Everyone Is Equal in the Grave

Kurt Vonnegut Jr.'s short story "Harrison Bergeron" contrasts the misunderstanding and perversion of equality with the true meaning of the word. Equality ought to be a philosophy and set of laws in which all people are given the same opportunity to achieve their own individual potential. In the U.S.A. of 2081, equality has become a philosophy and set of laws in which everyone is forced to be the same.   1

The Declaration of Independence presents the principle that "all men are created equal," and various laws attempt to put the principle into practice—laws about voting, employment, housing, and so on. "Equal before God and the law" in the second sentence of the story seems to show Vonnegut's approval of this approach. "Equal every which way" is another problem, though, and the story attempts to show that a government that interprets equality in that manner is going to be a slave state.   2

Giving people an equal opportunity to be the best they can be is not the same as forcing people to be like everyone else. Any person who wants to should have the   3 chance to study ballet. That represents equality. Letting poor dancers join the ballet company and "handicapping" good dancers so everyone will be the same is the corruption of equality that has taken place in 2081.

4   Instead of everyone with a good voice having the same chance to become an announcer if he or she wants to, all the announcers in the world of 2081 have speech impediments. Instead of the most skilled technicians competing for jobs on the television crews so that the best person will be chosen, the crews consist of people who cannot even hold cards right side up. Instead of admitting that smart people and dumb people are different even though they have the same worth as human beings, the government installs electronic equipment to prevent the smart people from using their brains for more than a few seconds at a time. Good-looking people wear masks to make them "equal" to ugly people. Strong people wear weights to make them "equal" to weak people.

5   Vonnegut's point is that this is not true equality, but tyranny. It is not just stupid to stifle exceptional people and create a world where being outstanding is a sin, but to do so requires a tremendous government agency whose job is to snoop and to control the smallest aspects of people's private lives. The Constitution has to be amended to make all this possible, and the Handicapper General has the authority to shoot criminals—that is, individuals—on sight.

6   Equality is and ought to be one of our most precious ideals. If it ever comes to mean sameness and conformity, it will not really be equality at all, only obedience and regimentation. Equality like that is the equality of the grave.

FOR WRITING OR DISCUSSION

1. What is the thesis of this paper?
2. Does Spense successfully achieve a one-sentence formal definition of the term? If so, what is it?
3. What methods of development does the writer use in advancing his definition? How do they help him make his idea clear?
4. From your reading of Vonnegut's story (pages 315–319), do you believe that the definition of equality presented in this paper is one of which Vonnegut would approve? Why, or why not?
5. Write your own definition of the term *equality*. You may draw on "Harrison Bergeron," some other story, or your own experience.

Student Writing: Informal Definition

In the following student paper, the writer provides fresh insights by informally defining familar words. Study the annotations.

Helen Fleming
The Grinnies

Until I was twelve years old, I thought everyone in the world knew about the grinnies, if I thought about the term at all—which is unlikely. After all, everyone in my family used the word quite naturally, and we understood each other. So far as I knew, it was a word like any other word—like *bath*, or *chocolate*, or *homework*. But it was my homework which led to my discovery that *grinnies* was a word not known outside my family.

My last report card had said that I was a "C" student in English, and my parents, both teachers, decided that no child of theirs would be just an average student of anything. So nightly I spelled words aloud and answered questions about the fine points of grammar. I wrote and rewrote and rewrote every composition until I convinced my mother that I could make no more improvements. And the hard work paid off. One day the teacher returned compositions, and there it was—a big fat, bright red "A" on the top of my paper. Naturally, I was delighted, but I didn't know I was attracting attention until the teacher snapped, "Helen, what are you doing?"

Called suddenly out of my happy thoughts, I said "Oh, I've got the grinnies!" The teacher and my classmates burst into laughter, and then I understood that grinnies were confined to my family. Other people were not so privileged.

And it is a privilege to have the grinnies, an emotional reaction showing an uncontrollable, spontaneous state of ecstasy. Grinnies appear on the outside as sparkling eyes and a wide, wide smile—not just any smile, but one that shows the teeth and stretches the mouth to its limits. A person experiencing the grinnies appears to be all mouth. On the inside, grinnies are characterized by a feeling of joyful agitation, almost a bubbly sensation. Grinnies usually last just a few seconds, but they can come and go.

1
Introduction provides necessary background as writer presents the term being defined.

2
Personal experience narrative helps reader see the word "grinnies" in action.

Transition paragraph links personal narrative with explanations and further examples.

3

Formal one-sentence definition, even though the essay itself is an *informal* definition.

4
Word "And" at beginning of paragraph serves as a transition and helps promote essay coherence.

Further details differentiate the term with precise characteristics.

Sometimes, when life seems just perfect, I have intermittent attacks of the grinnies for a whole day.

5   The term originated in my mother's family. Her younger sister, Rose, who had deep dimples, often expressed her pleasure with such a grin that the dimples appeared to become permanent. When Rose was about four, she started explaining her funny look by saying, "I have the grinnies." The term caught on, and it has been an important word in our family now for two generations.

Historical information further explains the term.

More examples to clarify the use of the term.

6   The occasion doesn't matter. Anything can bring on the grinnies—just so long as one feels great delight. When my brother finally pumped his bicycle—without training wheels—from our house to the corner and back, he came home with the grinnies. When I was little, my mother's announcement that we would have homemade ice cream for dessert always gave me the grinnies. My father had the grinnies when I was valedictorian. Grinnies can be brought on by a good meal, a sense of pride, a new friend, a telephone call from someone special, an accomplishment. Or sometimes one gets the grinnies for no reason at all: just a sudden sense of well-being can bring on a case. Whatever brings them on, an attack of the grinnies is among life's greatest pleasures.

Conclusion links to previous paragraph through transition "In fact" and to paragraph 2, contributing to the unity in the essay.

7   In fact, now that I look back on the experience, I feel sorry for my seventh-grade teacher. I think it's a pity that she didn't know the word *grinnies*. It's such a useful term for saying, "I'm really, really pleased!"

FOR WRITING OR DISCUSSION

1. What is the writer's attitude toward her subject?
2. What is her thesis in the essay? What transitions does the writer use to create coherence?
3. What methods of development does the writer use in defining the term?
4. What examples could you give—other than those used by the writer—of situations that could produce the grinnies?
5. Write an informal definition of a word or term used by some particular group or in a special region of the country. You might select a word like *wannabe, dude, honcho, hack,* or *dweeb*—or another of your own choosing.

Definition
in the World Around You

The language of law and commerce depends on a certain uniformity of definitions so that we have a common, understandable vocabulary. Examine any legal document and you will find it filled with definitions so that the signatories share familiar meanings. In this government agency Web site, note the effort of the Census Bureau to define a key word, poverty, which has dramatic implications for taxes, funding, and social legislation.

Thesis — The Census Bureau defines poverty as a function of money income.

Definition — The last paragraph of the introduction uses the word "definition" and points out the elements used in the Bureau's definition of poverty. Note the flexibility in the definition in order for it not to be too restrictive: "Many government aid programs use a different poverty measure...."

Audience and purpose — Anyone seeking to understand an official definition of poverty from the Census Bureau would find it here in relatively simple language. Public assistance policy, laws, housing requirements, taxation—all these elements rely on an agreed-upon definition, and the Census Bureau's is often used as a standard.

Details — The site identifies the specific details that make up the definition, including income used to compute poverty status and measure of need. You also see when the original poverty thresholds came into play.

Your Turn

Go online to find a definition of an important term, such as *democracy, addiction, wealth, fitness, depression,* or some such word or phrase. Then, write a definition of the word, drawing on the information you found at whatever sites you consulted. You might want to compare definitions or assert the superiority of one definition over the other according to your way of thinking.

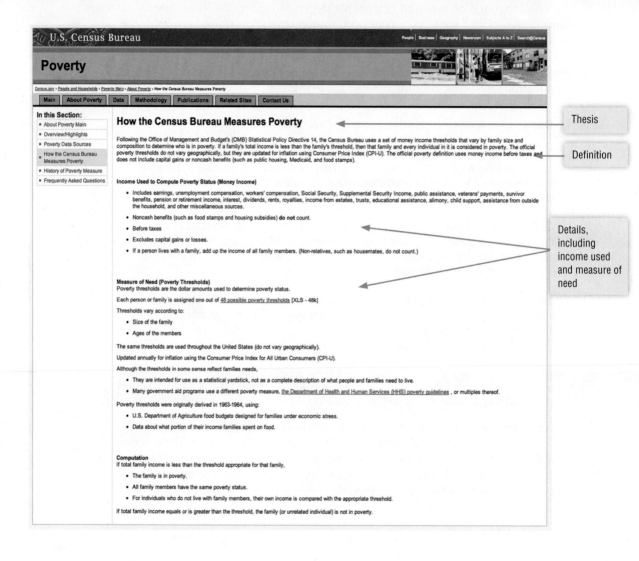

U.S. Census Bureau

People | Business | Geography | Newsroom | Subjects A to Z | Search@Census

Poverty

Census.gov › People and Households › Poverty Main › About Poverty › How the Census Bureau Measures Poverty

| Main | About Poverty | Data | Methodology | Publications | Related Sites | Contact Us |

In this Section:
- About Poverty Main
- Overview/Highlights
- Poverty Data Sources
- How the Census Bureau Measures Poverty
- History of Poverty Measure
- Frequently Asked Questions

How the Census Bureau Measures Poverty

Thesis

Following the Office of Management and Budget's (OMB) Statistical Policy Directive 14, the Census Bureau uses a set of money income thresholds that vary by family size and composition to determine who is in poverty. If a family's total income is less than the family's threshold, then that family and every individual in it is considered in poverty. The official poverty thresholds do not vary geographically, but they are updated for inflation using Consumer Price Index (CPI-U). The official poverty definition uses money income before taxes and does not include capital gains or noncash benefits (such as public housing, Medicaid, and food stamps).

Definition

Income Used to Compute Poverty Status (Money Income)

- Includes earnings, unemployment compensation, workers' compensation, Social Security, Supplemental Security Income, public assistance, veterans' payments, survivor benefits, pension or retirement income, interest, dividends, rents, royalties, income from estates, trusts, educational assistance, alimony, child support, assistance from outside the household, and other miscellaneous sources.
- Noncash benefits (such as food stamps and housing subsidies) **do not** count.
- Before taxes
- Excludes capital gains or losses.
- If a person lives with a family, add up the income of all family members. (Non-relatives, such as housemates, do not count.)

Details, including income used and measure of need

Measure of Need (Poverty Thresholds)
Poverty thresholds are the dollar amounts used to determine poverty status.

Each person or family is assigned one out of 48 possible poverty thresholds [XLS - 48k]

Thresholds vary according to:

- Size of the family
- Ages of the members

The same thresholds are used throughout the United States (do not vary geographically).

Updated annually for inflation using the Consumer Price Index for All Urban Consumers (CPI-U).

Although the thresholds in some sense reflect families needs,

- They are intended for use as a statistical yardstick, not as a complete description of what people and families need to live.
- Many government aid programs use a different poverty measure, the Department of Health and Human Services (HHS) poverty guidelines, or multiples thereof.

Poverty thresholds were originally derived in 1963-1964, using:

- U.S. Department of Agriculture food budgets designed for families under economic stress.
- Data about what portion of their income families spent on food.

Computation
If total family income is less than the threshold appropriate for that family,

- The family is in poverty.
- All family members have the same poverty status.
- For individuals who do not live with family members, their own income is compared with the appropriate threshold.

If total family income equals or is greater than the threshold, the family (or unrelated individual) is not in poverty.

Readings for Writing

The reading selections that follow provide examples of extended definitions.

DAVID OWEN

The Perfect Job

The perfect job—the one you would have if you could have any job in the world—what would it be?

The most nearly perfect part of any less-than-perfect job is usually the occasional hour in which you are able to pretend that you are doing the job when in fact you are reading a magazine and eating candy. The rest of the office is throbbing frantically, but you are sitting quietly at your desk and learning interesting facts about Fergie and that guy who put his wife in the wood chipper. The perfect job would feel like that, but all the time.

The trouble with less-than-perfect jobs is that they usually don't swoop you up and fling you through your day. That is, you don't very often look up at the clock to find out how many minutes past eleven it is and discover that it's five and time to go home. That's what the perfect job would be like. The time would zoom by, the way it does when you are going through some old boxes and suddenly discover that they are filled with artifacts from the Pilgrim days.

Well, I've thought about this a lot (while I was supposed to be doing something else), and I've narrowed down my choice of the perfect job to five possibilities:

- Doing an unbelievably great cleanup of my basement, and organizing my workshop so that I know exactly where everything is, and drawing up a lot of plans to show how I might expand my workshop so that it would fill the entire basement instead of only the third that it fills now, and buying every conceivable kind of woodworking tool and finding exactly the perfect place to keep each one, but never actually getting around to doing any woodworking projects.

- Doing the *Times* crossword puzzle and watching MTV while listening to people I knew in college discuss their marital problems on the other side of a one-way mirror.

- Sorting my children's vast Lego collection—by type, size, and color—into muffin tins and other containers while my children nearby happily build small vehicles and structures without hitting each other or asking me for something to eat.

- Setting the prison sentences of criminals convicted in highly publicized court cases; making all parole decisions for these people; receiving daily updates on how they spend their time in jail.

- Touring the houses of strangers and looking through their stuff while they're not there. If I were driving along and happened to see a house that looked interesting, I could pull over and let myself in with a set of master keys. If the people happened to be there, I could spray them with a harmless paralyzing gas that would prevent them from remembering that I had read their diaries and checked to see whether they were making efficient use of their limited amount of storage space, which they probably wouldn't have been.

10   All these jobs, as I see them, would require a full complement of office supplies: every conceivable kind of clip and clasp, name-brand ball-point pens, ungunked-up bottles of correction fluid, ammo-like refills for various desktop mechanisms, and cool, smooth, hard pads of narrow-lined paper. I guess I would also need a fax machine and a staff of cheerful recent college graduates eager to do my bidding. Plus a really great benefits program that would pay not only for doctors and prescription drugs but also for things like deodorant.

11   Recently I've begun to think that my *real* perfect job would probably consist of all five of my *possible* perfect jobs, one for each weekday. That way I would never have to lie awake at night wondering whether sorting my children's Legos would have made me happier than snooping through people's tax returns. Then, on weekends, I could hang around my house, drinking beer and watching golf tournaments on TV. I would seem to be having a really great time, but in reality I would be counting the hours until Monday and just itching to get back to work.

FOR WRITING OR DISCUSSION

1. How does paragraph 2 establish the humorous context of the essay? What other elements of humor do you find?

2. What important element of the perfect job does Owen establish in paragraph 3? Do you agree that for a job to be perfect, the time ought to "zoom by"? Why, or why not?

3. Outline the five possibilities in Owen's choice of the perfect job. You know that the writer is not serious about these elements. What, then, is he trying to accomplish?

4. Write a definition essay in which you answer the question posed in the first paragraph.

MARJORIE GARBER
What Is "Genius"?

1   The word "genius" derives from the same root as "gene" and "genetic," and meant originally, in Latin, a tutelary god or spirit given to every person at birth. One's genius governed one's fortune and determined one's character, and ultimately conducted one out of this world into the afterlife. The thinkers of antiquity suggested that every person had two geniuses, one good and one evil, which competed for influence. This concept was alive and well in Shakespeare's day, and survives in the expression "his better genius." The word "genius" soon came to mean a demon or spirit in general, as in the fairy-tale "genie" or "jinni." Genius thus conceived was part of a system that would later be called psychology, because it was thought of as residing somehow both inside and outside the individual,

and motivating behavior. Through the Renaissance and well into the eighteenth century the most familiar meaning of "genius" in English was something like "temperament" or "disposition": people were described as having a "daring genius" or an "indolent genius."

Joseph Addison's essay "On Genius," published in *The Spectator* in 1711, laid out the terrain of genius as we use the term today, to denote exceptional talent or someone who possesses it. According to Addison, there were two kinds of genius—natural and learned (the greatest of geniuses were the natural ones, whose inborn gifts freed them from dependence on models or imitation). Homer, Pindar, and Shakespeare were his examples of the first category, Aristotle, Virgil, Milton, and Francis Bacon of the second. In general terms this dichotomy—brilliant versus industrious—still underlies our notions of genius today, but despite Thomas Edison's oft quoted adage "Genius is one percent inspiration and ninety-nine percent perspiration," it's the inspiration that we dote on.

In Addison's day and for years after, the idea of the scientific genius was still for most people a contradiction in terms. Science, then and for years after, was more perspiration than inspiration. Genius was precisely what could never be quantified. As Immanuel Kant contended in his *Critique of Judgment,* genius is a talent for art, not for science, since "it is quite ridiculous for a man to speak and decide like a genius in things which require the most careful investigation by reason." The spontaneous generation of ideas that apparently characterizes genius seemed fundamentally at odds with the painstaking labor and analysis that characterize research. "We can readily learn all that Newton has set forth in his immortal work on the Principles of Natural Philosophy," Kant declared, "however great a head was required to discover it, but we cannot learn to write spirited poetry." But in England, in the novel *Tom Jones,* Henry Fielding had already poked fun at the notion of unschooled genius.

> As several gentlemen in these times, by the wonderful force of genius only, without the least assistance of learning, perhaps, without being well able to read, have made a considerable figure in the republic of letters; the modern critics, I am told, have lately begun to assert, that all kind of learning is entirely useless to a writer; and, indeed, no other than a kind of fetters on the natural spriteliness and activity of the imagination.

It was with the Romantic period that the true cult of the natural genius emerged. At the beginning of the nineteenth century poets and critics such as Coleridge and Shelley, perhaps self-interestedly, staked out genius as the territory of the poet. Shakespeare—or at least the Romantic period's fantasy of Shakespeare—was the quintessential genius, his brilliance and his inventiveness the results of attributes and resources that were innate rather than learned. "Sweetest Shakespeare, fancy's child, warbl[ing] his native woodnotes wild" Milton had called him, and this portrait of untutored genius had an enormous effect on critics in the centuries that followed. The less Shakespeare had been taught, the more genius he had—so ran the thinking then, and so, to a certain extent, it continues today. Thus some scholars exulted over Shakespeare's supposed lack of formal education: he attended only a rural grammar school, not a university; he had, as his admiring rival Ben Jonson indelibly phrased it, "small Latin and less Greek"—though in point of fact the curriculum of the Stratford grammar school, rich in history and mythology, offered a solid training in the classics.

5   The Romantics differed among themselves in their estimation of Shakespeare's style and his degree of learning, trying in various ways to explain the causes of the poet's supposed barbarisms, separating what they judged his timeless genius from the unfortunate fact that he lived and wrote in a cruder age. William Hazlitt, an influential critic and essayist, catalogued the playwright's imperfections, including his irritating fondness for puns and wordplay and his unaccountable willingness to alter chronology and geography to suit his dramatic purposes. But these flaws did not detract, in Hazlitt's view, from what he deemed Shakespeare's unique genius: "His barbarisms were those of his age. His genius was his own."

6   Coleridge, on the other hand, argued in a lecture forthrightly titled "Shakespeare's Judgment Equal to His Genius" that the plays were more than "works of rude uncultivated genius." Their form, he thought, was "equally admirable with the matter; the judgment of the great poet not less deserving of our wonder than his genius." Here the word "wonder" underscores Shakespeare's quasi-miraculous achievement. Judgment—in his case, unlike so many others—is not an element that contradicts genius but, rather, a virtue, equally unfathomable, that serves as its complement.

7   The cult of genius inherited from these Romantic writers, one that still has enormous force today, tells us that ordinary mortals can achieve many things by dint of hard work, but the natural and effortless gifts of a true genius (like Shakespeare) will forever elude the diligent overachiever. By this logic genius, and geniuses, cannot be made, only born.

FOR WRITING OR DISCUSSION

1. What is the thesis of this selection?
2. What two kinds for genius did Addison denote?
3. How does Garber use comparison-contrast strategies?
4. The writer uses many references to other writers and philosophers. Why? How do the quotations from other sources help her advance her point?
5. How does the last paragraph serve the essay?
6. Choose an abstract term like *genius—excellence, wealth, charity,* or *faithfulness,* for example—and write an essay to define it. Use library and online sources to develop a historical perspective and, like Garber, build toward a modern understanding of the word or term.

LORENZO ALBACETE

The Struggle With Celibacy

1   When I was in fifth grade and was invited to become an altar boy, my father would not allow it. He had made a promise to safeguard my faith, he explained, and if I got too close to priests, I might lose that faith, or—what seemed worse for him—I might become one of them. My father was born in Spain, and Spanish anticlericalism flowed through his veins.

His main objection was to priestly celibacy. He thought it divided priests into three kinds: saints who lived by it, rascals who took advantage of it to hide sexual desires of which they were ashamed, like homosexuality, and those who cheated. Since I gave no evidence of being saintly, I think he feared I might end up in one of the other categories.

I was angry and hurt by this response. I felt accused of something, though I wasn't sure exactly of what.

Eventually my father relented, and I became an altar boy. I tried hard to prove him wrong, and I resisted every indication of a priestly vocation. Many years later, though, having already begun my life as a secular adult, and on the verge of choosing a wedding date with my girlfriend, I found I could not resist anymore. My second Mass after ordination was at my father's grave. I hoped he would understand.

Now, with each new revelation of priestly pedophilia, in addition to shock and anger, I feel accused again. I worry that my altar boys and girls—not to mention their parents—are looking at me as a dirty old man, as a possible threat. When a case of abuse is exposed involving a married man, I doubt that most other married men feel implicated, embarrassed in front of their friends and relatives. They don't worry that the parents of their children's friends suspect them of horrible crimes. But because of my vow, even wearing my priestly garb has made me want to scream, "I'm not one of those!"

Like my father back then, an increasing number of people today think that celibacy must be blamed for this shameful situation. With none of the usual outlets, the theory goes, sexual energy inevitably explodes in manipulative forms based on the abuse of power.

This has not been my experience of celibacy. Still, I cannot help believing that there is some truth in the suspicion that celibacy is somehow related to the present crisis. There are those who use priestly celibacy to hide sexual desires. But I know a good many priests—in line, I believe, with the vast majority—who struggle to be faithful to a vow they hold dear and are appalled to see it abused by others. They wonder how the requirement can be maintained without facing these issues. We priests owe an answer to our scandalized people.

My opinion is that the problem lies not with celibacy as such, but with the way it is understood and lived. One standard defense of celibacy is that it frees priests from the obligations of marriage and thereby allows them to respond to the needs of the faithful without reservations. I believe this to be completely false. I think it is an insult to the countless married doctors, social activists, non-Catholic clergy and counselors whose dedication to others is second to none. In fact, there is the danger that celibacy will give priests a feeling of being separated from others, forming a caste removed from ordinary men and women. I think it is precisely because priests evoke this mysterious world of the sacred that pedophilia among them seems more despicable—and more compelling—than the same behavior among nonclerical men.

When I decided to go into the seminary at the age of 28, I broke up with my girlfriend—not because I was suddenly opposed to marriage, but because church law requires it. Asked whether I would have chosen a life of celibacy had it not been required, I have to admit that I would not have. But I experienced a profound call to follow without reservations or conditions, and in that spirit, I accepted the celibacy requirement with trepidation, but with the faith that I would be sustained in doing whatever it took to conform to it. Throughout the years, though, I have come to value the vow of celibacy highly.

10   I began to understand the meaning of celibacy, oddly, during a time when I was seriously questioning it. A dear friend of mine in Europe had sent his only son to study in the United States and asked me to watch over him. This friend told me how much he was suffering from this separation. I told him that at least he had a son, whereas I would never experience being a father. This aspect of celibacy, I said to him, was much more difficult than the lack of a sexual companion.

11   "But you have many sons and daughters," he said. "Look at the way young people follow you. You are a true father to them."

12   "Yes," I replied, "but let's be honest. They are not really my sons and daughters. Each one of them would have existed even if I had not. They are not mine as J. is your son."

13   "But Lorenzo," he said, "that is the point. J. is not my son. I do not own him. I must respect his freedom. And I thought that's why priests took a vow of celibacy, to help spouses and parents understand that to love is not to own, but to affirm, to help, to let go. I need this help now that J. has left home."

14   I understood then that celibacy has more to do with poverty than with sex. It is the radical, outward expression of the poverty of the human heart, the poverty that makes true love possible by preventing it from corrupting into possession or manipulation. That is why child abuse by priests is so shocking, so horrible, so destructive. It places celibacy at the service of power and lust, not of love.

15   In the future, the church may decide that particular pastoral situations require a change in the requirement of priestly celibacy. Still, I believe that even if priests marry, they are called to be witnesses of that "celibacy in the heart" that human love requires—namely, the absolute respect for the loved one's freedom. It's time for those of us who treasure priestly celibacy to live it in accordance with its intended message or else give it up as an obstacle to what we wish to say.

FOR WRITING OR DISCUSSION

1. What is the thesis of this essay, which appeared in "The Way We Live Now" segment of *The New York Times Magazine*?

2. The writer builds to a definition of *celibacy*. How does he ultimately define it? What is the dictionary definition of the word? How does it compare with Albacete's definition?

3. Why did the writer break off with his girlfriend?

4. Where does the writer use classification? Narration? Cause and effect?

5. Write a definition of some religious term that has important meanings to you. You might want to define spirituality, confirmation, baptism, synagogue, church, mosque, or some other word or phrase that has some religious significance.

KURT VONNEGUT JR.
Harrison Bergeron

The year was 2081, and everybody was finally equal. They weren't only equal before   1
God and the law. They were equal every which way. Nobody was smarter than anybody
else. Nobody was better looking than anybody else. Nobody was stronger or quicker than
anybody else. All this equality was due to the 211th, 212th, and 213th Amendments to
the Constitution, and to the unceasing vigilance of agents of the United States Handicapper General.

Some things about living still weren't quite right, though. April, for instance, still drove   2
people crazy by not being springtime. And it was in that clammy month that the H-G men
took George and Hazel Bergeron's fourteen-year-old son, Harrison, away.

It was tragic, all right, but George and Hazel couldn't think about it very hard. Hazel   3
had a perfectly average intelligence, which meant she couldn't think about anything except
in short bursts. And George, while his intelligence was way above normal, had a little mental handicap radio in his ear. He was required by law to wear it at all times. It was tuned to
a government transmitter. Every twenty seconds or so, the transmitter would send out some
sharp noise to keep people like George from taking unfair advantage of their brains.

George and Hazel were watching television. There were tears on Hazel's cheeks, but   4
she'd forgotten for the moment what they were about.

On the television screen were ballerinas.   5

A buzzer sounded in George's head. His thoughts fled in panic, like bandits from a   6
burglar alarm.

"That was a real pretty dance, that dance they just did," said Hazel.   7

"Huh?" said George.   8

"That dance—it was nice," said Hazel.   9

"Yup," said George. He tried to think a little about the ballerinas. They weren't really   10
very good—no better than anybody else would have been, anyway. They were burdened
with sashweights and bags of birdshot, and their faces were masked, so that no one, seeing a free and graceful gesture or a pretty face, would feel like something the cat drug in.
George was toying with the vague notion that maybe dancers shouldn't be handicapped.
But he didn't get very far with it before another noise in his ear radio scattered his thoughts.

George winced. So did two out of the eight ballerinas.   11

Hazel saw him wince. Having no mental handicap herself, she had to ask George what   12
the latest sound had been.

"Sounded like somebody hitting a milk bottle with a ball peen hammer," said George.   13

"I'd think it would be real interesting, hearing all the different sounds," said Hazel, a   14
little envious. "All the things they think up."

"Um," said George.   15

16   "Only, if I was Handicapper General, you know what I would do?" said Hazel. Hazel, as a matter of fact, bore a strong resemblance to the Handicapper General, a woman named Diana Moon Glampers. "If I was Diana Moon Glampers," said Hazel, "I'd have chimes on Sunday—just chimes. Kind of in honor of religion."

17   "I could think, if it was just chimes," said George.

18   "Well—maybe make 'em real loud," said Hazel. "I think I'd make a good Handicapper General."

19   "Good as anybody else," said George.

20   "Who knows better'n I do what normal is?" said Hazel.

21   "Right," said George. He began to think glimmeringly about his abnormal son who was now in jail, about Harrison, but a twenty-one-gun salute in his head stopped that.

22   "Boy!" said Hazel, "that was a doozy, wasn't it?"

23   It was such a doozy that George was white and trembling, and tears stood on the rims of his red eyes. Two of the eight ballerinas had collapsed to the studio floor, were holding their temples.

24   "All of a sudden you look so tired," said Hazel. "Why don't you stretch out on the sofa, so's you can rest your handicap bag on the pillows, honeybunch." She was referring to the forty-seven pounds of birdshot in a canvas bag, which was padlocked around George's neck. "Go on and rest the bag for a little while," she said. "I don't care if you're not equal to me for a while."

25   George weighed the bag with his hands. "I don't mind it," he said, "I don't notice it anymore. It's just a part of me."

26   "You been so tired lately—kind of wore out," said Hazel. "If there was just some way we could make a little hole in the bottom of the bag, and just take out a few of them lead balls. Just a few."

27   "Two years in prison and two thousand dollars fine for every ball I took out," said George. "I don't call that a bargain."

28   "If you could take a few out when you came home from work," said Hazel. "I mean— you don't compete with anybody around here. You just set around."

29   "If I tried to get away with it," said George, "then other people'd get away with it—and pretty soon we'd be right back to the dark ages again, with everybody competing against everybody else. You wouldn't like that, would you?"

30   "I'd hate it," said Hazel.

31   "There you are," said George. "The minute people start cheating on laws, what do you think happens to society?"

32   If Hazel hadn't been able to come up with an answer to this question, George couldn't have supplied one. A siren was going off in his head.

33   "Reckon it'd fall all apart," said Hazel.

34   "What would?" said George blankly.

35   "Society," said Hazel uncertainly. "Wasn't that what you just said?"

36   "Who knows?" said George.

37   The television program was suddenly interrupted for a news bulletin. It wasn't clear at first as to what the bulletin was about, since the announcer like all announcers, had

a serious speech impediment. For about half a minute, and in a state of high excitement, the announcer tried to say, "Ladies and gentlemen—"

He finally gave up, handed the bulletin to a ballerina to read. 38

"That's all right—" Hazel said of the announcer, "he tried. That's the big thing. He tried 39
to do the best he could with what God gave him. He should get a nice raise for trying so
hard."

"Ladies and gentlemen—" said the ballerina, reading the bulletin. She must have been 40
extraordinarily beautiful, because the mask she wore was hideous. And it was easy to see
that she was the strongest and most graceful of all the dancers, for her handicap bags were
as big as those worn by two-hundred-pound men.

And she had to apologize at once for her voice, which was a very unfair voice for a 41
woman to use. Her voice was a warm, luminous, timeless melody. "Excuse me—" she
said, and she began again, making her voice absolutely uncompetitive.

"Harrison Bergeron, age fourteen," she said in a grackle squawk, "has just escaped from 42
jail, where he was held on suspicion of plotting to overthrow the government. He is a genius
and an athlete, is under-handicapped, and should be regarded as extremely dangerous."

A police photograph of Harrison Bergeron was flashed on the screen upside down, 43
then sideways, upside down again, then right side up. The picture showed the full length of
Harrison against a background calibrated in feet and inches. He was exactly seven feet tall.

The rest of Harrison's appearance was Halloween and hardware. Nobody had ever 44
borne heavier handicaps. He had outgrown hindrances faster than the H-G men could
think them up. Instead of a little ear radio for a mental handicap, he wore a tremendous
pair of earphones, and spectacles with thick wavy lenses. The spectacles were intended to
make him not only half blind, but to give him whanging headaches besides.

Scrap metal was hung all over him. Ordinarily, there was a certain symmetry, a military 45
neatness to the handicaps issued to strong people, but Harrison looked like a walking junk-
yard. In the face of life, Harrison carried three hundred pounds.

And to offset his good looks, the H-G men required that he wear at all times a red 46
rubber ball for a nose, keep his eyebrows shaved off, and cover his even white teeth with
black caps at snaggle-tooth random.

"If you see this boy," said the ballerina, "do not—I repeat, do not—try to reason with 47
him."

There was a shriek of a door being torn from its hinges. 48

Screams and barking cries of consternation came from the television set. The photo- 49
graph of Harrison Bergeron on the screen jumped again and again, as though dancing to
the tune of an earthquake.

George Bergeron correctly identified the earthquake, and well he might have—for 50
many was the time his own home had danced to the same crashing tune. "My God—" said
George, "that must be Harrison!"

The realization was blasted from his mind instantly by the sound of an automobile 51
collision in his head.

When George could open his eyes again, the photograph of Harrison was gone. A liv- 52
ing, breathing Harrison filled the screen.

53   Clanking, clownish, and huge, Harrison stood in the center of the studio. The knob of the uprooted studio door was still in his hand. Ballerinas, technicians, musicians, and announcers cowered on their knees before him, expecting to die.

54   "I am the Emperor!" cried Harrison. "Do you hear! I am the Emperor! Everybody must do what I say at once!" He stamped his foot and the studio shook.

55   "Even as I stand here—" he bellowed, "crippled, hobbled, sickened—I am a greater ruler than any man who ever lived! Now watch me become what I *can* become!"

56   Harrison tore the straps of his handicap harness like wet tissue paper, tore straps guaranteed to support five thousand pounds.

57   Harrison's scrap-iron handicaps crashed to the floor.

58   Harrison thrust his thumbs under the bar of the padlock that secured his head harness. The bar snapped like celery. Harrison smashed his headphones and spectacles against the wall.

59   He flung away his rubber-ball nose, revealed a man that would have awed Thor, the god of thunder.

60   "I shall now select my Empress!" he said, looking down on the cowering people. "Let the first woman who dares rise to her feet claim her mate and her throne!"

61   A moment passed, and then a ballerina arose, swaying like a willow.

62   Harrison plucked the mental handicap from her ear, snapped off her physical handicaps with marvelous delicacy. Last of all, he removed her mask.

63   She was blindingly beautiful.

64   "Now—" said Harrison, taking her hand, "shall we show the people the meaning of the word dance? Music!" he commanded.

65   The musicians scrambled back into their chairs, and Harrison stripped them of their handicaps, too. "Play your best," he told them, "and I'll make you barons and dukes and earls."

66   The music began. It was normal at first—cheap, silly, false. But Harrison snatched two musicians from their chairs, waved them like batons as he sang the music as he wanted it played. He slammed them back into their chairs.

67   The music began again and was much improved.

68   Harrison and his Empress merely listened to the music for a while—listened gravely, as though synchronizing their heartbeats with it.

69   They shifted their weights to their toes.

70   Harrison placed his big hands on the girl's tiny waist, letting her sense the weightlessness that would soon be hers.

71   And then in an explosion of joy and grace, into the air they sprang!

72   Not only were the laws of the land abandoned, but the law of gravity and the laws of motion as well.

73   They reeled, whirled, swiveled, flounced, capered, gamboled, and spun.

74   They leaped like deer on the moon.

75   The studio ceiling was thirty feet high, but each leap brought the dancers nearer to it.

76   It became their obvious intention to kiss the ceiling.

77   They kissed it.

And then, neutralizing gravity with love and pure will, they remained suspended in air inches below the ceiling, and they kissed each other for a long, long time. 78

It was then that Diana Moon Glampers, the Handicapper General, came into the studio with a double-barreled ten-gauge shotgun. She fired twice, and the Emperor and the Empress were dead before they hit the floor. 79

Diana Moon Glampers loaded the gun again. She aimed it at the musicians and told them they had ten seconds to get their handicaps back on. 80

It was then that the Bergerons' television tube burned out. 81

Hazel turned to comment about the blackout to George. But George had gone out into the kitchen for a can of beer. 82

George came back in with the beer, paused while a handicap signal shook him up. And then he sat down again. 83

"You been crying?" he said to Hazel. 84

"Yup," she said. 85

"What about?" he said. 86

"I forget," she said. "Something real sad on television." 87

"What was it?" he said. 88

"It's all kind of mixed up in my mind," said Hazel. 89

"Forget sad things," said George. 90

"I always do," said Hazel. 91

"That's my girl," said George. He winced. There was the sound of a riveting gun in his head. 92

"Gee—I could tell that one was a doozy," said Hazel. 93

"You can say that again," said George. 94

"Gee—" said Hazel, "I could tell that one was a doozy." 95

FOR WRITING OR DISCUSSION

1. Vonnegut's story is one of the future in which he looks at trends today that disturb him and asks what life would be like if they continue for a hundred years or so. What other stories, novels, movies, and television programs can you think of that use the same approach?

2. What specifically is the author satirizing in modern America? Do you feel he has good cause to be upset? Why or why not?

3. What would the author feel is a correct definition of *equality*? How would Diana Moon Glampers define *equality*?

4. Why is the name Harrison Bergeron a better choice than a name such as John Smith or Bill Jones?

5. Name the different kinds of handicaps in the story. Does each attempt to solve a different problem?

6. Specifically, what are the bad results of the misunderstanding of equality?

7. What is symbolized by the soaring of Harrison and the ballerina to the ceiling?
8. Does the fact that Harrison declares himself an emperor justify the society's fear of him?
9. Write a paper in which you define *equality*.

Reading and Writing About Poetry

A poet captures the frustrations of unfulfillment in this brief, powerful poem.

LANGSTON HUGHES

Dreams

Hold fast to dreams
For if dreams die
Life is a broken-winged bird
That cannot fly.
Hold fast to dreams
For when dreams go
Life is a barren field
Frozen with snow.

5

FOR WRITING OR DISCUSSION

1. What is the main point of this poem?
2. What does Hughes mean by the first line of the poem? What is the effect of his repeating it in the fifth line?
3. Which of the two metaphors do you find more powerful? (See pages 392–393 for a definition of metaphor.) Or are they both equally strong? Why do you think so?
4. The poem operates through negation—that is, the poet tells us what life would be like without dreams. How do you think Hughes would define *dreams*? Or *life with dreams*?
5. Write an essay in which you define *dreams*. Or, you might define *life with dreams* or *life without dreams*. Use metaphors, where appropriate, to add pictorial strength to your paper.

STRATEGY CHECKLIST: Writing and Revising Your Definition Paper

Plan the paper.	☐ Have I selected a word or phrase that lends itself to an extended definition?
	☐ Is the word I've chosen too broad or too narrow, and how can I correct either of these two limitations?
	☐ Have I used one of the prewriting strategies to stimulate my thoughts?
	☐ Have I identified details and examples that support my understanding of the word?
	☐ Have I paid attention to peer comments about my prewriting?
	☐ Have I considered my audience and purpose?
	☐ Have I considered using an outline to plan my presentation?
Write a first draft.	☐ Have I written a thesis that expresses an opinion about the word I am defining?
	☐ For an extended formal definition, have I included a one-sentence definition with three major parts?
	▪ Term
	▪ Class
	▪ Differentiation
	☐ Have I written an introduction that states the term and provides some idea of why I'm choosing to define it?
	☐ Have I considered appropriate strategies to advance my definition?
	▪ Description ▪ Comparison and contrast
	▪ Narration ▪ Classification and division
	▪ Example ▪ Cause and effect
	▪ Process
	☐ Have I presented distinctive characteristics of the word in the body paragraphs?
	☐ Does my conclusion revisit the word or phrase, set a new context, or suggest that the reader take some action?

Revise and edit the paper.	☐ Do the characteristics I've identified suit the word I'm defining?
	☐ Should I add or remove some examples?
	☐ Is my definition complete?
	☐ Will readers understand my meaning of the word as opposed to meanings held by others?

| Proofread the paper. | ☐ Have I proofread for grammar, spelling, and mechanics? |

CROSSCURRENTS

David Owen in "The Perfect Job" (pages 309–310) and Nick Fiscina in "Dad's Disappointment" (pages 128–129) characterize work experiences from completely different perspectives. Write an essay in which you determine the definition of *job* or *work* advocated by the writers and compare and contrast their points of view.

COLLABORATIVE LEARNING

Once you decide on a topic, do prewriting (see pages 36–38) before you draft your definition essay. Come to class with your prewriting efforts and form groups of three to examine the work of each student in the group. Has each writer selected a term rich in meaning? What suggestions can you make about how to develop the thesis? Which patterns of essay development do you think will help each writer best define the word of choice? Where do you think the writer needs to provide details? Is the writer's intended purpose clear? What audience should the essay aim for, in your opinion?

When you produce the draft of your essay, take into account the comments you received from group members.

 For support in meeting this chapter's objectives, follow this path in MyCompLab: Resources ⇒ **Writing** ⇒ **Writing Samples: Descriptions and Definitions**. Review the Instruction and Multimedia resources about **definition**; then complete the Exercises and click on Gradebook to measure your progress.

CHAPTER **15**

Argumentation

An argumentation paper attempts to strengthen or change an attitude of the reader, or to persuade the reader to a particular point of view or to take some action. Although writers of argumentation papers may use emotional appeals, they place their principal faith in appealing to the intellects of their readers.

Argumentation has probably too often appeared in the combative context of a courtroom or debating society: right and wrong confront each other; one side wins, and one side loses. The victors gloat over the demolished points of their opponents or graciously accept their opponents' concessions of defeat and apologies for being so wrong. Many writers still do strive for total victory of this sort, of course, but argument also can be a matter of bringing opposing parties together, of showing the strengths and weaknesses of all points of view, of building consensus among former enemies. Argumentation can involve making peace as much as waging war.

In this chapter you will

- analyze the elements of logic and logical fallacies

- write appeals as part of an argument

- identify the strategies in writing a formal argument

- develop a debatable position and write your own argumentation paper

- analyze student argumentation essays

- explore the use of argumentation from the world around you

- analyze the use of argument in writing by professionals

Using Logic

Induction

Induction is the process of reasoning from the particular to the general. It is the process of arriving at a general conclusion about all the members of a group or class. Induction is a useful tool because it isn't always practical or possible to check every member of a group before drawing your conclusion. If, for example, you've noticed that for three Fridays in a row, Professor Hadley has given a pop quiz, you may draw the useful conclusion that Professor Hadley is likely to give pop quizzes on Fridays. You don't have to wait until the end of the term to see if you're right.

But induction is useful only if the conclusion about a class is drawn from a fair sampling of that class. What's fair depends on the class. You needn't stick your hand into twenty fires to conclude that fire burns; one or two fires will do. You should sample other classes more broadly. You should draw conclusions about groups of people, for example, from a large representative sampling and even then you should usually qualify statements with words like *tend, may, are likely,* and so on. (See "Hasty Generalization" and "Overgeneralization," page 326; see also Chapter 9, "Example.")

Deduction

Deduction is the process of reasoning from the general to the particular. You apply a generalization already established—by yourself or by someone else—to a specific case. Deduction, like induction, is a useful tool. You've concluded, for example, that Professor Hadley is likely to give pop quizzes on Fridays. As a result, you think twice about cutting Friday's class. You've applied your generalization (Fridays are likely days for quizzes) to a specific case (this Friday) and just may have assured yourself a passing grade in Professor Hadley's class.

The Syllogism

In its simplest form, the deductive process is stated as a *syllogism*: an argument consisting of a major premise, a minor premise, and a conclusion.

Major premise: Fridays are likely days for pop quizzes.

Minor premise: Today is Friday.

Conclusion: Therefore, today is a likely day for a pop quiz.

Perhaps a more sophisticated example is the syllogism implicit in the Declaration of Independence:

Major premise: Rulers who violate basic human rights should be overthrown.

Minor premise: King George III has violated basic human rights.

Conclusion: Therefore, King George III should be overthrown.

Syllogisms rarely appear in writing or conversation in their pure three-part form. It is far more common to find *enthymemes,* condensed syllogisms in which one or more parts are missing, the writer assuming that the missing parts are clearly understood and don't need to be stated directly.

It's Friday, so I'd better go to Professor Hadley's class. (*Missing premise:* Fridays are likely days for quizzes in Professor Hadley's class.)

I hate movies with violence, and this movie is teeming with violence.
(*Missing conclusion:* Therefore, I hate this movie.)

Syllogisms are worth serious study primarily because they enable readers and writers to examine the often unstated, and sometimes shaky, assumptions behind otherwise convincing arguments.

For a valid syllogism, both premises must be true. It's hard to imagine a syllogism that begins with the premise "The earth is flat" leading to any valid conclusion. But even if both premises are true, the reasoning process itself may be faulty and the conclusion invalid. Consider this syllogism:

Major premise: English majors read lots of books.

Minor premise: David reads lots of books.

Conclusion: Therefore, David is an English major.

Despite the true premises, the conclusion still doesn't follow. The major premise merely says, "English majors read lots of books"; it says nothing about other people who may also read books. Logically, David may be an English major, but he may also be a merchant marine or a grocery store clerk who loves books. The logical structure of the argument makes no more sense than this syllogism: grass is green; her hat is green; therefore, her hat is grass.

Using Induction and Deduction

Induction and deduction are not mutually exclusive. You will seldom engage in one kind of thought without using the other. When you use induction, you usually have a hunch about what generalization the facts will add up to. If you didn't, you wouldn't have a guideline for handling the facts. Consider, for example, that observation about Professor Hadley's quiz-giving tendency. If you hadn't already suspected that Hadley was a Friday quiz-giver, you might not have noticed that the pop quizzes did occur on Friday. Some deduction, therefore, was involved in the process of reaching the generalization about pop quizzes on Friday.

Similarly, in deductive reasoning you must also use induction. To ensure sound premises, you must be sure that your evidence is both adequate and fair, and that involves induction. Induction is important, too, when you present your material. Even if yours is the best of syllogisms, you probably won't convince a reader of its worth unless you offer support for it—reasons, statistics, facts, opinions of authorities, examples. In the Declaration of Independence, for example, Thomas Jefferson supported his case against George III by citing twenty-eight instances in which the king had violated basic human rights. The instances came from induction.

Avoiding Logical Fallacies

Whether your primary tool is induction or deduction, you need to make certain that the evidence you offer isn't based on errors in logic. In other words, you should avoid the following fallacies.

Post Hoc, Ergo Propter Hoc

This impressive Latin phrase means, "after this, therefore because of this." This fallacy takes for a cause an event that merely happened earlier; for example, *A black cat crossed my path and ten minutes later I broke my ankle; therefore, the black cat caused my broken ankle.* Unless the speaker tripped over the cat, such a statement is as unreasonable as *Night follows day; therefore, day causes night.*

Card Stacking

Card stacking means using only the evidence that supports a thesis and ignoring that which contradicts or weakens it. Card stacking is dishonest and can sometimes do serious damage. Suppose, for instance, that a popular newspaper columnist dislikes the mayor of the city. The columnist could prevent the mayor's reelection simply by emphasizing the administration's mistakes and playing down its accomplishments. Soon, the readers of the newspaper would begin to think of the mayor as a bungler who shouldn't be reelected.

Unfair? Of course. It's also unnecessary. A reasonable thesis doesn't require card stacking. A writer can make concessions and still advance the argument; for example, *Although the mayor has made some attempts to attract convention business, the efforts have been too few and too late.* If a thesis isn't reasonable, if it requires card stacking for support, it probably isn't worth defending and the writer should change it.

Slanting

A variation of card stacking is **slanting**, systematically using words whose connotations suggest extreme approval or disapproval of the subject. A person may be "a bag of bones" or have "a model's figure." In either case, the weight is the same, but one term suggests scorn and the other approval. The conscious use of slanting to sway opinion is, like card stacking, quite dishonest. But do not confuse slanting with a writer's legitimate efforts to convey admittedly personal impressions and emotions.

Hasty Generalization

One snowflake doesn't make a blizzard, nor does one experience make a universal law. That one student has cheated on the last five psychology quizzes doesn't mean that all psychology students in the school are cheaters; to say so is to make a **hasty generalization**, to draw a conclusion about a group that is based on insufficient evidence.

Overgeneralization

Overgeneralizations are similar to hasty generalizations. Overgeneralization occurs, regardless of how much "evidence" is available, when one assumes that all members of a group, nationality, race, or sex have the characteristics observed in some members of that group: "all feminists hate housework"; "the English are always cold and reserved"; "never trust a used-car salesperson." Surely it's possible that some feminists like to cook, that some English people are volatile, and that at least one or two used-car salespersons are trustworthy. Words such as *all, never, always, every, true,* and *untrue* are seldom justified when dealing with the complexities of human beings and human institutions. You would do well in writing your papers to qualify potentially troublesome generalizations with words such as *some, seldom, tend, sometimes, frequently, seem, appear, often, perhaps,* and *many.* Both hasty generalizations and overgeneralizations lead to prejudice and superstition and to theses that cannot be developed logically or effectively.

Non Sequitur

Meaning "it does not follow," a *non sequitur* is a conclusion that does not follow from the premises. For example:

> I was a volunteer worker this summer so now I am saving to go to medical school.

Usually, *non sequiturs* occur because the writer or speaker neglects to make the connection between the premises and the conclusion clear to readers. In the preceding example, the writer's thinking probably resembles this:

- I worked as a volunteer this summer for an organization that served men and women with serious diseases.
- These people suffered greatly.
- I felt that I was able to bring them some comfort from their pain and that this work gave me great satisfaction.
- I'd like to be able to help ill people.
- Therefore, I am saving to go to medical school so that I can become a physician and bring even more comfort to the sick.

Although the writer sees the connection easily, he has to reveal thought processes so that the audience may also see the connection.

Another kind of *non sequitur* occurs because the writer or speaker draws an incorrect or debatable conclusion:

> Jack is 6 feet, 7 inches tall; I want him on my basketball team.

The unstated syllogism that leads to the conclusion is

> Successful basketball players tend to be very tall.
>
> Jack is very tall.
>
> Therefore, Jack will be a successful basketball player.

Although both the major premise and the minor premise are true, the conclusion does not necessarily follow. Jack may be so awkward that he trips over his own feet; thus, not all tall people make good basketball players. The writer's conclusion is, therefore, questionable and perhaps should be rejected.

Ignoring the Question

In **ignoring the question**, the writer or speaker deliberately or unintentionally shifts emphasis from the topic under discussion. You can (but should not) ignore a question in several ways.

Ad Hominem Argument

Arguing *ad hominem* (literally, "against the man") means making an irrelevant attack on a person rather than dealing with the actual issue under discussion. Suppose, for example, that Senator Goodfellow, who has admitted to cheating on his income tax for the past five years, proposes a bill for welfare reform. It would be a fallacy to attack the bill by arguing that its proponent is guilty of tax evasion. The bill may be logical, humane, and in the best interest of the country. If it is not, what are its weaknesses? The bill, not Senator Goodfellow's problems with the Internal Revenue Service, should be the subject of discussion.

Not all personal attacks, of course, are necessarily irrelevant. If Senator Goodfellow were seeking reelection, one could logically approve of his ideas and still vote against him because his character defects indicate the danger of trusting him in a position of power and responsibility.

Straw Man Argument

The writer or speaker attributes to the opposition actions or beliefs of which the opposition is not guilty and then attacks the opposition for those actions or beliefs.

> Parents who boast of never having to spank their children should feel shame instead of pride. Discipline and socially responsible behavior are vitally important, and people who sneer at such things deserve the condemnation of all concerned citizens.

Some parents might very well be able to boast of not having to spank their children and yet also demand of their children discipline and socially responsible behavior.

Begging the Question

The writer or speaker assumes in the thesis something that really needs to be proved.

> Since students learn to write in high school, the college composition course is a waste of time and should be replaced by a more useful and stimulating course.

One who chooses to write a paper with that thesis has the obligation to prove that students do learn how to write in high school—a source of great controversy in all discussions of American education.

Shifting the Burden of Proof

Logic requires that *whoever asserts must prove*. It is not logical to say,

> I believe the flu epidemic was caused by a conspiracy of large drug companies, and you can't prove it wasn't.

For the assertion to be taken seriously, the writer must offer reasonable proof of a conspiracy.

Circular Argument

Arguing in a circle means simply restating the premise instead of giving a reason for holding the premise.

> I like detective novels because mystery stories always give me great pleasure.

All that sentence says is, "I like detective novels because I like detective novels." Of greater interest would be the characteristics of the detective novels the speaker does like. In other words, one needs a reason for liking detective novels, and to say that one likes them because they give pleasure is not to give a reason. Why do the novels give pleasure? An honest answer to that question will provide a workable thesis and prevent a circular argument.

Either/Or

In the **either/or fallacy**, the writer or speaker suggests that there are only two alternatives when, in fact, there may be more.

> Although I am quite ill, I must turn my term paper in tomorrow, or I will fail the course.

The writer presents only two alternatives; however, it is also possible that the instructor, recognizing the student's illness, might accept a late paper.

Of course, if one is cursed with a professor who does not accept late papers, regardless of circumstances, then one actually has only two alternatives, and no fallacy exists.

Argument by Analogy

An **analogy** is an extended comparison. It can clarify a difficult concept or dramatize an abstraction by comparing the unfamiliar with the familiar. But an analogy doesn't prove anything because, regardless of the number of similarities between two things, there are always some differences. One can't assume that because two things are alike in some respects, they are alike in all respects. Consider the following example.

> Learning to write a good essay is like learning to drive a car. Beginning drivers feel overwhelmed by the number of operations they must perform to keep a car moving—controlling the brake and the accelerator, staying in their lane, watching the cars in front of them while keeping an eye on the rear-view mirror. In addition, they must observe all traffic laws. The tasks seem insurmountable. Yet, in time, some of the operations become almost automatic and the drivers relax enough so that they can even look at the scenery now and then. So it is with beginning writers. At first, they wonder how they can make an outline for a paper, write clear topic sentences, develop paragraphs, provide transitions, write good introductions and conclusions, and still observe all the rules of English grammar. As with driving, part of the process eventually becomes automatic, and the writers relax enough to concentrate primarily on the ideas they wish to develop.

The comparison deals only with the similarities of feelings in the two experiences and is a successful analogy because it clarifies the experience of writing for the beginner. But if one extends the comparison to encompass other demands on drivers—checking antifreeze, repairing flats, maintaining brake fluid—the analogy falls apart.

Historical analogies present a similar problem. We can't assume that because two historical events are alike in some respects, the outcomes will inevitably be the same. You have probably heard the argument that the United States is on the verge of collapse because some conditions here—relaxed sexual mores, widespread demand for immediate pleasure, and political cynicism and corruption—parallel those of the Roman Empire just before its fall. The argument doesn't consider, among other things, that the forms of government differ, that the bases for the economy differ, or that the means of educating the population differ. The two societies are not alike in every respect, and one cannot assume that because one society fell, the other also will fall.

Analogy can be useful for clarifying an idea, but argument by analogy can be dangerous.

EXERCISE Following are examples of logical fallacies. Read them, and determine what type of fallacy each most strongly represents.

1. I lost my wallet yesterday. I knew that walking under that ladder in the morning would be trouble!
2. Yesterday, my neighbor's sixteen-year-old son zoomed out of the driveway in his new car and barely missed my daughter, who was riding her tricycle on the sidewalk. Last week, a seventeen-year-old girl hit the rear of my car when I had to stop suddenly for a traffic light. When are we going to come to our senses and raise the legal driving age to twenty-one?
3. How can she be guilty of that crime? She has such a lovely family—they go to church regularly and are such friendly people.
4. Of course she's poor. Look at that old torn coat she's wearing!
5. How can Senator O'Malley speak for labor? What does he know about the needs of the average worker? He was born rich.
6. I love visiting Wyoming because I really enjoy traveling out West.
7. We must change this unfair method of closing fire stations.
8. We should either pay our teachers better salaries or admit that we don't care about the quality of our children's education.
9. I don't understand why Abraham Lincoln is considered a great president. He was a warmonger who, by government proclamation, took away the property of a large number of citizens.
10. How do *you* know that life does not exist on other planets?

Making Appeals

In laying out your argument, you have to use details to back up your appeals. An appeal is simply your effort to get a reader to see that your ideas are valid, or at least more valid than someone else's. Students of argument as far back as the early Greek philosopher Aristotle have divided appeals into three categories:

- *Logos*, which means logical appeals
- *Pathos*, which means emotional appeals
- *Ethos*, which means ethical appeals

The strongest arguments usually draw on all three types of appeals and present supporting details that back up each kind. But pitfalls do exist in using these appeals, and you should find it useful to see the characteristics of each one and its potential misuse.

Kind of Appeal	Features	Potential for Abuse
Logos (logical appeals)	■ Clear reasoning ■ Reliable evidence—facts, data, statistics, expert testimony, personal experience, interviews, cases ■ Demonstrates any claim ■ Qualifies claims when needed ■ Acknowledges opposing arguments	■ Unexplained reasoning ■ Overgeneralization of assertions ■ Logical fallacies ■ Evidence left out ■ No opposing arguments considered
Pathos (emotional appeals)	■ Supports logical arguments ■ Language that influences readers ■ Verbal and (or) visual images ■ Balanced emotional language ■ Ideas stated fairly	■ Overuse of images ■ Replaces logical arguments ■ Stereotypes people ■ Takes advantage of emotional language (through hate, anger, fear, pity, prejudice, and so on) to manipulate rather than convince ■ Oversimplifies complex issues
Ethos (ethical appeals)	■ Appeals to reader's sense of fairness and realistic views ■ Sincerity and honesty ■ Humane and caring tone ■ Demonstrates understanding of reader's concerns ■ Confident in own credentials and those of experts used as supporting evidence	■ Apparent unfairness or dishonesty ■ Biased approach ■ Distortion of information ■ Intolerant of ideas of others ■ Advocates prejudiced viewpoints

Now look at the three kinds of appeals in action. If you were writing an argumentation paper that, for example, advocated the outlawing of tobacco sales, your appeals might draw on these kinds of evidence:

Appeals for Outlawing Tobacco Sales

Logos (logical appeals)	■ Present statistics on national sales of tobacco
	■ Present data on numbers of tobacco-related illnesses and deaths
	■ Show the long-term effects of tobacco use for current smokers
	■ Acknowledge the appeal of smoking to current users; then point out its irrelevance in the larger problem of health
	■ Indicate failing measures adopted in the past to cut cigarette use among Americans
Pathos (emotional appeals)	■ Present the anguished case of a long-suffering friend or family member seriously impaired by smoking habit
	■ Portray the effects of second-hand smoking on infants and children
	■ Cite interviews with nonsmokers who find smoking intolerable
Ethos (ethical appeals)	■ Show your sense of fairness by acknowledging financial effect on tobacco industry and tax receipts
	■ Counter the objection with suggestions on how tobacco farmers could raise productive crops or with recommendations for government tax subsidies
	■ Acknowledge cherished American value of free choice and individuality
	■ Cite experts who argue that outlawing sales is the best way to eliminate dire effects of smoking on health and health care

Writing Your Argumentation Paper

Argumentation papers must draw on controversial subject matter—that is, the possibility for a difference of opinion on the subject must exist. Otherwise, there would be no need to argue. In the sense that the purpose of an argumentation paper is to persuade a reader to a point of view, you have written argumentation papers since you began your study of English composition. In every paper, you have taken a position on a subject and have offered logical reasons for holding that position. Our "Having Your Say" exercises, appearing frequently throughout the text, further encourage you to write arguments.

Writing a Formal Argument

A formal argumentation paper has its own specific requirements. In a formal argument, the writer should follow certain guidelines.

 TIPS   for Writing a Formal Argument

- State the problem or issue, sometimes tracing its causes.
- In some cases, state the possible positions to be taken on the problem.
- State the position that the paper will take.
- Offer supporting detail that the position taken is the reasonable one to hold.
- Anticipate objections to the position and acknowledge or refute them.
- Affirm the position and make a final appeal.

All these requirements are important, but we want especially to note the importance of the next to the last point. Anticipating objections to your position, presenting them in your paper, and admitting or refuting them are key features of the strong argumentation essay.

Developing a Debatable Position

You know all about limiting a topic to suit the time and requirements of the assignment, but in an argumentation paper, there's another key element in regard to selecting your topic. Your topic and thesis must lend themselves to debate. If people can take sides on the issue, you've probably chosen a good topic. Of course, you have to know it well and be able to argue it convincingly. To check on whether your thesis is a good one, always ask yourself this question: Would anyone disagree with it?

Possible Thesis	Is It Debatable?
The scientific community should work hard to find a cure for cancer.	**No.** Who would dispute this statement? It's not a good topic for an argumentation paper.
We should stop using live animals for scientific testing.	**Yes.** Many disagree and feel that animal testing is essential if we are to make advances in medicine.
Gay couples should have the same marital rights as heterosexual couples.	**Yes.** This is a heated topic in today's society, and many people believe that laws should allow gay marriage.
People who own pets should clean up their animals' mess from city streets.	**Possibly but not probably.** Few would disagree that someone must clean up after pets; unless the argument is that someone other than the owners should address the problem or that city dwellers should not be allowed to own pets at all, this is not a viable argument.
We should provide high-quality schools for our children.	**No.** No one would debate this assertion.

ASSIGNMENT: ARGUMENTATION

Write an argumentation essay on a debatable topic that interests you. Use the tips on page 334 and the student model on pages 336–337 as a guide. Avoid logical fallacies: read carefully pages 325–330, which define and explain the most familiar forms of fallacious reasoning. Balance your appeals among logic, emotion, and ethics; examine the charts on pages 332–333. If you are having difficulty deciding on a topic for your argumentation paper, you might find help simply by choosing one of the following statements and arguing for or against that statement.

1. The media unfairly hound celebrities accused of crimes.
2. The United States government should reinstitute the draft for all men and women eighteen years and older.
3. Reality TV should really be called unreality TV.
4. The sale of tobacco should be made illegal.

5. Among the groups most unfairly discriminated against are overweight people.

6. If we require people to pass a driving test before licensing them to operate a car, we should require people to pass some kind of parenting test before allowing them to have children.

7. Marijuana should be legal for medicinal purposes.

8. As an exercise, swimming far exceeds running as a means to health and fitness.

9. The pollution of the world's oceans is a major threat to humanity.

10. Random drug tests of high school students are a violation of human rights.

Student Writing: Argumentation

Examine the following student argumentation paper, which includes annotations.

Sandra Travis-Edwards
The Right Not to Vote

1 — *Introduction: identifies opposing arguments*

I believe that the right to vote is one of the most important parts of being an American citizen. Our right to participate in choosing the leaders of our country ensures the continuance of our democratic system, and has protected this democracy and allowed it to flourish over the past two centuries. But, although I believe all this as firmly as it is possible to believe anything, I believe just as strongly in a citizen's right not to vote.

Thesis makes an arguable assertion: people have the right NOT to vote

2 Many people argue that not voting is sheer foolishness. They believe that not voting is a way of avoiding the responsibility of having a political opinion. They say that it is proof that a person has absolutely no interest in politics, and that a person who doesn't vote just doesn't care. While this may often be true, it is not always the case.

More opposing arguments

3 I have chosen not to vote twice in my life, both times for different, yet valid reasons. The first time I chose not to vote was when I was

Topic sentence of paragraph 3 with implied link to paragraph 4

Narration with clear chronology

Summary of main point of paragraph: forceful closing

Good phrase: "ineptness and idiocy"

Effective figurative expression: "staying home with me"

Conclusion: when not voting is justified and when not voting is unjustified

going through a three-year period in which I moved three separate times. I came into one community just in time to register for an extremely important and hotly contested mayoral election. Needless to say I was flooded with canvassers from various candidates, with flyers on my car's windshield, and with advice from my new neighbors. There were only a few short weeks until the election, and with a new job and a new apartment to get used to, I knew I would never have time to catch up with all the election details I needed. Instead of desperately attempting to become informed about my new neighborhood, its needs, and how each of the many candidates might or might not meet them, I chose not to vote. I believe that when one must choose between casting an ignorant, uninterested vote and casting no vote at all, the latter is the only responsible choice.

The second time I decided not to vote was a little later. I had finally gotten settled in the town which is still my home, and I had had time to get to know the community well enough to be an interested and excited participant in the various elections that had been held since I moved in. The most recent school board election was different, however. I hated the candidates. Everything I saw, heard, and read caused me to distrust their motives, suspect their honesty, and question their competence. The campaign was generally referred to as an attempt to determine the lesser of two evils. I was disgusted, as I believe that voting should be a matter of making a positive choice for a candidate, not being forced to choose between ineptness and idiocy. I chose, once again, not to vote. And when I was asked by anyone—friend, neighbor, or candidate—where my vote would be going, I explained that it would be staying home with me, and I explained why. Sometimes, the action of not voting is a stronger political move than voting is.

The right not to vote is as important as the right to vote. Properly thought out, in situations where it is logically seen to be the best possible option instead of the easy way out of an important responsibility, it can be a way of avoiding casting an ill-informed vote or a way of preserving one's personal integrity and making one's opinions known when faced with a bad slate of candidates.

Illustration: writer identifies the first time that she did not vote

Cause and effect: writer explains why she didn't vote

4

"The second time...": transition helps achieve unity and coherence by linking topic sentence to previous paragraph

Illustration: another example of when the writer didn't vote, followed by cause-and-effect analysis

5

Strong transition: connects final paragraph with last sentence of paragraph 4

FOR WRITING OR DISCUSSION

1. Of the two examples of deciding not to vote, which strikes you as more justified? Explain.

2. Does the writer try to consider possible arguments against her position? Are there reasonable and effective arguments that she does not consider? Explain your answer.

3. What kinds of appeals has the writer used? Support your answer with direct references to the essay.

4. Think of a current or recent candidate or proposed law and write an argumentation paper expressing your support or opposition.

Argumentation: Perspectives on Immigrants in America

In these selections about immigration—two Web sites, a cartoon, a current newspaper editorial and, finally, two student editorials from different college newspapers—note the argumentation strategies at play.

U.S. IMMIGRATION SUPPORT

"Illegal Immigration"

1   Illegal immigration continues to be a controversial and divisive topic, not only in the United States, but throughout the world. An individual who is residing in a country illegally is known as an "illegal immigrant." Other terms that are commonly used include: undocumented immigrant, illegal immigrant, undocumented alien, unauthorized migrant, illegal migrant, illegal alien, migrant, or undocumented worker. Illegal immigrants comprise a vast category. Some undocumented immigrants entered the country illegally and others entered legally but overstayed the number of days permitted on their visa or violated the terms of their permanent resident card or refugee permit. Regardless of how a migrant got to their new home country, they decided to take a risk and move to a foreign country in search of a better life. Many usually leave loved ones and valuable possessions behind. Some immigrants leave their home country due to political or economic reasons. Individuals generally choose to emigrate to countries that are more technologically advanced, have greater resources and offer more opportunities. Some immigrants also move to a foreign country to give their children a better life. In countries like the United States, children of illegal immigrants automatically gain citizenship. On the other hand, in other countries

such as France, children are not granted automatic citizenship. Instead, they must request citizenship from the government and fill out applicable documentation once they reach the age of 18. Failure to do so may result in illegal status and deportation.

As stated previously, many illegal immigrants obtain their "illegal" status by entering the country illegally. Throughout history, there continues to be a myriad of ways that immigrants cross the border in order to get into the United States. One method that is often popular with immigrants from the Caribbean is to cross the Atlantic Ocean to reach United States, often in a homemade boat or even a tube. Some immigrants from South America may fly into Mexico. Here they may elicit the assistance of a "coyote," or smuggler, to help them attempt to illegally cross the border into the United States. Other illegal immigrants may try to cross the border into the United States by cramming into shipping containers, trucks, or boxcars. They may be able to pay off corrupt authority figures to gain entry into a specific country. Most will find a way to get to their destination and oftentimes, it may involve grave risk to their life. Moreover, with increased security measures and improved technology, it has become even more difficult to cross the border and avoid detection. Immigrants sometimes try numerous times before successfully crossing the border. Political figures have also tried to reduce illegal immigration by passing legislation that would serve as a deterrent. For example, in France it is a crime to assist an illegal immigrant. However it is common for illegal immigrants to have family or friends in a foreign country, and this legislation is often ignored. In addition, in areas with high immigrant populations, cultural enclaves are formed which often offer support to new immigrants. Cultural enclaves offer an atmosphere, culture, and community for recent illegal immigrants much like in the home country. For example, Little Havana, located in Miami, Florida, is a cultural enclave that formed with the high rate of immigration from Cuba.

Once in the foreign country, illegal immigrants tend to become employed in what is known as "low skilled jobs." These jobs are often labor intensive and don't tend to attract many employees. In the United States for example, the landscaping and construction sectors tend to be popular with immigrants as there is generally no requirement to be fluent in the English language. Other employment sectors that attract illegal immigrants include restaurants, hospitality, prostitution, agriculture and domestic service. Some argue that illegal immigrants tend to take on the jobs that residents or citizens refuse while others argue that illegal immigrants take away jobs in general. Work regulations, specifically in the United States, prohibit employers from hiring illegal immigrants. However, this does not deter some employers. Unfortunately some employers even take advantage of an employee's "undocumented" status. An employer may pay below what the federal law requires and allow an employee to work in unsafe conditions. Some employers feel they could get away with these human rights violations with illegal immigrants because they wouldn't report their employer out of fear of deportation. Penalties exist for employers who hire illegal immigrants but they are not always enforced. However, the United States has seen a recent change in immigration enforcement. Companies have found themselves facing harsh penalties and getting negative publicity for hiring illegal workers. Legislation is also being proposed that offers even stricter penalties for employers who knowingly hire illegal immigrants as well as employers that don't support safe working conditions.

4   Not all individuals may be voluntarily entering the country illegally. During the 19th century many were brought into Europe and the United States during the slave trade. Over time, the importation of slaves was significantly reduced and has thankfully become nonexistent. Alarmingly, however, a common trend has emerged with the smuggling of young girls and women into what has become known as a "sex slave trade." Young females are sometimes approached and offered a job in a foreign country. They are deceived into thinking that this job promises sound financial opportunities, and due to their economic situation back home, this proposal seems highly attractive. For many of them, it is a way of getting out of poverty. However, after arriving in the foreign country, they shortly discover that they were brought into the country for the purpose of prostitution. Thousands of miles away from home and with nowhere else to go, they are very vulnerable and have nowhere to go for help. This problem has shown up in increasing numbers in the Middle East and Europe and on a smaller scale in the United States.

FACT VS. FICTION

U.S. Immigration and Customs Enforcement

Fiction: U.S. Immigration and Customs Enforcement (ICE) is aggressively dismissing cases.

1   FACT: Media have suggested that ICE is aggressively dismissing cases based on a directive from Director Morton. This just isn't true. ICE enforcement is alive and well. For two years in a row, ICE has removed a record number of illegal aliens from communities across the United States. The agency focuses limited resources on three high priority areas—the identification and removal of criminals and national security threats, fugitives, and recent border entrants and others who game the system. Last year, ICE removed substantially more criminal aliens than ever before.

2   On Aug. 20, 2010, Director Morton issued a memorandum that allows for the dismissal of a very narrow category of cases. The memorandum applies only to individuals who are about to receive an immigration benefit—namely lawful permanent residence—from U.S. Citizenship and Immigration Services. This is not backdoor amnesty. By dismissing these cases, ICE attorneys can use limited time before immigration judges to seek removal orders against aliens who are not about to receive a green card and can be removed from the country. Pursuing removal orders for aliens who are about to become lawful permanent residents doesn't make sense in terms of time or resources.

Fiction: ICE is pro-amnesty.

FACT: ICE does not engage in "backdoor" amnesty. For two years running, ICE has removed more aliens than it did under the prior Administration. In addition, ICE has removed more criminal convicts than ever before—rendering ICE's enforcement profoundly relevant to public safety. The agency also celebrated record-breaking enforcement against employers who violated the law. In fiscal year 2010, ICE arrested an unprecedented number of employers for illegal hiring and audited the records of more employers than ever before. ICE is committed to tough, sensible enforcement.

3

Fiction: ICE issues secret memos advocating administrative amnesty.

FACT: ICE is clear and upfront about its policies and procedures. ICE is not engaged in amnesty and the removal numbers speak for themselves. ICE has proceeded openly and candidly when considering policy changes. For instance, ICE posted a draft policy related to immigration detainers and solicited views from employees, Congress, law enforcement agencies and the public at large. ICE aims to be transparent in its decisions and policies and has not circulated or entertained secret memoranda about administrative amnesty. Beyond that, the agency's record of continued and serious enforcement speaks for itself. A summary of policy reforms can be viewed at ICE.gov.

4

Fiction: ICE is anti-enforcement.

FACT: ICE is serious about tough, sensible enforcement, and the facts speak for themselves. In a world of limited resources, ICE pursues rational priorities, namely public safety, border security, national security and maintaining the integrity of our immigration system.

5

For two years running, ICE has removed more aliens than it did under the prior Administration. Additionally, ICE removed 70 percent more convicted criminals than it did in 2008 under the prior Administration.

6

ICE is serious about enforcing the nation's immigration laws. ICE officers, attorneys and personnel report to work each day to advance the agency's enforcement mission. ICE's success is evident when criminal aliens are identified and removed from the United States rather than being released to our communities. Undoubtedly, ICE enforces the law—day in and day out.

7

Fiction: ICE runs secret detention facilities.

FACT: ICE is committed to transparency. This year, ICE launched an Online Detainer Locator System on its website, ICE.gov. Interested parties, counsel and family members can use this system to locate detainees. Additionally, visitors can find answers to frequently asked questions, locations of detention facilities, as well as contact information for the facilities on ICE.gov. ICE does not have any secret detention facilities.

8

J. B. HANDLESMAN
Undocumented Aliens

"*Well, they look pretty undocumented to me.*"

J.B. Handlesman/The New Yorker Collection/www.cartoonbank.com

ROCÍO

The Utah Compact

1   Not all the political news this year involves the rise of partisan extremism and government by rage. There has been lots of that. But maybe there is a limit, a point when people of good sense and goodwill band together to say no. As they have just done in Utah.

Political, business, law-enforcement and religious leaders there have endorsed what they call the Utah Compact. It is a statement of principles meant to address, with moderation and civility, "the complex challenges associated with a broken national immigration system." What a welcome contrast it draws with the xenophobic radicalism of places like Arizona.

2

The signers, who hope to influence the shape of state immigration policy, include the mayors of Salt Lake City and Salt Lake County, the state attorney general, two Republican former governors, a former United States senator, and the Roman Catholic Diocese of Salt Lake City, the Chamber of Commerce and a host of other civic groups and citizens. The prominent and powerful Mormon Church did not sign on but issued a "statement of support" calling the compact "a responsible approach to the urgent challenge of immigration reform."

3

A clearer expression of good sense and sanity than Utah's would be hard to find. It says immigration is an issue between the federal government and other countries—"not Utah and other countries." It says local police agencies should focus on fighting crime, "not civil violations of federal code." Because "strong families are the foundation of successful communities," it opposes policies that unnecessarily separate them. It recognizes immigrants' value as workers and taxpayers.

4

It ends by urging a humane approach to the reality of immigration: "Utah should always be a place that welcomes people of goodwill."

5

South of Utah in Arizona, the political establishment, top law-enforcement officers and voters have lined up behind a radical go-it-alone strategy to uproot and terrorize unwanted immigrants. That hard-line fever is spreading, with lawmakers in other states scrambling to pass their versions of the infamous Arizona law that empowers the police to demand people's papers.

6

Immigration hard-liners are used to using the harshest words possible for newcomers, and condemning calls for restraint and humane behavior—as the Utah Minutemen already have—as the same old liberal, pro-amnesty mush. But red-state Utah is nobody's idea of an open-borders fantasyland. The architects of the compact are conservative Republicans who have simply decided not to toe the simplistic party line.

7

This page has always insisted that reform can be—must be—pro-immigrant, pro-business, pro-family, pro-law-enforcement, all at the same time. These values are complementary. Law enforcement is strengthened by bolstering immigrants' rights. Assimilation is more American than mass expulsion. It is also cheaper: a new study by the liberal Center for American Progress calculated that Arizona had lost hundreds of millions of dollars in convention and other business, thanks to the notoriety from its immigration crackdown.

8

Nick Milano
Citizenship for Christmas

1   As the Christmas season arrives, stockpiles at food pantries fill up and help at shelters peaks; this time of the year really encourages people to treat others with sincere kindness. In this spirit, the debate on illegal immigration should be given a second look. From the moment Columbus stepped onto the shores of Hispaniola to this present day, the Americas, with the United States as no exception to the rule, have been marred by years of slavery, manipulation and racism.

2   The blatant exploitation of Native Americans went hand in hand with the importation of African slaves. The Civil War was followed by more wars with Native Americans, and Jim Crow ruled segregation. The human rights issue that plagues our generation is the treatment of illegal immigrants. Republicans on the national presidential stage and all across the country are calling for the construction of a magnificent wall across the border. Debates have seen other, more peculiar stances taken on the issue.

3   Mitt Romney and Rudy Giuliani take extreme measures to prove they each treated illegal immigrants worse than the other. But Romney continued to hire a landscaping company that was caught employing illegal immigrants while he was the governor of Massachusetts. For a man so gung-ho on tossing illegal immigrants out of the country, he was reluctant to double check on the men working on his own home. As with a multitude of other political positions Romney likes to take, it seems he only does so for the political gains.

4   Presidential candidate Tom Tancredo has led the charge against illegal immigration with tirades against the refusal of the people to learn English. In the Republican CNN/You Tube Debate, he refused to even allow for guest workers to come in and help small business owners who rely on their cheap labor. He claimed that there are plenty of Americans who would do the work, but for higher wages.

5   His is a common argument: the illegals are here to steal our jobs! But really, look at the situation logically. There are simple reasons we pay less than two dollars a pound at the grocery store for apples, bananas, oranges and other fruit and vegetables. The person picking the food is not making minimum wage. He does not have the right to limit himself to a humane 40-hour work week. He does not receive healthcare benefits. He most certainly is not going to collect social security or retirement benefits from his employer. They sacrifice a great deal, the least of which is their back from the strenuous labor of unskilled jobs.

Are they really taking jobs Americans would willingly work?   6

Lost in all the debate over who would treat illegal immigrants the worst is the fact   7
that they are very real people. Granted, they have broken the law by coming to the
United States. But for the most part these people embarked on a ruthless journey to
the United States in the hopes of giving their children a better shot at life. No doubt
there are some who harmed the image of the group as a whole by committing violent
crimes or joining gangs like MS-13. Every population has a group who breaks laws
and engages in criminal behavior. But just because some Italians may be in La Cosa
Nostra, not all Italians engage in bookmaking and drug running.

Illegal immigrants who commit violent crimes upon their arrival here should be   8
deported without a second thought. Those who get caught driving drunk should be
deported. Those who get caught running with gangs should be sent home. These are
simple straightforward guidelines, but it is just too much to stomach when politicians
dismiss illegal immigrants merely because they are seeking a new life.

It is the Christmas season, a time for reflection on how to better treat people   9
coming here in pursuit of the American Dream. As Mike Huckabee has mentioned
time and time again, the United States has a poor history when it comes to human
rights and "we're a better country than" one that punishes children. He has made
mention of his fear that there are people who want to treat these people poorly because they are different, for racist reasons.

The politicians hoping to lead this country into the future better take a step   10
back and consider the motivations for the animosity towards these migrant people
merely trying to better their lives. Is it really because they broke a law by coming to
the United States? Can we really blame them for wanting to become part of this great
country? The borders must be made secure, but the nation must also embark on a
journey towards granting amnesty and citizenship. The United States has a chance
to prove it is not a racist country. Let us not allow history to repeat itself yet again. Immigrants leave dire circumstances in the search of a more hopeful future. Who in their
shoes would not sacrifice so much for the betterment of their children's lives?

Quynh Nguyen
Being a Recent American

1   My mother, father and older siblings were all born in Vietnam and fled our homeland to the safety of U.S. soil. They were running away from mass murder, starvation and a Communist regime hell-bent on crushing those who opposed them. I'm the first in my family to be born in the United States, so the first and foremost thing my family taught me was to be grateful to be here.

2   All my life I have been told of the hardships of living in Vietnam—that I was lucky to have free education, health care, flushing toilets and running water. Every quarter I have spent playing an arcade game has been tempered with the knowledge that "25 cents could buy an entire bushel of cabbages in Vietnam that would feed a family for two weeks."

3   Imagine growing up feeling guilty for being so darn lucky, so spoiled with the finest amenities the likes of which your ancestors had never imagined. Then try reconciling that guilt with the drive to accomplish great things in college in order to make money to send home and spare family members from poverty.

4   Those expectations make going to college much more complicated than simply finding the major you love. It makes every selfish decision in college, any spare moment spent having fun, every poor grade feel like a wound to the family.

5   It's a common theme I see across students of all ethnicities who come to college—study hard, get a degree and make life better for your family and community. In spite of how pervasive that drive is, I never see this reflected in mainstream college culture. That lack of visibility makes it much harder to talk about the frustrations of reconciling family expectations with personal desires.

6   When we express that frustration, recent-American students like me are encouraged to be "more American." That means dropping the heavy burden of familial expectations and pursuing our personal, most selfish dreams.

7   Our non-immigrant peers have a hard time understanding the nature of self-sacrifice and familial dedication that is the backbone of our upbringing. They also struggle with the idea of ethnic student associations—why the need for ethnic student associations if we're all American and having a White Student Union would be taboo?

8   I have found it difficult to accommodate my culture and background with my identity as an American. In spite of the United States' long history with immigration, U.S. culture has not found a way to embrace other cultures and welcome them into

the fold. It is as if maintaining one's ethnicity is inherently un-American, and to forget it completely is the rite of initiation to Americanness.

The way I see it, everyone can benefit from the immigration experience, even the mainstream culture. My family has benefited greatly from adopting American values to replace some Vietnamese ones, i.e., feminism and that beating women and children is not OK. I think mainstream U.S. culture could benefit from learning things that my culture has to offer, like the fact that we Americans are probably the luckiest people on the planet.

9

I'm grateful, as all of us recent-Americans are, to be here and to experience the freedoms and the rich culture that the United States has to offer. I hope mainstream U.S. culture learns to cherish its immigrants and what we bring to the table (beyond our delicious cuisine).

10

FOR WRITING OR DISCUSSION

1. How do the titles of the two Web sites reflect their fundamental positions on the immigration issue? Which site makes the more powerful appeal? Where in the appeals of the sites do you find examples of pathos? Logos? Ethos?

2. What is the cartoonist's view of America's documentation demands? Why does he make such a serious issue the subject of a humorous appeal? Does the humor work? Why?

3. What is "The Utah Compact" in the title in the editorial? How does the Utah approach contrast with the approach by Arizona, according to the editorial? How does the editorial compare and contrast with the positions on the Web sites?

4. What is Milano's thesis? How does Nguyen's thesis add a personal dimension to the topic? Where does each writer use logos, pathos, and (or) ethos?

5. On the issues, has Milano convinced you that illegal immigrants are treated badly? Why or why not? How does the word "Christmas" used in the title and the essay strike you? Milano refers to a number of political figures in his essay. Who are they?

6. How does Nguyen accommodate her status as an American and her family's status as Vietnam immigrants? Do you agree with her argument that our "culture has not found a way to embrace other cultures and welcome them into the fold"? How does the writer support this assertion? Which details help you understand her point?

7. Select some aspect of the immigration issue in the United States and write an argumentation essay about it. You may draw on your own experience, your readings, your research, or even some of the points made in these essays.

Argumentation: Perspectives on the Death Penalty

In the selections following, you get a glimpse of the arguments in regard to both sides of the death penalty debate, which continues to draw advocates and opponents with every generation. Many arguments are forthright, as in the student essays you will read by Lauren Heist and Alex Shalom, both published in the same student newspaper on the same day. Mark Essig, author of *Edison and the Electric Chair* (2004), looks at the options for executing prisoners on death row and provides a chilling portrait regardless of one's point of view. Finally, Robert Mankoff's cartoon "Good News" is a subtle yet powerful argument for his position.

Lauren Heist
Capital Punishment: An Example for Criminals

1   A child looks around to see if anyone is watching him. When he's sure that the kitchen is empty, he opens up the cookie jar and smuggles a cookie up to his room. When his mother confronts him about the missing cookie, she tells him taking cookies is not very nice and says if he does it again he will be in trouble. A little while later the child sees the cookie jar again. Not seeing anyone around, he again takes a cookie. The mother tells him taking cookies is wrong again but does not punish him. Soon the child learns that because he hasn't gotten in trouble, taking cookies must not be that bad. Because the mother did not follow through on her threat, the child begins to take advantage of the mother, and the child gets away with whatever he wants.

2   That is what has happened to our police force today. Criminals do not take the law seriously. They do not fear the government. Criminals are taking advantage of us, and they are getting away with murder, literally.

3   The bottom line is people need to respect the law. Without laws, we would live in anarchy. But too many people feel that they are above the law and it does not apply to them. Because people feel alienated from the bureaucrats who make the laws, they simply choose to ignore the laws.

4   If we want to live in a peaceful society, we must enforce the laws, and that includes using the death penalty. Every criminal who commits a first-degree murder should receive the death penalty. The problem with the way the death penalty is used now is not that it is used too often, but rather that it is not used enough.

5   How many muggers actually think, "Man, I hope I don't get the death penalty," before they decide to hold a gun to the head of a person getting money out of an ATM machine? I can assure you that is not a thought that often crosses their minds. The death penalty is only used in extreme cases for infamous psychopaths and serial

killers. The average run-of-the-mill killer can get out of jail in no time flat. If the death penalty were employed more frequently, killers might actually take it into consideration before shooting someone.

The most common argument against the death penalty is that it is hypocritical. Critics ask, how can we claim that murder is wrong and then kill the killer? What most critics do not understand is that governments do not live by the same rules that individual people live by. Governments have powers that people do not have because people concede power to the government. 6

For example, governments have the power to confiscate houses by eminent domain if they are in the way of a road that is going to be built. An individual citizen cannot arbitrarily destroy a house or confiscate property, but governments can do these things because people entrust the government to act in the best interest of the majority of its citizens. The government has the right to use the death penalty because it has a responsibility to keep order in the society. 7

The other argument that people use to oppose the death penalty is that there is always a chance that an innocent person could be executed because the justice system is not perfect. Yes, it is true that the justice system is not entirely foolproof. Nothing is entirely foolproof. The founding fathers tried to ensure that the justice system would be fair by requiring all murder cases to be decided by a jury. People must have faith that their own peers will make fair, logical decisions. In addition, just as critics of the death penalty fear that innocent people might be executed, there is also the possibility that criminals will be set free and will endanger other innocent people. 8

Claiming insanity is no excuse for sparing someone from the death penalty. A murderer is a murderer, no matter who commits it or what mental state they claim to be in at the time. Milwaukee's Jeffrey Dahmer, who killed multiple victims and even admitted to practicing cannibalism, was not sentenced to the death penalty. Instead, he was sentenced to life imprisonment and was killed by a fellow inmate. Why was Dahmer not given the death penalty? Because he was determined to be insane. Susan Smith, the mother who drowned her two young sons in a car, also received life imprisonment instead of the death penalty because she pleaded temporary insanity. People who are clearly guilty of murder should be made examples. If Jeffrey Dahmer and Susan Smith do not receive the death penalty, why would any person ever have to fear the death penalty? 9

Finally, the death penalty should be used more often than it is today because it is economical. Keeping someone in a jail cell for years requires that taxpayers pay 10 for that criminal's food and shelter for the rest of the criminal's life, while he takes up a space that could be used by another criminal. Every day, guilty criminals leave the courthouse and head back out onto the street because the prisons and jails are overcrowded. Meanwhile, other criminals sit on death row, eating up the taxpayers' money and not contributing anything to society.

11   If we want to take this country back from the mobsters and the drug lords and put the power back in the people and the police, we need to use the death penalty. Using the death penalty will not only be economical for all taxpayers, but it will also deter future criminals from killing, which will make us all safer.

Alex Shalom
Abolish the Death Penalty

1   When a convicted murderer's head burst into flames in Florida's electric chair a few weeks ago, reactions varied. The state's Attorney General boasted that, due to problems with the lethal contraption, murderers should be particularly wary if they commit their crimes in Florida because they will suffer greatly before their lives are terminated by the state. Others reacted with disgust and concluded that the United States should abolish the death penalty. The latter is the appropriate response.

2   The U.S. would hardly be breaking ground by abolishing the death penalty. None of the nations of Western Europe practice capital punishment, nor do most of our Latin American neighbors. The reasons for the abolition of the death penalty are many; there are reasons why capital punishment is inherently unjust and there are also reasons why the death penalty, as practiced in the United States, is especially so. I will briefly address both of these categories of reasons. First, however, it will be useful to examine the problems with common justifications for state-sponsored killing.

3   Death penalty proponents generally extend support for capital punishment from both moral and practical perspectives. The pragmatic capital punishment advocates contend that the death penalty deters murder and that it costs less than keeping murderers incarcerated. The appropriate question, however, should not be whether or not the death penalty deters murder; surely it does. Rather, we should ask whether the death penalty deters murder better than life imprisonment, for no death penalty opponent advocates letting murderers walk free on the street.

Levels of deterrence are difficult to measure, but there are some ways to do   4
so. If one examines the states of Michigan and Illinois—two states with very similar
population, land, and demographic make-ups—one discovers something very interesting. Michigan has not executed anyone since it became a state over 150 years
ago, while Illinois has actively used the death penalty over the last 20 years. If the
death penalty were, in fact, a better deterrent than life imprisonment, then Illinois
should have a lower murder rate than Michigan. In reality, Michigan has a lower
murder rate than its southwestern neighbor.

Though it is ridiculous to put a price on human life, some people argue that   5
because prisons are too costly, murderers should be executed. This is a simplistic
answer. While the actual cost of a lethal injection is clearly cheaper than the cost of
a lengthy imprisonment, because death is the ultimate punishment, those facing the
death penalty are always entitled to many legal appeals. Oftentimes, because those
on death row are predominantly indigent, the state is forced to pay for both sides
of the appeals process. When the cost of appeals is factored into the equation, it
becomes evident that capital punishment is not a cost-effective solution.

All facts and figures aside, many people still attempt to justify the continued   6
practice of capital punishment, arguing both that the punishment should fit the
crime—that is, "an eye for an eye"—and that the families of the victims deserve
the peace of mind of having the murderer killed. Coretta Scott King, who lost both
a husband and a mother-in-law to assassination, offers an answer to both of these
statements: "I stand firmly and unequivocally opposed to the death penalty for
those convicted of capital offenses. An evil deed is not redeemed by an evil deed of
retaliation. Justice is never advanced by the taking of a human life. Morality is never
upheld by legalized murder."

In the United States, no crimes other than murder are met with punishments   7
that *imitate* the crime; they are answered with punishments that *fit* the crime. The
government does not burn the homes of arsonists, nor does it rape rapists. That
simply would not make for a just penal system.

There is no reason, moral or practical, to support the death penalty; there are,   8
however, several reasons why it should be abolished. Perhaps the best reason is that
no system of justice is infallible. As long as a state practices capital punishment, there is
always the possibility that an innocent person will be executed. A 1987 study published
by the Stanford Law Review showed that, despite our elaborate appeals system, at least
23 innocent people have been executed in the United States in this century.

9   Colonial Massachusetts is possibly best known for the numerous executions of the innocent during the Salem Witch Trials. The judge in many of those cases, Judge Suel, eventually realized the error of his ways. He made a public statement saying that it was wrong to execute the people that he had sentenced to death. I hope no more judges are forced to come to the dreadful conclusion that they are responsible for the murder of an innocent person.

10   Even when the question of innocence does not loom over a judge's head, there are still factors that make the death penalty inequitable and cruelly administered. The death penalty is a racist institution that disproportionately kills the poor. African Americans receive the death penalty somewhat more often than whites. However, the real injustice of capital punishment is that blacks who kill whites are more likely to receive the death penalty than whites who kill blacks. A study presented in front of the Supreme Court showed that murderers whose victims are white are 139 percent more likely to receive the death penalty than if their victim was black. Though it is clearly not the case that the life of a white person is more valuable than that of a black person, this is what our current system of capital punishment is saying.

11   Murderers who are unable to afford to pay for their own defense are far more likely to be executed than those who can afford a lawyer. In Texas, 75 percent of convicted murderers who had court-appointed attorneys received the death penalty, while only 33 percent of those with private attorneys were killed. According to former Supreme Court Justice Thurgood Marshall, "the burden of capital punishment falls upon the poor, the ignorant, and the underprivileged members of society." This is simply unfair, particularly when lives are at stake.

12   While the United States does not stand alone in the international community in continuing to practice capital punishment, the other countries that practice it are far from world leaders in the area of human rights. Only five countries execute criminals who committed their crimes while under the age of 18: Yemen, Saudi Arabia, Iran, Pakistan, and the United States. Strange bedfellows, indeed. Much of the rest of the world has realized the inhumanity of capital punishment and abolished it. How many more people will die at the hands of the state before the United States follows suit?

MARK ESSIG

Continuing the Search for Kinder Executions

In Tennessee, it is a crime to euthanize a cat with pancuronium bromide, but this doesn't   1
stop the state from using it to execute condemned criminals. Because the drug paralyzes
muscles but does not affect nerves, it may leave its victims wide awake but immobilized
as they painfully suffocate. So prisoners' advocates and medical experts are now trying
to persuade Tennessee—and the nearly 30 other states that use the drug—to choose
different poisons for lethal injection, thereby bringing euthanasia protocols for humans in
line with those for domestic animals.

And so continues the uniquely American habit of tinkering with the machinery of   2
death. For the past century and a half, America's capital punishment debate has resembled
a strange game of leapfrog: opponents of the death penalty claim that the current method,
whatever it may be, is barbaric, which prompts capital-punishment supporters to refine
that method or develop a new one.

Although 19th-century Americans tended to believe that justice and order demanded   3
the ultimate sanction, they were often shaken by graphic accounts of the pain suffered
by hanged men. In 1876, after an especially gruesome hanging, Maine abolished capital
punishment. Inspired by this victory, opponents of the death penalty began to emphasize
the cruelty of the gallows. But their effort was self-defeating: by claiming that the problem
with hanging was the suffering of the condemned, they simply challenged death penalty
advocates to find a better way to kill.

First came adjustments to the gallows. Hangmen created a formula in which rope   4
length was a function of the prisoner's weight—the heavier the victim, the shorter the
drop. But such delicate calculations of anatomy and gravity often failed to add up and
many prisoners slowly strangled to death. To dull the pain, Brooklyn officials in 1847
knocked a murderer cold with ether before hanging him, but this simply highlighted the
deficiencies of the gallows.

Then, in 1889, New York State built the first electric chair, a device championed   5
by Thomas Edison. Edison's advocacy was inspired in part by a wicked plan to hurt
his business rival, George Westinghouse—the chair was powered by Westinghouse's
alternating current, and Edison hoped consumers would begin to associate AC with
danger and death. But Edison had less cynical reasons as well: he was an opponent
of the death penalty—"an act of foolish barbarity," he called it—and he believed that
electrocution would be less barbaric than the noose. Many others agreed, and eventually
25 states and the District of Columbia installed electric chairs.

6   Electrocution remained the state of the art for three decades, until the public grew dismayed by bungled executions that required several shocks or set the prisoner on fire. Before long there was another scientific option: an airtight chamber filled with poison gas, adopted by Nevada in 1924 and then by 10 more states in the coming decades. Like all complex machines, however, these execution devices were prone to malfunction, and prisoners suffered the consequences.

7   So in 1977 Oklahoma began to poison condemned prisoners with a three-drug cocktail: sodium thiopental (to produce unconsciousness), pancuronium bromide (to paralyze the muscles) and potassium chloride (to stop the heart). Promising a clean, painless death, this protocol quickly gained widespread acceptance.

8   Until now that is. The next step seems obvious: states will adopt a different drug regimen, which, no doubt, will soon gain critics of its own.

9   However, it seems that many death-penalty opponents are realizing that technological leapfrog is a game they can't win, and are opting out of the latest debate. Amnesty International has issued this statement: "The search for a 'humane' way of killing people should be seen for what it is—a search to make executions more palatable." In Nebraska, the only state with the electric chair as its sole method of execution, State Senator Ernie Chambers has vowed to fight any attempt to "make executions easier." He hopes that the United States Supreme Court will one day declare electrocution unconstitutional, leaving Nebraska without a valid execution law.

10   Some of the condemned themselves have even sought a more painful death in order to highlight the hypocrisy of "painless execution." In 2001, John Byrd, a convicted murderer in Ohio, requested electrocution rather than the needle; when prison workers balked at using the chair, which had been idle for nearly 40 years, the Legislature abolished electrocution and forced Mr. Byrd to die by lethal injection. Earl Bramblett, a Virginia prisoner, had more success in his protest. "I'm not going to lay down on a gurney and have them stick a needle in my arm and make it look like an antiseptic execution," he said, and he died in the electric chair on April 9.

11   For too long, defenders of capital punishment, fearing that brutal killing methods might provoke public opposition, have found unwitting allies among their adversaries, anxious to relieve the suffering of the condemned. Now penalty opponents are realizing that scientific execution methods, ceaselessly refined, simply mask the barbarity of killing.

ROBERT MANKOFF

Good News

"*Good news. Your execution was overturned on appeal.*"

Robert Mankoff/The New Yorker Collection/www.cartoonbank.com

FOR WRITING OR DISCUSSION

1. What is the thesis of each student's paper? Where does Heist state the thesis most clearly? Shalom? What is the nature of the appeals in each essay?

2. How does each student writer treat the issue of the economics of the death penalty? In what ways do the presentations on the issue deal with opposing points of view? Where else do the writers treat opposing points of view?

3. What is Essig's thesis in "Continuing the Search for Kinder Executions"? How would you characterize the appeals he uses in the essay? In what ways does his closing paragraph suggest a new course of action for opponents of the death penalty?

4. How has Essig used illustration in making his argument? Comparison? Which cases do you find most convincing, if any? Why?

5. How has Essig produced a dramatic impact in the last line of the introduction? How does a phrase like "machinery of death" in paragraph 2 affect you as a reader?

6. The death penalty is no laughing matter—yet cartoonist Mankoff has used humor to provide a powerful statement of his position. How does the caption of the cartoon define the artist's argument and his thesis, so to speak? What is the setting of the cartoon, and why is it important? Who is the speaker? How does Mankoff in few words summarize one of the major objections held by those opposing the death penalty? And how does humor contribute to the success of the argument?

7. Identify some other government practice—the taxation system, adoption laws, job protection, wildlife protection, or affirmative action, to name just a few of many possibilities—and, after limiting your topic, write a well-reasoned argument, pro or con, that takes a firm position on the issue.

HAVING YOUR SAY

Consider the varied arguments in this section and write your own argumentation essay on the death penalty. You might read or reread George Orwell's essay "A Hanging" (pages 11–14) as another example of writing on capital punishment.

Argumentation in the World Around You

Some of the cleverest uses of argumentation appear in advertising, which draws on intense visual imagery and precise language to make a point quickly and indelibly. The argument can be transparent, especially in television and magazine ads at election time, when candidates trying to get your vote argue why you should choose them over others. But in many—even most—advertisements, the argument is more subtle, and as an active reader you have to tease out its meaning and to be aware of the strategies used to capture your attention and convince you that its message is valid. In this public service advertisement for an important cause, you can see how argumentative strategies help create intended meaning.

Thesis — People can do something specific to fight hunger in America. Note the induction-deduction elements. Hunger is bad; we should fight hunger; eat a Snickers bar and the manufacturers will donate a meal to a hungry person (and you won't be particularly hungry either, having eaten the candy bar).

Specific details — The ad's mixed ethnic and gender representation of the three people shown eating a Snickers bar suggests a wide acceptance of Snickers as a candy of choice, but also suggests that people everywhere are eager to "do good," as the ad states. The specific details of the Snickers bar and the people in a formal pose, as if looking to the future, one without hunger, help drive the point home.

Appeals — Your sense of fairness responds to *ethos* here: any effort to end hunger (most people want "to do good") is appropriate. The sentence "You can help us bar hunger in America" also makes an ethical appeal. For *logos*, you've seen the logic at play in the thesis: hunger is bad, and you can do something about it by eating a Snickers bar. For *pathos*, the tag line "It tastes good to do good" hints at emotional satisfaction derived from eating a Snickers bar. Eat one, and someone else won't go hungry. (Note the implied language play: eat a Snickers *bar* and you can *bar* hunger.) One may question whether the goal of 3.5 million meals is attainable, but it certainly is laudable. The phrases "Feeding America" and "Bar Hunger" have wide emotional and ethical appeal.

Audience and purpose — The ad appeared in *Rolling Stone*, a magazine devoted to music, liberal politics, and popular culture and directed at a young audience. Readers would know and buy Snickers, and the advertisement's purpose is to have more buyers buy even more—all for a notable cause.

Your Turn

Check the Internet for a "visual argument"—that is any photograph, cartoon, advertisement, or Web site that makes an argument in both visual and verbal terms. Write an essay in which you analyze your selection.

Specific details

Purpose

IT TASTES GOOD TO DO GOOD.

EVERY TIME YOU EAT A SNICKERS,* YOU CAN HELP US BAR HUNGER IN AMERICA. JUST ENTER YOUR WRAPPER CODE AND WE'LL DONATE A MEAL TO SOMEONE IN NEED. IT'S THE TASTIEST WAY TO DO SOME GOOD.

HELP US DONATE UP TO 3.5 MILLION MEALS.*
*Enter the code inside the wrapper of specially marked SNICKERS® at Snickers.com or text it to 45495.

FEEDING AMERICA

BAR HUNGER™

Ethical appeal

Thesis

Ethical and emotional appeal

SNICKERS® is a registered trademark of Mars, Incorporated. This trademark is used with permission. Mars, Incorporated is not associated with Pearson Education. The SNICKERS® advertisement is printed with permission of Mars, Incorporated.

Readings for Writing

The selections that follow are solid examples of argumentation writing. Drawn from popular periodicals, the pieces demonstrate argumentation writing on serious public issues.

STEPHANIE COONTZ

Till Children Do Us Part

Half a century ago, the conventional wisdom was that having a child was the surest way to build a happy marriage. Women's magazines of that era promised that almost any marital problem could be resolved by embarking on parenthood. Once a child arrives, "we don't worry about this couple any more," an editor at *Better Homes and Gardens* enthused in 1944. "There are three in that family now. . . . Perhaps there is not much more needed in a recipe for happiness." 1

Over the past two decades, however, many researchers have concluded that three's a crowd when it comes to marital satisfaction. More than 25 separate studies have established that marital quality drops, often quite steeply, after the transition to parenthood. And forget the "empty nest" syndrome: when the children leave home, couples report an increase in marital happiness. 2

But does the arrival of children doom couples to a less satisfying marriage? Not necessarily. Two researchers at the University of California at Berkeley, Philip and Carolyn Cowan, report in a forthcoming briefing paper for the Council on Contemporary Families that most studies finding a large drop in marital quality after childbirth do not consider the very different routes that couples travel toward parenthood. 3

Some couples plan the conception and discuss how they want to conduct their relationship after the baby is born. Others disagree about whether or when to conceive, with one partner giving in for the sake of the relationship. And sometimes, both partners are ambivalent. 4

The Cowans found that the average drop in marital satisfaction was almost entirely accounted for by the couples who slid into being parents, disagreed over it or were ambivalent about it. Couples who planned or equally welcomed the conception were likely to maintain or even increase their marital satisfaction after the child was born. 5

Marital quality also tends to decline when parents backslide into more traditional gender roles. Once a child arrives, lack of paid parental leave often leads the wife to quit her job and the husband to work more. This produces discontent on both sides. The wife resents her husband's lack of involvement in child care and housework. The husband resents his wife's ingratitude for the long hours he works to support the family. 6

When the Cowans designed programs to help couples resolve these differences, they had fewer conflicts and higher marital quality. And the children did better socially and academically because their parents were happier. 7

8   But keeping a marriage vibrant is a never-ending job. Deciding together to have a child and sharing in child-rearing do not immunize a marriage. Indeed, collaborative couples can face other problems. They often embark on such an intense style of parenting that they end up paying less attention to each other.

9   Parents today spend much more time with their children than they did 40 years ago. The sociologists Suzanne Bianchi, John Robinson and Melissa Milkie report that married mothers in 2000 spent 20 percent more time with their children than in 1965. Married fathers spent more than twice as much time.

10   A study by John Sandberg and Sandra Hofferth at the University of Michigan showed that by 1997 children in two-parent families were getting six more hours a week with Mom and four more hours with Dad than in 1981. And these increases occurred even as more mothers entered the labor force.

11   Couples found some of these extra hours by cutting back on time spent in activities where children were not present—when they were alone as a couple, visiting with friends and kin, or involved in clubs. But in the long run, shortchanging such adult-oriented activities for the sake of the children is not good for a marriage. Indeed, the researcher Ellen Galinsky has found that most children don't want to spend as much time with their parents as parents assume; they just want their parents to be more relaxed when they are together.

12   Couples need time alone to renew their relationship. They also need to sustain supportive networks of friends and family. Couples who don't, investing too much in their children and not enough in their marriage, may find that when the demands of child-rearing cease to organize their lives, they cannot recover the relationship that made them want to have children together in the first place.

13   As the psychologist Joshua Coleman suggests, the airline warning to put on your own oxygen mask before you place one on your child also holds true for marriage.

FOR WRITING OR DISCUSSION

1. What is the thesis of this essay? What is the purpose of the 1944 quote in paragraph 1 from an editor of a well-known magazine that still publishes today?

2. In what ways has Coontz chosen a debatable topic for this selection? What are its two sides?

3. How does Coontz deal with opposing arguments?

4. What is the essential nature of the appeals in this essay? Would you say that they are logical, emotional, or ethical—or a combination? Why do you feel as you do?

5. In what ways does the conclusion state the main point of the essay? What is the meaning of the last paragraph, which is only one sentence long?

6. Write an argumentation essay about the effects of children on a marriage. Be sure that you choose a debatable topic.

JAMES Q. WILSON

Just Take Away Their Guns

The President wants still tougher gun control legislation and thinks it will work. The public supports more gun control laws but suspects they won't work. The public is right. 1

Legal restraints on the lawful purchase of guns will have little effect on the illegal use of guns. There are some 200 million guns in private ownership, about one-third of them handguns. Only about 2 percent of the latter are employed to commit crimes. It would take a Draconian, and politically impossible, confiscation of legally purchased guns to make much of a difference in the number used by criminals. Moreover, only about one-sixth of the handguns used by serious criminals are purchased from a gun shop or pawnshop. Most of these handguns are stolen, borrowed, or obtained through private purchases that wouldn't be affected by gun laws. 2

What is worse, any successful effort to shrink the stock of legally purchased guns (or of ammunition) would reduce the capacity of law-abiding people to defend themselves. Gun control advocates scoff at the importance of self-defense, but they are wrong to do so. Based on a household survey, Gary Kleck, a criminologist at Florida State University, has estimated that every year, guns are used—that is, displayed or fired—for defensive purposes more than a million times, not counting their use by the police. If his estimate is correct, this means that the number of people who defend themselves with a gun exceeds the number of arrests for violent crimes and burglaries. 3

Our goal should not be the disarming of law-abiding citizens. It should be to reduce the number of people who carry guns unlawfully, especially in places—on streets, in taverns—where the mere presence of a gun can increase the hazards we all face. The most effective way to reduce illegal gun-carrying is to encourage the police to take guns away from people who carry them without a permit. This means encouraging the police to make street frisks. 4

The Fourth Amendment to the Constitution bans "unreasonable searches and seizures." In 1968 the Supreme Court decided (*Terry* v. *Ohio*) that a frisk—patting down a person's outer clothing—is proper if the officer has a "reasonable suspicion" that the person is armed and dangerous. If a pat-down reveals an object that might be a gun, the officer can enter the suspect's pocket to remove it. If the gun is being carried illegally, the suspect can be arrested. 5

The reasonable-suspicion test is much less stringent than the probable-cause standard the police must meet in order to make an arrest. A reasonable suspicion, however, is more than just a hunch; it must be supported by specific facts. The courts have held, not always consistently, that these facts include someone acting in a way that leads an experienced officer to conclude criminal activity may be afoot; someone fleeing at the approach of an officer; a person who fits a drug courier profile; a motorist stopped for a traffic violation who has a suspicious bulge in his pocket; a suspect identified 6 by a reliable informant as carrying a gun. The Supreme Court has also upheld frisking people on probation or parole.

7   Some police departments frisk a lot of people, but usually the police frisk rather few, at least for the purpose of detecting illegal guns. In 1992 the police arrested about 240,000 people for illegally possessing or carrying a weapon. This is only about one-fourth as many as were arrested for public drunkenness. The average police officer will make *no* weapons arrests and confiscate *no* guns during any given year. Mark Moore, a professor of public policy at Harvard University, found that most weapons arrests were made because a citizen complained, not because the police were out looking for guns.

8   It is easy to see why. Many cities suffer from a shortage of officers, and even those with ample law-enforcement personnel worry about having their cases thrown out for constitutional reasons or being accused of police harassment. But the risk of violating the Constitution or engaging in actual, as opposed to perceived, harassment can be substantially reduced.

9   Each patrol officer can be given a list of people on probation or parole who live on that officer's beat and be rewarded for making frequent stops to insure that they are not carrying guns. Officers can be trained to recognize the kinds of actions that the Court will accept as providing the "reasonable suspicion" necessary for a stop and frisk. Membership in a gang known for assaults and drug dealing could be made the basis, by statute or Court precedent, for gun frisks.

10   The available evidence supports the claim that self-defense is a legitimate form of deterrence. People who report to the National Crime Survey that they defended themselves with a weapon were less likely to lose property in a robbery or be injured in an assault than those who did not defend themselves. Statistics have shown that would-be burglars are threatened by gun-wielding victims about as many times a year as they are arrested (and much more often than they are sent to prison) and that the chances of a burglar being shot are about the same as his chances of going to jail. Criminals know these facts even if gun control advocates do not and so are less likely to burgle occupied homes in America than occupied ones in Europe, where the residents rarely have guns.

11   Some gun control advocates may concede these points but rejoin that the cost of self-defense is self-injury: Handgun owners are more likely to shoot themselves or their loved ones than a criminal. Not quite. Most gun accidents involve rifles and shotguns, not handguns. Moreover, the rate of fatal gun accidents has been declining while the level of gun ownership has been rising. There are fatal gun accidents just as there are fatal car accidents, but in fewer than 2 percent of the gun fatalities was the victim someone mistaken for an intruder.

12   Those who urge us to forbid or severely restrict the sale of guns ignore these facts. Worse, they adopt a position that is politically absurd. In effect, they say, "Your government, having failed to protect your person and your property from criminal assault, now intends to deprive you of the opportunity to protect yourself."

13   Opponents of gun control make a different mistake. The National Rifle Association and its allies tell us that "guns don't kill, people kill" and urge the Government to punish

more severely people who use guns to commit crimes. Locking up criminals does protect society from future crimes, and the prospect of being locked up may deter criminals. But our experience with meting out tougher sentences is mixed. The tougher the prospective sentence the less likely it is to be imposed, or at least to be imposed swiftly. If the Legislature adds on time for crimes committed with a gun, prosecutors often bargain away the add-ons; even when they do not, the judges in many states are reluctant to impose add-ons.

Worse, the presence of a gun can contribute to the magnitude of the crime even on   14
the part of those who worry about serving a long prison sentence. Many criminals carry guns not to rob stores but to protect themselves from other armed criminals. Gang violence has become more threatening to bystanders as gang members have begun to arm themselves. People may commit crimes, but guns make some crimes worse. Guns often convert spontaneous outbursts of anger into fatal encounters. When some people carry them on the streets, others will want to carry them to protect themselves, and an urban arms race will be underway.

And modern science can be enlisted to help. Metal detectors at airports have reduced   15
the number of airplane bombings and skyjackings to nearly zero. But these detectors only work at very close range. What is needed is a device that will enable the police to detect the presence of a large lump of metal in someone's pocket from a distance of ten or fifteen feet. Receiving such a signal could supply the officer with reasonable grounds for a pat-down. Underemployed nuclear physicists and electronics engineers in the post-cold-war era surely have the talents for designing a better gun detector.

Even if we do all these things, there will still be complaints. Innocent people will be   16
stopped. Young black and Hispanic men will probably be stopped more often than older white Anglo males or women of any race. But if we are serious about reducing drive-by shootings, fatal gang wars and lethal quarrels in public places, we must get illegal guns off the street. We cannot do this by multiplying the forms one fills out at gun shops or by pretending that guns are not a problem until a criminal uses one.

FOR WRITING OR DISCUSSION

1. What is the thesis of Wilson's essay? Where does he state it most directly?

2. What advantage does Wilson see in the police's using the "reasonable-suspicion test" over the "probable-cause standard"?

3. Why does Wilson support the value of self-defense with weapons? Where does he appeal to logic? To emotion? To ethics? Use the charts on pages 332–333 to help you determine the nature of Wilson's appeals. What arguments does he provide in opposition to his own point? Why does he use this strategy of presenting opposing arguments?

4. Write an argumentation essay in which you present your own views on gun control and the right to self-defense with weapons.

MEG GREENFIELD

In Defense of the Animals

1   I might as well come right out with it: Contrary to some of my most cherished prejudices, the animal-rights people have begun to get to me. I think that in some part of what they say they are right.

2   I never thought it would come to this. As distinct from the old-style animal rescue, protection, and shelter organizations, the more aggressive newcomers, with their "liberation" of laboratory animals and periodic championship of the claims of animal well-being over human well-being when a choice must be made, have earned a reputation in the world I live in as fanatics and just plain kooks. And even with my own recently (relatively) raised consciousness, there remains a good deal in both their critique and their prescription for the virtuous life that I reject, being not just a practicing carnivore, a wearer of shoe leather, and so forth, but also a supporter of certain indisputably agonizing procedures visited upon innocent animals in the furtherance of human welfare, especially experiments undertaken to improve human health.

3   So, viewed from the pure position, I am probably only marginally better than the worst of my kind, if that: I don't buy the complete "speciesist" analysis or even the fundamental language of animal "rights" and continue to find a large part of what is done in the name of that cause harmful and extreme. But I also think, patronizing as it must sound, that the zealots are required early on in any movement if it is to succeed in altering the sensibility of the leaden masses, such as me. Eventually they get your attention. And eventually you at least feel obliged to weigh their arguments and think about whether there may not be something there.

4   It is true that this end has often been achieved—as in my case—by means of vivid, cringe-inducing photographs, not by an appeal to reason or values so much as by an assault on squeamishness. From the famous 1970s photo of the newly skinned baby seal to the videos of animals being raised in the most dark, miserable, stunting environment as they are readied for their life's sole fulfillment as frozen patties and cutlets, these sights have had their effect. But we live in a world where the animal protein we eat comes discreetly prebutchered and prepacked so the original beast and his slaughtering are remote from our consideration, just as our furs come on coat hangers in salons, not on their original proprietors; and I see nothing wrong with our having to contemplate the often unsettling reality of how we came by the animal products we make use of. Then we can choose what we want to do.

5   The objection to our being confronted with these dramatic, disturbing pictures is first that they tend to provoke a misplaced, uncritical, and highly emotional concern for animal life at the direct expense of a more suitable concern for human suffering. What goes into the animals' account, the reasoning goes, necessarily comes out of ours. But I think it is possible to remain stalwart in your view that the human claim comes first and in your acceptance of the use of animals for human betterment and *still* to believe that there are some human interests that should not take precedence. For we have become far too self-indulgent, hardened, careless, and cruel in the pain we routinely inflict upon these creatures for the

most frivolous, unworthy purposes. And I also think that the more justifiable purposes, such as medical research, are shamelessly used as cover for other activities that are wanton.

For instance, not all of the painful and crippling experimentation that is undertaken in the lab is being conducted for the sake of medical knowledge or other purposes related to basic human well-being and health. Much of it is being conducted for the sake of super-refinements in the cosmetic and other frill industries, the noble goal being to contrive yet another fragrance or hair tint or commercially competitive variation on all the daft, fizzy, multicolored "personal care" products for the medicine cabinet and dressing table, a firmer-holding hair spray, that sort of thing. In other words, the conscripted, immobilized rabbits and other terrified creatures, who have been locked in boxes from the neck down, only their heads on view, are being sprayed in the eyes with different burning, stinging substances for the sake of adding to our already obscene store of luxuries and utterly superfluous vanity items.

Oddly, we tend to be very sentimental about animals in their idealized, fictional form and largely indifferent to them in realms where our lives actually touch. From time immemorial, humans have romantically attributed to animals their own sensibilities—from Balaam's biblical ass who providently could speak and who got his owner out of harm's way right down to Lassie and the other Hollywood pups who would invariably tip off the good guys that the bad guys were up to something. So we simulate phony cross-species kinship, pretty well drown in the cuteness of it all—Mickey and Minnie and Porky—and ignore, if we don't actually countenance, the brutish things done in the name of Almighty Hair Spray.

This strikes me as decadent. My problem is that it also causes me to reach a position that is, on its face, philosophically vulnerable, if not absurd—the muddled, middling, inconsistent place where finally you are saying it's all right to kill them for some purposes, but not to hurt them gratuitously in doing it or to make them suffer horribly for one's own trivial whims.

I would feel more humiliated to have fetched up on this exposed rock, if I didn't suspect I had so much company. When you see pictures of people laboriously trying to clean the Exxon gunk off of sea otters even knowing that they will only be able to help out a very few, you see this same outlook in action. And I think it *can* be defended. For to me the biggest cop-out is the one that says that if you don't buy the whole absolutist, extreme position it is pointless and even hypocritical to concern yourself with lesser mercies and ameliorations. The pressure of the animal-protection groups has already had some impact in improving the way various creatures are treated by researchers, trainers, and food producers. There is much more in this vein to be done. We are talking about rejecting wanton, pointless cruelty here. The position may be philosophically absurd, but the outcome is the right one.

6

7

8

9

FOR WRITING OR DISCUSSION

1. What is Greenfield's thesis?

2. The writer takes almost half the essay to support a key element in opposing arguments—that is, she defends the use of animals "in the furtherance of human welfare." Why does she give so much space to the other side of the argument? How is this use of logos helpful to Greenfield's argument? Where has she appealed to emotion? To ethics?

3. How does she say she came to her new realization that "some human interests . . . should not take precedence" over animal claims?

4. How does she defend her unwillingness to support all the claims of animal protection groups?

5. Select a controversial topic—gun control, prayer in the schools, flag-burning, or abortion rights, for example—and write a convincing argumentation essay about how you can accept only partially the arguments on one side of the issue and reject the others.

HAVING YOUR SAY

What is your view of animal rights and experimentation for human benefit? Choose one side of the issue and support it with concrete detail. Be sure to address the opposition's point of view by refuting it, by rejecting it completely, or by accepting only certain elements in the opposition's argument.

Reading and Writing About Poetry

Without the apparent strategies familiar to the argumentation essays we've been examining, Thomas Hardy, one of the prized poets of the nineteenth century, presents a strong argument here about war in his deceptively simple poetic idiom.

THOMAS HARDY

The Man He Killed

"Had he and I but met
By some old ancient inn,
We should have sat us down to wet
Right many a nipperkin!

"But ranged as infantry,
And staring face to face,
I shot at him and he at me,
And killed him in his place.

"I shot him dead because—
Because he was my foe,
Just so—my foe of course he was;
That's clear enough; although

"He thought he'd 'list perhaps,
Off-hand like—just as I—
Was out of work—had sold his traps—
No other reason why.

"Yes; quaint and curious war is!
You shoot a fellow down
You'd treat if met where any bar is,
Or help to half-a-crown."

FOR WRITING OR DISCUSSION

1. What is Hardy's main point—the argument—in this poem?
2. What comparisons are central to the poem? What is a nipperkin? A half-a-crown?
3. What is the purpose of the repetition in the second stanza?
4. Why does Hardy use the words "quaint" and "curious"—two odd words given the context—to describe war? How do they help the argument?
5. Write an argumentation essay about war or serving in the military.

STRATEGY CHECKLIST: Writing and Revising Your Argumentation Paper

Plan the paper.	☐ Have I identified a topic and a debatable position? Is there clearly one or more positions that might oppose mine?
	☐ Have I used prewriting to stimulate my thoughts?
	☐ Have I paid attention to peer comments about my prewriting?
	☐ Have I weighed my audience and purpose?
	☐ Have I done any necessary research at the library and online?
	☐ Have I considered using an outline to lay out my argument and the specific details to support it?

Write a first draft.	☐ Have I written a thesis that expresses my position on the debatable topic?
	☐ Have I developed an introduction to set the context for my position?
	☐ Have I used a tone suitable to my position on the topic?
	▪ Calm and reasonable ▪ Humorous ▪ Emotional ▪ Angry ▪ Ironic ▪ Other tone
	☐ Have I used appropriate strategies to advance my argument?
	▪ Description ▪ Comparison and contrast ▪ Narration ▪ Classification and division ▪ Example ▪ Cause and effect ▪ Process ▪ Definition
	☐ Have I used induction and deduction to make my points?
	☐ Have I weighed my use of appeals and strived for a balance among *logos*, *pathos*, and *ethos*?
	☐ Have I presented supporting details in the body paragraphs of my essay?
	▪ Relevant ▪ From credible sources ▪ Sufficient ▪ Documented if necessary
	☐ Have I anticipated and refuted opposing positions?
Revise and edit the paper.	☐ Do my examples and details properly support my argument?
	☐ Will the manner in which I've argued my position suit the audience I have in mind?
	☐ Are my inductions and syllogisms logical?
	☐ Are there any logical fallacies that I should revise?
	☐ Have I considered my opponents thoughtfully and courteously?
	☐ Have I made the argument successfully in the space and time I have available, or should I limit my topic further?
	☐ Should I add or remove supporting evidence?
	☐ Are my points logically connected through correct transitions?
	☐ Does my conclusion bring an appropriate end to my argument?
Proofread the paper.	☐ Have I proofread for grammar, spelling, and mechanics?

CROSSCURRENTS

Quynh Nguyen's "Being a Recent American" (pages 346–347) and Esmeralda Santiago's "A Blanco Navidad for New Yorikans" (pages 134–135) provide a personal window on the immigrant experience in America. How would the two writers react to the essay by Nick Milano (pages 344–345)?

COLLABORATIVE LEARNING

Bring the drafts of your argumentation essays to class. Form groups of three students to discuss the efforts of group members and to make recommendations for the next draft. Use the "Strategy Checklist: Writing and Revising Your Argumentation Paper" to guide your conversation.

PEARSON

For support in meeting this chapter's objectives, follow this path in MyCompLab: Resources ⇒ Writing ⇒ Writing Purposes ⇒ **Writing to Argue or Persuade.** Review the Instruction and Multimedia resources about **argumentation**; then complete the Exercises and click on Gradebook to measure your progress.

CHAPTER **16**

Mixing Methods of Development

In this chapter you will

- identify the strategies for writing a mixed-modes paper

- analyze student essays that mix modes of development

- identify a topic and write your own mixed modes paper

- analyze the use of mixed modes in writing by professionals

As you've worked your way through the chapters in this book, you've already seen in practice what we asserted at the outset: many writing efforts benefit from an intelligent mix of rhetorical methods. Although you've explored the options individually, you've seen that many writers combine rhetorical approaches for maximum effect.

So why, you're no doubt wondering, do we need a separate chapter on using mixed methods in writing? First, the chapter gives you an opportunity to address the topic consciously, not accidentally. We'll point out here through student samples and professional writing and accompanying annotations how and where the writers draw on multiple modes of development to advance their theses. Next, you'll have a chance to think critically about the multiple rhetorical perspectives as they emerge in a particular piece. And finally, you'll have the chance to incorporate mixed methods of development formally in your own writing.

Developing Your Paper Through Mixed Modes

When writing a paper using a variety of rhetorical modes, keep the following four strategies in mind.

TIPS for Developing a Mixed Modes Essay

- **Choose your topic carefully.** As you plan to write, consider which modes of development might help you best convince your readers. Do you want to write in support of one candidate for office over another? Contrast clearly would come into play, but, in considering actions taken by each candidate, you might explain the causes and effects of such actions. Drawing on sensory detail to describe the candidates might help you offer snapshots of the personalities with which your readers may be unfamiliar. Do you want to argue for a humane setting for emergency room care in local hospitals? Description would certainly help here, but you might also want to explain the process by which hospital staff admit patients and establish treatment programs or argue for a less-complicated and quicker admissions process.

- **Be familiar with the demands of the rhetorical strategies that you plan to use.** Recall, for example, the various options available if you want to develop part of your paper with contrast. Be aware of the various logical fallacies that can trip you up if you're developing your topic in part through argumentation. You should reexamine the "Strategy Checklist" at the end of each chapter in Part Two. Better yet, reread the chapters that deal with the rhetorical strategies your topic suggests you might use.

- **Pay particular attention to transitions.** Developing a coherent paper requires special attention in a mixed modes essay, and you want to be sure to lead the reader carefully from one part of the essay to another. The various elements of your paper must hold together. This does not mean a call for endless *therefores, in additions, moreovers*, and the like. It does mean that you should move your reader smoothly from one point to the other by means of logical connections and astute use of the rhetorical modes to make your point successfully. In Brian Jarvis's essay, which you will read here, note how he uses the word *commons* in both the first and the second paragraphs. The repetition helps him make a smooth transition from the description in the introduction to his definition of the word as it applies to his school. When he moves to a narrative approach in paragraph 4, he begins with "Ten years ago...." The time reference lends coherence to the essay.

- **Be reasonable in your choices for developing your essay.** Because you now understand all the rhetorical options open to you doesn't mean that you have to use them all at once. Your topic and your interest in it should dictate the strategies that will best serve your thesis. In other words, avoid drawing on too many modes of development just for the sake of using them.

Mixing Methods: Looking at Possibilities

Let's examine a topic close up to see how a variety of rhetorical approaches might work together to produce a strong paper.

Suppose you wanted to write about the need to improve voting in your community. These options (and many others, of course) are potentially available, based on your ultimate thesis and purpose.

Topic: Improve Voting in My Community

Rhetorical Strategy	Possible Approach
Description	Describe the broken and hard-to-use voting machines in your community.
Narration	Tell a story about a senior citizen who struggled to cast her vote.
Example	Give several examples of failed voting efforts.
Process	Explain how a local political party tries to get out the vote.
Comparison and contrast	Compare regular balloting and absentee balloting.
Classification and division	Describe the different categories of voters in your community.
Cause and effect	Explain why the voting board has done nothing to improve the ease of voting on election day.
Definition	Define "vote-getting."
Argumentation	Argue that without a proactive government plan to improve voting, elections will never be fair.

Do you see the possibilities? By combining two, perhaps three of these possible approaches, you could produce a paper that uses mixed modes of development. The specifics would depend on your thesis and purpose.

EXERCISE   Using the table above, explain how you would use two or more of the rhetorical strategies in an essay on improving local voting in your city or state.

EXERCISE   For the topics following identify at least two modes that you could use to develop a paper and explain how you would use them. "Television reruns" provides an example.

Topic	Modes	How to Use
Television reruns	Example	Provide illustrations of popular sitcom reruns.
	Comparison and contrast	Compare one or two old sitcoms and one or two new ones to show change in comedy values.

1. Cell phones
2. Smoking in public
3. Teenage alcohol use
4. Improving the economy
5. Greenhouse gases

ASSIGNMENT: MIXED METHODS OF DEVELOPMENT

Write an essay of your choice that draws upon at least two rhetorical strategies that you have examined in Part Two of this book. Think about your topic to see which methods of development will suit your essay. Use the Tips on pages 370–371 and the student and professional samples. Rely on the checklist on page 385. These suggestions for topics will help you develop a paper in which you draw on diverse methods of development. Of course, any topic of your own will do nicely as well: the point here is to integrate rhetorical modes so that they help you make your point successfully. An argumentation bent to your paper will help you draw on varied developmental strategies.

1. New Orleans returns
2. Addressing global warming
3. Pollution
4. Love redefined
5. Political corruption
6. Friends and enemies
7. Desert war
8. The night sky
9. Going home
10. Bible study
11. City transportation
12. Disciplining children
13. Sports rivalry
14. Consumerism
15. Auto trouble
16. Oceans
17. Confronting terrorism
18. Social media dangers
19. Prescription drugs
20. Censorship

Student Writing: Mixing Methods in Developing Your Essay

In this annotated paper by student writer Brian Jarvis, who wrote the essay for *Newsweek*, note the mixed modes of development that support the writer's thesis. Answer the questions after the piece.

Brian Jarvis
Against the Great Divide

Description: Helps establish details of the moment in the introduction to the essay and frames the problem that the writer will address in his paper.

1   I always notice one thing when I walk through the commons at my high school: The whites are on one side of the room and the blacks are on the other. When I enter the room, I think I'm at an African nationalist meeting. The atmosphere is lively, the clothes are colorful, the voices are loud, the students are up and about, the language is different, and there's not a white face to be seen. But the moment I cross the invisible line to the other side, I feel I've moved to another country. There are three times as many people, the voices are softer, the clothes more subdued. Everyone's sitting or lying down, and one has as much chance of seeing a black student as a Martian.

Note the repetition of the word "commons" here as a transition to the first paragraph, where we read the word for the first time in the essay.

2   The commons is a gathering spot where students relax on benches and talk with friends. They also buy candy and soda, watch TV, and make phone calls. It's a place where all sorts of things happen. But you'll never find a white student and a black student talking to each other.

Definition: Jarvis's meaning of "commons."

3   After three years, I still feel uncomfortable when I have to walk through the "black" side to get to class. It's not that any black students threaten or harass me. They just quietly ignore me and look in the other direction, and I do the same. But there's one who sometimes catches my eye, and I can't help feeling awkward when I see him. He was a close friend from childhood.

Example: From personal experience, the writer presents examples of a different relation between blacks and whites from relations identified at the writer's school.

4   Ten years ago, we played catch in our backyards, went bike riding, and slept over at one another's houses. By the fifth grade, we went to movies and amusement parks and bunked together at the same summer camps. We met while playing on the same Little League team, though we attended different grade schools. We're both juniors now at the same high school. We usually don't say anything when we see each other, except maybe a polite "Hi" or "Hey." I can't remember the last time we talked on the phone, much less got together outside of school.

Transition: "Ten years ago" helps lend coherence to essay.

Comparison and contrast: In paragraphs 5 and 6, Jarvis shows similarities and differences between friend and him.

Since entering high school, we haven't shared a single class or sport. He plays football, a black-dominated sport, while I play tennis, which is, with rare exception, an all-white team. It's as if fate has kept us apart; though, more likely, it's peer pressure. 5

In the lunchroom, I sit with my white friends and my childhood friend sits with his black ones. It's the same when we walk through the hallways or sit in the library. If Michael Jackson thinks, "It don't matter if you're black or white," he should visit my high school. 6

I wonder if proponents of desegregation realized that even if schools were integrated, students would choose to remain apart. It wasn't until 1983 that St. Louis's voluntary city-suburban desegregation program was approved. Today, my school has 25 percent black students. While this has given many young people the chance for a better education, it hasn't brought the two races closer together. 7

In high school, I've become friends with Vietnamese Americans, Korean Americans, Iranian Americans, Indian Americans, Russian Americans, and exchange students from France and Sweden. The only group that remains at a distance is the African Americans. I've had only a handful of black students in all my classes and only one black teacher (from Haiti). 8

Cause and effect: Here the writer explains the results of efforts to improve race relations at his high school.

In its effort to put students through as many academic classes as possible and prepare them for college, my school seems to have overlooked one crucial course: teaching black and white students how to get along, which in my opinion, would be more valuable than all the others. It's not that there haven't been efforts to improve race relations. Last fall, a group of black and white students established a program called Students Organized Against Racism. But at a recent meeting, SOAR members decided that the separation of blacks and whites was largely voluntary and there was little they could do about it. Another youth group tried to help by moving the soda machine from the "white" side of the commons to the "black" side, so that white students would have to cross the line to get a Coke. But all that's happened is that students buy their sodas, then return to their own territory. 9

Last summer, at a youth camp called Miniwanca in Michigan, I did see black and white teens get along. I don't mean just tolerate one another. I mean play sports together, dance together, walk on the beach together, 10

Example: Jarvis proposes a way to improve race relations and draws on examples from personal experience to support his point.

11

and become friends. The students came from all races and backgrounds, as well as from overseas. Camp organizers purposely placed me in a cabin and activity group that included whites, blacks, Southerners, Northerners, and foreigners, none of whom I'd met before.

For ten days, I became great friends with a group of strangers, at least half of whom were black. One wouldn't know that racism existed at that idyllic place, where we told stories around campfires, acted in plays, and shared our deepest thoughts about AIDS, parents, abortion, and dating. Everyone got along so well there that it was depressing for me to return to high school. But at the same time, it made me hopeful. If black and white teenagers could be friends at leadership camp, couldn't they mix in school as well?

12

Example: The illustrations continue as the writer first gives examples of joint activities at camp and then suggests ways to get "whites and blacks together as much as possible."

Schools need to make it a real priority to involve whites and blacks together as much as possible. This would mean more multicultural activities, mandatory classes that teach black history, and discussions of today's racial controversies. Teachers should mix whites and blacks more in study groups so they have to work together in and out of school. (Students won't do it on their own.) And most important, all students should get a chance to attend a camp like Miniwanca. Maybe the government could find a way to help finance other camps like it.

13

Conclusion: Provides a bird's-eye view of the problem and the writer's reaction to it.

As it is now, black and white teenagers just don't know one another. I think a lot about my friend from childhood—what he does on weekends, what he thinks about college, what he wants to do with his life. I have no answers, and it saddens me.

FOR WRITING OR DISCUSSION

1. What is Jarvis's thesis?
2. What is your reaction to the use of multiple modes of development in this essay?
3. Which details convince you most that the races do not get along harmoniously at Jarvis's school? Jarvis does not report any open conflict. Why, then, is he concerned?
4. Write an argumentation essay about race relations in your school, neighborhood, or place of business.

Critical Reading: Mixed Methods of Development

Experienced writers know that content drives the form of an essay, and they know how to integrate rhetorical strategies to suit their topics and purposes in writing. In the selection below, written by a professor of religion, marginal comments point to elements in the essay that a critical reader might highlight as well as to the varied rhetorical modes the writer draws on. Answer the questions after the selection.

TIMOTHY K. BEAL

Bibles du Jour

In introduction, writer immediately sets apart his bible topic from our more familiar understanding of the word "bible" through illustration— i.e., example.

Today we are witnessing a burgeoning of bibles. Not the kind you read in a synagogue or church, but the kind you read to master Java scripting. Or to get washboard abs. Or to create the perfect window dressing. From *The Internet Bible* to *The Golfer's Bible* to *The Body Sculpting Bible* (his and hers versions) to *The Curtain Bible*, from *The Runner's Bible* to *The Small Game and Varmint Hunter's Bible*, to *Cocktail: The Drinks Bible for the 21st Century*, there's a bible for anyone who wants to do or be anything. [1]

"du Jour" is French for "of the day" (e.g., soup du jour on restaurant menus).

Some historical background puts the topic in perspective, also through rhetorical strategy of example.

Calling these kinds of books bibles is not exactly new. *The Shooter's Bible* (previously *The Stoeger Gun Catalog and Handbook*, subtitled *The World's Standard*), appeared in 1940. But today we find more than ever. By my count, something like one in four books published in America over the past two years with "bible" in the title is this kind of bible. Indeed, you're likely to find more bibles in a bookstore's computer section than in its religion section. [2]

Why call these kinds of books bibles? Because it sells, of course. But why? What currency does it give a book to call it a bible? What does this title claim for a book? What does it promise? What does "bible" mean? [3]

Questions establish basic premise of thesis: Readers will expect answers to these questions.

Definition: What is a bible? Writer gives examples of what word means to him.

It means *comprehensive*. A book called a bible promises to cover all you need to know and understand about its subject, from A to Z, Genesis to Revelation. [4]

It means *authoritative*. A book called a bible claims to be the alpha and the omega, the first and last Word on all things golfing, draping, varmint hunting, whatever, dispensing all the right answers to all the right questions. [5]

It means *exclusive*. A book called a bible asserts itself to be the one and only, without serious competition. [6]

It means *practical*. A book called a bible promises to serve as a reference manual and a dependable guide for how to proceed on the path you've chosen. [7]

8   And it means *devotional*. A book called a bible treats its subject as something worthy of religious dedication and discipline from practitioners. Its subject literally becomes a religion of the book—*this* book. Take and read.

9   A book called a bible claims to be the one and only book for those who are devoted or who want to be devoted to its subject. Whether or not you know what a turbo charger is, you immediately understand that *Hot Rodder's Bible* is proclaiming itself the ultimate comprehensive authority, guide, and how-to manual for hot-rod devotees. That's what bible means.

True.

Many bibles.

10   That's what it means, but in fact there is no one bible, and there never has been. Even before this new generation of bibles came along, religious bibles were legion. The <u>Jewish Bible</u>, or Tanakh, includes the Torah (the first five books, Genesis through Deuteronomy), Neviim (Prophets), and Ketuvim (Writings), in that order. The <u>Protestant Bible</u> includes those same books, but in a different order, as well as the New Testament. The <u>Roman Catholic Bible</u> adds a number of Apocryphal scriptures. And many others reflect the biblical traditions of other forms of Christianity alive and well in America. In addition, <u>numerous translations exist of each of those bibles</u>. And behind each of those translations are literally hundreds of manuscripts written in many different languages and spanning centuries.

Argumentation: The writer has explained *bible* as "the one and only book"; now he challenges that idea with religious examples.

11   Neither is any one of the many Jewish and Christian bibles of one voice. Each is the product of multiple oral and literary traditions, multiple voices and pens speaking and writing within many different cultural contexts across hundreds of years. Every one of those bibles is more like a one-volume library than a single book.

Further details to support notion that a bible is not a one-and-only book.

"Bible-ness"—writer's own invented word. Legitimate? It works!

12   <u>As a result no single bible exemplifies our idea of bible-ness</u>. The prototype is a figment of our cultural imagination, revealing not what "the Bible" is but what we think or even wish it to be. *The Fly Fisherman's Bible* is not to fly fishing what "the Bible" is to religion. Rather, it purports to be to fly fishing what we imagine "the Bible" should be to religion.

Transition—summary (see paragraph 10).

Example to support writer's point that current use of word "bible" would have struck most readers in the 1900s as sacrilege.

13   A century ago, calling such books bibles would have struck most readers as inappropriate, even sacrilegious. Once I thought I had found a remarkably early example: In 1913 Nora Holm published *The Runner's Bible: Compiled and Annotated for the Reading of Him Who Runs*. But lo and behold, the book had nothing to do with breaking a sweat or beating the pavement. It was a Christian "prayer Bible," a compilation of biblical passages accompanied by Holm's devotional commentaries. Her title alludes to the New Testament use of competitive running as a metaphor for the Christian life—running to win "the imperishable" wreath of salvation, as the Apostle Paul puts it.

14   Holm's book is still in print and is well-known in Christian devotional circles. But these days its publishers must take care to distinguish it from Marc Bloom's better-known *The Runner's Bible* for competitive runners and joggers. Indeed, most readers today would assume that a book called *The Runner's Bible* is for someone who wants to win a 10K, not someone who wants to win

Paragraph 14, *comparison–contrast:* The Holm book vs. the Bloom book. Note the differences in the use of "bible" in title of each book.

Argumentation:
"mainstream
American culture
is now in many
respects post-
religious, indeed
post-Christian."

Example to
support idea
of flippancy—
Madonna and
Marilyn Manson,
popular culture
icons today.

Even when the
word "bible" is
used casually,
betrays nostalgia
for old-time reli-
gious authority.
Note use of cause
and effect: Why
is the market
for new kinds of
bibles growing?

Play on words
ends piece. "Bi-
ble" vs. "biblical
proportions." Is
this tongue in
cheek?

the imperishable wreath. The revised subtitle on the 1998 edition of Holm's *Runner's Bible* admits as much: *Spiritual Guidance for People on the Run*.

Nowadays calling a book about running a bible doesn't strike many of us as inappropriate, let alone sacrilegious. Maybe that's because mainstream American culture is now in many respects post-religious, indeed post-Christian. Images like crosses and Madonnas and terms like "salvation" and "bible" that were once set apart as sacred and handled exclusively within particular religious traditions have crossed over into mainstream consumer culture where they now circulate in countless new ways, primarily to sell stuff. Even those of us who are in fact religious (even Christian) have grown accustomed to seeing such images and words translated into new venues.

In this light, there is a bit of <u>sacrilegious flippancy</u> in calling these kinds of books bibles. Akin to Madonna's and Marilyn Manson's slight smirks as they don holy garb, we pronounce these books bibles with at least some tongue in cheek, aware that we can use the term that way because it has lost its traditional moorings in the sacred and is now floating freely down the mainstream.

But might there also be a bit of religious longing here? I have to wonder if the growing market for the new kinds of bibles betrays a bit of nostalgia, even amid the tongue-in-cheek flippancy, for that old-time kind of religious authority that "bible" stands for: a comprehensive, exclusive authority that gives guidance and calls for devotion. I say a bit of nostalgia. <u>Fundamentalism</u> is the name we give to movements ruled by that kind of nostalgia. Most of us know that we can't go back, and that the desire to do so can be a dangerous fantasy.

Still, what do we make of the increasing popularity of these newfangled bibles in our brave new post-religious world? One thing is for sure: Tongues in cheeks notwithstanding, a market still exists for authority of <u>biblical proportions</u>.

15

"Stuff":
informal
usage.

16
"sacrilegious
flippancy"—
interesting
phrase.

17

Writer's
conclusion
18 extends the
argument
further:
Popularity
of "bible"
books.

FOR WRITING OR DISCUSSION

1. How does the strategy of illustration serve the introduction? Cause and effect?

2. State the writer's thesis in your own words. How do the questions in paragraph 3 contribute to your understanding of the thesis?

3. Explain the writer's use of argumentation in paragraphs 10 and 15.

4. How do comparison and contrast serve the thesis of the essay?

5. Choose a key word used in many contexts in the way that Beal used the word *bible* to identify different types of books. For example, you may select *star*, *hero*, or *friend*. Then, define the word in an essay that uses a variety of rhetorical methods. Or, write your own definition of *bible*, also using a mixed modes approach in your paper.

Readings for Writing

Use the following selections as a stimulus for your own mixed modes writing and also as a means of examining the interaction among modes that the writers draw on to make their points.

HERBERT J. GANS

Fitting the Poor into the Economy

1   The notion of the poor as too lazy or morally deficient to deserve assistance seems to be indestructible. Public policies limit poor people to substandard services and incomes below the subsistence level, and Congress and state legislatures are tightening up even on these miserly allocations—holding those in the "underclass" responsible for their own sorry state. Indeed, labeling the poor as undeserving has lately become politically useful as a justification for the effort to eliminate much of the antipoverty safety net and permit tax cuts for the affluent people who do most of the voting.

2   Such misplaced blame offers mainstream society a convenient evasion of its own responsibility. Blaming poor men and women for not working, for example, takes the onus off both private enterprise and government for failing to supply employment. It is easier to charge poor unmarried mothers with lacking family values than to make sure that there are jobs for them and for the young men who are not marriageable because they are unable to support families. Indeed, the poor make excellent scapegoats for a range of social problems, such as street crime and drug and alcohol addiction. Never mind the reversal of cause and effect that underlies this point of view—for centuries crime, alcoholism, and single motherhood have risen whenever there has not been enough work and income to go around.

3   The undeserving underclass is also a useful notion for employers as the economy appears to be entering a period of long-term stagnation. Jobs are disappearing—some displaced by labor-saving technologies, others exported to newly industrializing, low-wage countries, others lost as companies "downsize" to face tougher global competition. Indeed, the true rate of unemployment—which includes involuntary part-time workers and long-term "discouraged" workers who have dropped out of the job market altogether—has remained in double digits for more than a generation and no longer seems to drop during times of economic strength. Labeling poor people as lacking the needed work ethic is a politically simple way of shedding them from a labor market that will most likely never need them again.

_____

Technology Review October 1995.

The most efficient antidote to poverty is not welfare but full employment. In the short 4
run, therefore, today's war against the poor should be replaced with efforts to create jobs
for now-surplus workers. New Deal–style programs of large-scale governmental employment, for example, can jump-start a slow economy. Besides being the fastest way to put
people to work, a public-works program can improve the country's infrastructure, including highways, buildings, parks, and computer databases.

In addition, private enterprise and government should aim to stimulate the most 5
promising labor-intensive economic activities and stop encouraging new technology
that will further destroy jobs—reviving, for example, the practice of making cars and
appliances partly by hand. A parallel policy would tax companies for their use of labor-
saving technology; the revenues from this tax would pay for alternative jobs for people in
occupations that technology renders obsolete. This idea makes good business as well as
social sense: human workers are needed as customers for the goods that machines now
produce.

To distribute the jobs that do exist among more people, employers could shorten 6
the work day, week, or year. Several large manufacturing companies in Western Europe
already use worksharing to create a 35-hour week. Making significant inroads on U.S.
joblessness may require reducing the work week to 30 hours.

A more generous welfare system would go a long way toward solving the problems of 7
the remainder: those who cannot work or cannot find jobs. By persisting in the belief that
poor people deserve their fate, society can easily justify a paltry and demeaning welfare
system that pays recipients only about one-quarter of the median income. A system that
paid closer to half the median income, by contrast, would enable those without work
to remain full members of society and thus minimize the despair, anger, and various illnesses, as well as premature mortality, distinctive to the poor.

For such antipoverty policies to gain acceptance, mainstream America will have 8
to unlearn the stereotype of poor people as immoral. Most of the poor are just as
law-abiding as everyone else. (While a minority of poor people cheat on their welfare
applications, an even larger minority of affluent people cheat on their tax returns—
yet the notion of undeservingness is never applied to the middle or upper classes.) In
admitting that the phenomena now explained as moral dereliction are actually trace-
able to poverty, Americans will force themselves to find solutions, not scapegoats, to the
country's problems.

Most of the people assigned to today's undeserving underclass are the first victims of 9
what is already being called the future "jobless economy." In the long run, if the cancer
of joblessness spreads more widely among the population, large numbers of the present
middle class will have to adapt to the reality that eventually most workers may no longer
be employed full time. In that case, more drastic job-creation policies will be needed,
including a ban on additional job-destroying technology and the establishment of permanent public employment modeled on the kind now associated with military spending.
Worksharing would most likely be based on a 24-hour week.

10   At that point, everyone would in fact be working part time by today's standards, and new ways to maintain standards of living would have to be found. One approach, already being discussed in Europe, is a universal, subsistence-level income grant. This "demo-grant," a twenty-first-century version of the $1,000-per-person allotment that presidential candidate George McGovern proposed in 1972, would be taxed away from people still working full time. In any case, private and government agencies should begin now to study what policies might be needed to preserve the American way of life when the full-time job will no longer be around to pay for the American Dream.

11   It is possible, of course, that new sources of economic growth will suddenly develop to revive the full employment and prosperity of the post–World War II decades. And some labor-saving technologies may, in the long run, create more jobs than they destroy; that may well be the case for computers, which have spawned a large sector of the economy. Such happy outcomes cannot be counted on to materialize, however, and there remains the danger that the war on the poor will continue as the politically most convenient path. We will undoubtedly find that when the economy begins to threaten the descendants of today's middle and even affluent classes with becoming poor, and then "undeserving," policies that today seem utopian will be demanded, and quickly.

FOR WRITING OR DISCUSSION

1. What is Gans' thesis in this essay? Where in the essay does he come closest to stating it for the reader?
2. Where does the writer use cause-and-effect strategies to advance his point?
3. In which paragraphs does Gans use process analysis? Example? Comparison and contrast?
4. Gans says people view the poor as "the undeserving working class." Write an essay called "The Deserving Working Class" and propose strategies for providing the poor with better services or for changing people's views of the poor so that society doesn't blame them for their fates.

RESHMA MEMON YAQUB

You People Did This

1   As I ran through my neighborhood on the morning of September 11th, in search of my son, who had gone to the park with his baby sitter, I wasn't just afraid of another hijacked plane crashing into us. I was also afraid that someone else would get to my son first, someone wanting revenge against anyone who looks like they're from "that part of the world." Even if he is just one and a half years old.

Rolling Stone 25 Oct. 2001.

I know I wasn't just afraid that the building where my husband works, a D.C. land-mark, might fall on him. I was also afraid that another American might stop him on the street and harass him, or hurt him, demanding to know why "you people" did this. As soon as we heard the news, 7 million American Muslims wondered in terror, "Will America blame me?"

When our country is terrorized, American Muslims are victimized twice. First, as Americans, by the madmen who strike at our nation, at our physical, mental and emotional core. Then we're victimized again, as Muslims, by those Americans who believe that all Muslims are somehow accountable for the acts of some madmen, that our faith—that our God, the same peace-loving God worshipped by Jews and Christians—sanctions it.

It didn't matter when the federal building in Oklahoma City blew up that a Muslim didn't do it. That a Christian man was responsible for the devastation in Oklahoma City certainly didn't matter to the thugs who terrorized a Muslim woman there, nearly seven months pregnant, by attacking her home, breaking her windows, screaming religious slurs. It didn't matter to them that Sahar Al-Muwsawi, 26, would, as a result, miscarry her baby. That she would bury him in the cold ground, alongside other victims of the Oklahoma City bombing, after naming him Salaam, the Arabic word for "peace."

But that travesty and hundreds like it certainly were on my mind that Tuesday morning. And they were reinforced every time a friend called to check on my family and to sadly remind me, "It's over for us. Muslims are done for."

Even as we buckled under the same grief that every American was feeling that day, American Muslims had to endure the additional burden of worrying for our own safety, in our own hometowns, far from hijackers and skyscrapers. Shots would be fired into the Islamic Center of Irving, Texas; an Islamic bookstore in Virginia would have bricks thrown through its windows; a bag of pig's blood would be left on the doorstep of an Islamic community center in San Francisco; a mosque near Chicago would be marched on by 300 people shouting racist epithets. A Muslim of Pakistani origin would be gunned down in Dallas; a Sikh man would be shot and killed in Mesa, Arizona (possibly by the same assailant who would go on to spray bullets into the home of a local Afghani family).

And those were just the cases that were reported. I know I didn't report it when a ten-year-old neighborhood boy walked by and muttered, "Terrorist," as I got into my car. My neurosurgeon friend didn't report that a nurse at the prominent Washington hospital where they both work had announced in front of him that all Muslims and Arabs should be rounded up and put into camps, as Japanese were in World War II. My family didn't report that we're sick with worry about my mother-in-law, another sister-in-law and my niece, who are visiting Pakistan, with their return uncertain.

In the days to come, in the midst of the darkness, there is some light. A neighbor stops by to tell me that he doesn't think Muslims are responsible for the acts of madmen. Strangers in Starbucks are unusually friendly to me and my son, reaching out as if to say, "We know it's not your fault." The head of a church told me his congregation wants to come and put its arms around us, and to help in any way possible—by cleaning graffiti off a mosque, by hosting our Friday prayers, whatever we needed. President Bush warns

9   Americans not to scapegoat Muslims and Arabs. He even visits a mosque, in a show of solidarity. Congress swiftly passes a resolution to uphold the civil rights of Muslims and Arabs, urging Americans to remain united. Jewish and Christian leaders publicly decry the violence against Muslims. At a mosque in Seattle, Muslim worshippers are greeted by members of other faiths bringing them flowers.

9   There's something America needs to understand about Islam. Like Judaism, like Christianity, Islam doesn't condone terrorism. It doesn't allow it. It doesn't accept it. Yet, somehow, the labels *jihad*, *holy war* and *suicide martyrs* are still thrown around. In fact, jihad doesn't even mean holy war. It's an Arabic word that means "struggle"—struggle to please God. And suicide itself is a forbidden act in Islam. How could anyone believe that Muslims consider it martyrdom when practiced in combination with killing thousands of innocents? Anyone who claims to commit a politically motivated violent act in the name of Islam has committed a hate crime against the world's 1.2 billion Muslims.

10   It is not jihad to hijack a plane and fly it into a building. But in fact there was jihad done that Tuesday. It was jihad when firemen ran into imploding buildings to rescue people they didn't know. It was jihad when Americans lined up and waited to donate the blood of their own bodies. It was jihad when strangers held and comforted one another in the streets. It was jihad when rescue workers struggled to put America back together, piece by piece.

11   Yes, there were martyrs made that Tuesday. But there were no terrorists among them. There were only Americans, of every race and religion, who, that Tuesday, took death for us.

FOR WRITING OR DISCUSSION

1. What is the meaning of the title? How does it engage the reader to want to read on? How does the first sentence provide the reader with the historical context needed to understand the essay?

2. What is Yaqub's thesis here?

3. How does the writer use quotations to good advantage? For example, what purpose does the quote serve in paragraph 5?

4. How does illustration serve the essay in paragraph 6? Paragraph 8? Paragraph 10? What is the effect on the reader of the accumulation of examples in those paragraphs? Where does Yaqub use contrast strategies? Cause and effect?

5. What steps would you propose for dealing with terrorism on American soil? Write an essay to address the topic, using a variety of rhetorical strategies.

STRATEGY CHECKLIST: Writing and Revising Your Mixed Modes Paper

Plan the paper.	☐ Have I identified a topic that lends itself to development through a variety of rhetorical modes?
	☐ Have I reviewed the methods of development so that I can use effectively whichever methods work for my topic?
	☐ Have I used one of the prewriting strategies to stimulate my thoughts?
	☐ Have I weighed my audience and purpose?
	☐ Have I considered using an outline to organize my thoughts?
Write a first draft.	☐ Have I written a thesis that expresses my opinion about or attitude toward the topic?
	☐ Have I developed an introduction to set the context for my paper?
	☐ Have I used appropriate rhetorical modes?
	■ Description ■ Comparison and contrast
	■ Narration ■ Classification and division
	■ Example ■ Cause and effect
	■ Process ■ Definition
	■ Argumentation
	☐ Have I integrated the mode strategies appropriately?
	☐ Have I presented sufficient supporting detail?
Revise and edit the paper.	☐ Have I paid attention to peer comments?
	☐ Do details I've presented support my thesis?
	☐ Does my use of varied modes reflect what I've learned about them in developing essays?
	☐ Have I checked carefully for the use—and not overuse—of transitions?
	☐ Have I made my point successfully in the space and time I have available, or should I limit my topic further?
	☐ Does my conclusion bring an appropriate end to my paper?
Proofread the paper.	☐ Have I proofread for grammar, spelling, and mechanics?

CROSSCURRENTS

Reread George Orwell's "A Hanging" on pages 11–14 and compare it with Reshma Memon Yaqub's "You People Did This" on pages 382–384. In what ways are they similar, if at all? In what ways are they different? How does the purpose of each piece differ?

COLLABORATIVE LEARNING

Bring to class your draft essays using mixed modes of development. Form groups of three students and read each other's papers, looking particularly at the thesis and how the writer used varied rhetorical strategies to address the topic. Has the writer succeeded in integrating the modes? What suggestions can you make for improvement?

 For additional help with writing, reading, and research, go to www.mycomplab.com

PART THREE

Special Writing

Literary Analysis

In this chapter you will

- explore ways of reading literature for analysis

- avoid common pitfalls in literary analysis

- analyze student essays that analyze literature

- analyze short stories for writing your own literary analysis

As you know, to analyze is to study a complex event, thing, or person by examining one or more of its parts and then showing the relationship of each part to the whole. When you receive an assignment such as "Trace the sequence of clues planted by the author so that we have a chance to anticipate the surprise ending in Jackson's 'Charles'" (pages 238–241), you are being asked to write a **literary analysis**. Sometimes instructors assign **explication**, a special form of literary analysis in which short works like poems or stories are examined word by word or paragraph by paragraph to show how each element fits into the general pattern and purpose of the entire work.

Writing Your Analysis of Literature

Reading Literature for Analysis

Reading literature for analysis is different from reading for information or for pleasure. Here are some suggestions for reading literary texts (see also Chapter 1).

TIPS for Reading Literature for Analysis

- **Read the material slowly.** When you are reading good or great literature, the intelligent approach is to read slowly. Any analysis involves a close examination of details. Fast reading can give you a general sense of the main points, but it can't prepare you to deal competently with all the concerns of a full-fledged analysis.

- **Reread.** When you read a piece for the first time, you're unlikely to have any valid notion of what the author is up to. When you read a selection again, all the ingredients will begin to register in a different way, a way that is emotionally and intellectually impossible to achieve in a first reading. The seemingly separate parts of the story can now come through to you as pieces within a logical pattern. Without a sense of that logical pattern and of how all elements are related to it, your analysis will be weak and incomplete.

■ **Assume that everything is significant.**   In good literature, nothing should be an accident. Each word, each character, each thought, each incident should make a contribution to the total effect the author is trying for. Assume that everything serves a purpose and that you have not reached a full understanding of the story, poem, or play until you see clearly the purpose that everything serves. Read closely, and give serious attention to details. When you get to the writing stage, make liberal use of the details to support your comments. No matter how much actual work you have done, if you do not rely heavily on references to details, your analysis will seem based on vague impressions.

■ **Do not study details out of context.**   Your response to the details of a work—a word, a phrase, a character, an incident—depends on the work as a whole. A sentence like "Mrs. Yee spent twenty minutes arranging the flowers in the vase" could appear in a satire of a neurotic fussbudget or a moving sketch of a mother preparing the house for her child's return from the army. Your analysis or interpretation of the flower arranging must obviously be in harmony with the rest of the work. Keep the intentions of the whole work in mind as you consider the proper approach toward one of its parts.

One more observation: try not to let your purely personal tastes or prejudices interfere with your responses to the work. An analysis explains what is going on in a piece of literature, not what your own philosophy of life may happen to be.

■ **Forget about "hidden meanings."**   No writer who is any good goes around hiding meanings. Writers have enough trouble expressing them openly, so that you should avoid the "hidden meanings" approach to literature. Never use the phrase, as many people do, to refer to an idea or emotion that the author had no intention of concealing but that you just didn't happen to notice on a first reading.

■ **Distinguish between moral and theme.**   Good literature, in general, is not pure art in the sense that a painting of a pretty landscape is pure art. Most literature attempts far more directly than such paintings to make a comment on life. In considering a story like Edgar Allan Poe's "The Tell-Tale Heart" (pages 402–405), we can and should discuss artistic elements such as plot construction and dialogue, but the story also provides a comment on human nature. If a work has something to say, we must ask ourselves what it is saying as well as how it is saying it.

Skipping the Hunt for Morals

A comment on life, however, is not necessarily a **moral**. In good literature, especially modern literature, it is almost never a moral. This fact confuses many inexperienced readers. For them the question of "what does it mean" or "what does it say" usually implies "what is the moral"—the direct, simple, short statement of a lesson or message to be drawn from the work. When they find no clear moral, they tend to feel cheated or frustrated. Why can't writers just come right out with it and say what they mean?

There are two ways of answering this question. First, morals have a way of being too tidy, too catchy, and dangerously superficial. They are fine in proverbs, children's stories, and five-minute sermons. But literature produced by a thoughtful writer attempts to capture some of the quality of life itself, and the preachy oversimplifications inherent in moralizing spring from distortions of life. *"He who hesitates is lost"; "Life begins at forty"; "It's no use crying over spilt milk"*—this stuff sounds good enough, but we all know that sometimes hesitation is advisable, that a significant life can begin at any age, and that crying over spilt milk has inspired, among many other things, some immortal poetry. When you look for neat little morals in literature, you cheat yourself and you are unfair to the writer.

Identifying Themes

As readers and critics we are much better off in dealing with a writer's something-to-say if we think not of the moral but the **theme**. A theme in literature is *the underlying issue, the basic area of permanent human experience treated by the author.* We can say that the theme or themes of *Romeo and Juliet*, for example, are love, and family, and fate, and conflicting loyalties, and reason versus passion. We could add to the list, and a good critic could probably then find a way of linking all the separate themes into one theme that covers them all. The author offers comments on these separate themes by creating certain characters who act in certain ways. Romeo and Juliet are individuals, not representatives of all young lovers. Their families are feuding, as most families are not. The characters in the play face issues that are permanent ingredients of human life and respond to these issues in their own way—and *that* is why the play has something to say, not because it gives us handy hints on how to live our own lives. Discussing the ideas in literature through the concept of *theme* enables us to escape the tyranny of moralizing.

Interpreting Symbols

A **symbol** is a person, place, or thing that stands for or strongly suggests something in addition to itself, generally an abstract idea more important than itself. Symbols are not exotic literary devices that readers have to wrestle with. In fact, the daily, nonliterary lives of readers are filled, quite comfortably and naturally, with more symbols than exist in any book ever written.

A Rolls Royce, for example, is an expensive car manufactured in Britain, but for many people it stands for something else: it is a symbol of success or status or good taste. Our lives are pervaded, perhaps dominated, by symbols. Think about the different symbolic meanings everyone gives to the following: a diamond ring, a new house, money, a police badge, a college diploma, a trip to Europe, a date with a rap star, the Confederate flag, Niagara Falls, a minivan.

Making symbols and reacting to symbols are such basic ingredients of the human mind that we should hardly be astonished to find symbols in literature. Symbols have an extremely practical value to a writer, however. They enable the writer to communicate abstract concepts with the vitality that can come only from specific details. Just as some people may be indifferent to abstract oratory about freedom's being a good thing but deeply moved by a visit to Ground Zero, a reader may be bored by or antagonistic to philosophical assertions about the passing of time but intensely impressed by the specific symbol of a ticking clock in a novel by Faulkner. Symbols of abstract ideas can often have a dramatic impact that the ideas themselves cannot, and sometimes in the hands of a master, symbols can express what might otherwise be almost inexpressible.

 **TIPS** for Avoiding Traps Involving Symbols

- **Remember that the symbol stands for or suggests something *in addition to* itself, not *instead of* itself.**   The symbolic level of a story or poem should never dwarf the other levels—especially the basic level of people and plot.

- **Keep in mind that symbols are usually obvious.**   If a critic has to struggle to establish that something functions as a symbol, it probably was not meant to be one. Stick to what the author clearly intends. In Hemingway's *A Farewell to Arms*, one of the characters says repeatedly that she is afraid of the rain because she dreams that it means her death. Then, when she does die and it is indeed raining, we can say that the rain is a symbol of death.

- **Do not confuse symbols with ordinary significant details.**   A symbol stands for or suggests something substantially different from itself. Rain may symbolize death. A veil may symbolize isolation. Springtime may symbolize youth, rebirth, longing, hope. If a man in a story, however, wipes his running nose with the back of his hand and doesn't cover his mouth when he coughs, we simply know that he has bad manners (in addition to a cold). The way he wipes his nose is not a symbol of bad manners, nor is the way he coughs; they *are* bad manners, details about the character that reveal something about him.

- **Do not be too eager to make a symbol stand for any one thing in particular.**   The most effective symbols often are not meant to work that way at all. They *stand for* nothing. They are meant to *suggest*—on an emotional level, at times a virtually subconscious level—a number of elusive concepts. That is precisely why symbols can be so valuable. Herman Melville's white whale in *Moby-Dick* becomes such a powerful symbol because it suggests so many ideas: evil, humanity's insignificance, the unchanging order of the universe, nature, God's will, and so on. Symbols are often a great writer's imaginative shortcuts for dealing with the imposing and frightening complexity of life as we know it.

Watching for Metaphors and Similes

Metaphors and similes are the two most common kinds of figurative language or figures of speech. A working definition of **figurative language** is "language that cannot be taken literally." In one way or another, figurative language departs from the conventional meaning and expression of words to bring about special effects, usually emotional. Figurative language is a common ingredient of our speech and writing; it is basic to almost all poetry, far more so than rhyme or meter.

A **simile** is a comparison using the word *like* or *as*.

The lecture was *as* dry as the dust on Grandpa's chicken farm.

All through that dreary summer weekend, we felt *as* if life had turned into a slow-motion movie.

A **metaphor** is a comparison that does without the word *like* or *as*, thus establishing a closer connection between the items compared.

Our lives that dreary summer weekend had turned into a slow-motion movie.

She had ice water in her veins.

Bill is the spark plug of his team.

As indicated by many of the preceding examples, metaphors fill our daily language. A number of them are so familiar that we have to struggle to recognize their metaphorical nature.

the arms of a chair	a wallflower
a clean sweep	the legs of a table
the traffic crawled	the heart of the matter
a poker face	peaches-and-cream complexion

Effective metaphors and similes, when fresh and original, enable writers to stimulate and direct the emotions of their readers, to communicate their own emotions with concrete images rather than flat, abstract statements, and thus to develop stylistic color and excitement. Readers and critics should pay particular attention to **metaphorical patterns**—metaphors sustained and developed through a whole work rather than dropped after one sentence. Many writers consciously use such patterns to achieve greater unity, consistency, and dramatic power, as you have seen in Shakespeare's sonnets (pages 244–245).

Avoiding Common Pitfalls in Literary Analysis

When writing your literary analysis, there are a couple of things you should *not* do, as the following list suggests.

 TIPS for Avoiding Common Pitfalls in Literary Analysis

- **Avoid plot summary.** Don't tell the story all over again. You have to assume that readers have read the piece, and they know the names of the characters, who's in love with whom, who lives and dies, and so on. You are writing an analysis, not a book report. Note how the student writer of the essay on Shirley Jackson's "Charles" (pages 238–241) doesn't hesitate to give away the surprise ending in her first sentence. Note how she uses all references to events in the story to remind readers of the events and to show how they relate to the thesis of the essay, not to inform readers that the events occurred in the first place.

- **Do not overuse direct quotations.** Unless you are writing about an author's style or explaining the meaning of some especially difficult lines, you should be cautious about direct quotations. Rely, for the most part, on references in your own words to the work you are discussing. True, a well-chosen direct quotation can add a strong dramatic touch to your introduction or conclusion. Moreover, direct quotations can sometimes be valuable if you feel your point might be questionable or controversial.

Student Writing: Literary Analysis

Now let's look at what happens when a student who is a careful reader and competent writer faces a literary work for analysis.

The following paper analyzes a Shirley Jackson short story that appears in an earlier section of this book (pages 238–341). Harriet McKay's assignment was to "Trace the sequence of clues planted by the author so that we have a chance to anticipate the surprise ending in Jackson's 'Charles.'"

Harriet McKay
The Beginning of the End

1   Until the last sentence of Shirley Jackson's "Charles," I had no idea that Charles, the terror of kindergarten, was an imaginary person created by Laurie and that Charles's little monster antics were really Laurie's own antics. The author fooled me completely, but I have to admit that she played fair. She gave her readers all the clues they needed to make a sensible guess about how the story would end.

2   Laurie's own personality offers one set of clues. Even before classes start, Jackson lets us know that Laurie might have a lot to overcompensate for. His mother has been dressing him in cute little boy clothes and thinking of him as a "sweet-voiced nursery-school tot." It is at Laurie's own insistence that he begins wearing tough-kid blue jeans. In addition, any boy nicknamed "Laurie" is due for some problems; one doesn't need to be a sexist pig to say that boys named "Laurence" ought to be called "Larry" and that "Laurie," to put it bluntly, is a sissy name. No wonder Laurie goes overboard. He's not a little boy anymore. He has hit the big time in kindergarten, and he begins "swaggering" even before his first class.

3   Laurie's behavior at home after school starts is another giveaway. Charles may be a monster at school, but Laurie isn't that much better at lunchtime. After only one class, he slams the door, throws his hat on the floor, shouts, speaks "insolently," makes deliberate mistakes in grammar, doesn't look at people when he talks to them but talks to the bread and butter instead, speaks with his mouth full, leaves the table without asking permission and while his father is still talking to him. This is no sweet little tot. His doting parents might try to pin Laurie's behavior on the bad influence of Charles, but that's certainly not the only possible explanation, and that's what doting parents have always tried to do. Besides, it would be stretching things to the limit to imagine that even Charles could have that great an influence after only one morning in the same classroom with him.

4   Still another giveaway is Laurie's explanation for being late. It's impossible to believe that a group of kindergarten kids would voluntarily stay after school to watch a child being punished. Laurie's parents swallow this story so easily that many readers probably didn't notice how fantastic the story really is—but an alert reader would have noticed.

5   The last clue I should have noticed is the way Laurie's parents look forward to the P.T.A. meeting so they can meet Charles' mother. They have been so poised and cool about everything that I really wonder why I did not realize that they would have to

be brought down a few pegs at the end of the story. Have they ever made a serious effort to correct their son's bad manners? Have they ever told him to stay away from a rotten kid like Charles? Heavens no, they're much too enlightened. The parents think Charles is amusing, and they can't wait to meet Charles' mother so they can feel superior to her. In simple justice they deserve what they get, and I should have seen it coming.

Laurie's personality and behavior, his unbelievable explanation for being late, and his parents' complacency all give readers the clues they need to predict the surprise ending.

6

FOR WRITING OR DISCUSSION

1. What is the thesis of this paper? Is the thesis stated in one sentence? If so, where?

2. What personality does the writer present to the reader? Is it appropriate to the subject matter?

3. Does the writer omit details from the story that could have strengthened her case?

4. Should the writer have devoted a separate paragraph to the issue of Laurie's lateness? If not, how could the issue have been treated more effectively?

5. Is the last paragraph too short? Too abrupt? Too dull?

6. Write a brief analysis of this student paper, discussing its strengths and making suggestions for any needed improvements.

EXERCISE Read or reread the student models "Enough Despair to Go Around" (pages 80–81) by Alan Benjamin and "Two Kinds of Love" (pages 245–246) by Julie Olivera. In what ways do these essays observe the principles of literary analysis that you have studied in this chapter?

Readings for Writing

The short stories that follow should stimulate you to find topics for your own papers of literary analysis. A checklist for writing and revising your literary analysis (pages 406–407) follows the stories. The checklist will help you review the important points in this chapter.

JAMAICA KINCAID

Girl

1   Wash the white clothes on Monday and put them on the stone heap; wash the color clothes on Tuesday and put them on the clothes-line to dry; don't walk barehead in the hot sun; cook pumpkin fritters in very hot sweet oil; soak your little cloths right after you take them off; when buying cotton to make yourself a nice blouse, be sure that it doesn't have gum on it, because that way it won't hold up well after a wash; soak salt fish overnight before you cook it; is it true that you sing benna in Sunday school?; always eat your food in such a way that it won't turn someone else's stomach; on Sundays try to walk like a lady and not like the slut you are so bent on becoming; don't sing benna in Sunday school; you mustn't speak to wharf-rat boys, not even to give directions; don't eat fruits on the street— flies will follow you; *but I don't sing benna on Sundays at all and never in Sunday school*; this is how to sew on a button; this is how to make a buttonhole for the button you have just sewed on; this is how to hem a dress when you see the hem coming down and so to prevent yourself from looking like the slut I know you are so bent on becoming; this is how you iron your father's khaki shirt so that it doesn't have a crease; this is how you iron your father's khaki pants so that they don't have a crease; this is how you grow okra—far from the house, because okra tree harbors red ants; when you are growing dasheen, make sure it gets plenty of water or else it makes your throat itch when you are eating it; this is how you sweep a corner; this is how you sweep a whole house; this is how you sweep a yard; this is how you smile to someone you don't like too much; this is how you smile to someone you don't like at all; this is how you smile to someone you like completely; this is how you set a table for tea; this is how you set a table for dinner; this is how you set a table for dinner with an important guest; this is how you set a table for lunch; this is how you set a table for breakfast; this is how to behave in the presence of men who don't know you very well, and this way they won't recognize immediately the slut I have warned you against becoming; be sure to wash every day, even if it is with your own spit; don't squat down to play marbles—you are not a boy, you know; don't pick people's flowers—you might catch something; don't throw stones at blackbirds, because it might not be a black-bird at all; this is how to make a bread pudding; this is how to make doukona; this is how to make pepper pot; this is how to make a good medicine for a cold; this is how to make a good medicine to throw away a child before it even becomes a child; this is how to catch a fish; this is how to throw back a fish you don't like, and that way something bad won't fall on you; this is how to bully a man; this is how a man bullies you; this is how to love a man, and if this doesn't work there are other ways, and if they don't work don't feel too bad about giving up; this is how to spit up in the air if you feel like it, and this is how to move quick so that it doesn't fall on you; this is how to make ends meet; always squeeze bread to make sure it's fresh; *but what if the baker won't let me feel the bread?*; you mean to say that after all you are really going to be the kind of woman who the baker won't let near the bread?

WILLA CATHER

A Wagner Matinee

I received one morning a letter, written in pale ink on glassy, blue-lined notepaper, and bearing the postmark of a little Nebraska village. This communication, worn and rubbed, looking as though it had been carried for some days in a coat pocket that was none too clean, was from my Uncle Howard and informed me that his wife had been left a small legacy by a bachelor relative who had recently died, and that it would be necessary for her to go to Boston to attend to the settling of the estate. He requested me to meet her at the station and render her whatever services might be necessary. On examining the date indicated as that of her arrival I found it no later than tomorrow. He had characteristically delayed writing until, had I been away from home for a day, I must have missed the good woman altogether.

The name of my Aunt Georgiana called up not alone her own figure, at once pathetic and grotesque, but opened before my feet a gulf of recollection so wide and deep that, as the letter dropped from my hand, I felt suddenly a stranger to all the present conditions of my existence, wholly ill at ease and out of place amid the familiar surroundings of my study. I became, in short, the gangling farm boy my aunt had known, scourged with chilblains and bashfulness, my hands cracked and sore from the corn husking. I felt the knuckles of my thumb tentatively, as though they were raw again. I sat again before her parlor organ, fumbling the scales with my stiff, red hands, while she, beside me, made canvas mittens for the huskers.

The next morning, after preparing my landlady somewhat, I set out for the station. When the train arrived I had some difficulty in finding my aunt. She was the last of the passengers to alight, and it was not until I got her into the carriage that she seemed really to recognize me. She had come all the way in a day coach; her linen duster had become black with soot, and her black bonnet gray with dust, during the journey. When we arrived at my boardinghouse the landlady put her to bed at once and I did not see her again until the next morning.

4   Whatever shock Mrs. Springer experienced at my aunt's appearance she considerately concealed. As for myself, I saw my aunt's misshapen figure with that feeling of awe and respect with which we behold explorers who have left their ears and fingers north of Franz Josef Land, or their health somewhere along the Upper Congo. My Aunt Georgiana had been a music teacher at the Boston Conservatory, somewhere back in the latter sixties. One summer, while visiting in the little village among the Green Mountains where her ancestors had dwelt for generations, she had kindled the callow fancy of the most idle and shiftless of all the village lads, and had conceived for this Howard Carpenter one of those extravagant passions which a handsome country boy of twenty-one sometimes inspires in an angular, spectacled woman of thirty. When she returned to her duties in Boston, Howard followed her, and the upshot of this inexplicable infatuation was that she eloped with him, eluding the reproaches of her family and the criticisms of her friends by going with him to the Nebraska frontier. Carpenter, who, of course, had no money, had taken a homestead in Red Willow County, fifty miles from the railroad. There they had measured off their quarter section themselves by driving across the prairie in a wagon, to the wheel of which they had tied a red cotton handkerchief, and counting off its revolutions. They built a dugout in the red hillside, one of those cave dwellings whose inmates so often reverted to primitive conditions. Their water they got from the lagoons where the buffalo drank, and their slender stock of provisions was always at the mercy of bands of roving Indians. For thirty years my aunt had not been further than fifty miles from the homestead.

5   But Mrs. Springer knew nothing of all this, and must have been considerably shocked at what was left of my kinswoman. Beneath the soiled linen duster which, on her arrival, was the most conspicuous feature of her costume, she wore a black stuff dress, whose ornamentation showed that she had surrendered herself unquestioningly into the hands of a country dressmaker. My poor aunt's figure, however, would have presented astonishing difficulties to any dressmaker. Originally stooped, her shoulders were now almost bent together over her sunken chest. She wore no stays, and her gown, which trailed unevenly behind, rose in a sort of peak over her abdomen. She wore ill-fitting false teeth, and her skin was as yellow as a Mongolian's from constant exposure to a pitiless wind and to the alkaline water which hardens the most transparent cuticle into a sort of flexible leather.

6   I owed to this woman most of the good that ever came my way in my boyhood, and had a reverential affection for her. During the years when I was riding herd for my uncle, my aunt, after cooking the three meals—the first of which was ready at six o'clock in the morning-and putting the six children to bed, would often stand until midnight at her ironing board, with me at the kitchen table beside her, hearing me recite Latin declensions and conjugations, gently shaking me when my drowsy head sank down over a page of irregular verbs. It was to her, at her ironing or mending, that I read my first Shakespeare', and her old textbook on mythology was the first that ever came into my empty hands. She taught me my scales and exercises, too—on the little parlor organ, which her husband had bought her after fifteen years, during which she had not so much as seen any instrument, but an accordion that belonged to one of the Norwegian farmhands. She would sit beside me by the hour, darning and counting while I struggled with the "Joyous Farmer," but she

seldom talked to me about music, and I understood why. She was a pious woman; she had the consolations of religion and, to her at least, her martyrdom was not wholly sordid. Once when I had been doggedly beating out some easy passages from an old score of *Euryanthe* I had found among her music books, she came up to me and, putting her hands over my eyes, gently drew my head back upon her shoulder, saying tremulously, "Don't love it so well, Clark, or it may be taken from you. Oh, dear boy, pray that whatever your sacrifice may be, it be not that."

When my aunt appeared on the morning after her arrival she was still in a semi-somnambulant state. She seemed not to realize that she was in the city where she had spent her youth, the place longed for hungrily half a lifetime. She had been so wretchedly train-sick throughout the journey that she bad no recollection of anything but her discomfort, and, to all intents and purposes, there were but a few hours of nightmare between the farm in Red Willow County and my study on Newbury Street. I had planned a little pleasure for her that afternoon, to repay her for some of the glorious moments she had given me when we used to milk together in the straw-thatched cowshed and she, because I was more than usually tired, or because her husband had spoken sharply to me, would tell me of the splendid performance of the *Huguenots* she had seen in Paris, in her youth. At two o'clock the Symphony Orchestra was to give a Wagner program, and I intended to take my aunt; though, as I conversed with her I grew doubtful about her enjoyment of it. Indeed, for her own sake, I could only wish her taste for such things quite dead, and the long struggle mercifully ended at last. I suggested our visiting the Conservatory and the Common before lunch, but she seemed altogether too timid to wish to venture out. She questioned me absently about various changes in the city, but she was chiefly concerned that she had forgotten to leave instructions about feeding half-skimmed milk to a certain weakling calf, "old Maggie's calf, you know, Clark," she explained, evidently having forgotten how long I had been away. She was further troubled because she had neglected to tell her daughter about the freshly opened kit of mackerel in the cellar, which would spoil if it were not used directly.   7

I asked her whether she had ever heard any of the Wagnerian operas and found that she had not, though she was perfectly familiar with their respective situations, and had once possessed the piano score of *The Flying Dutchman*. I began to think it would have been best to get her back to Red Willow County without waking her, and regretted having suggested the concert.   8

From the time we entered the concert hall, however, she was a trifle less passive and inert, and for the first time seemed to perceive her surroundings. I had felt some trepidation lest she might become aware of the absurdities of her attire, or might experience some painful embarrassment at stepping suddenly into the world to which she had been dead for a quarter of a century. But, again, I found how superficially I had judged her. She sat looking about her with eyes as impersonal, almost as stony, as those with which the granite Rameses in a museum watches the froth and fret that ebbs and flows about his pedestal-separated from it by the lonely stretch of centuries. I have seen this same aloofness in old miners who drift into the Brown Hotel at Denver, their pockets full of bullion, their linen soiled, their haggard faces unshaven; standing in the thronged corridors as solitary as though they were still in a frozen camp on the Yukon, conscious that certain experiences have isolated them from their fellows by a gulf no haberdasher could bridge.   9

10   We sat at the extreme left of the first balcony, facing the arc of our own and the balcony above us, veritable hanging gardens, brilliant as tulip beds. The matinee audience was made up chiefly of women. One lost the contour of faces and figures—indeed, any effect of line whatever-and there was only the color of bodices past counting, the shimmer of fabrics soft and firm, silky and sheer: red, mauve, pink, blue, lilac, purple, ecru, rose, yellow, cream, and white, all the colors that an impressionist finds in a sunlit landscape, with here and there the dead shadow of a frock coat. My Aunt Georgiana regarded them as though they had been so many daubs of tube-paint on a palette.

11   When the musicians came out and took their places, she gave a little stir of anticipation and looked with quickening interest down over the rail at that invariable grouping, perhaps the first wholly familiar thing that had greeted her eye since she had left old Maggie and her weakling calf. I could feel how all those details sank into her soul, for I had not forgotten how they had sunk into mine when. I came fresh from plowing forever and forever between green aisles of corn, where, as in a treadmill, one might walk from daybreak to dusk without perceiving a shadow of change. The clean profiles of the musicians, the gloss of their linen, the dull black of their coats, the beloved shapes of the instruments, the patches of yellow light thrown by the green- shaded lamps on the smooth, varnished bellies of the cellos and the bass viols in the rear, the restless, wind-tossed forest of fiddle necks and bows-I recalled how, in the first orchestra I had ever heard, those long bow strokes seemed to draw the heart out of me, as a conjurer's stick reels out yards of paper ribbon from a hat.

12   The first number was the *Tannhauser* overture. When the horns drew out the first strain of the Pilgrim's chorus my Aunt Georgiana clutched my coat sleeve. Then it was I first realized that for her this broke a silence of thirty years; the inconceivable silence of the plains. With the battle between the two motives, with the frenzy of the Venusberg theme and its ripping of strings, there came to me an overwhelming sense of the waste and wear we are so powerless to combat; and I saw again the tall, naked house on the prairie, black and grim as a wooden fortress; the black pond where I had learned to swim, its margin pitted with sun-dried cattle tracks; the rain-gullied clay banks about the naked house, the four dwarf ash seedlings where the dishcloths were always hung to dry before the kitchen door. The world there was the flat world of the ancients; to the east, a cornfield that stretched to daybreak; to the west, a corral that reached to sunset; between, the conquests of peace, dearer bought than those of war.

13   The overture closed; my aunt released my coat sleeve, but she said nothing. She sat staring at the orchestra through a dullness of thirty years, through the films made little by little by each of the three hundred and sixty-five days in every one of them. What, I wondered, did she get from it? She had been a good pianist in her day I knew, and her musical education had been broader than that of most music teachers of a quarter of a century ago. She had often told me of Mozart's operas and Meyerbeer's, and I could remember hearing her sing, years ago, certain melodies of Verdi's. When I had fallen ill with a fever in her house she used to sit by my cot in the evening—when the cool, night wind blew in through the faded mosquito netting tacked over the window, and I lay watching a certain bright star that burned red above the cornfield—and sing "Home to our mountains, O, let us return!" in a way fit to break the heart of a Vermont boy near dead of homesickness already.

14   I watched her closely through the prelude to *Tristan and Isolde*, trying vainly to conjecture what that seething turmoil of strings and winds might mean to her, but she sat mutely staring at the violin bows that drove obliquely downward, like the pelting streaks of rain in a summer

shower. Had this music any message for her? Had she enough left to at all comprehend this power which had kindled the world since she had left it? I was in a fever of curiosity, but Aunt Georgiana sat silent upon her peak in Darien. She preserved this utter immobility throughout the number from *The Flying Dutchman*, though her fingers worked mechanically upon her black dress, as though, of themselves, they were recalling the piano score they had once played. Poor old hands! They had been stretched and twisted into mere tentacles to hold and lift and knead with; the palms unduly swollen, the fingers bent and knotted—on one of them a thin, worn band that had once been a wedding ring. As I pressed and gently quieted one of those groping hands I remembered with quivering eyelids their services for me in other days.

Soon after the tenor began the "Prize Song," I heard a quick drawn breath and turned to my aunt. Her eyes were closed, but the tears were glistening on her cheeks, and I think, in a moment more, they were in my eyes as well. It never really died, then—the soul that can suffer so excruciatingly and so interminably; it withers to the outward eye only; like that strange moss which can lie on a dusty shelf half a century and yet, if placed in water, grows green again. She wept so throughout the development and elaboration of the melody.
 15

During the intermission before the second half of the concert, I questioned my aunt and found that the "Prize Song" was not new to her. Some years before there had drifted to the farm in Red Willow County a young German, a tramp cowpuncher, who had sung the chorus at Bayreuth, when he was a boy, along with the other peasant boys and girls. Of a Sunday morning he used to sit on his gingham-sheeted bed in the hands' bedroom which opened off the kitchen, cleaning the leather of his boots and saddle, singing the "Prize Song," while my aunt went about her work in the kitchen. She had hovered about him until she had prevailed upon him to join the country church, though his sole fitness for this step, insofar as I could gather, lay in his boyish face and his possession of this divine melody. Shortly afterward he had gone to town on the Fourth of July, been drunk for several days, lost his money at a faro table, ridden a saddled Texan steer on a bet, and disappeared with a fractured collarbone. All this my aunt told me huskily, wanderingly, as though she were talking in the weak lapses of illness.
 16

"Well, we have come to better things than the old *Trovatore* at any rate, Aunt Georgie?" I queried, with a well-meant effort at jocularity.
 17

Her lip quivered and she hastily put her handkerchief up to her mouth. From behind it she murmured, "And you have been hearing this ever since you left me, Clark?" Her question was the gentlest and saddest of reproaches.
 18

The second half of the program consisted of four numbers from the *Ring*, and closed with Siegfried's funeral march. My aunt wept quietly, but almost continuously, as a shallow vessel overflows in a rainstorm. From time to time her dim eyes looked up at the lights which studded the ceiling, burning softly under their dull glass globes; doubtless they were stars in truth to her. I was still perplexed as to what measure of musical comprehension was left to her, she who had heard nothing but the singing of gospel hymns at Methodist services in the square frame schoolhouse on Section Thirteen for so many years. I was wholly unable to gauge how much of it had been dissolved in soapsuds, or worked into bread, or milked into the bottom of a pail.
 19

The deluge of sound poured on and on; I never knew what she found in the shining current of it; I never knew how far it bore her, or past what happy islands. From the trembling of her face I could well believe that before the last numbers she had been carried out where the myriad graves are, into the gray, nameless burying grounds of the sea; or
 20

into some world of death vaster yet, where, from the beginning of the world, hope has lain down with hope and dream with dream and, renouncing, slept.

21   The concert was over; the people filed out of the hall chattering and laughing, glad to relax and find the living level again, but my kinswoman made no effort to rise. The harpist slipped its green felt cover over his instrument; the flute players shook the water from their mouthpieces; the men of the orchestra went out one by one, leaving the stage to the chairs and music stands, empty as a winter cornfield.

22   I spoke to my aunt. She burst into tears and sobbed pleadingly. "I don't want to go, Clark, I don't want to go!"

23   I understood. For her, just outside the door of the concert hall, lay the black pond with the cattle-tracked bluffs; the tall, unpainted house, with weather-curled boards; naked as a tower, the crook-backed ash seedlings where the dishcloths hung to dry; the gaunt, molting turkeys picking up refuse about the kitchen door.

FOR WRITING OR DISCUSSION

1. Where was Aunt Georgiana born? Where did she live at the time of the story? Why did she move there? Why did she seldom talk about music?

2. Who is Wagner? Which of his musical pieces does the orchestra play at the matinee? What is Aunt Georgiana's reaction to the pieces as she hears them?

3. What does Clark mean when he says near the end of the story, "It never really died, then"? What does the 'it' refer to? Do you believe that a love of any art never dies, even after a long absence from its spell?

4. What imagery do you find most visual? Look especially at the last sentence of the story. How in one sentence has Cather managed to convey the terrible desperation of Aunt Georgiana's life without music? What is your reaction to the image of turkeys "picking up refuse about the kitchen door"? Why is the word "refuse" so apt in light of the story's essential meaning?

5. Write an essay about the effect music had on you or someone you know at a concert or from a recording or computer transmission.

EDGAR ALLAN POE

The Tell-Tale Heart

1   True—nervous—very, very dreadfully nervous I had been and am; but why *will* you say that I am mad? The disease had sharpened my senses—not destroyed—not dulled them. Above all was the sense of hearing acute. I heard all things in the heaven and in the earth. I heard many things in hell. How, then, am I mad? Hearken! and observe how healthily— how calmly I tell you the whole story.

It is impossible to say how first the idea entered my brain; but once conceived, it haunted me day and night. Object there was none. Passion there was none. I loved the old man. He had never wronged me. He had never given me insult. For his gold I had no desire. I think it was his eye! Yes, it was this! One of his eyes resembled that of a vulture— a pale blue eye, with a film over it. Whenever it fell upon me, my blood ran cold; and so by degrees—very gradually—I made up my mind to take the life of the old man, and thus rid myself of the eye for ever.   2

Now this is the point. You fancy me mad. Madmen know nothing. But you should have seen *me*. You should have seen how wisely I proceeded—with what caution—with what foresight—with what dissimulation I went to work! I was never kinder to the old man than during the whole week before I killed him. And every night, about midnight, I turned the latch of his door and opened it—oh, so gently! And then, when I had made an opening sufficient for my head, I put in a dark lantern, all closed, closed, so that no light shone out, and then I thrust in my head. Oh, you would have laughed to see how cunningly I thrust it in! I moved it slowly—very, very slowly, so that I might not disturb the old man's sleep. It took me an hour to place my whole head within the opening so far that I could see him as he lay upon his bed. Ha!—would a madman have been so wise as this? And then, when my head was well in the room, I undid the lantern cautiously—oh, so cautiously—cautiously (for the hinges creaked)—I undid it just so much that a single thin ray fell upon the vulture eye. And this I did for seven long nights—every night just at midnight—but I found the eye always closed; and so it was impossible to do the work; for it was not the old man who vexed me, but his Evil Eye. And every morning, when the day broke, I went boldly into the chamber, and spoke courageously to him, calling him by name in a hearty tone, and inquiring how he had passed the night. So you see he would have been a very profound old man, indeed, to suspect that every night, just at twelve, I looked in upon him while he slept.   3

Upon the eighth night I was more than usually cautious in opening the door. A watch's minute hand moves more quickly than did mine. Never before that night had I *felt* the extent of my own powers—of my sagacity. I could scarcely contain my feelings of triumph. To think that there I was, opening the door, little by little, and he not even to dream of my secret deeds or thoughts. I fairly chuckled at the idea; and perhaps he heard me; for he moved on the bed suddenly, as if startled. Now you may think that I drew back—but no. His room was as black as pitch with the thick darkness (for the shutters were closed fastened, through fear of robbers), and so I knew that he could not see the opening of the door, and I kept pushing it on steadily, steadily.   4

I had my head in, and was about to open the lantern, when my thumb slipped upon the tin fastening, and the old man sprang up in the bed, crying out "Who's there?"   5

I kept quite still and said nothing. For a whole hour I did not move a muscle, and in the meantime I did not hear him lie down. He was still sitting up in the bed listening;— just as I have done, night after night, hearkening to the death watches in the wall.   6

Presently I heard a slight groan, and I knew it was the groan of mortal terror. It was not a groan of pain or of grief—oh, no!—it was the low stifled sound that arises from the bottom of the soul when overcharged with awe. I knew the sound well. Many a night, just   7 at midnight, when all the world slept, it was welled up from my own bosom, deepening, with its dreadful echo, the terrors that distracted me. I say I knew it well. I knew what the old man felt, and pitied him, although I chuckled at heart. I knew that he had been lying awake ever since the first slight noise, when he had turned in the bed. His fears had been ever since growing upon him. He had been trying to fancy them causeless, but could not. He had been saying to himself—"It is nothing but the wind in the chimney—it is only a mouse crossing the floor," or "it is merely a cricket which has made a single chirp." Yes, he has been trying to comfort himself with these suppositions; but he had found all in vain. *All in vain*; because Death, in approaching him, had stalked with his black shadow before him, and enveloped the victim. And it was the mournful influence of the unperceived shadow that caused him to feel—although he neither saw nor heard—to *feel* the presence of my head within the room.

8   When I had waited a long time, very patiently, without hearing him lie down, I resolved to open a little—a very, very little crevice in the lantern. So I opened it—you cannot imagine how stealthily, stealthily, until, at length, a single dim ray, like the thread of a spider, shot from out the crevice and full upon the vulture eye.

9   It was open—wide, wide open—and I grew furious as I gazed upon it. I saw it with perfect distinctness—all a dull blue, with a hideous veil over it that chilled the very marrow in my bones; but I could see nothing else of the old man's face or person: for I had directed the ray as if by instinct, precisely upon the damned spot.

10   And now have I not told you that what you mistake for madness is but overacuteness of the senses!—now, I say, there came to my ears a low, dull, quick sound, such as a watch makes when enveloped in cotton. I knew *that* sound well too. It was the beating of the old man's heart. It increased my fury, as the beating of a drum stimulates the soldier into courage.

11   But even yet I refrained and kept still. I scarcely breathed. I held the lantern motionless. I tried how steadily I could maintain the ray upon the eye. Meantime the hellish tattoo of the heart increased. It grew quicker and quicker, and louder and louder every instant. The old man's terror *must* have been extreme! It grew louder, I say, louder every moment!—do you mark me well? I have told you that I am nervous: so I am. And now at the dead hour of the night, amid the dreadful silence of that old house, so strange a noise as this excited me to uncontrollable terror. Yet, for some minutes longer I refrained and stood still. But the beating grew louder, louder! I thought the heart must burst. And now a new anxiety seized me—the sound would be heard by a neighbor! The old man's hour had come! With a loud yell, I threw open the lantern and leaped into the room. He shrieked once—once only. In an instant I dragged him to the floor, and pulled the heavy bed over him. I then smiled gaily, to defend the deed so far done. But, for many minutes, the heart beat on with a muffled sound. This, however, did not vex me; it would not be heard through the wall. At length it ceased. The old man was dead. I removed the bed and examined the corpse. Yes, he was stone, stone dead. I placed my hand upon the heart and held it there many minutes. There was no pulsation. He was stone dead. His eye would trouble me no more.

12   If still you think me mad, you will think so no longer when I describe the wise precautions I took for the concealment of the body. The night waned and I worked hastily, but in silence. First of all I dismembered the corpse. I cut off the head and the arms and the legs.

I then took up three planks from the flooring of the chamber, and deposited all between the scantlings. I then replaced the boards so cleverly, so cunningly, that no human eye— not even *his*—could have detected any thing wrong. There was nothing to wash out—no stain of any kind—no blood-spot whatever. I had been too wary for that. A tub had caught all—ha! ha!

13

When I had made an end of these labors, it was four o'clock—still dark as midnight. As the bell sounded the hour, there came a knocking at the street door. I went down to open it with a light heart—for what had I *now* to fear? There entered three men, who introduced themselves, with perfect suavity, as officers of the police. A shriek had been heard by a neighbor during the night; suspicion of foul play had been aroused; information had been lodged at the police office, and they (the officers) had been deputed to search the premises.

14

I smiled,—for *what* had I to fear? I bade the gentlemen welcome. The shriek, I said, was my own in a dream. The old man, I mentioned, was absent in the country. I took my visitors all over the house. I bade them search—search *well*. I led them, at length, to *his* chamber. I showed them his treasures, secure, undisturbed. In the enthusiasm of my confidence, I brought chairs into the room, and desired them *here* to rest from their fatigues, while I myself, in the wild audacity of my perfect triumph, placed my own seat upon the very spot beneath which reposed the corpse of the victim.

15

The officers were satisfied. My *manner* had convinced them. I was singularly at ease. They sat, and while I answered cheerily, they chatted familiar things. But, ere long, I felt myself getting pale and wished them gone. My head ached, and I fancied a ringing in my ears: but still they sat and still chatted. The ringing became more distinct:—it continued and became more distinct: I talked more freely to get rid of the feeling: but it continued and gained definitiveness—until, at length, I found that the noise was *not* within my ears.

16

No doubt I now grew *very* pale:—but I talked more fluently, and with a heightened voice. Yet the sound increased—and what could I do? It was a *low, dull, quick sound— much such a sound as a watch makes when enveloped in cotton*. I gasped for breath— and yet the officers heard it not. I talked more quickly—more vehemently; but the noise steadily increased. I arose and argued about trifles, in a high key and with violent gesticulations, but the noise steadily increased. Why *would* they not be gone? I paced the floor to and fro with heavy strides, as if excited to fury by the observation of the men— but the noise steadily increased. Oh God! what *could* I do? I foamed—I raved—I swore! I swung the chair upon which I had been sitting, and grated it upon the boards, but the noise arose over all and continually increased. It grew louder—louder—*louder*! And still the men chatted pleasantly, and smiled. Was it possible they heard not? Almighty God!— no, no! They heard!—they suspected!—they *knew!*—they were making a mockery of my horror!—this I thought, and this I think. But any thing was better than this agony! Any thing was more tolerable than this derision! I could bear those hypocritical smiles no longer! I felt that I must scream or die!—and now—again!—hark! louder! louder! louder! *louder!*—

17

"Villains!" I shrieked, "dissemble no more! I admit the deed!—tear up the planks!— here, here!—it is the beating of his hideous heart!"

18

FOR WRITING OR DISCUSSION

1. What is the narrator's mental state? How do you know? How does Poe's language help convey the mental state of the narrator?

2. What does the narrator say is the result of his disease? To whom is he speaking?

3. Sound plays an important part in the telling of this story. What images of sound can you identify here? What claim does the narrator make about sound in the first paragraph?

4. What do the frequent repetitions contribute to this story?

5. Do you trust the narrator? Why, or why not? Are his observations reliable?

6. Edgar Allan Poe, who wrote in the nineteenth century ("The Tell-Tale Heart" was published in 1843), continues to be an extremely popular writer. How do you account for his popularity? Write an essay in which you explain, on the basis of this short story, why Poe continues to have a hold on the American imagination.

STRATEGY CHECKLIST: Writing and Revising Your Literary Analysis Paper

Read the literary work.	☐ Have I read the work slowly? Have I reread it?
	☐ Have I read with the assumption that everything is significant?
	☐ Have I concentrated on *theme* rather than *moral*?
	☐ Have I been aware of any use of symbols?
	☐ Have I been alert to the use of metaphors and similes?
Plan the paper.	☐ Have I used prewriting to explore ideas for my analysis?
	☐ Have I thought about my purpose for writing?
	☐ Have I written for a general audience? If I am writing for a special audience, how will I make this clear to the reader?
	☐ Have I limited my topic?
	☐ Have I considered using an outline to organize my ideas?

Write a first draft.	☐ Have I established a clear thesis? ☐ Have I supported my thesis with details and examples?
Revise and edit the paper.	☐ Do I have enough support for my thesis? ☐ Have I remembered not to interpret details out of context? ☐ Have I avoided the "hidden meanings" fallacy? ☐ Have I been cautious about overreading and becoming a symbol hunter? ☐ Have I avoided writing a plot summary? ☐ Have I been cautious with direct quotations, using them only when they serve a specific, practical purpose?
Proofread the paper.	☐ Have I proofread for grammar, spelling, and mechanics?

 For additional help with writing, reading, and research, go to www.mycomplab.com

CHAPTER **18**

Writing Essay Exams

In this chapter you will

■ develop skills in preparing for exams

■ evaluate exam questions and cue words

■ analyze steps for planning and writing an exam essay

Essay examinations are an important part of college learning; they provide an excellent gauge of your knowledge of a subject. No doubt you have taken these kinds of tests before: you have one or more questions to answer in an in-class essay of several pages within a defined time frame—usually about an hour.

This general advice about how to prepare for and take essay exams for all your college courses should help you improve performance.

Preparing for the Exam

Always prepare carefully and well in advance of your test. If you've paid attention to lectures and class discussions during the semester, you'll have a good sense of your instructor's emphases. A useful way to begin is to make a table of topics and questions. First, develop a list of the key areas you believe might be covered on the exam. Then alongside the topics, indicate possible questions.

Look at this sample prepared by a student studying for a test on child development.

Table of topics and questions

Topic	Possible essay questions
Physical environment of the fetus	1. How does the physical environment of the fetus contribute to the psychological development of the child?
	2. Discuss the effects of drugs or alcohol on the fetus and explain some of the noticeable psychological results in the newborn.

Prenatal care

1. Explain the steps a caregiver can take to provide appropriate psychological care for the fetus.

2. Define *prenatal* and *neonatal* and give distinguishing characteristics of each.

Psychology of the newborn

1. What can parents do to provide a sound psychological environment for a newborn?

2. What are some possible effects on a child whose basic needs are not met in the first month after birth?

Evaluating the Question

Always read the entire test, and study each essay question carefully. A major complaint from teachers who grade essay exams is that students often do not answer the questions being asked. Read the question with care so that you know precisely what your instructor expects. Essay questions usually contain cue words that signal the specific requirements. The table below lists and explains some cue words and identifies the methods of essay development (explained in Part Two of this book) that you might use to write your answers. Keep in mind that some essay questions will ask for a combination of these methods. And you should refer especially to Chapter 16, "Mixing Methods of Development."

Strategies for Responding to Essay Exam Cue Words

Cue Words	What to Do	Method of Development
Describe, tell, discuss, trace	Give physical characteristics, provide details, indicate sequence, or explain features.	Description Narration
Explain, illustrate, give examples, identify	Make sense or order of, enumerate, or provide details and examples.	Example Definition

(continued)

Cue Words	What to Do	Method of Development
How? Explain how, show how, tell how	Explain a process or indicate chronology.	Process
Compare, contrast, compare and contrast	Indicate similarities and (or) differences.	Comparison–contrast
Why, tell why, analyze, explain the results (or effects) of, tell the consequences of	Show the relation between ideas or events; tell how one event influences, causes, or results from another; or draw conclusions.	Cause and effect
Agree or disagree, support, evaluate, judge, defend, argue	Provide logical support for your position on a topic; convince a reader that your position is correct.	Argumentation

The following chart presents, from courses across the disciplines, typical essay examination questions that use some of these cue words.

Typical Essay Exam Questions

Discipline	Essay Question
English Literature	Provide examples of Shakespeare's use of animal imagery in *The Tempest* and explain the meaning of several key images.
Biology	Explain the reproductive process of budding in yeast cells.
Sociology	Compare and contrast the conditions in state-run orphanages in California in the nineteenth and twentieth centuries.
Health Care	What are some effects of terminal illness on a patient's immediate family?
Psychology	Identify three personality disorders and describe the key features of each.
History	Describe the slave trade in America in the eighteenth century.

Planning and Writing Your Essay

Once you examine the question carefully and are confident that you understand the task, take time to plan the essay before you begin writing.

 TIPS for Planning and Writing Your Essay

- **Assess the expected length and range of your response.** Your teacher may indicate what she expects in the examination questions with statements like "Write a sentence or two" or "Write a paragraph." More often than not, however, you have to infer the length of your expected response. A question worth five or ten points demands a shorter answer—a few sentences or a paragraph, say—than a question worth twenty-five, fifty, or a hundred points.

- **Use the wording of the essay question to help get you started.** Use some of the language of the question in your response, especially in the introduction to your answer. Here are some possible opening responses to the questions above.

Opening Responses to Essay Questions

Essay Question	Opening Responses That Use Elements of the Questions
Provide examples of Shakespeare's use of animal imagery in *The Tempest* and explain the meaning of several key images.	In *The Tempest* we find many examples of animal imagery, especially regarding the character Caliban.
Explain the reproductive process of budding in yeast cells.	Yeast plants reproduce by a process of budding in which . . .
What are some of the effects of terminal illness on the patient's immediate family?	The effects of terminal illness on patients and their families can be devastating.

- **Budget your time.** For an hour's exam, reserve about forty-five minutes for writing and about fifteen to twenty minutes for planning, revising, and editing.

- **Follow the general guidelines for good writing.** You should express your thesis and purpose clearly and should support your assertions with concrete detail. Accuracy, specificity, completeness, and relevance are essential. Although verbatim citations are difficult unless you have a superb memory, you nevertheless should paraphrase key points carefully, identifying sources whenever you can. Write an introduction and a conclusion—brief as time may require them to be. Connect thoughts with necessary transitions within paragraphs; link paragraphs logically within the essay.

■ **Plan your essay carefully and make revisions and editorial changes as needed.**   Because of time pressures on an essay examination, you certainly will have to condense the steps we recommended that you take as writers. However, do not ignore basic features of the writing process, especially the prewriting and planning strategies.

Even with the clock ticking, take a few moments to plan. Use the margins or the inside or back cover of your exam booklet to jot down ideas and to develop a scratch outline. When you write, consider the effort as somewhere between a first draft and a revised and edited draft—that is, you cannot write your essay exam on scrap paper and expect to return later to make extensive revisions. Certainly, you must reread your first effort, deleting problematic sections, adding words and sentences as needed, and fixing errors. Write all additions clearly. Many students skip every other line as they write and leave large top and bottom margins to facilitate changes and insertions. Nevertheless, the press of time will prevent you from rewriting your essay entirely. Don't plan on it. Add key elements that you may have omitted; insert definitions or essential detail; correct mistakes. But unless you are sure that you have sufficient time to recopy a draft, or that your instructor expects a second draft, do not rewrite your essay examination.

STRATEGY CHECKLIST: Taking an Essay Exam

Study for the exam.	☐ Have I prepared well for the exam, studying notes and book chapters as assigned?
	☐ Have I anticipated the exam by listing the key areas and possible questions it may cover?
Plan your approach to the exam.	☐ Have I read all the questions carefully and made sure that I understand my task?
	☐ Have I determined the time allotted for the test? Have I budgeted the time carefully?

| Write the essay(s). | ☐ Have I used the language of the question to help me start writing my essay response? |
| | ☐ Have I used the strategies for good writing I learned throughout this book? |

| Revise and proofread the essay(s). | ☐ Have I made appropriate revisions? |
| | ☐ Have I proofread for grammar, spelling, and mechanics? |

For additional help with writing, reading, and research, go to
www.mycomplab.com

CHAPTER 19

Business Writing: An Overview

In this chapter you will

- analyze letters of inquiry and complaint
- analyze steps for writing and formatting a letter
- write a job application letter
- analyze steps in preparing a résumé
- write a hard-copy and an electronic résumé
- write memorandums and e-mails

The writing demands of the business world, complicated by widespread use of word-processing programs and other computer aids, build on certain formal conventions.

Writing Inquiry and Complaint Letters

Despite the easy access of e-mail (see page 422) and the availability of office phones, cellular phones, and text and voicemail messaging, letters continue to fuel the engine of most businesses. A letter is permanent and won't get wiped away by computer glitches and crashes; it provides an accurate record of transactions; it encourages the building of long-term relations among business partners; and it bears a signature that can carry legal weight. (We must note, however, that e-signatures are now as legal as more traditional "wet" ones.) As communications options expand endlessly, it seems, you often can convey the letter instantly via e-mail or fax, both of which provide quick and easy alternatives to the United States Postal Service and its competitors. Still, you never can go wrong by sending a letter in an envelope with a stamp affixed to it.

Letter of Inquiry

If you write a letter to *inquire* about or *request* something—cancellation of your subscription to *People* magazine, for example, information about the contents of makeup that causes your eyes to tear, or a self-charging mini dust buster that would be great for your dorm room—you want to make your request known as quickly as possible and to back it up with specific and accurate information needed to fulfill your request.

Letter of Complaint

If you write a letter to *complain* about something—incorrect billing for your tuition, for example, or the way airline personnel treated you when your flight was cancelled—your objective is to make your complaint known so that the respondent can redress it in some way. Your tone in a complaint letter is very important. Be firm and direct but not snide or insulting. Focus on the problem and your suggested resolution; don't condemn the whole company or castigate its leaders. State your charge. Provide all essential details (dates, prices, and place of occurrence as needed) without padding or drama. Remember, you want something in return, and you're writing to someone who may be in a position to give you what you want. Be courteous. Be straightforward. Stick to the facts (see the letter on page 416).

Letter Format

Most business letters follow the **block format**, which word processors now provide automatically as standard, and you can type in information swiftly without worrying about spacing. In the block format, all parts of the letter are flush with the left margin. You separate paragraphs by leaving a blank line between the last line of one paragraph and the first line of the paragraph that comes after it. In the **modified block format**, you indent by 25–30 spaces the inside address, the complimentary close, and the closing instead of placing them flush with the left margin. Note the labeled parts of the block format in the letter on the following page.

Print your letter on standard, 8½ × 11-inch unlined, heavy bond paper. Unless your letter is really short, use single space, with a blank space between paragraphs. Be sure to proofread your letter very carefully before sending it.

TIPS for Writing and Formatting a Letter

- **Heading.** Type your full street address flush left on the first line of the heading; your city, state, and ZIP code on the next; and the date on the last line. Letter conventions require that you avoid abbreviations (like *St.*, *Ave.*, and *Feb.*, to name a few) except for the name of a state, which should appear in the standard two-letter postal code abbreviation—CA, MD, NY, and CO, for example. Do not include your name anywhere in the heading. If you use letterhead stationery—paper that has the company logo and (or) name and the company address printed across the top, bottom, or side—your first typed entry is the date, beneath the letterhead after two or three line spaces.

Margin at least one inch from top of page

318 Walker Street
Boulder, CO 10036

Heading: your return address (omit if using letterhead stationery) and date

Comma here → April 7, 2011

Double space

Mr. Steve Kingsbury, General Manager
Customer Service Division
Bose Corporation   *Inside address*
The Mountain
Comma here → Framingham, MA 01701

Double space

Salutation   Dear Mr. Kingsbury: *Colon*

1-1¼ inch margin

Several months ago I received a gift of your Bose Wave radio, Model AWR1-1W, and have enjoyed using it. But I have encountered a problem for which I would like to request your help. *1¼ inch margin*

Double space between body paragraphs

I have misplaced the Wave radio remote control unit. It is a thin, black, rectangular object measuring approximately 1½ inches by 3 inches. Apparently it has no model or serial number. Is it possible to replace this item? If so, how much would it cost—and will you accept a credit card or do you require payment by check? How long do you think it would take for me to receive the remote control unit once I place the order? Would there be an extra charge for rapid delivery service? *Body*

Double space between body paragraphs

I would appreciate a prompt response so that I can enjoy my new radio more fully.

Double space between body paragraphs

Comma here → Sincerely,   *Complimentary close*

Quadruple space

William Cookson   *Signature*

William Cookson   *Typed name*

■ **Inside address.** Space two or three lines (more if you're writing a short letter) beneath the date and type the full name, title, and address of the person you're sending the letter to. It's correct to use abbreviations such as *Mr., Miss, Mrs., Ms.,* and *Dr.* If you don't know the name of the person you are writing to, start the inside address with the person's title or the department you're interested in—for example, *Director of Human Resources* or *Customer Relations Department.*

As with the inside address, you want to avoid most abbreviations other than the state and any abbreviation that appears as part of the company name.

If you want to make reference to previous correspondence or documents that will help the reader relate quickly to the issues in your letter, make reference to it a few spaces below the inside address. Type *Re* (an abbreviation for reference) followed by a colon and then indicate the document:

Re: Your letter of December 16, 2010

Re: Invoice Number 67843

- **Salutation.** In your greeting, after the word *Dear*, use the appropriate abbreviation for the person's title followed by the addressee's last name—*Dear Mr. Santiago, Dear Ms. Chin.* If you're writing to more than one person, use the abbreviations from the French: *Messrs.* for the plural of *Monsieur* and *Mmes.* for the plural of *Madame—Dear Messrs. Damon and Affleck, Dear Mmes. Schwartz and Murphy.* If you have not included a name in the inside address, do not use the word *Dear* in your salutation. Use *Gentlemen, Ladies*, or the combination *Gentlemen/Ladies.* This last combination has supporters among some letter writers, but it is not used widely.

- **Body.** The body of the letter is the content, the paragraphs in which you make your point. Keep your correspondence to about one page and your paragraphs short. Make your point concisely and without padding. Civility is essential—the reader of the letter does not have the added advantage of receiving your message with accompanying gestures, intonations, and facial impressions. The words on the page say everything, and you want to be relaxed and informal in your written language (not slangy), but not at the expense of courteous expression. You should avoid stilted (artificially formal and stiff) language and you should prune deadwood carefully. Chapters 22 through 24—that is, all of Part Five, Style, in the *Student's Book of College English*—can help you develop and sustain appropriate letter language and technique.

- **Complimentary close.** Use one of the following forms, which are most appropriate for and typical of business letters. The complimentary close always begins with a capital letter, ends with a comma, and appears on its own line in the letter.

Sincerely yours, Sincerely, Yours truly,

Leave three or four blank lines for your signature and type your name.

- **Notations.** Beneath the signature block you can make notations. If you want to indicate that you are enclosing something with the letter, usually a copy of a prior letter, document, or other reference material, note it beneath the signature as in the instances below.

Enclosures (2)

Encl.: Presbyterian Hospital medical file

If you want to indicate that you're sending a copy of the letter to someone, type the abbreviation *c.* (for copy) followed by the other recipient's name:

c. Mr. Steven Spielberg c. Dr. Ramona Leary

■ **Continuation pages.**   If your letter requires more than one page, do not use letterhead stationery on the second and subsequent pages. Instead, use plain white bond paper. In the block style, flush with the left margin, insert the page number, the name of the person you are writing to, and the date.

2

Mr. Steve Kingsbury

April 7, 2011

EXERCISE   Write a letter of inquiry or complaint to address one of the following situations. Figure out to whom you would write and use that information to construct the inside address and salutation.

1. You want information about a graduate program in physical therapy, including deadlines for applications, course requirements, fellowship availability, and any other related matters.
2. You have had your new automobile in the shop four times in the last two months for transmission problems and still it is not working right. You want a new transmission installed now; the existing transmission cannot be repaired, you believe.
3. You have had no success in raising cucumbers in your garden for the last few summers. They start off all right, but the fruits are distorted and not plentiful, and the foliage turns brown toward mid-season.

Writing a Letter to Apply for a Job

If you're using the more conventional route of responding to a classified advertisement or job posting at school, the job-seeking letter and accompanying résumé are a vital part of the employment process.

Many employers now require job candidates to submit all letters and résumés via e-mail. What passes for acceptable writing in informal e-mails to friends and family is thoroughly unacceptable in job applications. Clarity and correctness are essential. You'll be including your résumé with the letter, so avoid redundancy.

How do you make your letter stand out? Show the reader your special talents. Use specific examples to indicate relevant experience or to recount an incident that reflects your skills. Avoid the trite and careworn expressions that often infiltrate job letters: "Thank you in advance for your consideration," and "I look forward to hearing from you," and "I would be happy to meet with you at a convenient time," for example. Yes, it's a good idea to try to arrange for an interview, but you gain with a more forceful and direct statement, such as "May I call you next week to set up a meeting?" or "I'll call on Tuesday for an appointment at your convenience."

The sample letter appearing on page 420 is lucid and concise, yet forceful and infused with the writer's personality. The writer has chosen the block format.

Writing Your Résumé

A résumé is a summary of your education, job history, and accomplishments. Reflect on your past experiences and make a list of anything that seems relevant to displaying your character or giving any other valuable information about yourself. Think about any full- or part-time jobs you have held. Even if they are not in the field you're seeking to pursue, they can indicate ambition, ingenuity, strength of character, degree of responsibility, and so on. Think about honors and awards in school, on the playing field, or in some extra- or cocurricular enterprise. Even extracurricular work at high school, if it shows your skills in a positive light, can add useful information to your résumé.

Start the résumé with your name, address, and telephone number on the top of the page. Include a fax number and (or) an e-mail address, if you have one. Then, you want to establish categories to make it easier for the reader to identify related pieces of information. Some typical categories are *Job Objective, Education, Work Experience, Honors and Awards, Personal*, and *References*. Set off these categories in boldface type or by underlining them and place them at the left margin. Put relevant information beneath the categories, as shown in the Sanchez résumé on page 422. Use sentence fragments to indicate some of your responsibilities and use lively verbs and verb forms. Writing fragments helps you avoid the redundant "I"—*I* studied this, *I* did that, *I* did something else.

Present relevant information about yourself in each category, as appropriate, following reverse time order—that is, you list the most recent item first. Like the business letter, the résumé should follow accepted formatting conventions, although there is no absolute format that requires strict adherence. You should try to keep your résumé to a single page, if possible. To make the page

201 East 64th Street, Apt. 24J
New York, NY 10021
Phone: (212) 363-9999
E-mail: oscsan@tele.com

April 15, 2010

Key information complete in heading and inside address

Ms. Joyce Haberski, President
Web Designs, Inc.
1520 Commercial Drive
Sacramento, CA 95819

Salutation: use of <u>Ms.</u> to avoid indicating marital status for woman correspondent

Dear Ms. Haberski:

Purpose of letter stated directly and forcefully

I learned from a mutual friend, Brian O'Malley, that your new company is seeking web designers who can help put together commercial web pages for a variety of companies. I'm the person you are looking for.

Source of job announcement stated in first sentence

The keyboard is my soul mate. Although I wouldn't exactly call myself a computer nerd—I do like other things such as reading mystery novels, and fishing in Folsom Lake not far from our family home in Rancho Cordova—my laptop and I are inseparable. I never tire of exploring its potential. In high school I automated the production and design of our school newspaper, <u>Topics Weekly</u>, for which I served as managing editor in my senior year.

Friendly, informal style ("computer nerd"); personal information helps reveal writer's character

Block style followed throughout

After I moved East, I attended Mildred Elley College, where I completed studies in Informational Technology in 2003. Along with courses in computer repair, programming, and software applications, I studied visual programming, Internet design, and electronic commerce. After two years at the Wiles Corporation I decided that I liked the creative side of computer work and returned to college as a communication arts major.

Essential details from résumé highlighted without restating all points

Key courses identified to suggest essential training for position

As a student at Marymount, I now have many courses in visual design under my belt, and I earned a Certificate in Web Design and E-Commerce. As you can see from my enclosed résumé, I will complete my Bachelor of Arts degree this June. I love working with people and, as you can tell, I love working with computers. After an exciting few years in New York City I am eager to return permanently to California, where I was born and where my family lives.

I'll be back home in the Sacramento region after graduation on June 11 and would like very much to meet with you at your convenience soon after. May I call next week to set up an appointment?

Firm yet courteous effort to set up interview

Sincerely yours,

Oscar Sanchez

Oscar Sanchez

Complimentary close and signature

Encl.

look more attractive, you might want to vary typeface or type size, but you should resist overdoing design elements on your resumé. Look at the sample (page 422) prepared by Oscar Sanchez, and the accompanying annotations.

TIPS for Preparing a Résumé

- **Reflect on your past accomplishments.**   Make a list of any information that's relevant to the type of job you are seeking, including previous work experience, community service, and courses of study that show your preparation for the job.

- **Reflect on your character.**   Remember that personal characteristics like self-motivation, willingness to accept responsibility, and organization are qualities that employers look for. List key activities that suggest those and other important character traits.

- **Organize your information.**   Create categories for related information: for example, *Education, Work Experience*, and *Personal*.

- **Draft your résumé.**   Put your name and contact information at the top. Then draft each section. For work experience and education, present information in reverse time order, most recent first. To save space, use sentence fragments and active verb forms. Use the *Personal* category to highlight special interests and talents. Try to confine your entries to one page.

- **Format and finalize your résumé.**   Leave a 1-½ inch margin, and type the word *Résumé*, with your name and contact information directly below. Use underlining, boldface, or italics to set off the section headings, but don't be too fancy. Use a standard typeface like *Times New Roman* for the text. Your hard copy résumé will accompany your job application letter. If you are preparing a résumé to submit to a computerized database, do not use any special type formatting. If your résumé runs longer than a page, try to cut it back.

COLLABORATIVE LEARNING

In groups of three people each, exchange letters and résumés. Assume the persona of a job recruiter and, using the job listing to which the letter and résumé respond, tell each of your classmates what you see as the strengths and weaknesses of his or her submission.

RÉSUMÉ
OSCAR SANCHEZ

Home Address
318 Rose Hill Drive
Rancho Cordova, CA 95822
Phone: (916) 851-2345

Complete, relevant addresses for ease of contact

Campus Address
201 East 64th Street, Apt. 24J
New York, NY 10021
Phone: (212) 363-9999

E-mail: oscsan@tele.com

E-mail address

Category "Career Objective" set off in boldface

Career Objective   Web Designer/Web Master

Career objective stated simply and succinctly

Education
2007–2010

Date ranges indicated in chronologically reverse order

Marymount Manhattan College, New York, NY
Bachelor of Arts in Communication Arts Degree
expected: June 2010
Special courses: Advanced Animation, Desktop
Video, The Business of Media Arts, Desktop
Publishing, Electronic Newswriting
Gradepoint Average in Major: 3.2

Sanchez highlights GPA in major only because it is higher than his cumulative GPA

2002–2005

Mildred Elley College for Careers, Latham, NY
Associate in Occupational Studies in Information
Technology (O.A.S.) Degree conferred: June 1998
Special courses: Operating Systems, Software
Applications, Introduction to Visual Programming,
Electronic Commerce, Internet and Web Page
Design

Special education suited to the position

Work Experience
2005–2007

Category "Work Experience" includes full- and part-time work

Wiles Corporation, Brooklyn, NY
As Help Desk Manager, answered questions
about and repaired computer failures, installed
software programs, fixed faulty programs, and
offered ongoing workshops to a staff of 35

Sentence fragments with lively verb forms

**Summer 2004
and 2005**

The Computer Store, Sacramento, CA
Sold computers, did general troubleshooting for
repairs, advised on software purchase

**Personal
Background**

"References" category: reader will know how to get needed references

Born in California, grew up in Rancho Cordova
(near Sacramento). Moved east in 2002. Interests:
Fishing, anything high tech, action films, video
arcades, mystery novels, moving back west.

"Personal Background" category provides useful information about applicant

References   Furnished on request

EXERCISE	1. Prepare a résumé that highlights your character, education, and experience. Use the Sanchez résumé and the tips on page 422 as a guide.
	2. Check your local newspaper or familiar Web sites for job listings and write a letter applying for some current job that interests you. Attach the job listing with your letter.

Writing Memorandums and E-mail

The office memorandum (*memo*, for short) is a vital link between and among workers in an institution and provides a formal record of newly initiated activities and requests for information or action. An office manager may write a memo to all her employees about new safety regulations required by the state; a secretary may write to his boss requesting annual leave over Christmas and New Year; and a sales manager may write to a representative requesting explanations of weakening sales for an important product. Some memos are fairly long, but usually the most effective communication in this medium is brief and to the point—and dealing with an explicit topic. Memos never should go to people outside the organization; for such communication you need to write a letter. Look at the annotated memorandum on page 424.

Complementing the paper memorandum and letter as a means of business correspondence, e-mail continues to grow in popularity, and for good reason. It is quick; it is informal; and it can cover wide geographical territories without problems.

E-mail messages should be short and to the point and, despite the informality of the communication, should be error free. Most e-mail providers have built-in spell checks. Don't assume that e-mail is an open field for bad spelling and grammar; mistakes always diminish the impact of your message in any medium. And remember: Business e-mail is for doing business. If you want to pass along or receive jokes, local supermarket sales information, concert dates, and so on, be sure that you use your private e-mail account for such purposes, not the account established where you work. Many companies now monitor their employees' e-mail, and you want to be beyond reproach.

Look at the sample e-mail on page 425.

WALDORF CORPORATION

612 Super Highway

Milwaukee, Wisconsin 53201

MEMORANDUM

Date, including month, day, and year

Date: October 24, 2010

Person receiving memorandum

To: Mildred Greenberg-Stevens, Director of Human Resources

Sender's name and hand-written initials (indicating approval of the memorandum)

From: Roberta McAlister, Vice President for Administration (RM)

Subject: Day Care Center   *Topic of memorandum*

Purpose and desired outcome stated in the first paragraph

Many of our employees have asked us to establish a day care center for the children of Waldorf Corporation's workers. I think that this is a *Standard width* good idea, but we have far too little information to recommend the *typeface:* option to our Board of Directors. I have asked Winifred Rollison *12 point Times* and Roger Eggers to work along with you in developing by the *New Roman* end of next month a preliminary report that will guide a decision. Please address the following issues:

Double space between paragraphs

- **Space** Where would be the best place to establish a day care center in our building?
- **Regulations** What regulations—state, federal, local—exist to guide the construction of a day care center?
- **Cost** What would it cost to establish and maintain the day care center?
- **Need** Just how many Waldorf workers would take advantage of the Center? How many children would we expect to serve each day?

Double space between paragraphs

I'm sure that you will discover other key issues as well; feel free *Deadline for* to address them in your report.   *completion of stated task*

Recipients of copies of the memorandum

c. Winifred Rollison, Director of Personnel

  Roger Eggers, Eastern Regional Sales Manager

SAMPLE E-MAIL

Send to line routes message

Send to: Roberta McAlister   *Subject Line: reminds busy reader why you're writing*

Subject: MEMORANDUM OF OCTOBER 24, 2010

Date: 10/26/2010 10:37:16 A.M.   *Date and time will show automatically as part of e-mail format*

From: Mildred Greenberg-Stevens X 1565

Copy to: Winifred Rollison, Roger Eggers

I received your memo and am happy to take on this project. Day care comes up often in my conversations with our employees. Wini, Roger, and I have already met and given ourselves assignments. I'm sure we'll have a helpful report to you by the end of next month.   *Brief informal message*

I'll keep you posted on our progress.

EXERCISE

Write a memorandum or an e-mail on one of the following issues:

1. Announce to members of your class a trip to a local animal sanctuary; include the purpose of the trip, the day and time, the cost, the person in charge, and any other relevant details.
2. Assume that you are the office manager of an employee pool of twenty-five people and that you are writing to remind your workers of the importance of getting to work and getting to work on time. Sick-day call-ins seem excessive to you. Employees also have been clocking in beyond accepted arrival times.
3. Announce to members of your class a series of collaborative study sessions that you're trying to organize in preparation for the biology final.

For support in meeting this chapter's objectives, follow this path in MyCompLab: Resources ⇒ **Writing** ⇒ **Writing Samples: Technical and Workplace.** Review the Instruction and Multimedia resources about **letters and resumes**, then complete the Exercises and click on Gradebook to measure your progress.

PART FOUR

Research

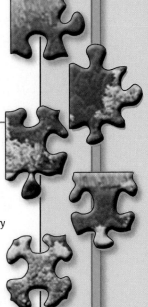

CHAPTER 20

Doing Research

A research paper (or research essay or library paper or term paper) is a nearly universal assignment in your first-year English course and in many other courses. In this chapter, you will see the evolution of a paper on lie detection.

Choosing Your Subject

As you think about formulating a subject for your research paper, follow some of the prewriting strategies you explored in Chapter 2. Surf the Web to examine a range of approaches to your subject. Make a rough list. Use free association. Brainstorm on a topic that seems even remotely interesting. Talk at length with roommates, friends, teachers, relatives, employers, coworkers—with anyone who will listen. Watch television talk shows or documentaries related to your subject. Browse in libraries and bookstores. Study newspapers, magazines, and journals; a word or two in a headline or title may catch your eye and get you thinking. Some background reading in a general encyclopedia like the *Encyclopaedia Britannica* may provide a useful overview of your topic.

Doing Preliminary Reading

Once you have an idea of the topic or topics you're interested in, it's time for a close look at reliable Web sites and a trip to the library. Your purpose now is to do some fairly easygoing "reading around." You want to make sure that the subject that seems so interesting when you think about it is still interesting when you read about it. You want to acquire enough of a general perspective on your subject to be able to limit it appropriately and to respond thoughtfully when you begin more serious and detailed reading.

Searching the Internet

As you know, the accessibility of source materials online has made Internet research not only convenient but also an invaluable supplement to conventional print sources available at your college or neighborhood public library. With the click of a mouse, you can retrieve material from library catalogs and Web sites created by corporations, professional organizations, government agencies, educators, colleges and universities, and too many other possible sources to mention. You can access full texts of books and periodicals, documents, articles and essays, television and radio programs, photographs, songs, symphonies, and cartoons, as well as information and critiques about all of these (and other) materials. If you have a home computer and can sign on to the Internet, you can bring libraries into your living room.

If you've done any research on the Internet, you're probably already familiar with search engines and directories like Yahoo!, Google, Bing, and Ask. These search tools are very useful in preparing a research paper. You access material by using a key word or phrase or by identifying a particular subject. The key words that you enter fit into directories arranged in a hierarchy. Each of the search tools, therefore, can provide broad subject directories in response to your key word, and you can explore the directories to find the limited area of your interest. Lists of pertinent Web sites will help you link to useful information.

"Googling" Your Subject

One of your first impulses regarding your research paper will no doubt send you to explore the topic through Google or some other search engine. We used the key words "lie detector" and brought up the first several entries, as shown on page 429.

First, you should note the overwhelming number of potential resources—more than two million (yes, million!) for someone researching this topic. Next, even on this first page of entries, you face an incredible mix of links for further information. The column to the right with the heading "Sponsored Links" is a list of advertisers, people and companies who pay to have their sites listed and have commercial services to offer. They want you to buy something from them.

As for the other entries, you have to judge the quality of the site before you can rely on it as a valid resource. In some cases you can tell the nature of the site from the descriptions below the highlighted link and can reject any that seem irrelevant to your purpose or you can go immediately to any that seem useful. In the section of this chapter called "Finding Articles," we explore some specialized search tools for locating resources in a range of disciplines.

Evaluating Online Sources

You may be tempted to do your research exclusively on the Internet. But at this very early stage of your investigations, you want to resist the temptation to

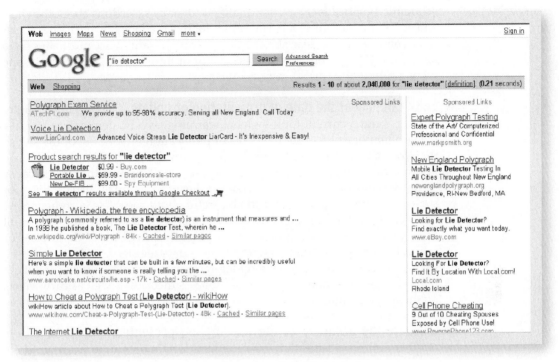

Google search results for "lie detector"

make the Web your only resource. At the outset, you need a clear, *reliable* overview of your topic. You probably know already how much rubbish is floating in cyberspace and how unreliable and downright wicked some sites, chat boxes, blogs, and e-mails are.

We've already explored ways of reading and evaluating Web sites in general (see pages 24–27, especially "Tips for Reading and Evaluating Web Sites," pages 24–25 and "Strategy Checklist: Reading and Evaluating Web Sites," page 27), yet we need to review that information in light of your online-based research efforts.

TIPS for Evaluating Web Sites Used in Your Research

■ **Identify the author and sponsor.** It's important to know about the person or people behind the site, and you want to find as much information as possible about the writers. Are the writer's credentials clear? Can you check them somewhere? Can you identify the writer's political, social, or economic agenda? Is the writer qualified to make assertions about the site's subject? If the author is a corporation, lobbyist, agency, group, or association, you have to be clear about what their biases are. Also, most sites have an "About Us" button that will reveal author information. Don't trust a site whose author and (or) sponsor is invisible!

■ **Look carefully at the date of presentation or update.**   Especially if you're writing about a current topic—global warming, say, or stem-cell research—it's very important to note the dates of publication or revision of the site so that you have access to the latest thinking on the matter. You usually can find relevant dates at the bottom of the site. Don't assume that just because the information appears on the Web that the information is current. Even for subjects in the past, you want to be careful about the site's currency. New theories about topics rooted in the past emerge all the time, and you want to be sure that you have access to the most recent views of the topic. For example, global warming sites present new data regularly and site sponsors frequently reevaluate current and long-term data. If you're writing about climate change, you should know about today's theories as well as early views on the phenomenon.

■ **Evaluate the accuracy of the information presented.**   Look for names of other authors or sites that validate the information you're reading. Many sites have links to similar sites, and it's worth taking time to look at some of them. If the information seems one-sided to you, be sure to seek sites that present opposing viewpoints.

■ **Evaluate the originality of the material.**   Is the site merely repeating exactly what appears somewhere else? Does the site indicate where it took its information from? The cut-and-paste function allows the all-too-easy transfer of material from one site to another, and you want to keep your guard up against possible plagiarism.

■ **Use the Web site address to help you determine reliability.**   Remember that Web addresses ending in *.gov*, *.org*, and *.edu* are usually reliable. Be cautious about sites ending in *.com*: many are reliable, but many are not, and you need to be sure that your *.com* site is dependable enough for use in your research.

Using General Encyclopedias

Usually, the most sensible place in which to begin reading hard copy is a recent edition of a general encyclopedia, such as the *Encyclopaedia Britannica* or the *Encyclopedia Americana*. The electronic encyclopedia *Encarta* also provides helpful background material. But, be careful about using Wikipedia, an online encyclopedia project written collaboratively by volunteers. Anyone with access to the Web site can edit or change any entry. Contributors' credentials may be suspect. Many entries are accurate, but some critics question its reliability, uneven quality, and inconsistency.

No significant research paper should use an encyclopedia article as a major source. The entry can offer only a broad survey of its subject, whereas a research paper explores its subject in depth. At this early stage, however, a broad survey is all you want. A good encyclopedia will suggest the appropriate parameters for your research and will help you later in the all-important task of evaluating Internet sources (see pages 24–27). If you are tethered to your computer, however, note that many encyclopedias are available online.

Using Specialized Reference Works

As good as or better than general encyclopedias for preliminary reading are specialized encyclopedias, dictionaries, and other reference works, many of which are updated and revised regularly. For example, if you are writing about an American who is no longer living, the *Dictionary of American Biography* may have an excellent article. The *Dictionary of National Biography* supplies similar information about British men and women who are no longer living. Your librarian can suggest which works to use for your area of interest and you should check the latest edition at your library. Specialized reference works are available for study in art, business, education, history, literature, music, philosophy, psychology, religion, science, social science, and politics, to name just a few. Your librarian also will help you find specialized reference works in online versions so that you can draw on the resources from your computer.

EXERCISE   Check your library and the Internet for resources, including computer search engines, to use for preliminary reading on your subject. Write the names of two Web sites and two specialized encyclopedias, dictionaries, or other reference works that you used for your preliminary reading.

Preparing Your Preliminary Outline

If all goes well in your preliminary reading, you should be in a position to draw up a **preliminary outline**, or **rough outline**, indicating the major divisions of your paper. You don't need anything elaborate; you will revise and expand the outline as you go along. In the meantime, the preliminary outline enables you to read and take notes as part of a systematic plan. You'll know what information is relevant and irrelevant, what divisions of the paper you need to work on more thoroughly, and so on.

Here is Elizabeth Kessler's rough outline for her research paper on polygraph testing:

<u>Topic/Thesis</u>: Polygraph Testing on the Job

1. Cost
2. Reliability
3. Accuracy
4. Relation between guilt and physical measures from test
5. Consequences of test on person's life

This outline, based on preliminary reading, guided Kessler's deeper probing into sources related to her topic and her ultimate writing of drafts for the paper. The outline changed many times—compare it with the items in her formal outline on page 491. At this stage, a preliminary outline is a useful guide to further thinking about your topic.

EXERCISE

Make a rough outline of the major divisions that you now think will structure your paper. (Remember: Your outline most likely will change as your research continues.)

Why Libraries?

The easy availability of information online probably has you wondering why you need to visit your college or community library at all. You can use online databases, find a range of resources for your research topic, take notes, record reference information, all without leaving your dorm room or home kitchen. And Web sources usually are very current, making them attractive options for modern works.

Yet your library has a major role to play in your research. Your library

- has volumes of texts that have not made it to electronic media.
- may have free research services available that you might have to pay for online.
- allows you to look at several resources at once. True, on your computer you can open a number of windows at the same time, but you face limited screen space for each entity, making it hard to read and tedious to follow.
- has experienced librarians available at all times who can guide you on the right path to your research, help you avoid pitfalls, and show you how to use specialized services, both at the library and online.

- has a uniform organization system. Using the Library of Congress classi-fication system (or, in some cases, the older Dewey decimal system), your library arranges its holdings consistently and systematically. You can find what you need easily and quickly.
- has chosen resources that have undergone some kind of review, whether editorial—most books have to pass through review hurdles before being published—or at the library itself through joint faculty–student–librarian committees that recommend new purchases. Online postings run the gamut from responsible to absurd, and you always have to worry about accuracy and reliability. Libraries also can house materials of questionable value, it is true, but the inherent review process usually validates most library resources.
- won't overwhelm you with a seemingly endless array of resources in the way that the Web does.

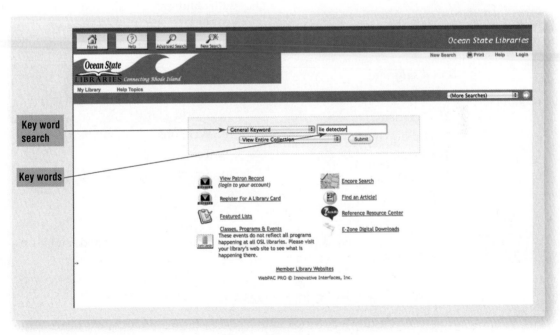

Library catalog search page

Limiting Your Research Topic

Once you have even a vague notion of a topic that interests you, think about it for a while. Consider whether it's too broad. Remember the importance of limiting your subject. "Custer's Last Stand" and "The Lizzie Borden Murder Case" might make good starting points for papers, but you could not write a good paper of reasonable length on a topic like "Famous Battles" or "Great Trials" because it's too broad.

One final suggestion: don't be too eager to settle on any single topic immediately. If you have two or three possibilities in mind, so much the better. There may not be as much information available on your first choice as you had hoped, and it's comforting to have something ready to fall back on.

EXERCISE

For the following broad subjects, indicate how you would limit each one to make it suitable for a research paper. Follow the format of the examples. (See pages 32–34 for more information on limiting topics.)

BROAD SUBJECT	⟶	LIMITED SUBJECT
Communication		The importance of regular conversation with children from six weeks to one year old
The solar system		Current theories on the sun's longevity

Broad subjects

1. Poverty
2. Terrorism
3. Hip-hop music
4. Climate
5. Immigration
6. Campaigning

7. The French underground in World War II
8. Weapons
9. Television programs
10. Smart phone apps

EXERCISE

Choose a broad subject from the list above or one of your own and limit it for a research paper.

Determining a Research Question

How can you turn your topic into a successful research paper? Many writers find it helpful to create a **research question** whose answer they can investigate through a variety of sources. You might need to do some elementary research before you are prepared to state a research question, but the advanced effort is worth it because of the help it can give you in defining your topic clearly.

Even the most limited topic can feel overwhelming at the outset. A research question helps you define the parameters of your investigation by forcing you to focus only on the question that you have established. Thus, if your topic is "The Lizzie Borden Murder Case," you might set this question: "Why was Lizzie Borden arrested in the gruesome murder of her father and stepmother?" The question helps you avoid a character study of Lizzie's sister; it helps you avoid the drama of the trial; it helps you avoid reporting at length on the missing evidence and excluded testimony. You might touch on any of those elements if it helped you answer your question, but your focus would remain on the reasons for Lizzie Borden's arrest.

Here are some other topics and possible research questions that could help a writer focus research.

Possible Topic	Limited Topic	Research Question
Famous battles	Custer's Last Stand	What other options did Custer have instead of making the Battle of the Little Bighorn a "last stand"?
Terrorism	Recruiting current terrorists in the Middle East	How do current terrorists attract people who become suicide bombers in the Middle East?
Hip-hop music	Teenage boys and hip-hop music	Why do teenage boys like hip-hop music?
Yellowstone National Park	Wolves in Yellowstone	What effects did the introduction of wolves have on the environment at Yellowstone?
Immigration	Effects of strict state laws on immigration	How has the Arizona immigration law affected commerce in the state?
Global warming	Climate change in Antarctica	How has climate change affected Antarctica wildlife?

There is nothing absolute in a research question, and if you choose to develop one, don't be surprised if it changes as you do your research. The point is that you can focus your initial research if you have a research question at hand.

Finding Sources and Developing a Working Reference List

When you're satisfied with the topic you've chosen, it's time for serious research and reading, and that brings us to the subject of the reference list or bibliography. When you write the final draft of your research paper, you'll have to include a list of works cited, which is an alphabetical list of the articles, books, and other sources that you refer to in the text of your essay. To prepare for that effort, you want to develop a **working reference list** that records key information about each source. For each article, book, and Web site that you find, you will need to note authors' names, titles, and publication data. Since you cannot know in advance which sources will contain useful information, you should record reference information for all of them.

We'll show you the information you will need for your working reference list later in the chapter, on pages 440–444. Now, let us discuss where you can find resources for your essay.

Finding Articles

To find magazine or journal articles, you will need to consult **periodical indexes**. Check your own college and public libraries to see which indexes they have in book form and which are online.

Periodical Indexes

One of the most frequently used indexes is *The Readers' Guide to Periodical Literature*, an index of articles that have appeared in popular American magazines during any given year since 1900. *The Readers' Guide* appears monthly in pamphlet form and is permanently bound every year. Like most indexes, the *Guide* has both an author and a subject listing, but you're more apt to look for titles under subject headings.

A helpful hint: don't use *The Readers' Guide* entries as models for entries on your own Works Cited list (see pages 468–470). Rather, use *The Readers' Guide* to find sources; once you have your sources in hand, copy reference information carefully from the sources themselves and according to the guidelines listed on pages 467–478.

The Readers' Guide is a good place to start, but it does, after all, index only popular American magazines. For most subjects, you will also want to read articles written by scholars in the field in order to get more specialized information. Almost every academic discipline has one or more journals to which specialists contribute, and you would certainly want to look at their articles. To find them, you would consult the special index and abstracts covering your subject. Your librarian will direct you to the special indexes in your field of interest. Many indexes are now available electronically.

Newspaper Indexes

The *New York Times Index* provides a complete listing, by year, of every article that has appeared in its newspaper. The *Times* has been thoroughly indexed since 1913. If you need newspaper articles from local papers, you often must page through or scan on microfilm the newspapers issued during the period your subject covers. The *New York Times* Web site provides articles in an extensive database, as does *AP Online* (an electronic source for the Associated Press) and the *Washington Post* Web site. Newspaper databases can provide helpful indexes for articles on key topics.

EXERCISE

Identify two or three indexes that you could use to find periodical articles related to your subject. Examine two of these indexes carefully and list several articles from them that seem useful to you as you explore your topic.

Finding Books: The Online Library Catalog

Most libraries have turned their paper card catalogs into computerized catalogs. These catalogs list books, reference works, audio and video materials, and periodicals that are available through the library.

You can search a library catalog for useful sources by entering key terms. You can search by the author's name, by the title of the work, by key words, and by subject. Your search will result in a list of possible titles; to see more about an entry, click on it. This will bring up a screen that shows more detailed information about the work. As an example, when Elizabeth Kessler did research in her library's online catalog, she first chose to do a key word search using the term "lie detector," as shown here.

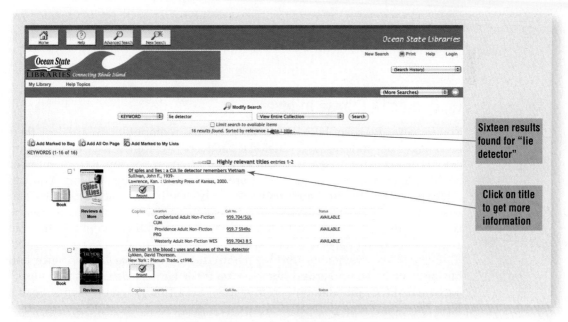

Library catalog search results for "lie detector"

Kessler thought the first item in the results list, *Of Spies and Lies* by John F. Sullivan, looked promising. She clicked on the title to get more information, as shown below. She noted the call number and went to the stacks to find the book.

Library catalog entry for *Of Lies and Spies* by John F. Sullivan

Electronic Database Indexes

You've already seen how some libraries use computers to catalog their holdings. Like indexes and catalogs, *databases*—reference lists available on computer—provide extensive reference information for topics in a number of disciplines. Essentially, databases are specialized catalog systems. You can retrieve lists of titles and authors in a variety of subjects covered by the database—and with some databases, such as *Infotrac* and *EbscoHost*, you can use the computer to retrieve the works themselves. At your library you may have to pay a fee for using particular databases.

In the fields of humanities, government, education, science, social science, and business, many computerized libraries use other familiar databases like Lexis/Nexis, DIALOG, Bibliographic Retrieval Services (BRS), and Academic Search Elite. The Educational Research Information Center (ERIC) provides a wide range of information on education. Newspaper Source via EbscoHost provides full text for many U.S. newspapers as well as international newspapers and newswires.

You can search periodical databases by author, title, or subject. Many databases have a list of subject headings that you must use as search terms; others allow you to search by key words. If you are not sure how the database is organized, look for a list of subject headings, or experiment entering key words and then narrowing your search. Your librarian can help you find appropriate subject headings for your research topic.

When Elizabeth Kessler searched the EbscoHost database for her research paper, she first used the key words "lie detectors" (see below). EbscoHost returned results along with the option of narrowing the search by subject headings. Kessler narrowed the search by choosing "lie detection and employee testing." The first two entries of her final search results appear on page 440. Kessler thought the first item, "Challenging Interviewees During Interviews," would be useful, so she clicked on the title to get the full entry. As you can see on page 441, this entry has full publication information. If Kessler wants to see the whole article, she can click on "PDF Full Text." Not all articles are available in PDF format online; you may have to track down the published journals in the library stacks to see the full articles.

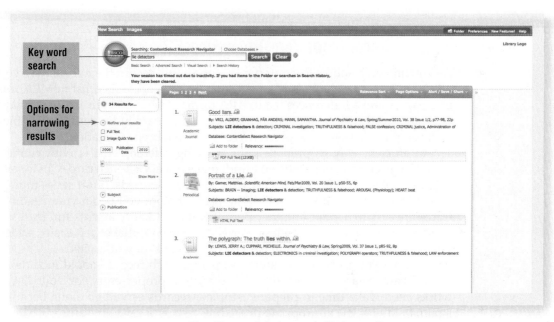

EbscoHost search for key words "lie detectors"

Search narrowed by subject headings

Click on title to see full entry

EbscoHost search results narrowed by subject

Keeping Records for Your References

As you find each source for your paper, you should record the information you will need to prepare your reference list (called a Works Cited list in MLA format papers and a References list in APA format papers). There are many ways you can record bibliographic information. You can use index cards, Word files on a computer, a notebook, or even Web sites that prepare citations.

An efficient way to prepare your working reference list is with citation cards. For each promising title you find, make out a 3 × 5-inch card. Obviously, you will not use all the sources for which you make cards, but it saves time to make cards for any title that might be useful before you begin your reading. Cards are easy to handle, and they permit you to add new sources and to delete sources that turn out to be useless. Cards can also be alphabetized easily, which will save you time when you make up your final list of works cited.

Whether you use cards or another method, each record should include all the relevant data that you will need to write a proper entry for your list of works cited. Take time to prepare complete records as you go along because, again, following the appropriate procedure now will save time and frustration when you write your paper later on. Follow the format of the samples here as you prepare your own reference records.

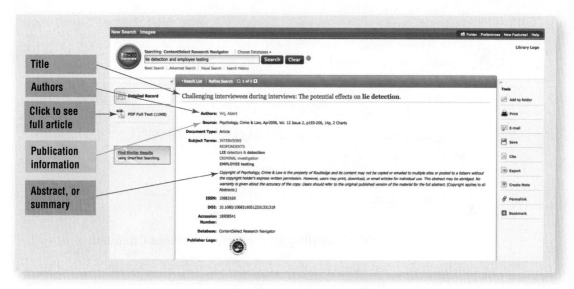

EbscoHost entry for journal article

Reference Records for Periodical Print Articles

Bibliography records for periodicals should include the following information. A sample record appears on page 442.

- The author's name, if one is given
- The title of the article
- The name of the magazine, journal, or newspaper
- The publication date
- The inclusive page numbers
- For a newspaper, the section number or letter and the edition, when given on the masthead
- For a scholarly journal article, the volume and issue numbers, when given
- For a scholarly journal article from an online database, the database name and date of access
- For APA style citations, record the DOI (digital object identifier) when given

Reference Record for a Journal Article from an Online Database

Authors ————————➤	Grubin, Don & Madsen, Lars
Title of article ————————➤	"Lie Detection and the Polygraph: A Historical Review"
Periodical name ————————➤	*Journal of Forensic Psychiatry & Psychology*
Date of publication ————————➤	June 2005
Volume and issue numbers ———➤	Vol. 16, Issue 2
Page numbers ————————➤	357–69
Database name ————————➤	*ContentSelect Research Navigator*
DOI (needed for APA style citations) ————————➤	10.1080/14789940412331337353
Medium of publication ————➤	Web
Date accessed ————————➤	17 Mar. 2010

Corresponding MLA citation in Works Cited list:

Grubin, Don, and Lars Madsen. "Lie Detection and the Polygraph: A Historical

Review." *Journal of Forensic Psychiatry and Psychology* 16:2 (2005):

357–69. *ContentSelect Research Navigator*. Web. 17 Mar. 2010.

Pages 468–470 provide examples of the different formats used for citing articles in the list of works cited. Examine these examples carefully as you prepare your citation records.

Reference Records for Books

Reference records for books should include the following information. A sample record appears on page 443.

- The author's name
- For an essay, poem, short story, or a play in a collection, the title of the relevant selection, enclosed in quotation marks
- The title of the book
- The city in which the book was published
- The name of the publishing company
- The copyright date
- The complete call number of the book. You do not have the correct call number, you will not be able to locate the book
- Edition and revision information, if any
- For multivolume works, the overall number of volumes and the specific number used

- If the book is edited, the editor's name
- If the book is translated, the translator's name

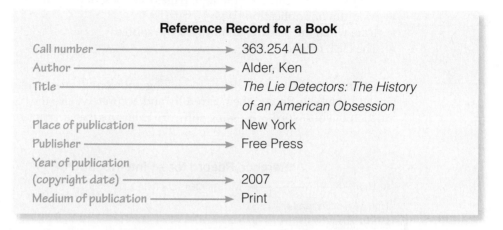

Reference Record for a Book

Call number ⟶	363.254 ALD
Author ⟶	Alder, Ken
Title ⟶	*The Lie Detectors: The History of an American Obsession*
Place of publication ⟶	New York
Publisher ⟶	Free Press
Year of publication (copyright date) ⟶	2007
Medium of publication ⟶	Print

Corresponding MLA citation in Works Cited list:

Alder, Ken. *The Lie Detectors*: *The History of an American Obsession*.

New York: Free P, 2007. Print.

Look ahead to pages 470–473 for the various Works Cited formats required for a wide variety of books that you might find in your research. These formats tell you what information to include on your bibliography cards.

Reference Records for Internet Sources

If you are taking material from the general access portion of the Internet, record information using the format in the sample that follows. The following list indicates most parts of an entry for an Internet publication as well as their order in an entry. Some information you record may not appear in the entry in your Works Cited list but will help you find your source again.

- Author's name—or the name of the editor, compiler, or translator
- Document title (article, poem, essay, or other short work) *or* title of posting to discussion list or forum (taken from subject line)
- Title of book or periodical, if any
- Name of editor, compiler, or translator of text, if relevant
- Publication information of the print version of the source, if any
- Title of site—online periodical, scholarly project, *or* personal or professional site (italicized)—or, if a personal or professional site without a title, some description such as *Home page*
- Name of site's sponsor
- For an article, volume and issue numbers, or the version number of the source if not part of the title

- Date of electronic publication, latest update, or posting
- For a posting to a discussion list or forum, name the list or forum
- Number range or total number of pages, sections, or paragraphs, if numbered
- Medium of publication (Web)
- Date when the researcher accessed the source
- The URL for the source

An important caution: URLs can be long and complicated in their use of letters and symbols. Record them carefully and accurately. Use the copy and paste function in your word processing software to ensure the accuracy of the URL.

Reference Record for an Internet Source

Author ⟶	Motsinger, David L.
Title of article, page, or document ⟶	"History"
Web site name ⟶	*Indianapolygraphassociation*
Web site sponsor ⟶	LaFayette Instrument Co., Inc.
Date of posting or copyright ⟶	2006–2010
Medium of publication ⟶	Web
Date accessed ⟶	17 Mar. 2010
URL ⟶	www.indianapolygraphassociation.com/history.asp

Corresponding MLA citation in Works Cited list:

Motsinger, David L. "History." *Indianapolygraphassociation.* Lafayette

Instrument, 2006–2010. Web. 17 Mar. 2010.

EXERCISE

Produce a working reference list by preparing reference records for your subject. Record at least ten books, periodicals, and Internet or other sources. Your instructor may wish to examine your bibliography records before you move ahead with your research.

Taking Notes

What do you look for when taking notes? You should look for any fact, idea, or opinion not generally known that appears to relate to your topic. It's easier to take a few extra notes than it is to go back to a source when you discover, after you start writing the paper, that you don't have enough evidence to make a point.

Nevertheless, you should not simply take notes at random. You have begun your research with at least a vague idea of what you want to say. The sooner the idea becomes definite, the more directed and less time-consuming your note taking will become. But don't worry if you find yourself taking many notes from the first sources you read. After all, the subject is fairly new to you, and everything about it may seem important. You should soon get a focus on the material, and then you can become more selective in the notes you take.

When Elizabeth Kessler started taking notes for her paper on polygraph testing (see paper on pages 490–511), she was intrigued at first by the technology of the equipment, and she took notes on every aspect of the lie-detecting mechanism itself. But soon she realized that she didn't want to write a paper about the history of lie detector machines. Rather, she wanted to understand the pros and cons of polygraph testing so that she could form her own opinion about the procedure. Kessler's reading and note taking became much more focused at this point. She was able to concentrate on the views of critics and supporters. As her reading advanced further, she discovered that polygraph testing is used in many arenas—police work, government, the armed forces, and job hiring. To manage her subject, Kessler limited it even further by concentrating on lie detector tests and requirements for employment.

Since the advent and development of polygraph testing spans decades, Kessler explored readings both from current sources such as Web sites and an electronic encyclopedia and from current books and articles and those going back to the 1970s.

Limit your subject and your approach to it as soon as you can, so you can perform the job of note taking efficiently.

Note-Taking Options: Pencils or Keyboards?

Many people feel most comfortable with tried and true note-taking options: index cards, available in many sizes; tablets of lined white or yellow paper; photocopies with notes scribbled in the margins. Elizabeth Kessler took notes on index cards; she liked being able to shuffle the cards to experiment with ordering her information.

Many online applications now exist for note taking, and you might want to explore commercial sites like *Evernote, Ubernote, NoodleBib,* or *WebAsyst Notes* for taking down information electronically. Many of these programs are free for their most basic uses, which have valuable features, and some libraries own more comprehensive versions. You can search the Web with them and copy relevant quotations and even whole articles. You can send yourself e-mails. You can tag your notes and organize them according to your own plan. And you can share notes with fellow students for helpful online collaboration. Some programs will format Works Cited lists if you supply the appropriate reference information. Perhaps most important, you'll be recording your notes through a keypad, and you won't have to worry about illegible jottings.

The temptation with online note-taking programs is to record too much information. You want to be sure not to overwhelm your research plan with long articles and chapters you've cut and pasted from your readings. As you will see, much of your paper will rely on quoting and paraphrasing (see pages 448–449), and the more selectively you take down information, the easier it will be to write your paper, and the less likely you'll be to fall into the trap of plagiarism (see pages 460–462).

Evaluating Sources

You must assure that all your sources are valid, and that means some legwork before you waste time taking notes from material that may prove unreliable later on. The tips below will help you evaluate your sources before you're too heavily invested in them. You'll find many of these recommendations familiar: we proposed them when we presented cautions for using online sources.

 TIPS for Evaluating Your Sources

- **Check the level of presentation.** Is your source suitable for an academic research paper? Examine the bibliography and citations to determine the range of research that went into the book or article. If you can't see any sources—or if the sources seem skimpy—think twice about using the piece in your paper.

- **Use the title as a good starting point before you take notes.** Before you get busy recording information, check the title of the source against any table of contents, index, preface, or chapter names. Book titles can deceive you, and sometimes they don't match your expectations. It's all right to reject a source if you find that it's not relevant to your research.

- **Find out about the author.** Use a search engine to find out more about the author. Or, you can check your library's online catalog. What other publications has the author produced? What is her reputation among her peers? Is she often quoted by other writers on the same or a related topic? You may not find answers to all these questions, but some answers may give you important insights into the writer's credentials.

- **Look for bias in your sources.** You should be able to determine any deeply held prejudices if the writer presents information only to back up a fixed opinion reached in advance. A writer arguing against stem cell research, for example, should present (and try to refute) those who see its potential in curing many medical problems. Biased writing is often highly charged emotionally, and the writer often ignores opinions that challenge or contradict her own. Political, industrial, and religious groups often write from a biased point of view. But don't take a strongly worded assertion as always biased. If the argument is fair, the facts not misrepresented, and opposing views presented honestly, the writer's strong opinions may be justified.

■ **Know your own biases.** You may have chosen a topic about which you believe passionately, but don't let your passion skewer your evaluation of other sources. If you believe that firm antidrug abuse laws are not working, don't let your prejudice rule out books, articles, or Web sites making the opposite claim.

■ **Consider when the source appeared.** The dates of your sources are very important in your understanding of your topic. Your subject itself will help you determine whether or not a source is out of date—or at least needs a balanced view from a previous or later source. If Lincoln is your subject, Carl Sandburg's 1926 biography is essential reading; but you'd probably want to look at "When Lilacs Last in the Dooryard Bloom'd," Walt Whitman's poem of 1865, written soon after Lincoln's assassination. James McPherson's 2008 biography explores why Lincoln remains a hero two hundred years after his birth—a viewpoint neither of the earlier works could provide.

Recording Quotations

When you **quote** a source, you use the exact wording from that source to convey facts or ideas contained in it. Quotation marks must enclose the material that you quote. It may be a month or more between the time you take the note and the time you write your paper, and you don't want any uncertainty about which words are yours and which are those of the original author. Many researchers use a special mark—an asterisk, a checkmark, an X—in the margin to distinguish their own words from the words of the source. Be certain, too, that you copy the quotation *exactly* as it appears in the original. If the original contains an obvious error, copy the error and follow it with *sic* (the Latin word for "thus") in brackets.

Occasionally, you may want to quote only parts of an entire passage. If you leave out a whole paragraph or more, indicate the omission by placing spaced dots all the way across the note. If you leave out a part of a sentence or one or two sentences, use three spaced dots (an *ellipsis*) to indicate the omission. For an ellipsis within a sentence, use a space before the first period and after the last period as well. If you omit the beginning of a sentence, place the quotation mark before the ellipsis. If you omit the end of a sentence, place the quotation mark after the ellipsis and the end punctuation (period, question mark, or exclamation point).

A few words of caution about using the ellipsis: never alter the meaning of the original by using an ellipsis. If the original statement reads, "This is not the most exciting movie of the year," using an ellipsis to omit the word *not* would be dishonest. Second, be sure that you still have a complete sentence when you use the ellipsis. Don't omit from the sentence important elements such as subjects and verbs.

When quoting, you may find it necessary to clarify a word or date in the original quotation because you are taking the words out of context. Pronouns, for example, may need clarification. In context, "He suffered extreme hardships" may be perfectly clear. Isolated in a note, however, you might need to explain the pronoun *he*. If you want to insert a word, phrase, or figure into the quotation, do so by putting the information in brackets: "He [Lincoln] suffered extreme hardships." Or the original might read, "in that year, he faced the greatest crisis of his life." The sentence, taken out of context, does not identify the year. You would want to insert it: "in that year [1839], he faced the greatest crisis of his life."

Summarizing and Paraphrasing in Your Notes

Despite this advice on how to use quotations in your research and note taking, you should quote sparingly. In your notes you should summarize or paraphrase most of the original material.

A **summary** is a short restatement of the original source in your own words. A **paraphrase** is a more expanded summary, often contains words taken from the original, and generally follows both the sequence and the logic of the original source. Often, paraphrase and summary work hand in hand. Of course, if you are in a hurry and don't have time to think about the best way to summarize or paraphrase a note, rather than risk plagiarism (see "Avoiding Plagiarism," pages 460–462), do quote the material and later decide how best to convey it in your own words.

When Elizabeth Kessler researched her topic, she found the following passage useful (from page 132 of *Science vs. Crime: The Hunt for Truth* by Eugene B. Block).

Original Source

In the first part of the nineteenth century, Cesare Lombroso pioneered in experiments with the heartbeat as a means of detecting lying, an interesting forerunner of today's polygraph, which has now advanced far beyond the early concepts of the distinguished Italian, utilizing not only heartbeats but changes in respiration and blood pressure to determine the truth or falsity of an answer.

Proud of his success and certain of the soundness of his theories, Lombroso recorded numbers of effective tests, including one concerning a notorious thief whose heartbeat reactions proved him guilty of one crime and innocent of another. It was on the early Lombroso principle that later criminalists like Vollmer, Keeler, and Larson based their developments of the lie detecting machine, but progress was slow and many methods and theories were tried and abandoned.

In her notes, shown below, she recorded the exact words of the original source enclosed in quotation marks. The ellipsis—the three spaced dots following the word *polygraph*—indicates that Kessler omitted a portion of the quote from the original (the words "which has now advanced far beyond the early concepts of the distinguished Italian"). Further, she uses an asterisk to flag concerns that she will consider later on, when she reviews her note cards.

NOTE CONTAINING A DIRECT QUOTATION

Block, Science vs. Crime *132*

"In the first part of the nineteenth century, Cesare Lombroso pioneered in experiments with the heartbeat as a means of detecting lying, an interesting forerunner of today's polygraph . . . utilizing not only heart-beats but changes in respiration and blood pressure to determine the truth or falsity of an answer."

*Check earlier work on lie detection. 18th century? earlier?

In a paraphrase of the original source, Kessler uses her own language, blending in some of Block's words and enclosing them in quotation marks.

NOTE CONTAINING A SUMMARY/PARAPHRASE OF THE ORIGINAL MATERIAL

Block, Science vs. Crime *132*

In the early 1800s, Cesare Lombroso used heartbeats in experiments to detect lies; his work anticipated the modern polygraph, which measures heartbeats as well as "changes in respiration and blood pressure to determine the truth or falsity of an answer."

Lombroso's experiments included one on a thief whose heartbeat showed he had committed one crime but not another. Later developments of the polygraph were based on Lombroso's principle.

Combining paraphrases and direct quotations is a good note-taking strategy. It allows you to capture the writer's main idea in your own language and to record some of the writer's own words for possible quotation in your paper.

Disagreements: Distinguishing Between Facts and Opinions

One final warning on note taking: as you take notes, don't assume that just because something is in print, it must be true. Be careful to distinguish between a writer's statement of fact and expression of opinion. There is a world of difference between saying that Aaron Burr was the vice president of the United States and saying that Aaron Burr was a scoundrel. In rare cases in which you note an outright disagreement among authors on matters of fact, slam on your mental brakes and do some checking. One of the standard reference works or encyclopedias might be a good source for resolving such disagreements or disputes. When you cannot determine which opinion is correct, acknowledge frankly in your paper the difference of opinion and present both opinions as honestly as possible.

EXERCISE   Take notes as you read your sources. Your instructor may wish to examine your notes for one or more of your readings.

Developing Your Thesis

Virtually every research paper requires that you gather facts and opinions (sometimes conflicting) from a variety of sources and that you organize and present them in your own words and style through your own hard work. Every research paper also requires that you document whatever sources you have used. When you document a source, you tell the reader where you found information taken from someone else's writing. Typical documentation includes the author's name, the title of the selection, and important publication data. You'll read more about documentation in Chapter 21.

However, the most important kind of research paper does more than cite sources—it has as its basis a **thesis**. Most teachers want students to use research in order to develop opinions of their own and to present those opinions in a carefully documented paper. Hence, in a research paper with a thesis, you do extensive investigation to find facts, but you also interpret those facts and you try to persuade the reader that your interpretation or opinion is correct. Rather than merely stating the facts, you use them to support your opinion. The thesis drives the research you present to your readers. As noted before, you might use your research question as the basis for your thesis.

Developing a thesis is critical to writing a successful research paper. This book pays considerable attention to writing a thesis, and you may wish to review the general steps for developing a powerful thesis in Chapter 3.

Your thesis for a research paper will grow and take shape as you investigate your resources. Your research almost certainly will cause you to change or modify your original thesis as you progress from prewriting to rough draft to final draft.

For the sample paper "The Banning of the Polygraph," which appears in Chapter 21, student writer Elizabeth Kessler arrived at this thesis after conducting some research on her topic.

Thesis 1

Many employers have used polygraph testing as a means for determining the honesty of future employees.

As Kessler considered this thesis, she realized that it makes a simple assertion of fact but offers no opportunity for interpretation or judgment. She then revised her thesis as follows:

Thesis 2

Supporters and critics battle the merits and drawbacks of lie detector tests.

We see a clear topic statement in this sentence and, on the surface, what seem to be strong opinions about the topic. Yet the more Kessler thought about the topic, the more she realized that her own opinion was absent from the thesis. She again had made an assertion of fact: some people supported the polygraph test and others opposed it. As she pondered the question "How do I feel about using the polygraph test in job-related situations?" and started shaping an early draft, Kessler wrote this thesis:

Thesis 3

My own research indicates that the polygraph test as a condition of

employment is highly unfair.

Here Kessler's interpretation of the topic is clear: required polygraph testing for a job is not fair. As you will see when you examine her paper, as Kessler continued her research, she changed her thesis again.

EXERCISE Write a tentative thesis for your limited subject. Consider what you will try to assert about your subject. Remember that your thesis may change considerably, especially after you do preliminary (and then sustained) reading and research for your paper.

Preparing Your Formal Outline

Start by reading and rereading all your notes carefully. You have accumulated the notes over a period of weeks, and you may not know precisely what material you have gathered.

Making a Slug Outline

Set aside those notes that seem irrelevant to your current idea of the paper. Among those you keep you should see a pattern; you may have several groups of notes with each group relating to a particular aspect of your topic. When you are familiar enough with your notes that you can arrange them according to single headings, you are ready to write a **slug**—that is, a brief heading that indicates the content of each note. Don't try to be creative here and write a different heading for each note; you should have several notes with the same slug.

Some of the slugs that Elizabeth Kessler developed for her paper on polygraph testing include mechanical features, training of examiners, accuracy of readings, and legal support for lie detector tests. These and other slugs on her note cards allowed Kessler to classify her ideas and, ultimately, to produce a formal outline for her paper.

Writing a Formal Outline

If you have succeeded in putting slugs on each note, the outline will almost write itself. Either a topic outline or a sentence outline is acceptable (see Chapter 4). Observe all the conventions of good outlining as you write, using the slugs in your notes as rough guides for topics and subtopics. (See the outline on page 491 and the sample paper that follows.) For a long and complex paper, it's usually a good idea to add a category labeled *Conclusion* to your formal outline.

Look at the topic outline for Elizabeth Kessler's paper, which appears below. After her thesis statement, which is a complete sentence, note the three major divisions, each labeled with a roman numeral—I, II, III. First-level subdivisions appear beside uppercase letters—A, B, C, and so on. Second-level subdivisions appear beside arabic numbers—1, 2, 3. Note, too, the full-sentence statement of a conclusion here. Readers of this outline see at a glance where Kessler wants to take her topic. For Kessler herself, the outline served as a starting point for the paragraphs she developed in an early draft. Ultimately, she decided to produce a sentence outline for submission along with her paper (see page 491), and she made a number of changes in the order of the elements and in the language of the various outline points. Like your thesis, your outline will change as your thoughts develop on your topic.

Topic Outline: Polygraph Testing

<u>Thesis</u>: The polygraph test should not be used as part of employment decisions.

   I. Arguments of polygraph test supporters

      A. Inexpensive and valid way to identify potential thieves on the job

      B. Reliable findings

      C. Well-trained examiners

  II. Arguments of those who oppose polygraph tests

      A. "Toothless" laws

      B. Examiners poor

      C. Inaccurate readings

      D. Physiological displays of guilt not measurable

      E. Human rights violations

         1. Loss of employment

         2. Invasion of privacy

         3. Reputations destroyed

III. Federal legislation against polygraph testing

    A. No polygraph screening for employment

    B. Defined testing procedures

    C. Employee rights

<u>Conclusion</u>—In spite of a recent national law, polygraph testing should be banned in the workplace.

EXERCISE

1. Compare the formal topic outline with Kessler's preliminary rough outline on page 432. How are they similar? Different?
2. Compare the topic outline with the sentence outline (page 491) Kessler ultimately submitted. How are the two outlines alike? different? Why do you think Kessler decided to produce a sentence outline after all?
3. After you complete your research and note taking, reread your notes carefully and identify a pattern among them. Arrange your notes according to headings and develop a slug outline. (You may find it helpful to review the preliminary outline that you developed for the exercise on page 432.) As you continue planning your paper and writing your drafts, develop a formal outline.

STRATEGY CHECKLIST: Doing Research

Choose your subject.	☐ Have I chosen an interesting subject?
	☐ Have I surfed the Web, brainstormed, and done prewriting to discover approaches to the topic?
	☐ Have I narrowed the topic so it's suitable for a research paper?

Do preliminary reading.	☐ Have I consulted general encyclopedias?
	☐ Have I used specialized reference works?
	☐ Have I searched the Web using Google or another search engine?
	☐ Have I evaluated Web sites carefully?

Prepare a preliminary outline.	☐ Have I identified major divisions of my paper? ☐ Have I drafted a rough outline?
Limit your research topic.	☐ Have I avoided a topic that is too broad? ☐ Have I narrowed my topic sufficiently? ☐ Have I established a research question?
Find sources and develop a working reference list.	☐ Have I looked for books and other sources online and in my library catalog? ☐ Have I looked for articles in periodical indexes and databases? ☐ Have I made reference records for all my sources?
Take notes.	☐ Have I taken notes on all my sources? ☐ Have I evaluated my sources carefully? ☐ Have I recorded quotations carefully? ☐ Have I summarized and paraphrased my sources? ☐ Have I distinguished between facts and opinions?
Develop your thesis.	☐ Have I written a preliminary thesis statement? ☐ Does my thesis statement express my own opinion about the topic? ☐ Have I revised my thesis to suit the direction of my research?
Prepare a formal outline.	☐ Have I reviewed my notes and made a slug for each relevant note? ☐ Have I sorted my notes and made a slug outline? ☐ Have I written a formal outline for my paper?

For support in meeting this chapter's objectives, follow this path in MyCompLab: Resources ⇒ Research ⇒ The Research Assignment. Review the Instruction and Multimedia resources about **finding and evaluating sources**, then complete the Exercises and click on Gradebook to measure your progress.

CHAPTER **21**

Writing Your Research Paper

Writing a research paper involves all the same challenges as writing an essay, and a few additional challenges as well. In writing the paper, you will need to blend quotations and paraphrases of your sources into your own writing, avoid plagiarism, document your sources according to MLA or APA style, and prepare the final copy using conventional MLA or APA formats. We'll begin this chapter with an overview of the research paper writing process and then fill in the details.

In this chapter you will

- write drafts of your research paper
- quote and paraphrase sources correctly
- analyze ways to avoid plagiarism
- analyze methods of documenting sources in MLA and APA styles and create a list of works cited for your research paper
- analyze steps for preparing the final copy of your research paper
- review frequently asked questions about research papers
- analyze a student's research paper

Writing Your Research Paper: An Overview

It's time to set your notes aside, put your outline in front of you, and start writing.

The First Draft

In the first draft, the point is to get your ideas down. Don't worry about grammar or punctuation. Don't try to work in quotations from your sources. You should be familiar enough with the contents of your notes by now to remember the general ideas they contain. Just write.

Subsequent Drafts

Now, write the paper again. Consult your notes to add quotations where appropriate and to fill in facts you might not have remembered when writing the first draft (see pages 39–40). You should check your notes, too, to be sure that the facts, ideas, or opinions you have reported are accurate. And, in this second effort, you should make some attempt to correct any grammar or punctuation errors you made in the first draft and to rephrase awkward sentences. Then you should add documentation (see pages 463–479).

Once you have completed this draft, go back through it several times to make certain that you have quoted accurately, that you have documented every source properly, and that you have polished your language as well as you can. Don't hesitate during this process to use your computer's cut and paste function to add, delete, or shift passages as you go along.

Using Explanatory Notes

If you need to explain some point or add information but feel that what you want to say really doesn't fit smoothly into the text of your paper, use a footnote or an endnote. Place a raised number (superscript) after the word where you'd like the reader to consider this additional material. Then, on a separate page called "Notes," use the corresponding number and provide the necessary information. If you use a footnote, place it at the bottom of the page on which your superscript appears.

Look at the next example, from the essay "Nathaniel Hawthorne, Una Hawthorne, and *The Scarlet Letter*," by T. Walter Herbert, Jr.

> This is not the occasion for a detailed treatment of the pattern of solicitude and discipline that the Hawthornes organized about their baby daughter,[3] but crucial issues of the selfhood they sought to impart are disclosed in their naming her Una, after Spenser's maiden of holiness. This decision provoked a controversy among family and friends that illuminates the large cultural processes of gender definition that were then taking place.
>
> [3]A discussion of Sophia Hawthorne's role in the formation of Una's mental life lies beyond the scope of this essay. Sophia's exceptional response to the emerging norms of gender, the marriage she made to Nathaniel, and her place in the constellation of family relations are complex subjects that bear on this question, which I will treat in a forthcoming book.

The footnote here discusses Sophia Hawthorne's role in Una's mental life—additional information that the writer chose not to include in the text of his essay.

Toward the Final Copy

If you think you have polished the paper as much as you can, make yet another copy, complete with quotations and appropriate documentation (see pages 463–479). Many instructors will not accept a final copy of a paper unless they have seen and approved a draft. If your instructor falls into this category, this draft is the one you should submit. Your instructor will make suggestions, point out stylistic problems, and indicate the parts of your paper that are not developed as fully as they might be. Conscientious students heed their instructors' suggestions and make the appropriate changes on the third draft before preparing the final paper.

Also, before printing your final copy, pay attention to editing details. Proofread carefully. By now you should be familiar with your characteristic errors, and you should comb your paper to find and correct them before submitting your work for evaluation. (See the checklist on page 121 and the discussion of proofreading on pages 119–120.)

Quoting and Paraphrasing Your Sources

Your outline is a kind of X-ray of your awaiting paragraphs—only the bare bones showing. Consider how to flesh out the sentences and develop the paragraphs of your research essay. To support the points made in your paper, you need to quote or paraphrase the information you found in other sources. Most important, however, you need to connect your own writing style smoothly with the comments drawn from other writers.

Quoting an Original Source

Following is a quote from Bennett H. Beach's article "Blood, Sweat and Fears," which appeared in *Time* magazine.

> The FBI uses polygraphs mostly to probe leads and verify specific facts, areas in which, experts concede, the machines are at their best. The agency also employs highly trained examiners, who usually spend half a day on each session (compared with an average of an hour in private industry). Tests given to Jeb Magruder and Gordon Strachan led to evidence of the Watergate cover-up. Right now, Justice Department investigators are using polygraphs extensively in their search for the source of Abscam leaks. Attorney General Benjamin Civiletti has ruled that an "adverse inference" may be drawn if an employee of the FBI or any other part of the Justice Department balks at submitting to the machines.

Assume that you want to use some of this material in your paper. You might want to quote the source exactly—using one or more phrases to several sentences to even the whole paragraph, depending on your purpose. In the following example, note the smooth connection between the student Elizabeth Kessler's words and Beach's words:

Agencies of the United States government have relied on lie detector tests in important legal matters:

The FBI uses polygraphs mostly to probe leads and verify specific facts. . . . The agency also employs highly trained examiners, who usually spend half a day on each session. . . . Attorney General Benjamin Civiletti has ruled that an

> "adverse inference" may be drawn if an employee of the
>
> FBI or any other part of the Justice Department balks at
>
> submitting to the machines. (Beach 44)

The writer introduces the long supporting quotation with a sentence of her own. The **block format** is used to set off a quotation of four or more typed lines from the text of the essay. The ellipsis (. . .) allows the writer to omit a portion of the quotation. Quotation marks are not used in a block quotation; rather, a ten-space indentation at the left margin sets off the quote. However, when quotation marks appear in the original, as in "adverse inference" in the preceding example, the quotation marks are included in the block quotation as well.

In the following example, Kessler uses shorter quotations from the same source to support her point. However, here the quotations are carefully integrated with the writer's own words and are in each case enclosed by quotation marks.

> Not only does private industry use lie detectors but the federal
>
> government does also. "The FBI," reports Beach, "uses polygraphs mostly
>
> to probe leads and verify specific facts, areas in which, experts concede,
>
> the machines are at their best." To assure a higher degree of accuracy
>
> than in other testing situations, no doubt, the FBI "employs highly trained
>
> examiners, who usually spend half a day on each session (compared with
>
> an average of an hour in private industry)" (44).

Paraphrasing an Original Source

You may also choose to paraphrase the source material. In the following example, Kessler skillfully expresses Beach's point in her own words. Quotation marks surround the phrase "balks at submitting to the machines" because it is quoted from the original source. Note how Kessler attributes the information to Beach and cites the page number for the material she uses.

> As Beach points out, the FBI (as might be expected) uses polygraph
>
> testing to aid in major investigations. Yet employees also are expected to
>
> take the test. It is clear that the FBI views in a negative light any employee
>
> who "balks at submitting to the machines" (44).

Direct Quotations: How Many?

The research paper presents a special challenge: you must make borrowed material a part of your own statement. If, you simply string quotations together, you will not be writing a research paper; you will be merely transcribing your notes. The paper must be yours—your idea, your organization, and, for the most part, your words. You should use the notes to support your ideas, which means that you should integrate the notes into your own statements. Otherwise, you do not have an honest research paper.

In the following excerpt from a student paper, the writer merely strings quotations together:

> W. E. B. DuBois said in *The Souls of Black Folk* that "the problem of the twentieth century is the problem of the color line" (xiv).
>
> DuBois felt that dreams of opportunities and fulfillment were reserved solely for whites.
>
> DuBois became aware of racial differences at an early age. He related this experience vividly:
>
>> The shades of the prison-house closed around about us all: the walls strait and stubborn to the whitest, but relentlessly narrow, tall, and unscalable to sons of night who must plod darkly on in resignation, or beat unavailing palms against the stone, or steadily, half hopelessly, watch the streak of blue above. (16)

The student here has simply copied her notes into the paper. She could make the point more clearly if she phrased it largely in her own words, as in this example:

> W. E. B. DuBois, who said in *The Souls of Black Folk* that "the problem of the twentieth century is the problem of the color line" (xiv), came to believe that dreams of opportunities and fulfillment were reserved solely for whites, and he compared the life of blacks in America with that of prison inmates (16).

In this version, the writer composed a unified paragraph that makes the point clearly without the overuse of quotations. (A good, safe rule of thumb is, unless the subject of your paper is an author's style, quote no more than 10 percent of your paper.) This version shows a much greater mastery of the material than does the first version.

EXERCISE

Read the following passage from page 52 of Megan McArdle's essay "Can GM Get Its Groove Back?" in the November 2010 issue of *Atlantic*, a monthly magazine. Then write a paragraph in which you both quote directly from the selection and paraphrase it.

> Factories are shuttering across the Rust Belt, but at the General Motors plant in Lansing, Michigan, the assembly lines are still rolling. This plant is supposed to showcase the "new GM": no sullen human cogs tightening bolts on an endless stream of indifferent cars, but small autonomous teams working together to produce top-quality automobiles. A massive, multi-building affair with a gleaming white exterior, the facility has been recently refurbished. It looks like what a car dealership might want to be when it grows up.
>
> Then you go inside, and you are peering into the innards of the American auto industry. For as many times as I am reminded about the facility's new bells and whistles and environmental certifications, this still looks a lot like the old GM. A stamping machine the size of a summer cabin turns sheets of metal into body parts. Incomplete autos with their gray-metal bones half exposed roll down the line, one every 72 seconds. At regular intervals, robot arms seem to jump out of nowhere, unerringly delivering dozens of precision spot welds in a few seconds. Workers step out onto the line with the rapid-but-casual grace that comes from long repetition, tighten here and fill there, then step back to let the next car roll forward.

Avoiding Plagiarism

Unless the material you borrow is as well known as the Gettysburg Address, when you take facts or ideas from someone else, you must credit the source. Such a statement often frightens students because their first assumption is that they will have to credit almost every sentence in their papers. That is not the case.

You should, of course, give a citation for all direct quotations that are not well known. You should also cite all facts and opinions that are not common knowledge—*even when you have put the facts or opinions into your own words*. Two kinds of facts or opinions come under the heading *common knowledge*: (1) facts everyone in our culture is expected to know (George Washington was the first president of the United States, for example), and (2) facts that are common knowledge in the field you are investigating. Suppose you are writing a paper on Custer's last stand. You might not have known, when you began reading, the name of the Indian tribe that fought Custer and his men. If every source you read, however, says that it was the Sioux tribe, you would not need to give a citation for that fact. Your wide reading lets you know the fact is commonly known to historians. Nor would it be necessary to credit the opinion that Custer blundered; most historians agree that he did. But any theories about why Custer led his men into such a trap should be credited.

If you do not pay careful attention to the techniques of quoting and crediting sources, you run the risk of being accused of plagiarism. **Plagiarism** is the use of facts, opinions, and language taken from another writer without acknowledgment. At its worst, plagiarism is outright theft or cheating: a person has another person write the paper or simply steals a magazine article or section of a book and pretends to have produced a piece of original writing. Far more common is plagiarism in dribs and drabs—a sentence here and there, a paragraph here and there. Nonetheless, small-time theft is still theft, and small-time plagiarism is still plagiarism. For your own safety and self-respect, remember the following rules—not guidelines, *rules*:

- The language in your paper must be either your own or a direct and credited quote from the original source.
- Changing a few words or phrases from another writer's work is not enough to make the writing "your own." Remember rule 1: the writing is either your own or the other person's; there are no in-betweens.
- Documentation acknowledges that the fact or opinion expressed comes from another writer. If the language comes from another writer, quotation marks are necessary in addition to documentation.

Now for a detailed example. Look at this excerpt from an "About.com" Web site.

Police Technology and Forensic Science:
History of the Lie Detector or Polygraph Machine
Mary Bellis

An earlier and less successful lie detector or polygraph machine was invented by James Mackenzie in 1902. However, the modern polygraph machine was invented by John Larson in 1921.

John Larson, a University of California medical student, invented the modern lie detector (polygraph) in 1921. Used in police interrogation and investigation since 1924, the lie detector is still controversial among psychologists, and is not always judicially acceptable. The name polygraph comes from the fact that the machine records several different body responses simultaneously as the individual is questioned.

The theory is that when a person lies, the lying causes a certain amount of stress that produces changes in several involuntary physiological reactions. A series of different sensors are attached to the body, and as the polygraph measures changes in breathing, blood pressure, pulse and perspiration, pens record the data on graph paper. During a lie detector test, the operator asks a series of control questions that set the pattern of how an individual responds when giving true and false answers. Then the actual questions are asked, mixed in with filler questions. The examination lasts about 2 hours, after which the expert interprets the data.

Student version	**Comment**
When a person lies, the lying causes a certain amount of stress that produces changes in several involuntary physiological reactions. A series of different sensors are attached to the body, and as the polygraph measures changes in breathing, blood pressure, pulse and perspiration, pens record the data on graph paper.	**Obvious plagiarism**. Student version contains word-for-word repetition without acknowledgment.
The theory is that when a person lies, the lying causes a certain amount of stress that produces changes in several involuntary physiological reactions (Bellis).	**Still plagiarism**. *The documentation alone does not help.* The language is the original author's, and only quotation marks around the whole passage plus documentation would be correct.
The theory is that lying causes a certain amount of stress that produces changes in involuntary physiological reactions, and pens record the data on graph paper.	**Still plagiarism**. The writer has changed or omitted a few words, but by no stretch of the imagination is the student using his or her own language.
"Lying will cause stress, which then produces changes in involuntary physiological reactions. Sensors are attached to the body, and as the polygraph machine measures changes in breathing, blood pressure, pulse and perspiration, it records the data on graph paper" (Bellis).	**Not quite plagiarism**, but incorrect and inaccurate. Quotation marks indicate exact repetition of what was originally written. The student, however, has changed some of the original and is not entitled to use quotation marks.
"The theory is that when a person lies, the lying causes a certain amount of stress that produces changes in several involuntary physiological reactions. A series of different sensors are attached to the body, and as the polygraph measures changes in breathing, blood pressure, pulse and perspiration, pens record the data on graph paper" (Bellis).	**Correct**. The quotation marks acknowledge the words of the original writer. The documentation is also needed, of course, to give the reader specific information about the source of the quote.
The polygraph can record multiple responses at the same time, and when a person lies, the stress causes "changes in several involuntary physiological reactions" like heart rate and blood pressure. The machine has pens which "record the data on graph paper" (Bellis).	**Correct**. The student writer uses his or her own words to summarize some of the original passage. The documentation shows that the ideas expressed come from the original writer, not from the student. The few phrases kept from the original passage are carefully enclosed in quotation marks.

EXERCISE Look at the passage below and the students' efforts to use the passage in their own papers. Comment on each student's work. Which are examples of plagiarism?

Original Passage

Certainly there was nothing genteel about Dreiser, either as man or novelist. He was the supreme poet of the squalid, a man who felt the terror, the pity, and the beauty underlying the American dream. With an eye at once ruthless and compassionate, he saw the tragedy inherent in the American success ethic; the soft underbelly, as it were, of the Horatio Alger rags-to-riches myth so appealing to the optimistic American imagination. (Richard Freedman, *The Novel* [New York: Newsweek Books, 1975], 104–05)

1. There was nothing genteel about Dreiser, either as man or novelist. He was the supreme poet of the squalid, a man who felt the terror, the pity, and the beauty underlying the American dream.
2. There was nothing genteel about Dreiser, either as man or novelist. He was the supreme poet of the squalid, a man who felt the terror, the pity, and the beauty underlying the American dream (Freedman 104).
3. "Certainly there was nothing genteel about Dreiser, either as man or novelist. He was the supreme poet of the squalid, a man who felt the terror, the pity, and the beauty underlying the American dream" (Freedman 104).
4. Nothing was genteel about Dreiser as a man or as a novelist. He was the poet of the squalid and felt that terror, pity, and beauty lurked under the American dream.
5. "Nothing was genteel about Dreiser as a man or as a novelist. He was the poet of the squalid and felt that terror, pity, and beauty lurked under the American dream" (Freedman 104).
6. By 1925 Dreiser's reputation was firmly established. The reading public viewed Dreiser as one of the main contributors to the downfall of the "genteel tradition" in American literature. Dreiser, "the supreme poet of the squalid," looked beneath the bright surface of American life and values and described the frightening and tragic elements "in the American success ethic" (Freedman 104).

Documenting Sources in the Humanities: MLA Style

The Modern Language Association (MLA) style documentation guidelines presented here follow the *MLA Handbook for Writers of Research Papers*, 7th ed. (2009).

Parenthetical Citations

Documenting or **crediting** or **citing** a source simply means letting the reader know where you found another's quotation, fact, idea, or opinion that appears in your paper. Most current style manuals, including the influential Modern Language Association's *MLA Handbook for Writers of Research Papers*, recommend the efficient method of **parenthetical documentation**.

In this method, the last name of the author and the page number on which the material appears are placed within parentheses immediately after the information or quotation. Or, if you can integrate the author's name conveniently in the text itself, only the page number appears in parentheses. (If you refer to a whole work, however, no page reference is necessary.) Readers interested in finding the work cited then consult the bibliography, titled "Works Cited," at the end of the paper for further information about the source. In parenthetical documentation, footnotes and endnotes are used only to provide additional information or commentary that might otherwise interrupt the flow of the text.

The following examples of parenthetical documentation reflect the Seventh Edition MLA style, used widely in the humanities and in other disciplines as well.

Work by One Author

The most common citation is for a work written by a single author. It contains the author's last name and the page number from which the material is taken, unless the citation is of an entire work.

> "The problem of the twentieth century is the problem of the color line" (DuBois xiv).

> Indeed, he grew so bitter about the plight of blacks that he rejoiced when his infant son died because the child would never have to experience the prejudice that he had felt (DuBois 155–56).

> In *The Souls of Black Folk*, DuBois shows in dramatic personal terms the effects of prejudice in America.

Work by Two or More Authors

If the work has two or three authors, use the last names of all the authors as they appear on the title page.

If the work has more than three authors, name them all in the order in which they appear on the title page, or use the last name of only the first author and follow the name with *et al.*, the abbreviation for the Latin *et alia*, "and others."

Note the period after *al.*, which is an abbreviation for *alia*; and note that no period follows *et* because it is not an abbreviation. (*Et* means *and*.)

> A wide range of job opportunities is available to adventurous travelers
> (Krannich and Krannich 1–3).

The example preceding refers to the book *Jobs for People Who Love to Travel* by Ronald L. Krannich and Caryl Rae Krannich.

> Heller, Heller, and Vagnini see carbohydrates as part of a healthy
> diet (2).

The work cited, *The Carbohydrate Addict's Healthy Heart Program*, is by three authors, Richard F. Heller, Rachael F. Heller, and Frederic J. Vagnini.

> Teachers in all courses should determine the writing skills levels of
> their students (Anderson et al. 4).

> Anderson and her coauthors insist that teachers in all courses
> determine the level of writing skills for their students early in the
> semester (4).

Anderson and three coauthors wrote *Integrated Skills Reinforcement*. A full reference for this book appears on page 472.

More than One Work by the Same Author

> He learned as a child that he could be rejected simply because of the
> color of his skin (DuBois, *Souls* 16).

Because the researcher cites more than one work by DuBois in the paper, an abbreviation of the title, *The Souls of Black Folk*, serves to distinguish this work by DuBois from other works by the same author.

More than One Volume of a Work

> Although he had urged conscientious objection during World War I,
> his views changed gradually, and by 1940, he concluded that he
> must support the war against the Nazis (Russell 2: 287–88).

The Autobiography of Bertrand Russell has more than one volume; thus, the information cited comes from the second volume, pages 287–288.

Work for Which No Author Is Given

Frequently, the author of a work is not given or is not known. In such a case, do not use the word *anonymous* or its abbreviation, *anon*. Instead, put in parentheses the title or an abbreviated title and the page number, as in this example:

> Supporters of the polygraph test point out that to help alleviate pos-
>
> sible nervousness, the subject is given access to the questions he will
>
> be asked during the test for as long as he desires ("What's It Like" 8).

Information About a Work or Author Already Given in Sentence

Many of your sentences may already contain enough information about a work that the parenthetical documentation can be made even shorter than in the examples given so far.

> W. E. B. DuBois said in *The Souls of Black Folk* that "the problem of
>
> the twentieth century is the problem of the color line" (xiv).

Because the writer names the author and title in the sentence, only the page number appears in parentheses.

The following sentence is from a paper that cites more than one work by DuBois. Since the author's name is used in the sentence, you need not repeat it in the documentation. However, an abbreviated title of the book distinguishes this work by DuBois from other works by the same author.

> W. E. B. DuBois, who believed that "the problem of the twentieth cen-
>
> tury is the problem of the color line" (*Souls* xiv), learned as a child that
>
> he could be rejected simply because of the color of his skin.

There are even times when you don't need to use parenthetical documentation. For example, if a writer says, "DuBois devotes his entire *Souls of Black Folk* to the subject," a reader need simply turn to the Works Cited list to find the remaining facts of publication. However, if you need to cite a section of a work, rather than the entire work, use one of the following forms:

> This point has been made before (DuBois 16–156).

> or

> DuBois has made this point before (16–156).

If the section is in a work of more than one volume, you might write

> Russell has detailed the kind of opposition to the war made by pacifists in England (2: 3–128).

or

> In the second volume of his work (3–128), Russell has detailed the kind of opposition to the war made by pacifists in England.

In other words, the more skillfully you construct your sentences, the less information you need to include in your parenthetical documentation.

EXERCISE   Return to the exercise on page 460 and reread the passage. In only one sentence, summarize the passage and provide parenthetical documentation according to the guidelines you just learned.

A List of Works Cited

Parenthetical documentation requires a **list of works cited**, an alphabetical listing of the sources cited in the paper. This list appears on a separate page at the end of the paper and is headed "Works Cited." The list of works cited contains full references to all sources used in the paper.

Different types of sources require somewhat different treatment. The examples that follow are typical MLA-style entries for the list of works cited. For entries that do not appear here, consult the *MLA Handbook for Writers of Research Papers*, 7th ed. (2009), or some other research style manual that your instructor recommends.

Here's an important caution: if you use an autocite program like NoodleBib or Easybib for your Works Cited list, watch out for potential pitfalls. If you feed the wrong information into the program, you'll have a mess. For a periodical entry, for example, you'll have to distinguish carefully between the name of the article and the name of the publication from which it comes. An autocite program can easily confuse the two entities, especially if your punctuation is not perfect. It's a good idea to check with your instructor to see how she feels about your use of one of these programs. In any case, for the sake of accuracy, you should check any citation list against the various entries we've provided here.

Standard Periodical Entry for the Works Cited List
Article with one author

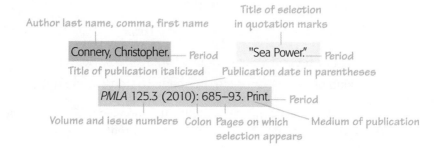

To see where this information comes from, refer to the illustration on page 469.

The entry for a journal article contains three major divisions: (1) the author's name, (2) the title of the work, and (3) the publication data. For journal articles, both the name of the article (in quotation marks) and the name of the journal (italicized) are included.

As in the example on the next page, many journals use continuous pagination throughout the year—for example, if the first issue ends on page 280, the second issue will begin on page 281. To cite journals that use continuous pagination, place the volume and issue numbers before the year of publication, which is given in parentheses. The month is not needed. A colon precedes the inclusive page numbers on which the selection appears.

Other Periodical Entries for the Works Cited List
Article in a journal that numbers pages in each issue separately

Risen, Clay. "Spies Among Us." *American Scholar* 78.1 (2009): 49–60. Print.

The issue number follows the volume number, and a period separates them (78.1 in the preceding example refers to volume 78, issue 1). If only an issue number appears, include it as you would a volume number.

Selection in a monthly (or bimonthly) magazine

Smith, Patti. "The Crowded Mind of Johnny Depp." *Vanity Fair* Jan. 2011: 48+. Print.

The entry includes the month (abbreviated) instead of a volume number. Only the months May, June, and July are not abbreviated. The plus sign means that the article is not printed on consecutive pages.

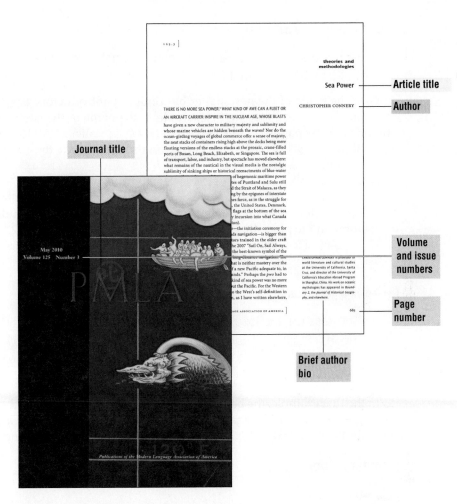

Journal title

Article title

Author

Volume and issue numbers

Page number

Brief author bio

Connery, Christopher. "Sea Power." *PMLA* 125.3 (2010): 685–93. Print.

Source information from a journal

Selection in a weekly (or biweekly) magazine

Klein, Ezra. "Tax Cutters for Truth." *Newsweek* 20 Dec. 2010: 18. Print.

Unsigned selection in a magazine

"Lutheran Defectors Plan New Church Body." *Christian Century* 29 Dec. 2009: 14. Print.

When no author is given, the entry begins with the title of the article. Do not use the word *anonymous* or its abbreviation, *anon.*

Unsigned article in a daily newspaper

> "Financial Bailout May Cost Less Than Thought." *New York Times* 12 Dec. 2010, late ed.: B2. Print.

Give the name of the newspaper but omit any introductory article, such as *The* from *New York Times* in the example. If the name of the city is part of the title of the newspaper, as in the *New York Times*, italicize it. However, if the name of the city is not part of the newspaper's title, include the city in brackets and do not italicize it: *Star-Ledger* [Newark].

Some newspapers print more than one edition a day, and the contents of the editions may differ. In such cases, include the edition you used. In addition, newspapers often indicate section numbers, and you should include them in the citation. In the preceding example, B2 refers to section B, page 2.

Use a plus sign after the page number when the entire selection does not appear on consecutive pages.

Review in a periodical

> Rev. of *Trespass*, by Rose Tremain. *New Yorker* 1 Nov. 2010: 109. Print.
>
> Flanagan, Caitlin. "The Age of Innocence." Rev. of *College Girls: Bluestockings, Sex Kittens, and Coeds, Then and Now*, by Lynn Peril. *Atlantic* Apr. 2007: 107–11. Print.

In the first example, the book review is unsigned. In the second, the review is both signed and titled: Flanagan's review of the book *College Girls: Bluestockings, Sex Kittens, and Coeds, Then and Now* is called "The Age of Innocence."

Standard Book Entry for the Works Cited List

Book with one author

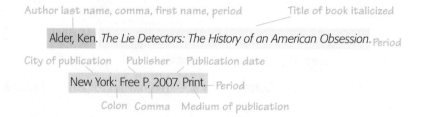

To see where this information comes from, refer to the illustration on page 471. Double-space the entry. Invert the author's name and place a period after it, after the title of the book (which is in italics), and after the publication date. A colon separates the city of publication and the name of the publisher. A comma separates the publisher's name—written in a shortened form (and without *Inc.*, *Company*, and the like)—and the year of publication. *Free P* here refers to the Free

Press and *Print* is the medium of publication. The first line of the entry begins at the left margin. Indent all subsequent lines of the entry one-half inch from the left.

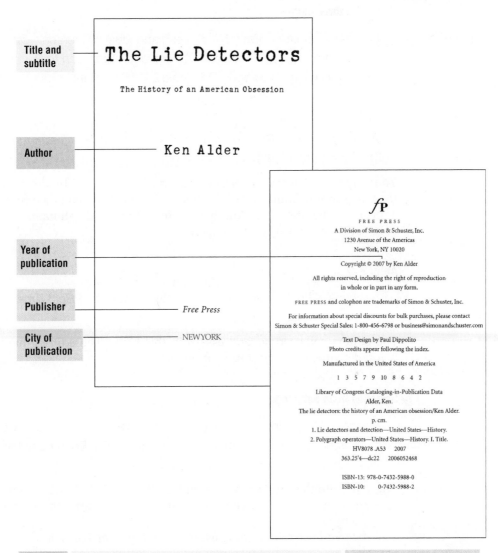

Title and subtitle — The Lie Detectors

The History of an American Obsession

Author — Ken Alder

*f*P

FREE PRESS
A Division of Simon & Schuster, Inc.
1230 Avenue of the Americas
New York, NY 10020

Copyright © 2007 by Ken Alder

All rights reserved, including the right of reproduction
in whole or in part in any form.

FREE PRESS and colophon are trademarks of Simon & Schuster, Inc.

For information about special discounts for bulk purchases, please contact
Simon & Schuster Special Sales: 1-800-456-6798 or business@simonandschuster.com

Text Design by Paul Dippolito
Photo credits appear following the index.

Manufactured in the United States of America

1   3   5   7   9   10   8   6   4   2

Library of Congress Cataloging-in-Publication Data
Alder, Ken.
The lie detectors: the history of an American obsession/Ken Alder.
p. cm.
1. Lie detectors and detection—United States—History.
2. Polygraph operators—United States—History. I. Title.
HV8078 .A53   2007
363.25'4—dc22   2006052468

ISBN-13: 978-0-7432-5988-0
ISBN-10:   0-7432-5988-2

Year of publication

Publisher — Free Press

City of publication — NEW YORK

Alder, Ken. *The Lie Detectors: The History of an American Obsession*. New York: Free P, 2007. Print.

Other Book Entries for the Works Cited List
Book with two authors

Haynes, William O., and Rebekah H. Pindzola. *Diagnosis and Evaluation in Speech Pathology*. New York: Allyn, 2007. Print.

Invert only the name of the first author. The order of the names is the same as that on the title page of the original source.

Book with three authors

> Longhofer, Jeffrey, Paul M. Kubek, and Jerry Floersch. *On Being and Having a Case Manager: A Relational Approach to Recovery in Mental Health.* New York: Columbia UP, 2010. Print.

Book with more than three authors

> Anderson, JoAnn Romeo, et al. *Integrated Skills Reinforcement.* New York: Longman, 1983. Print.

You may use the name of the first author only, followed by the notation *et al.,* the Latin abbreviation for "and others." The name given is the first name that appears on the title page. Another option is to provide all names in full in the order in which they appear on the title page.

Anthology

> Hitchens, Christopher, and Robert Atwan, eds. *The Best American Essays 2010.* Boston: Houghton, 2010. Print.

The editors collected several essays in this book. The editors' names appear before the title, with the abbreviation *eds.*

Selection in an anthology

> Driscoll, Mary Erina. "Choice, Achievement, and School Community." *School Choice: Examining the Evidence.* Ed. Edith Rasell and Richard Rothstein. Washington: Economic Policy Inst., 1993. 147–72. Print.

The page numbers given at the end of the entry indicate where the essay appears in the anthology. The editors' names appear after the abbreviation *Ed.* ("edited by").

When you use two or more essays from the same collection, you may *cross-reference* them, as in this example:

> Witte, John F. "The Milwaukee Parental Choice Program." Rasell and Rothstein 69–109.

The reference "Rasell and Rothstein" is to the anthology *School Choice: Examining the Evidence.* A citation for the anthology itself must then be included in the Works Cited list.

Special edition of an author's work

Thoreau, Henry David. *Walden*. Ed. Jeffrey S. Cramer. New Haven: Yale UP, 2006. Print.

Editions other than the first

Raimes, Ann. *Keys for Writers*. 5th ed. Boston: Houghton, 2008. Print.

For a revised edition, the abbreviation *Rev. ed.* appears after the title.

Translated work

Keilson, Hans. *Comedy in a Minor Key*. 1947. Trans. Damion Searls. New York: Farrar, 2010. Print.

Multivolume work

Adams, Wallace E. *The Western World*. 2 vols. New York: Addison, 1968. Print.

Pamphlet

Treat a pamphlet like a book, using the name of the committee or organization that created the pamphlet as the author if no author's name is provided.

Helsinki Summer School 2010. Helsinki: U of Helsinki, 2010. Print.

Selection in an encyclopedia

Kaeliinohomoku, Joanh W. "Hula." *Encyclopedia Americana*. 2006 ed. Print.

It is not necessary to give full publication information for a well-known reference work. If the article is signed only with the initials of the author, the rest of his or her name—the parts usually included in brackets—can be found by consulting the index volume. In some encyclopedias, the full name of the author can be found in the frontmatter section of the encyclopedia.

"Georgetown." *Encyclopaedia Britannica: Micropaedia*. 2007 ed. Print.

When no author is given, the entry begins with the title of the article. *The Encyclopaedia Britannica* has two parts: the *Micropaedia*, which contains short articles on the subject and cross-references to the *Macropaedia*, which contains longer articles on the subject, generally written by important scholars in the field.

Unpublished dissertation

Lu, J. "A Reexamination of the Career Factors Inventory." Diss. Purdue U, 2010. Print.

Standard Entry for an Online Source

Source information from an online document

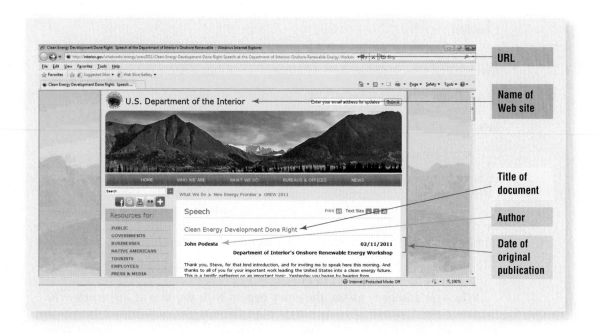

To see where this information comes from, refer to the illustration above.

For Web sources, give as much information as you can, including the original publication information if the source was published elsewhere first. If you cannot find the sponsor or publisher of the site, use *N.p.* (for "No publisher").

If the document does not have a date of posting, use *n.d.* (for "no date"). You do not have to include a URL unless you think readers will have difficulty finding the source by searching. If you must divide a URL at the end of a line, divide it only after a slash mark.

Document within an information database, a scholarly project, or Web site

> "Homer." *Encyclopaedia Britannica Online*. Encyclopaedia Britannica, 2007. Web. 18 Feb. 2010.
>
> Webster, Augusta. "A Castaway." *Portraits*. London, 1870. *Victorian Women Writers Project*. Ed. Perry Willett. Indiana U, 24 Apr. 1998. Web. 13 Apr. 2010.

Entire Internet site, such as an online scholarly project, information database, or professional or personal site

> Willett, Perry, ed. *Victorian Women Writers Project*. Indiana U, 1995–2003. Web. 13 Apr. 2010.
>
> Boyle, T. C. Home page. N.p., n.d. Web. 19 June 2007.
>
> *CBS.com*. CBS, 2007. Web. 23 July 2010.

Home page for a course

> Wild, Larry. Theater 241: Stagecraft. Course home page. Dept. of Theater, Northern State U, Fall 2006. Web. 12 Aug 2010.

No component of the entry requires italicizing.

Online book

> Anderson, Sherwood. *Winesburg, Ohio*. 1919. *Bartleby.com: Great Books Online*. Bartleby.com, 1999. Web. 11 Dec. 2010.
>
> Webster, Augusta. *Portraits*. London, 1870. *Victorian Women Writers Project*. Ed. Perry Willett. Indiana U, 24 Apr. 1998. Web. 20 Apr. 2010.

The Webster example is a book that is part of a scholarly project.

Part of an online book

> Anderson, Sherwood. "Hands." *Winesburg, Ohio*. 1919. *Bartleby.com: Great Books Online*. Bartleby.com, n.d. Web. 9 Oct. 2010.

Online article from a scholarly journal

> Rist, Thomas. "Religion, Politics, Revenge: The Dead in Renaissance Drama." *Early Modern Literary Studies* 9.1 (2003): 20 pars. Web. 19 June 2010.

The item *20 pars* in the reference indicates the total number of paragraphs in the selection. The online article numbered the paragraphs. If the selection numbers pages or sections instead, indicate the number range or total number of pages or sections.

Online article from a journal database

> Grubin, Don, and Lars Madsen. "Lie Detection and the Polygraph: A Historical Review." *Journal of Forensic Psychiatry and Psychology* 16.2 (2005): 357–69. *ContentSelect Research Navigator*. Web. 17 Mar. 2011.

Online article from a magazine

> Indiviglio, Daniel. "Why Is the Recovery Ignoring Men?" *TheAtlantic.com*. Atlantic Publishing Group, 14 Dec. 2010. Web. 20 Jan. 2011.

Online article from a newspaper

> Schiesel, Seth, and David Leonhardt. "Justice Dept. Acts to Block Proposed WorldCom-Sprint Deal." *New York Times*. New York Times, 28 June 2000. Web. 19 May 2010.

Online television program

> "Injury List." *Friday Night Lights. NBC.com*. WNBC, New York, 23 July 2010. Web. 15 Dec. 2010.

When you watch a program or video or listen to a recording online, the medium of publication is *Web*. See also *Films and television (or radio) programs*, page 478.

Nonperiodical publication on CD-ROM, diskette, or magnetic tape

> Mann, Ron. *Emile De Antonio's Painters Painting*. Irvington: Voyager, 1996. CD-ROM.

Selection from a periodically published database on CD-ROM

> "Polygraph." *Encarta Reference Lib*. 2005. CD-ROM. Microsoft, 2005.

Item from a personal subscription service

"Circe." *Compton's Encyclopedia Online*. Vers. 2.0. America Online, 1997.
Web. 3 Feb. 2010.

E-mail communication

Kane, Joshua. Message to the author. 2 Aug. 2010. E-mail.

Smith, Johnson C. "Re: Critique of Marx's Views." Message to Ramon
Vargas-Llosa. 23 June 2000. E-mail.

Wright, John. E-mail interview. 7–9 Apr. 2010.

The Kane entry illustrates an untitled e-mail message sent directly to the
writer of the paper at hand; the Smith entry illustrates a titled e-mail message
originally sent to someone else. The entry for Wright shows an e-mail interview over a number of days and indicates the inclusive dates.

Online posting to an e-mail discussion list

McCarty, Willard. "Humanist's 20th!" *Humanist Discussion Group*. N.p., 7
May 2007. Web. 28 Jan. 2011. <http://www.digitalhumanities.org/
humanist/Archives/Virginia/v21/0000.html>.

Synchronous communication on a MUD or MOO

Online Forum for Educational MOO Administrators. LinguaMOO. N.p., 6 July
1995. Web. 20 June 2008. <http://www.pub.utdallas.edu/~cynthiah/
lingua_archive/edumoo-7-6-95.txt>.

MUD is the acronym for multiuser domain; MOO is the acronym for multiuser domain, object oriented. Both are forums for posting synchronous
communication.

Other Types of Works Cited Source Entries

Recordings, tapes, and compact discs

Groban, Josh. *Illuminations*. Reprise/WEA, 2010. CD.

The entry includes the name of the artist, the title of the recording, the
manufacturer, and the date. The recording is a compact disk. If the piece is
in another medium, use *LP* (long-playing record), *Audiocassette*, or *Audiotape*
(reel-to-reel tape) at the end of the entry.

Films and television (or radio) programs

The Social Network. Dir. David Fincher. Perf. Jesse Eisenberg, Andrew Garfield, and Justin Timberlake. Columbia, 2010. Film.

"Lillian Gish: The Actor's Life for Me." Narr. Eva Marie Saint. Prod. and dir. Terry Sanders. *American Masters*. PBS. WNET, New York, 11 July 1988. Television.

Cartoons

Smaller, Barbara. Cartoon. *New Yorker* 22 Nov. 2010: 54. Print.

Schulz, Charles. "Peanuts Classic." Comic strip. *Daily News* [New York] 21 Nov. 2005: 43. Print.

Interviews

Fraser, Brendan. Interview. *Tavis Smiley*. PBS. WNET, New York, 16 Jan. 2008. Radio.

Hawke, Ethan. Personal interview. 11 Mar. 2010.

Performances

South Pacific. By Richard Rodgers and Oscar Hammerstein. Dir. Bartlett Sher. Perf. Kelli O'Hara and Paulo Szot. Vivian Beaumont Theater, New York. 12 Dec. 2009. Performance.

Preparing the Works Cited List

In preparing your list of works cited, follow these guidelines for the correct format.

TIPS for Preparing the Works Cited List

- **Prepare the list on a separate page headed "Works Cited."** Place the heading about an inch from the top and center it. (Do not underline the heading; use uppercase letters only for the first letter in each word.) The Works Cited page appears at the end of the paper.

- **Double-space before typing the first entry.** Begin each entry flush with the left margin, and indent all other lines of each entry five spaces. Use double-spacing throughout your list of works cited.

- **Arrange the entries alphabetically, according to the authors' last names.** Do not separate books and periodicals. For entries without authors, use the first word in the title (other than *A*, *An*, or *The*) to determine alphabetical order.

- **When you cite two or more books by the same author, arrange them alphabetically by title.** Give the author's full name only in the first entry. In subsequent entries, replace the author's name with three hyphens. For example:

  > Geertz, Clifford. *The Interpretation of Cultures.* New York: Basic, 1973. Print.

  > —. *Local Knowledge: Further Essays in Interpretive Anthropology.* New York: Basic, 1983. Print.

- **Use autocite programs with caution.** Check carefully all computer-generated Works Cited lists for errors.

See pages 508–510 for a complete, formatted Works Cited list.

EXERCISE Write entries for a list of works cited according to the MLA-style system of documentation for two sources you will use in your research paper.

Documenting Sources in the Social Sciences: APA Style

Writers in the social sciences use the system of documentation set forth in the *Publication Manual of the American Psychological Association* (APA), 6th ed. (2010). Since your instructors in psychology, sociology, and other courses may require you to follow APA guidelines, you should be familiar with this system. Like the MLA style, **APA-style documentation** uses parenthetical citations supported by a separate list of sources headed "References," which appears at the end of the research paper.

Parenthetical Citations

A typical APA-style text citation includes the author's name and the date of publication, separated by a comma.

> Lower species of animals use only a few signs in their communication systems. For example, the rhesus monkey uses only about 37 different signals (Wilson, 1972).

As with MLA-style documentation, the APA system aims to integrate references smoothly with the text of the paper. Here are some further examples:

> In 1972 Wilson showed that the rhesus monkey uses only about 37 different signals in its communication system.

> According to Wilson (1972), rhesus monkeys use only 37 signals. Communication systems that rely on only a few signs are typical of lower animal species.

When quoting a passage from a source, the page number on which the passage appears follows the publication date. Note the required use of the abbreviations *pp.* for "pages" and *p.* for "page." Separate the date and the page information by a comma.

> Creative people use divergent thinking to their advantage and "prefer complexity and some degree of apparent imbalance in phenomena" (Barron, 1963, pp. 208–209).

When citing more than one work by the same author published in the same year, use an *a* after the date for the first publication, a *b* after the date for the second, and so on. The citations on the References list should also include these letters. In the following example, the reference is to the second 1971 article by Schacter, "Some Extraordinary Facts About Obese Humans and Rats." This reference is marked *b* on the References list. Schacter's first 1971 article, "Eat, Eat," would be marked *a* on the References list (see page 483).

> Researchers have identified important similarities for obesity in rats and humans (Schacter, 1971b).

The examples that follow show how to cite multiple authors in the APA system. Note that the ampersand (&) replaces the word *and* between authors' names in the parenthetical citation (see the first example). If the authors' names are not given parenthetically, as in the second example, use the word *and*.

> Famous studies of the chimpanzee Washoe demonstrated that animals other than humans could learn and use language (Gardner & Gardner, 1969).

> Rumbaugh, Gill, and von Glaserfeld (1973) studied the language skills of the chimpanzee Pan.

When citing works by three to five authors, use all authors' names (followed by the date) for the first reference, but in the second and subsequent text references use the abbreviation *et al.* after the first author's name.

> Rumbaugh et al. (1973) have documented certain levels of reading
>
> and the ability to complete sentences among chimpanzees.

EXERCISE   Return to pages 457–459. Revise any two MLA-style citations there so that they reflect the APA style of parenthetical citation.

A List of APA References

APA-style documentation requires that a list of the references cited in the paper appear on a separate page at the end. The heading "References" is typed at the top of the page and is not underlined (see page 483). Titles of books, newspapers, journals, and magazines appear in italics. On the following pages are sample references in the APA format.

Standard Periodical Entry for the References List

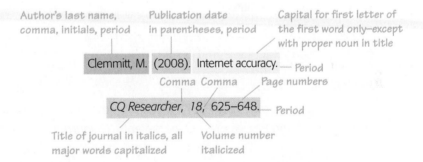

Article in a journal that numbers the pages in each issue separately

Eubanks, W. R. (2009). Affirmative action and after. *American Scholar*, *78*(1), 41–48.

The notation refers to volume 78, issue 1.

Article in a monthly (or bimonthly) magazine

Ward, L. (2010, November). Shooting for the sun. *The Atlantic*, *306*, 90–96.

In a monthly or bimonthly magazine, the month of publication is given after the year in parentheses. A comma separates the year and the month. The volume number follows the magazine title. Use the abbreviation *p.* for page and *pp.* for pages only for newspaper entries.

Article in a daily newspaper

> Meier, B. (2010, December 17). The implants loophole. *The New York Times*, p. B1.

Standard Book Entry for the References List

Book with one author

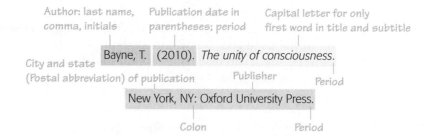

Book with two or more authors

> Hick, S. F., & McNutt, J. G. (2002). *Advocacy, activism, and the Internet.* Chicago, IL: Lyceum Books.

Electronic Sources

> Dyer, J., & Findlay, B. (2007). Psychocardiology: Advancing the assessment and treatment of heart patients. *E-Journal of Applied Psychology, 3*(2), 3–12. Retrieved from http://ojs.lib.swin.edu.au/index.php/ejap/article/view/88/120
>
> Grubin, D., & Madsen, L. (2005). Lie detection and the polygraph: A historical review. *Journal of Forensic Psychiatry & Psychology, 16*(2), 357–369. doi: 10.1080/14789940412331337353
>
> Hinshelwood, R. O. (2007). Intolerance and the intolerable: The case of racism. *Journal for the Psychoanalysis of Culture and Society, 12*(1), 1–20. Retrieved from http://palgrave-journals.com/pcs/journal/v12/n1/full/2100103a.html
>
> Sengupta, S. (2008, January 17). Push for education yields little for India's poor. *The New York Times.* Retrieved from http://www.nytimes.com

Use the models above to develop citations for a range of electronic sources that you might cite in a paper. Note that in APA style, the words "Retrieved from" precede the URL and a period does not appear at the end of the URL. If you need to break a URL from one line to the next, break *before* the slash (/) or other major puncuation mark, but break *after* the double slash (//). Dates of retrieval appear only if you reference a draft version of the article; final versions of articles require no retrieval dates in the citation. Finally, if an article is assigned a digital object identifier (DOI) in a database, as in the Grubin entry above, use this number in place of database names and URLs.

The *APA Style Guide to Electronic References* (2010) provides more information and a comprehensive collection of sample references for electronic sources.

Preparing Your APA References List

If your instructor asks you to prepare your paper in APA format, here is a sample References list for you to examine and some tips for preparing the References list.

References

Bayne, T. (2010). The unity of consciousness. New York, NY: Oxford University Press.

Chase, A. (2000, June). Harvard and the making of the Unabomber.
     Atlantic, 282, 41–65.

Eubanks, W. R., (2009). Affirmative action and after. *American Scholar,*
     78(1), 41–48.

Gardner, R. A., & Gardner, B. T. (1969). Teaching sign language
     to a chimpanzee. *Science, 165*, 664–672.

Hinshelwood, R. O. (2007). Intolerance and the intolerable: The case of racism.
     Journal of the Psychoanalysis of Culture and Society, 12(1), 1–20.
     Retrieved from htttp://palgrave-journals.com/pcs/journal/v12/n1/full/2100103a.html

Schacter, S. (1971a, November). Eat, eat. *Psychology Today, 5*, 44–47, 78–79.

Schacter, S. (1971b). Some extraordinary facts about obese humans and rats.
     American Psychologist, 26, 129–144.

TIPS for Preparing an APA References List

- **Type the heading "References" at the top of a new page.** On a separate page that will appear at the end of the paper, type the heading centered on the line. Do not underline it; do not enclose it in quotation marks. List all the sources cited in the text. Double-space from the heading to the first entry.

- **Arrange all entries alphabetically.** Without separating books from periodicals, arrange all entries alphabetically according to the author's last name (or, according to publication dates—earliest to most recent—for works by the same author).

- **Double-space within and between all entries.**

- **The first line of each entry is flush with the left margin.** Indent second and subsequent lines of each entry five spaces.

- **Number the References page.**

Be sure to check the APA Web site (www.apastyle.org/elecref.html) for more information about APA style requirements.

EXERCISE   Select reference notes (for books, periodicals, and online sources) that you prepared for your research paper and write an APA-style References list for them.

Preparing Your Manuscript

Before you begin to prepare your final copy, make sure your printer has ink or toner and is in good working order. Since you have put so much work into writing the paper, you don't want to spoil the final product by presenting your instructor with a hard-to-read, smudged copy. Avoid unusual typefaces like script or italic. Times New Roman is standard for formal documents. Set the type size at 10- or 12-point.

Good bond paper gives a more attractive appearance than less expensive types. White, 8½ x 11-inch, twenty-pound bond paper is usually recommended. Avoid using erasable paper because it smudges and will not take corrections made in ink. Corrections are easy to make on a computer, but don't neglect to reread your paper carefully before you submit it. Check for careless errors like unnecessary spaces and repeated words. Follow these guidelines as you prepare the final copy:

TIPS for Preparing the Final Copy

■ **Double-space.** Double-space the paper throughout, including long quotations and notes, except as indicated in the following discussion of margins.

■ **Use one-inch margins.** Leave margins of one inch at the top, bottom, and both sides of the text. If you are not using a title page, type the centered title two inches from the top of the page, and double-space between the title and the first line of the text. Indent the first word of each paragraph five spaces from the left margin. Indent a block quotation ten spaces from the left margin.

■ **Format the title.** MLA guidelines call for a heading on the first page instead of a separate title page. The writer's name, instructor's name, course number, and date appear flush left on the first manuscript page, spaced as shown in the example below.

However, many instructors prefer a title page, especially if an outline or table of contents precedes the first page of text. If your instructor calls for a title page, it should contain the title of your paper, your name, the course name and number, the name of your instructor, and the date. Neatly center this information on the page, as shown on page 490.

Whichever form you use, remember that you should never put your own title in quotation marks, underline it, or use all capital letters. Underline words in the title only if you would underline them in the text also.

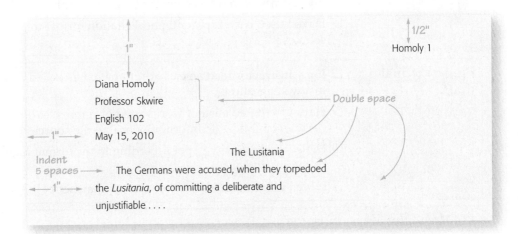

■ **Pagination.** Number all pages consecutively (except the title page and any prefatory material) in the upper-right-hand corner. Just type the number; don't punctuate it with a period, hyphens, or parentheses. In addition to putting the number in the upper-right-hand corner, you may want to type your name right before the page number to ensure against misplaced pages. (See the pagination of "The Banning of the Polygraph," page 492, for example.) Number prefatory materials, such as your outline, acknowledgments, or preface, with lowercase Roman numerals—i, ii, and so on.

STRATEGY CHECKLIST: Writing Your Research Paper

Note: This checklist begins with the first draft. For a research and planning Strategy Checklist, see Chapter 20.

Write the first draft.	☐ Is my thesis clear and limited? Does it state or suggest an interpretation or judgment on the topic? ☐ Does the body of the paper develop the thesis?
Write subsequent drafts.	☐ Are my ideas logically developed and connected with clear transitions? ☐ Have I supported my points with quotations and paraphrases from my sources? ☐ Following my intructor's guidelines, have I acknowledged all my sources even when summarizing or paraphrasing? ☐ Have I used correct parenthetical citation format for all sources?
Prepare a final draft.	☐ If my instructor read an early draft, have I attended carefully to any suggestions? ☐ Have I prepared a list of works cited or references, including complete publication information for all the sources I used? ☐ Have I prepared my paper according to the format required by my instructor? ☐ Have I followed guidelines for correct manuscript preparation?
Proofread the paper.	☐ Have I proofread for grammar, spelling, and mechanics?

EXERCISE   Using your formal outline as your guide, write the necessary drafts of your research paper. Document all sources. Prepare a list of works cited. Be sure to study the student sample and the accompanying commentary on the following pages.

Frequently Asked Questions About Writing Research Papers

How do I find a good topic?
As with any paper, identify areas that interest you. Baseball? Fashion? TV programming? Prewrite. Browse your library's catalog. Surf the Web. Rent movies and watch relevant TV. Talk to friends, teachers, coworkers, and family. Think about your topic.

When I have decided on a topic, what do I do next?
Limit your topic so that it is suitable for a research paper of the scope and length defined by your instructor. *Baseball* might become *how Hollywood presents baseball heroes in film*; *TV programming* might become *violence in television cartoons for children* (see pages 32–34).

How do I develop a thesis for my topic?
Once you have limited your topic by browsing and discussing your ideas, you must make some assertion about your topic, and that will be your tentative thesis (see pages 49–50). Each thesis below grew from the limited topics above:

- Hollywood films idealize baseball heroes, who never correspond in fact to the real, troubled athletes playing the game.
- Students of the media may disagree on the long-term effects of TV violence on children, but the graphic images of brutality in popular cartoons cause deep psychological problems for young viewers.

Expect to revise your thesis many times as your research progresses and your ideas take shape.

How do I begin my reseach?
Develop a general perspective on your topic by relaxed "reading around." Look up your topic in a recent edition of a general or specialized encyclopedia (see pages 430–431). Use library catalogs; browse bookshelves; use search engines to identify Web sources that might stimulate your thinking at this stage simply by their names or home pages.

What if I can't find any good sources?
Talk to a librarian. Talk to your teacher. Talk to classmates.

How can I organize my thoughts at this point?
Develop an informal outline (see pages 66–67) to help you read and take notes in a systematic way.

How do I identify the sources of my quotes and paraphrases?
Most papers for English courses require documentation in the MLA style (see pages 463–479). Name your source exactly and provide some identifying information in the body of the paper as you present quotes or paraphrases; name your source more completely in a list of works cited at the end of your paper (see pages 478–479).

What documentation style do I use for writing social science papers?
Use the format described in the *Publication Manual of the American Psychological Association* (see pages 479–484) and the *APA Style Guide to Electronic References*.

How do I do the kind of serious research that will help me write about my topic?
Read selections from books you've identified. To find current periodical selections (an important source of current information), use the *Reader's Guide*, newspaper indexes, or other periodical indexes useful to your topic (see page 436). Do an electronic search (see page 428). Read reliable Web sources carefully (see pages 24–26).

How do I record information?
Reproduce information carefully and use quotation marks on your research notes around *anything* you copy word for word from a source. Separate your own thoughts carefully from quotes. (Use special marking or another color ink.) Use ellipses (spaced dots) to indicate words you've left out of a quote (see pages 447–448). Use paraphrasing and write summaries to record most of the information you're extracting from your readings (see pages 448–449).

Once I start accumulating notes from my reading, how can I organize them when I'm ready to write my paper?
Give each note a topic slug and then sort the notes by topic. Make an outline. (See Chapter 4 as well as pages 451–453.) Develop a sentence outline.

What if my teacher doesn't require an outline?
You probably should do one anyway, just to make sure that you're organizing the points in your paper logically.

How do I actually use someone else's words or ideas in my own paragraphs?
Learn to integrate smoothly any quotations you take from sources, use quotation marks where needed, and cite the sources correctly (see pages 457–459). If you paraphrase, make sure that it's clear—through correct citation—which thoughts are yours and which are those of your source. Use quotation marks around any set of words within your paraphrase that come directly from the source. Ignoring citation risks plagiarism, a very serious offense (see pages 460–462).

How many quotations should I use in my paper?
Be careful not simply to string quotations together as you write your paper. Use quotes to support your ideas, which means that you have to integrate the quotes into your own statements. Often paraphrasing makes the point as well as lengthy quotes (see page 459).

Sample MLA-Style Research Paper

The following sample research paper shows how one student, Elizabeth Kessler, managed to blend a variety of elements successfully. The commentary that appears on the pages facing the paper highlights its key features and calls attention to special issues. The paper uses MLA-style documentation.

TITLE PAGE, IF REQUIRED

Title begins one-third down page.

The Banning of the Polygraph

Double-space
between the title
and the next line.

by

Elizabeth Kessler

English 102, Section 18

Professor D. Skwire

15 January 2011

Writer's name, course and section, instructor's name,
and date of submission are all double-spaced.

OUTLINE, IF REQUIRED Kessler i

Formal sentence outline observes format described in Chapter 4.

Outline

Thesis: The polygraph test as an element in employment decisions should be banned.

First major division

I. Those who argue in favor of the polygraph feel it should be used as a criterion for employment.

A. Supporters claim that the examiners are adequately trained.

First-level subdivisions

B. Supporters claim that polygraph findings are reliable.

C. Supporters argue that it is an inexpensive and effective method to avoid hiring potential thieves.

II. Those who oppose the polygraph test correctly believe it should not be used as a criterion for employment.

A. Opponents believe the examiners are uneven in quality.

B. Opponents believe the readings are not accurate.

C. Opponents believe there is no clear-cut physiological indication of guilt.

D. Opponents believe the laws regarding the use of the polygraph are "toothless."

E. Opponents believe the test violates basic human rights.

1. The test can lead to loss of employment and damage to reputation.

Second-level subdivisions

2. The test is an invasion of privacy.

III. The 1988 Polygraph Protection Act restricts lie detector use.

Conclusion: Despite legislation restricting polygraph use nationally, continuing abuses and potential abuses in the future argue forcefully against the lie detector test in the workplace.

Conclusion

■ 1

■ 2

■ 3

The polygraph (lie detector) monitors physiological change.[1] The subject, while attached to the polygraph machine, must answer a series of questions to measure the person's honesty. Any physiological change "such as a faster heart rate, higher blood pressure, increased perspiration" during a particular question is

■ 4

believed to show "that the person is lying" ("How Does?"). Employers use polygraphs to weed out dishonest current or prospective employees and "as a means of curbing employee thefts, a

■ 5

multibillion-dollar-a-year headache" (Gugas 6). By the 1980s, two million Americans a year were tested. "By then," writes Ken Alder, "one-fourth of all U.S. firms used the technique for preemployment screening or systematic checkups on honesty" (254). Banks, police departments, and guard agencies have made similar demands ("Tests Untrustworthy" 16).

■ 6

Despite wide use much debate surrounds testing. Supporters praise it, it is true.[2] Yet critics argue strongly against its use. Merely a machine, the polygraph simply registers a person's emotional reactions. One psychiatrist insists that "there is no such thing as a

■ 7

■ 8

lie detector" ("Truth" 76). A syndicated columnist reminded readers of the "foolishness of dependence" on the polygraph (Safire A39). Indeed, on the evidence, one must agree with the 1988 Employee Polygraph Protection Act, which attempts to ban the polygraph test as a criterion for most employment. Lie detectors have no place in the

■ 9

work environment.

Those who favor the polygraph test claim that it is accurate because those who administer it are adequately trained. The examiner "must be consistently objective and should be thoroughly

1. The page number appears in the upper right-hand corner of each page one-half inch from the top. The writer's last name is optional.
2. Begin the first paragraph about two inches from the top of the page.
3. The raised numerals 1 and 2 correspond to notes 1 and 2 on page 1 of the research paper. Such notes provide explanatory information that doesn't fit smoothly into the paper.
4. Quotation marks surround the statement that Kessler copied, word for word, from the electronic source "How Does a Lie Detector (Polygraph) Work?" The article appears on a Web site, which she identifies clearly on the list of works cited (page 508 of the research paper). She shortened the long title to "How Does?" Here is the language from which the quoted material comes, with the words Kessler used highlighted:

   > Both during and after the test, a polygraph examiner can look at the graphs and can see whether the vital signs changed significantly on any of the questions. In general, a significant change (such as a faster heart rate, higher blood pressure, increased perspiration) indicates that the person is lying.

   Note, first, how Kessler chose to use only a small part of the statement on the Web site and, next, how she integrated the quote with her own language. She eliminated the word "indicates" and substituted "is believed to show" because she wanted to establish some doubt about the polygraph's use right from the start of the paper. Her own words do not appear in quotations.

5. The parenthetical citation (Gugas 6) refers to the work named with all the appropriate publishing data in the list of works cited (see page 508 of the research paper). No comma separates the author's name and the page number. No abbreviation for *page* or *pages* is used. Quotation marks surround the words beginning with *as* and ending with *headache* because Kessler copied the statement exactly from Gugas' book *The Silent Witness* (see page 508 for the complete citation). Here is part of the paragraph as it appears in Gugas; Kessler extracted only the small piece that would serve her purpose.

   > Business and industry use the polygraph examination widely in screening job applicants and as a means of curbing employee thefts, a multibillion-dollar-a-year headache. Our Army, Navy, Air Force, and Marines all use polygraph testing.

6. Note how the introduction calls attention to both supporters and critics of polygraph testing. The paper itself expands on these issues.
7. The citation ("Truth" 76) indicates that the quotation appears on page 76 of an unsigned piece. Kessler shortened the full title "The Truth About Lie Detectors, Says David Lykken, Is That They Can't Detect a Lie." See the list of works cited on page 11.
8. The citation (Safire A39) refers to a column in section A, page 39 of the *New York Times*. The complete reference appears in the list of works cited on page 11 of Kessler's paper.
9. The thesis makes a forceful assertion: keep polygraphs out of the workplace.

trained in scientific interrogation to reduce the inherent human error"

■ 10   ("Polygraph"). In fact, many states demand education and other

■ 11   requirements for the licensing of polygraph examiners ("In Ohio" F4).
The training supposedly enables the examiner to distinguish between
nervousness and actual deception ("What's It Like" F8).

■ 12   Supporters of the test believe that the training equips examiners
to make accurate distinctions. Using control questions, an examiner
can determine a person's normal emotional reaction. Then, the
examiner can detect deception, which reveals itself in an abnormal
response (Inbaw 44). Supporters of the test point out that to reduce
nervousness, the subject has access to the questions on the test for
as long as he desires ("What's It Like" F8).

■ 13   Supporters of the polygraph further argue that it is "a valuable

■ 14   tool for an employer in... investigating workplace crime" ("How
to Comply" 36). Each year theft exceeds twenty billion dollars
(Beach 44). Therefore, employers enlist the aid of the polygraph
and with it can reduce employee theft by as much as 50 percent

■ 15   (Flaherty 31). Interestingly, at numerous Chicago banks during the
1930s, employees who failed lie detector tests and remained on
the payroll became "The banks' most honest employees. . . . The

■ 16   lie detector become [*sic*] a psychological deterrent as much as a
catcher of thieves" (Alder 124).

10. Kessler cites a quotation from another electronic source. The "Polygraph" piece appears in *Encarta*, an encyclopedia on CD-ROM. See page 11 of the research paper for the exact source.

11. "In Ohio" is a shortened title for "In Ohio, Anyone May Run Lie Detector," which refers to an unsigned article that Kessler identifies fully in the list of works cited. The full title appears in the Works Cited list on page 10.

12. Here Kessler uses an important strategy in writing arguments: She presents her opponents' views clearly and fairly. She herself does not approve of polygraph testing, but she does not ignore the issues put forth by those who support the test. The paragraph expands on point I. B. in Kessler's outline on page i.

13. Kessler begins to explore additional views of her opponents, using the phrase *further argue* to signal the transition to a new point.

14. The ellipsis points (three spaced periods) indicate that Kessler omitted from the quotation the words she felt were not relevant. As indicated on the list of works cited, the source is an article called "How to Comply with the Polygraph Law," which appeared in Nation's Business. (See full details in the list of Works Cited on page 10.) If the original source itself contains an ellipsis, place brackets around the ellipsis you have inserted to distinguish it from the ellipsis in your source. Kessler remembered to use a space before and after the three spaced periods.

15. The statistical data are impressive. Even though Kessler is arguing a point opposite to what she believes, she marshals substantial evidence to show the other side of the issue. To help readers draw thoughtful conclusions on their own, writers should present opposing arguments fairly.

16. The Latin abbreviation *sic* means "thus" or "so." It tells readers that Kessler knows that the correct verb form here is past tense—*became*, not *become*—but that she is reporting the text exactly as it appeared in Alder's book, with the error intact.

■ 17   Supporters argue, too, that the polygraph test is much quicker, more efficient, and less expensive than background checking. As Beach indicates, using the polygraph costs about $35 to $150; doing a background check on a potential employee costs significantly more, an average of $300 (44).

And, of course, federal support for polygraph testing has added validity to their use. Agencies of the United States government have relied on lie detector tests in important legal matters:

■ 18   The FBI uses polygraphs mostly to probe leads and verify specific facts. . . . The agency also employs highly trained examiners, who usually spend half a day on each session. . . . an "adverse inference" may be drawn if an employee of the FBI or any other part of the Justice Department balks at submitting to the machines. (Beach 44)

The supporters of the polygraph believe its efficiency and low cost justify its use.

■ 19   Those who favor the polygraph in the workplace, then, argue that adequately trained examiners produce reliable findings at low cost. These are strong arguments. However, those who oppose the test question the claims made by its supporters, and they are right to do so.

■ 20   Despite assertions that examiners are adequately trained, Beach points to regular reports by employees that examiners browbeat them during polygraph testing (44). And "about 90% of the damaging

■ 21   reports made to employers are based not on physiological reactions but on the examiners' assumptions, or on incriminating confessions

17. Here Kessler integrates into her sentence the name of the author whose work she paraphrases. The parenthetical reference (44) tells readers the page number in Beach's article "Blood, Sweat and Fears," which Kessler paraphrased. The full citation appears on page 10 of Kessler's paper. Note throughout this paragraph the consistent use of numbers, all written as numerals. See page 592.

18. Kessler sets off this quotation ten spaces from the left margin because it takes more than four lines. The parenthetical citation of Beach comes after the last line of the quotation. See page 457 for the complete paragraph as it appears in Beach's article.

19. The transitional paragraph neatly connects the two major sections of the essay. In the first part of the paragraph, Kessler summarizes the issues advanced by polygraph test supporters. The word *then* in the first sentence connects the ideas expressed here with the preceding paragraphs. With the word *However*, Kessler signals her opposition to the strong arguments put forth by those who support the test. Notice how the last sentence connects to the thesis sentence on page 1 of the research paper.

20. Kessler shows why she believes that the training of polygraph examiners is uneven. Readers must weigh the assertions in this paragraph against the arguments by those who say that examiners are well trained.

21. Kessler has paraphrased the statement for which she credits Beach. Here is the selection exactly as it appears in Beach's article:

> Lie detector tests, either to screen job applicants or to uncover theft by employees, have become big business: hundreds of thousands are given each year, and the number is rising steadily. But despite technical improvements in the equipment, the accuracy of the results is often open to question, and there are persistent reports of browbeating by examiners....

Even though she uses her own language to restate Beach, Kessler attributes the source of her ideas with the page reference (44). The author's name appears in the sentence; hence, it is excluded from the parenthetical citation.

Kessler 4

made during an interview" ("Truth" 76). These findings suggest that the quality of operators in the polygraph industry is uneven at best.

Furthermore, critics say that the test is accurate only 60 to 75 percent of the time, and many variants have never been checked for validity ("Tests Untrustworthy" 16). Error is more likely to occur when a truthful person is shown to be deceptive (Beach 44). Readings do not always indicate deception; people who do not believe that the machine can detect dishonesty feel no stress when lying: therefore, no great physiological response will indicate

■ 22
deception on the readings (Flaherty 32). Clinical tests suggest that tranquilizers can reduce the physiological response that accompanies deception (Ward et al. 74). Also, those who are "really clever . . . can

■ 23
fool the machines" ("Rights Abuse" 10).

When seven FBI agents with access to high-secret information failed polygraph tests not long ago, the director at that time, Robert S. Mueller III, said the failed polygraphs did not automatically mean that the agents were suspected of spying. He said that "a follow-up investigation could exonerate" all the employees (Johnston, A18).

■ 24
So much for accuracy! One must question the value of readings that may be unreliable.

■ 25
Nor does a clear-cut physiological indication of guilt seem to be as certain as supporters of the test claim. Often, heightened feelings bring about physiological responses that are similar to those caused by deception. According to David Lykken, a psychiatrist and professor of psychology, people who run a special risk include those who get upset if someone accuses them of something they did not do, those with short tempers, and those who tend to feel guilty

22 Flaherty and Ward are sources for the paraphrases included in this paragraph. See the list of works cited on pages 10 and 11 of the paper for the complete citations.

23 Kessler uses ellipses to indicate that she has left out words in this quotation taken from an editorial called "Rights Abuse," in the *Christian Science Monitor*. (See reference in Works Cited list, page 11.)

24 Kessler uses a sentence fragment as an exclamation ("So much for accuracy!") to make a sharp commentary on the meaning of Mueller's statement. Once again, she offers her own opinion, based on an element in her research.

25 This paragraph develops point II. C. in the outline (page i). The transition *Nor* connects the ideas of this paragraph to those in the paragraph before it.

anyway. Lykken believes that the polygraph machine detects not
only the physiological responses that accompany lying but also the
nervousness people feel when strapped to a machine. The polygraph
confuses guilt with fear, anger, and other emotions that can alter heart
rate, breathing, and perspiration. Each person varies in physiological
responses to these emotions ("Truth" 79).

■ 26   Moreover, until now, polygraph laws tended to be "toothless."
Some laws prohibit requiring employees to submit to a polygraph;
however, businesses are still free to make the request (Flaherty 34).
Private companies can advertise job-related lie-detection services
even now. One company, for example, asserts that its polygraph
test is a valuable 'investigative tool'" and that its expert examiners
"can help 'clear' loyal staff members while resolving open issues
during a non-accusatory interview and examination process" ("Dallas

■ 27 Polygraph Services"). If a current or prospective employee refuses
to take the test, employers may interpret the refusal as an admission
of guilt ("Truth" 79). In fact, refusal may mean the loss of a job

■ 28 (Beach 44). This is unfair: the burden lies entirely on the employee's
shoulders. Further, some laws free only present, not prospective,
employees from a polygraph test. Finally, the fines and jail terms
for violating these laws rarely have risen above misdemeanor level.
Fines, which seldom exceed $1,000, do not hinder "deep-pocketed"
employers from using the polygraph (Flaherty 34). Such laws, test
opponents argue, have not protected employees.

    One must also consider the problem of human rights violation
("In Ohio" F4). Polygraph testing "unjustly robs suspects of

26 This paragraph develops point in the outline.

27 The information about the company comes from the company's Web site. Kessler provides the full Internet source on her list of works cited, page 10. "Dallas Polygraph Services" is the name of the page she used from the Web site http://dallaspolygraph.com.

28 Kessler reflects on her findings, inserting her own opinion on the information she presents. Writers of research papers should do more than simply summarize, paraphrase, or quote acknowledged experts.

Kessler 6

■ 29

their innermost secrets," and courts have ruled that the test illegally forces people to testify against themselves (Block 131). Several experts claim that the lie detector, with all its apparatus, constitutes a "modern third degree" and may intimidate a subject into blurting out a false confession before the test begins (Beach 44). They argue, also, that an unfavorable reading, whether accurate or not, could result in damage to an employee's reputation and the inability to obtain new employment, especially since, in many states, a person must sign a form before taking the test that allows any individual access to the test results ("Lie Detectors Raise" F7). Thus, one can, in effect, be found guilty and be punished—having committed no crime—without the traditional protections of presumption of innocence until guilt is proved, trial by jury, and the right to confront accusers. The polygraph test, then, can be an infringement on individual rights.

■ 30

      A further infringement on individual rights, according to opponents of the test, is invasion of privacy. Many examiners have probed into personal affairs (Beach 44). The examiners ask questions pertaining to political, sexual, and union matters. As a result, many large non-governmental employers avoid polygraph testing. A retired director of personnel at Schlumberger Limited, a large multinational corporation, believes that potential employees would prefer to work in organizations that valued "personal impressions and evaluations of candidates rather than the 'answer'

29   Kessler smoothly integrates the quote from Block with her own language. Look at the statement from Block and then at the note Kessler prepared as she read the source material.

> Some sociologists and theologians question the fairness of the lie detector, arguing that it unjustly robs suspects of their innermost secrets, and some courts have held that to some extent it illegally compels defendants to testify against themselves. Yet modern police authorities insist that many baffling cases have been solved only because such a test, taken voluntarily by a suspect, has proved scientifically that he or she lied in answering key questions pertinent to the case.

Block, Science vs. Crime, 131

"Some sociologists and theologians question the fairness of the lie detector, arguing that it unjustly robs suspects of their innermost secrets, and some courts have held that to some extent it illegally compels defendants to testify against themselves."

Police say, however, that polygraphs help solve puzzling cases by giving scientific proof of lying.

*Focus here is on criminal cases.

Kessler has copied one sentence exactly and has enclosed it in quotation marks on her note card. She has also paraphrased the rest of the paragraph—the sentence starting with the words *Police say* on the notes. In addition, she has written a brief note to herself on the card—the sentence beginning with the word *Focus*. She uses an asterisk to highlight the statement as her own, so that she will not mistakenly attribute it to Block when she reviews the note cards later on and chooses information to include in her essay.

When Kessler draws on the material from this note card to make her point in the paper, she uses only one part of the quotation from Block. Kessler paraphrases the portion of the quote that reads "and some courts have held that to some extent it illegally compels defendants to testify against themselves." In her paper, this part of the quote becomes "courts have ruled that the test illegally forces people to testify against themselves (Block 131)." The parenthetical documentation tells readers that both the quote and the paraphrase are from Block.

30   Note the smooth transition. Kessler writes "A further infringement on individual rights," repeating exactly a phrase from the last sentence of the previous paragraph, adding the word "further." This paragraph develops point II. E. 2. in the outline.

■ 31   provided by a machine" (Alexander). Invasions of privacy are
violations of constitutional rights and should not be tolerated.

■ 32   Fortunately, the government heeded the chorus of voices
against the lie detector over the years. In 1988, Congress passed
the Polygraph Protection Act, which, according to an article called
"How to Comply with the Polygraph Law" in *Nation's Business*,
finally prohibits polygraphs to "screen job applicants or investigate

■ 33   employees . . ." (36). The law defines proper testing procedures and
gives employees a wide range of rights, including notice in advance
of the time and place of the examination, its scope, and the reasons
the employer has for suspecting the employee in some specific
incident "involving economic loss or injury to the business" (36). In
addition, the law spells out "procedural requirements" with guidelines
for the examiners' qualifications. Some good sense has prevailed
here; many workers now have protection against offensive testing.

■ 34   Yet despite restrictions in the 1988 law, the polygraph is highly
unpopular with workers. Scientists at national weapons laboratories
recently walked off the job to protest "congressionally mandated lie
detector tests" (Wilson 42). And many civil rights advocates are still
unhappy. In fact, some are vicious in their attack against polygraph
use. *AntiPolygraph.org* argues that "Our government's stubborn
reliance on this pseudoscience poses clear and present danger:
make-believe science yields make-believe security." Advertising claims
like those of the James W. Bassett Company in 2010 have not abated
("Polygraph Testing Services"). The legal system in the past has not
protected employees well against abusive polygraph testing, and the
Polygraph Protection Act allows too many exceptions, particularly
the "reasonable suspicion" feature. Employers bent on using the test
no doubt can develop charges of suspicion against employees

31 The citation ("Alexander") is to another electronic source, this one an e-mail Kessler received from a former employee of a multinational corporation. See page 10 for the full citation of this e-mail.

32 Kessler draws to a close by bringing the topic up to date in light of current law. She treats fairly the positive provisions of the new bill, even though they might challenge her own position. This paragraph expands on point III in Kessler's outline.

33 Note punctuation with ellipsis at the end of a sentence. Three spaced periods indicate an omission at the end of the *Nation's Business* quote. The parenthetical reference here follows the quotation mark after the ellipsis; a sentence period follows the final parenthesis.

34 The opening sentence of the conclusion reestablishes one of the basic themes of the paper—the ongoing debate about polygraph testing. Kessler here states strongly her own opinions, raising again what she sees as the key issues in the dispute—the test's unreliability and its encroachment on civil rights. She provides a powerful quotation from an established Web site (*AntiPolygraph.org*) to debunk lie detection as a science. Her conclusion does not simply restate the essential points of the paper, nor is it a shorter version of the introduction. Rather, Kessler uses the conclusion to reassert her own beliefs sharply and clearly.

they dislike. Additionally, federal, state, and local governments
are exempt from the law, as are several private-sector employers,
including security companies and many drug companies. Ultimately,
the poor accuracy record of the tests in general condemns them, no
matter how much they are restricted. As a result of these weaknesses
in the law and of other major issues, polygraphs should have no
place in any employee judgments.

Notes

■ 35   [1]These physiological changes in the body functions are measured by the use of special apparatus: a rubber tube placed around the chest, a pressurized cuff around one arm, and several sensors taped to the skin (Dunn 85).

[2]Although efforts to detect lies go back to ancient times, the modern history of polygraph testing starts with Cesare Lombroso and his experiments with human heartbeats. After him, Hugo Munsterberg, "Harvard's pioneer in criminal psychology" (Block 132), advanced efforts to develop a reliable lie detector. In 1920, criminologists August Vollmer, John A. Larson, and Leonardo Keller developed a machine that could record "on paper with up-and-down lines a subject's changes in heartbeat, blood pressure, and respiration under steady questioning" (134).

35   Note 1 refers to the superscript[1] on page 1 of Kessler's paper. It adds information that is not essential to the paper but that is nonetheless instrumental in helping readers understand how the polygraph equipment may be used. Kessler does not want to focus on the mechanical features of the polygraph in the text of her paper, which concentrates on the unfairness of using the device.

Indicate the note number as a superscript; indent five spaces and double-space all lines of the note. Place the notes on a separate page headed "Notes," typed one inch from the top and centered. The Notes page appears directly before the Works Cited list. (Your instructor may prefer that you type each footnote at the bottom of the page on which the superscript appears in the text.)

Note 2 refers to the superscript[2] on page 1 of the paper.

■ 36

■ 37

■ 38

■ 39

■ 40

■ 41

■ 42

■ 43

■ 44

Kessler 10

Works Cited

Alder, Ken. *The Lie Detectors: A History of an American Obsession.* New York: Free P, 2007. Print.

Alexander, Arthur. "Re: Polygraph Examinations in Employment." Message to the author. 15 Oct. 2010. E-mail.

AntiPolygraph.org. Antipolygraph.org, 2007. Web. 15 Nov. 2010.

Beach, Bennet H. "Blood, Sweat and Fears." *Time* 8 Sept. 1980: 44. Print.

Block, Eugene B. *Science vs. Crime: The Evolution of the Police Lab.* San Francisco: Cragmont, 1979. Print.

"Dallas Polygraph Services." *DallasPolygraph.com.* Michael D. Park and Associates Polygraph, 2007. Web. 12 Oct. 2010.

Dunn, Donald. "When a Lie Detector Test Is Part of the Job Interview." *Business Week* 27 July 1981: 85–86. Print.

Flaherty, Francis. "Truth Technology." *Progressive* June 1982: 30–35. Print.

Gugas, Chris. *The Silent Witness: A Polygraphist's Casebook.* Englewood Cliffs: Prentice, 1979. Print.

"How to Comply with the Polygraph Law." *Nation's Business* Dec. 1989: 36–37. Print.

"How Does a Lie Detector (Polygraph) Work." *Science. How StuffWorks.com/question123.* How Stuff Works, 01 April 2000. Web. 18 Nov. 2010.

"In Ohio, Anyone May Run Lie Detector." *Dayton Daily News* 31 Mar. 1982: F4. Print.

Inbaw, Fred. "Polygraph Test." *Encyclopedia Americana.* 1993 ed. Print.

Johnston, David. "Seven F.B.I. Employees Fail Polygraph Tests for Security." *New York Times* 4 Apr. 2002, late ed.: A18. Print.

36 The references appear on a separate page headed "Works Cited" and are listed alphabetically by the authors' last names (or, if the work is unsigned, by the first key word in the title). Put the heading "Works Cited" about an inch from the top of the page. Center it. Do not separate entries for books, periodicals, and Web sources.

37 This is an entry for a book with one author. If a reference runs to a second line, indent it five spaces. *P* is an acceptable abbreviation for *Press*.

38 The reference is to an electronic source, an e-mail Kessler received from a retired director of personnel (see pages 6–7 of the paper itself).

39 The reference is to a Web site accessed by the writer through a Google search. AntiPolygraph.org is "dedicated to the abolishment of polygraph testing." The name of the site is italicized. The year 2007 indicates the online publication date; 15 Nov. 2010 is the date Kessler accessed the material online.

40 The reference is to an article in a weekly periodical.

41 The reference is to another electronic source, a Web site called *Dallaspolygraph.com*. Michael D. Park and Associates Polygraph is the site's sponsor. *Dallaspolygraph.com* is a commercial site that strongly supports the use of polygraph testing. Note how Kessler has balanced her electronic sources here. See notes 38 and 39 above.

42 This is another standard entry for a book. *Prentice* is an acceptable abbreviation for Prentice Hall, the publisher.

43 Because this newspaper article is unsigned, Kessler alphabetizes it according to the word *In*, the first word in the title.

44 The entry is standard for a signed article in a daily newspaper. David Johnston is the reporter whose name appears in the byline. The item *A18* means that the article appears in section A, page 18, of the newspaper. The notation *late ed.* after the date indicates the particular edition in which the article appeared. (Different editions of a newspaper often contain different material.) Note the comma before the specified edition.

Kessler 11

"Lie Detectors Raise Personal Rights Issue." *Dayton Daily News*
　　29 Mar. 1982: F6–8. Print.

"Lie Detector Tests Untrustworthy." *USA Today* 20 Feb. 1981:
　　16. Print.

"Polygraph." *Microsoft Encarta Premium 2008*. CD-ROM.
　　Microsoft, 2008.

"Polygraph Testing Services." *Theftstopper.com*. James W.
　　Bassett, 2008. Web. 18 Oct. 2010.

■ 45　"Rights Abuse." Editorial. *Christian Science Monitor* 20 Oct.
　　1999: 10. Print.

Safire, William. "Lying 'Lie Detectors.'" *New York Times* 10 Oct.
　　2002, late ed.: A39. Print.

■ 46　"The Truth about Lie Detectors, Says David Lykken, Is That They
　　Can't Detect a Lie." *People* 11 May 1981: 75+. Print.

■ 47　Ward, William, et al. "Meprobamate Reduces Accuracy of
　　Physiological Detection of Deception." *Science* 3 Apr.
　　1981: 73–74. Print.

"What's It Like to Take a Lie Detector Test?" *Law and Order*
　　[Columbia] 5 July 1981: F7–8. Print.

Wilson, Jim. "Truth, Lies and Polygraphs." *Popular Mechanics*
　　Oct. 2001:42. Print.

45. Kessler indicates that this source is an editorial with the word *Editorial* right after the title of the selection.

46. This article from a weekly magazine appears on interrupted pages; the selection starts on page 75 and continues on pages 76 and 79. The pages on which the selection continues do not appear in the citation.

47. Since there are more than three authors for this magazine article— William Ward, Emily Carota Orne, Mary R. Cook, and Martin T. Orne— the citation names only the first author, followed by the Latin abbreviation *et al.*, meaning "and others." However, you may choose to give all names in full in the order in which they appear. Invert the first and last names of only the first author, placing the last name first. For all other authors in a multiple author citation, place the first name before the last name.

For support in meeting this chapter's objectives, follow this path in MyCompLab: Resources ⇒ **Research** ⇒ **The Research Assignment.** Review the Instruction and Multimedia resources about **integrating sources,** then complete the Exercises and click on Gradebook to measure your progress.

PART FIVE

Style

CHAPTER 22

Proper Words in Proper Places

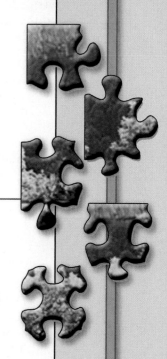

Jonathan Swift, the author of *Gulliver's Travels*, once defined good style as "proper words in proper places." Gustave Flaubert, the great French novelist, felt that the writer's craft was embodied in the quest for *le seul mot juste*, "the single right word." Nearly all writers can learn to hit the right word simply by becoming more alert to the possibilities of language and the need for thoughtful revision.

In this chapter you will

- identify denotation and connotation in words
- review the differences between abstract writing and concrete writing
- analyze the use of specific details
- write specific words and phrases in place of abstractions
- explore the use of comparisons to improve your writing

Denotation and Connotation

Traditionally, the most logical way to begin thinking about right and wrong words is through the distinction between denotation and connotation:

- The **denotation** of a word is its explicit, surface meaning, its bare "dictionary meaning."
- The **connotation** of a word is its implicit meaning, the meaning derived from the emotions associated with the word in people's minds.

Words like *Las Vegas* or *Ireland*, for example, simply denote a particular city or country—a mere geographical location—but for many people, they also have an emotional significance that has nothing to do with geography. The connotative meanings of a word do not always appear in a dictionary, but they are as vital a part of the word's full meaning as are denotations.

The Importance of Connotation

Let's take a simple example. Suppose you are the head of a successful advertising agency, and a major motor corporation wants you to handle the campaign

513

introducing a new car. Would you recommend calling the car the Giraffe, the Porcupine, or the Hawk?

We all probably agree that among Giraffe, Porcupine, and Hawk, the last name is the only reasonable choice for the new car. For most people, the idea of a hawk carries with it connotations of power, speed, and perhaps freedom and beauty. These are concepts that motivate people who buy cars, no matter how loudly they may claim that their sole interests are economy and "just transportation." Consider the animal names in use for car models and notice how many connote power, speed, or both: Bronco, Mustang, Jaguar, Rabbit, Thunderbird, Firebird, Ram. The name Hawk, then, has certain connotations that might be helpful in marketing the car.

Word Sensitivity

Developing a sensitivity to the connotations of words, then, is an invaluable asset for all writers. The right word will be the one with the right connotations—the connotations that most precisely reflect the writer's intended meaning and produce the desired reaction from the writer's audience. Was the person who had too much to drink *inebriated, intoxicated, drunk, looped, smashed, tipsy, high, crocked, pickled, loaded,* or *blotto*? Was the overweight person *plump, fat, pudgy, obese, chubby, portly, chunky, corpulent, stout,* or *stocky*? Few greater compliments can be paid to writers than to say that they have a knack for choosing the right words. That knack does not come simply from having a large vocabulary. Rather, it comes mainly from thinking about the fine distinctions in connotation that separate words with similar denotation.

EXERCISE

Rearrange each group of words by connotation, from the least favorable term to the most favorable. In many cases, opinions will differ; there are few purely right and purely wrong answers.

1. unromantic, realistic, pragmatic, hardheaded
2. thin, skinny, slender, bony, emaciated
3. weep, cry, blubber, bawl
4. squabble, disagreement, quarrel, brawl
5. knowledgeable, bright, shrewd, smart, brainy
6. pretty, gorgeous, lovely, stunning, beautiful
7. miserable, blue, depressed, sad, unhappy
8. look, ogle, stare, glower, gaze
9. strut, swagger, stride, pace
10. gripe, complain, squawk, bellyache

EXERCISE   *All the words in parentheses make sense in the sentences that follow. How does the meaning of the sentence change, depending on which word you use?*

1. The minister strikes me as (an idealist, a dreamer).
2. The criticisms of the new health care proposal are mostly (uninformed, foolish, idiotic).
3. We have (loud, raucous, noisy) neighbors.
4. The salesperson at the bookstore seemed (reserved, aloof).
5. The astronauts' mission was (challenging, laborious).
6. I was (apprehensive, terrified) about beginning a new career.
7. My grandfather says that as a young man he (loved, adored) Marilyn Monroe.
8. He was as smart as (a fox, a trained dog in a circus, Albert Einstein).
9. Congresswoman Saunders is a gifted (speaker, talker, orator).
10. Sometimes (solitude, loneliness, isolation) can be good for the soul.

Abstract Writing and Concrete Writing

Although the distinction between denotation and connotation is valuable to writers, it is sometimes easier to see the immediate, practical consequences of a writer's quest for the right word in the distinction between abstract writing and concrete writing:

■ **Abstract writing** is writing that lacks specific details and is filled with vague, indefinite words and broad, general statements.
■ **Concrete writing** is characterized by specific details and specific language.

Every piece of writing needs generalizations, of course, and vague words such as *nice* and *interesting* can be useful. But writing that is dominated by such words is abstract writing, and abstract writing is the main cause of bored readers. It is often a reflection of lazy or careless thinking. It can interfere with full communication of meaning. It prevents many students from developing their writing adequately.

Consider the following examples of abstract and concrete writing.

ABSTRACT $\longrightarrow$	CONCRETE
Too much poverty exists in this country.	I see one-third of a nation ill-housed, ill-clad, ill-nourished.
Mr. Jones is a tough grader.	Mr. Jones flunked 75 percent of his class and gave no higher than a C to the students who passed.

(continued)

ABSTRACT ⟶	CONCRETE
Computers now execute many of the tasks that only humans could do many years ago.	Today's technology allows computers to perform tasks like processing banking transactions, obtaining research from thousands of sources, and sending information overseas.
The story is quite amusing in places, but basically is very serious.	Underneath the slapstick humor, the story presents a bitter attack on materialism and snobbishness.
Religious faith is important, but practical considerations are also important.	Trust in God, and keep your powder dry.

Nothing is technically wrong with all these examples of abstract writing, but we need only compare them to the rewritten concrete versions to see their basic inadequacy. They convey less information. They are less interesting. They have less impact.

Using Specific Details

The use of specific details is the most direct way to avoid abstract writing. Unfortunately, much of the material we read every day is abstract. The sports columnist writes, "The team should do better this year," and leaves it at that, instead of adding, "It should finish in third or fourth place and even has a fighting chance for the pennant." The teacher writes an angry letter saying, "This school ignores all vital needs of the faculty," and sounds like just another crank unless the letter goes on and points to *specific* needs that have in fact been ignored.

Student writing—from essay exams to themes in composition courses—would improve considerably if students paid more attention to eliminating excessive abstractions and adding specific details. Our use of language, not to mention our level of thought, would probably improve a hundredfold if we established an informal rule:

Never make an unsupported general statement, a general statement not backed up by specific details.

This rule sounds easy enough, but it means what it says. It means a writer should never try to get by with sentences such as, "The day was too hot"; "The hero of the story was very ambitious"; "The administration is corrupt";

"The Industrial Revolution brought about many changes." These sentences are neither ungrammatical nor necessarily incorrect in what they say, but without specific details they are worthless. "The day was too hot" is uninteresting and unpersuasive. *Back it up.* The reader should know that the temperature was 93 degrees, that Bill's sweaty glasses kept slipping off his nose, that a cocker spaniel who had managed to find a spot of shade was too exhausted and miserable to bother brushing away the flies. Whatever the piece of writing— a letter of application for a job, an analysis of a short story, a final exam in history—specific details give the writing life and conviction that abstractions alone can never achieve.

Within reason, *the more specific the better.* As long as the detail is relevant— as long, that is, as it supports the generalization and is not instantly obvious as too trivial for consideration—the writer is unlikely to go wrong by being too specific. On a history exam, a student may generalize, "In the Revolutionary War, the Americans had many difficulties." As specific support for that statement, the student may go on to write, "The number of Tories was quite large." But better in all respects would be, "Tories numbered as much as 30 percent of the population." Eventually, it is true, one can defeat one's purpose; it would be a mistake to give the reader the names and addresses of all the Tories during the Revolutionary War. The writing would then become so overwhelmed by specifics that the major point would be lost.

To summarize: support all your generalizations with relevant, specific details. Remember that, within reason, the more specific the details, the better the writing.

Abstract (weak)

The telephone is a great scientific achievement, but it can also be a great inconvenience. Who could begin to count the number of times that phone calls have come from unwelcome people or on unwelcome occasions? Telephones make me nervous.

More specific (better)

The telephone is a great scientific achievement, but it can also be a great pain. I get calls from bill collectors, hurt relatives, salespeople, charities, and angry neighbors. The calls always seem to come at the worst times, too. They've interrupted my meals, my baths, my parties, my sleep. I couldn't get along without telephones, but sometimes they make me a nervous wreck.

Still more specific (much better)

The telephone is a great scientific achievement, but it can also be a great big headache. More often than not, that cheery ringing in my ears brings messages from the Ace Bill Collecting Agency, my mother (who is feeling snubbed for the fourth time that week), salespersons of encyclopedias and magazines, solicitors for the Police Officers' Ball and Disease of the Month Foundation, and neighbors complaining about my dog. That's not to mention frequent wrong numbers—usually for someone named "Arnie." The calls always seem to come at the worst times, too. They've interrupted steak dinners, hot tubs, Friday night parties, and Saturday morning sleep-ins. There's no escape. Sometimes I wonder if there are any telephones in padded cells.

EXERCISE   Invent two or three specific details to back up each of the following generalizations. Use your imagination. Remember, the more specific the better. Don't settle for a detail like "He reads many books" to support the statement "My teacher is very intellectual."

1. Some television commercials are extremely entertaining.
2. Some television commercials are extremely irritating.
3. Most people are foolish about their own health.
4. After enough time goes by, anything can become a bore.
5. Thundershowers are dangerous.
6. It's hard to keep up with Gretchen.
7. When it comes to driving, slowpokes are as bad as speed demons.
8. Iraqis are trying to build a democracy in their country.
9. A photograph can capture the emotions of a moment.
10. Going on a picnic is asking for trouble.

Using Specific Words and Phrases

For most writers, the biggest challenge is learning to recognize when a particular word or phrase is not specific enough, and why. Often the first word that pops into our heads doesn't really work as effectively as it should. "He smiled," for example, may seem the natural way to describe a common facial expression. But have we truly conveyed the exact expression we are trying to write about? Wouldn't our readers get a clearer picture of the face we have in mind if we tried to pin down the word that best describes *this* smile: He grinned? Smirked? Sneered? Leered? Simpered? Turned up the corners of his mouth? Smiled half-heartedly? Smiled broadly? Once we develop the habit of checking our original word choices carefully, making sure we've come as close to our precise meaning as possible, our style will become at once more specific and more colorful. Revision, as you have seen throughout this book, then, is not an inconvenience; it's an essential tool of the trade.

Nobody, it is true, will ever be ridiculed or exposed to public disgrace for writing, "She went to the door." But surely our readers deserve to be told, and surely we should want them to know, if she ran or walked or strolled or strutted or shuffled or limped or stumbled or sauntered or trotted or tiptoed to that door. Only one abstract word needs to be changed here, but the person who habitually recognizes that abstract word, refuses to let it pass, and selects a specific word to replace it is no longer just someone who writes, but a *writer*.

Using specific words is a different matter from supporting generalizations with details, though specific words may sometimes help give us a more detailed picture. Selecting specific words is primarily a means of expression, a way of putting things, a style. "He wore a hat" becomes, "His top hat tilted jauntily over one eyebrow." We are not backing up a previous statement about someone's clothing preferences here—we are making a statement that has a specific meaning in and of itself. Together, specific details and specific words are the primary means of eliminating boring and dreary abstractions from our writing.

EXERCISE

In the sentences that follow, the italicized words or phrases are abstract and dull. Find a specific word or short phrase that can substitute for the abstract one without changing the meaning of the sentence.

1. The *car moved slowly* down the road.
2. The *pet* was *poorly trained*.
3. My aunt *made a nice profit* on *that investment*.
4. The guest brought a *small gift* for the party's *host*.
5. My parents gave me a *nice watch* for the *great event*.
6. The articles in that *publication* discussed very *timely issues*.
7. Unless you make *payment promptly*, we will take *legal action*.
8. The *school official* commented that *technology* is a valuable tool in education.
9. *Traveling by air* makes me *slightly uncomfortable*.
10. I planted some *beautiful flowers outside*.

Using Comparisons

Another way of avoiding abstract writing and increasing the liveliness of concrete writing is to use effective figures of speech, particularly **comparisons** (see pages 392–393 for a discussion of metaphors and similes). Sometimes a writer may have a hard time coming up with a forceful substitute for a humdrum expression like "it was very easy." There are plenty of synonyms for "very easy," of course, but the writer's best bet might be a comparison: "It was as easy as (*or* It was so easy it was like) drinking a second glass of beer," or like "splattering toothpaste on the bathroom mirror," or like "forgetting the car keys." Good comparisons are attention-getters. They can add a helpful spark to otherwise pedestrian writing.

Two cautions are in order. First, use comparisons in moderation. The more comparisons a piece of writing contains, the less impact each one is likely to have. Second, and more important, avoid the routine, trite comparisons that fill our language. Don't write "It was as easy as pie" or "It was as easy as taking candy from a baby." Try to be fresh and different. Rather than be trite, avoid comparisons altogether.

Make sure, too, that you phrase your comparisons correctly, whether you are using them for lively specific detail or as a simple means of making a point—"Alice is smarter than Sally," for example. But beware of illogical sentences like those that follow.

INCORRECT $\longrightarrow$	IMPROVED
Some of these horror stories are very similar to Edgar Allan Poe. [Intending to compare the horror stories of one author to the horror stories of another author, the writer instead compares the horror stories of one author to another author.]	Some of these horror stories are very similar to Edgar Allan Poe's. *or* Some of these horror stories are very similar to those of Edgar Allan Poe.
His appetite was as huge as a pig.	His appetite was a huge as a pig's. *or* His appetite was as huge as that of a pig. *or* His appetite was as huge as a pig's appetite.
The new supermarket's prices are higher than the competition.	The new supermarket's prices are higher than the competition's. *or* The new supermarket's prices are higher than those of the competition.

Another kind of illogical comparison unintentionally excludes an item of comparison from the group that it belongs to through the omission of the word *other*.

INCORRECT	IMPROVED
Lincoln had more detailed knowledge of the Bible than any American president.	Lincoln had more detailed knowledge of the Bible than any other American president.
My high school paid less attention to sports than any school in the city.	My high school paid less attention to sports than any other school in the city.

Sometimes, too, improper phrasing can result in confusion. What did the writers of these sentences want to say?

I like him more than you.	Did the writer mean "I like him more than you like him" or "I like him more than I like you"?
Hemingway is more indebted to Mark Twain than anyone else.	Did the writer mean "Hemingway is more indebted to Mark Twain than to anyone else" or "Hemingway is more indebted to Mark Twain than anyone else is"?

EXERCISE Make up *two* logical phrases to complete each of the following comparisons. Be prepared to tell which of your phrases is better and why.

1. I have no more chance of passing this course than . . .
2. My brother is more dependable than . . .
3. The congressman's explanation was as plausible as . . .
4. If you'd buy an insurance policy from him, you're the kind of person who . . .
5. I haven't had a more hectic day since . . .
6. The National Parks are as majestic as . . .
7. The police officers chased the speeding car like . . .
8. The burning sun made my skin feel like . . .
9. Waiting in line is more boring than . . .
10. I trust her so much that I would . . .

   Rephrase the following sentences where necessary.

1. The judge was less harsh on me than my friend.
2. Eminem's music was more relevant to our lives than Elvis Presley.
3. Legalized abortions arouse stronger emotions than any controversial issue.
4. The way he talks is like my teacher.
5. I prefer 7-Up commercials to Coke.
6. Our gross national product is substantially larger than Germany.
7. *South Pacific* has a better score than any Broadway musical.
8. The incumbent's campaign is more radical than her opponent.
9. This soap opera has more agony per character than any show on television.
10. The fans swarmed around the rock star like bees to honey.
11. The administration's proposal for reducing the deficit is less drastic than the opposition.
12. Andrew, I love you more than any man.
13. Ricardo liked the *paella* more than his brother.
14. The leopard is more beautiful and more powerful than any animal.
15. My medical plan is better than my sister's.

CHAPTER **23**

Effective Sentences

The stylistic considerations we have discussed so far—denotation and connotation, specific details, specific language—require decisions about individual words. In this chapter we consider elements of style more closely related to entire sentences and groups of sentences than to single words.

Wordiness and Economy

Many human individuals use more words in their sentences than are absolutely necessary and essential to express the thoughts and ideas that they (the human individuals) are attempting to communicate. They repeat the same thing constantly and say the same thing over and over again. Sometimes instead of actually repeating themselves they merely substitute various and sundry long phrases for a simple word due to the fact that it is their opinion that readers will be impressed by this writing method of procedure. But in the modern contemporary world of today, good writing should never be wordy. It should be economical—that is, it should say what it has to say, and then stop, cease, and desist.

In case you haven't noticed, the sentences you just read violate all of their own good advice. They contain numerous examples of wordiness: "human individuals" instead of "people," "thoughts and ideas" instead of "thoughts" *or* "ideas," "due to the fact that" instead of "because," "it is their opinion" instead of "they think." We could cut these sentences to half their length without losing anything but a mass of nonfunctioning words:

> Many people use more words than are necessary to express their thoughts. They repeat the same things constantly or substitute long phrases for a simple word because they want to impress their readers. But good writing should never be wordy: it should say what it has to say, and then stop.

Wordiness is a major writing problem. It is hard to avoid because it can turn up for any number of reasons, and writers usually don't realize that they are

In this chapter you will

- examine the differences between wordiness and economy in writing

- analyze verbs in the active and passive voice

- examine and correct faulty parallelism

- examine and correct faulty subordination and sentence combining

- use sentence variety to avoid monotony in your writing

being wordy. Nobody wants to be a windbag, yet unneeded words sneak into nearly everyone's writing.

Before discussing the different kinds of wordiness, we should clear up one point: wordiness results from using words that don't do anything—it has no direct connection to the number of words. A poor writer can produce a wordy paragraph on the meaning of freedom; a good writer can produce a whole book on the same subject that is not wordy. If the words contribute to the effect the writer wants, if eliminating any of them would sacrifice something valuable, then the writer is *not* being wordy. Only when words can be eliminated without any harm being done do we find real wordiness.

There are four major sources of wordiness: deadwood, pointless repetition of meaning, inadequate clause cutting, and delay of subject.

Cutting Deadwood

Some words are like dead wood on a tree or bush—unless you remove them, they sap the strength of the healthy words around them. Moreover, an attentive writer can remove **deadwood** with little or no tampering with the rest of the sentence, as in the examples that follow.

DEADWOOD ⟶	IMPROVED
Pollution conditions that exist in our cities is disgraceful.	Pollution in our cities is disgraceful.
The building has a height of 934 feet.	The building rises 934 feet.
She was in a depressed state of mind.	She was depressed.
In this day and age we live in, people seem totally apathetic about everything.	People today seem totally apathetic.
The hero of the story was an individual in the high-income bracket.	The hero of the story was wealthy.
The validity of such statements should not be adhered to.	Such statements are invalid.
He spoke to her in a harsh manner.	He spoke to her harshly.
Because of the fact that my teacher disliked me, he gave me a bad grade.	Because my teacher disliked me, he gave me a bad grade.
Sometimes the moral of a story is a very important factor.	Sometimes the moral of a story is very important.

Deadwood infiltrates nearly everyone's first draft, but there is no room for these tiresome words-without-purpose in a finished composition. As a general rule, it is safe to assume that if words can be removed without harming anything—as in the preceding examples—they should be removed.

Avoiding Pointless Repetition of Meaning

Pointless repetition of meaning is a special kind of deadwood. Aside from adding useless words, such repetition reflects writers' lack of confidence in themselves—their fear that their point will not be clear unless they make it twice. Unfortunately, this overemphasis usually suggests sloppy thinking to the reader, rather than a desire for accuracy.

POINTLESS REPETITION	IMPROVED
Our streams are filthy and dirty.	Our streams are filthy.
This approach could end in a catastrophic conclusion.	This approach could end catastrophically.
The author gives examples of different and varied criticisms of the novel.	The author gives examples of different criticisms of the novel.
Some early critics of Jonathan Swift called him an insane madman suffering from the symptoms of mental disease.	Some early critics of Jonathan Swift called him insane.
There is no question about the worth and value of an education.	There is no question about the value of an education.
He has no emotional feelings.	He has no feelings.
Each and every person ought to read a newspaper.	Everyone ought to read a newspaper.

EXERCISE   Point out any instances of deadwood and pointless repetition in the following sentences.

1. At this point in time, we have no travel plans.
2. In my opinion, I think depression is a terrible kind of illness.
3. We have ignored and neglected the basic fundamental essentials for too long a period of time.
4. Men and women of both sexes must join the combat to fight for a better world.
5. Rebecca Lobo is an individual who excels in the area of basketball.
6. Sleepy and tired, he looked drained and exhausted.

7. A healthful lifestyle can help prevent many different kinds of diseases and illnesses.
8. As far as jewelry is concerned, my favorite jewelry is a simple string of pearls.
9. With bright, vivid colors and hues, Georgia O'Keeffe made American modern painting a beautiful kind of art.
10. I pledge to oppose the forces of godless atheism and disloyal treason.

Cutting Wordy Clauses

One of the most effective ways of reducing wordiness is to cut a cumbersome clause into a shorter phrase or, if possible, a single word. This **clause cutting** can result in a tighter, more economical structure, with the phrase or word more firmly incorporated into the sentence than the original clause ever was.

WORDY CLAUSE ⟶	IMPROVED
The woman who had red hair was afraid.	The red-haired woman was afraid.
Some of the students who were more enthusiastic wrote an extra paper.	Some of the more enthusiastic students wrote an extra paper.
The story was very exciting. It was all about ghosts.	The ghost story was very exciting.
Alexander the Great was a man who tried to conquer the world.	Alexander the Great tried to conquer the world.
The applause, which sounded like a thunderclap, shook the auditorium.	The applause shook the auditorium like a thunderclap.
Passionate love is a feeling that has inspired many great writers and artists.	Passionate love has inspired many great writers and artists.

Avoiding Delay of Subject

The phrases *there is*, *there has*, *it is*, and *it has*—in all tenses—are frequent causes of wordiness. Nothing is wrong with these phrases in themselves; they are necessary parts of the language, and some thoughts might be inexpressible without them. Too often, however, they are used carelessly and delay a sentence or clause from getting down to business. In the following examples, the original sentences begin with words that have no more purpose than the throat-clearing noises made by a speaker before a talk. The revised sentences begin with important words, words that communicate the central concern of each sentence.

WORDY DELAY ⟶	IMPROVED
There are too many people who care only for themselves.	Too many people care only for themselves.
It has often been commented on by great philosophers that philosophy solves nothing.	Great philosophers have often commented that philosophy solves nothing.
There have been a number of conflicting studies made of urban problems.	A number of conflicting studies have been made of urban problems.
It was on December 7, 1941, that the Japanese attacked the U.S. fleet at Pearl Harbor.	On December 7, 1941, the Japanese attacked the U.S. fleet at Pearl Harbor.

EXERCISE   Rewrite these sentences to make them more economical, cutting clauses and eliminating wordy delay of subject wherever possible.

1. The man who lives next door to me walks his two poodles every morning that it is cool and sunny.
2. There have been many complicated plans that have been proposed to reduce the number of nuclear weapons that are stationed in Europe.
3. Many people who frequently travel by plane may experience some delays, which are caused by new airport security measures recently put in place.
4. The idea of a guaranteed annual wage is a notion that conflicts with many traditional middle-class values.
5. Another time, when he was shown the list of the names of the officers who had been appointed to serve under him at the Battle of Waterloo, the Duke commented, "I don't know if they will frighten the French, but, by Gad, they terrify me!"
6. People who do not know any better unthinkingly use chemicals that can be harmful to health on their backyard flowers and vegetables.
7. There has been much disagreement among people who produce television programs about giving shows ratings to tell audiences which are programs that contain violence and explicit subject matter.
8. People who play practical jokes are people who are basically insecure.
9. Cars that are made in Germany do not have the reputation for good workmanship that they used to have.
10. It was an agonizingly difficult decision to make.

Passive and Active Verbs

In most English sentences, the subject performs an action.

> John likes this poem.
> The critic saw the movie.
> The senator is going to vote for the bill.

The verb in such sentences is said to be in the **active voice**. The active voice is direct, clear, and concise; in most sentences, it is what we expect.

Too often, however, instead of using the active voice, writers substitute the more stilted **passive voice**. A verb in the passive voice combines a form of *to be* with the past participle of the verb: *is given, has been delivered, was mailed*. Thus, instead of *acting*, the subject of the sentence is *acted upon*.

> This poem is liked by John.
> The movie was seen by the critic.
> The bill is going to be voted for by the senator.

Compared to the active voice, the passive is generally awkward, exceedingly formal, and wordy. It is better to write "This paper will analyze the story" than "The story will be analyzed in this paper." It is better to write "My sociology teacher offered some challenging insights into contemporary problems" than "Some challenging insights into contemporary problems were offered by my sociology teacher."

On occasion, the passive voice doesn't sound bad, of course. Such occasions may arise when the actor is unknown, insignificant, or nonexistent, or when a deliberately impersonal tone is required. Don't be afraid of the passive when it seems normal and unforced—as in the last part of the preceding sentence—but always be alert to its dangers. When you use the passive voice, you should always have a reason for choosing it over the active voice.

Here are a few examples of perfectly acceptable passives:

> The game was delayed because of rain.
> The eighteenth century has been called the Age of Enlightenment.
> Your prompt attention to this request for payment will be appreciated.

EXERCISE   Change the passive voice to the active voice wherever appropriate in the following sentences.

1. Fewer novels are being read by teenagers these days.
2. At the corner restaurant, all of the tacos are freshly made each day.
3. The director was convicted of embezzling funds and using the money for herself.
4. The doctor was advised to get malpractice insurance by his lawyer.
5. The victim was pronounced dead on arrival by the coroner.

6. The causes of greenhouse emissions are being studied by researchers at major universities.
7. Your child should be hugged and kissed by you frequently.
8. Legislation to raise taxes is being considered in a joint meeting of the House and Senate.
9. Two suspects were interrogated by Officer Chan.
10. The course syllabus was handed out by Professor Sharp and was read by all of the students.

Faulty Parallelism

What Is Parallelism?

Essentially, **parallelism** means expressing ideas and facts of equal (or coordinate or "parallel") importance in the same grammatical form. We do it all the time, almost unconsciously.

The store was filled with *chairs, tables, sofas,* and *lamps*.	(a group of four nouns)
He *came home, ate dinner*, and *went to bed*.	(three verb phrases)
You can get there by *car, bus,* or *plane*.	(three nouns)
I thought the climactic episode in the story was *shocking, offbeat*, and *amusing*.	(three adjectives)

Parallel grammatical structure reinforces a writer's thoughts by stressing the parallel importance of the various sentence elements, and so makes life easier for the reader. Many of the most famous phrases in our language draw strength in part from effective use of parallelism:

. . . *life, liberty*, and the *pursuit* of happiness.	(group of three nouns)
. . . *of the people, by the people*, and *for the people*.	(three prepositional phrases)
Love me or *leave me*.	(two imperatives)
Early *to bed* and early *to rise*/Makes a man *healthy*, and *wealthy*, and *wise*.	(two infinitives/three adjectives)
I come *to bury Caesar*, not *to praise him*.	(two infinitives with objects)
I came, I saw, I conquered.	(three independent clauses)
Better be *safe* than *sorry*.	(two adjectives)

Avoiding Faulty Parallelism

Now notice how faulty parallelism or lack of parallelism can sabotage a sentence.

INCORRECT	⟶	CORRECT

INCORRECT	CORRECT
You can get there by *car*, *bus*, or *fly*. (noun, noun, verb)	You can get there by *car*, *bus*, or *plane*. (noun, noun, noun)
I thought the climactic episode in the story was *shocking*, *offbeat*, and *I found it very amusing*. (adjective, adjective, independent clause)	I thought the climactic episode in the story was *shocking*, *offbeat*, and very *amusing*. (adjective, adjective, adjective)
She *liked* people and *was liked* by people. (active voice, passive voice)	She *liked* people and people *liked* her. (active voice, active voice)
The teacher told us *to work* fast and *that we should write on only one side of the paper*. (infinitive, clause)	The teacher told us *to work* fast and *to write* on only one side of the paper. (infinitive, infinitive)

Descriptive words added to some of the parallel elements do not break the basic parallelism and can be valuable in avoiding monotony.

Judith had *brains*, *talent*, and an extremely charming *personality*.	(still parallel: a group of three nouns, even though one is modified by an adjective, and the adjective is modified by an adverb)
The man owned a *mansion* and a fine *collection* of modern etchings.	(still parallel: two nouns, even though one of them is modified by an adjective and followed by a prepositional phrase)
The baby has now learned how to *whimper*, *shriek*, *yell* loudly, and *cry* its head off.	(still parallel: four infinitives, even though one is modified by an adverb and one is followed by an object)

Parallelism, then, is an indispensable aid to style and meaning, but keep in mind that its value is limited to cases in which the various elements are of equal importance. If we try to parallel unequal elements, we can wind up with startling calamities, unless we are being intentionally humorous:

She had wealth, vitality, sophistication, and a short nose.
My friend John is a revolutionary activist and a former Cub Scout.
We must all work together to eliminate war, disease, hunger, and dirty movies.

EXERCISE   Which of the following sentences use faulty parallelism? Which use parallelism correctly? Which use inappropriate parallelism? Make corrections in the sentences that need them.

1. She enjoys running, mountain climbing, and the movies.
2. Some day I will go bungee jumping, parasailing, and buy a boat.
3. The principal said the main issues were discipline, academic achievement, and good attendance at the pep rally.
4. Percy Bysshe Shelley wrote some of the greatest poems in the English language, lived a spectacularly scandalous private life, and had a weird middle name.
5. Steven Yip's résumé shows that he is hardworking, responsible, and an experienced manager.
6. Alfred Hitchcock had a nearly unbroken record of directing films that were suspenseful, original, and great successes.
7. Magazines, newspapers, and reading books are some possible pastimes when you have to wait to see the doctor.
8. Portuguese *Fado* music touches the heart, stirs the mind, and captures the trials of love.
9. My sister's doctor told her to eat a lot of leafy vegetables, fruits, and not to smoke.
10. Faith, hope, and charity are three classic virtues.

Faulty Subordination and Sentence Combining

Which of the following observations on that great new epic movie, *The Return of the Hideous Vampire*, is likely to be most significant?

It was produced by Paramount.
It is one of the best horror movies of the last ten years.
It was filmed in Technicolor.

Which of these facts about Earnest N. Dogood deserves the most emphasis?

He is a Republican.
He has announced his candidacy for president of the United States.
He is a senator.

The answers are obvious; in both cases, the second item is the one you should have chosen. Neither set of statements provides parallel thoughts—because ideas and facts are not all created equal. Treating each set of items as parallel in a sentence, giving equal weight to each fact, would create a monotonous stream of unfiltered data.

A skillful writer will **subordinate** some of those facts, arranging the sentence or paragraph so that some parts are clearly secondary to others. This process is sometimes called **sentence combining**.

Look again at the beginning of this section on subordination above. We have three pieces of information about a movie. The writer with no sense of subordination merely smacks down each point as it comes to mind, without attempting to differentiate between major and minor items, giving each item a sentence to itself.

The Return of the Hideous Vampire was produced by Paramount. It is one of the best horror movies of the last ten years. It was filmed in Technicolor.

By contrast, with proper subordination the writer collects the three related observations, reserves the independent clause for the most important one, and tucks away the rest in a less conspicuous place.

The Return of the Hideous Vampire, a Technicolor film produced by Paramount, is one of the best horror movies of the last ten years.

We can see the same principle at work with the sentences about Earnest N. Dogood that also begin this section.

UNSUBORDINATED	→	SUBORDINATED
Earnest N. Dogood is a Republican. He has announced his candidacy for president of the United States. He is a senator.		Senator Earnest N. Dogood, a Republican, has announced his candidacy for president of the United States.

Remember that related ideas can often be combined in a way that shows their relations more clearly. Remember, too, that an independent clause, whether it stands alone as a single sentence or is incorporated into a complex sentence, is a loud cry for attention and should generally be saved for matters of importance.

Here are a few examples of how subordination can improve writing:

UNSUBORDINATED	→	SUBORDINATED
Jane is a wonderful person. She is very shy. She is extremely kind to everybody.		Although very shy, Jane is a wonderful person who is extremely kind to everybody.
This play explores the fate of love in a mechanized society. It is highly symbolic, and it has two acts.		This highly symbolic play of two acts explores the fate of love in a mechanized society.
Professor Jones is terribly sarcastic. He is also a tough grader. It is true that he knows his subject. Most students dislike him, however.		Despite Professor Jones' knowledge of his subject, most students dislike him because of his terrible sarcasm and tough grading.

EXERCISE Rewrite the following sentences, making effective use of subordination.

1. Some scientists are skeptical about life on other planets. Astronomers calculate that there are many Earth-like planets. Some evidence exists that microbes once survived on Mars.
2. The nuclear age is in its seventh decade. We should reevaluate atomic energy. People are very emotional about it.
3. Bicycle riding is an exhilarating and challenging sport. It is also great exercise. It tones muscles. It builds stamina.
4. It was sad to hear him say such harsh things about poor people. He had once been poor himself.
5. Good writing does not happen by accident. Inexperienced writers believe in inspiration. Professionals know that good writing requires hard work.
6. Everything I like to eat is fattening. Everything I like to eat is also unhealthy. I know I should eat more salads and fresh vegetables. I hate them, however. I don't think I will ever be able to change.
7. "Ping-Pong" is a childish name for a real sport. It shows that most Americans look down on it. The grown-up name is "table tennis." It is a sport that is taken seriously almost everywhere else in the world, and it is played with great skill and ferocity.
8. My mother is a bundle of nerves. My mother is afraid of dark rooms. She also fears insects. Some of her other fears are directed toward heights, dogs, door-to-door salespeople, and doctors.
9. Most Texans know what to do in case of a tornado. They have endured more tornadoes in the last forty years than any other state.
10. Sara just got a golden Labrador retriever. He is the color of honey. He is just ten weeks old. He is not yet trained. Sara thinks he knows his name already since he runs to her when she calls, "Tyler!"

Sentence Monotony and Variety

Readers frequently find themselves struggling to concentrate on a string of sentences even though nothing obvious seems to be wrong. Sentence by sentence, in fact, the author may be writing perfectly well. Put the sentences together, though, and monotony sets in. The monotony can usually be attributed either to a series of sentences that are all, or nearly all, of the same *length* or the same *structure*.

Varying Sentence Length

Sentences come short, medium, and long—and the simple principle for effective writing is to try for variety. Don't take this principle more rigidly than it's intended. Don't assume, for instance, that every single short sentence must be followed by a long one, and vice versa. A string of short or long sentences can sometimes be effective, providing that it is eventually followed by a sentence that varies the pattern. Common sense and alertness will tell you when variety is needed. Just remember that too many sentences of the same length bunched together can create a monotonous style and a restless reader.

MONOTONOUS ⟶	**IMPROVED**
He told us the car got good mileage. He said the tires were excellent. The engine was supposed to be quiet. The transmission was supposed to be smooth. He stressed that the brake linings still had plenty of wear. Everything he said was a lie.	He told us the car got good mileage and that it had excellent tires, a quiet engine, a smooth transmission, and sound brake linings. In other words, he lied.
I thought the course was going to be easy, but I was wrong, because after a two-week sickness early in the term I could never find the time to catch up with the assignments, and I kept getting poor grades. I wish I had had the foresight to see what was coming and had taken the initiative either to drop the course or to ask the teacher for an incomplete, but pride or vanity kept me plugging away, and nothing did any good.	I thought the course was going to be easy, but I was wrong. After a two-week sickness early in the term, I could never find the time to catch up with the assignments, and I kept getting poor grades. Why didn't I drop? Why didn't I ask for an incomplete? If I'd known for sure what was coming, I probably would have done one or the other. Pride or vanity kept me plugging away, however, and nothing did any good.

Varying Sentence Structure

Regardless of sentence length, a group of sentences can become monotonous if each sentence uses the same basic structure. All the sentences may begin with a present participle (*-ing* endings), for example, or the first word of each sentence may always be the subject of the sentence, or the first word may never be the subject. Perhaps every sentence turns out to be a compound sentence (two or more independent clauses) or a complex sentence (one independent clause and one or more dependent clauses).

Now forget about the grammatical terms. Remember only that there are many different ways of structuring a sentence, and wise writers never limit themselves to one method. Variety is again the key.

MONOTONOUS ⟶	IMPROVED
Entering the personnel manager's office, Bill wanted to make a good impression. Smiling, he shook hands. Sitting down, he tried not to fidget. Answering the questions politely, he kept his voice low and forced himself not to say "uh." Being desperate for a job, he had to be at his best. Wondering if his desperation showed, he decided to risk a little joke.	Entering the personnel manager's office, Bill wanted to make a good impression. He smiled, shook hands, and tried not to fidget when he sat down. He answered questions politely, keeping his voice low and forcing himself not to say "uh." Bill was desperate for a job. He had to be at his best. Wondering if his desperation showed, he decided to risk a little joke.
Red wine goes best with meat, and white wine goes best with fish. Red wine should be served at room temperature, and white wine should be chilled. Red wine should usually be opened about a half hour before serving, and the accumulated gases should be allowed to escape from the bottle. These rules are not meaningless customs, but they are proven by centuries of experience, and they improve the taste of the food as well as the wine.	Red wine goes best with meat, and white wine goes best with fish. Unlike white wine, which should be served chilled, red wine should be served at room temperature. Red wine also benefits from being opened about a half hour before serving to allow the accumulated gases to escape from the bottle. Proven by experience, these rules improve the taste of the food as well as the wine. They are not meaningless customs.

EXERCISE

The following groups of sentences are monotonous. Rewrite them to add greater variety in sentence length and structure.

1. Tired and bored, I gazed vacantly out the window. Energetic and powerful, a robin dug for worms. Cheerful and bright, a cardinal chirped melodiously in a treetop. Ashamed and humbled, I watched their total involvement in life.

2. Certificates of deposit from local banks are insured by a federal agency, so they are extremely safe investments, but your money is tied up in them for long periods of time unless you are willing to accept stiff penalties for early withdrawal, and they also do not always pay particularly high rates of interest. You may find it more beneficial to invest in a conservative mutual fund specializing in government bonds, which will give you great safety, too, but it also offers excellent returns on your money and permits you to withdraw money by check any time you wish.

3. Eager to begin their vacation, the family loaded the minivan. Filled with enthusiasm, they drove for twenty-five minutes. Shocked by the sudden failure of the engine, they pulled the car to the side of Interstate 90. Horrified at their poor planning, they realized they had forgotten to fill the tank with gas.

4. Going shopping with my sister is lots of fun. Walking around the mall, we go into almost every store. Making decisions is easier with her along, too. Keeping each other from buying useless or silly items is part of our game plan.

5. Recycling cans, glass, paper, and plastic is very important for the human race because if we keep making more trash we will run out of places to put it, and then we will suffocate ourselves and our planet under piles of junk. Don't let this happen because it would be a terrible tragedy, and all we have to do to prevent it is remember to recycle.

For support in meeting this chapter's objectives, follow this path in MyCompLab: Resources ⇒ Grammar ⇒ **Usage and Style**. Review the Instruction and Multimedia resources about **redundancy and wordiness,** then complete the Exercises and click on Gradebook to measure your progress.

CHAPTER 24

Additional Style Problems and Solutions

We discussed individual word choices in Chapter 22 and effective sentences in Chapter 23. In a sense, style has to be a matter of words and sentences, of course, but some issues are best approached from a wider perspective. Writers who frequently use trite expressions or sexist language, for example, are not merely creating ineffective sentences but are creating an image of themselves in the reader's mind that can have a far more devastating impact than a wordy phrase or an error in parallelism. Writers who overindulge themselves in showing off large vocabularies or familiarity with current slang can antagonize a reader and risk ruining a whole essay. In this chapter, we define and describe these problems and others that are most likely to arise so that you can either avoid them completely or recognize and correct them if they do appear in your writing. We also explain which of these stylistic elements can serve a valid purpose when used consciously and carefully.

In this chapter you will

- identify and avoid triteness in your writing
- identify and avoid euphemisms in your writing
- analyze examples of good and bad repetition
- identify and avoid slang
- identify and avoid fancy writing
- identify and avoid sexist language
- review miscellaneous strategies to improve your writing

Triteness

A **trite expression**, or **cliché**, is a word or phrase that has become worn out through overuse. Many trite expressions may once have been original and even brilliant, but through constant repetition they have lost whatever impact they once had. If a writer uses many trite expressions, a reader may be tempted to assume that the thoughts are as secondhand as the language.

Triteness generally calls attention to itself in some way. Words like *the, a, man, woman, come,* and *go* are not trite even though we tend to use them all the time, because they are simple, direct, and not self-conscious. Trite expressions seem, on the surface, to convey a thought or feeling particularly well, and people who haven't read enough to recognize them sometimes think them clever, or elegant, or lively. Experienced readers, however, interpret them for what they usually are—evidence of a writer's laziness and lack of imagination.

The best way to handle triteness is to eliminate it. Apologetic little quotation marks do not help. If the writer has been trite, quotation marks call even more attention to the fault and let the reader know that the triteness was no accident.

The following list contains a number of trite expressions. Avoid them. Choose ten from the list and try to think of original and effective ways to express the same ideas.

Trite Expressions

- more fun than a barrel of monkeys
- worth its weight in gold
- over the hill
- stop on a dime
- fresh as a daisy
- happy as a lark
- hard as nails
- have someone in a corner
- make a long story short
- no use crying over spilled milk
- a penny saved is a penny earned
- cool as a cucumber
- pretty as a picture
- in the pink
- apple-pie order
- under the weather
- devil-may-care attitude
- go at it tooth and nail
- generation gap
- broaden one's horizons
- peer pressure
- do unto others
- flat as a pancake

- armed to the teeth
- flattery will get you nowhere
- dumb as an ox
- turned on
- red as a rose
- tired but happy
- a good time was had by all
- white as snow
- black as pitch
- put it in a nutshell
- spread like wildfire
- the crack of dawn
- spring chicken
- dog-eat-dog
- survival of the fittest
- every cloud has a silver lining
- sick as a dog
- work like a dog
- easy as pie
- sweet as sugar
- quick as a wink
- greased lightning
- a matter of life and death

- tender loving care
- sly as a fox
- stubborn as a mule
- rat race
- struggle for existence
- the bigger they are, the harder they fall
- sad but true
- south of the border

- a bolt from the blue
- signed, sealed, and delivered
- open-and-shut case
- flash in the pan
- not a cloud in the sky
- feathered friends
- slow as molasses
- last but not least

In addition to these phrases, we express some familiar—and important—ideas in the same language so often that the ideas themselves seem trite unless we word them differently. No matter how much we believe in the need for stable human relations, we are not going to get very excited when someone tells us "People must learn to get along with one another." If we are presenting one of these ideas, we must express it in a dramatic, forceful way, or at least show that we do not regard it as a profound new insight. Here is a partial list of such potentially trite ideas.

Trite Ideas

The older generation has made a mess of things.
A good marriage involves more than sex.
Getting to know people of different backgrounds is a good thing.
College is more difficult than high school.
Pollution is a major problem in the United States.
Education is necessary for many jobs.
We live in a technological society.
This problem could have been avoided by better communication.
This problem will be solved by better communication.
We need to think more about people who are less fortunate.
It is possible to have different opinions about a poem.
Nature is beautiful.
Adults have more responsibilities than children.
This issue is very complicated.

Euphemisms

A **euphemism** is a word or phrase used as a polite substitute for a more natural but less refined word or phrase. Euphemisms can be handy to have around, especially in social situations. For example, chances are that the parents of Suzy or Jerry will be more comfortable to hear that their child is "not working up to full capacity" than to be told that their child is "lazy."

As a rule, though, you should avoid euphemisms, especially in your writing. They generally seem pretentious, fussy, and old-fashioned. The natural, honest word is usually the best one, so long as honesty is not confused with exhibitionistic crudeness or vulgarity. In most cases, then, avoid writing both "He passed on to a better world" and "He croaked." Try instead "He died."

EUPHEMISMS ⟶	DIRECT LANGUAGE
low-income individual	poor person
urban poverty area	slum
sanitation worker	trash collector
custodian *or* superintendent	janitor
mortician *or* funeral director	undertaker
conflict	war
distortion of the facts	lie
casualties	dead and wounded
senior citizen	old person
powder one's nose	go to the bathroom
financially embarrassed	in debt
reconditioned	used
to pass on	to die

EXERCISE Locate the trite expressions and euphemisms in the following sentences and suggest alternatives.

1. He had once established a meaningful relation with a member of the fair sex, but time flies, and she moved on to greener pastures.
2. When the senior citizen stepped into the street and began walking as slow as molasses, I had to stop my car on a dime to avoid an unfortunate incident.
3. Excessive ingestion can significantly increase adipose tissue.
4. The army executed a strategic withdrawal.
5. It made my blood boil to hear that officers of the law were accused of assaulting an unarmed gentleman who was as helpless as a kitten.
6. Mr. Abdul's immediate superior told him that his services would no longer be required.

7. Mrs. Chung's recent generous donations to various philanthropic organizations suggested that she was rolling in dough.
8. The unruly child screamed like a banshee and ran around like a bull in a china shop, his face turning beet red and his hair sticking up in all directions.
9. Gina's hair is jet black, her skin is smooth as silk, and her evening gown fits her like a glove, but she doesn't hold a candle to my betrothed.
10. The firms need some new blood, so they will employ several up-and-coming young lawyers.

Repetition, Good and Bad

Repetition can help or hurt your writing depending on how you use it. When used to add clarity or dramatic impact, repetition is a major stylistic resource. At other times, however, repetition can interfere with good style, and writers need to be aware of its dangers.

Repetition for Clarity

Repetition can help to clarify meaning and get the writer and reader from one sentence or clause to another. One of the simplest and most valuable transitional devices for a writer is the repetition of a key word or phrase, sometimes in slightly altered form, from a preceding sentence or clause:

> Five drug *companies* have been accused of misleading advertising. The first of these *companies* is. . . .

> Critics tend to make too much of a fuss about *symbols*. *Symbols* are not obscure artistic tricks. Our own daily lives are filled with *symbols*.

Repetition for Impact

Repetition can often add effective dramatic impact, as in the following examples.

> We've shrugged at scandals. We've shrugged at violence. We've shrugged at overpopulation and pollution and discrimination. Now it's time to stop shrugging.

> When she lost her husband, she lost her friend, lost her lover, lost her confidant. She lost everything that had given meaning to her life.

> The decision must be made this week—not this year, not this month, not early next week, but this week.

If not handled skillfully and tastefully, repetition for impact can also lead to foolish emotionalism or unnecessary stress on the obvious:

> Must cruel developers have their way forever? What of the flowers? What of the trees? What of the grass? What of the homeless birds and squirrels and bunnies?

> There is too much violence on television. Bang, bang, bang, bang, bang— that's all we ever hear. Bang, bang, bang.

Undesirable Repetition of Meaning

Avoid restating a point that is already sufficiently clear. For example:

> The American flag is red, white, and blue *in color*.

> She was remarkably beautiful. *She was, in fact, quite exceptionally good-looking*.

> The effect *and outcome* of all this was most unfortunate.

> In today's *modern contemporary* world. . . .

(See the discussion of wordiness in Chapter 23.)

Undesirable Repetition of the Same Word

Although repetition of a word or word form can help to clarify a point or serve as a transitional device, if used too often it can become monotonous and irritating. This is especially true if the word itself is not crucial to the meaning of the passage; words such as *very*, *really*, and *interesting* are major offenders.

> I am *very* pleased to be here on this *very* distinguished occasion. Your *very* kind remarks and your *very* generous gift have left me *very* much at a loss for words, but *very* deeply appreciative.

> I *really* enjoyed reading this story. It was a *really* exciting story with *real* people in *real* situations. The suspense was *really* terrific.

Beware of using different forms of the same word through carelessness. The result can be an awkward and confusing sentence.

> We had a *wonderful* time seeing the *wonders* of Florida.

> The *beauties* of Shakespeare's sonnets are outstandingly *beautiful*.

> People must be made more *aware* of the need for increased *awareness* of our environment.

Undesirable Repetition of Sounds

Save rhymes for poetry. Avoid horrors like these:

The condemnation of the administration was brought about by its own lack of ability and student hostility.

The church is reexamining its position on the condition of the mission.

Go easy on **alliteration**, the repetition of sounds at the beginning of words. Every once in a while, alliteration can be effective, but when a writer is obviously pouring it on, the results are silly at best.

We must toss these sneering, snickering, swindling swine out of office.

The orchestra's bold blowing of the brasses thrilled me to the bottom of my being.

EXERCISE

Point out any undesirable repetition in the following sentences and make the necessary corrections.

1. Endless streams of tourists threaten to ruin our state's rivers, brooks, and streams.
2. Despite efforts to forget, I find that the mind will remind us of our errors.
3. I am sure that avarice adds fuel to his already active aspirations for advancement.
4. The carpenter has such energy and drive that it's a pleasure just to watch him drive a nail into a piece of wood.
5. At this point in time I am looking for an assistant.
6. Bill Hawkins was a tragic figure—tragic in school, tragic in business, tragic in marriage, tragic in life.
7. The president squandered and foolishly spent the company's money until he had to declare bankruptcy.
8. I love you, my love, with a love that surpasses the love of all the greatest lovers in history.
9. The fantastic fragrance of the field filled with wildflowers made me feel faint.
10. It seems that Professor Reames had great dreams.

Slang

A carefully chosen, appropriate **slang** expression can sometimes add interest and liveliness to writing. Slang can help to establish a humorous or casual tone. More significantly, in a few cases, it can suggest an attitude or a shade of meaning that a more conventional expression could not.

By and large, however, slang is inappropriate for the comparatively formal, analytical writing that college courses most often demand. But when you feel sure that a slang expression can genuinely communicate something you could not otherwise convey as well, don't be afraid to use it. When you do use it, avoid the coy quotation marks that some writers put around slang to show that they are really sophisticated people who could use more formal language if they wanted to. Good slang should seem natural, and if it is natural, it doesn't need quotes.

Once thought of as the intellectual leader of a generation, Thompson turned out to be just another jerk with the gift of gab.

Billed as a luxury resort, the hotel was a high-priced dump.

Be careful about using slang, however. Don't use it to show how up-to-date you are; slang changes so fast that what seemed current yesterday is often embarrassingly old-fashioned tomorrow. Don't use slang to show your reader what a folksy person you are; that technique almost always fails. Avoid crude sentences like these:

In *Hamlet*, Hamlet's girlfriend, Ophelia, goes nuts.

This profound political allegory really turned me on.

Albert Einstein was one of the big brains of the twentieth century.

Fancy Writing

For every writer who uses slang to show off, there are probably a dozen who show off by habitually using big or unfamiliar words. A large vocabulary is an asset for any writer, of course, but that fancy word or phrase should be used only when it adds something valuable to tone or meaning that a more familiar word or phrase could not add. If the familiar word will do the job as well, use it; the unfamiliar word will seem stilted and pretentious. (See the discussion of jargon on page 549.)

FANCY	→	IMPROVED
Many of our new buildings suffer from inadequate fenestration.		Many of our new buildings have too few windows.
They raised their hands in the time-honored gesture of respect to the emblem of their nation's sovereignty.		They saluted their country's flag.
Charles Dickens' novelistic achievements are veritably unrivaled in English letters.		Charles Dickens wrote better novels than any other English writer.

Be particularly careful about mixing slang and fancy writing unless you are deliberately trying for a humorous effect. Tuxedos and sweatshirts are both wearable articles of clothing, but they do not go well together.

POOR MIX	→	IMPROVED
Also listed as available options on this formidable contender for car-of-the-year honors are cruise control, power sunroof, tape deck, and zillions of other gizmos.		Also listed as available options on this formidable contender for car-of-the-year honors are cruise control, power sunroof, tape deck, and a host of other luxuries.
With its vulgarity masquerading as wit, its tired stereotypes masquerading as characters, and its disjointed episodes masquerading as plot, this new play is totally yucky.		With its vulgarity masquerading as wit, its tired stereotypes masquerading as characters, and its disjointed episodes masquerading as plot, this new play is a dismal failure.

EXERCISE

Correct any inappropriate use of slang or fancy writing in the following sentences.

1. The cacophony emanating from the foyer indicated to us an altercation among our offspring.
2. Good writers eschew prolixity.
3. Through all the vicissitudes of life, Benjamin Franklin kept his cool.
4. Little Billy became lachrymose when his mother turned off the boob tube.
5. Many liberal policy makers concur with welfare recipients who express sentiments indicating their desire to obtain employment as long as it isn't flipping burgers at some burger joint.
6. The mobster's hortatory remarks were intended to placate his minions but only exacerbated long-simmering tensions.
7. My previous employer was a birdbrain.
8. My colleague's perpetual obsequiousness makes me want to crack up.
9. The vocalist's melodious utterances lulled me into a slumber.
10. Geometry is difficult, but interesting. Algebra is the pits.

Sexist Language

Sexist language is language that displays prejudice and stereotyped thinking about the roles, character, and worth of both sexes, though women have most frequently been its victims. Avoiding sexist language is a moral issue, of course—the sexist bigot is no more appealing than the racial, religious, or ethnic bigot. It is also a stylistic issue because language reflects social realities, and habits of language may continue long after the social realities have changed. Sexist language is sometimes more the product of habit than of intention.

To prevent or eliminate sexist language, pay particular attention to the following suggestions.

 **TIPS** for Avoiding Sexist Language

■ **Avoid stereotypes in occupations.** The notion of distinctive man's work and woman's work has by and large become outdated.

SEXIST LANGUAGE ⟶	IMPROVED
A nuclear physicist needs to take his environmental responsibilities seriously.	Nuclear physicists need to take their environmental responsibilities seriously.
Adele is hoping to become a policeman.	Adele is hoping to become a police officer.
Carla Rodriguez is an outstanding lady doctor.	Carla Rodriguez is an outstanding doctor.
Our file clerk quit yesterday, and we need a new woman for the job.	Our file clerk quit yesterday, and we need to find someone new for the job.

■ **Avoid stereotypes in character and social behavior.** Not all women giggle, gossip, and want to have babies any more than all men swear, drink beer, and overdose on football.

SEXIST LANGUAGE ⟶	IMPROVED
A good cook always seems to have a secret recipe for her Thanksgiving stuffing.	A good cook always seems to have a secret recipe for Thanksgiving stuffing.
Her woman's heart melted when she saw her new grandson.	Her heart melted when she saw her new grandson.

■ **Avoid insulting and condescending language.** Some sexist words are obvious insults and easy enough to recognize: *babes, dames, dolls, broads,* and the like. Other words and phrases masquerade as affectionate tributes or compliments but can, in fact, be extremely patronizing: *the fair sex, the gentle sex, my better half, girl* (when used to describe a grown woman), and so on. Avoid both types.

SEXIST LANGUAGE ⟶	IMPROVED
When Jenny left the company, it was hard to find another girl to replace her.	When Jenny left the company, it was hard to find anyone to replace her.
My aunt was thoughtful, helpful, and compassionate—a truly gracious lady.	My aunt was thoughtful, helpful, and compassionate—a truly outstanding person.

■ **Avoid using *man*, *men*, and *mankind* as synonyms for *humanity*, *people*, and *the human race*.**

SEXIST LANGUAGE	→	IMPROVED
Man's future is uncertain.		Humanity's future is uncertain.
Men must first learn to love themselves before they can love anyone else.		People must first learn to love themselves before they can love anyone else.
Are you telling me that mankind is on the brink of doom? What else is new?		Are you telling me that the human race is on the brink of doom? What else is new?

■ **Avoid using the pronoun *he* when sex is unknown or irrelevant.**

SEXIST LANGUAGE	→	IMPROVED
We need a person who can offer a few hours of his time each week.		We need a person who can offer a few hours of time each week.
A liar needs to make sure that he has a good memory.		Liars need to make sure that they have good memories.

(For a more detailed discussion of nonsexist pronoun use, see page 594 of the Handbook and page 642 of the Glossary.)

EXERCISE

Rewrite the following sentences to eliminate sexist language.

1. After moving from her neighborhood of the past twenty-five years, Julie most missed the girls' nights out every Tuesday.
2. A collegiate athlete must be able to manage his time well.
3. A parent concerned about her child's progress in school should first arrange for a conference with her child's teacher.
4. With both of them working, they thought they were at last in a position to pay for a cleaning lady.
5. Forget about elections and wars. The fate of man is determined more by climate than by anything else.
6. Alan so urgently needs a male authority figure to enforce discipline and teach him right from wrong.
7. She shouldn't let these disappointments bother her pretty little head. All she really needs is a good cry.
8. Every company should have a day for fathers to bring their daughters to work with them.

9. Our postal service has become most erratic. I'm not sure that mailmen still take pride in their work.
10. Mothers who attend PTA meetings may feel more involved in their children's education.

Miscellaneous Dos and Don'ts

Some special stylistic problems common to classroom writing don't fit conveniently under any of the main labels, so we've included brief comments about them here.

 TIPS for Writing in an Academic Style

- **Don't write a personal letter to your instructor.**
  This assignment at first confused me, but after several cups of coffee, I began to get an idea: I remembered that last week you said something about certain kinds of literature depending on formal patterns, and I think I've come up with an interesting notion about the two stories we just read. See what you think.

If that paragraph were read by anyone other than the teacher or the members of the class that discussed the stories, it would make almost no sense. What difference does it make to a general reader—or teacher—how much coffee the student drank? What assignment does the student refer to? What stories did the class just read?

- **Don't make formal announcements of what you are going to do.**
  In this paper I am going to prove that, far from being ignored, the elderly have received special privileges for decades.
  The thesis that I shall attempt to establish in this paper is that crime rates have gone down because of broad social patterns, not because of better police work.

It's distracting and unnecessary to begin a paper with a trumpet fanfare. Don't tell the reader what you are going to do. Get down to business and do it.

Far from being ignored, the elderly have received special privileges for decades. Crime rates have gone down because of broad social patterns, not because of better police work.

- **Avoid a speechmaking tone.**
  In conclusion, let me simply say that. . . .
  With your permission, I'd like to make a few observations on that point.

Such sentences introduce an irritating artificial quality into written English.

■ **Don't shilly-shally.**

In my opinion, the Industrial Revolution was a major chapter in the history of civilization.

I think that Dr. Watson is childishly impressed by Sherlock Holmes.

Go easy on terms such as *in my opinion, I think,* and the like. An apologetic or uncertain tone suggests that you do not have faith in your ideas, and if you do not believe in what you say, your audience probably won't either. Of course, you would not state a personal theory as a universal truth; but don't weaken solid ideas by shilly-shallying, and don't expect an *in my opinion* to make a shaky idea more acceptable.

■ **Don't bluster.**

Anyone but an idiot can see that Hughes' poem protests the treatment of African Americans.

Legalized prostitution is opposed mainly by neurotic hypocrites and religious nuts.

Blustering is the opposite of shilly-shallying. Its effect on an intelligent audience is just as negative.

■ **Be careful about using the word *you* as an indefinite pronoun.**

Even though you are a drug addict, you are not necessarily an evil person.

Your constant arguments with your parents are part of the process of growing up.

You is the pronoun of direct address. In this book, for example, we, the authors, write to you, the students in a composition course, and thus address you directly. But in writing aimed at a general audience, it is preferable to use the indefinite pronouns *anyone, one, each, either, neither, another, anybody, someone, somebody, everyone, everybody,* and *nobody.* And *you* cannot be substituted for *the speaker, the character, the average citizen, people, the student, the author, the reader,* and so on. Since you cannot be sure of the age, class, sex, or living conditions of your readers, you will not want to chance offending or unintentionally amusing them by attributing to them attitudes, strengths, vices, or talents they may not possess.

Drug addicts are not necessarily evil.

Constant arguments with parents are part of the process of growing up.

■ **Define unfamiliar terms.** This advice is especially important in any paper on technical subjects. An audience of nonspecialists can be expected to have the general knowledge of educated citizens, but nothing more. Avoid **jargon**—the special language of particular professions and activities—whenever you can. When you can't, see to it that your reader understands you. A paper on automobile repairs, for instance, would need to define terms such as *universal joint* and *differential.* A paper on legal problems would need to define *tort* and *writ of mandamus.* A paper on finance would need to define *cash flow* and *price-earnings ratio.*

EXERCISE   Comment on the stylistic problems in each of the following sentences, and rewrite the sentences where necessary.

1. Your ugly buck teeth can now be corrected more quickly and economically than was once the case.
2. This paper will demonstrate that Beyoncé is more than just a pretty face.
3. Cobalt treatment engendered remission.
4. In my opinion, I believe that George W. Bush will go down in history as an extremely controversial president.
5. Any intelligent person knows that seatbelt laws violate your right to privacy.
6. Recent government funding cuts mean that you may no longer be able to feed your hungry children.
7. Thus the poem clearly shows, in my humble opinion, that Dickinson was a shrewd observer.
8. The focus of this paper will be the explanation of the pros and cons of nuclear power.
9. The caesura in the fourth stanza of the sestina is effected by the poet's scrupulous diction.
10. Sitting here, crouched before my laptop, I wonder how to begin this essay.

For support in meeting this chapter's objectives, follow this path in MyCompLab: Resources ⇒ **Grammar** ⇒ **Usage and Style.** Review the Instruction and Multimedia resources about **bias in language and sexist language**, then complete the Exercises and click on Gradebook to measure your progress.

PART SIX

Handbook, Glossary, and ESL Pointers

Handbook

Glossary of Problem Words

ESL Pointers: Tips for Non-Native Writers

Part Six is a quick guide to basic writing skills. Use it to check on grammatical points, to answer simple questions that may occur to you while writing or revising, to correct any mechanical errors that your instructor finds in your work, and to guide you in appropriate word choice. Most English teachers assume that you have already mastered the basics, and your instructor probably will devote only limited classroom time to mechanics. It is your responsibility to make your papers grammatically correct. The Handbook, Glossary, and ESL Pointers can help you do that.

Both the Handbook and the Glossary follow an alphabetical arrangement. The Handbook presents the most common areas of trouble: comma splices, fragmentary sentences, and so on. You will find a number of exercises on more difficult points so that you can test your understanding of them. The Glossary of Problem Words explains specific words and phrases that frequently confuse writers. ESL Pointers: Tips for Non-Native Writers addresses major areas of difficulty for English Language Learners writing in English for their courses.

We have tried to keep our explanations as free as possible of specialized grammatical terminology. When such terminology is necessary, we have strived to make our explanations self-contained. For example, in our treatment of adjective-adverb confusion, we work definitions of adjectives and adverbs into the discussion. Some separate definitions have proven essential, however, and it's wasteful to define overwhelmingly common terms such as *subject, noun,* and *verb* every time we mention them. Definitions of such common terms appear alphabetically in the Handbook.

Handbook

Abbreviations.   As a rule, avoid abbreviations.

Wrong	**Right**
NYC and other municipalities can cure their financial ills only by aid from the federal gov't.	New York City and other municipalities can cure their financial ills only by aid from the federal government.
Thanksgiving comes on the fourth Thurs. of Nov.	Thanksgiving comes on the fourth Thursday of November.
I had trouble finding the proper st. & had to ask a taxi driver for directions.	I had trouble finding the proper street and had to ask a taxi driver for directions.

Even when abbreviations are permissible, it is nearly always acceptable in standard English to spell a word in its entirety; therefore, when in doubt, spell it out.

However, in cases like the following, abbreviations are required or preferred. In general, the trend in abbreviations is not to use periods after letters or spaces between letters, especially when all letters of an abbreviation are capital letters (FBI, CD-ROM, NY).

- *Standard forms of address.* Before a person's name, it is standard usage to write *Mr., Mrs., Ms., Dr.,* or *St.* (for Saint, not street).
- *Titles.* If both a person's surname (last) and given name (first) or initials are used, then it is acceptable to write *Rev., Hon., Prof., Sen.*

   Rev. John Yip, Prof. A. J. Carr (but not Rev. Yip or Prof. Carr)

- *Degrees.* After a name, abbreviate academic degrees, *Jr.,* and *Sr.* Academic degrees may also be abbreviated when used by themselves.

   Marion Jonas, MD
   He is now studying for a BA after completing his AAS degree.

- *Organizations.* The names of many organizations and some countries are commonly abbreviated, without periods.

   NATO   NAACP   OPEC   UN   USA   AFL-CIO   MLA

■ *Other*. Traditional footnote references and bibliographical terms (many no longer in common use) are nearly always abbreviated, as are a few familiar words.

etc.	pp. 137–40
ibid.	vol.
et al.	TNT
p. 23	DNA

EXERCISE   Replace unnecessary abbreviations in the following sentences.

1. After the Aug. 2005 hurricane Katrina hit New Orleans, the La. gov't provided $$ and drs.
2. Many U.S. airlines have flights from L.A. to N.Y.
3. Mr. Dowd always complains that there is nothing to watch on t.v. on Tues. nights.

ad

Adjective-Adverb Confusion

Adjectives modify nouns.

Getting a diploma takes *hard* work.

The boxer's *left* jab is his *strongest* weapon.

The *better* team won.

The porridge was *hot*.

Adverbs modify verbs, adjectives, or other adverbs.

We walked *carefully*.

Foolishly, we kept arguing until midnight.

The porridge was *very* hot.

The doctor had to cut *quite* deeply.

Form most adverbs by adding *-ly* to adjectives:

Adjective	Adverb
nice	nicely
strong	strongly
poor	poorly

When an adjective already ends in *y* or *ly*, you may have to change the *y* to an *i* before adding the adverbial *-ly* ending. A few of the resulting adverbs may sound so awkward that an adverbial phrase is the preferred form.

Adjective	**Adverb**
pretty	prettily
messy	messily
nasty	nastily

but

Adjective	**Adverbial Phrase**
friendly	in a friendly way
lovely	in a lovely way
heavenly	in a heavenly way

A few adjectives and adverbs are identical in form:

Adjective: He is a *better* person for the experience.

                     Fast drivers are dangerous drivers.

Adverb: He did *better* than I.

                     I can type *fast*.

Some words are adverbs in themselves—adverbs to start with—and do not spring from adjectives: *very, quite, rather, somewhat*. Other adverbs are irregular; the adjective *good*, for example, is expressed as an adverb by the word *well*.

Adjective: He was a *good* worker.

Adverb: He did the work *well*.

Confusion of adjectives and adverbs is among the most common grammatical errors and is likely to turn up from one of the following causes.

- *Misuse of an adjective to modify a verb.*

Wrong	**Right**
I wish she acted *different*.	I wish she acted *differently*.
Bill did *good* on his examination.	Bill did *well* on his examination.
Let's speak *direct* to each other.	Let's speak *directly* to each other.

- *Misuse of an adjective to modify an adverb or other adjective.*

Wrong	**Right**
The price was *sure* very expensive.	The price was *surely* very expensive.
The patient is *considerable* worse today.	The patient is *considerably* worse today.
My teacher is *real* strict.	My teacher is *really* strict.

- *Misuse of an adverb after a linking verb.* The correct modifier after a linking verb is an adjective. The single most common linking verb is *to be* (*am, is, are, was, were, will be,* and so on). Verbs dealing with the senses—sight, touch, taste, smell, hearing—are often used as linking verbs: *feel, look, sound, taste, appear.* Other verbs frequently serving as linking verbs are *get, seem, remain, become.* (See also *good, well* in the Glossary.)

Wrong	**Right**
The music sounds *beautifully*.	The music sounds *beautiful*.
The food tastes *badly*.	The food tastes *bad*.

Some verbs, including many of those just listed, may be used as transitive or intransitive verbs, as well as linking verbs. In such cases, note how an adjective or adverb determines meaning.

I smell bad. (I need to buy deodorant.)

I smell badly. (My sinuses are stuffed up.)

He looks evil. (He looks like a wicked person.)

He looks evilly. (His glances are frightening.)

I feel terrible. (I am depressed or in ill health.)

I feel terribly. (My sense of touch has deserted me.)

EXERCISE

Choose the correct adjective or adverb in the following sentences.

1. If you act (quick, quickly), you will receive a free bonus gift.
2. Thunder rattled (angry, angrily) in the hills.
3. Some frozen foods are (real, really) tasty.
4. The international news sounds (explosive, explosively).
5. If you speak (hasty, hastily), you may repent (hasty, hastily).
6. Feeling (thirsty, thirstily), he drank (noisy, noisily).
7. Driving too (slow, slowly) can cause as many accidents as driving too (fast, fastly).

8. Writing (concise, concisely) helps to prove a point more (effective, effectively).
9. Though he appeared (calm, calmly) his heart thumped (rapid, rapidly).
10. My sister looks (splendid, splendidly) in her new three-piece suit.

EXERCISE   Find the errors in the following paragraphs.

1. My Florida vacation went terrible! It rained the entire time I was there. I had planned to get a suntan, go snorkeling, and hopefully see some dolphins, but all my plans went sourly. Instead, I wandered unhappy through the hotel hallways, wishing I had stayed at home. The worst part of all was that the sun shone down brilliant as I boarded the plane to go home.

2. You can make linguine with clam sauce much more easy than you might expect. Prepare the linguine as you would normally. Then, fry some onions and garlic in butter. Add the juice from a can of clams and a little parsley and simmer the mixture gentle. Add the clams and, after they have heated, mix the linguine in real good. This dish tastes great with a little Parmesan cheese.

3. A curving path wound through the forest. Carlos and Bryna walked down it slow, admiring the scenery and enjoying the cool shade. They spotted a doe and her fawn hiding among the trees. They moved closer, but the animals ran away too quick to follow.

Adjectives, comparative and superlative forms.   See *Comparative and superlative forms*.

Adjectives, coordinate.   See *Commas, E.*

Adverbs.   See *Adjective-adverb confusion.*

Adverbs, comparative and superlative forms.   See *Comparative and superlative forms*.

Agreement.   See *Pronoun agreement; Subject-verb agreement.*

Antecedent.   The noun or pronoun to which a pronoun refers.

   Richard Yee left *his* lunch at home.

Here, the pronoun *his* refers to its noun antecedent, *Richard Yee.*

Apostrophe.   Use the apostrophe to form contractions, plurals, and possessives.

- *Contractions.* In contractions, the apostrophe indicates that a letter or letters have been left out.

it is = it's	she is = she's	who is = who's	you will = you'll
let us = let's	you are = you're	do not = don't	she would = she'd

- *Plurals.* Use the *'s* to form the plural of letters: *a*'s, *x*'s, *B*'s, *C*'s. You need only an *s* to form the plurals of abbreviations and numbers.

the 1930s	the &s (*or* the &'s)	two *c*'s in *occupy*
DAs	POWs	

- *Possessives.* Use an apostrophe to form the possessive of nouns and indefinite pronouns. The first task is to determine whether you need a possessive apostrophe. If you do, the second task is to use it correctly.

  Difficulties for many people begin with the confusion of speaking with writing. In speech, *cats*, *cat's*, and *cats'* all sound identical. The meanings are all different, however, and in writing, those differences show up immediately. *Cats* is a simple plural—add an *s* to the singular without the use of an apostrophe.

The cats howled all night.
Purring is a way cats have of showing affection.

Cat's is a possessive singular, another way of expressing the thought *of the cat*. *Cats'* is a possessive plural, another way of expressing the thought *of the cats*. Note the simplicity of determining whether a word with a possessive apostrophe is singular or plural: just look at the part of the word *before the apostrophe*.

Singular	**Plural**
cat's claws	cats' claws
machine's speed	machines' speed
Mr. Smith's home	the Smiths' home

Note, too, that in a phrase like *of the cats*, the word *of* takes care of the idea of possession, and no apostrophe is used.

Possessives with *of* (no apostrophe)	**Possessives with apostrophes**
The claws of a cat are sharp.	A cat's claws are sharp.
The name of my cat is Tigger.	My cat's name is Tigger.
The hunting abilities of cats are well known.	Cats' hunting abilities are well known.
The mysterious glow in the eyes of cats can be frightening.	The mysterious glow in cats' eyes can be frightening.

One more observation is necessary. Possessive pronouns—*my, mine, our, ours, your, yours, his, her, hers, its, their, theirs*—are already possessive in themselves and *never take apostrophes.*

When a possessive apostrophe is required, the rules are relatively simple.

1. Singular or plural nouns that do not end in -*s* form their possessives by adding *'s.*

Ivan's car	Arlene's book	Women's Liberation
the teacher's notes	New York's mayor	children's games

2. Plural nouns that end in -*s* form their possessives by adding only an apostrophe:

the students' teacher	Californians' freeways
oil companies' profits	the two boys' mother
automobiles' engines	the two teachers' classes

3. Singular nouns that end in -*s* ordinarily form their possessives by adding *'s*. Some writers make exceptions of words that already have so many *s* or *z* sounds in them (for example, *Massachusetts, Jesus*) that pronunciation of a final *'s* could create awkward hissings and buzzings. You can form the possessive of such words by adding only an apostrophe. Both methods are correct, and writers can use their own judgment as long as they are consistent.

the octopus's tentacles	the press's responsibilities
Dickens's novels	the business's profits
Charles's bowling ball	Jesus's disciples (*or* Jesus' disciples)
Mr. Jones's new roof	Moses's journey (*or* Moses' journey)

4. Indefinite pronouns form their possessives by adding *'s*:

nobody's fool	someone's knock
anyone's guess	everybody's business

5. In the case of joint possession—possession by two or more—the possessive is formed by adding an apostrophe or *'s*, as appropriate, to the last noun:

the girls and boys' school	Jill and Bob's car

   NOTE: To show individual possession, write "Jill's and Bob's cars" and "the girls' and boys' schools." Here Jill has a car and Bob has a car; the girls have a school and the boys have a school.

EXERCISE   Rewrite the following phrases to form possessives, using only an apostrophe (') or an apostrophe plus the letter *s* ('*s*) as appropriate.

1. The wail of the saxophone
2. The wail of the saxophones
3. The president of the country
4. The presidents of the countries
5. The checking account of Mr. James
6. The checking account of the Jameses
7. The suspense of the story
8. The suspense of the stories
9. The leaves of the birch tree
10. The leaves of the birch trees
11. The choice of the person
12. The choice of the people
13. The mother of Sarah and Jess
14. The mothers of Sarah and Jess (*two mothers—individual possession*)
15. The title of the book

EXERCISE   In the following sentences, decide which of the italicized words ending in -*s* are simple plurals or verbs and which are possessives. Then make the necessary corrections and be prepared to explain them.

1. *Managements problems* with the *unions* derive more from *misunderstandings* than from genuine conflicts of interest.
2. The *prison guards* ignored the *inmates complaints* about their *cells* filthy conditions.
3. *Joggings* appeal *eludes* me. There must be less boring exercises.
4. That ancient *trees* gnarled *branches* only add to *its* beauty.
5. Your behavior is worse than *theirs*; *yours* can't be excused by your *fathers* neglect.
6. The *Lees* joined the *Sepulvedas* for dinner at *Psaros* Restaurant.
7. The *actors* constant bickering forced the *shows producers* to choose which one of the *performers* would leave.
8. After *years* of happiness, *Frances* and *Roberts* marriage is on the *rocks*.
9. Many of our *universes* greatest *mysteries*, like the *causes* of aging and the *reasons* we need sleep, have baffled the *worlds scientists* for *centuries*.
10. *Hundreds* of *customers complaints* filled the *companys* mail room.

Appositive.   See *Commas, F.*

Block quotations.   See *Quotation marks.*

Brackets. Use brackets ([ ]) to enclose comments or added information that you have inserted into a direct quotation. Do not use parentheses instead of brackets because the reader will assume that the inserted material is part of the original quotation.

> "While influenced by moral considerations, Lincoln signed it [the Emancipation Proclamation] primarily to further the war effort."

> "The music column had the altogether intimidating title of *Hemidemisemiquavers* [sixty-fourth notes]."

Capital letters. Use a capital letter for the first word of a sentence or direct quotation, the first word and all important words of titles, the first word and all nouns of a salutation, the first word of a complimentary close, some pronouns, and all proper nouns—the names of particular persons, places, or things.

■ *The first word of a sentence or direct quotation.*

A popular early television show featured a detective whose most characteristic line was, "We just want the facts, ma'am."

■ *The first and all important words of titles of books, movies, radio and television programs, songs, magazines, plays, short stories, poems, essays, and chapters.* Unimportant words (for example, *a, an, and, the*) and prepositions (e.g., *of, in, to, with, about*) are not capitalized unless they are the first word.

A Streetcar Named Desire [play]	"Ode to a Nightingale" [poem]
Time [magazine]	"Gifts" [essay]
Roget's College Thesaurus [book]	"Basin Street Blues" [song]

■ *The first word and all nouns of a salutation.*

Dear Sir:	My dear Ms. Hunt:	Dear Bill,

■ *The first word of a complimentary close.*

Sincerely yours,	Yours truly,

■ *Some pronouns.*

1. First-person singular: *I.*
2. References to the Judeo-Christian Deity, where necessary to avoid confusion:

   God told Moses that he must carry out His commandments.

- *Proper nouns.*
  1. Names and titles of persons and groups of persons:
     a. Persons: Martin Luther King Jr., President Barack Obama, Oprah, Hillary Rodham Clinton.
     b. Races, nationalities, and religions: Caucasian, Chinese, Catholic (but *black, white*).
     c. Groups, organizations, and departments: League of Women Voters, Ford Motor Company, United States Senate, Department of Agriculture.
     d. Particular deities: God, Allah, Buddha, Zeus.
  2. Names of particular places:
     a. Cities, counties, states, and countries: Cleveland, Cuyahoga County, Ohio, United States of America.
     b. Particular geographical regions: Europe, Pacific Northwest, the South.
     c. Streets: East Ninth Street, El Cajon Avenue.
     d. Buildings: Empire State Building, Union Terminal.
     e. Heavenly bodies (except the sun and moon): Mars, Milky Way, Andromeda, Alpha Centauri.
  3. Names of particular things:
     a. Days and months: Friday, August.
     b. Holidays: Easter, May Day.
     c. Historical events and periods: the Civil War, the Middle Ages.
     d. School courses: Biology 101, History 102 (but a *history* course).
     e. Languages: English, Russian.
     f. Schools: Cornell University, Walt Whitman High School (but "I graduated from *high school*").
     g. Brands: Buick, Peter Pan Peanut Butter (but "I had a *peanut butter* sandwich for lunch").

EXERCISE Capitalize words as needed in the following sentences.

1. my best subject in high school was mathematics, but my tenth grade english teacher really taught me to enjoy classics like *jane eyre* and *the grapes of wrath*.
2. every saturday in july the arthur taylor jazz quartet performs concerts in grant park.
3. my friend suzy yip swoons when josh groban sings "to where you are."
4. ellen hasn't decided whether to spend christmas in chicago with her grandparents or in seattle with her aunt felice and uncle gregg.
5. mr. tanner's third graders at pine street elementary school planted daffodils in the park in honor of mother's day.
6. according to the food and drug administration, genetically altered crops are entirely safe.

7. drive south on sumpter street and park across from home depot, the largest store in our town.
8. director steven spielberg won wide acclaim for *saving private ryan, schindler's list*, and *munich.*
9. have you seen the two-headed turtle at the nature museum in charlotte, north carolina?
10. painting 101 will meet on tuesdays and thursdays beginning this fall.

Clause. A group of words with a subject and predicate. A clause can be independent or dependent. An *independent clause* stands alone as a separate sentence.

Maria went home.

A *dependent clause* cannot stand alone; rather, it must depend on an independent clause to complete its meaning.

After I came home, I took a nap.

The man *who lived next door* died.

Collective nouns. See *Subject-verb agreement.*

Colon. A colon (:) commonly appears after a clause introducing a list or description, between hours and minutes, in the salutation of a formal letter, between biblical chapter and verse numbers, and between the title and subtitle of a book. Less commonly, a colon may separate independent clauses and appear before quotations.

- *List.* A colon appears between a general statement and a list or description that follows:

We shall never again find the equals of the famous three *B*'s of music: Bach, Beethoven, and Brahms.

He plans to take five courses: history, English, psychology, French, and physical education.

NOTE: A colon should appear after a complete statement. Do not use a colon after a form of the verb to be (*be, am, is, are, was, were, been,* etc.) or after a preposition.

Wrong	**Right**
Perennial contenders for the NFL championship are: San Francisco, New England, Dallas, and Buffalo.	Several teams are perennial contenders for the NFL championship: San Francisco, New England, Dallas, and Buffalo.
	or
	Perennial contenders for the NFL championship are San Francisco, New England, Dallas, and Buffalo.

- *Time.* When recording a specific time in numerals, use a colon between hours and minutes:

8:00 p.m.   8:10 a.m.

- *Salutation.* In formal letter writing, use a colon after the salutation:

Dear Ms. Johnson: Dear Sir:

- *Biblical references.* To separate chapter from verse, use a colon:

Genesis 1:8 (chapter 1, verse 8)

- *Title and subtitle.* A colon separates the title and subtitle of a book:

Johnson's Dictionary: A Modern Selection

- *Independent clauses.* A colon may appear between independent clauses when the second clause explains the first:

They reared their children on one principle, and one principle only: do unto others what they would like to do unto you—and do it first.

- *Quotations.* A colon sometimes introduces a short quotation and often introduces a long block quotation:

Whenever I try to diet, I am reminded of the bitter truth of Oscar Wilde's epigram: "I can resist everything but temptation."

In commenting on his function as a writer, Joseph Conrad put every writer's dream into words:

> My task which I am trying to achieve is, by the power of the written word to make you hear, to make you feel—it is, before all, to make you *see*. That—and no more, and it is everything. If I succeed, you shall find there according to your deserts: encouragement, consolation, fear, charm—all you demand—and, perhaps, also that glimpse of truth for which you have forgotten to ask.

NOTE: No quotation marks surround a long block quotation.

EXERCISE

Correct any errors by adding or removing colons. One sentence is already correct.

1. Sponsored public service announcements achieve two goals they deliver important messages and create goodwill for the advertisers.
2. Karl's new job brought him to cities he had never visited, like: Milan, London, Santiago, and Tokyo.
3. Because my father is always looking at his watch, for Father's Day I bought him the book *Keeping Watch A History of American Time.*

4. Gina's delectable brownies are the perfect dessert: sweet, rich, gooey, and chocolatey.

5. I hate to admit it, but my mother's favorite saying was true "Give some people an inch, and they'll take a mile."

Commas. Using a comma correctly is almost never a matter of taste or inspiration. It is even less a matter of following the ancient junior high school formula of tossing in a comma "to indicate a pause." Different people pause for breath and emphasis in different places, and nearly *every* mark of punctuation indicates some kind of pause—periods, semicolons, and dashes no less than commas. When errors in comma usage occur, they are most often the result of the writer's being comma-happy—putting in too many commas. Our basic rule, then, is *never use a comma unless you know it is necessary.* A comma is necessary in the following cases:

- Between elements in a list or series
- Between independent clauses joined by *and, but, or, nor, for, yet, so*
- After introductory elements
- Before and after interrupting elements
- Between coordinate adjectives
- Before and after nonrestrictive elements
- Before and after phrases that express a contrast
- Before and after words of direct address, interjections, and *yes* and *no*
- Between certain words to prevent misreading
- In conventional elements such as dates, numbers, addresses, titles, correspondence, and direct quotations

A. *Series.* Separate three or more items in a list or series by commas for the sake of clarity.

The potential buyer should take special care to inspect the roof, basement, and ceilings.

Make sure you read parts one, two, and three before completing the assignment.

The three novels in Dos Passos's *USA* trilogy are *The 42nd Parallel, Nineteen Nineteen,* and *The Big Money.*

NOTE: In all three examples, the comma before *and* is optional. Most experienced writers use the comma, however, because it reinforces the idea of a series in the reader's mind.

B. *Independent clauses.* Two independent clauses (a group of words that can stand alone as a complete sentence) joined by a coordinating conjunction—*and, but, or, nor, for, yet, so*—require a comma *before* the conjunction:

Barack Obama fought hard for votes, and he impressed people all over the country.

Each writing assignment requires a different kind of organization, but each may require a different length.

Use no comma if there is only one independent clause:

> Barack Obama fought hard for votes and impressed people all over the country.

> Each writing assignment requires a different kind of organization and may require a different length.

EXERCISE   Add or remove commas as needed in the following sentences. Some sentences may be correct.

1. I decided against taking the new job yet I suspected I would always be grateful for the offer.
2. Marie knew that the book would sell but never dreamed of its record-breaking success.
3. I have traveled extensively throughout the United States but I have never been abroad.
4. The manager told the division heads that they must all work together or she would fire them all separately.
5. Hand-held phones are smaller than ever, and provide more, and more services than in the past.
6. Nothing made any sense in my income tax forms so I decided I needed to consult an accountant.
7. Florida held its 2008 Presidential primary in January and the Democratic National Committee punished the state by disallowing its delegates.
8. Martin was restless and he thought about giving Pamela a call.
9. Martin was restless and thought about giving Pamela a call.
10. The English partly destroyed the Spanish Armada, but the weather played an even larger destructive role.

C. *Introductory elements.* In general, use a comma after an introductory element:

> *Because the students were having trouble with commas*, they read the section on punctuation.

> *In good writing*, there are few punctuation errors.

The italicized parts of these two sentences are introductory elements. When the introductory element is extremely short—one word, for example—you can omit the comma if the meaning remains clear: "*Soon* the term will end."

Poor	Correct
Because this is an introductory element it should have a comma after it.	Because this is an introductory element, it should have a comma after it.
Despite the best efforts of both parties no agreement was reached.	Despite the best efforts of both parties, no agreement was reached.

Never having seen her before I expected the worst.	Never having seen her before, I expected the worst.
As soon as he had showered he went straight to bed.	As soon as he had showered, he went straight to bed.

However, if the introductory element is moved so that it appears *after* the independent clause (and thus no longer introduces anything), do not use a comma:

No agreement was reached despite the best efforts of both parties.

He went straight to bed as soon as he had showered.

EXERCISE   Insert a comma after the introductory element as needed.

1. Finished at last with work she looked forward to an evening on the town.
2. Because Carmela forgot to set her alarm she missed her nine o'clock appointment.
3. Having decided that both sides had presented excellent cases I then concluded that my only reasonable vote was an abstention.
4. To learn more about Cuba we attended a lecture at our local community college.
5. After a long introductory clause or phrase use a comma.
6. Use a comma after a long introductory clause or phrase.
7. Now I feel better prepared.
8. Considering my shortcomings I have been luckier than I deserve.
9. Bored and disgusted with the ball game I thought bitterly that there were some peanut vendors in the stands who were better athletes than anyone on the field.
10. Whenever I hear someone suggest that love is the answer to our problems I wonder why love has usually made me miserable.

D. *Interrupting elements.* A comma should be used before and after an interrupting element. Interrupting elements, while often needed for clarity and continuity, are those that break the flow of words in the main thought of a sentence or clause. In the previous sentence, *while often needed for clarity or continuity* is an interrupting element. Some writers find it helpful to think of interrupting elements as asides to the audience or parenthetical insertions. Interrupting elements may be words such as *indeed, however, too, also, consequently, therefore, moreover, nevertheless* and phrases such as *as the author says, of course, after all, for example, in fact, on the other hand*.

Wrong	**Right**
Suppose for example that you decide to write about your own life.	Suppose, for example, that you decide to write about your own life.
We must bear in mind too that even the best system is imperfect.	We must bear in mind, too, that even the best system is imperfect.

Wrong	**Right**
Punctuation as we can see is not exactly fun.	Punctuation, as we can see, is not exactly fun.
The only thing wrong with youth according to George Bernard Shaw is that it is wasted on the young.	The only thing wrong with youth, according to George Bernard Shaw, is that it is wasted on the young.
His pledges for the future however could not make me forget his broken promises of the past.	His pledges for the future, however, could not make me forget his broken promises of the past.

E. *Coordinating adjectives.* Use a comma to separate coordinating adjectives—adjectives of equal rank—that come before the nouns they modify.

Wrong	**Right**
This poet uses concrete believable images.	This poet uses concrete, believable images.
Her warm enthusiastic energetic behavior was often mistaken for pushiness.	Her warm, enthusiastic, energetic behavior was often mistaken for pushiness.

You can identify coordinating adjectives in two ways: (1) the word *and* may be used to join them (concrete *and* believable, warm *and* enthusiastic *and* energetic) or (2) they may be reversed (believable, concrete; enthusiastic, energetic, warm). Compare these examples to "This poet uses several concrete images." We cannot say "several and concrete" or "concrete several." Therefore, we do not use a comma between them. Note, too, that if the coordinate adjectives had originally been joined by *and*, no commas would have been necessary: "Her warm *and* enthusiastic *and* energetic behavior was often mistaken for pushiness."

EXERCISE   Add commas as needed around the interrupting elements and between the coordinating adjectives in the following sentences. Also remove any incorrectly placed commas. Some sentences may be correct.

1. The student's sincere deep apology fell on deaf ears.
2. The teacher's apology I am sorry to say seemed less sincere.
3. Protracted, municipal efforts to expand the airport, are at a standstill.
4. The mayor keeps insisting however that efforts will continue.
5. Drinking a glass of cool refreshing water can energize you.
6. Always make certain, in addition, to check your manuscript for careless errors.
7. Dogs too can get sunburns.
8. The so-called, good, old days were often actually bad, old days.
9. Turner's theory to put it bluntly was wrong.
10. Her inherent bad vertebral structure inhibited her career as a gymnast.

F. *Nonrestrictive elements.* A comma should be used before and after a nonrestrictive element.

Nonrestrictive modifiers. Commas are used before and after nonrestrictive modifiers. A nonrestrictive modifier gives additional information about the noun it modifies but is not necessary to identify or define that noun:

The Empire State Building, *which I visited last year*, is a most impressive sight.

My father, *who has worked in a steel foundry for thirty years*, has made many sacrifices for me.

A *restrictive modifier* is not set off by commas. It is a necessary part of the meaning of the noun it modifies:

A person *who is always late for appointments* may have serious psychological problems.

The novel *that Professor Higgins praised so highly* is very disappointing.

People *who live in glass houses* shouldn't throw stones.

Many jobs *for highly skilled technicians* are still available.

Proper punctuation of restrictive and nonrestrictive modifiers often can affect meaning:

The sofa, with those huge armrests, is an eyesore.	(The writer sees just one sofa. The nonrestrictive modifier merely conveys more information about it.)
The sofa with those huge armrests is an eyesore.	(The writer sees more than one sofa. The restrictive modifier is necessary to distinguish this sofa from the others.)

A special type of nonrestrictive element is called the *appositive*—a word or group of words that means the same thing as the element that precedes it. In the sentence, "Joseph Terrell, *mayor of Greenville*, will speak at graduation," the italicized phrase is an appositive—that is, it has the same basic meaning as the first element, *Joseph Terrell*. The rules governing the punctuation of modifiers also govern the punctuation of appositives.

Nonrestrictive appositives. Commas are used before and after nonrestrictive appositives. A nonrestrictive appositive gives additional information about the noun it follows but is not necessary to identify that noun:

Ms. Susan Swattem, *my high school mathematics teacher*, was the meanest person in town.

Thomas Jefferson, *third president of the United States*, also founded the University of Virginia.

A *restrictive appositive* is not set off by commas. It is necessary to identify the noun it follows:

> The expression *hitch your wagon to a star* was first used by Emerson.

> He spoke to Susan *my sister*, not Susan *my wife*.

As with modifiers, proper punctuation of nonrestrictive and restrictive appositives often can affect meaning.

My brother, George, is a kindly soul.	(The writer has only one brother, so the word *brother* is sufficient identification. *George* is nonrestrictive.)
My brother George is a kindly soul.	(The writer has more than one brother, so the name of the specific brother is a necessary part of the meaning. *George* is restrictive.)

EXERCISE Add commas where necessary to set off the nonrestrictive elements in the following sentences. Also remove any commas that have been incorrectly placed. Some sentences may be correct.

1. Anyone who hates loud music cannot appreciate a Metallica concert.
2. The Smurfs, elflike blue creatures of spectacular cuteness, won the hearts of America's children during the early 1980s.
3. A person who cares about the future cannot be indifferent to the proliferation of nuclear weapons.
4. The highway repair project which the department scheduled for completion in two years now will need double that time to be completed.
5. The film that my cousin Stefan loved, bored me so much, that I fell asleep.
6. Albert Einstein that legendary figure of modern science was a notable underachiever during his school days.
7. Exxon which is the largest oil company in the world used to be known as Standard Oil Company of New Jersey.
8. The man who picked up the packages for the old woman had his wallet stolen when he bent over.
9. Harold Arlen who wrote such songs as "Stormy Weather" and "Let's Fall in Love" also composed the classic score for the film *The Wizard of Oz*.
10. The star of the *High School Musical* films, Zac Efron who has an unbelievable following among teenage girls appeals to many adult women too.

G. *Contrast.* Commas should be used to set off phrases expressing a contrast.

> She told him to deliver the furniture on Wednesday, not Tuesday.

> Hard work, not noble daydreams, is what I believe in.

> The money did not bring hope, but anxiety.

NOTE: The comma can sometimes be omitted before contrasting phrases beginning with *but*: "We have nothing to fear *but* fear itself."

H. *Direct address, interjections,* yes *and* no. Commas separate words and phrases of direct address, interjections, and the words *yes* and *no* from the rest of the sentence.

1. *Direct address:*

I tell you, ladies and gentlemen, that this strategy will not work.

Jim, you're still not following the instructions.

2. *Interjections:*

Well, it appears that the committee has finally issued its report.

Oh, I'd say the new car should arrive in about three weeks.

Although commas are generally used with mild interjections, more dramatic interjections may take exclamation points:

Well! It was the worst mess I'd ever seen.

Oh! How could she have made such a contemptible remark?

3. Yes *and* no:

Yes, I plan to vote for Ruppert.

I have to tell you plainly that, no, I cannot support your proposal.

I. *Misreading.* Apart from any more specific rules, commas are sometimes necessary to prevent misreading. Without commas, the following examples would be likely to stop readers in midsentence and send them back to the beginning.

Confusing	**Correct**
High above the trees swayed in the wind.	High above, the trees swayed in the wind.
At the same time John and Arnold were making their plans.	At the same time, John and Arnold were making their plans.
Hugging and kissing my half-smashed relatives celebrated the wedding.	Hugging and kissing, my half-smashed relatives celebrated the wedding.

J. *Conventions.* Use commas in such conventional elements as dates, numbers, addresses, titles, correspondence, and direct quotations.

1. *Dates.* Commas separate the day of the month and the year:

April 24, 1938   January 5, 1967

If you write only the month and year, you can omit the comma:

April 1938   April, 1938

If the year is used in midsentence with the day of the month, follow it by a comma. With the month only, you may omit the comma:

World War II began for the United States on December 7, 1941, at Pearl Harbor.

World War II began for the United States in December 1941 at Pearl Harbor.

World War II began for the United States in December, 1941, at Pearl Harbor.

In Works Cited entries, use European or military date order, where no commas are necessary (see pages 467–479):

7 December 1941

15 March 2008

2. *Numbers.* Use commas to group numbers of more than three digits to the left of the decimal point:

| $5,280.00 | 751,672.357 | 5,429,000 | 5,280 |

However, commas are not used for page numbers, addresses, or years:

page 4233   1236 Madison Ave.   1989

3. *Addresses.* Use commas to separate towns, cities, counties, states, and districts:

Cleveland, Ohio

Brooklyn, Kings County, New York

Washington, D.C.

NOTE: Do not use a comma to separate the ZIP code from the state.

Pasadena, California 91106

4. *Titles.* A comma often separates a title from a name that precedes it:

Harold Unger, MD   Julia Harding, PhD

5. *Correspondence.* Use a comma after the salutation in informal letters and after the complimentary close:

Dear John,   Dear Jane,

Respectfully yours,   Sincerely yours,

6. *Direct quotations.* See *Quotation marks.*

EXERCISE Insert commas as needed in the following sentences. Remove any unnecessary commas.

1. My brother Choon, was born in Shanghai China on September 8 1958.
2. Yes I do hope that my activism will help change government policies.
3. Emily is this your sweater?
4. At the moment, we are compiling, a guest list for our New Year's Eve bash.

5. Savoring each delicious bite she wanted the meal to go on forever.
6. Below the bridge looked like a tiny road as our plane gained height.
7. Apply sunscreen liberally and spend your summer romping in the sun not indoors cringing from the discomfort of sunburn.
8. Susan's reaction, was one not of outrage but of resignation.
9. Beginning July 12 2009 we will accept applications for the position of Assistant Director of the Milton School.
10. You must understand my friend that this is not easy for me.

Comma splice.   Often considered a special kind of *run-on sentence* (for which the Handbook provides a separate entry), a *comma splice* is a punctuation error that occurs when two independent clauses are joined only by a comma. You can correct a comma splice by (1) using both a comma and a coordinating conjunction or (2) replacing the comma with a semicolon or a period.

There are only seven coordinating conjunctions: *and, but, or, nor, for, yet,* and *so.* When you use these between independent clauses, in formal usage, precede them by a comma.

CS

Wrong	**Right**
The boy had been physically disabled since infancy, he still tried to excel in everything he did.	The boy had been physically disabled since infancy, but he still tried to excel in everything he did.
	or
	The boy had been physically disabled since infancy; he still tried to excel in everything he did.
	or
	The boy had been physically disabled since infancy. He still tried to excel in everything he did.
Each writing assignment requires a different kind of organization, each may be a different length.	Each writing assignment requires a different kind of organization, and each may be a different length.
	or
	Each writing assignment requires a different kind of organization; each may be a different length.
	or
	Each writing assignment requires a different kind of organization. Each may be a different length.

It is often tempting to use words such as *however, therefore, nevertheless, indeed,* and *moreover* after a comma to join independent clauses. Don't! The only words following a comma that can join two independent clauses are the seven coordinating conjunctions.

Wrong	**Right**
We started with high hopes, however, we were disappointed.	We started with high hopes; however, we were disappointed.
She had been hurt many times, nevertheless, she always seemed cheerful.	She had been hurt many times; nevertheless, she always seemed cheerful.

Although any choice among coordinating conjunctions, semicolons, and periods will be technically correct, the best choice often depends on complex issues of style and thought. If the independent clauses under consideration are surrounded by long sentences, for example, the writer might choose to break the monotony with a period, thus creating two short sentences. If the independent clauses are surrounded by short sentences, the writer can sometimes achieve variety by creating a long sentence with a coordinating conjunction or semicolon. In addition, the more closely connected the thoughts in two independent clauses, the more likely the writer will be to show that connection by using a coordinating conjunction or semicolon. In such cases, two separate sentences would indicate too great a separation of thought. Obviously, no easy rules work here, and the writer's intentions have to be the main guide.

A somewhat more sophisticated way to correct a comma splice is often the best way: since the comma splice is created by connecting two independent clauses with a comma, change one of the independent clauses into a phrase or dependent clause. Notice how this technique works with the preceding sample sentences.

Physically disabled from infancy, the boy still tried to excel in everything he did.

Although he had been physically disabled from infancy, the boy still tried to excel in everything he did.

While each writing assignment requires a different kind of organization, each may be a different length.

We started with high hopes but were disappointed.

Despite her being hurt many times, she always seemed cheerful.

NOTE: Comma splices can be acceptable in standard English when each clause is unusually short and when the thought of the whole sentence expresses an ongoing process.

I came, I saw, I conquered.

Throughout the interview, she squirmed, she stammered, she blushed.

EXERCISE Rewrite the following sentences, correcting the comma splices where necessary. Some sentences are correct.

1. General Electric is a widely diversified company, it makes everything from light bulbs to airplane engines, refrigerators to medical scanning devices.
2. It is allergy season again, I can't stop sneezing from the pollen and ragweed.
3. Trash talk is a disgrace to professional sports, therefore it should be outlawed.
4. Although I am no cook myself, I love to study the gourmet recipes.
5. Fear can prevent a person from acting, hate, on the other hand, will often cause action.
6. She was a human being: she was born, she lived, she suffered, she died.
7. Nothing matters more than your own personal integrity, never surrender your principles.
8. Most daytime talk shows allow people to air their dirty laundry in public, however, *The View* contains relevant topics for intelligent viewers.
9. Do not join two sentences with just a comma, use a comma and a conjunction, a semicolon, or a period to separate sentences.
10. My uncle believes that loyalty is rarely rewarded as much as it should be in the business world, he tells me therefore, not to be afraid or ashamed of changing jobs.

EXERCISE Correct the comma splices in the following paragraphs.

1. Desperately searching the kitchen for something to eat, I found nothing. A little milk, some leftover macaroni, and one beet were the only things in the refrigerator, I saw that the situation was hopeless, I knew I would starve. In my anguish I thought about competing with the puppy for his food, but that seemed a little extreme. There was no escape, I would have to shop.
2. Air travel gets more and more expensive and less and less comfortable all the time, moreover, in order to give travelers in first class more room, airlines have moved the less expensive seats even closer together. This change leaves travelers almost no leg room at all, it's ridiculous. Even a short flight leaves one with numb feet and aching knees. Unless airlines make considerable improvements, they may find that people are choosing slower, but more comfortable, ways to travel.
3. The children ran wild through the neighborhood that summer they chased each other up and down the streets on roller skates, skateboards, and bicycles. Their games of tag engulfed block after block in the town. It was glorious. It seemed as if the long, sunny days would never end,

school would never start. But the weather began to cool, and the leaves began to change. Back to school they went. The streets were quiet and a little lonely without them.

Comparative and superlative forms. Comparative forms of adjectives and adverbs are used to compare or contrast groups of two—and only two. The comparative form of regular adjectives is formed by adding *-er* to the ending of the adjective or by using the word *more* before the adjective: *nicer, sweeter, more dramatic, more beautiful.* (Some adjectives are irregular: the comparative of *good* is *better*; the comparative of *bad* is *worse.*) The comparative form of adverbs is formed by using *more* before the adverb: *more nicely, more sweetly, more dramatically, more beautifully.*

Superlative forms of adjectives and adverbs compare or contrast groups of three or more. The superlative form of regular adjectives is formed by adding *-est* to the ending of the adjective or by using the word *most* before the adjective: *nicest, sweetest, most dramatic, most beautiful.* (Some adjectives are irregular: the superlative of *good* is *best*; the superlative of *bad* is *worst.*) The superlative form of adverbs uses *most* before the adverb: *most nicely, most sweetly, most dramatically, most beautifully.*

In summary, comparative forms apply to two, and superlative forms apply to more than two.

Wrong	**Right**
If I had to choose between Reese Witherspoon and Renee Zellweger, I would have to say that Witherspoon is the *best* actor.	If I had to choose between Reese Witherspoon and Renee Zellweger, I would have to say that Witherspoon is the *better* actor.
The high school girl and the junior high school girl competed on the parallel bars. The junior high school girl was given the *higher* scores.	The high school girl and the junior high school girl competed on the parallel bars. The junior high school girl was given the *highest* scores.
I like many people, but I like Betsy *more.*	I like many people, but I like Betsy *most.*
Although my first and second themes both required hard work, I wrote the second *most* easily.	Although my first and second themes both required hard work, I wrote the second *more* easily.

EXERCISE   Correct any errors in comparative and superlative forms. Some sentences are correct.

1. Comparing travel by cars to travel by planes, I enjoy cars most.
2. Rockefellers and Kennedys are both rich, but Rockefellers are probably richer.

3. The new Corvette is the most beautiful car I have ever seen.
4. Jenny won first prize for her watercolor landscape, but Elizabeth's painting was better.
5. One needs both love and friendship in marriage. Friendship could easily be the most important.
6. Among all my friends, I believe Karen is the one more likely to help in a crisis.
7. Though I adore both chocolate and strawberry ice cream, I enjoy strawberry the most.
8. At the moment, I feel more inclined toward a career in medicine than in law.
9. Most complicated choices depend on luck as well as on intelligence.
10. Dreiser was a great writer in many respects, but of all the giants of American literature he probably had less basic talent.

EXERCISE   Correct any errors in comparative and superlative forms in the following paragraphs.

1. Hansel and Gretel stopped just outside the gingerbread house. It was the most wonderful thing they had ever seen. Every bit of the house was made out of something delicious: candy, cookies, or cake. The children were very hungry, and the house smelled very good. They decided to break off small pieces to eat. Hansel was oldest, so he went first.
2. My mother and father shop very differently. Mom goes out for an entire day, looks in every store, and sometimes comes home with nothing. She shops to see what is available and to think about what she might want to buy. Dad goes out for twenty minutes, shops in one place, and always brings home what he set out to buy. He shops for one reason: he needs something. Dad is certainly more efficient, but Mom probably has the most fun.
3. Writing business letters can be very difficult. It is a real challenge to find the appropriate tone. One must be formal yet friendly, brief yet thorough. Even the more experienced writers may have great trouble composing a really good business letter. Perhaps this widespread difficulty is the reason that form letters have become so popular.

Comparisons.   Comparisons must be both logical and complete.

comp

- *Logical.* Do not compare items that are not related. For example, you would not compare horses to safety pins because they have nothing in common. Not all illogical comparisons are this obvious, however, since it is usually the phrasing rather than the thought behind it that is at fault.

Wrong	Right
His appetite is as huge as a pig. (Here the comparison is between *appetite* and *pig*.)	His appetite is as huge as a pig's. *or* His appetite is as huge as a pig's appetite. *or* His appetite is as huge as that of a pig.
Mark Twain is more amusing than any American writer. (Here Mark Twain is excluded from the group that he belongs to.)	Mark Twain is more amusing than any other American writer.

■ *Complete.* A comparison must be complete; that is, the items being compared must be clear, and both items must be stated.

   1. Clarity:

       Poor: I like him more than you.

       Right: I like him more than I like you.

                                 or

                                 I like him more than you like him.

   2. Both items stated:

       Poor: Old Reliable Bank has higher interest rates. (Higher than it had before? Higher than other banks have? Higher on deposits or higher on loans?)

       Right: Old Reliable Bank has higher interest rates on savings accounts than any other bank in the city.

(For further discussion of comparisons, see Chapter 22, pages 520–521.)

EXERCISE   Correct any faulty comparisons in the following sentences.

   1. George W. Bush's political philosophy is not too unlike his father.
   2. Hitchcock's *Psycho* is still the most frightening movie.
   3. I like meeting strangers more than my husband.
   4. Her marks were higher than anyone in the class.
   5. My new television's reception is better than my old TV.
   6. *Hamlet* is more interesting than any play ever written.

7. His great big sad eyes are like a cocker spaniel.
8. Curious, bouncy, and not too bright, he was as out of place at the meeting as a kangaroo.
9. Wah Lee's kitchen is cleaner than his sister.
10. Stephen Hawking can explain physics better than any scientist today.

Complement.   Usually a noun, pronoun, or adjective that follows a linking verb and is necessary for logical completion of the predicate.

Marilyn Monroe was an *actor*.

Who are *you*?

That proposal seems *sensible*.

Compound subjects.   See *Subject-verb agreement*.

Conjunction.   A word used to join parts of sentences or clauses. *Coordinating conjunctions* (joining words or clauses of equal importance) are *and, but, or, nor, for, yet, so; subordinating conjunctions* (linking dependent and independent clauses) are *because, while, when, although, until, after*, and so on.

Conjunctions, coordinating.   See *Commas, B; Comma splice*.

Conjunctions, subordinating.   See *Fragmentary sentences*.

Coordinating adjectives.   See *Commas, E*.

Coordinating conjunctions.   See *Commas, B; Comma splice*.

Dangling modifier.   See *Modifiers*.

Dash.   A dash (—) serves to emphasize a parenthetical or otherwise nonessential word or phrase. It can also highlight an afterthought or separate a list or series from the rest of the sentence. An introductory list or series may be separated by a dash from the rest of the sentence if it is summarized by a word that serves as the subject of the sentence.

- *Parenthetical word or phrase.*

    Only when politicians are exposed to temptation—and rest assured they are almost always so exposed—can we determine their real worth as human beings.

- *Afterthought.*

    The only person who understood the talk was the speaker—and I have my doubts about her.

- *List or series.*

    The great French Impressionists—Manet, Monet, Renoir—virtually invented a new way of looking at the world.

The Scarlet Letter, Moby-Dick, Walden, Leaves of Grass, Uncle Tom's Cabin—these American classics were all published during the incredible five-year span of 1850–1855.

NOTE: Use dashes sparingly, or they lose their force. Do not confuse a dash with a hyphen (see *Hyphen*). In typing, indicate a dash by striking the hyphen key twice (--), leaving no space between the dash and the two words it separates.

Dependent clause. See *Clause*.

Direct object. See *Object*.

Double negative. Always incorrect in standard English, a double negative is the use of two negative terms to express only one negative idea. Remember that in addition to obvious negative terms such as *no, not,* and *nothing,* the words *hardly* and *scarcely* are considered negatives.

Wrong	**Right**
I don't have no memory of last night.	I don't have any memory of last night.
	or
	I have no memory of last night.
For truly religious people, money cannot mean nothing of value.	For truly religious people, money cannot mean anything of value.
	or
	For truly religious people, money can mean nothing of value.
His mother couldn't hardly express her feelings of pride at his graduation.	His mother could hardly express her feelings of pride at his graduation.
Our troubles had not scarcely begun.	Our troubles had scarcely begun.

Ellipsis. An ellipsis (. . .) shows omission of one or more words from quoted material. If the ellipsis occurs at the end of a sentence, four spaced dots are used; one dot is the period for the sentence.

Original	**Use of ellipsis**
"The connotation of a word is its implicit meaning, the meaning derived from the atmosphere, the vibrations, the emotions that we associate with the word."	"The connotation of a word is its implicit meaning, . . . the emotions that we associate with the word."
"We had a drought in 1988 and major floods in 1989. Statistics can be deceptive. The two-year statistics for rainfall look totally normal, but the reality was wildly abnormal."	"We had a drought in 1988 and major floods in 1989. . . . The two-year statistics for rainfall look totally normal, but the reality was wildly abnormal."

End marks. The three end marks are the period, question mark, and exclamation point.

■ *Period.* A period is used at the end of complete sentences, after abbreviations, and in fractions expressed as decimals.

1. *Sentences.* If a complete sentence makes a statement, use a period at the end:

Please give unused clothing to the Salvation Army.

Place pole *B* against slot *C* and insert bolt *D.*

The class wants to know when the paper is due.

2. *Abbreviations.* Use a period after some abbreviations:

Mr. R. P. Reddish   Mt. Everest   p.m.

A period is not used in abbreviations such as UNESCO, NAACP, FCC, MLA, and AARP. See *Abbreviations.*

3. *Decimals.* Use a period before a fraction written as a decimal.

¼ = 0.25   ¹⁄₂₀ = 0.05

NOTE: If you use a decimal point to indicate money, you also need a dollar sign: $5.25.

■ *Question mark.* A question mark indicates a direct question or a doubtful date or figure.

1. *Direct question.* Use a question mark at the end of a direct question. Do not use a question mark with indirect questions such as "They asked when the paper was due."

When is the paper due?

Did the teacher say when the paper is due?

You need to use a question mark when only the last part of a sentence asks a question, and when a quotation that asks a question is contained within a larger sentence.

I know I should go to college, but where will I get the money for tuition?

The student asked, "When is the paper due?"

After asking, "When is the paper due?" the student left the room.

In the last example, the question mark replaces the usual comma inside the quotation.

2. *Doubtful date or figure.* After a doubtful date or figure, use a question mark in parentheses. This does not mean that if you are giving an approximate date or figure you should use a question mark. Use it only if the accuracy of the date or figure is doubtful.

> The newspaper reported that the government said it cost $310 (?) to send a person to the moon. (Here a question mark is appropriate because it is doubtful if $310 is the figure. Perhaps there has been a misprint in the paper.)

> Chaucer was born in 1340 (?) and died in 1400. (Here historians know when Chaucer died but are doubtful of exactly when he was born, even though most evidence points to 1340. If historians were completely unsure, they would simply write, "Chaucer was born in the mid-1300s and died in 1400.")

A question mark in parentheses should never be used to indicate humor or sarcasm. It is awkward and childish to write, "He was a good (?) teacher," or, "After much debate and cynical compromise, the legislature approved a satisfactory (?) state budget."

- *Exclamation point.* An exclamation point is used at the end of emphatic or exclamatory words, phrases, and sentences. In formal writing, exclamation points are rare. They most often occur in dialog, and even there they should be used sparingly lest their effect be lost.

  1. *Word or phrase:*

     My God! Is the paper due today?

     No! You cannot copy my exam.

  2. Sentence:

     The school burned down!

     Stop talking!

     NOTE: Comic book devices such as !?! or !! should be avoided. Words, not the symbols after them, should carry the primary meaning.

EXERCISE Add periods, question marks, and exclamation points as needed in the following sentences.

1. Every newspaper delivery driver must have dependable transportation and a reliable backup driver
2. Who will wait in line for tickets to the charity concert
3. Ling wondered if her fax machine was malfunctioning again
4. Last May I got a job with a nonprofit consumer advocacy organization based in Washington, DC

5. Did you know that a ten-foot high razor wire fence surrounds Melilla on the coast of Morocco

6. The receptionist asked when I could come in for an interview

7. "Why do you insist on taking my things without asking" she demanded angrily

8. I believe that we must hold HMOs accountable for any decisions that affect patients' health

9. The candidate claims that he favors hate-crimes legislation, but why did he never propose such legislation when he was a congressman

10. Don't you think it's time you moved into your own apartment

Exclamation point.   See *End marks*.

Fragmentary sentences.   A fragmentary sentence (also called a sentence fragment) is a grammatically incomplete statement punctuated as if it were a complete sentence. It is one of the most common basic writing errors.

To avoid a sentence fragment, make sure that your sentence contains at least one independent clause. If it does not contain an independent clause, it is a fragment.

Here are some examples of sentences with the independent clause italicized; sometimes the independent clause is the whole sentence, and sometimes the independent clause is part of a larger sentence.

Jack and Jill went up the hill.

He sees.

If you don't stop bothering me, *I'll phone the police.*

Tomorrow at the latest, *we'll have to call a special meeting.*

He straightened his tie before he entered the room.

Discovering that she had lost her mother, *the little girl started to cry.*

An *independent clause* is a group of words that contain a subject and verb and express a complete thought. This traditional definition is beyond criticism except that it can lead to messy discussions about the philosophical nature of a complete thought. You can avoid such discussions by concentrating on the practical reasons for a missing independent clause. There are three major reasons: omission of subject or verb, confusion of verb derivatives (verbals) with verbs, and confusion of a dependent (subordinate) clause with an independent clause.

- *Omission of subject or verb.* This is the simplest kind of fragment to spot:

    There are many events that take place on campus. *Such as plays, concerts, and innumerable other activities.*

    My father finally answered me. *Nastily and negatively.*

Mr. Jones has plenty of interests to keep himself busy. *Nagging, scolding, snooping, and drinking.*

The new department head had a brand-new pain in the neck. *In addition to the old ones.*

We had many blessings. *Like love, nature, family, God, and television.*

These fragments should be obvious even without the italics, and the remedies should be just as obvious. Simple changes in punctuation will solve the problems. Here are the same sentences with the fragments eliminated:

There are many events that take place on campus, such as plays, concerts, and innumerable other activities.

My father finally answered me nastily and negatively.

Mr. Jones has plenty of interests to keep himself busy: nagging, scolding, snooping, and drinking.

The new department head had a brand-new pain in the neck in addition to the old ones.

We had many blessings, like love, nature, family, God, and television.

- *Confusion of verb derivatives (verbals) with verbs.* Verbals are words derived from verbs. Unlike verbs, they cannot function by themselves as the predicate of a sentence. Infinitive forms are verbals (*to do, to see, to walk*). So are gerunds and present participles (*-ing* endings: *doing, seeing, walking*). Study the italicized sentence fragments that follow.

I decided to take her to the game. *Susan enjoying football with a passion.*

Nobody ought to vote. *The government being corrupt.*

We should take pleasure in the little things. *A boy petting his dog. Lovers holding hands. Soft clouds moving overhead.*

To *make the world a better place. To help people be happy.* These are my goals.

In the last example, the fragments lack subjects as well as verbs and can readily be identified. Inexperienced writers, however, looking at the fragments in the first three examples, see a subject and what appears to be a verb. They assume, consequently, that the words make up an independent clause. They are wrong. A present participle by itself cannot serve as a verb, and an independent clause must have a verb. Study these corrected versions of the fragments.

I decided to take her to the game. Susan has been enjoying football with a passion.

Nobody ought to vote. The government is corrupt.

We should take pleasure in the little things: a boy petting his dog, lovers holding hands, soft clouds moving overhead.

I want to make the world a better place. I want to make people happy. These are my goals.

- *Confusion of a dependent (subordinate) clause with an independent clause.* All clauses contain a subject and a verb. Unlike an independent clause, however, a *dependent* or *subordinate clause* does not express a complete thought and therefore cannot function as a sentence. A subordinate clause at the beginning of a sentence must always be followed by an independent clause. A subordinate clause at the end of a sentence must always be preceded by an independent clause. Fortunately, subordinate clauses can be readily identified if you remember *that they always begin with subordinating conjunctions—*a much easier approach than trying to figure out whether your sentence conveys a complete thought. Here, in alphabetical order, is a list of the subordinating conjunctions you are most likely to encounter. Whenever one of these words immediately precedes a clause (subject + verb), that clause becomes a subordinate clause and cannot stand alone as a complete sentence.

after	as soon as	even though	provided that	unless
although	as though	how	since	until
as	because	if	so that	whenever
as if	before	in order that	than	wherever
as long as	even if	once	though	while

NOTE: Except when used as question words, *who, which, when,* and *where* also introduce a subordinate clause.

In the left-hand column below, examples of subordinate clauses used as sentence fragments are italicized. In the right-hand column, italics indicate corrections to repair these sentence fragments.

Fragments	**Corrected**
If I ever see home again.	If I ever see home again, *I'll be surprised.*
Keats was a great poet. *Because he was inspired.*	*Keats was a great poet because* he was inspired.
I will never apologize. *Unless you really insist.*	*I will never apologize unless* you really insist.
Provided that the contract is carried out within thirty days.	Provided that the contract is carried out within thirty days, *we will not sue.*
This is the person who will be our next governor. *Who will lead this state to a better tomorrow.*	*This is the person who will be our next governor, who* will lead this state to a better tomorrow.

The major difficulty anyone is likely to have with sentence fragments is in identifying them. They are usually easy to correct. Sentence fragments occur, in many cases, because of a misunderstanding of complex grammatical issues, but they can almost always be corrected with elementary revisions in punctuation.

Sentence fragments should nearly always be avoided. In rare situations, they can sometimes be justified, especially if the writer wants a sudden dramatic effect.

I shall never consent to this law. Never!

Death to the tyrant!

Scared? I was terrified.

Lost. Alone in the big city. Worried. The boy struggled to keep from crying.

EXERCISE Some of the following are sentence fragments. Rewrite them to form complete sentences. You may have to supply additional information.

1. Trying to follow Professor Garcia's lecture.
2. After majoring in English at the University of Southern California.
3. Who will send the invitations?
4. Although I admired her greatly and thought she deserved a chance.
5. Dressed in jeans and a torn tee shirt.
6. Because the senator planned to pursue some other interests.
7. Although improving many people's appearance, contact lenses are far less convenient than traditional eyeglasses.
8. To make a long story short.
9. To mention just a few items of relatively minor importance.
10. A person who can approach problems with a unique combination of vision and practicality.
11. Unless we all work together for a better world, we may have no world at all.
12. Who was that masked man?
13. Until the orchestra plays more popular selections.
14. Angry and screaming at the top of their lungs.
15. In addition to dwindling market share, mounting losses, and falling stock prices.

EXERCISE Find and correct the sentence fragments in the following paragraphs.

1. Yu-lin had several errands to run that afternoon. Going to the shoe repair store, stopping off at the bank, and dropping off a few books at the library. He had no idea if he could finish in time. Thinking carefully, he made a plan. He would stop at the bank, then pick up his shoes. And then drive all the way across town to the library. If he drove quickly and didn't get stopped by any red lights, he could be home in time to start supper and do a few loads of laundry.
2. Scrabble is a game that requires intelligence, skills, and almost infinite patience. A single game can take as long as three hours and can get very dull at times. While you wait for your opponent to think of a word.

There isn't much for you to do but look at the ceiling, try to remember how to spell *syzygy*, and hope that your opponent doesn't play a word in the space you hope to use. Beyond these few diversions, all you can do is wait. And wait.

3. My favorite way to spend an evening. To curl up on the couch with a big bowl of popcorn and watch old movies. Black-and-white movies are best. I munch my popcorn and let myself get pulled into a fantasy. Where people have doormen, where everyone wears hats and gloves, where chivalry is not dead. Romance, too. I love the movies where the hero and heroine fall desperately and hopelessly in love. Films like that are always wonderfully sad and romantic, and if I cry, the popcorn just gets a little extra salt. Of course, I also like the old comedies and suspense thrillers. There's just no way for me to go wrong with a night filled with comfort, snack food, and entertainment.

Fused sentence.   See *Run-on sentence.*

Hyphen.   A hyphen (-) is used to form some compound words and to divide words at the end of a line.

- *Compound words.*

  1. As a general rule, you should consult a recent dictionary to check the use of the hyphen in compound words. Many such words that were once hyphenated are now combined. The following are some compound words that are still hyphenated:

mother-in-law	court-martial
knee-deep	water-cooled

  2. All numbers from twenty-one to ninety-nine (except multiples of ten) are hyphenated:

forty-three	one hundred fifty-six

  3. A hyphen joins two or more words that form an adjective before a noun:

a well-known teacher	a first-rate performance
but	*but*
The teacher is well known.	The performance was first rate.

- *Divided words.* Divide words at the end of a line by consulting a dictionary and following accepted syllabication. A one-syllable word cannot be divided. In addition, a single letter cannot be separated from the rest of the word; for example, *a-bout* for *about* would be incorrect. The hyphen should come at the very end of the line, not at the beginning of the next line.

Independent clause.   See *Clause*.

Indirect question.   See *End marks*.

Infinitive.   Simple form of a verb preceded by the word *to*—for example, *to come, to go*.

Intransitive verb.   See *Verb*.

Italics (underlining).   In handwriting, underlining represents printed italics. The rules for underlining and italics are the same. Underline or italicize titles of complete works; most foreign words and phrases; words used emphatically; and letters, words, and phrases pointed to as such. If you are preparing an essay based on MLA or APA style, use italics.

> Handwritten:
>
> I love <u>Star Wars</u>.
>
> Print generated:
>
> I love *Star Wars*.
>
> *NOTE:* When a word or phrase that would usually be italicized appears in a section of text that is already italicized, the word or phrase is typed or written with no italics.

- *Titles of complete works.*

    1. Books: *The Great Gatsby, Paradise Lost, The Hitchhiker's Guide to the Galaxy*
    2. Newspapers and magazines: *New York Times, Chicago Tribune, Newsweek*
    3. Plays and movies: *A Raisin in the Sun, Macbeth, Win Win, Sleepless in Seattle*

    Enclose the titles of poems in quotation marks, except for book-length poems such as Milton's *Paradise Lost* and Homer's *Iliad*. Use quotation marks to enclose the titles of small units contained within larger units—such as chapters in books, selections in anthologies, articles or short stories in magazines, and individual episodes of a television series. (See *Quotation marks*.)

- *Foreign words and phrases not assimilated into English.*

vaya con Diós	*paisano*	*auf Wiedersehen*	
but			
cliché	genre	laissez-faire	taco

- *Words used emphatically.*

    Ask me, but don't *tell* me.

    Under *no* circumstances can we permit this to happen.

    She didn't really know *everything*, although it seemed that way.

Except in special situations, good word choice and careful phrasing are far more effective than italicizing or underlining to show emphasis.

- *Letters, words, and phrases pointed to as such.*

    Do not use words such as *however* and *therefore* as coordinating conjunctions.

    The letter *x* is often used in algebra.

    The phrase *on the other hand* anticipates contrast.

    A *proton* is a positively charged particle in the nucleus of an atom.

Check with your instructor about his or her preference for italics or underlining.

Linking verb.   See *Verb; Adjective-adverb confusion.*

Misplaced modifier.   See *Modifiers.*

Modifiers.   The most frequent errors involving modifiers are dangling modifiers and misplaced modifiers.

- *Dangling modifiers.* A *dangling modifier* is a group of words, often found at the beginning of a sentence, that do not refer to anything in the sentence or that seem to refer to a word to which the dangler is not logically related. Dangling modifiers usually include some form of a verb that has no subject, either implied or stated. This construction results in statements that are sometimes humorous and always illogical. To correct a dangling modifier, either change the modifier into a subordinate clause, or change the main clause so that the modifier logically relates to a word in it. On occasion, you may have to change both clauses.

dm

Incorrect	Correct
Climbing the mountain, the sunset blazed with a brilliant red and orange. (This sentence says that the sunset is climbing the mountain.)	As we were climbing the mountain, the sunset blazed with a brilliant red and orange. (Subordinate clause) *or* Climbing the mountain, we saw the sunset blazing with a brilliant red and orange. (Main clause)
After looking in several stores, the book was found. (In this sentence, the book is looking in several stores.)	After looking in several stores, we found the book.

To become an accurate speller, a dictionary is very helpful. (In this sentence, the dictionary is becoming an accurate speller.)

If you want to become an accurate speller, a dictionary is very helpful.

or

To become an accurate speller, you should use a dictionary.

While talking and not paying attention, the teacher gave the class an assignment. (This sentence says that the teacher is talking and not paying attention while giving an assignment. If that is what the writer meant, then this sentence is correct. If, however, the writer meant that the class was talking and not paying attention, then it is incorrect.)

While the class was talking and not paying attention, the teacher gave an assignment.

or

While talking and not paying attention, the class was given an assignment by the teacher.

mm

- *Misplaced modifiers.* Since part of the meaning of the English language depends on word order—some other languages depend mostly on word endings—you must make sure that phrases serving as modifiers and adverbs such as *only, always, almost, hardly,* and *nearly* are placed in the position that will make the sentence mean what you intend. *Misplaced modifiers,* unlike dangling modifiers, can almost always be corrected simply by changing their positions.

    1. Phrases serving as modifiers:

       The teacher found the book for the student in the library.

       This sentence indicates that the student was in the library. If, however, the writer meant that the book was found in the library, then the modifier *in the library* is misplaced. The sentence should read:

       In the library, the teacher found the book for the student.

       The writer of the following sentence seems to be saying that the college is near the lake:

       His parents met his friend from the college near the lake.

       If, however, the writer meant that the meeting took place near the lake, the modifier is misplaced and the sentence should read:

       Near the lake, his parents met his friend from the college.

2. Adverbs like *only, always, almost, hardly,* and *nearly* usually qualify the word that comes after them. Therefore, the position of these words depends on what the writer wishes to say.

The adverb *only* is a notorious troublemaker. Observe how the sentence "*I want a son*" changes meaning significantly with the change in position of *only:*

I *only* want a son.	(I don't yearn for or long for a son; I only want one.)
I want *only* a son.	(I have no other wants.)
I want an *only* son.	(One son is as many as I want.)
I want a son *only.*	(I do not want a daughter.)

EXERCISE Rewrite the following sentences as necessary to correct any dangling or misplaced modifiers.

1. Racing down the street, our books fell out of the bag.
2. My history professor spoke passionately about the evils of cheating on Tuesday.
3. Carve the roast after standing at room temperature for a few minutes.
4. I baked special cookies for the minister with chocolate chips.
5. The quarterback was removed from the game before he was permanently injured by the coach.
6. Singing in a soft voice, the acoustical system made it possible for all to hear.
7. Erica bikes well on the mountain trails with powerful leg muscles.
8. Running toward second base, we saw the runner make a daring slide.
9. Juan wants Judy to love him badly.
10. While driving through Yosemite, a bear stopped our car.

EXERCISE Correct any dangling or misplaced modifiers in the following paragraphs.

1. The weather was beautiful that day, and everyone tried to make the most of it. The park was filled with people playing catch, flying kites, or simply lying in the grass and soaking up the sun. Chirping happily in the trees, numerous picnickers were entertained by choruses of birds. Swimming was a popular way to spend the day, too. The river overflowed with kids of all ages taking their last summer swim.
2. Everyone knew the house was haunted. Looming ominously in the distance, it overshadowed the whole town. No one had been inside for

years. Everyone had been afraid since that fateful day when, shrieking and hollering, the house was rapidly vacated by the family that owned it. They all said they had seen a ghost in frightened voices. No one believed them, not at first. Then, the noises began.

3. Football fans sometimes seem a little crazy to the rest of the world. They love their teams so much and want them to win so badly that these fans will do just about anything. Cleveland is just one example. Wearing dog masks, barking, and throwing dog bones at the opposition, the town goes wild. All of this silliness springs not from insanity, but from love and devotion. It's just the fans' way of saying, "We're behind you all the way. Win one for us!"

Modifiers, nonrestrictive.   See *Commas, F.*

Modifiers, restrictive.   See *Commas, F.*

Nonrestrictive modifiers.   See *Commas, F.*

Noun.   Traditionally defined as the name of a person, place, thing, or concept, nouns are generally used as the subject, object, or complement of a sentence: *Roosevelt, Bill, accountant, California, Lake Ontario, Boulder Dam, desk, car, freedom, love.*

Numerals.

- *Numerals are used to indicate dates, times, percentages, money, street numbers, and page references.*

  On January 21, 2003, at 5:00 a.m., a fire broke out at 552 East 52nd Street, and before the Fire Department brought the flames under control, the fire had destroyed 75 percent of the building.

- *In other cases, if a number is one or two words, spell it out; if it is over two words, use the numeral.*

  In the big contest forty-five young boys won ribbons. William ate 152 hot dogs.

- *Opt for ease and consistency when you refer to different numbers in one sentence.*

  In the big contests yesterday 45 young boys won ribbons and William ate 152 hot dogs in 2 minutes.

- *Spell out all numbers that begin a sentence.*

  Four thugs assaulted an old woman last night.

  Three hundred thirty-one traffic deaths happened nationwide during the Labor Day weekend.

Object.   The person, place, or thing that receives the action of a verb, or the noun or pronoun after a preposition.

George shot *Joe*.

Florence kissed *him*.

All motives are suspect to *them*.

You'll find your *gloves* in the car.

Parallelism. Express ideas and facts of equal importance in the same grammatical form. See pages 529–530 for a fuller treatment of parallelism.

Parentheses. Parentheses can enclose incidental comments, provide explanatory details, sometimes set off numerals that accompany the points of a paper, and enclose source information in research papers. In largely outdated citation formats, parentheses enclose information in footnotes. In many cases, parentheses serve to mark afterthoughts that probably should have been incorporated into the writing elsewhere. Use parentheses sparingly.

- *Incidental comments.*

  The movie *The Killers* (its plot had little resemblance to Hemingway's short story) won an award.

- *Explanation of details.*

  The cornucopia (the horn of plenty) is a Thanksgiving symbol.

- *Enumerated points.*

  This essay has four main pieces of advice: (1) know your professors as people, (2) attend college-sponsored events, (3) attend student-sponsored events, and (4) use the library.

- *Source material.*

  [1]Peter Straub, *Shadowland* (New York: Coward, 1980), 10. (Straub 10.)

Passive voice. See *Voice*. Also see Chapter 23, page 528.

Period. See *End marks*.

Person. The form of pronouns and verbs that indicates the speaker (*first person*), the person or thing spoken to (*second person*), or the person or thing spoken about (*third person*).

	Pronoun	**Verb**
First person	I, we	go
Second person	you	go
Third person	he, she, it	goes
	they	go

Possessives.   See *Apostrophe*.

Predicate.   The part of a clause that tells what the subject does, or what is being done to the subject.

> Sal *went home*.

> The child *will be punished*.

See also *Subject*.

Preposition.   A connecting word such as *in, by, from, on, to,* or *with* that shows the relation of a noun or a pronoun to another element in a sentence.

> The man *with* the gun shot the deer.

Pronoun.   A word that takes the place of a noun. It may be personal (*I, you, he, she, it, we, they, me, him, her*), possessive (*my, mine, your, yours, his*), reflexive or intensive (*myself, yourself, herself*), relative (*who, which, that*), interrogative (*who, which, what*), or indefinite (*anyone, somebody, nothing*).

Pronoun agreement.   A pronoun must agree with its antecedent both in gender (masculine, feminine, or neuter) and number (singular or plural). The antecedent of a pronoun is the word or words to which the pronoun refers. For example, in the sentence "Jason lost his book," the pronoun *his* refers to the antecedent *Jason*. Another example is "Jason could not find his book. He had lost it." In the second sentence, there are two pronouns—*he* and *it*. The antecedent of *he* is *Jason*, and the antecedent of *it* is *book*. With the exception of constructions such as *it is nearly eight o'clock*, in which *it* has no antecedent, all pronouns should have antecedents.

- *Gender.* When the gender of a singular antecedent is unknown, irrelevant, or general (as in *student* or *person*, for example), be sure to avoid sexist language. The traditional rule calling for the masculine pronoun to take precedence in such situations is now outdated and has been rejected by all or nearly all publishers of books, magazines, and newspapers as well as English instructors.

  If the singular antecedent is retained, sexist language can be avoided by using a form of *he or she*, though this phrasing can often be awkward and excessively formal.

> A student needs to turn in his or her work on time.

> A person who truly likes others will find that others will like him or her.

  The most effective way of avoiding sexist language is usually to change the singular antecedent to plural.

> Students must turn in their work on time.

> People who truly like others will find that others will like them.

  (See *he, his, him, himself* in the Glossary and pages 545–547 in Chapter 24.)

■ *Number.* Most pronoun agreement errors occur when the pronoun does not agree with its antecedent in number. If the antecedent is singular, the pronoun must be singular; if the antecedent is plural, the pronoun must be plural.

1. *Indefinite pronouns.* Words like *anybody, somebody, everybody, nobody*, and *each* are always singular. Others like *few* and *many* are always plural. Indefinite pronouns such as *all, any, most*, and *more* can be either singular or plural, depending on the object of the preposition that follows them: "All of my concern is justified"; but, "All of my concerns are justified."

Incorrect:	Everybody missed the deadline for turning in their paper.
	Each employee was told that they represented the company, not just themselves.
Correct:	Everybody missed the deadline for turning in his or her paper.
	Each employee was told that he or she represented the company, not just himself or herself.

   NOTE: Overuse of the *he or she* approach can lead to awkwardness. It's a good idea to see if changing to a plural antecedent can create a more effective sentence.

   All the students missed the deadline for turning in their papers.

   The employees were told that they represented the company, not just themselves.

2. *Collective nouns.* Some singular nouns refer to more than one thing: *group, youth, family, jury*, and *audience*, for example. If the noun acts as a unit, it takes a singular pronoun. If the individuals within the unit act separately, the noun takes a plural pronoun.

   The jury reached *its* decision.

   The jury divided bitterly on *their* decision.

   The audience rose to *its* feet to show *its* approval.

   The audience straggled to *their* seats through the entire first act.

3. *Antecedents joined by* either . . . or *and* neither . . . nor. When two antecedents are joined by *either . . . or* or *neither . . . nor*, the pronoun agrees with the antecedent closer to it:

   Either Ruby or Jan lost *her* album.

   Either the mother or the daughters lost their albums.

   Either the daughters or the mother lost her album.

   Neither the boys nor the girls lost *their* albums.

4. *Compound antecedents.* Except when the words function as a single unit—such as in "Macaroni and cheese *is* my favorite dish"—antecedents joined by *and* take a plural pronoun:

The owl and the pussycat shook *their* heads sadly.

EXERCISE Correct any errors in pronoun agreement in the following sentences.

1. No one at the meeting knew what they might expect the mayor to say.
2. Everyone remembered their lines in last night's performance.
3. Both my brother and my sister brought their children to the party.
4. Every student needs to understand the importance of coming to their classes on time.
5. The crowd of sport fans shouted their disapproval of the umpire's decision.
6. Everybody I know talks about their birthplace with great affection, but almost nobody ever goes back.
7. Neither Win Hou nor his brother Shing wore their jacket, though the air was chilly.
8. All of the soup was tainted, so they were recalled by the manufacturer.
9. Either the boss or the workers will have to make up his mind about medical benefits.
10. The team celebrated their victory.

EXERCISE Correct any pronoun agreement errors in the following paragraphs.

1. At the end of the show we will have a curtain call and a company bow. The chorus will bow first. Then, the supporting cast will take their bows in a group. The two leads will meet center stage and receive their applause. Finally, everyone will take their neighbors' hands and the entire company will bow together. Please, don't forget to bow quickly and smile.
2. The jury debated for a long time. Could they convict this man of murder? Such a conviction would mean at least life imprisonment, if not the death penalty. Were they positive he was guilty? For five hours the jury argued among themselves. Finally, a verdict was reached. Together, the jury filed back into the courtroom and prepared to give the decision they had reached.
3. Going to the laundromat is no fun at all. It takes forever, and inconsiderate people make it take even longer. There is always someone who has saved up his laundry for an entire year and is using five washers and six dryers. People with less laundry have to wait hours for an empty machine. Then there are the kids who have never done laundry before. They wash their socks and their underwear with their

blue jeans and complain when their whites get dingy. The rest of us have to wait while these fools relaunder all their clothes. I am so tired of it all that I just might start doing my laundry in my dishwasher.

Pronoun case. *Pronoun case* refers to the change in form of pronouns that corresponds with their grammatical function. There are three cases, and their names are self-explanatory: *subjective* (when the pronoun acts as a subject), *objective* (when the pronoun acts as an object), and *possessive* (when the pronoun acts to show possession). Following is a list of case changes for the most common pronouns:

Subjective	Objective	Possessive
I	me	my, mine
you	you	your, yours
he	him	his
she	her	her, hers
it	it	its
we	us	our, ours
they	them	their, theirs
who	whom	whose

- *Compound subjects and objects (subjects and objects connected by* and*)*. Do not be misled by a compound subject or object. Use the pronoun case that shows the pronoun's grammatical role.

Wrong	**Right**
My father scolded Jim and *I*.	My father scolded Jim and *me*.
Betty and *her* had many good times.	Betty and *she* had many good times.

A simple test for getting the right word is to eliminate one of the compound terms and see which pronoun works better. No one would write "My father scolded I"—so "My father scolded me" is correct. No one would write "Her had many good times"—so "She had many good times" is correct.

- *Object of a preposition.* In a prepositional phrase, any pronoun after the preposition always takes the objective case.

Wrong	**Right**
This match is just between you and *I*.	This match is just between you and *me*.
I went to the movies with Ramona and *she*.	I went to the movies with Ramona and *her*.
This present is for John and *he*.	This present is for John and *him*.

ca

- *After forms of* to be (is, am, are, was, were, has been, had been, might be, will be, *etc.*). A pronoun after forms of *to be* is always in the subjective case. This rule still applies rigorously in formal written English. It is frequently ignored in informal English and has all but disappeared from most conversation.

  It was she.

  This is he.

  The winners will be they.

- *After* as *and* than. In comparisons with *as* and *than*, mentally add a verb to the pronoun to determine which pronoun is correct. Should you write, for example, "Bill is smarter than I," or, "Bill is smarter than me"? Simply complete the construction with the "understood" verb. You could write, "Bill is smarter than I am," but not, "Bill is smarter than me am." Therefore, "Bill is smarter than I" is correct.

Wrong	**Right**
I am just as good as *them*.	I am just as good as *they*.
Her mother had more ambition than *her*.	Her mother had more ambition than *she*.
Bill liked her more than *I*.	Bill liked her more than *me*. (Meaning *Bill liked her more than he liked me*.)
Bill liked her more than *me*.	Bill liked her more than *I*. (Meaning *Bill liked her more than I liked her*.)

- We *or* us *followed by a noun.* Use *we* if the noun is a subject, *us* if the noun is an object. If ever in doubt, mentally eliminate the noun and see which pronoun sounds right. Should you write, for example, "The professor had us students over to his house," or, "The professor had we students over to his house"? Mentally eliminate *students*. No one would write, "The professor had we over to his house," so *us* is correct.

Wrong	**Right**
After the final exam, *us* students were exhausted.	After the final exam, *we* students were exhausted.
The company's reply to *we* consumers was almost totally negative.	The company's reply to *us* consumers was almost totally negative.

- *Gerunds.* A gerund is an *-ing* verb form that functions as a noun. In "Swimming used to be my favorite sport," *swimming* is a gerund. A pronoun before a gerund takes the possessive case.

Wrong	**Right**
Us nagging him did no good.	*Our* nagging him did no good.
His parents do not understand *him* reading so poorly.	His parents do not understand *his* reading so poorly.
Them believing what she says does not mean that she is telling the truth.	*Their* believing what she says does not mean that she is telling the truth.

- Who *and* whom. See the Glossary, pages 659–660.

EXERCISE   Choose the correct pronoun in each of the following sentences. Be prepared to explain your choice.

1. He cared about money every bit as much as (I, me), but he was a more successful hypocrite than (I, me).
2. For (he and she, him and her), divorce might have been the only practical choice.
3. Will you accompany Sally and (I, me) to the movies?
4. (She, Her) and I took the same courses last semester.
5. (Him, His) lying has become part of his character.
6. (He and I, Him and me) decided that we would adopt a beagle from our local shelter.
7. I honestly don't know what he expects (we, us) poor students to do.
8. The judge then assessed an additional fine for (them, their) resisting arrest.
9. The winning contestants were no brighter or quicker than (I, me).
10. Bennett hated Stephen and (she, her) with a jealous passion.

EXERCISE   Find and correct any errors in pronoun case in the following paragraphs.

1. Jack Fitzwilliam, master thief, strolled calmly down the street. In his pockets were the diamonds and pearls that, until recently, had been the sacred treasure of the Montgomery family. Now they were Jack's. He knew the police were only moments behind him. However, with his false beard and moustache, he had no fear of being recognized, and if he ran from the police they might think of him running as an admission of guilt.
2. Just between you and I, I've never been very fond of Ann Pickett. It's not that she's cruel or nasty; we just have so little in common. For some reason, we are always expected to be best friends and exchange cozy confidences. To me, that is unthinkable. We just never have anything to talk about.
3. We are tired of this abuse, and we just won't take it any longer. Us poor kids do all the work around here. We mow the lawn, take out the trash, do the dishes, feed and walk the dogs, fold the laundry, and wash windows. You adults just sit around and do nothing. When are you going to start

taking some responsibility for yourselves? When are you going to become mature and capable? We're tired of waiting. Us kids are on strike.

ref

Pronoun reference. A pronoun must not only agree with its antecedent, but that antecedent must be clear as well. An ambiguous antecedent is as bad as no antecedent at all. Generally, two types of ambiguity occur: a pronoun with two or more possible antecedents, and one pronoun referring to different antecedents.

- *Two or more possible antecedents.* In the sentence, "When Stanton visited the mayor, he said that he hoped his successor could work with him," the pronouns *he, his,* and *him* can refer to either the mayor or Stanton. This problem can be avoided by making the antecedent clear: "When Stanton visited the mayor, Stanton said that he hoped his successor could work with the mayor." Here the pronouns *he* and *his* clearly refer to Stanton. Be particularly careful of the potential ambiguity in vague use of the word *this.*

Ambiguous	Improved
I received an *F* in the course and had to take it over again. This was very unfair. (Was the *F* unfair or having to take the course again? Were both unfair?)	I received an *F* in the course and had to take it over again. This grade was very unfair.
Young people are unhappy today and are demanding change. This is a healthy thing. (What is healthy—being unhappy, demanding change, or both?)	Young people are unhappy today and are demanding change. This demand is a healthy thing.

- *One pronoun referring to different antecedents.* "Mark received an *F* on his term paper and had to write a revision of it. It took a long time because it had many errors." In these sentences, the first *it* refers to the paper, the second to the revision, and the third to the paper. A reader could easily become confused by these sentences. In that case, simply replacing the pronouns with their antecedents would solve the problem: "Mark received an *F* on his term paper and had to write a revision of it. The revision took a long time because the paper had many errors."

EXERCISE Rewrite the following sentences by correcting any errors in pronoun reference. Some sentences are correct.

1. Scuba diving and snorkeling are very popular in Palau, but it can be dangerous.
2. The fans cheered the performers hysterically, and they didn't leave the hall for another hour.
3. The students left the rooms in their usual order.
4. Jim told his father that he ought to put his funds into a money-market account.

5. Anita Sanchez inspected the carburetor and distributor. It needed several adjustments.

6. Emma's coach told her that she needed to see some more plays before she could leave for the day.

7. Zoe received her citizenship papers and registered to vote. This made her very happy.

8. The animals clawed and rattled their cages. They were filthy and their stench was horrifying.

9. The prosecutor disagreed with the judge. He felt he was guilty.

10. His final grades were an *A* and a *C*. This really saved him.

EXERCISE   Find and correct the pronoun reference errors in the following paragraphs.

1. The old Road Runner and Coyote cartoons are popular with just about all children. The shows have no plot to speak of, just lots of random silliness. This is what makes them so much fun for kids to watch. It's always amazing to see the endless schemes the Coyote will use to try to catch the Road Runner, and it's even more fun to try to guess how it will fail. These cartoons certainly aren't edifying or educational, but it's so much fun that no child really minds.

2. Sir William Gilbert and Sir Arthur Sullivan are famous for writing some of the greatest operettas in the history of music. Although the two men never got along personally (perhaps because of his infamous temper), their words and music blended harmoniously. Extremely popular, if slightly shocking in their time, Gilbert and Sullivan's operettas are just as popular today. Everyone from the Met to the smallest community theater has a Gilbert and Sullivan show in their repertoire. *Topsy-Turvey*, a successful film, made the two writers come alive for audiences. They still dazzle with their words and music.

3. A three-year-old's idea of the perfect lunch is a peanut butter and jelly sandwich. Do not, however, make the mistake of thinking you can slap a little PB and J on some bread, toss it to a kid, and be left in peace. Three-year-olds are picky. They must be made to precise specifications or they won't eat them. Use white bread, the squishier the better. Little kids don't eat whole wheat. Use creamy peanut butter, not chunky. Little kids don't like food with texture. Use grape jelly. Don't mess with exotic alternatives. Little kids can't say *marmalade* and won't eat it. Cut the sandwich into four triangles; remove the crusts; serve; and breathe a sigh of relief.

Question marks.   See *End marks.*

Questions, indirect.   See *End marks.*

99 99

Quotation marks.   Quotation marks are used to indicate material taken word for word from another source; to mark the title of a poem, song, short story, essay, and any part of a longer work; and to point out words used in a special sense—words set apart for emphasis and special consideration, slang and colloquial expressions, and derisively used words.

- *Direct quotations.* Quotation marks indicate what someone else has said in speech or writing:

  The mayor said, "The city is in serious financial trouble if the new city income tax does not pass."

  "No man is an island," John Donne once wrote.

  "The world," said the senator, "is growing smaller and smaller."

  If there is a quotation within a quotation, use single marks for the second quote:

  The mother commented wryly, "I wonder if Dr. Spock and the other great authorities on bringing up kids have ever seen you, calm as can be, say, 'I don't wanna.'"

  Observe the following rules in punctuation of direct quotations.

  1. *Block quotation.* If a direct quotation other than dialog is more than four lines long, it should be blocked. Block quotations *do not* take quotation marks and are indented ten spaces from the left margin.

     > In the section of the text on quotation marks, the authors make the following observation:

     >> Use quotation marks to indicate material taken word for word from another source; to mark the title of a poem, song, short story, essay, and any part of a longer work; and to point out words used in a special sense—words set apart for emphasis and special consideration, slang and colloquial expressions, and derisively used words.

  2. *Periods and commas.* Periods and commas at the end of quotations always go inside the quotation marks.

     "The city will be in serious financial trouble if the city income tax does not pass," said the mayor.

     The film was widely considered pornographic although to describe it, the producer used the word "art."

  3. *Other punctuation.* An exclamation point or question mark goes inside the quotation marks if it is part of the quotation. If it is part of a longer statement, it goes outside the quotation marks.

     The student asked, "Is this paper due Friday?"

     Did Robert Frost write "Mending Wall"?

A colon or a semicolon always goes outside the quotation marks.

The text says, "A colon or a semicolon always goes outside the quotation marks"; this rule is simple.

- *Titles.* Use quotation marks to indicate the title of a work—a poem, a song, a short story, a chapter, an essay—that is part of a larger whole, or a short unit in itself.

    John Collier wrote the short story "The Chaser."

    The chapter is called "Stylistic Problems and Their Solutions."

- *Words used in a special sense.* Quotation marks are sometimes put around words used in a special sense, but these quotation marks are often over-used. Pay close attention to the cautionary statements that accompany the following examples.

    1. *Words used as words.*

        I can never tell the difference between "affect" and "effect."

        "Really" and "very" are frequently overused words.

        Underlining or italicizing is usually preferable to quotation marks in sentences of this kind. (See *Italics (underlining)*.)

    2. *Words used as slang and colloquial expressions.*

        The speaker gave me good "vibes."

        I wonder what's on the "tube."

        This usage is almost always undesirable. (See Chapter 24, pages 543–544.)

    3. *Words used derisively.* The use of quotation marks to indicate sarcasm or derision is generally a primitive means of showing feelings and, as a rule, should be avoided:

        The "performance" was a collection of amateurish blunders.

        This "dormitory" is unfit for human habitation.

EXERCISE

Add quotation marks (or italics: see pages 588–589) as needed in the following sentences. In some cases you will need to add capitals and commas as well.

1. Coach Sharif reminded us I expect all of my players to remain prepared and flexible, including those of you who may be on the bench.
2. Did you read The Girl with the Dragon Tattoo?
3. Though he hasn't repaid the $50 he borrowed, using the word crook to describe him is much too harsh.
4. The teacher reminded her kindergarten class, don't forget that Officer Torres said, Always hold a grown-up's hand when you cross the street.
5. We'll never forget the cheers of joy when Professor Kwan said, Tomorrow's test is cancelled.

6. Eric Carle's The Very Hungry Caterpillar is a longtime favorite storybook for many children.
7. The more my neighbor referred to her party as her soireé, the less I wanted to attend it.
8. Jermaine wondered why the map didn't show the fork in the road that he had just reached.
9. A Midsummer Night's Dream is Shakespeare's most hilarious comedy.
10. The Secretary of Labor said learning about safety may be the most important lesson of a teen's summer job.

Run-on sentence.   A *run-on sentence* or *fused sentence* is two or more sentences written as one, with no punctuation between them. It is most commonly corrected by rewriting the run-on sentence as separate sentences, by placing a semicolon between the sentences, or by placing a comma and a coordinating conjunction between the sentences. A comma alone would create a comma splice, often considered a special kind of run-on sentence. (See *Comma splice.*)

Incorrect	**Correct**
This rule sounds easy enough putting it into practice is not so easy.	This rule sounds easy enough. Putting it into practice is not so easy.
	or
	This rule sounds easy enough; putting it into practice is not so easy.
	or
	This rule sounds easy enough, but putting it into practice is not so easy.

EXERCISE   Correct the following run-on sentences by using a comma and a coordinating conjunction (*and, but, or, nor, for, yet, so*), a semicolon, or a period.

1. The music of Queen is still popular I didn't realize that the group boasts the longest running fan club in history.
2. It is possible to "zap" almost anything in a microwave, however roasts still require conventional cooking.
3. The fear of being buried alive is universal the fear may first have been expressed in writing by Poe.
4. Make sure you separate sentences with a conjunction, a semicolon, or a period never just run them together.
5. Drunk drivers are dangerous they killed thousands of people last year.
6. Many houses have hidden defects for example, the plumbing may be bad.

7. Medical literature lists more than three hundred causes for hiccups so-called everyday hiccups can result from inhaling too much air, eating spicy foods, and drinking too rapidly, among other causes.

8. It's all very well to say that we need new carpeting it's just that we don't have the funds.

9. Your new sweater is lovely I think that the color is perfect.

10. Waking early has never agreed with me it leaves me sulky and disagreeable.

11. A knowledge of classical mythology is a valuable part of anyone's educational background it can not only add a spark to one's own writing but can enable one to get more out of one's reading.

12. I don't know how anyone can possibly dislike chocolate it's my favorite food.

13. My sister can't sit still for more than a few minutes she can barely sit through her favorite sitcom she certainly can't concentrate on a novel.

14. They boarded the airplane with a sense of fear and trepidation then they noticed the pilot was reading an instruction book.

15. Spinach is the best vegetable Popeye claimed it gave him his incredible strength.

Semicolon. Use a semicolon between two independent clauses when the coordinating conjunction has been left out and between separate elements in a list or series when the elements contain punctuation within themselves.

- *Between independent clauses.*

  Stating the problem is simple enough; solving it is the tough part.

  Roberta wasn't precisely sure what the bearded stranger wanted; all she knew was that he made her nervous.

  Observe that in both of these cases a coordinating conjunction preceded by a comma could be used to replace the semicolon. Under no circumstances could a comma alone be used between these independent clauses. In order to use a comma, you must also have a coordinating conjunction (*and, but, or, nor, for, yet, so*) between independent clauses. (See *Comma splice.*)

- *Between separate elements that contain commas in a list or series.*

  The following American cities have grown enormously in recent years: Houston, Texas; Dallas, Texas; Phoenix, Arizona; and Denver, Colorado.

Sentence. A group of words beginning with a capital letter and ending with a period, question mark, or exclamation point that contains at least one independent clause.

> Birds sing.
>
> Do birds sing?
>
> Shut up, all you birds!

(See *Clause; Predicate; Subject.*)

shift

Shifts in time and person.   Do not unnecessarily shift from one tense to another (past to present, present to future, and so on) or from one person to another (*he* to *you*, *one* to *I*).

- *Tense shifts.* If you begin writing in a particular tense, do not shift to another unless a change in time is logically necessary. The following paragraph breaks this rule:

  > In William Carlos Williams's "The Use of Force," a doctor *was called* to examine a young girl. The doctor *was concerned* about diphtheria and *needs* to examine the girl's throat. The girl *is* terrified and *begins* to resist. As her resistance *continues*, the doctor *is compelled* to use more and more physical force. Though he *knows* the force *is* necessary, the doctor, to his horror, *found* that he *enjoyed* it and really *wanted* to hurt the girl.

  Here the writer starts in the past tense (*was called, was concerned*), shifts to the present tense (*needs, is, begins, continues, is compelled, knows, is*), and then shifts back to the past tense (*found, enjoyed, wanted*). Why? There is no reason. No change in time is needed. If writers view the events of a story as happening in the present, they should use the present tense consistently. Writers could also view the events as past actions—over and completed—and write entirely in the past tense. In either case, writers should decide which view they prefer and stick to it throughout.

All verbs in present tense	**All verbs in past tense**
In William Carlos Williams's "The Use of Force," a doctor *is called* to examine a young girl. The doctor *is concerned* about diphtheria and *needs* to examine the girl's throat. The girl *is* terrified and *begins* to resist. As her resistance *continues*, the doctor *is compelled* to use more and more physical force. Though he *knows* the force *is* necessary, the doctor, to his horror, *finds* that he *enjoys* it and really *wants* to hurt the girl.	In William Carlos Williams's "The Use of Force," a doctor *was called* to examine a young girl. The doctor *was concerned* about diphtheria and *needed* to examine the girl's throat. The girl *was* terrified and *began* to resist. As her resistance *continued*, the doctor *was compelled* to use more and more physical force. Though he *knew* the force *was* necessary, the doctor, to his horror, *found* that he *enjoyed* it and really *wanted* to hurt the girl.

- *Shifts in person.* Write from a consistent point of view, making sure that any change in person is logically justified. If, for example, you begin expressing your thoughts in the third person (*he, she, it, they, one, the reader, the student, people,* and so on), avoid sudden shifts to the first person (*I, we*) or to the second person (*you*). Similarly, avoid sudden shifts from third- or first-person singular to third- or first-person plural.

Poor	**Improved**
Most *average citizens* think *they* are in favor of a clean environment, but *you* may change *your* mind when *you* find out what it will cost. (Shift from third-person *average citizens* and *they* to second-person *you, your*.)	Most *average citizens* think *they* are in favor of a clean environment, but *they* may change *their* minds when *they* find out what it will cost.

Poor	Improved
The teenager resents the way *he* is being stereotyped. *We're* as different among *ourselves* as any other group in the population. *They* are tired of being viewed as a collection of finger-snapping freaks who say "cool" all the time. (Shift from third-person singular *teenager* and *he* to first-personplural *we* to third-person plural *they*.)	*Teenagers* resent the way *they* are being stereotyped. *They* are as different among *themselves* as any other group in the population. *They* are tired of being viewed as a collection of finger-snapping freaks who say "cool" all the time.
Readers will find this suspense-filled mystery irresistible, just as *they* have found P. D. James's previous efforts. *You* should have a real battle keeping *yourself* from looking ahead to the last page. (Shift from third-person *readers* and *they* to second-person *you, yourself.*)	*Readers* will find this suspense-filled mystery irresistible, just as *they* have found P. D. James's previous efforts. *They* should have a real battle keeping *themselves* from looking ahead to the last page.
One wonders what is going on at City Hall. *We* have put up with flooded basements and lame excuses long enough. (Shift from third-person *one* to first-person *we.*)	*We* wonder what is going on at City Hall. *We* have put up with flooded basements and lame excuses long enough.

EXERCISE Correct any illogical shifts in tense or person in the following sentences.

1. You can never tell when one needs a friend's help.
2. Chapter 1 introduces us to a scientist who is devoted to making the world a safer place. In Chapter 2, the scientist turned into a werewolf.
3. Teenage parents get the worst of both worlds. We didn't have the temperament or finances for adulthood, and we had too many responsibilities to enjoy what remained of our youth.
4. The two thugs drive up to the door of the diner. They walk in, sit down, and pick up a menu. They look at Nick coldly. "What's the name of this dump?" they asked.
5. You need to be careful about shopping at discount stores. First, a person needs to check the quality as well as the price. Even cheap is too expensive if your purchase self-destructs after a few days.
6. Many of John Grisham's books involve a lawyer who became disillusioned with the judicial system or who is forced to give up a position as an attorney.
7. The snow is falling, and we were getting ready for another winter.
8. The company is going to introduce its new line of luxury cars this weekend. We decided two years ago that we would have to be represented at the high end of the market to stay fully competitive.
9. A person who is contemplating buying a new washing machine must take into account your types of clothing and your washing habits.
10. Finding a one hundred dollar bill in the park was a problem. My girlfriend wants to give it to charity. I wanted to turn it in to the ranger.

Spelling.   Poor spelling can seriously damage an otherwise fine paper. Faced with any significant number of spelling errors, readers cannot maintain their original confidence in the writer's thoughtfulness and skill.

The one spelling rule every writer needs to know is very simple: *use a dictionary*. Rules for spelling specific words and groups of words almost always have exceptions and are difficult to learn and remember. Good spellers, almost without exception, turn out to be people who read a great deal and who have the dictionary habit, not people who have memorized spelling rules. The most important spelling rule, then, as well as the quickest and easiest one, is use the dictionary.

Yet it can sometimes be handy to have available a list of frequently misspelled words. For quick reference, we include such a list. Note that words spelled the same as parts of longer words are not usually listed separately: for example, the list has *accidentally* but not *accident*, *acquaintance* but not *acquaint*.

Frequently misspelled words

absence	arithmetic	commission	disastrous
accidentally	ascend	committee	discipline
accommodate	athletic	conscience*	dissatisfied
accumulate	attendance	comparative	dormitory
achievement	beginning	compelled	effect
acquaintance	balance	conceivable	eighth
acquire	belief	conferred	eligible
acquitted	believe	conscientious*	eliminate
advice*	batallion	conscious*	embarrass
advise*	beneficial	control	eminent
all right	benefited	controversial	encouragement
amateur	boundaries	controversy	encouraging
among	Britain	criticize	environment
analysis	business	deferred	equipped
analyze	calendar	definitely	especially
annual	candidate	definition	exaggerate
apartment	category	describe	excellence
apparatus	cemetery	description	exhilarate
apparent	changeable	desperate	existence
appearance	changing	dictionary	existent
arctic	choose	dining	experience
arguing	chose	disappearance	explanation
argument	coming	disappoint	familiar

*See the Glossary.

Frequently misspelled words   (continued)

fascinate	laboratory	particular	prophecy (noun)
February	laid	pastime	prophesy (verb)
fiery	led	performance	pursue
foreign	lightning	permissible	quantity
formerly	loneliness	perseverance	quiet*
forty	lose	personal*	quite*
fourth	losing	personnel*	quizzes
frantically	maintenance	perspiration	recede
generally	maneuver	physical	receive
government	manufacture	picnicking	receiving
grammar	marriage	possession	recommend
grandeur	mathematics	possibility	reference
grievous	maybe	possible	referring
height	mere	practically	repetition
heroes	miniature	precede*	restaurant
hindrance	mischievous	precedence	rhythm
hoping	mysterious	preference	ridiculous
humorous	necessary	preferred	sacrifice
hypocrisy	ninety	prejudice	sacrilegious
hypocrite	noticeable	preparation	salary
immediately	occasionally	prevalent	schedule
incidentally	occurred	principal*	seize
incredible	occurrence	principle*	sense
independence	omitted	privilege	separate
inevitable	opinion	probably	separation
intellectual	opportunity	procedure	sergeant
intelligence	optimistic	proceed*	severely
interesting	paid	profession	shining
irresistible	parallel	professor	siege
judgment	paralysis	prominent	similar
knowledge	paralyze	pronunciation	sophomore

*See the Glossary.

Frequently misspelled words   (continued)

specifically	surprise	tragedy	usually
specimen	technique	transferring	village
stationary*	temperamental	tries	villain
stationery*	tendency	truly	weather
statue	than, then*	tyranny	weird
studying	their, they're, there*	unanimous	whether
succeed	thorough	undoubtedly	woman, women
succession	through	unnecessary	writing
supersede	to, too, two*	until	

*See the Glossary.

EXERCISE   Correct the misspelled words in the following sentences. Numbers in parentheses indicate the number of incorrectly spelled words.

1. In February he generaly feels disatisfied with the whether. (3)
2. When you are referring to the commission on attendance, don't exagerate their excellence. (1)
3. You can succeed at writting if you persue your goal to elimenate grammar errors. (3)
4. Ocasionally a beleif can controll your existance and sieze your good sense. (5)
5. I usualy recomend that you truely seperate the salery issue from the more intresting challanges you will face by working in a foreign country. (7)

Subject.   A word, phrase, or clause that names the person, place, thing, or idea that the sentence is about. (See also *Predicate*.)

> *Sal* went home.

> The president's *speech* was heard by 100,000 people.

Subject-verb agreement.   A verb must agree with its subject in number and person. This rule has most practical meaning only in the present tense; in other tenses, the verb forms generally remain the same regardless of number or person. (The exception is in the past tense of *to be*; in that instance the verb forms do change: *I was, you were, he was, we were, they were.*)

In the present tense, the third-person singular verb usually differs from the others—most often because an *-s* or *-es* is added to the verb stem. A third-person singular verb is the verb that goes with the pronouns *he, she,* and *it* and with any singular noun.

to dream

	Singular	Plural
First person	I dream	we dream
Second person	you dream	you dream
Third person	he she }dreams it	they dream

The lovers *dream* of a long and happy future together.

The lover *dreams* of his sweetheart every night.

People often *dream* about falling from great heights.

Jennifer *dreams* about being buried alive.

to miss

	Singular	Plural
First person	I miss	we miss
Second person	you miss	you miss
Third person	he she }misses it	they miss

The children *miss* their father more than they thought they would.

The child *misses* her friends.

The commuters *miss* the bus almost every morning.

The left fielder *misses* more than his share of easy fly balls.

Even with highly irregular verbs, the third-person singular in the present tense takes a special form (always with an *-s* at the end).

to be

	Singular	Plural
First person	I am	we are
Second person	you are	you are
Third person	he she }is it	they are

to have

	Singular	**Plural**
First person	I have	we have
Second person	you have	you have
Third person	he she }has it	they have

The clowns *are* happy.

Erica *is* sad.

The Joneses *have* a lovely new home.

Mr. Jones *has* a lot to learn.

The few cases in which a present tense verb in the third-person singular has the same form as in the other persons come naturally to almost every writer and speaker: *he can, he may, he might*, and so on.

Once a writer realizes the difference between third-person singular and other verb forms, the only problem is likely to be deciding which form to use in a few tricky situations.

■ *Compound subjects.* If the subject is compound (joined by *and*), the verb is plural unless the two words function as a single unit—"Pork and beans *is* an easy dish to prepare," for example—or unless the two words refer to a single person, as in "My cook and bottle washer *has* left me" (one person performed both jobs).

Wrong	**Right**
Writing and reading *is* necessary for success in college.	Writing and reading *are* necessary for success in college.
The introduction and conclusion *does* not appear in an outline.	The introduction and conclusion *do* not appear in an outline.

■ *Neither . . . nor, either . . . or, nor, or.* If two subjects are joined by any of these terms, the verb agrees with the closer subject.

Wrong	**Right**
Neither the students nor the teacher *are* correct.	Neither the students nor the teacher *is* correct.
Either the supporting details or the thesis statement *are* wrong.	Either the supporting details or the thesis statement *is* wrong.
Snowstorms or rain *cause* accidents.	Snowstorms or rain *causes* accidents.
Rain or snowstorms *causes* accidents.	Rain or snowstorms *cause* accidents.

- *Time, money, weight.* Words that state an amount (time, money, weight) have a singular verb when they are considered as a unit even if they are plural in form.

Wrong	Right
Two semesters *are* really a short time.	Two semesters *is* really a short time.
Five dollars *are* a modest fee for credit by examination.	Five dollars *is* a modest fee for credit by examination.
Five kilos of soybeans *are* about eleven pounds.	Five kilos of soybeans *is* about eleven pounds.

- *Titles.* Titles of songs, plays, movies, novels, or articles always have singular verbs, even if the titles are plural in form.

Wrong	Right
The Wings of the Dove were made into a movie.	*The Wings of the Dove was* made into a movie.
"The Novels of Early America" *were* published in *American Literature.*	"The Novels of Early America" *was* published in *American Literature.*

- *Collective nouns.* Collective nouns such as *family, audience, jury,* and *class* have singular verbs when they are considered as a unified group. If the individuals within the unit act separately, the verb will be plural.

Wrong	Right
The family *plan* a vacation.	The family *plans* a vacation.
The jury *is* divided on the verdict.	The jury *are* divided on the verdict.
The audience *are* going to give this show a standing ovation.	The audience *is* going to give this show a standing ovation.
The audience *is* divided in their opinion of the show.	The audience *are* divided in their opinion of the show.

- *Indefinite pronouns.* Indefinite pronouns such as *one, no one, someone, everyone, none, anyone, somebody, anybody, everybody, each, neither,* and *either* take singular verbs:

Wrong	Right
None of the ideas *are* correct.	None of the ideas *is* correct.
Each of the students *have* the time to study.	Each of the students *has* the time to study.
Either *are* a valid choice.	Either *is* a valid choice.

- *Intervening elements.* No matter how many words, phrases, or clauses separate a subject from its verb, the verb must still agree with the subject in number.

    1. Separated by words:

Wrong:	Many state capitals—Carson City, Augusta, Jefferson City, Olympia—*is* only small towns.
Right:	Many state capitals—Carson City, Augusta, Jefferson City, Olympia—*are* only small towns.

    Here the plural *capitals*, not the singular *Olympia*, is the subject.

    2. Separated by phrases:

Wrong:	A crate of oranges *are* expensive.
Right:	A crate of oranges *is* expensive.

    Here *crate*, not *oranges*, is the subject.

Wrong:	Agreement of subjects with their verbs *are* important.
Right:	Agreement of subjects with their verbs *is* important.

    Here *agreement*, not *subjects* or *verbs*, is the subject.

    3. Separated by clauses:

Wrong:	Reading well, which is one of the necessary academic skills, *make* studying easier.
Right:	Reading well, which is one of the necessary academic skills, *makes* studying easier.

    Here *reading*, not *skills*, is the subject.

- *Reversed position.* If the subject comes after the verb, the verb must still agree with the subject.

    1. *There.* If a sentence begins with *there* and is followed by some form of *to be* (*is, are, was, were,* etc.), the number of *be* is determined by the subject. *There* is never the subject (except in a sentence like this one).

Wrong:	There *is* five students in this class.
Right:	There *are* five students in this class.

    Here *students* is the subject, and it is plural. Therefore, the verb must be plural.

2. *Prepositional phrases.* Sometimes a writer begins a sentence with a prepositional phrase followed by a verb and then the subject. The verb must still agree with the subject.

Wrong:	Throughout a grammar book *appears* many helpful writing hints.
Right:	Throughout a grammar book *appear* many helpful writing hints.

Here *hints*, not *book*, is the subject.

EXERCISE   Correct any subject-verb agreement errors in the following sentences. Some sentences are correct.

1. Every pair of glasses Rosa owns are scratched.
2. The twists and turns of international espionage are the main themes of the novels of Alan Durst.
3. My school, as well as hundreds of others all over the country, are trying to tighten academic standards.
4. Disagreement among highly trained economists about budgetary deficits of hundreds of millions of dollars are causing the public to become more confused every day.
5. Neither John nor Esteban have enough money to buy textbooks.
6. Peeling all of those nasty carrots are making me sick.
7. Each of the celebrities' houses are more extravagant than the next.
8. Federal judges and the president constitute the judicial and executive branches of government.
9. The heavenly fragrance of the roses and gardenias were my reward for having coaxed them into bloom.
10. Although I can't see the bells, their clanging and chiming rouses me from my idle daydreams.

EXERCISE   Find and correct any subject-verb agreement errors in the following paragraphs.

1. Lobsters are great for a special dinner, but you have to work for what you eat. You'll need to crack the claws of your lobster with a pair of nutcrackers, which are the only tool for the task. Once the claws are cracked, you can pull out the meat with a nutpick. After consuming the claws, you will want to attack the tail, the smaller legs, and the actual body of the lobster. Proper consumption requires experience gained only through years of practice. So, if you're a first-timer, bring a veteran along for guidance.

2. Balancing checkbooks aren't really very difficult. Problems arise only because of carelessness or inattention. Forgetting to note the amount and number of each check that has been written, neglecting to write down automatic teller transactions, and assuming that bank statements are always correct are major causes of checkbook imbalances. All that are required for balanced checkbooks is attention. Pay attention to every transaction, and write everything down immediately. Assuming that things can be taken care of later will result in checkbook chaos.

3. In fairy tales, the beautiful princess was always locked up in some high stone tower. She didn't do much. She didn't say much. She just waited to be rescued. I want to know why the princesses never bothered to try to escape. Were they too stupid? Were they too weak? I bet that half of the tower doors were left unlocked, and that those two dragons guarding the gate was no more than baby dragons. Any princess worth her salt would have tried to escape. Why didn't a single one even consider it?

Subjunctive mood.   Once far more common in English than it is now, the subjunctive mood is still sometimes used to express "conditions contrary to fact"—hypothetical conditions, conditions not yet brought about, suppositional ideas, and the like. In the subjunctive, the verb form is usually plural even though the subject is singular.

> She wished she *were* here.

> If I *were* you, I would turn down the latest offer.

> I move that the chairperson *declare* the meeting adjourned.

> He looked as if he *were* going to be sick.

Subordinating conjunctions.   See *Fragmentary sentences*.

sub

Subordination.   The most important idea in a sentence should be in an independent clause. Lesser ideas, explanations, qualifying material, and illustrations should be in subordinate clauses or phrases. (See also Chapter 23, pages 531–532.)

Poor	Improved
John is a wonderful person. He is very shy. He is extremely kind to everybody.	Although very shy, John is a wonderful person who is extremely kind to everybody. (The main idea is that John is a wonderful person.)
	or
	Although he is a wonderful person who is extremely kind to everybody, John is very shy. (The main idea is that John is very shy.)

Professor Jones is terribly sarcastic. He is also a tough grader. It is true that he knows his subject. Most students dislike him, however.

Despite Professor Jones' knowledge of his subject, most students dislike him because of his terrible sarcasm and tough grading.

I am going to start on my new job, and I am very optimistic.

I am very optimistic about starting on my new job.

Superlative forms.   See *Comparative and superlative forms.*

Tense shifts.   See *Shifts in time and person.*

Titles, punctuation of.   See *Italics (underlining); Quotation marks.*

Transitive verb.   See *Verb.*

Underlining.   See *Italics (underlining).*

Verb.   A word that expresses an action, an occurrence, or a state of being. Verbs may be divided into three classes: *transitive verbs*, which require objects to complete their meaning (Mary *admires* him); *intransitive verbs*, which are complete in themselves (John *trembled*); and *linking verbs*, which join a subject to its complement (Phyllis *is* a beauty; Their actions *were* cowardly).

In sentences, a complete verb often consists of a *main verb* (marked in grammatical abbreviation as MV) and a *helping verb* (HV). Sometimes a complete verb is a single-word verb. Helping verbs, or auxiliaries, work along with principal parts or other verb forms (like present participles, the *-ing* form of a verb) to express appropriate action.

Helping Verbs

be	are	does	might	should
being	was	has	must	will
been	were	have	can	would
is	do	had	could	
am	did	may	shall	

The nine helping verbs in boldface print—*must, may, can, shall, will, might, could, would,* and *should*—constitute an important subgroup of helping verbs, called modals. Modals tell what the writer believes about the action and express probability, ability, or need or obligation. (She *may drive* the motorcycle. She *can drive* the motorcycle. She *must drive* the motorcycle.)

Verbs: principal parts. The form of most verbs changes according to which tense is being used, and to get the correct form a writer needs to know the principal parts of each verb. There are generally considered to be three principal parts: the *stem* or *infinitive* (the stem is the present tense form of the verb, and the infinitive is the stem preceded by *to*), the *past tense*, and the *past participle*. The past participle is the form used with helping verbs in perfect tenses (*I have seen, I had seen, I will have seen*) and in the passive voice (*I am seen, I was seen, I will be seen, I have been seen*), and in modal verb structures (*I can see, I should see, I may see*).

The principal parts of regular verbs are formed by adding *-ed* or *-d* to the stem: *rush, rushed, rushed; love, loved, loved; drag, dragged, dragged.* The past tense and past participle of regular verbs are always the same.

The principal parts of *irregular verbs* need to be learned separately—and even for the most experienced writer sometimes require checking in a dictionary or handbook. For quick reference, here is an alphabetical list of the principal parts of the most common irregular verbs.

Stem	Past tense	Past participle
arise	arose	arisen
be	was	been
bear	bore	borne, born
begin	began	begun
bind	bound	bound
blow	blew	blown
break	broke	broken
bring	brought	brought
burst	burst	burst
buy	bought	bought
catch	caught	caught
choose	chose	chosen
come	came	come
creep	crept	crept
deal	dealt	dealt
dig	dug	dug
dive	dived, dove	dived
do	did	done
draw	drew	drawn
drink	drank	drunk
drive	drove	driven

eat	ate	eaten
fall	fell	fallen
flee	fled	fled
fly	flew	flown
forbid	forbad, forbade	forbidden
freeze	froze	frozen
give	gave	given
go	went	gone
grow	grew	grown
hang	hung	hung
hang (execute)	hanged	hanged
know	knew	known
lay	laid	laid
lead	led	led
lend	lent	lent
lie	lay	lain
lose	lost	lost
mean	meant	meant
ride	rode	ridden
ring	rang	rung
rise	rose	risen
run	ran	run
see	saw	seen
seek	sought	sought
send	sent	sent
shake	shook	shaken
shine	shone, shined	shone, shined
shrink	shrank	shrunk
sing	sang	sung
sink	sank, sunk	sunk
sleep	slept	slept
sneak	sneaked	sneaked
speak	spoke	spoken
spin	spun	spun
spit	spat	spat
spread	spread	spread

steal	stole	stolen
teach	taught	taught
stink	stank	stunk
swear	swore	sworn
swim	swam	swum
swing	swung	swung
take	took	taken
teach	taught	taught
tear	tore	torn
thrive	thrived, throve	thrived, thriven
throw	threw	thrown
wear	wore	worn
weep	wept	wept
write	wrote	written

Confusion of the past tense and past participle of irregular verbs is a frequent cause of writing errors. Remember that the past participle is the correct form after *has*, *have*, and *had*.

Wrong	**Right**
The mountaineers *had froze* to death.	The mountaineers *had frozen* to death.
The sprinter *has* just *broke* another track record.	The sprinter *has* just *broken* another track record.
I *begun* the book yesterday.	I *began* the book yesterday.
We *seen* that movie when it first came out.	We *saw* that movie when it first came out.

EXERCISE   Correct any errors in verb form in the following sentences.

1. The police finally apprehended Gus. He had stole his last Ferrari.
2. They flown nonstop around the world. Now they begun nonstop appearances on television.
3. I have wrote on this painful subject before, but your negligence has drove me to distraction.
4. The phone must have rang thirty times last night.
5. I have swore on the altar of the gods to do my duty even unto death.
6. Yesterday Priscilla swum thirty laps. Her recovery seems complete.

7. The eagle flown away over the tall pines.
8. The quarterback had threw the ball at least fifty yards down the field.
9. The wide receiver had blew another great opportunity and snuck away before the crowds attacked him.
10. My mother insisted that she had wore that winter coat for the last time.

EXERCISE

Find and correct any errors in verb form in the following paragraphs.

1. Ella loved watching her older sisters get ready to go out at night. It was always fun to watch women who were working all day transform themselves into beautiful butterflies. They were so quick to change, too! Off came the dingy work clothes and the everyday shoes and socks, and on went the delicate dresses, tiny dance slippers, and silky stockings. Suddenly, her sisters weren't the people she fighted with over the telephone and the bathroom. They were beautiful, elegant, sweet-smelling strangers.

2. Every once in a while, monks who worked on transcribing manuscripts couldn't resist adding their own words to the books they were copying. Because transcribing was hard, dull, and tiring work, the words the monks added were often words of complaint. Scribbled in the margins of some old books are messages praying that the work day would end soon, or saying that the monks would have froze to death without a miracle. Sometimes these marginal notes are more interesting than the books that hold them. The notes are a window into the monks' lives and a way for modern readers to personalize the Middle Ages.

3. It was a creepy kind of night. The wind blown fiercely through the streets. We shivered in our flimsy Halloween costumes. We weren't scared, of course. We were too old to be scared. If we walked a little more quickly and clung more closely than usual, it was for warmth, not protection. The moon shined down from behind the clouds. It gave a softened light. We admired it, picked up our candy bags, and continued down the block.

Verbs: tenses.   What is the difference between *I eat* and *I am eating*? What is the difference between *I passed* and *I have passed*? Most verbs can be expressed in any tense, and the many different tenses enable the writer to present fine shades of meaning with great accuracy.

There are six tenses. Most verbs can take either the *active voice* or the *passive voice* in any tense (see page 625). To make matters even more varied, *progressive constructions* can be used for all tenses of active verbs and some tenses of passive verbs.

to save

Tenses	Active voice	Progressive
Present	I save	I am saving
Past	I saved	I was saving
Future	I will (*or* shall) save	I will be saving
Present perfect	I have saved	I have been saving
Past perfect	I had saved	I had been saving
Future perfect	I will (*or* shall) have saved	I will have been saving

Passive voice

Tenses	Active voice	Progressive
Present	I am saved	I am being saved
Past	I was saved	I was being saved
Future	I will (*or* shall) be saved	
Present perfect	I have been saved	
Past perfect	I had been saved	
Future perfect	I will (*or* shall) have been saved	

to drive

Tenses	Active voice	Progressive
Present	I drive	I am driving
Past	I drove	I was driving
Future	I will drive	I will be driving
Present perfect	I have driven	I have been driving
Past perfect	I had driven	I had been driving
Future perfect	I will have driven	I will have been driving

Passive voice

Tenses	Active voice	Progressive
Present	I am driven	I am being driven
Past	I was driven	I was being driven
Future	I will be driven	
Present perfect	I have been driven	
Past perfect	I had been driven	
Future perfect	I will have been driven	

A. *Present tense.* The present tense indicates present action, of course, especially continuing or habitual action:

I *save* ten dollars every week.
I *eat* a good breakfast each morning.
She *drives* carefully.

The present is also used to express permanent facts and general truths, and is usually the preferred tense for discussing literary actions:

The speed of light *is* faster than the speed of sound.

Truth *is* stranger than fiction.

In *The Great Gatsby*, all the events *take* place during the 1920s.

Nick Carraway *is* the only character in the novel who *understands* Gatsby.

The present can even be called upon to deal with future action.

Tomorrow she *drives* to the convention.

The *present progressive* indicates actions occurring—actions "in progress"—at the specific instant referred to.

I *am eating* a good breakfast, and I do not want to be interrupted.

She *is driving* too fast for these icy roads.

The same principle of action in progress at the time applies to all progressive tenses:

Past Progressive:	The criminal *was shaving* when the police arrested him.
Future Progressive:	At this time next week, I *will be surfing* in Hawaii.

B. *Past tense.* The past tense describes previous actions, generally actions over and done with:

The lifeguard *saved* two children last week.

She *drove* to Florida three years ago.

C. *Future tense.* The future tense describes actions after the present:

From now on, I *will save* fifteen dollars every week.

Marlene says that her in-laws *will drive* her to drink.

D. *Present perfect tense.* The present perfect tense (*have* or *has* plus the past participle) refers to past actions, generally of the fairly recent past, that still go on or have bearing on the present:

I *have saved* over one thousand dollars so far.

She *has driven* this short route to work many times.

The preceding sentences expressed in the simple past would suggest different meanings. "I saved over one thousand dollars" would suggest that the saving has now stopped. "She drove this short route to work many times" would suggest that some other route is now being used.

E. *Past perfect tense*. The past perfect tense (*had* plus the past participle) is employed for actions previous to the simple past—"more past than past."

The lifeguard saved two children last week and *had saved* three adults the week before.

She *had driven* to Florida three years ago, so she felt quite confident about making the trip again.

F. *Future perfect tense*. The future perfect tense (*will have* or *shall have* plus the past participle) expresses action that will be completed before some future time:

By this time next year, I *will have saved* two thousand dollars.

When she gets to Florida, she *will have driven* through three time zones.

The proper sequence of tenses within a sentence or series of sentences when different verbs refer to different time periods is an important consideration for all writers. The simple rule that verb tenses need to express precisely the intended period of time is not always simple to apply to one's own writing.

Improper sequence	**Correct sequence**
The witness *told* [past] the court that on the night of the crime he *saw* [past] the accused break the window of the liquor store.	The witness *told* [past] the court that on the night of the crime he *had seen* [past perfect] the accused break the window of the liquor store. (The past perfect *had seen* refers to events "more past than past.")
When I *will get* [future] to the lake, you *will* already *be* [future] there for two weeks.	When I *will get* [future] to the lake, you *will* already *have been* [future perfect] there for two weeks. (The future perfect *will have been* refers to events that will be completed before some future time.)
Although the coach *has set* [present perfect] new curfew hours, the players still *have refused* [present perfect] to comply.	Although the coach *has set* [present perfect] new curfew hours, the players still *refuse* [present] to comply. (The coach's rules were set a while ago. The present tense *refuse* is necessary to show that the players' refusal to follow the rules is current.)

EXERCISE   Make any necessary corrections in verb tenses in the following sentences.

1. The candidate had promised that she will never increase taxes, but she did.
2. The doctor says that when he first saw the patient, the patient was suffering for two weeks with severe migraine headaches.
3. When the book will be released, the competition will already be on sale for a month.

4. Lei Feng saved half of each paycheck for two years, but then he had blown it all on one trip to the casino.

5. Soledad has taken all the abuse she can. She felt a legal separation was the only course open to her.

6. Brian still says that he really loves her, but Joan had declared that he has said that many times before.

7. The long-awaited report is going to be printed next week. It will have shown a long pattern of misappropriation of public funds.

8. At the hearings, the admiral insisted he did not receive any warning of the enemy attack.

9. When I will finally visit England, all my friends will be there dozens of times.

10. I did not want my nephew to play that horrible music again. I heard it many times before.

Voice. The quality of a verb that tells whether the subject *acts* or is *acted upon*. A verb is in the *active voice* when its subject does the acting, and in the *passive voice* when its subject is acted upon.

Active:	The Senate passed the new law.
Passive:	The new law was passed by the Senate.

Wordiness. *Wordiness* means using more words than are necessary. Wordiness never makes writing clearer, more convincing, more interesting, or more graceful—just longer. Be sure to examine your work for wordiness before turning it in. (For exercises and more detailed information, see Chapter 23.)

Glossary of Problem Words

A, an. Use *a* when the next word begins with a consonant sound. Use *an* when the next word begins with a vowel sound.

a book	an urgent request
a rotten apple	an added attraction

Note that it is the sound that counts, not the actual letter.

a hasty decision	an unusual picture
an hour	a usual routine

Accept, except. *Accept* is a verb meaning "to receive, to agree to, to answer affirmatively." *Except* is usually a preposition meaning "excluding." It is also used infrequently as a verb meaning "to exclude."

I accepted the parcel from the mail carrier.

Senator Jones hoped they would accept his apology.

I liked everything about the concert except the music.

I except you from my criticism.

Adapt, adept, adopt. *Adapt* means "change or adjust in order to make more suitable or in order to deal with new conditions." *Adept* means "skillful, handy, good at." *Adopt* means "take or use as one's own" or "endorse."

The dinosaur was unable to adapt to changes in its environment.

The new textbook was an adaptation of the earlier edition.

Bill has always been adept at carpentry.

They had to wait six years before they could adopt a child.

The Senate adopted the new resolution.

Adolescence, adolescents. *Adolescence* refers to the teenage years. *Adolescents* are teenagers.

My adolescence was marked by religious questioning, parental snooping, and skin problems.

Adolescents pay outrageous rates for automobile insurance because, as a group, they have outrageous numbers of accidents.

Adverse, averse to. *Adverse* means "hostile, difficult, unfavorable." *Averse to* refers to someone's being unwilling or reluctant.

Adverse weather conditions have tormented farmers for the past decade.

John has always been averse to accepting other people's ideas.

Advice, advise. *Advice* is a noun. *Advise* is a verb.

My advice to you is to leave well enough alone.

I advise you to leave well enough alone.

Affect, effect. If you are looking for a noun, the word you want is almost certainly *effect*, meaning "result." The noun *affect* is generally restricted to technical discussions of psychology, where it means "an emotion" or "a stimulus to an emotion." If you are looking for a verb, the word you want is probably *affect*, meaning "impress, influence." The verb *effect* is comparatively uncommon; it means "bring about, accomplish, produce."

Many of our welfare programs have not had beneficial effects.

This song always affects me powerfully.

The crowd was not affected by the plea to disband.

We hope this new program will effect a whole new atmosphere on campus.

Pete's affect was always sullen and perverse.

Affective, effective. The word you are after is almost certainly *effective*, meaning "having an effect on" or "turning out well." *Affective* is a fairly technical term from psychology and semantics meaning "emotional" or "influencing emotions."

Only time will tell if Federal Reserve policy is effective.

The affective qualities of sound are difficult to evaluate in laboratory conditions.

Aggravate. The original meaning of *aggravate* is "worsen" or "intensify." The more common meaning of "irritate" or "annoy" is also acceptable in all but the fussiest formal writing.

Ain't. *Ain't* should never be used in written English except in humor or dialogue. Use of the phrase *ain't I*, when asking a question in conversational English, is undesirable, as is the supposedly elegant but totally ungrammatical *aren't I*. *Am I not* is grammatically correct, but awkward and stuffy. The best solution to the problem is to avoid it by expressing the thought differently.

All ready, already. *Already* means "previously" or "by the designated time." *All ready* means "all set, all prepared."

Professor Wills has already told us that twice.

The plane is already overdue.

The meal was all ready by six o'clock.

All right, alright.   *Alright* is often considered nonstandard English. It is good policy to use *all right* instead.

All together, altogether.   *All together* means "joined in a group." *Altogether* means "thoroughly" or "totally."

For once, the citizens are all together on an important issue.

The character's motivations are altogether obscure.

Allusion, illusion.   An *allusion* is "an indirect mention or reference," often literary or historical. The verb form is *allude*. An *illusion* is "an idea not in accord with reality."

The nominating speech alluded to every American hero from Jack Armstrong to Neil Armstrong.

The patient suffered from the illusion that he was Napoleon.

A lot of.   This phrase is more appropriate in conversation than in general written English. Use it sparingly. Remember that *a lot* is *two* words. Do not confuse it with *allot*, meaning "to give out" or "apportion."

Already.   See *All ready, already.*

Alright.   See *All right, alright.*

Altogether.   See *All together, altogether.*

A.M., a.m., P.M., p.m.   These are Latinate abbreviations used with time; A.M. means *ante meridiem* (before noon); P.M. means *post meridiem* (after noon). Either capitals or lowercase letters are acceptable, but you should not alternate between the two in any one piece of writing. Always precede these abbreviations with specific numbers. Don't use "in the morning," "in the afternoon," or "in the evening" along with these abbreviations. Use one or the other.

Wrong:	Her office hours start at 7:00 A.M. in the morning.
	Pick me up at 6:15 P.M. in the evening.
	We expect her sometime in the a.m.
Right:	Her office hours start at 7:00 A.M. *or* Her office hours start at 7:00 in the morning.
	Pick me up at 6:15 P.M. *or* Pick me up at 6:15 in the evening.
	We expect her sometime in the morning.

Among, between.   Use *between* when dealing with two units. Use *among* with more than two.

> *Wrong:*   The company president had to make an arbitrary decision among the two outstanding candidates for promotion.
>
> Tension has always existed between my mother, my father, and me.
>
> *Right:*   The company president had to make an arbitrary decision between the two outstanding candidates for promotion.
>
> Tension has always existed among my mother, my father, and me.

Amount, number.   Use *amount* to refer to quantities that cannot be counted. Use *number* for quantities that can be counted.

> No amount of persuasion will convince the voters to approve the new levy, though the mayor has tried a number of times.

An.   See *A, an.*

And etc.   *Etc.* is an abbreviation of *et cetera,* meaning "and so forth" or "and other things." Using the word *and* in addition to *etc.* is therefore repetitious and incorrect. See *Etc.*

Anxious, eager.   *Anxious* suggests worry or fear, as in anxiety. *Eager* suggests enthusiasm.

> *Wrong:*   I am anxious to see you again at our reunion next week.
>
> *Right:*   I am eager to see you again at our reunion next week.
>
> *Wrong:*   The whole town waited anxiously for the triumphant hockey team.
>
> *Right:*   The whole town waited eagerly for the triumphant hockey team.

Anyone, any one.   Use *anyone* when you mean anybody at all. Use *any one* when you are considering separately or singling out each person or thing within a group.

> Anyone can learn how to do simple electrical wiring.
>
> Any one of these paintings is worth a small fortune.

The same principle applies to *everyone, every one* and *someone, some one.*

Anyways.   Not standard written English. Use *anyway.*

As.   Do not use *as* as a substitute for *because* or *since.*

> *Poor:*   I was late for my appointment as I missed the bus.
>
> As I am a shy person, I find it hard to make new friends.
>
> *Better:*   I was late for my appointment because I missed the bus.
>
> Since I am a shy person, I find it hard to make new friends.

As far as.   This phrase should be followed by a noun and a verb. Without the verb, it is incomplete.

> *Poor:*   As far as religion, I believe in complete freedom.
> *Better:*   As far as religion is concerned, I believe in complete freedom.

Askance.   This word is an adverb meaning "suspiciously, disapprovingly"— used for looks, glances, and the like. It should never be used as a noun.

> *Wrong:*   The sportswriters looked with askance at the coach's optimistic prediction.
> *Right:*   The sportswriters looked askance at the coach's optimistic prediction.

Aspect.   An overused, pseudoscholarly word. Try to avoid it wherever possible. Where you feel you must use it, try to preserve the concept of *looking* as part of the implicit meaning of the word.

> We viewed the problem in all its aspects.

As to.   Stuffy. Change to *about*.

> *Poor:*   We need to talk more as to our late deliveries.
> *Better:*   We need to talk more about our late deliveries.

Averse to.   See *Adverse, averse to*.

Awful.   The original meaning of *awful* is "awe-inspiring, arousing emotions of fear." Some people insist that this is still its only valid meaning. We see nothing wrong, however, when it is also used to mean "extremely bad, ugly, unpleasant." The word *dreadful* has evolved in the same way, and we know of no objections to that word. See *Awfully*.

Awfully.   Does not mean "very."

> *Poor:*   He's an awfully nice person.
>   I'm awfully impressed by what you said.
> *Better:*   He's a very nice person.
>   I'm impressed with what you said.

A while, awhile.   *A while* is a noun. *Awhile* is an adverb.

> I thought I saw her a while ago.
>
> Take it easy for a while.
>
> Success comes only to those who are prepared to wait awhile.

Bad, badly.   *Bad* is the adjective, *badly* the adverb. In some sentences, the verbs *look*, *feel*, and *seem* function as linking verbs and must be followed by the adjectival form.

I play badly.

but

I feel bad.

She looks bad.

The idea seems bad.

Watch the location of *badly* when you use it to mean "very much." It can often be misread as having its more familiar meaning, and comic disaster can occur.

> *Incorrect:*   I want to act badly.
>
>   He wanted her to love him badly.

Be.   Not standard written English in constructions like *I be going* and *They be ready*. Use *I am going* or *They are ready* instead.

Being as, being as how, being that.   Not standard written English. Use *because* or *since*.

Beside, besides.   *Beside* means "alongside of." It can also mean "other than" or "aside from."

> He pulled in beside the Buick.
>
> Your last statement is beside the point.

Besides means "in addition to" or "moreover."

> I'm starting to discover that I'll need something besides a big smile to get ahead.
>
> Besides, I'm not sure I really liked the dress in the first place.

Between.   See *Among, between.*

Brake, break.   *Brake*, whether a verb or noun, has to do with stopping a vehicle or other piece of machinery. For additional meanings, see a dictionary.

> Frantically, he slammed on the brake.
>
> She braked her car to a complete stop.

Break, whether a verb or noun, has many meanings, most commonly "to destroy, damage, exceed, interrupt." The simple past is *broke*; the past participle is *broken*.

> Porcelain can break, so be careful.
>
> Her left arm was broken.
>
> Hank Aaron broke Babe Ruth's home-run record.
>
> The committee took a ten-minute break.
>
> The attempted jail break was unsuccessful.
>
> The brake of the school bus has been broken.

Breath, breathe.   *Breath* is a noun. *Breathe* is a verb.

His statement is like a breath of fresh air.

The soprano drew a deep breath.

In some cities it can be dangerous to breathe the air.

The soprano breathes deeply.

But however, but nevertheless, but yet.   All these phrases are guilty of pointless repetition of meaning. Rewriting helps the logic and eliminates wordiness.

Poor:	Inflation is horrible, but however, the remedies are sometimes even more horrible.
	She loved her husband, but yet she feared him.
	Failure may be inevitable, but nevertheless we will do our best.
Better:	Inflation is horrible, but the remedies are sometimes even more horrible.
	Inflation is horrible; however, the remedies are sometimes even more horrible.
	She loved her husband, yet she feared him.
	Failure may be inevitable, but we will do our best.

But that, but what.   Not standard written English. Use *that*.

Wrong:	I don't question but that you have good intentions.
	I don't question but what you have good intentions.
Right:	I don't question that you have good intentions.

Can, may.   In formal English questions, *can* asks if the ability is there, and *may* asks if the permission is there.

Can your baby speak yet?

May I intrude on your conversation? (Not *can*—anyone with a voice has the ability to intrude.)

Outside of formal contexts, few people worry about the distinction.

Can't hardly.   A double negative. Use *can hardly*.

Can't help but.   Wordy and repetitious. Avoid this phrase in written English.

Poor:	I can't help but worry about what winter will do to my old car.
Better:	I can't help worrying about what winter will do to my old car.

Capital, capitol.   *Capital* refers to money, uppercase letters, and cities that are seats of government. A *capitol* is a building in which major legislative bodies meet. With an uppercase *C, Capitol* refers to the building in Washington, DC.

Investments in Compucorp, though highly speculative, offer excellent opportunities for capital gains.

The poet e. e. cummings had an aversion to capital letters.

Madison is the capital of Wisconsin.

Madison's capitol closely resembles the Capitol in Washington, DC.

Casual, causal. These lookalike words are often misread. *Casual* means "informal" or "unplanned." *Causal* means "having to do with a cause," "constituting a cause," and so on.

Bill is entirely too casual about his financial future.

Karen understands the causal connection between cigarettes and lung disease, but she keeps smoking anyway.

Censor, censure. *Censor*, as a verb, means "to examine mail, art, etc., to see if it should be made public," or "to cut out, ban." As a noun, *censor* means "a person engaged in censoring." *Censure* can be a verb or noun meaning "condemn" or "condemnation," "criticize adversely" or "adverse criticism."

Parts of the movie have been censored.

The prison censor examines all mail.

The Citizens Committee recently censured the mayor.

Dickens's deathbed scenes have long been singled out for censure.

Center around. Since a center is a single point in the middle of something, *center around* is an illogical phrase. Use *center on* instead.

The discussion centered on ways to increase productivity in the coming year.

Cite, site, sight. *Cite*, a verb, means "mention." *Site*, a noun, means "location." *Sight*, also a noun, means something viewed, the ability to see, or the foreseeable future.

He cited many examples to prove his point.

The site of a new housing project has been debated for more than a year.

In her feather hat and seashell earrings, she was quite a sight!

There's no cure in sight for advanced stages of brain cancer.

Climactic, climatic. *Climactic* is the adjectival form of *climax*.

The hero's death is the climactic moment of the story.

Climatic is the adjectival form of *climate*.

Climatic conditions in the Dakotas go from one extreme to the other.

Complected. Not standard English. *Complexioned* is preferable, but it's better to reword your sentence so you can avoid using either term.

Acceptable: He was a light-complexioned man.

Better: He had very fair skin.

Complement, compliment. The verb *complement* means "to complete" or "bring to perfection." The noun *complement* means "the full amount." *Compliment* means "praise" (noun or verb).

Cheese and wine complement each other.

The ship had its required complement of officers.

I don't appreciate insincere compliments.

Don't compliment me unless you mean it.

Compose, comprise. *Compose* means "to make up, to constitute."

Thirteen separate colonies composed the original United States.

Comprise means "to be made up of, to encompass."

The original United States comprised thirteen separate colonies.

If the distinction between these two words gives you trouble, forget about *comprise* and use *is composed of* instead.

Conscience, conscientious, conscious. *Conscience* is the inner voice that tells us right from wrong. *Conscientious* means "painstaking, scrupulous, ruled by conscience," as in *conscientious objector. Conscious* means "aware."

No one should ask you to act against your conscience.

I've tried to do this work as conscientiously as possible.

Jerry became conscious of a subtle change in Mary's attitude.

Console, consul, council, counsel. *Console*: As a verb (accent on second syllable)—"to sympathize with, to comfort." As a noun (accent on first syllable)—"a radio, phonograph, or television cabinet, usually a combination, resting directly on the floor"; also "a small compartment, as found in an automobile between bucket seats"; for other meanings, see a dictionary.

Consul: A representative of a nation, stationed in a foreign city, whose job is to look after the nation's citizens and business interests.

Council: A governing body or an advisory group.

Counsel: As a verb—"to advise, to recommend." As a noun—"advice, recommendation, exchange of ideas."

I could find no words to console the grieving widow.

I've lived with this portable stereo too long. I want a console.

The French consul will answer any of your questions on import duties.

The council met last week in a special emergency session.

The tax expert counseled him on medical deductions.

Sarah knew she could rely on her father's friendly counsel.

Contemptible, contemptuous. Use *contemptible* to describe something or someone deserving of scorn. Use *contemptuous* to describe the expression of scorn.

Few crimes are more contemptible than child abuse.

Instead of shaking hands, she thumbed her nose and stuck out her tongue. Her contemptuous attitude was clear.

Continual, continuous. *Continuous* means "completely uninterrupted, without any pause."

The continuous noise at the party next door kept us awake.

The patient received continuous round-the-clock care.

Continual means "frequently repeated, but with interruptions or pauses."

He had a bad cold and blew his nose continually.

She changed jobs continually.

Costume, custom. *Costume* refers to style of dress. *Custom* refers to conventional practice. See a dictionary for other meanings.

He decided to wear a pirate's costume to the masquerade.

Trick or treat is an old Halloween custom.

Could care less. See *Couldn't care less.*

Couldn't care less. Means "utterly indifferent to." The phrase *could care less* is sometimes mistakenly used to mean the same thing. It does not mean the same thing; it makes no sense at all.

Wrong: I could care less about her opinion of me.

Right: I couldn't care less about her opinion of me.

Couldn't hardly. See *Can't hardly* and *not hardly.*

Could of, should of, would of. Not standard written English. Use *could have, should have, would have.*

Council.   See *Console, consul, council, counsel.*

Counsel.   See *Console, consul, council, counsel.*

Credible, creditable, credulous.   *Credible* means "believable." *Creditable* means "worthy of praise." *Credulous* means "gullible, foolishly believing."

> Their lame excuses were not credible.
>
> Adam's behavior since his parole has been creditable.
>
> She's so credulous she still believes that the stork brings babies.

Criterion.   This word (plural: *criteria*) is overused and frequently stuffy. Use *standard* instead.

Custom.   See *Costume, custom.*

Cute.   An overused word. Avoid it wherever possible in written English.

Data.   Technically, a plural word, the singular form of which is *datum.* The word's Latin origins, however, have nothing to do with its current usage. We believe that *data* can be treated as singular in all levels of English—and probably should be.

> *Correct:*   This data is accurate and helpful.
>
> *Correct (but very formal):*   These data are accurate and helpful.

Decompose, discompose.   *Decompose* means "to rot or break into separate parts." *Discompose* means "disturb, fluster, unsettle."

> When the police found the body, it had already begun to decompose.
>
> His drunken foolishness discomposed all of us.

Definitely.   Nothing is wrong with this word except that it is used far too often (and often misspelled) to add vague emphasis to weak thoughts and weak words.

Detract, distract.   *Detract* means "belittle." *Distract* means "divert, confuse."

> Almost everyone tries to detract from television's real accomplishments.
>
> A mosquito kept distracting her attention.

Device, devise.   *Device* is a noun meaning, among other things, "mechanism" or "special effect." *Devise* is a verb meaning "to invent" or "to plot."

> The safety pin is a simple but extraordinarily clever device.
>
> The person who devised the safety pin is one of humanity's minor benefactors.

Dialog.   Alternative spelling for *dialogue.* In general, save this word for references to conversation in literary works.

No creative writing class can give a writer an ear for good dialog.

Proper punctuation of dialog requires knowledge of many seemingly trivial details.

Some critics assert that Eugene O'Neill's plays have many great speeches but almost no believable dialogue.

Martin Buber, the great twentieth-century theologian, expanded the meaning of *dialog* to refer to an intense, intimate relationship that can sometimes take place between God and human beings. Buber's influence, unfortunately, has led many people who should know better to corrupt the term into a pretentious, sometimes self-serving, synonym for normal conversation. Avoid this usage.

Poor: At its meeting last week, the committee engaged in effective dialog.

The Singles Club provides its members with many opportunities for meaningful dialog.

As if that corruption were not enough, the word has been virtually destroyed through its faddish use as a verb. *Dialog* is not a verb in standard written English. Never use it that way.

Wrong: We dialogued about politics until two in the morning.

Professor Biggs said that she enjoyed dialoging with her students after class.

Different than, different to.   *Different from* is preferable in all circumstances.

Discompose.   See *Decompose, discompose.*

Discreet, discrete.   *Discreet* means "tactful," "reserved." *Discrete* means "separate," "distinct."

Discreet silence is sometimes the most effective reply to an insult.

Rising interest rates have several discrete effects on the economy.

Disinterested, uninterested.   Don't confuse these words. *Disinterested* means "impartial, unbiased." *Uninterested* means "bored, indifferent." An audience is uninterested in a poor play. A disinterested judge is necessary for a fair trial.

Disorientate, disorientated.   Awkward variations of *disorient* and *disoriented.*

Distract.   See *Detract, distract.*

Each.   Takes a singular verb and a singular pronoun. See *He, his, him, himself.*

Each breed of dog has its own virtues.

Each dancer was told to practice her bows.

Each of the Cleveland Indians is taking his turn at batting practice.

Eager.   See *Anxious, eager.*

Economic, economical.   Use *economic* for references to business, finance, the science of economics, and so on. *Economical* means "inexpensive" or "thrifty."

>   Economic conditions are improving in the textile industry.

>   The economical shopper looks hard for bargains.

Effect.   See *Affect, effect.*

Effective.   See *Affective, effective.*

Either.   Use *either* only when dealing with two units.

>   *Wrong:*   Either the Republican, the Democrat, or the Independent will be elected.
>   *Right:*   Either Elaine or Tom will get the job.

When *either* is the subject, it takes a singular verb and pronoun.

>   The men are both qualified. Either is ready to give his best.

See *Neither.*

Elicit, illicit.   *Elicit* means "to draw out." *Illicit* means "improper" or "prohibited."

>   The interviewer was unable to elicit a direct answer.

>   Where would our modern novelists turn if they were suddenly prohibited from writing about illicit romance?

Eminent, imminent.   *Eminent* means "distinguished" or "noteworthy." *Imminent* means "about to happen."

>   The eminent speaker delivered a disappointing address.

>   After years of frustration, a peace treaty is imminent.

Ensure, insure.   Both words are often used interchangeably, but use *insure* for references to financial guarantees against loss of life, health, and property.

>   The new screens should ensure that insects stay outside where they belong.

>   Authorities say that if you insure your home or apartment, you should take photographs of all your most valuable possessions.

>   Our state has just made it mandatory for motorists to insure their own vehicles.

Equally as.   Not a standard English phrase. Eliminate the *as* or substitute *just as.*

>   *Poor:*   My grades were equally as good.
>   The style was equally as important as the plot.

> *Better:*   My grades were equally good.
>
>   The style was just as important as the plot.

Etc.   Abbreviation of *et cetera* (Latin for "and so forth," "and other things"). Except where brevity is a major concern, as in this glossary, avoid *etc.* It tends to convey the impression that the writer doesn't want to be bothered with being accurate and specific. See *And etc.*

Every.   This adjective makes the noun it modifies take a singular verb and a singular pronoun. See *He, his, him, himself.*

> Every woman leader needs to learn how to deal with the prejudices of her male counterparts.
>
> Every Denver Bronco is required to report his weight upon arrival at training camp.
>
> Every idea has been put into its proper place in the outline.

Every day, everyday.   *Every day* is the common phrase used for references to time.

> He loved her so much that he wanted to see her every day.
>
> Every day that we went to the pond that summer, we saw new signs of pollution.

Everyday is an adjective meaning "normal, ordinary, routine."

> After the interview, Bill looked forward to changing into his everyday clothes.
>
> The everyday lives of many everyday people are filled with fears, tensions, and the potential for tragedy.

Everyone, every one.   See *Anyone, any one.*

Except.   See *Accept, except.*

Expand, expend.   *Expand* means "to increase, enlarge, fill out." *Expend* means "to spend, use up."

> The company needs to expand its share of the market.
>
> The student fell asleep during the final examination because he had expended all his energy in studying.

Explicit, implicit.   *Explicit* means "stated or shown directly." *Implicit* means "implied, not stated or shown directly."

> Cheryl's mother gave explicit instructions to be home before dark.
>
> Even by current standards, the movie goes to extremes in its explicit presentation of sex.

My wife and I have an implicit understanding that the first one who can't stand the dirt any longer is the one who does the dishes.

The diplomatic phrasing does not hide the implicit threat of war.

Facet. An overused, pseudoscholarly word. Avoid it wherever possible.

Farther, further. Use *farther* for geographic distance, *further* for everything else.

Allentown is five miles farther down the road.

Further changes improved the curriculum.

Jim kissed her, but they were further apart than ever.

We need to go further into the subject.

Faze, phase. *Faze* means "disconcert, fluster."

Critical sneers will not faze a great artist.

Phase means "a stage in development." It is an overused word. Limit it to contexts in which the passage of time is especially significant.

Poor: One phase of the team's failure is poor hitting.

Better: The history of the team can be divided into three phases.

Fellow. As an adjective, *fellow* means "being in the same situation" or "having the same ideas." Make sure you do not use it to modify a noun that already implies that meaning.

Wrong: My fellow colleagues have been hasty.

Right: My fellow workers and I voted to strike.

Fewer, less. Use *fewer* for references to amounts that can be counted individually, item by item. Use *less* for general amounts or amounts that cannot be counted or measured.

Joe earned fewer dollars this year than he did five years ago.

Joe made less money this year than he did five years ago.

Figurative, figuratively. See *Literal, literally*.

Flaunt, flout. *Flaunt* means "show off arrogantly or conspicuously." *Flout* means "treat scornfully, show contempt," mostly in attitudes toward morality, social customs, or traditions.

They lost no opportunity to flaunt their newfound wealth.

Those hoodlums flout all the basic decencies and then complain that we misunderstand them.

Foreword, forward.   A *foreword* is a preface or introduction. *Forward* is the opposite of backward. It can also mean "bold" or "impertinent."

The only interesting part of the entire book was the foreword.

Our mistakes are part of history. We must now look forward.

Amy's old-fashioned grandfather told her that she was a forward hussy.

Formally, formerly.   *Formally* means "in a formal manner." *Formerly* means "in the past."

We dressed formally for Pedro and Olga's wedding.

People formerly thought that the automobile would become just another fad.

Former.   Means "the first of two." Don't use *former* when dealing with more than two items or persons.

Wrong:	Grant, McKinley, and Harding were poor presidents. The former was the poorest.
Right:	Grant, McKinley, and Harding were poor presidents. The first was the poorest.
	Grant and McKinley were poor presidents. The former was the poorer.

See *Latter*.

Further.   See *Farther, further*.

Good, well.   The adjective *good* modifies a noun. The adverb *well* modifies a verb, adjective, or other adverb.

Mary was a *good speaker*.

She *spoke well*.

The speech *went well*.

After a linking verb, always use *good*. Common linking verbs are *to be* (in all forms and tenses—*am, is, are, was, were, have been, has been, had been, would be, will be*, and so on), *feel, look, sound, taste, appear, smell*, and the like.

Her voice sounded good.

The speech was good.

Mary felt good.

See the discussion of adjective-adverb confusion, pages 554–556.

Hanged, hung.   Both are past participles of *hang*; technically, they are interchangeable. Traditionally, however, *hanged* is reserved for references to executions and *hung* is used everywhere else.

The spy was hanged the next morning.

All the pictures hung crookedly.

He, his, him, himself.   English has no distinct singular pronoun to refer to both sexes. In the past, the masculine pronoun was used to refer to a singular subject of either sex or when sex was irrelevant or unknown.

The used-car buyer needs to be careful. In fact, *he* can hardly be too careful, for many dealers are waiting for the opportunity to swindle *him*.

Each citizen can make *his* choice known on Election Day.

Everybody should protect *himself* from the dangers of alcoholism.

However, increased sensitivity to sexist language (see pages 545–547) has caused this usage to disappear from contemporary published writing. The easiest and most common way to avoid sexist language is to change singular phrasing to plural whenever possible.

Used-car buyers need to be careful. In fact, *they* can hardly be too careful, for many dealers are waiting for the opportunity to swindle *them*.

All citizens can make *their* choice known on Election Day.

People should protect *themselves* from the dangers of alcoholism.

Rephrase sentences that do not lend themselves to a plural approach. See *He/she, his/hers, him/her, he or she, his or hers, him or her.*

He/she, his/hers, him/her, he or she, his or hers, him or her.   Though often convenient and sometimes indispensable, these efforts to achieve sexual equality in language are usually best saved for legal contracts. The phrasing is generally strained and pompous. Use a plural subject and pronoun whenever possible, or recast the sentence to eliminate sexist language (see pages 545–547).

Poor:	Everyone needs to make early plans for his/her career.
	In cases of fatal illness, should a patient be told the truth about what is wrong with him or her?
Better:	People should make early plans for their careers.
	In cases of fatal illness, should patients be told the truth about what is wrong with them?

Hoard, horde.   *Hoard* is a verb meaning "amass" or a noun meaning "a large, hidden supply." *Horde* is a large throng or crowd.

As rumors of war increased, some citizens began to hoard food.

The old man's hoard of gold was concealed beneath the floorboards.

The horde of locusts totally destroyed last year's grain crop.

Hopefully. *Hopefully* is an adverb, which means that it modifies and usually appears next to or close to a verb, adjective, or another adverb.

The farmers searched hopefully for a sign of rain.

Hopefully, the children ran down the stairs on Christmas morning.

Hopefully does *not* mean "I hope, he hopes, it is hoped that. . . ." Avoid using it in sentences like the following:

Hopefully, we can deal with this mess next weekend.

The new driver's training program, hopefully, will cut down on traffic fatalities.

In fairness, so many educated writers and speakers mishandle *hopefully* that the incorrect usage is likely to worm its way into standard English someday.

Human, humane. *Humane* means "kind, benevolent." *Human* means "pertaining to *man-* and *womankind*."

Humane treatment of prisoners is all too rare.

The human condition is frail at best.

I, me. *I* functions as the subject of a sentence or clause, and as a complement in the extremely formal but grammatically correct *It is I*. *Me* is the object of a verb or preposition.

He gave the book to me.

He gave me the business.

For me, nothing can beat a steak and French fries.

Why does she like me so much?

To determine which word to use in sentences like "Nobody is more enthusiastic than I" or "Nobody is more enthusiastic than me," simply complete the sentences with a verb and see which makes sense.

Wrong: Nobody is more enthusiastic than me (am).

Right: Nobody is more enthusiastic than I (am).

Idea, ideal. An *idea* is a concept or notion. An *ideal* is a model of perfection. As an adjective, *ideal* means "perfect."

A new idea for solving the problem suddenly occurred to Linda.

Lofty ideals need to be tempered by common sense.

Ideal children exist only in books.

Illicit. See *Elicit, illicit*.

Illusion. See *Allusion, illusion*.

Imminent.   See *Eminent, imminent*.

Implicit.   See *Explicit, implicit*.

Imply, infer.   To *imply* means "to suggest or hint at something without specifically stating it."

> The dean implied that the demonstrators would be punished.

> The editorial implies that our public officials have taken bribes.

To *infer* means "to draw a conclusion."

> I inferred from her standoffish attitude that she disliked me.

> The newspaper wants its readers to infer that our public officials have taken bribes.

Incredible, incredulous.   *Incredible* means "unbelievable." *Incredulous* means "unconvinced, nonbelieving."

> The witness gave evidence that was utterly incredible.

> I was incredulous at hearing those absurd lies.

Indict.   To *indict* means "to charge with a crime." It does not mean to arrest or to convict.

> The grand jury indicted Fields on a gambling charge.

Individual.   Often contributes to stuffiness and wordiness.

> *Bad:*   He was a remarkable individual.
> *Better:*   He was a remarkable man.
> *Best:*   He was remarkable.

Infer.   See *Imply, infer*.

Inferior than.   Not standard English. Use *inferior to*.

Ingenious, ingenuous.   *Ingenious* means "clever." *Ingenuous* means "naive, open."

> Sherlock Holmes was an ingenious detective.

> Nothing could rival the ingenuous appeal of the little child's eyes.

The noun forms are *ingenuity, ingenuousness*.

In reference to.   Stuffy business English. Use *about*.

In spite of.   *In spite* is two separate words.

Insure.   See *Ensure, insure*.

Inter-, intra-. *Inter-* is a prefix meaning "between different groups." *Intra-* is a prefix meaning "within the same group."

> Ohio State and Michigan fought bitterly for intercollegiate football supremacy.

> The English faculty needs a new department head who can control intradepartmental bickering.

Irregardless. Not standard English. The proper word is *regardless*.

Irrelevant, irreverent. *Irrelevant* means "not related to the subject." *Irreverent* means "scornful, lacking respect."

> Your criticisms sound impressive but are really irrelevant.

> America could use some of Mark Twain's irreverent wit today.

Confusion of these words may be responsible for the frequent mispronunciation of *irrelevant* as *irrevelant*.

Its, it's. *Its* is the possessive of *it*. *It's* is the contraction for *it is*.

> The cat licked its paws. It's a wonderfully clean animal.

Its' is not a word. It does not exist in current usage, and it never has.

Job. Frequently overused in student writing. *Job* is probably most effective when reserved for simple references to employment for wages.

> *Poor:* Shakespeare does a great job of showing Hamlet's conflicting emotions.
>
> *Better:* Our economy needs to create more jobs.

Kind of. Means what it says—"a type of, a variety of." It does *not* mean "somewhat" or "rather" except in the most informal writing.

> *Poor:* She was kind of eccentric.
>
> I was kind of curious about his answer.
>
> *Better:* He suffered from an obscure kind of tropic fever.
>
> She had a kind of honest stubbornness that could be very appealing.

Latter. Means "the second of two." Don't use *latter* when dealing with more than two items or people.

> *Wrong:* Washington, Jefferson, and Lincoln were great presidents. The latter was the greatest.
>
> *Right:* Washington, Jefferson, and Lincoln were great presidents. The last was the greatest.
>
> Washington and Lincoln were great presidents. The latter was the greater.

See *Former*.

Lay, lie.   *Lay* is a transitive verb. It always takes an object *or* is expressed in the passive voice.

Present	Past	Past participle	Present participle
lay	laid	laid	laying

Lie is an intransitive verb. It never takes an object and never is expressed in the passive voice. This problem-causing *lie*, by the way, means "recline," not "fib."

Present	Past	Past participle	Present participle
lie	lay	lain	lying

I lay my burden down forever.

The hen laid six eggs yesterday.

The mason has laid all the bricks.

Our plans have been laid aside.

The porter is laying down our suitcases.

Now I am going to lie down.

Yesterday he lay awake for five hours.

The refuse has lain there for weeks.

Homeless people are lying on the park benches.

Lead, led.   As a noun, *lead* has various meanings (and pronunciations).

The student had no lead for his pencil.

The reporter wanted a good lead for her story.

Which athlete is in the lead?

The past of the verb *lead* is *led*.

The declarer always leads in bridge.

I led an ace instead of a deuce.

Is it possible to lead without making enemies?

Grant led the Union to triumph at Vicksburg.

Leave, let.   *Leave* means "to depart." *Let* means "to allow, permit."

Wrong:	Leave us look more closely at this sonnet.
Right:	Let us look more closely at this sonnet.

Lend, loan.   *Lend* is a verb; *loan* is a noun.

Jack was kind enough to lend me ten dollars.

High interest rates have interfered with loans.

Less.   See *Fewer, less.*

Liable, libel.   *Liable* means "likely to" or "legally obligated." *Libel* is an unjust written statement exposing someone to public contempt.

> After a few drinks, that man is liable to do anything.
> The owner of the dog was liable for damages.
> Senator Green sued the newspaper for libel.

Libel, slander.   *Libel* is written injustice. *Slander* is spoken injustice.

Lie.   See *Lay, lie.*

Like, as.   In agonizing over whether to use *like* or *as* (sometimes *as if*), look first at the words that follow. If the words make up a clause (subject plus verb) use *as*; if not, use *like*.

> Even philosophers can sometimes act like fools.
> Even philosophers can sometimes act as fools would act.
> The painting made the sunset look like a double-cheese pizza.
> The painting made the sunset look as if it were a double-cheese pizza.
> My boss treated me like dirt.
> My boss treated me as if I were dirt.

This rule is not foolproof, but it will solve most practical problems. *Like* in place of *as* is now fairly well accepted outside of formal written English.

Literal, literally.   These terms mean "in actual fact, according to the precise meaning of the words." Some people use *literal, literally* when they mean the opposite: *figurative, figuratively.*

> *Wrong:*   He literally made a monkey of himself.
>
> Some of our councilmen are literal vultures.
>
> I literally fly off the handle when I see children mistreated.
>
> *Right:*   The doctor said Karen's jealousy had literally made her ill.
>
> We were so lost that we literally did not know north from south.
>
> A literal translation from German to English rarely makes any sense.

Loan.   See *Lend, loan.*

Loath, loathe.   *Loath* is an adjective meaning "reluctant." *Loathe* is a verb meaning "hate."

> I am loath to express the full intensity of my feelings.
> I loathe people who use old-fashioned words like *loath.*

Loose, lose.   *Loose* is the opposite of *tight. Lose* means "to misplace."

Mad.   Use *mad* in written English to mean "insane," not "angry."

Poor: Please don't be mad at me.

Better: Shakespeare tends to be sympathetic to his mad characters.

The current trade policy is utterly mad.

Majority, plurality.   A candidate who has a *majority* has more than half of the total votes. A candidate who has a *plurality* has won the election but received less than half the total votes.

Masochist.   See *Sadist, masochist.*

Massage, message.   A *massage* makes muscles feel better. A *message* is a communication.

May.   See *Can, may.*

May be, maybe.   *May be* is a verb form meaning "could be, can be." *Maybe* is an adverb meaning "perhaps."

I may be wrong, but I feel that *Light in August* is Faulkner's finest novel.

Maybe we ought to start all over again.

Me.   See *I, me.*

Medal, metal, mettle.   A *medal* is awarded to heroes and other celebrities. *Metal* is a substance such as iron or copper. *Mettle* refers to stamina, enthusiasm, or vigorous spirit.

The American team won many Olympic medals in swimming.

Future metal exploration may take place beneath the sea.

Until the Normandy invasion, Eisenhower had not really proved his mettle.

Medium.   An overused word in discussing communications. The plural of *medium* is *media*. See a dictionary for its many meanings.

Mighty.   Use *mighty* to mean "powerful" or "huge." Do *not* use it as a substitute for *very*.

Poor: I was mighty pleased to meet you.

Better: I was very pleased to meet you.

Moral, morale.   *Moral*, as an adjective, means "having to do with ethics" or "honorable, decent, upright." As a noun, it means "lesson, precept, teaching." *Morale* refers to one's state of mind or spirit.

Not all moral issues are simple cases of right and wrong.

The story has a profound moral.

The new coach tried to improve the team's morale.

More, most. Use *more* when two things are being compared. For any number over two, use *most*.

Between Sally and Phyllis, Sally was the more talented.

Of all my teachers, Mr. Frederic was the most inspired.

Never use *most* as a synonym for *almost*.

Wrong: Most everyone showed up at the party.

I'll be home most any time tomorrow.

Mr., Mrs., Miss, Ms. These titles should not be used in referring to figures from the historical, cultural, and scientific past. With living figures, the titles should be used in moderation; the better known the person, the less need for the title.

Poor: Mr. John Adams was the second president of the United States.

Mr. Nathaniel Hawthorne wrote *The Scarlet Letter*.

Mr. Yeltsin's speech received worldwide press coverage.

Better: John Adams was the second president of the United States.

Nathaniel Hawthorne wrote *The Scarlet Letter*.

Yeltsin's speech received worldwide press coverage.

Ms. Now standard usage as a title for women, though *Miss* and *Mrs.* are still used.

Myself. Use *myself* to reinforce and stress the pronoun *I*, not as a replacement for it or the word *me*.

Wrong: Make an appointment with José and myself next week.

Right: I myself made that fudge.

Natural. Means "unartificial," among other things. It is overused as a term of vague praise. It might be applied to someone's voice or manner, but it sounds absurd in a sentence like this:

Brand X eyelashes will give you that natural look.

Neither. Use only when dealing with *two* units.

Wrong: I like neither collies nor poodles nor dachshunds.

Right: I like neither dogs nor cats.

When *neither* is the subject, it takes a singular verb and pronoun.

> Both nations are responsible. Neither is doing its best for the environment.

See *Either*.

Nice.   An overused word, generally too vague in meaning to have much value. Try to find more specific substitutes.

None.   Means "no one" or "not one" and takes a singular verb and pronoun.

> None of these women understands that she is a public servant.

> None of those men is willing to accept his responsibilities.

Not hardly.   A double negative. Not standard English. Use *hardly*.

Wrong:	He couldn't hardly see his hand in front of his face.
Right:	He could hardly see his hand in front of his face.

Number.   See *Amount, number*.

Oftentimes.   Wordy and pointless version of *often*.

Only.   A tricky word in some sentences. Make sure that it modifies what you really want it to.

Poor:	I only felt a little unhappy. (Only *felt?* Are we meant to assume that the writer did not consciously *think* this way?)
	I only asked for a chance to explain. (Are we meant to assume that the writer did not insist on or strongly desire that chance?)
Better:	I felt only a little unhappy.
	I asked only for a chance to explain.

Orientate, orientated.   Awkward variations of *orient* and *oriented*.

Passed, past.   *Passed* is the past participle of pass. *Past* is used mainly as an adjective or a noun. Never use *passed* as an adjective or noun.

> We passed them on the highway.

> Valerie had a mysterious past.

> History is the study of past events.

Patience, patients.   *Patience* has to do with not being in a hurry. *Patients* are people seeking medical care or under medical attention.

> We expect the delivery tomorrow; our patience is almost at an end.

> The patients nervously waited in the doctor's office.

Perpetrate, perpetuate. *Perpetrate* means "to commit an evil, offensive, or stupid act." *Perpetuate* means "to preserve forever."

> He perpetrated a colossal blunder.

> We resolved to perpetuate the ideals our leader stood for.

Persecute, prosecute. *Persecute* means "to oppress or pick on unjustly." *Prosecute* means "to carry forward to conclusion or bring court proceedings against."

> Persecuting religious and racial minorities is an ongoing folly of the human race.

> The general believes that the war must be prosecuted intensely.

> We must prosecute those charged with crimes as rapidly as possible.

Personal, personnel. *Personal* is an adjective meaning "private, individual." *Personnel* is a noun referring to the people employed in an organization. It can also refer to a department in the organization that oversees employee-based issues such as hiring and firing, morale, and processing of claims for benefits.

> My love life is too personal for me to discuss.

> There is no point to arguing about matters of personal taste.

> The company's personnel increased more than 10 percent in the past year.

> Address all inquiries to the Personnel Department.

Perspective, prospective. *Perspective* has various meanings, most commonly "the logically correct relationships between the parts of something and the whole" or "the drawing techniques that give the illusion of space or depth." *Prospective* means "likely to become" or "likely to happen."

> Inflation is not our only problem; we need to keep the economy in perspective.

> Medieval painting reveals an almost complete indifference to perspective.

> The prospective jurors waited nervously for their names to be called.

> None of the prospective benefits of the merger ever materialized.

Phase. See *Faze, phase.*

Phenomenon. Singular; the standard plural form is *phenomena.*

Plurality. See *Majority, plurality.*

Plus. Do not use *plus* between clauses as a substitute for *and.*

> *Poor:*   I had to buy groceries, plus I had to study for a test.
> *Better:* I had to buy groceries, and I had to study for a test.

Precede, proceed.   *Precede* means "to go before." *Proceed* means "to go on." See a dictionary for other meanings.

> Years of struggle and poverty preceded her current success.
>
> Let us proceed with our original plans.

Prejudice, prejudiced.   *Prejudice* is ordinarily used as a noun. *Prejudiced* is an adjective.

> *Wrong:*   John is prejudice.
>
>   The neighborhood is filled with prejudice people.
>
> *Right:*   John is prejudiced.
>
>   Legislation alone cannot eliminate prejudice.

Prescribe, proscribe.   *Prescribe* means "to order, recommend, write a prescription." *Proscribe* means "to forbid." See other meanings in a dictionary.

> The committee prescribed a statewide income tax.
>
> The authorities proscribe peddling without a license.

Prescription.   *Prescription* is often misspelled "perscription"—there is no such word.

Principal, principle.   As an adjective, *principal* means "foremost, chief, main." As a noun, it can refer to a leading person (as of a school) or the amount owed on a loan exclusive of interest. For other meanings see a dictionary. *Principle* is a noun meaning "a fundamental doctrine, law, or code of conduct."

> The principal conflict in the novel was between the heroine's conscious and subconscious desires.
>
> For the third time that week, Jeff was summoned to the principal's office.
>
> The interest on a twenty-five- or thirty-year mortgage often exceeds the principal.
>
> Be guided by one principle: "Know thyself."
>
> The candidate is a woman of high principles.

Prioritize.   This overused word is often a pretentious and awkward substitute for *set up priorities*.

Pronunciation.   Note the spelling. There is no such word as *pronounciation*.

Quiet, quite, quit.   *Quiet* means "silence, to become silent, to make silent." *Quite* means "rather" or "completely," in addition to its informal use in expressions like "quite a guy." *Quit* means to stop, to terminate.

> The parents pleaded for a moment of peace and quiet.
>
> Throughout the concert, I tried to quiet the people behind me.

April was quite cold this year.

When the job was quite finished, Mary felt like sleeping for a week.

Quit looking at me as if I did something wrong.

Did you quit your job yesterday?

Raise, rise.   *Raise* is a transitive verb. *Rise* is an intransitive verb and never takes an object.

I always rise at 8:00 a.m.

The farmer raises corn and wheat.

Rationalize.   This word is most effective when used to mean "think up excuses for." It can also mean "to reason," but in this sense it is just a stuffy word for a simple idea. The noun form is *rationalization.*

The gangster tried to rationalize his behavior by insisting that his mother had not loved him.

All these rationalizations conceal the unpleasant truth.

Really.   An overused word. It is especially weak in written English when it serves as a synonym for *very* or *extremely.*

Poor: We saw a really nice sunset.

That was a really big show.

When you do use *really,* try to preserve its actual meaning, stressing what is *real* as opposed to what is false or mistaken.

The noises were really caused by mice, not ghosts.

He may have been acquitted through lack of evidence, but everyone knew that Bronson was really guilty.

Reason is because.   Awkward and repetitious. Use *reason is that.* Even this phrase is awkward and should be used sparingly. Never repeat *is* as many speakers and writers do.

Wrong: The reason is is that. . . .

Poor: His reason for jilting her was because his parents disapproved of older women.

Better: His reason for jilting her was that his parents disapproved of older women.

Even better: He jilted her because his parents disapproved of older women.

Relevant.   An overused word, frequently relied on to express shallow thought: "Literature is not relevant to our needs," for example. See *Irrelevant, irreverent* for a note on pronunciation.

Respectfully, respectively. *Respectfully* means "with respect." *Respectively* means "each in the order named."

Everyone likes to be treated respectfully.

The speaker discussed education, medical research, and defense spending, respectively.

Sadist, masochist. A *sadist* enjoys hurting living creatures. A *masochist* enjoys being hurt.

Seeing as how. Not standard English. Use *since* or *because*.

Seldom ever. *Ever* is unnecessary in this phrase. Avoid it.

Poor: He was seldom ever angry.

Better: He was seldom angry.

Sensual, sensuous. *Sensuous* is the usually positive word referring to physical pleasure. The negative word is *sensual*, suggesting gross overindulgence in physical sensations.

Jane felt that a hot tub and a cold martini were among life's great sensuous delights.

Two years of unlimited sensual abandon were directly responsible for Ben's early death.

Set, sit. To *set* means "to place" or "to put." A dictionary gives dozens of other meanings as well. Our main concern is that *set* does not mean *sit* or *sat*.

Set the table.

We sat at the table. (*Not* "We set at the table.")

Set down that chair.

Sit down in that chair. (*Not* "Set down in that chair.")

Shall, will. Elaborate rules differentiate between these words. Few people understand the rules, and no one remembers them. Our advice on this subject is to use *will* all the time except when *shall* obviously sounds more natural, as in some questions and traditional phrases. Examples: "Shall we dance?" "We shall overcome."

Share. *Share* is an excellent word to indicate what generous children do with candy bars and what generous adults do with their last five dollars. In recent years, the word has sometimes been abused as a pretentious and sentimental synonym for *show* or *tell about*.

Poor: Joan shared her snapshots of her summer vacation with us.

Better: Joan showed us her snapshots of her summer vacation.

Poor: I asked him to share his innermost thoughts with me.

Better: I asked him to tell me his innermost thoughts.

Shone, shown. *Shone* is the alternate past tense and past participle of *shine*. Same as *shined*. *Shown* is the alternate past participle of *show*. Same as *showed*.

> The sun shone brightly.

> More shocking films are being shown than ever before.

Should of. See *Could of, should of, would of*.

Sic. Means *thus* or *so* in Latin. *Sic* is used in brackets within quoted material to indicate that an obvious error or absurdity was actually written that way in the original.

> The author tells us, "President Harold [*sic*] Truman pulled one of the biggest political upsets of the century."

Site. See *Cite, site, sight*.

Slander. See *Libel, slander*.

So. When *so* is used for emphasis, the full thought often needs to be completed by a clause. See *Such*.

Poor:	The coffee was so sweet.
	My sister is so smart.
Right:	The coffee was so sweet that it was undrinkable.
	My sister is so smart that she does my homework for me every night.

So-called. This word has a specific meaning. Use *so-called* to complain about something that has been incorrectly or inaccurately named. Do not use it as a simple synonym for *undesirable* or *unpleasant*.

Wrong:	These so-called jet planes make too much noise.
	She wore a so-called wig.
Right:	Many of our so-called radicals are quite timid and conservative.
	These so-called luxury homes are really just mass-produced bungalows.

Someone, some one. See *Anyone, any one*.

Somewheres. Not standard English. Use *somewhere*.

Sort of. Means "a type of, a variety of." Do not use as a substitute for *somewhat* or *rather*. See *Kind of*.

Stationary, stationery. *Stationary* means "unmoving, unchanging." *Stationery* is paper for letter writing.

Story.   A *story* is a piece of short prose fiction. Do not use the word when referring to essays and articles, poems, plays, and novels. Remember, too, that the action in any work of literature is *plot*, not story.

Such.   When *such* is used for emphasis to mean "so much" or "so great," the full thought usually needs to be completed by a clause. See *So.*

Poor:	He was such a wicked man.
	We had such fun at the picnic.
Right:	He was such a wicked man that everyone feared him.
	We had such fun at the picnic, we had to force ourselves to go home.

Supposed to.   Don't forget the *d* in *supposed*.

This poem is supposed (not *suppose*) to be one of the greatest ever written.

The students are supposed (not *suppose*) to have a pep rally tomorrow night.

Sure and.   *Sure to* is preferable in writing.

Poor:	Be sure and cancel newspaper deliveries before leaving for vacation.
Better:	Be sure to cancel newspaper deliveries before leaving for vacation.

Than, then.   *Than* is the word for expressing comparisons and exceptions. *Then* is the word for all other uses.

Florida is more humid than California.

At first Roberta thought the story was funny. Then she realized its underlying seriousness.

Their, they're, there.   *Their* is the possessive form of *they*.

They took their seats.

They're is the contraction of *they are.*

The defensive linemen say they're going to do better next week.

For all other situations, the correct word is *there.*

They.   Often used vaguely and meaninglessly, as in "They don't make things the way they used to," or "They really ought to do something about safety." Nowhere is the use of *they* more meaningless and weird than when applied to an individual writer. *Never* write:

This was an excellent mystery. They certainly fooled me with the solution.

I think it was sad that they had Othello die at the end of the play.

This, these. Frequent problem-producers when used imprecisely. Make certain that no confusion or vagueness is possible. To be on the safe side, many writers make a habit of following *this* and *these* with a noun that clarifies the reference: "this idea, these suggestions, this comment."

Through, thru. *Through* is the standard spelling except, perhaps, on road signs where space and reading time merit special consideration.

> We drove straight through to Buffalo.
>
> Thru Traffic Keep Left.

Thusly. Not standard English. Use *thus*.

To, too, two. *To* is the familiar preposition used in diverse ways. *Too* means "also" or "excessively." *Two* is the number.

Try and. Acceptable in conversation, but undesirable in print. Use *try to*.

> *Poor:* We must all try and improve our environment.
>
> *Better:* We must all try to improve our environment.

Type of. This phrase frequently contributes to wordiness.

> *Wordy:* He was an interesting type of artist.
>
> I enjoy a suspenseful type of novel.
>
> *Better:* He was an interesting artist.
>
> I enjoy a suspenseful novel.

Under way. Two words, except in special technical fields.

Uninterested. See *Disinterested, uninterested*.

Unique. This word means "one of a kind"; it cannot be made stronger than it already is, nor can it be qualified. Do not write "very unique, more unique, less unique, somewhat unique, rather unique, fairly unique."

Used to. Don't forget the *d* in *used*.

> I used (not *use*) to like the tales of Jules Verne.
>
> We are used (not *use*) to this kind of treatment.

Vain, vane, vein. *Vain* refers to vanity or futility. *Vane* is most commonly another word for "weathervane." *Vein* is a blood vessel but has many figurative meanings as well.

Jim is so vain that he dyes the gray hairs on his chest.

Betty's efforts to control her temper were mostly in vain.

You can recognize the house by the rooster vane near the chimney.

The vein carries blood to the heart.

Beneath the teasing runs a vein of deep tenderness.

At first the miners thought they had found a vein of gold.

Very.   One of the most overused words in the language. Try to find one *exact* word for what you want to say instead of automatically using *very* to intensify the meaning of an imprecise, commonplace word.

very bright	*could be*	radiant
very bad	*could be*	terrible
very sad	*could be*	pathetic, depressed
very happy	*could be*	overjoyed, delighted

Weather, whether.   *Weather* has to do with climate. *Whether* has to do with choices and alternative possibilities.

The dark clouds indicate that the weather may soon change.

Anita needs to decide whether to accept the most recent job offer.

I can never recall whether the bank is closed on Monday or Wednesday.

When.   In using this word, make sure it refers to *time*, as in "It was ten years ago when we first fell in love."

Wrong:	Basketball is when five men on opposing teams . . .
Right:	Basketball is a game in which five men on opposing teams . . .
Wrong:	New York is when the Democratic Convention was held.
Right:	New York is where the Democratic Convention was held.

Where.   In using this word, make sure it refers to *place*, as in "This is the house where I used to live."

Wrong:	I'm interested in seeing the movie where the motorcycle gang takes over the town.
Right:	I'm interested in seeing the movie in which the motorcycle gang takes over the town.
Wrong:	The class is studying the time where the Industrial Revolution was beginning.
Right:	The class is studying the time when the Industrial Revolution was beginning.

Where . . . at, where . . . to.   The *at* and the *to* are unnecessary. They show how wordiness can often sneak into our writing almost subconsciously.

Poor:	Where are you staying at?
	Where is he going to?
Better:	Where are you staying?
	Where is he going?

Whether or not.   The one word *whether* means the same as *whether or not*, and is therefore preferable.

Poor:	We wondered whether or not it would snow.
Better:	We wondered whether it would snow.

Who, that, which.   Use *who* or *that* for people, preferably *who*, never *which*. Use *which* or *that* for things, preferably *that*, never *who*.

Keats is one of many great writers who died at an early age.

There's the woman that I was telling you about.

Podunk is a town that people always ridicule.

The play which we are now studying is incredibly difficult.

Who, whom.   Although the distinction between *who* and *whom* is no longer a major issue in the conversation of many educated speakers and in much informal writing, formal English still fusses about these words—and perhaps your instructor does, too. We first discuss the traditional rules; then we consider more casual approaches.

Formal English requires *who* to serve as the *subject* of verbs in dependent clauses:

He is a fine man who loves his family.

She is a person who should go far in this company.

I dislike people who can't take a joke.

Formal English uses *whom* as the *object* in dependent clauses:

The drunk driver whom Officer Jerome had ticketed last night turned out to be Judge Furness.

The teacher whom I feared so greatly last term has now become a good friend.

Note that it is the role played by *who* or *whom* in the *dependent clause* that determines which word is right; don't be distracted by the connections that *who* or *whom* may appear to have with other parts of the sentence. In cases of doubt, a sometimes effective tactic is to substitute *he, she, they* or *him, her, them* for the word in question and see which makes better sense. If *he, she, they* works, use *who*. If *him, her, them* works, use *whom*.

> I dislike people (who, whom) can't take a joke.

Take the dependent clause *(who, whom) can't take a joke*. Clearly, *they can't take a joke* works, and *them can't take a joke* does not work. Use *who*.

> The drunk driver (who, whom) Officer Jerome had ticketed last night turned out to be Judge Furness.

Take the dependent clause *(who, whom) Officer Jerome had ticketed last night*. *Officer Jerome had ticketed him last night* makes sense; *Officer Jerome had ticketed he last night* does not make sense. Use *whom*.

Special problems pop up when words intervene between *who* or *whom* and its verb. Don't be misled by expressions like *I think, they say, it seems, she feels*, and so on. These expressions should be thought of as interrupting words and do not affect the basic grammar of the clause.

> The minority leader is the man who I think should be the next president. (*Who* is the subject of *should be*.)

> No artist who he said was brilliant ever impressed us. (*Who* is the subject of *was*.)

Through the years, the complex traditional rules have confused many people, and we've tried to explore only the most frequent complexities. As teachers, we confess that we feel distinctly uncomfortable when the old rules are broken. We also confess, however, that Theodore Bernstein, late stylist-in-chief of the *New York Times*, makes a strong case in declaring that the rules are more trouble than they are worth. Check with your own instructor, and then consider the following guidelines and shortcuts:

1. Immediately after a preposition, use *whom*.

> He asked to whom I had been speaking.

> This is the person in whom we must place our trust.

2. At other times, use *who*.

> In my home, it's the man who does the cooking.

> Fred Smiley is the man who Ethel chose.

3. If *who* sounds "wrong" or unnatural, or if you are in a situation that demands formal writing and feel uncertain about the formal rules (the sample sentence about Fred and Ethel breaks the rules), try to eliminate the problem with one of these techniques:

   a. Change *who* or *whom* to *that*.
   Fred Smiley is the man that Ethel chose.

   b. Remove *who* or *whom*.
   Fred Smiley is the man Ethel chose.

Who's, whose.   *Who's* is a contraction of *who is* or *who has. Whose* is the possessive form of *who.*

> Who's going to get the promotion?
>
> Fenton is a man who's been in and out of jail all his life.
>
> Whose reputation shall we attack today?
>
> Kennedy was a president whose place in history is assured.

Will.   See *Shall, will.*

Would of.   See *Could of, should of, would of.*

Your, you're.   *Your* is the possessive form of *you. You're* means "you are."

> You're certain to get caught in rush-hour traffic.
>
> All of your suggestions are excellent.
>
> Your attitude shows that you're not truly interested.

EXERCISE   Make any changes necessary to correct the following sentences containing problem words. Numbers in parentheses refer to the number of errors in each item.

1. She should of left the cite earlier but refused to except her own advise. (4)
2. Miss Chien was unaccustomed to receiving complements on her wardrobe from her kindergarten students, but however, she excepted this complement gracefully anyways. (5)
3. Given a choice between chicken, fish, or beef, I usually pick fish, being that its so healthful. (3)
4. My nephew literally drives me up a wall when he repeatedly asks whether or not we're going to the park. (2)
5. The whether this winter has been awfully bitter, so I'm glad I bought alot of wool sweaters, heavy pants, and etc. (4)
6. The cable television network announced that it's restructuring now underway would center around integrating its t.v. and Internet operations to insure quality service. (4)
7. Maria was all together alright this a.m. but by evening she felt so badly she couldn't hardly breath. (6)
8. I could care less as to her advise anyways. (4)
9. The reason she disliked him was because he was equally as vein as his boss, the principle. (4)
10. Hopefully next year there will be less people sent to prison seeing as how the nation's prison population is so high. (3)

EXERCISE   Correct any incorrect words in the following phrases and sentences.

1. can't hardly talk
2. an exciting type of film
3. drive thru the park
4. a more unique idea
5. Did you except her suggestion?
6. between you, Chung Woo, and me
7. mighty tasty enchilada
8. Pedro and myself made a crumb cake.
9. I like neither dogs, cats, nor birds as pets.
10. suppose to leave early
11. keep quite in the church
12. over their
13. disinterested in the speaker's lecture
14. ate less M & Ms
15. hung the murderer
16. leave us study the homework
17. laid in the sun at the pool
18. a lose knot
19. paid her a complement
20. different than her friend

ESL Pointers: Tips for Non-Native Writers

Speakers of other languages bring to the study of English a range of knowledge and skills linked to the grammar system of their native tongues. Although many grammatical systems have similar features, learning to read and write in a new language has many challenges. Reading and writing English to meet the demands of an academic community are not easy even for native speakers. Those who learn English as a second or third language must deal with a number of common issues, and these next few pages attempt to address some of the most important ones. We have built instruction around basic parts of speech and fundamental concepts in grammar, many of which you saw in Part Six.

Verbs and Helping Verbs, Including Modals

English verbs, as those of other languages, have several forms—called the **principal parts** of verbs (see pages 618–620)—that work independently or cooperatively with familiar helping verbs (also called **auxiliary verbs** or simply **auxiliaries**). The infinitive *to be* is highly irregular and appears below the main examples for *to look* and *to speak*.

Summary Checklist: Principal Parts and Auxiliaries for Three Sample Verbs

Infinitive—the base form of the verb (always includes the word *to*)	Present tense form (infinitive without the word *to*)	Past tense	Past participle (used with helping verbs to form perfect tenses and passive voice)	Present participle (used with helping verbs to form progressive tenses)
to look [Regular verb]	I **look** He, she, it **looks** You, they **look**	I **looked**	I **have looked** He, she, it **has looked** You, we, they **have looked**	I am **looking** He, she, it **is looking** You, we, they **are looking** I, he, she, it **was looking** You, we, they **were looking**
to speak [Irregular verb]	I **speak** He, she, it **speaks** You, they **speak**	I **spoke**	I **have spoken** He, she, it **has spoken** You, we, they **have spoken** The words **were spoken**	I am **speaking** He, she, it **is speaking** You, we, they **are speaking** I, he, she, it **was speaking** You, they **were speaking**
to be [Irregular verb]	I **am** He, she, it **is** You, they **are**	I, he, she, it **was** You, they **were**	I **have been** He, she, it **has been** You, we, they **have been**	I am **being** He, she, it **is being** You, we, they **are being** I, he, she, it **was being** You, we, they **were being**

A subgroup of helping verbs, called **modals**, also works with principal parts of verbs (see pages 617–618). Because the modals do not identify actual events—you remember that they indicate probability, ability, or need or obligation—they can cause confusion.

Follow these guidelines for using helping verbs, including modals.

Using Helping Verbs and Modals with Principal Parts of Verbs

- Use *has, have,* and *had* with the past participle to form the perfect tenses: *has driven; has eaten; has, have been.* Do not use these helping verbs with the infinitive (or base form) of the verb:

Incorrect:	He has speak. They have look.
Correct:	He has spoken. They have looked.

- Use the modals with the infinitive (or base form) of the verb: *can run, should rest, might be.*

Incorrect:	He can speaking. They should looks.
Correct:	He can speak. They should look.

- Use *do, does,* and *did* with the infinitive (or base form) of the verb. Modals include *do begin, does work, did fly.*

Incorrect:	I do speaks. She does speaking. They did looked.
Correct:	I do speak. She does speak. They did look.

- Use the various forms of the verb *to be* with present or past participles, depending on your intended meaning:

  Present participles: **am** running, **is** singing, **are** laughing, **was** working, **were** studying. Verbs that express states of being (*appear, become, be, believe, seem*), sensory awareness (*feel, hear, see, smell, taste*), and emotion or feeling (*dislike, hate, imagine, intend, know, like, prefer, realize, suppose, think, understand, want, desire, wish, wonder*) do *not* usually appear in the progressive tenses. (There are some exceptions.)

Incorrect:	The chili was tasting bad.
	Liu and Cal are appearing ready.
	The professor is preferring my answer.
Correct:	The chili tasted bad.
	Liu and Cal appear ready.
	The professor prefers my answer.

  Past participles: **is** produced, **was** forbidden, **were** frozen. With the *to be* verb, past participles form the passive voice. Do not use the simple past form of the verb to form the passive voice. (In general, you should avoid the passive voice in writing and use the active voice instead. See page 625.)

Incorrect:	The important words were spoke.
	The door was close to the visitors.
Correct:	The important words were spoken.
	The door was closed to the visitors.

Phrasal Verbs

Some verbs in English combine with prepositions (see page 669) and some-times adverbs to form **phrasal verbs**. Phrasal verbs are two- and three-word expressions, generally with a new and different meaning from the original verb's meaning.

Verb:	He *ran* down the street. [*Ran* here means moved quickly.]
Phrasal Verb:	He *ran into* his former girlfriend. [*Ran into* means met unexpectedly.]
Phrasal Verb:	She *ran out of* patience. [*Ran out of* means came to an end, finished.]
Verb:	Juanita *kept* the book. [*Kept* here means held on to or set aside.]
Phrasal Verb:	Juanita *kept off* the grass. [*Kept off* means avoided, did not touch.]
Phrasal Verb:	Juanita *kept to* her story. [*Kept to* means did not change.]

Phrasal verbs play an important part in daily conversation and informal writing, and although they appear less frequently in academic writing, you need to learn them. As common idiomatic expressions, they contribute to your fluency and confidence as an English language user.

Tips and Pointers for Phrasal Verbs

- You can separate the parts of some phrasal verbs, but not others. There is no general rule.

Separate:	*Take out* the garbage.	*Take* the garbage *out*.
	Tear the wallpaper *down*.	*Tear down* the wallpaper.
Do Not Separate:	*Keep up* with your sister. NOT Keep with your sister up.	
	Look after the child. NOT Look the child after.	

- Place a pronoun object between the words of phrasal verbs you can separate:

  The police *took* **him** *away*. NOT The police took away him.

- You usually have the option of placing a phrase object between the words of or after a separable phrasal verb.

  The police *took* **the criminal** *away*. The police *took away* the **criminal**.

- When the object is a *clause*, do not place the clause so it separates the parts of a phrasal verb.

Incorrect:	The police took the criminal who had escaped them for years away.
Correct:	The police took away the criminal who had escaped them for years.

- Here are some familiar phrasal verbs. You should not separate the phrasal verbs that appear in boldface print:

ask out	fill out, fill up, fill in	**go over**	make up (with), make over
break up (with), break down	find out	**grow up**	run out (of), run over, **run across, run into**
bring up, bring about		hand in, hand over, hand out	
call back, call off, call in	**get along with**, get back, get away,	keep out, keep off, **keep up with**	**speak to, speak with**
drop off, drop in, **drop out (of)**	get in, get out, get on, **get off**	leave out	turn in, turn on, turn off, turn down
figure out		look around, look up, look over, **look after, look into, look out for**	wake up

Nouns: Countable and Uncountable

Some English nouns—words for things, people, places, or ideas—cannot be counted separately and, almost invariably, cannot show plurality. Other nouns can be counted separately.

Examples of Nouns You Cannot Count

Sports, games, and other activities	football, checkers, homework, studying, reading, soccer
Languages	Spanish, Chinese, Vietnamese, Creole
Courses and study fields	history, biology, math, psychology
Foods	bok choy, lettuce, pork, spaghetti, milk
Liquids, particles, grains, powders, gases	coffee, water, dust, sand, sugar, air, oxygen, fog, steam, water
Natural events	rain, weather, lightning, sunshine, gravity
Abstract ideas and emotions	beauty, fun, peace, hatred, truth, information, fear
Other uncountable nouns	luggage, money, furniture, news information, clothing, equipment, vocabulary, mail, jewelry

Remember, you can't make most of these uncountable nouns plural.

Incorrect: Our furnitures finally arrived.
Correct: Our furniture finally arrived.

Incorrect: Our luggages broke on our trip.
Correct: Our luggage broke on our trip.

You can use most of these uncountable nouns with words or phrases that do indicate separate units (these phrases are called *partitives*): *piece of* pie, *slice of* bread, *quart of* milk, for example. Even when the partitive is plural, keep the uncountable noun singular.

Incorrect:	We ate four pieces of pies.
Correct:	We ate four pieces of pie.

Incorrect:	We drank three glasses of milks.
Correct:	We drank three glasses of milk.

The Articles *a, an,* and *the*

- Avoid using the **indefinite article** *a* or *an* with most uncountable nouns.

Incorrect:	A luggage is on the airport scale.
Correct:	Luggage is on the airport scale.

- Use the **definite article** *the* or the word *some* when the uncountable noun has an explicit identity known to your reader.

Incorrect:	I saw a lightning last night.
Correct:	I saw some lightning last night.
	I saw the lightning last night.

- Use *a* before words that start with a consonant sound and *an* before words that start with a vowel sound. With words beginning with the letter *h*, use *a* before a consonant sound (*a* ham sandwich) and *an* before a vowel sound (*an* hour).

a pencil	an apple
a union	an express train
a year ago	an age ago

- The articles *a* and *an* do not work successfully with all nouns. With singular countable nouns, use the indefinite articles *a* or *an* only when you don't identify which particular one you mean. Use the definite article *the* when you specify which one among several.

  Maria bought *a* dress for her daughter. [one dress among several]

  He dropped *an* egg on the floor. [no particular egg]

  Maria bought *the* dress for her daughter. [the reader knows which dress]

  He dropped *the* egg on the floor. [a particular egg that the reader knows about]

- Be sure not to leave out the articles.

Incorrect:	Maria bought dress for her daughter.

- Use the definite article *the* if you repeat a noun you already have mentioned.

  Carlos gave *milk* to William's baby. *The* milk was warm and sweet.

- Use the definite article *the* to identify a unique event, occasion, or other one-of-a-kind reference.

  The Declaration of Independence was signed in 1776 on a day we now celebrate as *the* Fourth of July.

When Not to Use the Definite Article *The*

- **Most geographical places**: Europe, Fifth Avenue, Texas, Bismarck, Italy, Mount Rushmore, Lake Como, South America, Jamaica
- **Names of people**: John F. Kennedy, Madonna
- **Academic subjects and languages**: algebra, French, sociology
- **Holidays**: Christmas, Thanksgiving, Veteran's Day
- **Businesses, stores, universities, and colleges**: IBM, Walmart, Cisco Systems, Princeton University, LaGuardia Community College
- **Exceptions**: Use the definite article *the* for oceans, deserts, and mountain ranges (the Gobi Desert, the Rockies); geographical regions (the Western Hemisphere, the Far East, the Great Lakes); rivers, gulfs, and canals (the Hudson River, the Gulf of Tunis, the Suez Canal)

Prepositions

Prepositions are words that show relations between other words and function with those words in prepositional phrases. As modifiers, prepositional phrases tell when (*in* the morning), where (*on* the boat), or how (*by* airplane). English has many prepositions; some common prepositions are *about, above, after, against, along, among, at, because of, before, behind, below, between, by, by means of, except (for), from, in, in addition to, inside, into, near, next to, off, on, out, past, through, to, toward, until, up, upon, with*, and *without*. The uses of *in, at*, and *on* can seem complicated to speakers of other languages. And many prepositions are part of idiomatic expressions whose meanings you simply must memorize in order to use correctly.

Using *in, at,* and *on*

Use *in*:
- to show time in a year, month, or period

  in 2004   in March   in a week's time   in the evening
- to show certain places that are usually parts of larger entities

  in your basement   in the refrigerator   in Miami   in Hollywood

Use *at:*
- to identify a specific location

  at the dentist's   at the supermarket
- to indicate a specific time period

  at two o'clock   at noon   at 1:00 a.m.   at lunch

Use *on:*
- to indicate a specific day or date

  on July 5   on Wednesday   on your day off
- to refer to a surface

  on the desk   on Route 66   on the street

EXERCISE   Correct any errors that you find in the following sentences. Numbers in parentheses indicate the number of errors in each sentence.

1. He has try to keep up his friend with in their jogging every morning. (2)
2. David Kee's luggages had break when he flown from LA to Chicago in bad weathers. (4)
3. They were have funs in Wilson College along the Fifth Avenue in the downtown San Francisco. (4)
4. Loiza arrive to the supermarket to buy a sugar at Wednesday in the March of last year. (5)
5. Mayor did speaks, and he went the budget items over for audience. (4)
6. Alphonso was wanting cold drink in July afternoon, as he was appearing tired in the Yellowstone National Park. (5)
7. The children were dress up when they seen a elephant at zoo relaxing in a sunshine. (5)
8. Waters in the glasses were froze at refrigerator. (5)
9. At wrong stop she got the bus off and had look around for taxi. (4)
10. David had ask the girl who was smiling to him out on date. (3)
11. Mustafa and Lila did begins dating and they were wanting to go movies on the Saturday night. (4)
12. My teacher was disliking my report on the Europe where I spoke my grandmother to after very long time. (4)
13. In the October the weathers had turning very cold. (3)
14. Augusta has went to bakery for two loaf of breads. (4)
15. She have work at the IBM where she manage shippings department. (4)
16. Betty Fong had broke plate to floor when she hear a lightning the last night. (7)
17. Professor can speaking Russian but do uses language only at class in the Webster Community College. (5)
18. My uncle was wanting visit museum but main door was close after the five o'clock. (6)
19. She have go the test over many the times, but at Saturday on Chicago, classmates were hold study session in public library. (9)
20. "Look child after," she had scream to friend Beverley, "or he can fallen big puddle into and can getting very wet." (8)

Credits

Index

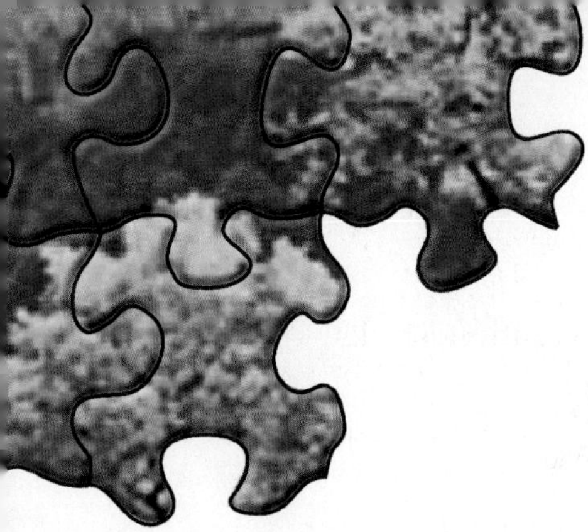

Correction Symbols and Abbreviations

Your instructor may use these symbols and abbreviations on your papers. Page numbers refer you to appropriate sections of the text.

ab	Incorrect abbreviation (553–554)
abst	Too abstract (516–521)
ad	Adjective, adverb confusion (554–556)
agr	Subject–verb agreement (611–615) or pronoun agreement (594–596)
awk	Awkward style
cap	Capitalize (561–562)
ca	Pronoun case (597–599)
comp	Faulty comparison (520–521, 577–578)
cs	Comma splice (573–574)
dm	Dangling modifier (589–590)
esl	English as a Second Language issue (663–670)
frag	Fragmentary sentence (583–586)
fs	Fused sentence or run-on sentence (604)
glos	See Glossary (626–662)
gr	Obvious error in grammar
lev	Inappropriate level of usage: too colloquial (543–544) or too fancy (544–545)
log	Faulty logic (326–330)
mm	Misplaced modifier (590–591)
pass	Awkward use of passive verb (528, 625)
p	Error in punctuation
ref	Faulty pronoun reference (600)
rep	Undesirable repetition of meaning (541), words (541), or sounds (541–542)
ro	Run-on sentence or fused sentence (604)
sexist	Sexist language (545–547)
shift	Illogical shift in tense or person (606–607)
sp	Spelling error (608–610)
sub	Faulty subordination (531–532, 616–617)
trans	Transition (97–99)
var	Sentence variety (533–535)

vb	Error in verb form (617–620)
vt	Error in verb tense (621–624)
wc	Poor word choice: see dictionary or Glossary (626–662)
wordy	Wordiness (625)
wr	Write out whole word (553–554) or spell out numeral (592)
ww	Wrong word: see dictionary or Glossary (626–662)
⊙	Insert period (581)
?	Question mark (581–582)
!	Exclamation point (582)
^	Insert comma (565–572)
;	Insert semicolon (605)
:	Insert colon (563–564)
“ ”	Insert quotation marks (602–603)
’	Insert apostrophe (558–559)
-	Insert hyphen (587)
…	Insert ellipsis (580)
()	Parentheses (593)
[]	Brackets (561)
ital	Use italics (underlining) (588–589)
//	Faulty parallelism (529)
|	Separate letters or words
⊂⊃	Bring together letters or words
¶	Start new paragraph
No ¶	No paragraph
∿	Transpose letters or words
/	Do not capitalize (561–562)
˘	Careless error
?	Illegible or meaning unclear
ℓ	Delete

Guide to the Handbook and Glossary

Handbook

The Handbook provides practical guidance on grammar, punctuation, and mechanics. Consult the appropriate text pages for discussion, explanation, and practice exercises.

Glossary of Problem Words

The Glossary of Problem Words explains specific words and phrases that frequently confuse writers. The Glossary begins on page 626. Some commonly consulted Glossary entries follow for easy reference.